Mapping a Northern Land
The Survey of Canada, 1947–1994

Canada was a difficult land to map. Planning, effort, and overall cost of obtaining a complete mapping were comparable to other national efforts, such as building the Canadian Pacific Railway and the St Lawrence Seaway. *Mapping a Northern Land* details the last half century of immense human effort necessary to define and describe this vast territory. Twenty-three specialists, many of whom were key players in the events they recount, describe developments in the fields of geodesy, topographic mapping, remote sensing, navigational charting, and geographic information systems during a period of tremendous technological change.

The book provides an excellent description of the birth and development of remote sensing, especially valuable in Canada because of its many areas of difficult access, and of geographical information systems, a Canadian innovation. For those interested in maps themselves rather than the techniques of gathering the necessary information, there are chapters on the development of federal and provincial map and chart styles, the wealth of atlases, and the numerous thematic maps produced in Canada as well as on how this spatial information has been marketed. For the surveyor there are chapters on the contributions of geodesy, cadastral surveying, and engineering surveying. The photogrammetrist's interests are addressed by chapters on federal mapping, Canada's air survey industry, and photogrammetric research. There are also chapters on education, the naming of Canada's places and features, and Canada's international role in mapping and surveying.

A conclusion to Don Thomson's three-volume *Men and Meridians, Mapping a Northern Land* will be an essential reference not only for those who work in the field of geomatics but for those interested in maps, charts, and atlases and in the adoption of new technology for surveying and mapping this northern land.

GERALD MCGRATH is professor emeritus of geography, Queen's University, and previously held the chair of cartography at the International Institute for Aerospace Survey and Earth Sciences, The Netherlands. Louis Sebert, before his retirement, worked for the Army Survey Establishment, DND, and then was head of the Mapping Programme Section at the Surveys and Mapping Branch of Energy, Mines, and Resources.

Mapping a Northern Land
The Survey of Canada, 1947–1994

Edited by

Gerald McGrath and
Louis M. Sebert

McGill-Queen's University Press
Montreal & Kingston • London • Ithaca

Reproduced with the permission of PWGSC –
Publishing Services, Public Works and Government Services Canada.

Legal deposit first quarter 1999
Bibliothèque nationale du Québec

Printed in Canada on acid-free paper

McGill-Queen's University Press acknowledges the financial support of
the Government of Canada through the Book Publishing Industry
Development Program for its activities. We also acknowledge the support
of the Canada Council for the Arts for our publishing program.

Canadian Cataloguing in Publication Data

Main entry under title:
Mapping a northern land: the survey of Canada, 1947–1994
Includes bibliographical references and index.
ISBN 0-7735-1689-1
1. Surveying – Canada – History. 2. Cartography – Canada – History.
3. Canada – Surveys – History. 3. Surveyors – Canada.
I. McGrath, Gerald, 1932–   . II. Sebert, L.M.
TA523.A1M36 1999   526.9'0971   C98-901047-3

Typeset in Times 10/12
by Caractéra inc., Quebec City

Contents

Foreword

Thirty years after the three volumes of *Men and Meridians* were published, as the author of that series I was gratified to learn that a fourth volume, continuing the story beyond 1947, was in the works. Astonishing to me was its ambitious scope consisting of nineteen chapters written by at least that many highly knowledgeable professionals. On reading the manuscript I noted with special interest that a good number of them were persons with whom I was closely associated in the writing of *Men and Meridians*, most prominent among them L.M. Sebert. The meticulous research work of these authorities, along with their skilful descriptions, embellish the vast scope of the periods covered. It is a mammoth project and most impressive in every way.

True, I would have preferred to have this new volume entitled *Men and Meridians, Volume 4*. But the world has changed greatly during the last half of the twentieth century. So many women, for example, are now engaged in nearly every aspect of surveying and mapping in Canada that a different title is required.

In fieldwork alone, for example, dramatic changes have taken place in surveying since the Second World War. In much of the *Men and Meridians* story, field parties worked on foot with packhorses, fighting hordes of insect pests and extreme heat or cold, and doing a great deal of tree-cutting in forested areas. All this became obsolete with the increasing use of planes, helicopters, motor boats, motorized vehicles, tractors, and bulldozers. In addition new electronic systems for measuring distances came into common use. All these improvements served to more than double production in the field.

When, in 1967, I was invited to address American professionals in Washington, D.C., on the history of surveying and mapping in Canada, I encountered at that conference, for the first time, the new age of computers. This fourth volume demonstrates how quickly Canadians adapted to computer use. In doing so they showed strength of commitment, variety, and innovation, all hallmarks of Canada's national and international role in surveying, mapping, and remote sensing, and in the provision of geographic information in atlases and otherwise.

In 1988 the establishment of the National Topographic Data Base (NTDB) with its three levels of map data made possible the build-up of a digital capability. Another important change in Canadian surveying and mapping was the substitution of metric for imperial scales. All these changes proved revolutionary in nature. Geodesists devised means of positioning offshore oil wells and photogrammetrists produced medium-scale federal maps for pipeline routes. Aerial photography and air surveys proved highly useful in timber assessment work as well as in the surveying and mapping of the northern wilderness areas of Canada. The St Lawrence Seaway as well as major hydroelectric projects required hydrographic surveys and topographic mapping for planning purposes. All industry was greatly aided by GIS, a significant pioneering effort by Canadians. In chapter 12, part two, the major part played by the National Research Council, especially in the development of photogrammetry, fills a void left in *Men and Meridians* by the rigid time frames imposed on that series.

An important new addition is the excellent chapter on the progress in Canada since 1960 in educating students in surveying, mapping, and remote sensing. The chapter describes, as a basis for future development in such education, the evolution of important centres, namely the Laval University, the University of New Brunswick, Erindale College, and the University of Calgary, supplemented by the Royal Military College at Kingston.

In the 1950s, 1960s, and into the 1970s Sam Gamble, during his illustrious tenure as director of the Surveys and Mapping Branch in Ottawa, provided invaluable leadership and diplomacy in fostering friendly cooperation between federal and provincial surveying and mapping organizations.

This new volume, as a whole, salutes those Canadians whose boundary lines, nationally and internationally, have served to secure peace without conflict and whose special abilities have helped develop potentialities into production. In all parts of Canada and in many parts of the world, on water, by land, and in the air, the contribution made to nation building by all who have sought out, measured, or portrayed the earth's domain is beyond any measurement. Long may their works thrive.

Don W. Thomson, LL.D., F.R.G.S.

Preface

In 1962 Don W. Thomson was commissioned to write the history of surveying and mapping in Canada from the sixteenth century to 1947. His work was called *Men and Meridians*, and was published in three volumes by the Queen's Printer in 1966, 1967, and 1969. They were acclaimed widely for their scholarship and well-balanced treatment of the subject.

In mid-1992 Hugh O'Donnell, then assistant deputy minister of the Surveys, Mapping, and Remote Sensing Sector of the federal government's Energy, Mines, and Resources (EMR), invited us to produce a fourth volume to bring Thomson's work up to the present. This period has been one of profound change in the political, economic, financial, and technological contexts for all forms of surveying and mapping. It has also seen a rapid growth of remote sensing, and the innovation of geographic and land information systems. We pointed out to O'Donnell that due to the enormous technical changes it would be virtually impossible for any two authors to cover the necessary fields with sufficient authority. We proposed recruiting a team of authors, each known and respected in his or her field. This suggestion was accepted. A list of the authors and their contributions is given in the table of contents, and biographic notes on each are provided in appendix A.

We submitted an outline of the work in September 1992, and based on this outline a contract was awarded in April 1993 to Queen's University at Kingston for the necessary research and writing to be undertaken. The university then subcontracted with each author to write the appropriate part of the text. The text of all chapters and appendices was delivered to EMR in March 1995, a month ahead of schedule. As co-editors we acknowledge with deep gratitude the financial support of EMR, which made possible the project of research and writing, and the unfailing interest and commitment of our fellow professionals, the authors. It has been a pleasure to work with both.

National events then took control. As part of government restructuring following the federal budget of February 1995, EMR ceased to exist and was replaced by Natural Resources Canada (NRCan). On 16 August 1995 the Surveys, Mapping, and Remote Sensing Sector became part of the Earth Sciences Sector of NRCan under M.D. Everell as assistant deputy minister. Later that year the sector's budget was reduced substantially, and it was announced that no further public funds could be committed to the publication of the book.

Discussions with McGill-Queen's University Press revealed its interest in publishing the book, with two provisos: release of the manuscript from NRCan had to be negotiated, and due to the length of the work, and the necessity to avoid undue financial risk, a subvention of $25,000 had to be found. Negotiations for the release of the manuscript were carried out successfully by Donald Akenson, the senior editor of McGill-Queen's University Press in Kingston, whose continued interest, support, and equanimity have been appreciated. There was one important condition: that the book should not carry the title of *Men and Meridians*, Volume 4. A major role in fund-raising was played by Ed Kennedy, president of the Geomatics Industry Association of Canada, Don McLarty, Earl Schaubel, and George Zarzycki. Through their collective efforts, and the generous support of the following donors, the subvention was raised by March 1997. Without this generosity this book could not have been published.

Alberta Land Surveyors Association
Angus C. Hamilton
Association of New Brunswick Land
    Surveyors
Association of Ontario Land Surveyors
George Babbage
Carl Zeiss Bio+Med Systems Ltd
ESRI Canada Limited
George Falconer
D.H. Gray
Leica Photogrammetry
Leica Surveying Division

Marshall Macklin Monaghan
McElhanney Land Surveys Ltd
Gerald McGrath
Donald McLarty
North West Geomatics Ltd
Saskatchewan Land Surveyors Association
L.M. Sebert
SHL VISION Solutions
Terra Surveys Limited
The Orthoshop
UMA Geomatics

We are deeply indebted to the two reviewers to whom the press referred the manuscript in 1996, and to the helpful suggestions that they made. These were taken up with individual authors, and many are reflected in the text. We also acknowledge the substantial assistance we have received from colleagues in the Departments of Geography and Information Technology Services at Queen's University, and the Canadian Institute of Geomatics. Not the least, we also owe much to the sustained encouragement of our wives throughout a longer period than had been expected.

Gerald McGrath, Kingston
Louis M. Sebert, Ottawa

CHAPTER ONE

Surveying and Mapping:
The Era of Change

Gerald McGrath and Louis M. Sebert

The period of the history of the surveying and mapping of Canada covered in this volume, 1947 to 1994, coincides to a large extent with the period of the Cold War. During this period of extended international tension life went on, but there were adjustments in the industrial world that favoured research and development in spheres of special interest to defence and space exploration. This was particularly true in the U.S. and USSR where funds seemed almost limitless for projects that would put them ahead in the so-called arms and space races. Although most of the research undertaken for defence and space needs was funded by defence departments, the majority of the work was done in civilian laboratories. Equally important was industry's commitment to research and development independent of defence and space requirements. This saw innovations such as the transistor. Although this was not initially connected to improved weaponry, it took its place quickly in many military and civil applications. The Canadian research centres of Bell Northern, Alcan, Du Pont, and other large companies bear testimony to industry's commitment. So also was fundamental and applied research carried out at government laboratories and centres such as those of the National Research Council and Agriculture Canada, and by a growing number of small and active companies. By no means the least was the expanding contribution of universities, with financial support from the research councils that were established after the Second World War.

The Cold War was also the beginning of the age of the computer. The early fragile computers, with their unreliable vacuum tubes, were made sturdy and more dependable by the transistor. The improved ruggedness of the computer made it applicable to the guidance systems of missiles, and in turn the reliable missiles opened the space age. Eventually navigation by computers became so precise that the position fixes of marine and air navigation became the precise positions of satellite geodesy. There were many other trails such as this, leading from research to development in the military field, then on to civilian applications in the field of surveying, mapping, and remote sensing. It was indeed an era of change.

Surveying and mapping is central to defining the extent and portraying the topographic and geological complexity of the Canadian land mass and Canadian waters. Techniques have been found, and are now being employed, for keeping this geographic information up to date, and for making it available in suitable forms to a wide variety of users. But before describing the advances and accomplishments of the Cold War era, it is appropriate to start with an examination of the mapping situation at the beginning of this period.

THE MAPPING AND SURVEYING SITUATION IN 1947

The 1947 Federal Mapping Plan

Work on the mapping of Canada by the two federal mapping agencies, Topographical Survey and the Army Survey Establishment (ASE), entered a new era in 1947. During the war Canadian military mapping units had been introduced to the instruments and techniques used to compile topographic maps from vertical air photos. Before the war some work of this type had been done in Ottawa by the army's Geographical Section of the General Staff (GSGS, predecessor of the ASE), but this had been experimental in nature and covered at best a few dozen square miles. The Topographical Survey used the plane table for most of its large-scale mapping and oblique air photography for the smaller scales. As late as 1939 vertical photography was considered too expensive for mapping the great expanses of Canada, and vertical photogrammetry much too slow. When the efficient wartime mapping methods were brought back to Canada it was obvious to all concerned that they were the answer to the country's mapping needs. Even the most reactionary member of the mapping fraternity could see that with these techniques it was possible, within the foreseeable future, to cover the whole of the country with good contoured topographic maps.

In 1946 William Miller, director of Topographical Survey, and Lt-Col Cyril Smith, the commanding officer of the ASE, devised a completely new programme for the modern mapping of Canada. This new plan was remarkable both in its scope and in its optimism. It was based on a previous plan drawn up in 1927 that gave the country its National Topographic System (NTS).

The main purpose of the NTS in 1927 was to coordinate the topographic mapping efforts of the three federal mapping agencies. (Before 1936 the Topographic Section of the Geological Survey was separate from Topographical Survey.) In short the NTS set out the sheet-lines, symbols, colours, and other specifications for modern topographic mapping. There were four scales in the system, at one-, two-, four- and eight-miles to the inch. Maps at each scale would cover the same area as four sheets at the next larger scale. In the original plan field mapping would be done by plane table at the two largest scales and the other two scales would either be derived from the larger coverage or compiled from existing maps at any available scale, from oblique aerial photography, or from any other pertinent information. The 1927 plan contained neither scheduling nor deadlines, and the mapping agencies were left to set their own priorities.

The 1947 plan was completely different. Among other commitments it called for the completion of the Four-Mile Series* in 918 sheets within twenty years, and the One-Mile Series of some 13 000 sheets within about fifty years. Areas of responsibility were set out.

---

* In this book the terms One-Mile, Four-Mile, et cetera, are used to designate the scale of the map in miles to the inch. Unfortunately in the 1930s many of the One-Mile sheets carried the scale statement "One Inch to One Mile," and the terms One-Inch and One-Mile were used interchangeably to describe these maps. In the British Ordnance Survey (OS) the terms One-Inch, Half-Inch, Quarter-Inch, and Eighth-Inch were used to describe the equivalent scales. The very popular OS One-Inch maps were well-known in Canada, and unfortunately this scale designation slowly entered Canadian usage. The conversion of 1:50 000 in 1950 ended the confusion.

For example in mapping the arctic at the Four-Mile scale, ASE would take the western Arctic and Topographical Survey the eastern half. Approval for long-range funding was obtained through the Cabinet Defence Committee. This was not difficult because there was a strong defence commitment to the mapping of northern Canada. The necessary personnel were hired and the plan was put in motion in 1947.

In retrospect it can be seen that the planned programme was very optimistic. To meet the deadlines that were set, the planners were counting on the development of a number of highly technical inventions and innovative mapping techniques. Without Electromagnetic Distance Measurement devices, helicopters for transport, and computers for survey calculations and photogrammetric adjustments (to name just a few), meeting the deadlines would have been impossible. The story of the working out of the 1947 plan is covered in the mapping chapters of this book.

Existing Federal Mapping in 1947

As the period of Canada's mapping history covered in this book begins in 1947, it is proper to start with a short description of the mapping situation in that year.

THE NATIONAL TOPOGRAPHIC SYSTEM

The specifications of the NTS were accepted completely in the Miller-Smith Plan. The existing NTS sheets therefore became its foundation. The state of the different NTS scales in that year is interesting. Despite over forty years of work, the One-Mile scale provided coverage of less than 2 percent of the country. Figure 3-11 shows this coverage in 1950, the year in which all these sheets were converted to the equivalent metric scale of 1:50 000. The coverage in 1947 was not much different. It can be seen that the mapping is concentrated in the settled areas of eastern Canada, southern British Columbia, and a few of Canada's mining centres. These were good maps with accurately drawn contours, but they were few in number.

Work at the Two-Mile scale was even less advanced. In 1947 sheets of this series fell into three categories. About one-third were derived maps* produced by GSGS from its One-Mile coverage. These were excellent maps. Another third were drawn by Topographical Survey directly from plane table sheets. GSGS rarely did Two-Mile mapping by plane table, but Topographical Survey used it very successfully in Nova Scotia. These maps were also first-class. The third category were maps compiled from existing surveys of various degrees of reliability. These maps were generally poor, and were considered stopgaps until something better was produced. In all classes the total coverage was less than seventy sheets.

In 1947 only six sheets of the Four-Mile Series had been published with contours. These were Kingston, Kitchener, Lake Simcoe, Montreal, Ottawa, and Toronto, all of which had been derived from One-Mile coverage by GSGS. Another forty-five had been compiled from existing maps and oblique aerial photography, but these contained no height information and were of low accuracy.

The Eight-Mile Series was the pride of the Topographical Survey. With massive help from the U.S. Army Air Force, it had been completed by 1944 in 220 sheets. For the first time Canada had a topographic series covering the whole country, but pride in this accomplishment was really misplaced. Almost half the sheets were uncontoured, and throughout the northern part of the country the horizontal accuracy was far below specifications.

---

* See the glossary in appendix E for a definition of this and other terms.

In the original NTS mapping plan the Eight-Mile sheets were to be compiled from existing map sources. The first sheet appeared in 1929. This was 94SE Hudson Hope, which had been compiled from a combination of Dominion Land Survey plans and sketch maps drawn by the Geological Survey. Experimental colours and symbols were tried out, and although they received general approval no further work was done on the series until 1933.

In 1933 airfield construction was underway on the Trans-Canada Airway, which ran from Halifax to Victoria, and there was an urgent need for air charts to cover the route. The Eight-Mile Series was chosen to provide the topographic base for these charts. As this work is described in detail in chapter 9, it is sufficient to say here that the Eight-Mile Series received a tremendous elevation in importance in 1933. After war was declared the completion of the Eight-Mile Series became the major mapping activity in the country. Due to wartime pressure and virtually unlimited funds, the last sheet was printed in July 1944 but, as has been mentioned, many of the sheets were seriously deficient in both horizontal accuracy and height information. The publication of air charts without contours or spot elevations was accepted as a wartime necessity. Nevertheless in 1947 a major initiative was the start of work on the second editions of this series with height data provided by either barometer surveys or Airborne Profile Recorder (APR) data.

In addition to the NTS mapping, two old series were in use and were being kept reasonably up to date. These were the Three-Mile sectional maps of the Prairies and the Chief Geographer's Series of south-eastern Canada. No new mapping was being done for these series, but new editions were being published from time to time that had a large and enthusiastic following.

THE THREE-MILE SECTIONAL MAPS

The older of the two series is the Three-Mile Series of the Canadian prairies. This series was started in 1892 to help control the settlement of the prairies. It was drawn at the three-mile scale so that the townships of the Dominion Land Survey System (which are six-mile squares) could be shown as two-inch squares on the map. As the land was surveyed the Three-Mile maps were drawn and revised to show the progress of the land survey. New sheets were derived from the survey plans, and in the land offices hand amendments were made to show land that had been granted and land still available for homesteading. Settlers could obtain copies so they could see where their land was in relation to other farms, local roads, railroads, and nearby towns.

As settlement progressed many facilities developed that improved the life on the prairie homesteads, but these were not shown on the original rather bleak outline maps. In 1919 it was decided to convert the original planimetric maps to true topographic maps. Contours were surveyed, roads were classified, and much cultural detail was added (for example farmsteads, schools, and churches). These new-style maps were published in five colours with a fine and delicate cartography. The three-mile scale was ideally suited to the broad expanse of the prairies. Revision of these sheets was carried on until 1955.

THE CHIEF GEOGRAPHER'S SERIES

In 1903 the usefulness of the western Three-Mile Series was noted in the Department of the Interior, and it was decided that similar coverage should be provided in the East. The decision was made that maps at both 1:250 000 and 1:500 000 would be compiled from existing maps and surveys with absolutely no expenditure for fieldwork. A search was made for any mapping that could provide data for these sheets. County maps were a mainstay, railroad plans were used extensively, and the work of the Geological Survey of Canada provided much needed data, especially in the parts of Ontario and Québec that lay to the north of county surveys. Coverage was extended north to 51° north latitude.

In the 1920s the collective name of these two mapping scales was changed to the Standard Topographic Maps of Canada. As far as can be determined today, this was done simply to give some artificial prestige to the work. They were certainly not topographic maps as they had no contours or any other height information other than the elevation of railroad stations taken from the railroad plans. In many respects they had an old-fashioned look. Only three colours were used: black for land detail, blue for open water, and orange to accentuate county, provincial, and international boundaries. Roads were not classified, which made them useless as road maps, and the rather slavish depiction of township land patterns obscured much of the minor cartographic detail. Despite their shortcomings these maps were popular in schools, county and township administrative offices, and many business establishments. Revision was stopped in 1948.

In summary it can be seen that in 1947 the maps available for development and other purposes were a mixture of old and new, good and bad. It is easy to be critical of the work done by topographical surveyors in the pre-war years, but it must be remembered that in 1939 the combined establishments of the GSGS and Topographical Survey totalled less than 150 people. Their area of responsibility covered half a continent. They did the best they could, but this was not good enough for a country that by 1947 had become a major industrial nation.

Provincial and Municipal Mapping

In 1947 only British Columbia was engaged in topographic surveys. The terrain of the province is so rugged that maps without contours can be very misleading. Thus in 1912 the Geographic Division was established within the provincial government to provide the maps needed for settlement and resource development. British Columbia had its own set of topographic scales, but in 1938 found that the NTS One-Mile specifications suited certain provincial needs. From that year until 1968 the provincial mapping agency cooperated with the Topographical Survey in producing sheets of the One-Mile (later the 1:50 000) Series.

In the other provinces mapping in 1947 consisted mainly in providing planimetric maps for resource development. The setting out of mining claims and timber rights was done by some provinces on its own mapping or on federal mapping adapted for provincial use by enlarging, overprinting, or other alterations. The work of the provincial mapping agencies is covered in chapter 4.

All cities and major towns in Canada had their own survey departments for the planning and control of city works and the provision of urban utilities. These were independent activities, and to a large extent each municipality set its own standards and specifications for its urban surveying and city mapping.

Surveying in Canada in 1947

In the actual practice of surveying the instruments and techniques used in Canada were, in 1947, not much different from those in use at the end of the nineteenth century. The Geodetic Survey had adopted the European optical reading theodolite in 1936, but such instruments were rare indeed throughout Canada. In 1946 the first major advance in surveying technology occurred. This was the testing of Shoran for the surveying of geodetic monuments throughout northern Canada. This was the beginning of electronic surveying, and as shown in chapter 2 new instruments and new techniques arrived with bewildering frequency over the next few years.

The Overall Picture

It can be seen from the preceding accounts that if Canada intended to compete on the world stage in the fields of mapping and surveying, a dramatic change from pre-war methods and habits would have to be made. Systems that were barely adequate in the Canada of 1930, when the country was hardly considered an industrial nation, would not serve in 1947. The Second World War was, however, a period of vast improvement in Canada's industrial stature. The knowledge and abilities of those in the surveying and mapping business were equally advanced by their war experiences. In short, by 1947 the country was ready to take its place in the forefront of the surveying and mapping industry, worldwide. The account given in this volume tells how this goal was to a large extent achieved.

POSTWAR CANADA:
THE PERIOD OF CHANGE AND CHALLENGE

The period covered by this book has been one of profound change worldwide in politics, economics, demography, social services, and many other aspects of daily life. Such changes provide the background against which the policies of successive governments, and the programmes that are based on those policies, can be viewed.

Postwar Political Spheres and Defence Alliances

Before the Second World War Canada's military planners were frustrated by not having any apparent enemy to justify a need for defence. The United States was too powerful to fill the role, and all other countries were too remote to be a credible threat. Canada's defence policy was therefore aimed at having a small defence force for local emergencies, and to have it trained to become a useful ally should it be needed in more distant altercations.

Canada emerged from the Second World War as a state positioned geographically between the two prime world powers. Detailed knowledge of the geography of the land between became a military necessity, and Canada's military planning became inextricably linked to that of the Americans. This led to bipartite mapping agreements as described in chapter 5, then tripartite (U.S., U.K., and Canada), and eventually multinational within NATO. One important outcome was a series of standardization agreements designed so that the maps of one country could be used readily by the military forces of the others. It was not long before they affected civilian mapping in the member states. An example in Canada is the relatively early change from imperial to metric scales in Canada's national mapping. This was caused partially by experience during the war, but more directly by military agreements with the United States in 1949 in which metric mapping scales were deemed essential to military cooperation. Canada could not afford to produce both imperial and metric scales, and thus the change to metric was made.

Table 1-1
The Growth of the Canadian Population

Decade	Population at End of Decade	Increase in Decade	Natural Increase	Net Immigration Positive	Net Immigration Negative
1851	2 436 297				
1851–61	3 229 633	793 336	641 000	152 000	
1861–71	3 689 257	459 624	651 000		−191 000
1871–81	4 324 810	635 553	723 000		−87 000
1881–91	4 833 239	508 429	714 000		−206 000
1891–1901	5 371 315	538 076	718 000		−180 000
1901–11	7 206 643	1 835 328	1 120 000	716 000	
1911–21	8 787 949	1 581 306	1 230 000	351 000	
1921–31	10 376 786	1 588 837	1 360 000	229 000	
1931–41	11 506 655	1 129 869	1 222 000		−92 000
1941–51	14 009 429	2 502 774	1 972 000	* 169 000	
1951–61	18 238 247	4 228 818	3 148 000	1 081 000	
1961–71	21 586 311	3 330 064	2 608 000	722 000	
1971–81	24 343 180	2 774 869	1 920 000	855 000	
1981–91	27 108 000	2 764 820	1 973 000	792 000	

* Population at end of decade includes Newfoundland, but figures for natural increase and net immigration do not.
Source: *The Canadian Encyclopaedia* and *The Canada Yearbook* for 1994

The development of strategic weapons certainly emphasized the need for military cooperation. Strategic planning required complete map coverage of Canada at medium scale. This military requirement paved the way for the cabinet's approval of funds for a twenty-year programme to complete national coverage by the 1:250 000 map series of the NTS.

Postwar Immigration and Population Growth

Immigration into Canada between 1861 and 1901 added just over 1.75 million to the population, the majority of whom came from the U.K. and Europe. But during the same period 2.4 million emigrants, almost all of whom left for the U.S., more than counterbalanced the new arrivals. The net immigration was therefore negative, as table 1-1 shows. The net number of immigrants was about 1.25 million during the period 1901–41, with negative immigration of 92 000 being experienced between 1931 and 1941 due to the Depression and the Second World War. Immigration resumed after 1946 with the arrival of many from war-torn Europe and the U.K., though arrivals from the then Iron Curtain countries virtually ceased until 1956. The peak of net immigration (1 080 000) occurred during the period 1951–61. The principal sources of later waves of immigrants have been the West Indies, the Indian subcontinent, and South-east Asia respectively.

Net immigration as a component of population growth has depended on government policies, both in Canada and the U.S. These have been influenced largely by the variable state of the Canadian economy and political circumstances outside Canada. The natural increase in the population has been a more significant component than net immigration, as table 1-1 shows. Clearly evident is the so-called postwar Baby Boom, but so also is the later slowing in natural growth caused by changing views on the sizes of families and employment. The overall effect of both components has been almost a doubling of Canada's

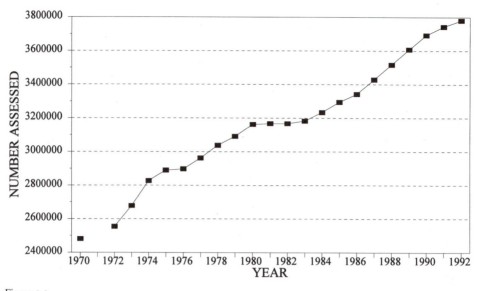

Figure I-I
Province of Ontario – number of assessed properties.
Source: Ministry of Revenue

population since 1951. The spatial distribution of growth has, however, been very uneven. The urban population increased substantially whilst the rural declined, and Ontario remained a magnet to many immigrants until the 1970s. All have had an impact on surveying and mapping. One indication is the number of dwellings on which construction was started each year. The annual starts almost doubled between 1966 and 1971 (from 134 474 to 233 653), but dropped substantially during the recessions of the 1980s. Each property was surveyed and registered, and each was assessed for property taxation. The growth of the latter is illustrated by Ontario, where assessed properties increased by 48 percent during the twenty-year period commencing 1972 (see figure 1-1).

Urbanization

Internal migration away from rural areas to the cities started after the First World War, and increased during and after the Second. This was caused by better employment opportunities in the cities, the reorganisation of agricultural production on larger farms, and the reduced need for farm labour. Immigration, the natural increase in population, increased industrialization, and an expanding service and business sector have also contributed to growing urbanization. There have, however, been significant counter-flows from city centres to rapidly expanding suburbs, flows that have abated only recently. For the most part these flows have been caused by the increased availability of the automobile, and to a much smaller extent by improved public transport. In almost every case the enlarged cities have taken over farm land. Figure 1-2 shows the total rural land converted to urban uses in urban-centred regions (UCRs) during twenty years starting in 1966. Of the 301 440 ha total rural land converted in seventy UCRs across Canada, some 175 000 ha were classed as

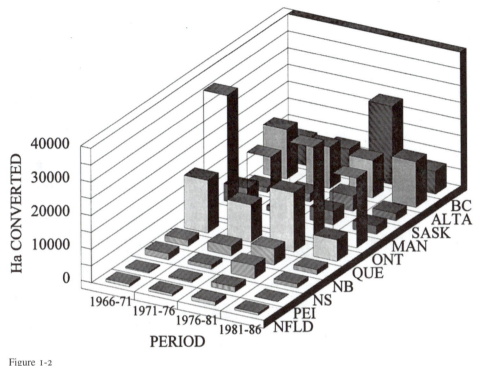

Figure 1-2
Total rural land converted to urban in UCRs.
Source: Environment Canada, 1989

"prime agricultural land."[2] The conversion of farm land and the aggregation of people in cities were not experienced uniformly across the country, as figure 1-3 reveals. It can be seen that during the same period (1966–86) the areas and populations of cities with more than 500 000 inhabitants grew more rapidly than those of smaller cities, and that smaller cities urbanized land more rapidly than the larger cities. Thus the ambition of most Canadians to own their own house on their own parcel of land has caused significant loss of agricultural land, great urban spreading with low-density residential subdivisions and shopping malls, and the accompanying high cost of providing municipal services.

Urbanization has placed great demands on planners, cadastral surveyors, and land registrars to design, lay out, and register the new subdivisions and the individual parcels of land within them. Subsequent changes in ownership have also had to be registered, along with mortgages and any necessary surveys. Designing, surveying, and building the urban infrastructure of roads and the networks for water, sewerage, electricity, gas, and telephones have added to the engineering surveyor's tasks. Large-scale mapping undertaken by the air survey industry or by a provincial government has been an essential part of urban expansion, and municipal land information or facilities management systems have been constructed recently in more than 100 cities to help integrate land-related data. The changes in urban land use throughout Canada have had to be monitored, for which remote sensing has been utilized.

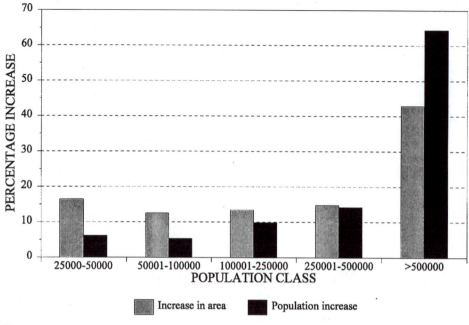

Figure 1-3
Canada: urban-centred regions, 1966–86. Increase in area/population growth.
Source: Environment Canada, 1989

As the ownership of property has been under provincial jurisdiction from the time of Confederation, all provinces have developed active legal survey establishments. In 1947 this activity was controlled in some provinces by self-regulating associations, but in others it was under the control of the provincial directors of survey. The surveyor general in the Department of Mines and Resources continued to head the Dominion Land Survey System for cadastral surveys in the territories and on federal lands in the provinces.

Natural Resource Exploration and Exploitation

Canada has been known for the wealth of its natural resources since the days of the first explorers. The fur trade opened the north-west. Subsequently the forest industry supported settlement, and then went on to become a resource industry of tremendous importance. The Geological Survey of Canada was the first government scientific agency. Upon confederation the natural resources of southern Canada came under provincial control, but support for development continued from Ottawa.

The forestry and mining industries have grown substantially since the Second World War. The former has provided lumber and a wide range of derivatives to help house the greatly expanded populations of Canada and the U.S. Pulp and paper products have been in increased demand for both domestic and foreign markets. Long-established precious and other metals have generally prospered, the production of iron ore and zinc, for example, having more than doubled between 1961 and 1966. The precious metals and some of the base metals have, however, been affected by wide fluctuations in market prices and substantially increased competition from producers overseas. Overall this has not prevented further exploration. One of the more obvious changes in the postwar years has been the explosive growth in the consumption of oil, gas, and oil-based products by a wide variety of users. This prompted the successful exploration of potential basins in the Arctic by Canadian companies, and offshore along the east coast. Further exploration in the 1980s was dampened by the prevailing low price per barrel.

The forestry and mining industries have presented significant challenges to those in surveying, mapping, and remote sensing. For example, geodesists have had to devise ways of positioning oil wells offshore, the photogrammetrists were asked to produce medium-scale federal maps for exploration and planning pipeline routes, and the air survey industry undertook aerial photography and airborne geophysical surveys. Tree species were identified by interpreting aerial photographs, and the quantity and quality of marketable timber was assessed. Satellite data were used together with new techniques of computer processing. More recently Geographic Information Systems (GIS) have been pressed into use by the forest industry and government forest departments to help manage increased volumes of forest data collected by remote sensing and ground surveys, and to facilitate spatial analysis. Similar advances have been made in airborne geophysical exploration. Canada has been a pioneer in both remote sensing and GIS, and in the integration of the two methodologies.

The Changing Nature of Agriculture

Whilst the number of census farms in Canada declined from about 733 000 in 1941 to 338 500 in 1976 (see figure 1-4), the average size of farm rose from 96 ha to 202 ha during the same period (see figure 1-5).[3] These changes were by no means uniform. The Maritimes suffered the most severe reductions in the number of farms (a decline of between 70 and 85 percent), compared with 38 to 49 percent in the three Prairie provinces. The largest average sizes of farms in 1941 were 176 ha and 175 ha in Alberta and Saskatchewan respectively. By 1976 the average size of farm in Saskatchewan was 374 ha. Overall the total area of farm land declined only marginally from 70 million ha in 1941 to 68.5 million ha in 1976, whilst the area of improved farm land increased from 37 million ha to 44 million ha during the same period. Although the numbers of farms and persons employed in agriculture declined, with a 50 percent reduction in the latter between 1951 and 1971, the output from most forms of agriculture has increased. The internal markets for Canadian farm produce have grown, and the export markets have become increasingly significant to the economy – particularly in grains and dairy produce.

From its inception the federal Department of Agriculture has been concerned with determining the suitability of land for specific types of agriculture, promoting good farming practice and control of disease, and improving plant stock through breeding at its research stations. Aerial photographs became an indispensable tool in agriculture after the Second World War. The nationwide Canada Land Inventory programme of thematic mapping owes much to the interpretation of aerial photographs, as chapter 11 shows. The land inventory maps have also been used for studies in land suitability, soil moisture, drainage, determining the identities of crops, measuring areas under specific crops in a programme to reduce crop inventories, forecasting production, and monitoring crop health. In conjunction with the

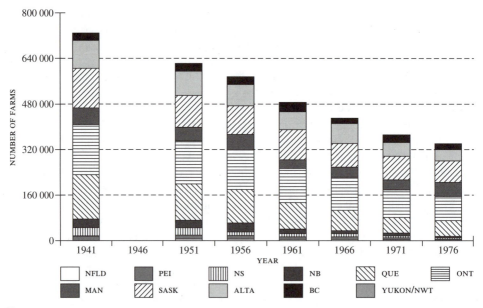

Figure 1-4
Number of census farms, 1941–76.
Source: Environment Canada, 1982

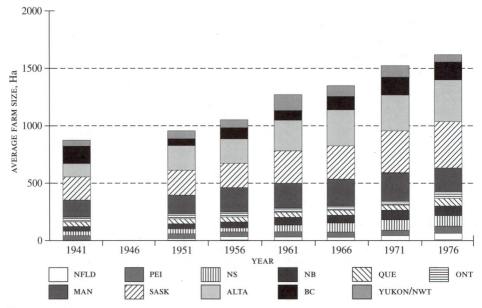

Figure 1-5
Average size of census farms, 1941–76.
Source: Environment Canada, 1982

Canada Centre for Remote Sensing, the department was an early user of satellite data for these and other purposes as chapter 14 describes. The provinces, too, have been active in this field and there have been valuable flows of information between the two levels of government.

Engineering in the Era of Change

The famous spiral tunnel on the Canadian Pacific's main line through the Rocky Mountains, which had a flawless breakthrough, and several Canadian mines that have vertical shafts of over a mile in depth are examples of early achievements in engineering surveying. Before the First World War Canada's communities were like beads along the string of the national railways which provided coast-to-coast service in this vast country. Between the wars major improvements were made to the highway system, and in 1938 Trans-Canada Air Lines began service. These were of great assistance in drawing the country together, but still a feeling of local isolation persisted. To a great extent this has been rectified since 1947, and Canadian engineering has played a leading role in making this possible. The provincial highway systems were expanded between 1950 and the 1970s with modern divided highways. Pipelines for oil, gas, and water were added to the traditional transportation systems. Microwave, and more recently satellite, communication have made interprovincial connections cheap and effective. Improvements to railways have been made by doubling tracks and by reducing grades in the mountainous areas through massive tunnelling projects. Thus the efficiency of the rail network has been increased, and the cost of moving agricultural, mining, and manufacturing products to market and for export has been reduced.

One of Canada's major postwar engineering projects saw the St Lawrence Seaway built to give ocean-going vessels access to Great Lakes ports, and permit larger lake vessels to be employed. Others include the construction of major oil and gas pipelines from Alberta and the Northwest Territories to Canadian and U.S. markets, and the building of major dams for hydroelectric generation at Manicouagan and James Bay. All of these engineering developments have required medium- and large-scale topographic maps for planning, cadastral surveys for defining the legal limits, and engineering surveys for setting out the new works. Some have required hydrographic surveys. The newly constructed dams have been subjected to high-precision surveys to measure the small deformations of the dam structures after construction. The part played by surveyors in these projects is explained in chapter 16.

Improving Knowledge of the Seabed and Inland Waters

In 1947 the Canadian Hydrographic Service (CHS) was in comparatively good shape so far as the ports on Canada's East and West Coasts were concerned. Though the war years had been times of frantic activity with traffic in 1945 being at least three times its 1939 level, CHS was able to keep abreast of the demands for both charts and new surveys. Despite this reassuring picture, CHS was about to confront major challenges.

By 1947 the possibility of Newfoundland joining Confederation was becoming a probability, and if that happened the CHS would be faced with a greatly enlarged area of responsibility. In the aftermath of the Second World War the political situation demanded that increased attention be paid to the Arctic and its waters, the charts of which were mainly British and mostly over 100 years old. Establishing sovereignty was an early challenge, together with supplying coastal stations of the new early warning radar system that was built across Canada, and other communities. Scientific studies in the North also had to be supported. Anti-submarine defensive measures on both coasts needed much improved knowledge of the whole seabed and its topography. Throughout the period maritime commerce has remained vital to the economy of Canada, as have the sea lanes converging upon the main ports of Halifax, Montreal, and Vancouver. Yet major changes have occurred to the sizes and functions of cargo vessels. The smaller, wartime vessels of 10 000 to 15 000 tonnes were replaced by larger and deeper draught vessels. Gradually the latter were replaced by very large crude carriers (the "super tanker"), container vessels, and other specialized carriers. Each had a deeper draught than before, and each required more exact information on the depths of channels and the clearance over underwater obstacles. The opening of the Great Lakes to ocean-going vessels and larger lakers in 1959 introduced similar requirements to inland waters. Commercial fishing became more sophisticated as technological improvements were made to positioning devices and depth sounding. And by no means the least, augmented leisure time and higher disposable incomes gave many Canadians the opportunity to take their leisure on the water in small boats, both power and sail.

The CHS has had to respond to this wide variety of challenges. Just as the Royal Navy has been known as the "Silent Service," this term could equally be applied to the CHS. Its work is rarely in the public eye. Yet it covers the three coasts of Canada and its inland waterways, and has been successful in helping to keep marine disasters to a minimum. The accomplishments of the Service in hydrographic surveying and charting since the Second War World are described in chapter 8. In addition to techniques that are unique to hydrographers, the CHS has integrated many of the developments that have occurred in surveying and mapping on land, specifically in positioning systems, photogrammetry, computer mapping, and remote sensing.

Environmental Concerns

Concern about the environment has increased exponentially in the last fifty years. Throughout history it has been almost impossible to develop a mine or open a smelter without causing some local degeneration of the environment. In the past this was accepted as the price for developing a natural resource. Today this has changed. When a new ore body is discovered, or a smelter is being planned, the cost of reducing or containing pollution is entered into the overall development costs. This allows the economic viability of the project to be determined, and monitoring and control mechanisms to be implemented. The causes of environmental deterioration are manifold. Vehicles emit atmospheric pollutants. Sewage is discharged untreated into rivers and lakes, as is effluent from manufacturing pulp, cooling water from power stations, and fuel oil from ships' bunkers. Septic systems fail. Garbage landfill sites release leachate. Fires occur in tire dumps. Noise emanates from busy airports. Changes to vegetation are caused by forest clear-cutting, as are interruptions to natural drainage and the dispersal of the wildlife population.

Aerial photography, specialized airborne sensors, and data from satellite sensors have played critical roles in helping to detect and monitor sources of environmental deterioration. Private industry was in the forefront of environmental monitoring in Canada during the late 1960s, and government institutions have also contributed their expertise in the development of appropriate sensors and methodologies for specific applications. Geographical information systems have been used more recently to help manage the growing volume of data on environmental degradation collected through remote sensing and ground surveys. Attention is also being directed to modelling the impact of a specific pollutant or hazardous action.

Structural Change

The movement of people to urban centres has been accompanied by alterations in employment patterns. Those in agriculture have already been noted. There have also been shifts from primary resource extraction and heavy industry towards lighter manufacturing and the service sector. This sector includes finance, insurance, real estate, trade, education, health and welfare, and public administration. Certain of these alterations were evident before 1960. Others became prominent afterwards. Some are still occurring, particularly the growth of what might be described as an "information sector." Such changes undoubtedly bring new opportunities to some sectors and reduce expectations in others.

One other feature must be mentioned. Much greater emphasis has been placed in Canada on university and college education since the 1950s, and the increased level of government funding has reflected this. Educational standards are much higher today, consistent with the advances that have been made in theory, methodology, and technology during the past fifty years. Surveying is recognized as a separate post-secondary academic discipline, and is offered as such by several Canadian universities – though the term "geomatics" is now being applied to embrace surveying, photogrammetry, cartography, remote sensing, the cadastre, and spatial information systems. In other institutions some or all of these fields remain as a component of an engineering or earth sciences discipline. The changes in survey education are described in chapter 13.

RESPONDING TO THE CHALLENGES: CANADA'S SURVEYING AND MAPPING ORGANIZATIONS

In the areas of concern to this volume, the division of responsibilities between federal, provincial, and private agencies in Canada has been fairly clear-cut. Defence, national mapping, ocean resources, and foreign aid have been areas of federal jurisdiction. Provincial governments have been responsible for land, natural resources, and education. The private sector has contributed by conducting business for profit and licensing professionals. Contributions to training, research, and development have been made by all three and by the educational sector. An outline follows of the principal government agencies in the surveying and mapping fields.

Federal Agencies

NATURAL RESOURCES CANADA
When this department was formed as the Department of Mines and Resources in 1936 on the disbandment of the Department of the Interior, it absorbed the resource development functions of the latter. In 1950 it became the Department of Mines and Technical Surveys

(DMTS)* and in 1966 Energy, Mines and Resources (EMR). Finally, in 1993, it underwent one more change of name to Natural Resources Canada (NRCan). Throughout these changes the principal function of the department has been resource development, but there have been changes in emphasis. Energy was a less important resource in 1947 than it is today. Forestry was transferred to the department in 1993 as an element of major restructuring of government. Some see the fact that for the first time the word "Mines" does not appear in the department title as an indication that this industry is not quite as important as it once was.

Responsibilities for surveys and mapping within DMTS and later EMR were assigned to the Surveys and Mapping Branch (SMB). This branch operated under several federal statutes and orders in council.[4] The branch was under a director (latterly director general), and was organized internally into divisions or directorates that, for much of the period, included the Geodetic Survey, Topographical Survey, Geographical Services, Reproduction and Distribution, Legal Surveys, and the International Boundary Commission. A more complete description of each division and its work can be found in the report of a task force published in 1978.[5] Changes in name and emphasis have occurred. Topographic mapping has always been important, but in recent years more resources have been allocated to creating a national digital topographic database and map revision than to new mapping. In 1966 responsibility for hydrographic charting was passed to the Department of the Environment, and eventually, in 1979, to the Department of Fisheries and Oceans. Aeronautical charting has assumed greater importance over the years. In all aspects of surveying and mapping, contracting work to the private sector has increased. Unchanged is the critical role that the National Air Photo Library has fulfilled in housing and indexing all federal aerial films and photography.

In 1987 a major reorganization dissolved the divisions and directorates within the SMB and replaced them with a series of centres in a new Surveys, Mapping and Remote Sensing Sector (SMRSS): the Canada Centre for Surveying, Canada Centre for Mapping, the Geographic Information Systems Division, and the Cartographic Information and Distribution Centre. The Canada Centre for Remote Sensing, which had been created within EMR in 1972, was also incorporated in the SMRSS, and the new Canada Centre for Geomatics was added later. The SMRSS came under the direct supervision of a newly appointed assistant deputy minister (ADM), Hugh O'Donnell. This grouping of responsibilities under an ADM greatly improved the planning of work in each centre, and ensured that such planning was consistent with the overall planning of the department. The federal budget of 26 April 1993 saw the SMRSS embark on a new journey into relatively uncharted territory when it was transformed, on a trial basis, into a Special Operating Agency within Natural Resources Canada. This transformation began with the development of a business plan for the agency, and the creation of "an advisory board of outside members and senior management ... to assist SMRSS management with strategic, business and marketing advice, to provide knowledge of the client sector and to offer technical expertise."[6] Not the least was the establishment of a revolving fund with which to finance certain of the SMRSS's activities. The most recent step has been the renaming of the sector as Geomatics Canada.

---

* The acronyms DMTS, EMR, and NRCan are used frequently throughout this volume, together with SMB for the Surveys and Mapping Branch of DMTS (and later EMR) and SMRSS for the Surveys, Mapping and Remote Sensing Sector of EMR (and later NRCan). Appendix F provides a full list of acronyms.

The Geological Survey of Canada is also an important mapping agency within Natural Resources Canada, but since 1936 has not been active in topographic mapping. It uses the maps produced by the Canada Centre for Mapping as bases for its geological and geophysical maps.

THE DEPARTMENT OF NATIONAL DEFENCE (DND)
The second federal department that contributed to national mapping for a long period is the DND. The Canadian military has produced topographic maps since 1904, and its contributions are described in chapter 5. Although the directorate involved has also undergone a series of name changes (for example, the Directorate of Cartography), the mission has remained the same. It has been charged with defining and collating the military requirements for maps, charts, and geographical information, and satisfying these wherever possible. The agency for producing maps and charts was the ASE, which was created in October 1946 as the successor to the First Field Survey Company of the Royal Canadian Engineers. It was renamed the Mapping and Charting Establishment (MCE) in 1966.

Originally the military mapping unit assisted in the production of maps of the NTS, but in 1966 its role was changed abruptly to assisting the American military mapping agency in producing 1:250 000 maps of the whole world, especially of places where there might be military involvement. This change of direction removed a valuable contributor to the basic mapping of Canada, but provided the Canadian military with access to foreign mapping, geographic information, and American mapping technology.

OTHER FEDERAL DEPARTMENTS WITH A MAPPING
OR CHARTING ROLE
Mention has been made of the Department of Fisheries and Oceans, which, in 1979, took over responsibilities for hydrographic charting and the CHS. In addition to the Geological Survey, a number of agencies have been active in thematic mapping in which specialist information relevant to the work of the department is portrayed on maps at a variety of scales. In many respects mapping is the best way of educating the public in their areas of research, and over the years they have published maps that illustrate their work brilliantly. The agencies include Agriculture, Environment, and Statistics. Subsequently the first two became major users of remotely sensed data, and played significant roles in the development and application of GIS. Computer cartography was adopted at an early stage by Statistics Canada, and it remains a leading exponent of these techniques. But mapping is such a convenient way of portraying a theme or message that all government departments have at times published maps. In some cases the Canada Centre for Mapping has acted as a consultant, and at times an active participant, in the project. For most of the period the National Research Council was a fund of innovation in the development of photogrammetric plotting instruments and software, but in addition it supported photogrammetric research and cadastral projects overseas.

Provincial Agencies

The topographic mapping and cadastral agencies of the provinces are described in Chapters 4 and 7. For the most part these are in provincial ministries responsible for provincial natural resources. Table 1-2 lists the ministries, and the section or division responsible for

Table 1-2
Provincial Agencies Responsible for Surveys and Mapping

Newfoundland	Land Branch, Department of Natural Resources
Nova Scotia	Geomatics Centre, Land Information and Management System, Department of Municipal Affairs
New Brunswick	New Brunswick Geographic Information Corporation
Prince Edward Island	Geomatics Information Centre, Fiscal Management Division, Department of the Treasury
Québec	Le Service de la Cartographie, Direction des Relevés Techniques, Ministère des Ressources Naturelles
Ontario	Provincial Mapping Office, Ministry of Natural Resources
Manitoba	Manitoba Land Information Centre, Department of Natural Resources
Saskatchewan	Central Survey and Mapping Agency, Saskatchewan Property Management Corporation
Alberta	Information Resources Management Service, Alberta Environmental Protection Ministry
British Columbia	Department of Surveys and Resource Mapping, Ministry of Environment, Lands and Parks
Yukon	Yukon GIS Coordinating Unit, Land Interest Management System
Northwest Territories	Department of Municipal and Community Affairs

surveys and mapping. Although the statutes governing land registration and property assessment vary considerably from province to province, those that deal with surveys and surveyors represent common themes – the conduct of land surveys, and the licensing and regulation of surveyors.

THE ORGANIZATION OF THIS BOOK

Chapters 2 to 5 cover the fundamental sciences of geodesy and photogrammetry by which the basic data on the size, shape, and topography of Canada are collected and processed. The roles and programmes of the federal and provincial agencies that work in these fields are described, and chapter 6 points out the important contribution that private companies make in these operations.

Cadastral surveys, which are the basis of land ownership, are described in chapter 7. Hydrographic charting has its own very specialized requirements for survey, and these are covered in chapter 8. Aeronautical charting, on the other hand, is no longer involved in acquiring topographical information but, as described in chapter 9, uses current topographical maps to produce base maps on which to display navigational data.

The text then deals with the fields of atlas and thematic mapping in chapters 10 and 11. This is followed by chapter 12, which reviews the important contributions Canadians have made to research in surveying, photogrammetry, and cartography. Chapter 13 explains the substantial changes that have occurred in survey education and training over the years, and in recent times in the newer subjects of photogrammetry and remote sensing.

Canada has had long experience in obtaining specialized information on the terrain through the interpretation of aerial photographs, and more recently by using remotely sensed data from aircraft and satellites. These are reviewed in chapter 14. The Canadian innovation of the 1960s, the GIS, is considered in chapter 15.

Then follows chapter 16 on engineering surveys, a type of survey so widespread that it is hardly noticed by the public. The chapter is focused on some of the numerous major engineering projects that have been completed in Canada since the Second World War, and the very high-precision surveys needed to monitor major structures to detect any deformations that might be taking place.

Chapters 17 and 18 deal with what might seem to be the more abstract subjects of marketing spatial information (mapping, survey data, etc.), and Canada's contributions to international development through surveying and mapping. The volume concludes with a retrospective look at the period covered (1947 to 1994), and a brief assessment of future prospects.

NOTES

1 Thomson, Don. W. *Men and Meridians*. Ottawa: Queen's Printer. Vol 1, 1966; vol. 2, 1967; and vol. 3, 1969.

2 1989. *A State of the Environment Fact Sheet. Urbanization of Rural Land in Canada, 1981–86*. Ottawa: Environment Canada.

3 McCuaig, J.D., and E.W. Manning. 1982. *Agricultural Land-Use Change in Canada: Process and Consequences*. Ottawa: Lands Directorate, Environment Canada. Appendix A.

4 *Order in Council 766 of 20 April 1909*, which established the Geodetic Survey as a unit in the Department of the Interior.

Order in Council 180 of 7 February 1925, which established the National Air Photo Library in the Department of the Interior.

Mines and Resources Act, 1936.

Order in Council 37/4433 of 1 November 1947, which established the Surveys and Mapping Bureau with five divisions: Geodetic Survey, Topographical Survey, Legal Surveys, Hydrographic Service, and Map Compilation and Reproduction.

Order in Council 3397 of 3 August 1948, which established the Canadian Board on Geographic Names.

Department of Mines and Technical Surveys Act, 1949, which created the department and the Surveys and Mapping Branch (from the existing Surveys and Mapping Bureau), and defined "technical surveys" as including geographical, geological, geodetic, topographical, and hydrographic surveys.

The *Canada Lands Surveys Act*, 1951 and amended in 1977, which established the basis in law for the Surveyor General of Canada Lands, cadastral surveys of Crown lands in the territories and federal lands, and other surveying responsibilities.

International Boundary Commission Act, 1960 and amended in 1970, which provided the basis in law for the International Boundary Commissioner and the maintenance of the boundary between Canada and the U.S.

Representation Commissioner Act, 1963, which required the preparation of electoral maps needed by the commissioner for federal elections.

Order in Council 318 of 1964, which transferred the Air Photo Production Unit, RCAF to Surveys and Mapping Branch, Mines and Technical Surveys.

Electoral Boundaries Act, 1964–65, which specifies the responsibility of Surveys and Mapping Branch for electoral boundary mapping.

Government Organization Act, 1966–67, which created the Department of Energy, Mines and Resources, repealed the previous Department of Mines and Technical Surveys Act, 1949, and substituted an act respecting resources and technical surveys (noted below).

Resources and Technical Surveys Act, 1966–67, which defined the responsibilities of the minister for "technical surveys."

Department of Energy, Mines and Resources Act, 1966-7, which defined the work of the new department created during government reorganization to include "technical surveys."

Official Languages Act, 1968–69, which required the Surveys and Mapping Branch to prepare bilingual district maps needed by the Commissioner for Official Languages.

Order in Council 1458 of 22 July 1969, which assigned to Surveys and Mapping Branch secretariat support for the Canadian Permanent Committee on Geographical Names.

Government Organization Act, 1970, which again defined "technical surveys," and provided for a "geographic service" including geographic names, and "support to other agencies" in the federal and provincial governments.

5 Lapp. P.A., A.A. Marsan, and L.J. O'Brien. 1978. *Report of the Task Force on National Surveying and Mapping*. Study conducted for the Department of Energy, Mines and Resources, Surveys and Mapping Branch under contract OSQ77-0013. Ottawa: Surveys and Mapping Branch, EMR.

6 1993. *Special Operating Agency.* Statement by J.H. O'Donnell.

CHAPTER TWO

Geodesy in Canada, and International and Interprovincial Boundaries

George Babbage and Allen C. Roberts

PART I   GEODESY IN CANADA*

Introduction

The word "geodesy" has Greek roots and means literally "to divide the earth." A normal dictionary definition would be "the applied science that deals with the determination of the size and shape of the Earth and its associated gravity field." To simplify the presentation in this chapter, geodesy has been divided into three specialties and two time periods: positioning, gravimetry, and physical geodesy (the determination of crustal movements and gravity variations), and the electronic era (1947–72) and the satellite era (1973–onwards).

Geodesy provides essential basic information for a host of technical and scientific endeavours that benefit Canada in an immediate, practical way. Geodesy answers the question "where am I?" The answer, with an emphasis on precision, is provided through the establishment and maintenance of a national network of geodetic reference stations, marked on the ground, whose positions and heights have been determined accurately. The positions are usually expressed in latitudes and longitudes, and the heights in metres or feet above mean sea level. All are expressed in a uniform, unique frame of reference commonly called a datum. These reference (control) stations on the ground can easily be identified and connected to by those seeking positional anchors for their work.

The national geodetic reference system therefore serves as a framework for such essential, practical activities as navigation, the mapping of the natural features and resources of Canada, and the planning and building of major engineering works such as hydroelectric dams, oil and gas pipelines, seaways, railways, and highways. In addition it greatly facilitates the determination of the various jurisdictional boundaries of Canada, ranging

---

* Part I of the chapter was contributed by George Babbage.

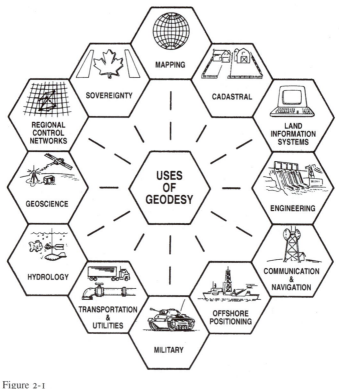

Figure 2-1
Uses of Geodesy.
Source: Geodetic Survey of Canada

from the International Boundary and the offshore limits for oil exploration and fishing to boundaries between individual private properties or land parcels.

The national geodetic reference system is also an essential foundation for numerous scientific endeavours. Currently the most demanding is the monitoring of the Earth's crustal movements, to enable geophysicists to improve their earthquake predictions and, consequently, provide the public with better forewarning of disaster. Figure 2-1 illustrates some of the many activities that depend on the geodetic reference system for an accurate, unique framework of position and height.

Through connections to the system the various sets of spatial data for a given area or project can be gathered on a common datum. Therefore these sets can easily be compared, superimposed, or dealt with in various combinations to suit particular information needs. This capability is vital today for computerized Geographical Information Systems, which feature the digitization and computer manipulation of numerous, large spatial data sets.

Apart from the positioning network there also exists a national network of gravity stations, which provides additional public benefits. A knowledge of gravity contributes greatly to our understanding of the composition of the Earth's crust, which is the repository of important commercial minerals, including oil and gas. Gravity measurements, combined with geodetic measurements of surface movements, also serve to improve the accuracy of earthquake predictions. There are also military interests. A knowledge of gravity is vital for estimating accurately the trajectories of ballistic missiles, and for refining the orbits of earth satellites.

Regarding the quantifiable benefits of geodetic systems, a research study by the University of Maine in 1984 estimated the ratio of benefits to cost to be, conservatively, in the range 1.7 to 4.5.[1]

Most pre–Second World War geodetic work was done in Canada by two organizations in the federal government: the Geodetic Survey of Canada, which was created in 1908 and is responsible for positioning horizontal and vertical control, and an organization known today as the Gravity Section of the Geological Survey of Canada, which is responsible for gravity data. A full and interesting account of Canadian geodetic activities prior to the end of the Second World War is available.[2,3]

By 1946 the national geodetic reference system consisted of a horizontal control network of about 19 400 km of triangulation, and a vertical control network of some 63 000 km of precise levelling. In addition numerous baselines and astronomic stations had been established (see figures 2-2 and 2-3). Only fair progress had been made by 1946 in the establishment of a national gravity network. This was due in part to the usual lack of money and personnel, but also to the necessity of having to make gravity measurements slowly and laboriously with pendulum-type gravimeters. After the Second World War the use of the new spring-type gravimeter would greatly increase productivity.

At the end of the war horizontal control was still being propagated by traditional triangulation in the form of cross-braced quadrilateral figures. Angles were being measured with precise, compact glass-circle theodolites that had replaced the original, ponderous silvered-circle instruments in the late 1920s and early 1930s. Sightings were being made to battery-powered electric target lamps, operated by timers, which had replaced acetylene lamps in 1921. Progress was still limited, however, by the frequent need to construct towers at observation stations so that intervisibility between stations could be achieved. This was done laboriously from lumber and local timber. Another enduring problem was the inability to measure long distances accurately, and the consequent need for time-consuming baselines and their extension networks. Later, electronics would solve this problem.

At this time the national levelling network was still being extended by precise levelling. The basic technique had not changed much since 1909. The instruments were a little different: the original U.S. Coast and Geodetic type levels had been replaced, starting in 1923, by more modern units of European design. The earlier wooden rods had been replaced in 1925 by rods of invar.

Geodetic computations were still laborious, although the introduction of mechanical calculators had lessened the drudgery. Logarithms were still not extinct. Great increases in computational speed and reductions in drudgery would have to await the coming of the electronic computer, still about ten years away.

In 1946 Canada was poised for an economic boom and for the taking of a huge inventory of its natural resources. For this inventory much of the 10 million km^2 of the country's land mass still had to be surveyed and mapped. In addition the bed of the offshore area, which was equivalent to some 38 percent of the land mass in area, had to be explored. The role of Canadian geodesy in meeting these and other important challenges will now be described.

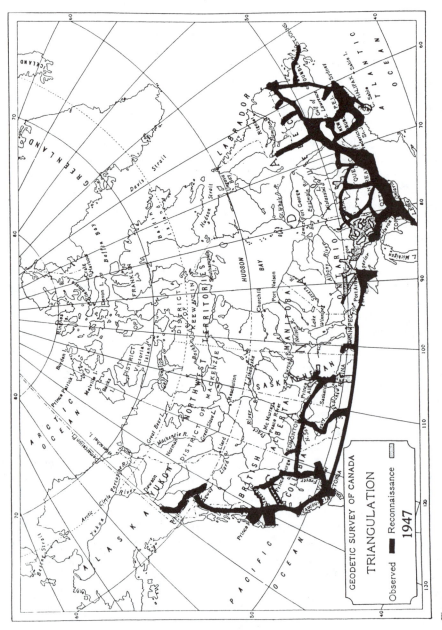

Figure 2-2
Status of triangulation, 1947.
Source: Geodetic Survey of Canada

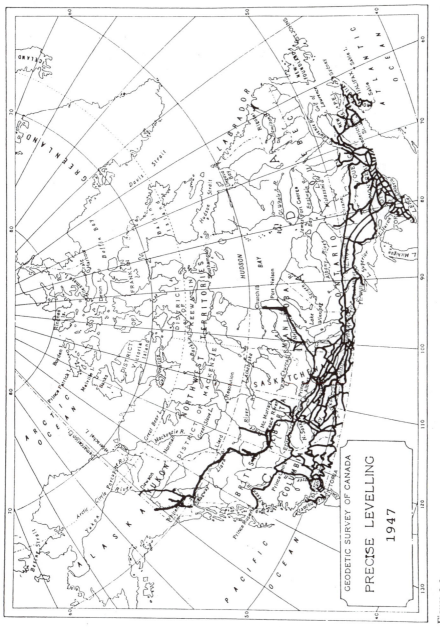

Figure 2-3
Status of precise levelling, 1947.
Source: Geodetic Survey of Canada

POSITIONING

Canadian geodesy was to be revolutionized by electronic developments during this period. Two inventions produced the main effects: the electronic distance measurer and the electronic computer. The former would be the answer to the field geodesist's prayer: it would allow long distances to be measured quickly, accurately, and economically. Its use, combined with that of the newly arrived helicopter, would greatly facilitate the extension of the national horizontal control network. The computer would greatly increase the accuracy and speed of computations, and provide welcome relief from numerical drudgery. It would also allow the introduction of more rigorous, mathematically correct methods of treating the observational data and of estimating their soundness through the use of mathematical statistics. These methods had been shelved hitherto in favour of semi-precise methods because of the enormous amount of computational labour involved. Some of the more important geodetic achievements made possible by electronic aids follow.

SHORAN (1947–57)

John Leslie Rannie succeeded Noel Ogilvie as dominion geodesist and head of Geodetic Survey in 1947. Coincident with Rannie's appointment there was a need to establish control in remote areas, particularly in the north. This was mainly for the new National Topographic Series (NTS) of 1:250 000 scale maps destined, eventually, to cover all of Canada. For this series the astronomic control methods used earlier were not accurate enough; a better solution had to be found.

Geodetic Survey's solution was Shoran (Short Range Aid to Navigation). This radar navigation system had been developed during the Second World War to improve bombing accuracy. In its military application a bomber was continually positioned, enroute to its target, by the continuous measuring by radar of its distance from two transponders on the ground. The proposed geodetic application was an extension of this. The Shoran aircraft would make a number of passes across the centre of the imaginary line between the two ground stations, measuring the left and right distances to them as it approached and crossed the line. The distance between the ground stations would then be calculated from the minimum sum of the pairs of distances recorded on each pass. When these measured lines are arranged to form a trilateration network (as in figure 2-4), a control system can be introduced across the terrain.

Development of the geodetic application of Shoran took place in 1947 and 1948. It was a joint effort by Geodetic Survey, the National Research Council, the Royal Canadian Air Force, and the Army Survey Establishment. By 1950 a Shoran control net some 1900 km long had been established successfully between existing triangulation stations in Manitoba and Saskatchewan.

During the next seven years, under the direction of J.E.R. Ross, who succeeded Rannie as dominion geodesist in 1951, the Shoran network was extended northwards across most of northern Canada up into the Arctic islands. Planning and logistical tasks were formidable because of the large scope of the operation, the wide dispersal of field units, the short field season (particularly in the Arctic islands), and the ever-variable and often inhospitable weather. A typical field season would feature two to four Lancaster line-crossing aircraft, which were modified Second World War bombers. Operating and maintenance bases were needed. So also were seven other aircraft helping to establish, supply, and withdraw some

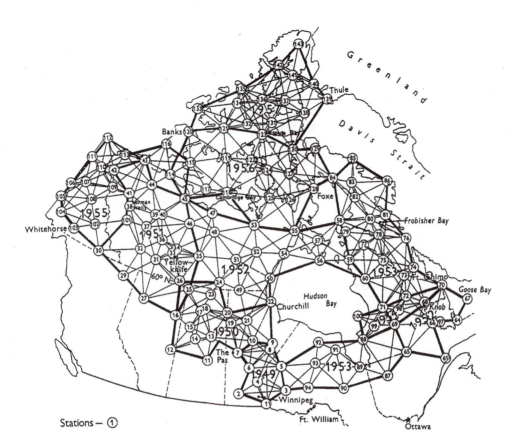

Figure 2-4
The Shoran Network.
Source: Geodetic Survey of Canada

ten three-person ground stations spaced some 400 km apart, and needing three to four tons of supplies each. Use would be made of virtually every other form of transport known in the North. The number of personnel per season varied from 75 in 1949 to some 280 in 1957. Most of these people were from the RCAF, and it is estimated that during the whole project some 1000 people came from that source.

Upon completion in 1957 the total Shoran network consisted of 501 measured lines (averaging 400 km in length) and 119 stations.[4] These stations were spread over some 6.5 million km² – roughly 65 percent of Canada's land mass. Generally, third-order survey accuracy standards were achieved where the network could be anchored by conventional triangulation stations, and fourth-order standards in areas far removed from such stations. (See appendix E under "Survey Accuracies" for an explanation of accuracy standards.) The Shoran achievements were a fitting tribute to the hard-working participants and to the leadership exhibited by Ross, who retired in 1957 and was succeeded by J.E. Lilly.

During the period 1947–57 good progress had been made elsewhere in extending the geodetic networks, in addition to the Shoran operation. About 7300 km had been added to

Figure 2-5
An early model Tellurometer in action. This portable electronic instrument enabled long distances to be measured easily and accurately for the first time.
Photo: Geodetic Survey of Canada

the conventional triangulation network, making the total some 26 700 km. Meanwhile about 13 000 km had been added to the precise levelling net to raise the total to some 76 000 km.

A very important scientific event occurred in October 1957, the launching of Sputnik. Few could foresee then the profound effect artificial earth satellites would have on the sciences, including geodesy.

THE ARRIVAL OF PRECISE ELECTROMAGNETIC DISTANCE MEASUREMENT (EDM)

Two important instruments arrived on the Canadian surveying scene in the early and mid-1950s. Named the Geodimeter and the Tellurometer, they were destined to revolutionize field operations because both were portable and capable of measuring long distances quickly and accurately. The Geodimeter, invented by Dr Bergstrand of Sweden, used light waves for this purpose, while the Tellurometer (figure 2-5), invented by Dr Wadley of South Africa, employed microwaves.

The principle of EDM is as follows. A modulated beam of light or microwaves, the frequency of which is known accurately, is emitted from one end of the line to be measured. The beam is returned back from the other end, and the phase difference of the returning modulation is recorded. The total double-distance measurement therefore comprises a fixed number of multiples of the modulation wavelength, together with the fraction of the wavelength that corresponds to the recorded phase difference outgoing and returning.. The number of full wavelengths and the fraction can be determined from measures of the phase differences on other frequencies. The fraction is measured by passing a sample of the transmitted modulation through a delay line and measuring the amount of phase change required to complete a full wavelength. Since the speed of transmission of the beam is known, the length of the line can be calculated.

The Geodimeter Model 2 was first used by Geodetic Survey in 1956 to measure triangulation baselines. Baseline lengths had hitherto been measured laboriously using invar tapes, and the savings in time and effort now made possible by EDM were substantial. In 1958 the Tellurometer made its geodetic debut in Canada. Because this instrument had a long range, the triangulation sides could be measured directly and the need for special baselines disappeared. Furthermore the design of the triangulation networks, normally in the form of chains of cross-braced quadrilaterals, could now be simplified to single chains of abutting triangles. This speeded up the work without loss of accuracy. Productivity increased further in 1959 when Geodetic Survey started using portable, steel Bilby towers. In 1959 a triangulation milestone was reached with the completion of work in Manitoba: Canada now had a continuous coast-to-coast triangulation network.

Even though the use of EDM proved very advantageous in first-order work, the benefits were even greater in second- and lower-order operations because the simplest method of propagating field control, traversing, could now be conducted speedily and accurately. Theodolite-Geodimeter traversing rapidly became the most cost-effective method of providing accurate control in urban areas, while the theodolite-Tellurometer combination excelled on longer lines in wilderness areas, especially when helicopters were used.

Although EDM was a great boon it also brought some bad news. It revealed that the scale of the older geodetic triangulation nets, which were dependent on short invar baselines, was much weaker than had been supposed. Accordingly Geodetic Survey set about strengthening these older nets by measuring selected sides with the new EDM instruments, a process known as "scale control."

By 1963 triangulation consisting of a chain of single, abutting triangles of which all angles and sides were measured had largely replaced the original system of cross-braced quadrilaterals. This change was induced by the relative ease with which high-accuracy Geodimeter and Tellurometer measurements could be made. This form of triangulation featured prominently in the most northerly first-order triangulation ever conducted in Canada. This was a net from Yellowknife to Coppermine, and thence Cambridge Bay and Fort Reliance. This was established under the able direction of A.D. Selley between 1961 and 1964.

Those who laboured on geodetic computations also had their turn to benefit from electronics. An IBM 650 electronic computer at the University of Ottawa was used for the first time in 1957 to process geodetic data. By 1961 H. Klinkenberg and J. Wickens had developed the first comprehensive Canadian computer program for this purpose, called GROOM, which greatly reduced the drudgery inherent in geodetic computations. GROOM was followed in 1969 by GALS, a sophisticated program designed by C.D. McLellan, A.E. Peterson, and G. Katinas. GALS was capable of adjusting horizontal control networks of triangulation, traversing, or trilateration, or any combination of these. It also enabled geodesists to design and test networks "on paper" in advance of fieldwork, thereby improving operational efficiency. Like its predecessor GROOM, GALS was also used extensively outside Geodetic

Survey, both in Canada and abroad. The principle of survey adjustments is covered in appendix E under "Least Squares."

AERODIST (1962–73)

Aerodist is the airborne version of the Tellurometer. The method of measurement is similar to Shoran. A "master" Tellurometer-type microwave transmitter-receiver is mounted in an aircraft, which is flown across a line joining two ground stations occupied by transponders. A carrier wave is emitted from the master unit during flight and is returned by these transponders, resulting in continuous recording of the ranges from the aircraft to the ground stations. As for Shoran, a minimum-sum distance is obtained for each crossing. Repeated crossings are made to improve the accuracy by averaging. From these minimum-sum determinations the chord distance can be computed, given associated meteorological data and the heights of the aircraft and ground stations. For most Canadian operations the lines were arranged in networks in the form of cross-braced quadrilaterals.

The first Aerodist equipment in Canada was acquired by Topographical Survey, Geodetic Survey's sister organization, in 1962. (Just prior to this an airborne Tellurometer system had been devised and tested in 1961 by P. Atkinson of Topographical Survey with assistance from the National Research Council, but it was never fully developed.) This new equipment was put to immediate use that year to establish a second-order trilateration net along the southern and western shores of James Bay and Hudson Bay. The success of this initial project, despite numerous teething problems, encouraged development of the system for the production of more accurate primary geodetic control. In 1963 further testing showed that this was indeed feasible.

Aerodist proved its geodetic capability in 1965 when Geodetic Survey and Topographical Survey joined forces to establish a primary network across Hudson Strait between northern Québec and Baffin Island, and across the mouth of Hudson Bay from northern Québec to Southampton Island. In 1968 the field, computations, and field records staff of Topographical Survey were transferred to Geodetic Survey, which now assumed the additional responsibility of supplying control for the 1:50 000 NTS mapping programme. Aerodist operations continued in Geodetic Survey until 1973, by which time the original equipment was showing its age and its eventual replacement, the new satellite Doppler positioning system (TRANSIT), was already demonstrating great potential.

During the period 1962–73 the Aerodist system had established some 219 primary stations, with an average spacing of about 100 km, over some 2.6 million km^2 or about 26 percent of the total land area of Canada (see figure 2-6). Moreover most of this control had been established in inhospitable areas of muskeg, wooded swamps, and the like that had hitherto defied conventional methods of surveying. In addition Aerodist had provided in-flight positioning for many thousands of kilometres of aerial photography. The general accuracy of the Aerodist stations was high second-order, and the cost per station much less than with Shoran.

GEODETIC CONTROL SURVEYS IN URBAN AREAS

Geodetic Survey's first activities in urban areas occurred in the 1910s, when it occasionally assisted municipalities by conducting triangulation and levelling needed for the production of city maps and plans. It provided professional staff and equipment, and the municipalities paid for materials and labour.

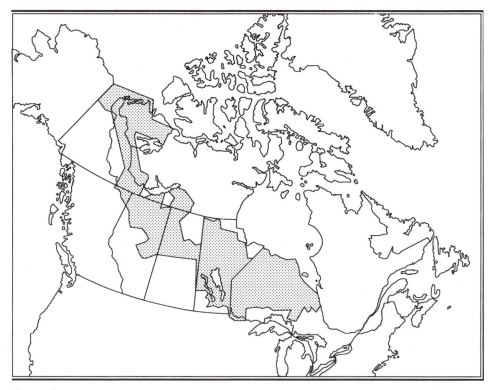

Figure 2-6
The Aerodist Network.
Source: Geodetic Survey of Canada

Urban involvement remained minimal until about 1961, when the Geodetic Survey commenced a long-term programme of establishing horizontal and vertical control in municipalities. This programme, which commenced with work in Metropolitan Toronto that year, continued until 1970. During this period first-order control was established in some thirty municipalities. This work provided the basic "anchors" of position and height for part of a large programme of second- and third-order surveys to increase the density of control. These were conducted by Topographical Survey in more than fifty municipalities during the same period. This work of densification would be continued by provincial and municipal surveying and mapping agencies, as they developed expertise and obtained funding. Today this control work is the foundation of many urban geographic information systems.

LEVELLING OPERATIONS (1947–72)
There were many notable events in precise levelling during the early and middle 1950s. In 1953 special fieldwork was done in Ontario and Québec to accommodate the needs of the then new St Lawrence Seaway Project. This was accompanied by parallel actions by the U.S. Coast and Geodetic Survey in the state of New York. Special levelling was done in 1955 to complete a more accurate connection between Pointe-au-Père, Québec, and Kingston,

Ontario. It was the culmination of work started in 1945. All this work, together with other re-levellings done by Canada and the U.S. around the Great Lakes, formed the basis for a special datum declared by both nations in 1955 and named the International Great Lakes Datum (IGLD). The main purpose of this datum was to improve consistency in monitoring post-glacial rebound in the Great Lakes area, and to facilitate the construction and regulation of various water works. For these reasons a dynamic height system was adopted instead of the usual geodetic system of orthometric heights. The dynamic system better reflected the effects of small but important gravitational variations that might influence water levels and flow.

Because of its very nature, precise levelling fieldwork is slow to benefit from new technology. Moreover during the electronic era referred to here, few benefits attributable to electronics were realized in levelling. A great improvement in the ease with which level sightings could be made came about, however, with the introduction of the automatic level in 1955. In this type of level the line of sight is kept horizontal automatically by a special mechanical compensator, usually in the form of a freely suspended prism mounted in the telescope. The need to keep the line of sight level by constant reference to a conventional bubble tube is dispensed with. This type of instrument became popular immediately despite some initial problems. It was as accurate as the normal spirit levels then in use, and setups and rod sightings could be made much more quickly and with less strain. The pace of precise levelling work is, however, dictated more by how quickly the rods can be moved than by rapid setups and readings of instruments. Therefore the daily rate of advance in most production work did not increase substantially.

After the Second World War new precise levelling lines were to follow the developing highways of the nation, away from the relatively unchanging railways. Canada's first national highway, the Trans-Canada Highway joining St John's and Victoria, was opened in 1963. By 1971 a second transcontinental precise level line of some 6400 km had been completed along this highway. Comparison with the transcontinental railway level line of 1916 revealed a difference of about 1.5 metres. This was a disappointing result and to date, despite much head scratching, no satisfactory explanation has been found. The U.S. National Geodetic Survey (USNGS) experienced a similar result but it, too, is none the wiser.

Levelling operations took a novel turn in 1972. A level line was started along the banks of the Mackenzie River northerly from Great Slave Lake. The normal techniques of precise levelling, designed to follow fairly smooth and level roads and railways, now had to be adapted to the rugged terrain of the Mackenzie Valley. This was accomplished very successfully, and during the next four summer seasons the line was extended some 1200 km down the Mackenzie to reach Arctic Red River in 1976. This was a notable achievement and marked the first time that Canadian geodetic levelling had been extended north of the Arctic Circle.

CONTROL SURVEY ACCURACY SPECIFICATIONS

Since its founding Geodetic Survey had followed international accuracy standards in establishing its first-order control networks. There were in Canada, however, no generally accepted standards, international or national, for second- and lower-order control surveys. In the 1950s it became clear that control survey activity by various federal and provincial agencies was increasing significantly, and that the adoption of national standards would be of general benefit. Accordingly, in 1961, the Surveys and Mapping Branch (SMB) of the federal Department of Mines and Technical Surveys issued Canada's first comprehensive set of accuracy specifications for its use. These were the work of an SMB committee headed by Lilly as dominion geodesist, and were adopted immediately by the SMB. Many other surveying and mapping organizations followed suit, thereby making these specifications de facto national guidelines for the next twelve years.

GRAVIMETRY (1947–72)

In Canada, unlike most other countries, gravity measurements were not made in the Geodetic Survey. Originally they were the responsibility of the Observatories Branch of Energy, Mines and Resources. In 1970 the astronomic duties of the Observatories Branch were transferred to the National Research Council, and the remaining facility was renamed the Earth Physics Branch. In a government reorganization in 1986 the Observatories Branch was dissolved, and the responsibility for gravity was passed to the Geophysics Division of the Geological Survey.

In the period 1947–72, referred to in this chapter as the electronic era, there was a huge increase in the pace with which gravity measurements were made. However, little of this increase could be attributed to electronics. It stemmed principally from the further development and greater use of the portable, spring-type gravimeter first introduced in 1944. This device resembles a spring balance so constructed that any small change in gravity will induce a relatively large movement in the sensing mass. It interpolates gravity, and an observation can be made within minutes. It must be calibrated frequently against a known gravity difference to provide a gravity conversion factor for the spring movement, and to minimize the effects of changes in spring characteristics.

Some 10 000 gravity observations had been made by 1951 with an average spacing of 50 to 80 km. Of these some 1500 were on the Canadian Shield. By 1956 annual production was averaging about 1100, and the total had increased to 15 000. Spacing varied between 15 and 50 km. The programme was made more systematic in 1957, and dovetailed with the NTS 1:250 000 mapping programme being conducted by the SMB. Spacing was reduced to a maximum of 15 km. Beginning in 1958 there were good gains in productivity, particularly in remote areas, through the greater use of fixed-wing aircraft equipped with floats. This productivity received a substantial additional boost in 1960 with the introduction of helicopters.

By the late 1950s the increasing delays in the processing of the flood of field data became a matter of concern. Fortuitously the electronic computer had just appeared on the scene and by 1962 computer programs had been developed in the Observatories Branch and were reducing the computational backlog.

During the period 1958–67 there was extensive coverage of the Canadian Shield and of the Arctic islands and seas. Arctic coverage was facilitated through logistics support provided by the Polar Continental Shelf Project (PCSP). This special unit was created in 1958 within the then Department of Mines and Technical Surveys to promote and coordinate scientific research in the far north. It also helped, by "showing the flag," to strengthen Canada's claims to sovereignty in the Arctic. During the next thirty years it would support over 3000 northern research projects.

At the heart of these gains in productivity was the LaCoste-Romberg gravimeter, introduced in 1960. This remarkably versatile instrument, notable for its excellent range and low drift rate, became a reliable and very adaptable workhorse in gravity work. It was used not only on land but, with suitable modifications, also for ice-surface and underwater measurements that commenced in 1961. It is still in use today.

The flood of data that resulted from the introduction of the gravimeter in 1944 focused attention on the need for calibration lines, and a national network of base stations. These would help ensure that measurements would be made consistently, and would be correlated properly through a common datum. The first gravimeter calibration line was established in 1950 between Prescott, Ontario, and Maniwaki, Québec. In 1954 it was extended to Senneterre, Québec, and by 1955 to Washington, D.C. Mainly to meet a need that arose from the subsequent widespread use of long-range gravimeters, which were introduced in the early 1960s, other longer lines were established later.

The first network of base stations was established in Ontario and Québec during 1951. From this start the network would be expanded nationwide, eventually to form the Canadian Gravity Standardization Network (CGSN) comprising some 3400 control stations. Twenty stations of the CGSN would be tied securely to the International Gravity Standardization Net in 1971, thereby making Canadian gravity values much more useful for international studies in geodesy and geophysics. The official adoption of the net by the International Union of Geodesy and Geophysics (IUGG) in 1971 was in no small measure due to the efforts of J.G. Tanner and R.K. McConnell of the Observatories Branch.

As mentioned above, gravity measurements were confined in Canada initially to the land mass. They were then extended to cover ice-surface and underwater work in accordance with demand, and as suitable instrumentation and methods of operation could be devised to meet these new challenges. Another important step was taken in 1964 in this process of extension when a programme of sea-surface gravity measurements was initiated by the Atlantic Geoscience Centre at Dartmouth, Nova Scotia. In this technique the gravimeter has to be mounted on a special gyro-stabilized platform designed to minimize the effects of the ship's motion on the gravity readings. The platform provided for testing was one salvaged from the ill-fated Avro Arrow jet interceptor project, the cancellation of which by the government in 1959 caused a national furore. Some 4800 observations were made in 1964. During the next eighteen years some 295 000 sea-surface measurements would be made in this programme alone, a major contribution to Canadian knowledge of gravity off the eastern and Arctic seaboards.

Unacceptable errors can be introduced into geodetic precise levelling lines when they pass over mountainous or rolling terrain, if gravity measurements are not made at bench-marks between which large differences of height exist. Accordingly at the request of Geodetic Survey the Observatories Branch commenced a joint programme of making gravity measurements at such marks in 1964. Between 1964 and 1970 some 3400 measurements were made and added to the National Gravity Data Base (NGDB).

In 1967 and 1969 gravimetry took a novel turn when expeditions to the North Pole were mounted, with strong logistic support provided by the PCSP. One of the aims of these expeditions was to develop techniques for using sea ice as a floating, moving platform for geophysical measurements. Both expeditions provided the participants with good, practical experience in the conduct of scientific investigations in polar regions that would pay dividends in future years.

In the late 1960s the flood of gravity data, coupled with rapid advances made in computational, storage, and access devices, dictated a major revamping of gravity data processing methods. By 1970 a new system designated POGO (Processing of Gravity Observations) had been designed and was operational.

PHYSICAL GEODESY

The period 1964–67 saw Geodetic Survey placing emphasis on special high-accuracy surveys to monitor earth crustal movements. Formerly this type of work had been carried out intermittently, as resources could be spared from the main tasks of extending and maintaining the primary geodetic networks of the country. This emphasis stemmed from a need to assist geophysicists in predicting earthquakes and tremors, thereby helping to reduce future loss of life and property damage.

A small, special network to measure horizontal earth movement was remeasured near Québec City in 1964, the original measurements having been made in 1926, but no appreciable changes could be detected. In 1965 a special network was established to monitor possible relative movement between opposite shores of the St Lawrence River, between Québec City and Tadoussac. This movement was suspected from earlier seismo-logical observations. A similar network was established the same year across the Strait of Georgia in British Columbia, and in 1967 a ten-station network was established across Robeson Channel, between northern Ellesmere Island and Greenland.

Some interest had already been generated in the 1950s regarding vertical movements in the Great Lakes area, as described above. Further interest was stimulated by the accidental discovery in 1962, from records of re-levelling done near the Saguenay River, that move-ments were occurring in the Lac St Jean area of Québec. In addition to these vertical movements from natural causes, there was concern about movements induced, unnaturally, by the huge weight of water trapped when large dams were built. Between 1959 and 1964, in response to concerns expressed by provincial hydro authorities in Saskatchewan, Québec, and British Columbia, Geodetic Survey established special level lines in the vicinity of three new dams then under construction. These were the Gardner Dam on the South Saskatchewan River, Manicouagan V on the Manicouagan River in Québec, and the Bennett Dam on the Peace River in British Columbia. A similar level line was established in 1970 near the Mica Dam on the Columbia River in British Columbia. The purpose of these lines was to determine how much the earth's crust would be deformed by hydraulic loading. In general, subsequent re-levelling of all these lines showed significant crustal deformation under the initial loadings, with some rebound later as the crust accommodated this unfa-miliar burden. However none of these movements was considered large enough to be dangerous.

The Satellite Era (1973 Onwards)

POSITIONING

The successful launching of the Soviet Union's Sputnik in October 1957 was a notable technological achievement and a spectacular news item. It was also an historic event, marking the beginning of the Space Age. Media attention focused initially on the Cold War military ramifications and superpower pride and rivalry. After the furore had died down the scientific applications became more apparent. In the early 1960s there was a rapidly growing awareness among geodesists of the very substantial advantages offered by satellites, particularly in geodetic positioning. However a readily available, practical means to bring this about was lacking. The solution arrived in 1963 in the form of the U.S. Navy Navigation Satellite System, called TRANSIT. Designed initially for military navigation purposes, it was in 1967 made available for civilian use and appeared to be readily adaptable for geodetic positioning.

The system originally featured five satellites, to which a sixth was added in 1975. They followed nearly circular polar orbits at an altitude of about 1100 km and with a period of about 107 minutes. The method of observation consisted of recording the Doppler shift (the apparent change in frequency of the radio signal emitted by the satellite) as it passed overhead. The rate of change of this shift is a function of the receiver's distance from the satellite. Since the satellite's position is known at all times from independent tracking at known locations, the receiver's position can be determined from multiple Doppler shift measurements to the satellite and its companions.

Interest in TRANSIT was high in Canada, particularly because of offshore positioning needs, and because there were still large gaps in the control coverage on land in remote areas. Starting with the pioneering work of Shell Canada (A. Hittel) and the Bedford Institute of Oceanography (D. Wells), development proceeded steadily. In 1972 H.E. Jones of the Geodetic Survey and E. Krakiwsky of the University of New Brunswick collaborated in field tests that demonstrated that first-order geodetic horizontal control accuracies could be achieved. Accordingly in 1973 Geodetic Survey adopted satellite Doppler methods officially for that purpose. It proceeded immediately to establish a fundamental first-order national framework of 196 Doppler stations spaced some 300 to 500 km apart. These stations were planned as anchors for the proposed North American Datum 1983 (NAD83) project, and also to serve as the basis for a Doppler densification programme designed to cover Canada with stations about 80 km apart.

Satellite positioning methods characteristically produce a flood of data that must be gathered, vetted, and processed systematically, accurately, and quickly. (In one early test supervised by Krakiwsky, which featured seven receivers, paper-tape recording, and observations spread over a few days, a total of 60 000 feet or 11.4 miles of punched tape was needed to record the data!) A number of sophisticated computer programs were designed to treat the flood of Doppler data. Of these the Canadian programs GEODOP (J. Kouba) and GDLSAT (A. Peterson) became very popular and were eventually used around the world.

As expected, Doppler positioning methods took hold very rapidly in Canada, not only for first-order work but for a host of other control requirements. By 1981 first-order stations alone numbered more than 800. There were also many hundreds of lower-order stations that had been established for mapping, resource exploration and development, and numerous other purposes by federal and provincial surveying and mapping agencies, and by private industry. Industry was always in the forefront of Canadian Doppler development.

In the meantime control propagation by conventional methods continued. The flexibility afforded by EDM encouraged the use of traversing and trilateration in addition to triangulation, as the terrain dictated. Productivity increased with the adoption in 1975 of a new, portable, lightweight tower invented by F. Lambert, Canada's International Boundary Commissioner. However, satellite Doppler methods developed quickly and became so cost-effective that in 1977 Geodetic Survey decided to discontinue the use of conventional methods for propagating first-order horizontal control, except in urban areas. In these areas the spacing of stations was relatively dense, and the required relative accuracy could still be achieved by conventional means.[5]

Figure 2-7
A typical satellite Doppler station in northern Canada.
Photo: Geodetic Survey of Canada

By 1977 satellite Doppler, and the new Inertial Survey System (ISS) described below, were becoming a very useful combination. The first was capable of supplying on-the-spot framework control quickly when needed, and the second of densifying between this control as appropriate. This enabled Geodetic Survey to be much more flexible and prompt in responding to control requests.

In about 1980 a promising new satellite navigation system being developed by the U.S. Department of Defense had begun to attract the attention of geodesists. Called the Global Positioning System (GPS), it showed immense potential for rapid, highly accurate geodetic positioning. GPS (also known as NAVSTAR for Navigation Satellite Timing And Ranging) was intended as a replacement for TRANSIT, and superficially is similar in principle – orbiting satellites emitting signals and modulated information on their whereabouts, for reception by ground receivers. However the details are different. The GPS constellation, only recently completed, consists of twenty-one satellites and three active spares circulating in near-circular orbits about 20 000 km above the Earth. These satellites are distributed in three orbital planes at sixty-degree inclinations to the equator, so that at least four are available at all times to provide a position fix. Each receives and stores information from special controlling ground stations, carries very accurate atomic clocks, and emits signals on two carrier frequencies intended for ground receivers. Code and satellite messages are superimposed on these frequencies by modulation. Distances or ranges between satellites and receivers are derived either by measuring the travel time of the coded signal, or by measuring the phase of the signal received in a manner similar to EDM determinations. The position of the receiver is determined at the intersection of the ranges. To obtain geodetic accuracies differential observing techniques must be employed. A very comprehensible explanation of GPS for the uninitiated is given in Geodetic Survey's *GPS Positioning Guide*.[6]

Tests of special American-built GPS receivers were being undertaken in Canada by 1983. These tests produced excellent results despite the fact that only a few of the planned twenty-one GPS satellites were then in orbit. Software development was proceeding in parallel with this testing in government, universities, and private industry. One commercial surveying company had even managed successfully to perform a number of practical tasks using the embryonic system. The days of satellite Doppler control were clearly numbered. The last major use of Doppler by Geodetic Survey occurred in 1985, when some fifty-eight stations were established in British Columbia and the Northwest Territories for the purpose of first-order densification. The best Doppler accuracies were about 50 cm for position and 70 cm for spheroidal heighting. The cost per station was about 25 percent of that of Aerodist, and some 50 percent of that of conventional triangulation.

The year 1985 also marked the end of first-order field astronomy in Geodetic Survey when the contribution of stations measuring deflection (of the plumb-line) to the refinement of the geoid was judged to be not worth the high cost: the funds could be better spent on acquiring gravity data. Laplace observations had virtually ceased earlier, after the extra stations needed to strengthen conventional networks had been installed. This strengthening was needed for the conversion to the NAD83.

By 1984 GPS was being used for a variety of positioning tasks on land, at sea, and in the air. The accuracy and speed of positioning were improving rapidly due to research efforts. First-order GPS stations were established for the first time in 1985 by Geodetic Survey in southern Ontario in order to strengthen existing networks.

The concept of the Active Control System (ACS) was advanced in Geodetic Survey during 1985, principally by R. Steeves. This concept envisaged the establishment of a national network consisting of widely separated, accurately positioned tracking stations. These stations would record continuously and automatically the passes of GPS satellites, and transmit these data to a central processing facility. The objectives of ACS were to monitor the integrity of the GPS orbits, to improve the accuracy of orbit predictions, to serve as control and calibration sites for GPS users, and to distribute differential corrections to these users . A favourable "proof of concept" study was made that year. The equipment for a prototype station had been assembled by 1987 and was functioning well. Although much more development work remained, the feasibility of the system was no longer in question.

During 1986 and 1987 Canadian use of GPS increased greatly, even though few satellites were available and observing periods were limited. Geodetic Survey's output alone exceeded 400 stations. Virtually all federal and provincial surveying and mapping agencies were either experimenting or doing practical work with the system. Four universities were engaged in research and development, and many of the leading commercial surveying firms were routinely providing GPS control, both in Canada and overseas.

Some of the tasks performed by governments and private industry using GPS included control to densify the first-order network, the positioning of hydrographic launches, general mapping control, control to position islands in Hudson Bay, multipurpose control along main highways in the Yukon and Northwest Territories, and control to monitor tectonic plate movements on the west coast. GPS was running rampant, and for good reason. Despite the limitations imposed by a lack of satellites, its cost-effectiveness was already impressive and expected to increase greatly with further development.

Canadian expertise in GPS became even more evident in 1986. At the Fourth International Symposium on Satellite Positioning held at Austin, Texas, no fewer than ten Canadian papers on GPS were delivered. That year also featured the publication of *The Guide to GPS Positioning*, a 600-page book co-authored by eleven Canadian experts under the leadership of Wells of the University of New Brunswick, which dealt with all aspects of the subject.[7]

Early in 1987 Geodetic Survey established a GPS station at Yellowknife as part of an international network. Data from this station contributed to improvements in predictions of system orbits. Later in 1987 Geodetic Survey started a ten-year campaign of making measurements with GPS at selected benchmarks of the first-order levelling network. There were three objectives: to make control more accessible to users, to refine the geoid (see Physical Geodesy below), and to monitor systematic levelling errors. By the end of 1993 some 2000 measurements had been made.

The GOTEX project in 1988 provided Geodetic Survey and the provinces with the opportunity to conduct a joint GPS observing campaign. The aim of this international project was to improve knowledge of the orbits of GPS satellites by means of a series of coordinated, systematic, high-accuracy observations at selected stations around the world. Canada's contribution of twenty-eight stations, spread across the country, helped significantly to improve the utility of the system. In addition these Canadian stations became eligible for future incorporation in the Canadian ACS project, still undergoing development.

A report delivered in 1989 by a leading consulting firm, charged with determining the cost-effectiveness of the ACS project, recommended that the system be implemented in stages in close cooperation with the provinces and private industry. This is now being done and, to help bring it about, a special working group named Team ACS (TACS) was formed in 1990, with representatives from federal and provincial governments and industry. By the end of 1993 seven prototype automated tracking stations were operating. Called Active Control Points (ACPs), they are located at St John's, Algonquin Park, Churchill, Yellowknife, Penticton, Victoria, and Holberg, British Columbia. Each ACP is equipped with a high-precision, dual-frequency GPS receiver and an atomic clock, and there is continuous recording of carrier phase and pseudo-range measurements to all GPS satellites in view. These and other data are transmitted daily, by phone or satellite, to a central data processing facility in Ottawa. There they are analysed and validated to check GPS performance before being made available to GPS users.

The ACS provides two main benefits to Canadian GPS users. First, the ACP tracking data is fed back into GPS to produce better determinations of satellite orbits, particularly over Canada. This improves the accuracy with which GPS positioning can be done. Second, the differential corrections derived from ACP data enable users to save time and improve accuracy when establishing GPS project control in regions around ACPs. Another ACP function is to detect and inform users about Selective Availability (SA). SA is a quaint euphemism for a process whereby GPS signals are deliberately upset, by the U.S. authorities, to deny full GPS accuracy to unauthorized users. ACP data are also provided to the International GPS Service for Geodynamics. Thereby valuable information is contributed to worldwide studies of Earth movements, polar motion, and other geodynamic phenomena.

In 1992 a use was made of GPS not anticipated by its designers – the determination of the height of Canada's highest mountain, Mount Logan. GPS receivers were backpacked to the summit by a fifteen-person expedition headed by M. Schmidt of the Geological Survey of Canada. The expedition was a partnership between the Royal Geographical Society of Canada, Geological Survey, Geodetic Survey, and the National Parks Service. Despite numerous hardships the expedition was able to make measurements on 6 and 8 June. The result was a new official height of 5959 m (19550 ft) above mean sea level. The previous official value was 5951 m.[8]

One of the geodetic highlights of 1993 was the completion of the full GPS constellation of twenty-one satellites and three active spares. This means that a position fix can now be made at any time, anywhere on Earth, regardless of weather – the geodesist's and navigator's dream come true. The full impact of GPS on geodesy and surveying becomes clearer when its performance is compared with that of its predecessor, satellite Doppler. The most accurate Doppler position fixes attained an accuracy of about 50 cm. This required measurements to be spread over at least forty-eight hours (sometimes twice that), made with equipment costing some $40,000. By comparison, in 1993, GPS relative position fixes good to 2 cm or better could be made routinely, well within an hour, using equipment costing about $10,000 (in depreciated dollars). Fixes of lesser accuracy can be made within a few minutes. Alternatively, millimetre accuracies are possible with special effort over longer periods.

The usefulness of GPS is spreading well beyond the domain of geodesy. For those users who do not need high accuracy, such as forest rangers, fishermen, and prospectors, small hand-held GPS receivers are now available for less than $300. These are capable of providing, almost instantaneously, fixes good to about 100 metres. Towards the end of 1993 a number of leading automobile manufacturers in Japan and the United States announced that GPS receivers would soon be offered as optional extras in their cars.

SECONDARY CONTROL

As mentioned earlier, Geodetic Survey assumed an additional responsibility in 1968 when the field, computations, and field records staff of Topographical Survey were transferred to the division. The main responsibility was to supply control for the NTS 1:50 000 scale mapping programme. Other implicit responsibilities attended the transfer, such as providing the Yukon and Northwest Territories with the secondary control needed to facilitate resource exploration and general development, and meeting the various miscellaneous secondary control requirements of other federal government departments. As a consequence Geodetic Survey's secondary control fieldwork has featured a wide variety of methods, equipment, and transportation. These methods have included EDM traversing, Aerodist, satellite Doppler, astronomical determinations, spirit levelling, altimetry, trigonometric levelling, heights by Ground Elevation Meter (GEM), inertial systems (elaborated upon below), and finally GPS. Unlike the first-order geodetic field operations, which generally follow set procedures, secondary work requires a great deal of flexibility in planning and execution.

Geodetic Survey made one of the most expensive capital purchases in its history when it bought a Litton Autosurveyor in 1975. This equipment was an aircraft inertial navigation system that had been adapted to surveying. The main reason for the purchase was to improve the cost-effectiveness of providing ground control for the 1:50 000 scale mapping programme. Later it would prove very useful to the provinces in meeting their local requirements for multipurpose control.

An intriguing and unique aspect of inertial positioning is that the accuracy is independent of atmospheric conditions. Virtually all other systems of geodetic positioning – even the latest satellite systems – are limited in their accuracy by how well tropospheric refraction can be determined.

In lay terms the working principles of geodetic positioning by the inertial method are as follows. Consider a platform, mounted on gimbals, that can be levelled and oriented by gyroscopes and, during transportation, can be kept level and pointed in the same direction by these gyroscopes. Accelerometers are attached to the platform and are capable of measuring accelerations, during transportation, in each of the three main directions: north-south, east-west, and up-down. While the platform is being transported these accelerations are recorded and transmitted every sixteen milliseconds to an onboard computer where they are integrated (summed) to produce the corresponding velocities in the three main directions. These velocities are, in turn, integrated to produce the corresponding distances travelled in each of the main directions. Therefore as the system is moved from point to point, the differences of position and height between these points are determined.

Geodetic's system became known as the ISS, and after testing was used for some production work in 1975, being mounted in a motor vehicle. Helicopter-mounting proved necessary for maximum effectiveness, however, and this form of transport was used almost exclusively thereafter. To minimize the accumulation of certain inherent systematic errors when operating ISS, it is necessary for the helicopter to proceed in a series of hops, landing about every four minutes to carry out a "zero velocity and alignment update" (ZUPT). Fortuitously the 10 km (6-mile) distance traversed by the helicopter during a hop would match the spacing necessary for 1:50 000 mapping control. This distance, a township width in the Prairie provinces, also satisfied the control needs of these provinces for their own multipurpose control and resource mapping programmes.

Accordingly, starting in 1976, many joint projects were undertaken by Geodetic Survey and the surveying and mapping agencies of Manitoba, Saskatchewan, and Alberta. These projects shared the necessary labour. The provinces attended to the preparation, monumentation, targeting, and photo-identification of control stations, while Geodetic Survey made the ISS measurements and undertook the computations. During the period 1976–86 about 10 000 stations were established in this cooperative and very cost-effective manner across the townships of the Prairie provinces.

Generally the ISS control was established along helicopter-flown traverse lines that conformed to the prairie township pattern and were arranged in the form of rectangular grids with 10 km spacing. All lines were flown in the forward and reverse directions to minimize systematic errors. Because the ISS is an interpolator, it must work between fixed "anchor" points. In the work on the prairies these anchors were about 80 km apart and consisted of both first-order Doppler satellite stations (established in advance for the purpose) and older existing first-order geodetic control stations.

New ISS units (Litton LASS II) were purchased in 1984 to replace the well-worn originals bought nine years earlier. One unit was purchased by Geodetic Survey and another by the Mapping and Charting Establishment (MCE) of the Department of National Defence. By agreement these units were loaned to the other organization as the need arose. This was just as well, since neither unit was very reliable initially.

The ISS proved to be very versatile.[9] Apart from the prairie grid control it provided mapping control for numerous federal projects, multipurpose control along the main highways in the Yukon and Northwest Territories, and control for gravimetry. One unusual task featured three-dimensional control on the Columbia Icefield to aid researchers in determining the rates of ice creep and melt.

The ISS lived a charmed life, surviving many serious helicopter crashes and a number of minor mishaps. The worst of these crashes occurred in October 1979 near Jenpeg, Manitoba. On returning from a mission the helicopter snapped a tail rotor coupling and plunged into the Nelson River. The field officer, M. Strutt, and pilot J. Ryan were able to swim to an island nearby, and waited for four hours in below-freezing temperatures before being rescued. After the helicopter was salvaged a few days later, the ISS unit was removed, sprayed with distilled water, and dried. After some electronic boards were replaced it was made to function again. It was returned to the factory later for a complete inspection and repair. But the best was yet to come. ISS units survived a serious crash in Alberta in 1983, crashes in Saskatchewan and the Yukon in 1984, and, in 1985, two more in Québec. Miraculously no personnel were killed or seriously injured in these accidents, but many helicopters had to be replaced.

Most of the prairie grid work had been completed by the end of 1985. Geodetic Survey was then emphasizing the refinement of the geoid so as to realize the full potential of the new, rapidly developing GPS for providing accurate heights as well as positions. Furthermore there were still large gaps in the basic gravity coverage, mainly in the Western Cordillera. For these reasons EMR's Earth Physics Branch and Geodetic Survey concentrated more on completing this coverage, using the ISS to provide positions and heights for the gravimeter points. The height accuracy required in the western mountains could not then be attained by any other method that was more cost-effective.[10]

ISS was still being used for mapping control, and one of the operational highlights occurred in 1987 when it was used to establish control in the Arctic islands above latitude 72 degrees. Despite the dire predictions of theorists that the accuracy of gyroscopes near the pole would be reduced drastically, the system continued to function more or less normally. By 1990 an important milestone had been reached, namely the completion of all necessary control required for the NTS 1:50 000 scale mapping programme. ISS use thereafter was almost wholly devoted to supporting gravity work.

In 1991 an intensive three-year gravity data-gathering campaign, called Operation Bouguer, was launched jointly by the MCE and the Geophysics Division, in conjunction with the U.S. Defense Mapping Agency (DMA).[11] Although ISS provided control for this operation in 1991, it could no longer compete with GPS, which was used for control in 1992 and 1993. During these last two years the MCE and Geodetic Survey inertial units remained indoors, and only underwent periodic cycling in the laboratory.

LEVELLING OPERATIONS (1973 ONWARDS)

Contracting federal government work to the private sector was first emphasized in 1975. Consequently Geodetic Survey let its first contract for precise levelling in 1976 for work on Prince Edward Island. Thereafter the amount of contracting gradually increased until the only work retained in-house was special-order levelling to monitor earth movements. Despite some early start-up problems the work contracted has generally been done well and at reasonable cost.

During the 1970s there were a number of notable achievements in precise levelling in remote areas. One of these, mentioned earlier in this chapter, was the extension of a level line along the banks of the Mackenzie River in the Northwest Territories from Great Slave Lake to Arctic Red River. In 1978 a line of levels was carried along the newly built Dempster Highway (Canada's first highway north of the Arctic Circle), from Dawson in the Yukon Territory north to Arctic Red River, to complete a giant levelling loop of over 5500 km.

Another important loop was completed in 1978 in the Yukon Territory, when some 180 km of levelling was done from Tetlin Junction in Alaska through to the Alaska-Yukon boundary, following the Taylor Highway. This completed a comparatively small loop with a periphery of only 1300 km! This project featured an amusing incident. The first 150 km of levelling from Tetlin Junction would pass through Alaska, and permission was obtained in advance from the USNGS for this work to be done. USNGS wanted its own benchmarks used and agreed to supply them to the Canadian party. When it became clear that their arrival would be long delayed, the party chief, M. Berrigan, was compelled to use hastily modified standard Canadian benchmarks. However only minor modifications could be made with the equipment on hand. Consequently this unique U.S. line of levels today sports benchmarks with caps carrying inscriptions in Canada's two official languages.

An important link in Canadian northern levelling was completed in 1980 when a Geodetic Survey field party headed by J.G. Perron connected levelling at Macmillan Pass on the Yukon–Northwest Territories boundary to the Mackenzie River line. This was done by running a 390 km line that generally followed the old, disused Canol Road and pipeline through the Mackenzie Mountains to Norman Wells. The road and pipeline had been constructed hastily in 1943 and 1944 to meet a wartime crisis in oil supply, only to be abandoned in 1949.[12] During the levelling the party came across many abandoned, but surprisingly well-preserved, vehicles, tools, and other items of equipment. The party was able to make use of one of the abandoned camps for accommodation.

Bad news arrived on the international geodetic levelling scene in 1981. Investigations in Europe confirmed that precise levelling done with most makes of automatic levels suffered from systematic errors caused by the Earth's magnetic field acting on the compensators. Only lines running north-south or close to it were affected, and the size of the error varied with the make of level. The average error (about 1 mm per km) was tantalizing. It was very small, but just large enough to warrant, for first-order levelling, attention and expensive correction. Geodetic Survey investigated those lines in the Canadian network likely to be affected. The result was that over the next ten years some 20 000 km of levelling would be redone, and an empirically determined correction factor would be applied to other lines to correct matters.

Precise levelling during a Canadian winter is best avoided, particularly in remote areas. Sometimes, however, the terrain is such that there is no other practical alternative. Normally a levelling party must work briskly to make good progress, yet not act too hastily for fear of making some small slip, often not immediately detectable, that might ruin a section and result in an expensive rerun. In winter this challenge to efficient, accurate operation becomes much greater. Because of the cold the level is sluggish and harder to operate, breath freezes on the eyepiece, gloved hands are clumsy in manipulating the level and recording the rod readings, and the tripod and rod footplates are often resting on ice or on unstable, compacted snow. In addition the continual battle against the cold spoils concentration and the daylight hours are limited. Special care must be taken to ensure that benchmarks remain stable and there is the ever-present risk of a sudden snowstorm or squall disrupting the work or, worse still, causing a whiteout and preventing a return to base camp. Despite these inherent difficulties a number of very successful precise levelling operations have been conducted in the dead of a Canadian winter.

A severe test of winter levelling skills occurred in northern Québec in the winters of 1982 and 1983. A Geodetic Survey levelling party under Perron ran a line from Schefferville, Québec, northerly to Ungava Bay following the Swampy Bay, Caniapiscau, and Koksoak Rivers. This is a total distance of about 540 km, all through wilderness. This work had been requested by the Québec Geodetic Service, which needed the line as a datum reference to link together numerous lower-order lines. Perron's party encountered, in addition to the usual winter temperatures and snowstorms, very high winds for days on end, frequent patches of thin ice through which skidoos often broke, nearly drowning their drivers, and numerous gorges, rapids, and waterfalls that had to be outflanked. To cap it all, just before reaching its destination the party found itself in the middle of a 60 000-head caribou herd. Apart from interruptions caused by animals crossing lines of sight, the party was faced with an irate game warden from Fort Chimo who threatened to shut the levelling operation down, but who was eventually persuaded to allow it to continue. Despite all this, levelling progress for the 1983 work averaged about 6 km per working day.

The most recent winter precise levelling project of note occurred in the Northwest Territories in 1988, above the Arctic Circle. The requirement was to run a line of levels for about 220 km from Inuvik to a tide gauge at Tuktoyaktuk, following a sinuous winter "ice" road that wound its way across part of the Mackenzie River delta. There was an important objective: to make the first connection of the national levelling network to a mean sea level reference at the Arctic Ocean. This would provide a vital tidal gauge anchor for many thousands of kilometres of levelling established in western and north-western Canada. At that time the nearest tidal reference for this levelling was the gauge at Prince Rupert. The work commenced in late February as soon as enough daylight was available. The party was accommodated in cat-train cabooses (see figure 2-16). Despite bitter cold, a lack of cover in the bleak terrain, and the aggravation of high winds the line was completed on 22 April. The party, headed by D. Erickson, had averaged some 6 km of levelling per day, very good progress in the circumstances.

About 1980 Geodetic Survey became interested in motorized precise levelling. Experience in Sweden indicated that it could be very productive. Motorized levelling is an arrangement whereby the level and two rods are each mounted on a motor vehicle, and conveyed by this means between set-ups. At each set-up the rods and level are lowered to the ground, and readings are taken in the usual way. Then they are all raised again and transported to the next set-up. Along roads with moderate traffic, progress is usually much quicker than normal levelling on foot.

In 1981 and 1982 a prototype system was built and tested, featuring three four-wheel drive vehicles. Production work was started in 1983 with the system equipped with an automated data recording system. After early development problems had been solved, the unit's greater productivity in comparison with levelling on foot (about 40 percent) soon became apparent. However this extended only to operations along fairly open, wide-shouldered roads with light to moderate traffic. In cities and suburban areas there were few or no gains in productivity; sometimes levelling on foot was better. In some provinces, for example British Columbia, provincial regulations regarding the use of vehicles for levelling were so restrictive as to nullify any advantages motorized levelling might offer. Despite these drawbacks Geodeticm Survey persevered with its system until 1987. By then the vehicles were wearing out, and most levelling was being contracted to private industry. During the field seasons of 1986 and 1987 the system was operated by private contractors, and Geodetic Survey attempted to interest private industry in building and operating a replacement system. No interest was displayed, however, and the original motorized levelling system was retired.

Two priority items claimed much of Geodetic Survey's levelling resources during the 1980s. The first was the re-levelling needed for the North American Vertical Datum (NAVD) 88 readjustment project.[13] The second was special work to monitor earth movements in cooperation with the then Earth Physics Branch (now Geophysics Division of Geological Survey). The NAVD 88 priority came about in 1981, when Geodetic Survey agreed formally to cooperate with the USNGS in this important project. This was followed by a commitment to provide, by 1990, "clean" data for a Basic Net comprising some 56 000 km of post-1960 first-order levelling. The fieldwork needed to groom this net started about 1982, and became more focused and intensive from 1985. By the end of 1989 the grooming was virtually complete, and comprised more than 24 000 km of modern re-levelling, which represented about 80 percent of Geodetic Survey's total levelling output for that period. This accommodated an increase in the total Basic Net requirement, which in the meantime had grown from 56 000 km to some 76 000 km. The remaining 60 000 km of the national network is to be incorporated soon, in and around the kernel of the Basic Net. Most of the resources previously devoted to the Basic Net have now been diverted to the grooming of the remainder through re-levelling under contract.

The special work for earth movement monitoring came about more gradually. As mentioned earlier in this chapter, Geodetic Survey was undertaking levelling in the late 1960s in the vicinity of a number of major dams in order to monitor the effects of hydraulic loading. This work continued until about 1982. Then Geodetic Survey withdrew its support to the provincial hydro authorities concerned, because this type of work could now be done by private industry. Meanwhile in 1976 Geodetic Survey and the Earth Physics Branch decided to cooperate closely in monitoring larger-scale earth crustal movements. This was the start of a programme of cooperation between the two organizations that, at the end of 1993, still continued. Most work in the programme has been concentrated on Vancouver Island. It will be described later in this chapter in the section on physical geodesy.

CONTROL SURVEY STANDARDS AND SPECIFICATIONS

In 1973 the federal Surveys and Mapping Branch adopted a new set of accuracy specifications for its control survey operations. The levelling requirements were similar to those contained in previous specifications issued in 1961. However, the accuracy criterion for horizontal control was quite different. The 95 percent error ellipse criterion (see appendix E under "Survey Accuracies") replaced the maximum anticipated error, the mainstay of the 1961 specifications. Greeted initially with dismay by many in the Canadian surveying community because of this novelty, these specifications eventually became popular. They were widely adopted outside the SMB and eventually became de facto national guidelines. The SMB issued a special supplement in 1975 that modified the criterion slightly so as to accommodate better the error characteristics of short lines. Three years later the SMB published a revised edition that amalgamated the contents of the 1973 and 1975 documents in one publication. This publication was still widely used in 1993.[14]

Thought has been given recently to abandoning the present method of classifying horizontal control rigidly by orders of accuracy according to the 95 percent criterion, in favour of a more flexible criterion based on statistical reliability. However this thinking has not yet crystallized in the form of an official publication.

In 1981 Geodetic Survey published guidelines and specifications for satellite Doppler surveys that found widespread acceptance. More recently, in December 1992, it published guidelines and specifications for GPS surveys. During the past few years some provincial surveying and mapping agencies have designed and published control specifications and guidelines for their own operations, thereby continuing a trend away from a single set of national specifications.

CALIBRATION ACTIVITIES

The precise calibration of geodetic measuring equipment is obviously essential for proper performance. Before EDM the only geodetic equipment needing calibration was Geodetic Survey's invar measuring tapes and invar levelling rods. This work was done by the National Research Council.

With the arrival of EDM equipment in about 1957 a need arose for calibration baselines. The first of these was laid out in the basement of the Surveys and Mapping Branch building in Ottawa, soon after its opening in 1960. The short length limited the usefulness of this baseline, however, and in 1970 an outdoor baseline 2.4 km long was constructed at Shirley's Bay near Ottawa. The latter was measured with invar tapes in 1971, 1972, and 1973 and pronounced stable. Called the National Geodetic Baseline (NGBL), it has served as the national standard for EDM calibrations ever since.

By 1973 EDM use was commonplace in the surveying community, and there was a growing need for similar baselines elsewhere in Canada to serve the calibration needs of surveyors and engineers. In that year there appeared on the market a special EDM instrument designated the Kern Mekometer ME 3000. It was designed to measure short distances of up to 2 km very accurately. (The accuracy has been rated at between 1 and 2 mm over a distance of 2 km.) In response to the above need Geodetic Survey bought a Mekometer and, in 1974, started what became known as the EDM baseline programme. Under this programme, which still continues, Geodetic Survey and various provincial surveying and mapping agencies have cooperated in the establishment of calibration baselines, usually located in or near cities and large towns. The provincial agencies choose the sites and construct the reference piers. Geodetic Survey then makes the measurements over two successive years using the Mekometer or one of its successors. The measuring instruments are usually checked on the NGBL before, during, and after a summer measuring campaign. By the end of 1993, forty-five such baselines had been established.

From about 1985 the use of GPS in Canada increased greatly and the need for calibration facilities became apparent. In response Geodetic Survey started a cooperative programme with provincial agencies to establish GPS basenets, similar to the baseline programme. Generally a basenet consists of six or more stations. These form a local network with inter-station distances close to 2, 10, 40, and 50 km, and sometimes with additional distances of 100 and 150 km. Most basenets incorporate previously established baselines, thereby also providing a selection of shorter distances if needed. The purpose of a basenet is to facilitate the testing, under operating conditions, of a complete assembly of GPS equipment (including software) intended for use in production work. This is to determine its reliability and accuracy. The first basenet was established in 1988, and by the end of 1993 a total of nine had been completed.

Invar rod calibration for levelling continues, and procedures have remained much the same. The only difference is that calibration is now done in Geodetic Survey, using its own laser interferometer equipment, because of the cessation of the service provided by the National Research Council.

DATUMS AND ADJUSTMENTS OF OBSERVATIONS

The end-products of routine geodetic control survey operations are identifiable, permanently marked monuments, the coordinates of which are known and expressed with reference to a common national datum. Given these coordinates and monument descriptions, users can go about their business. Geodetic field measurements normally contain numerous redundancies. These redundant measurements are made deliberately to improve accuracy, to check against blunders, and to provide data from which inferences can be drawn about the precision of the work. To arrive at the coordinates one must treat the measurements mathematically, in a manner that reconciles the various redundancies to produce the best coordinate values. In geodetic parlance this treatment is usually referred to as a least squares adjustment.

In 1972 Geodetic Survey and the USNGS entered into a cooperative agreement to update their horizontal control networks and adopt a revised North American datum. These networks were no longer up to par, and their deficiencies were becoming more evident in the face of increasing user demands for more accurate and consistent coordinate values. In some parts of Canada network deficiencies had been mitigated by a series of makeshift regional adjustments: however these only postponed the inevitable.

The cooperative agreement put in motion the very important NAD83, which would continue into the 1990s. Some of the many tasks to be tackled were converting all old data to a form in which they could be processed by computer; analysing and evaluating these data to determine their accuracy and reliability; making extra field measurements to strengthen the networks and relate them to a new datum; purchasing computer hardware and designing sophisticated computer software to process enormous amounts of data; and the necessary research and development, and the training of professional and technical staff.

Readjustment of the Canadian networks was planned to be done in stages: first, a joint readjustment with the U.S. that would include some 7000 Canadian primary stations; and second, the subsequent integration, within this readjusted primary network, of all secondary stations (some 100 000). All coordinates were to be based on a new North American datum.

Some strengthening of the network had been done before 1972 in anticipation of the need for readjustment. Further strengthening got under way, in the field, with the filling in of some gaps in the network and the completion of some essential links, as well as the addition of scale control and extra Laplace observations. The evaluation and digitization of data proceeded apace in the office. In 1974, when satellite Doppler positioning methods had become accurate enough to provide first-order control, a special Doppler field campaign was launched to expand, strengthen, and anchor the primary network in preparation for the readjustment. By this time various NAD83-related research and development activities were under way. These were given further impetus from two international symposia on NAD83: the first at the University of New Brunswick in Fredericton during 1974, and the second in Arlington, Virginia, in 1978.

Despite much activity during the first few years of the project, the matter of the new datum had not been resolved in Canada. Some authorities and advisers favoured retaining the existing NAD27 datum in order to minimize the size of the coordinate shifts and subsequent technical and administrative disruption. Others favoured taking a bolder step and adopting a geocentric datum, arguing that the larger initial disruption would be more than counterbalanced by the long-term advantages of a datum much better suited to satellite positioning methods – the wave of the future. The debate on the datum came to a head in 1977. At a special meeting of the Canadian Council on Surveying and Mapping (CCSM), held in Ottawa in January, there was a consensus that Canada should go geocentric. The only debatable issue was whether Canada should proceed immediately with an independent readjustment based on a geocentric datum, or wait for a geocentrically based adjustment with the U.S., as planned under the joint NAD83 agreement. Most council members favoured waiting, and this became the official Canadian position.

A notable exception to this was the position taken by the Land Registration and Information Service (LRIS), which was responsible for, *inter alia*, control surveys in New Brunswick, Nova Scotia, and Prince Edward Island. LRIS believed that the momentum of its surveying and mapping programmes would be greatly reduced by having to wait for NAD83 to be completed. Therefore it proceeded with an independent, regional readjustment of control in the Maritime provinces on a geocentric datum. This was named the Average Terrestrial System 1977 (ATS 77), and was adopted officially by LRIS in 1979.

By 1985 the preparatory work for the adjustment of the Canadian primary networks was nearing completion. Virtually all the data preparation had been done, the sophisticated software was designed and refined, and four test adjustments completed. The project had by now been delayed some two years beyond its original target date. However, the delays also brought some good, allowing the late inclusion of net-strengthening GPS and Very Long Baseline Interferometry (VLBI) data. (See chapter 12, part 1, for an explanation of VLBI.)

Anticipating that new primary coordinates would soon be available, CCSM passed a resolution in 1985 that the general release of these coordinates be withheld deliberately until after the Canadian secondary networks had been integrated. The reason was that the process of integration was expected to change the new primary values, except at the junction points with the U.S.

In June 1986 the NAD83 Continental Adjustment was finally completed, and the new Canadian primary coordinates became available as input for the integration process, expected to be completed in late 1987. Since it was now likely that the general release of new NAD83 values would occur within a year or two, CCSM focused its attention in 1986 on action to inform users about the ramifications of NAD83. A resolution was passed that year encouraging members to hold user seminars and, for emphasis, a similar resolution was passed at the next annual meeting in 1987.

By this time secondary integration had been under way for about two years through an informal, cooperative effort between Geodetic Survey and most of the provincial surveying and mapping agencies, LRIS excepted. Their respective roles needed to be clarified. Accordingly the following division of responsibilities was confirmed by CCSM at its 1988 meeting. The provinces participating would be responsible for all their secondary stations established by conventional means. Geodetic Survey would attend to the secondary networks in the Yukon and the Northwest Territories, and to those stations in the provinces established by VLBI, GPS, ISS, and Doppler methods. The work, which took longer than expected, was treated in three large blocks or regions – eastern, western, and northern. By 1989 the work on the eastern region, comprising some 57 000 stations, had been completed. The two remaining regions were completed in June 1990 for a grand total of about 105 000 stations. This marked the end of the NAD83 project, started about eighteen years before. An indication of the computational labour involved is provided by the integration of the combined western and northern regions. There were some 48 000 stations, and the adjustment required the simultaneous solution of about 350 000 linear equations.

During 1990 and 1991 a series of informative seminars was held under the auspices of the then Canadian Institute of Surveying and Mapping (now the Canadian Institute of Geomatics) to brief users on the technical ramifications of NAD83.

The federal Department of Energy, Mines and Resources (now Natural Resources Canada) and the British Columbia Ministry of Crown Lands and Parks adopted NAD83 officially in May 1990. They were followed by the Québec Department of Energy and Resources and Forests on 1 August of that year, and on 1 January 1993 by Newfoundland. Alberta, Saskatchewan, and Ontario were expected to adopt NAD83 officially in 1994. Figure 2-8 depicts the extent of the geodetic primary horizontal control network in Canada in 1993.

Although the NAD83 project as such is officially complete in Canada, the task of fitting lower-order surveys remains. Transformation methods appear to be the most practical for most, but not all, of these surveys. To assist the provinces Geodetic Survey designed a transformation software package that was released in 1993 for general use.

Another datum and adjustment project of major importance is the NAVD 88.[15] Started about 1978 and still under way, this project deals with the Canadian primary vertical control network, which comprises some 135 000 km of geodetic spirit levelling. Like NAD83 this project stemmed from the realization in the early 1970s, both in Canada and the U.S., that their existing vertical control networks were no longer able to meet user demands for more accurate and consistent heights.

In Geodetic Survey these concerns resulted in the appointment in 1976 of a special group to look into the matter. The report of this group, together with the results of an associated research contract performed by the University of New Brunswick, confirmed the need for remedial action. Since the USNGS had reached the same conclusion earlier regarding its own network, the two national geodetic organizations agreed, in 1978, to cooperate in a North American readjustment of the vertical network and a redefintion of the datum.

To stimulate thought and discussion and to bring international expert knowledge to bear on the problem, two symposia were held. The first, held in 1979 at Fort Clayton in the Panama Canal Zone, was attended by 32 participants from twelve countries; the second, held in Ottawa in 1980, attracted some 160 participants from twenty-one countries.

The cooperation between USNGS and Geodetic Survey was recognized officially in 1981 by the signing of a Memorandum of Understanding. It soon became clear that Canada could not upgrade its entire primary network in time for the continental adjustment, tentatively scheduled for 1990. Accordingly it was decided that the Canadian adjustment would be done in two stages. The first would consist of treating data for about 40 percent of the total network. This portion, to be known as the Canadian Basic Net, would comprise

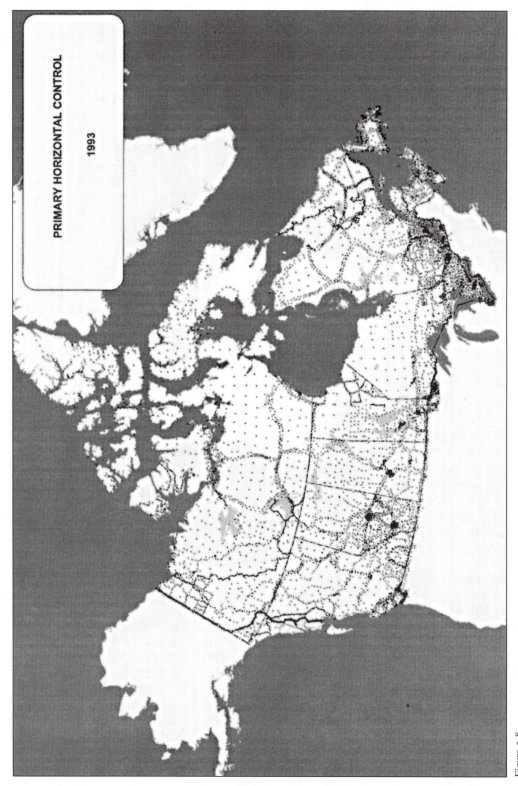

PRIMARY HORIZONTAL CONTROL

1993

Figure 2-8
Primary horizontal control, 1993.
Source: Geodetic Survey of Canada

some 56 000 km of post-1960 first-order levelling. The second stage would consist of a separate, Canadian adjustment of the remainder, based on the adjusted heights of the Basic Net obtained from the continental adjustment.

To better concentrate on the task Geodetic Survey formed a special NAVD 88 project section in 1981. Fieldwork needed for the grooming of the Basic Net began in earnest in 1982, becoming more intensive from 1985 on.

Further impetus was given to the project in 1985 by the holding of a third symposium in Rockville, Maryland, which drew some 110 participants from nineteen countries. By the end of 1989 the extra fieldwork had been completed, as had the automation and verification of the Basic Net data. By this time the Canadian Basic Net total had increased to 76 000 km. The continental adjustment was finally done in 1991, completing the first stage of the Canadian adjustment. Work is now proceeding on preparing the remainder of the Canadian network for adjustment in 1994. The new vertical datum agreed to by the U.S. and Canada (but not yet adopted officially) is based on the mean sea-level height of only one point, the Canadian tide gauge benchmark at Rimouski, Québec. Figure 2-9 depicts the extent of the geodetic precise levelling network in Canada in 1993.

GRAVIMETRY (1973 ONWARDS)

In the early 1970s gravity measurements continued at a brisk pace. The sea-surface surveys were conducted in 1972 on a more systematic basis leading to a flood of data. By 1976 the NGDB contained over 345 000 stations.[16] The Earth Physics Branch improved the methods of data storage, retrieval, and display to the point at which, by the late 1970s, it was one of the world's leading authorities in database applications of gravity data.

In the late 1970s and early 1980s the main efforts in the field were directed towards surveys in the Western Cordillera, the Arctic, and the eastern and western continental shelves. During the period 1979–82 about 8500 static gravity stations were observed, and over 58 000 line miles of ship-borne dynamic gravity profiling completed.

The year 1982 marked the completion of a four-year campaign of regional coverage of the Western Cordillera up to latitude 54 degrees, roughly the latitude of Terrace, British Columbia. The average spacing of stations was about 12 km. During this campaign airborne ISS were used to advantage to position gravity stations in three dimensions.

The period 1979–82 also saw a reobservation and readjustment of some 260 first-order stations of the CGSN. These stations serve as the reference anchors for regional gravity coverage and for various local surveys such as those for mineral exploration, including oil and gas.

In 1979 the Earth Physics Branch led and coordinated the polar expedition LOREX (Lomonosov Ridge Expedition). This was followed in 1983 by its leadership and coordination of CESAR (Canadian Expedition to Study the Alpha Ridge). These expeditions, both on sea ice, were sponsored by the federal Department of Energy, Mines and Resources, and were supported by the PCSP and the Canadian Armed Forces. Conducted by several Canadian government agencies and by Canadian and U.S. universities, the scientific programmes for both expeditions were similar and mainly devoted to geophysical and marine geological investigations.

Buoyed by the successes of these two expeditions and benefiting from the experience gained, the PCSP embarked in 1984 on a more ambitious polar project. It established a research station on an ice island. Dubbed "Hobson's Choice" (a humorous reference to

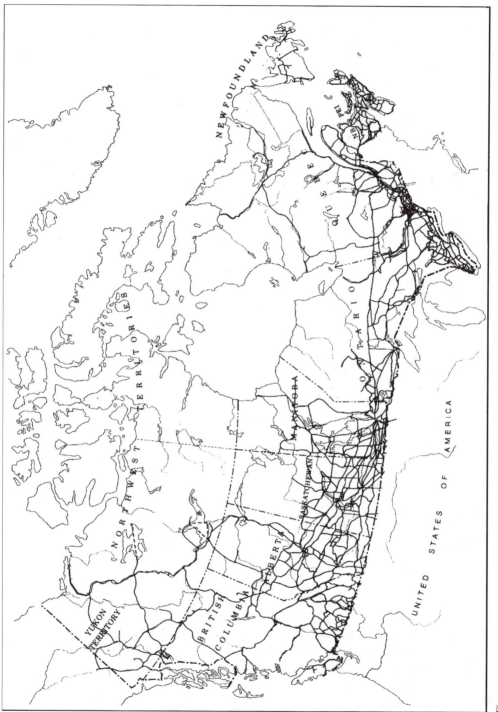

Figure 2-9
Precise levelling, 1993.
Source: Geodetic Survey of Canada

George Hobson, then director of PCSP), this tabular ice island, measuring some 4 by 6 km and about 45 m thick, had broken off from the Ward Hunt Ice Shelf. It was then located near the entrance to Nansen Sound, floating among sea ice some 2 m thick. A substantial camp was established, and over the next few years the ice island would become a floating platform for a host of geophysical and marine geological research activities. It would also serve as a base for bathymetric and gravity surveys over the continental shelf and margin. Satellite Doppler and GPS methods would be used to ascertain its wayward drifting pattern. Later, in 1987, the ice island would serve as a base for a gravity operation that would result in the establishment of some 1900 stations on Arctic sea ice. This would complete gravity coverage of the polar shelf from the Beaufort Sea to the Lincoln Sea, the culmination of twenty-five years of effort.

A major organizational change occurred in 1986. The Earth Physics Branch as such was dissolved, and the component divisions became part of Geological Survey. The responsibility for gravity rested with the Gravity Section of the Geophysics Division. By 1987, with further progress, and thanks to additional contributions of gravity data from private industry and from some universities and provinces, about 85 percent of the Canadian land mass and 75 percent of the offshore had been covered at a spacing of 15 km or closer.

A significant gravity field operation took place from 1991 to 1993. Called Operation Bouguer, it was mounted by the MCE of the Department of National Defence, with financial support from both the U.S. Defense Mapping Agency and the Geophysics Division of Geological Survey. Geodetic Survey provided inertial system equipment and staff training. During three summers over 5100 gravity observations were made in the south-west corner of the Northwest Territories, in southern and south-western Yukon, and in north-western British Columbia. This work virtually completed the regional gravity coverage of the Western Cordillera.

By the end of 1993 the NGDB contained data on more than 700 000 stations (see figure 2-10). One of the gravity programme's long-range objectives, that of completing regional gravity coverage of the total Canadian land mass and offshore by the year 2005, now appears achievable. The current main gaps are in the Arctic islands and channels, and across Great Bear Lake. Another objective is to provide more accurate and denser coverage of the Canadian Shield, Canada's rich mineral storehouse, in order to reveal hidden economic potential that cannot be discerned from the existing old, relatively sparse coverage. A third objective is to provide more accurate and denser coverage to improve the computation of the geoid over Canada.

PHYSICAL GEODESY (1973 ONWARDS)

Two topics were emphasized in physical geodesy in Canada during this period. The first was improved modelling of the geoid (geoid refinement), whilst the second was monitoring of regional crustal movements. By contrast Geodetic Survey's programme of monitoring local earth movements in the vicinity of some of the principal dams, which had been started in the late 1960s in response to requests from provincial hydroelectric authorities, tapered off. It stopped in the early 1980s when it became clear that this service could be provided directly by private industry.

For a host of practical purposes it is necessary to know which way fluids, and chiefly water, will flow. Therefore any practical geodetic system of heights must take gravity into account. Accordingly it is common sense to adopt equipotential surfaces as the basis for

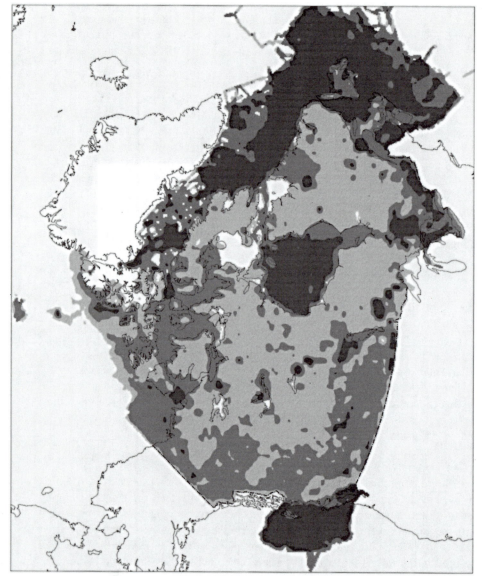

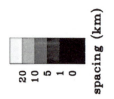

spacing (km)

20
10
5
1
0

Figure 2-10
Gravity station spacing.
Source: Geodetic Survey of Canada

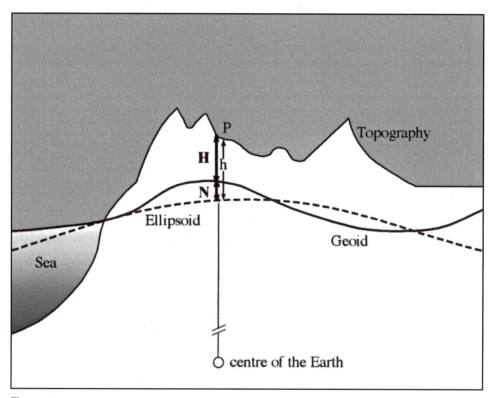

Figure 2-11
Geoid undulation.
Source: Geodetic Survey of Canada

such a system. An equipotential surface is one on which the gravity potential is constant. The Earth may be regarded as being enveloped by an infinite number of such surfaces, rather like the layers of an onion. It is also common sense to choose one of these layers or surfaces as the basic reference or zero of the system. The common practice in geodesy is to choose that surface which corresponds most closely to mean sea level, and to call it the geoid. The geoid is intangible and must be defined mathematically.

Interest in a better definition of the geoid was stimulated by the continuing development of satellite Doppler methods that, by 1974, could provide heights accurate to about 1 m. Thus a new tool was available to provide heights of sufficient accuracy to meet a number of practical needs, particularly in the Canadian hinterlands. However there was a snag: satellite heights are referred to a reference spheroid. To be useful they must be referred to mean sea level (i.e., the geoid). This requires an accurate estimate of the difference in height between the spheroid and geoid, known in geodetic parlance as the geoid separation (see N in figure 2-11).

Refining the geoid is a complicated, ongoing process of research and development that features a mathematical "stew" comprising copious amounts of satellite, gravity, astronomic, geodetic, and topographic data. If underlying theory is sound, the quality of the result will depend largely on the quantities of the various types of data available, and how judiciously they have been selected and mixed. From the mid-1970s onwards most Canadian research on geoid refinement would be performed in three places: the universities of New Brunswick and Calgary, and in Geodetic Survey. A brief account of geoid-related events during the past twenty years follows.

In 1974 L.J. O'Brien succeeded L.A. Gale as dominion geodesist and director of Geodetic Survey. A reorganization followed and in 1975 a new Physical Geodesy Section was created in recognition of the growing importance of this specialty. This soon paid dividends. By 1977, G. Lachapelle of the section had developed an improved method of estimating geoid undulations using a combination of satellite, gravity, astronomic, and geodetic data. The accuracy was generally about 1 m, except in the Western Cordillera where it deteriorated to about 2 m.

Geoid research proceeded apace. Further improvement was achieved by using additional satellite, gravity, and astronomic data. Better mathematical treatment was given to these data, particularly the combination of satellite and gravity data. Some of the achievements during this period were a Canadian gravimetric geoid produced at the University of New Brunswick by P. Vanicek in 1986, and geoids produced at the University of Calgary by K.-P. Schwarz, for Alberta in 1986 and for British Columbia in 1989.

In the mid-1980s the use of GPS was increasing rapidly, and the better heighting accuracies possible with this new system emphasized the need for matching refinement of the geoid. The quest for refinement was given a boost in 1987 by the start of Geodetic Survey's GPS-on-Benchmarks Programme. In this programme GPS three-dimensional positioning would be done at selected benchmarks of the national first-order levelling network. Among other benefits, this would enable direct comparisons to be made of measured differences between spheroidal and sea-level heights at these points, and those estimated according to the latest theory of geoid refinement. By the end of 1993 some 2000 benchmarks had been treated in this way, including a high priority trans-Canada line.

A new International Geoid Commission was established in 1988 within the International Association of Geodesy. The increasing importance of geoid studies in Canada was recognized through the creation of a geoid working group by the National Advisory Committee on Control Surveys and Mapping (NACCSM). Shortly afterwards this working group proposed the design of a Canadian national standard geoid. This was intended for general application, with geoid data to be issued in tabular form accompanied by interpolative software. This proposal was accepted by Geodetic Survey, and further development proceeded under the direction of A. Mainville. A national geoid prediction package, called GSD91, was released by the Geodetic Survey for general use in June 1992. The accuracy is about 5 to 10 cm in elevation for most regions of Canada, deteriorating to about 25 cm in mountainous areas. Research and development continues and with the availability of more gravity and topographic data, the use of more powerful computers, and more sophisticated interpolative procedures, accuracies will continue to improve, particularly in the mountains.

As indicated above, in physical geodesy from 1973 onwards emphasis was also put on monitoring regional earth movements. One of the chief concerns was tectonic plate interaction on Canada's west coast near Vancouver.

In the first half of this century geologists were reluctant to accept the fact that the Earth's crust could drift. Up and down motion was fine, but sideways motion was scientific heresy. The theory of continental drift, advanced by German geophysicist Alfred Wegener in 1912, was greeted initially with scorn or, by the more polite, with a crescendo of one-handed applause. This reluctance, which stemmed from a lack of global research in undersea geology and a failure to envisage a suitable mechanism that could move continents thousands of kilometres, would eventually disappear as evidence of drift mounted.

In the 1960s it was discovered that the sea floor was spreading in the vicinity of the major ocean ridges, leaving gaps that were filled by new crust formed of material supplied by the underlying mantle. This led to the re-examination of the theory of continental drift, and to the eventual development of the modern theory of plate tectonics. The late J. Tuzo Wilson, the distinguished Canadian geophysicist, was a strong advocate of plate tectonic theory and did much to convince others of its validity. According to this theory the lithosphere, the first 100 km or so in depth of the earth's crust, is divided into seven major plates and a number of smaller ones. These plates move about very slowly, driven by convection currents below. They can move apart, collide, slide by, or move under each other.

On Canada's west coast near Vancouver there are three plates: two are large, the Pacific and North American Plates, and the third is a much smaller plate known as the Juan de Fuca Plate. The Juan de Fuca Plate has slid below the North American and appears to be stuck there at the moment, straining to break free. Scientists believe that when it does, the resulting jolt will contribute to a major earthquake with appalling consequences for this densely populated region.

A long-term study of the geodynamics of the region was started in the mid-1970s by the Earth Physics Branch in an attempt to discover what was going on, and to try to provide advance warning of any impending disaster. Geodetic Survey made its first contribution to this study in 1976 by undertaking special-order precise levelling on Vancouver Island, between Campbell River and Gold River. This marked the start of a period of close cooperation between Geodetic Survey and the Earth Physics Branch (now the Geophysics Division of Geological Survey) in earth-movement monitoring. This cooperation continues.

By 1985 GPS methods were approaching the very high accuracies needed for earth-movement detection. Thereafter most line measurements were made using both EDM and GPS methods. By about 1991, however, the superiority of GPS had been established, and the accompanying measurements by EDM ceased. More recently a network consisting of automated GPS stations has been established to provide continuous monitoring of any movements, as well as to provide a continuous, common, very precise regional reference frame for all geodetic and surveying work.

To date all these very precise geodetic measurements have helped confirm that the two plates are indeed stuck, and that the brittle rupture zone is about 60 km wide and underlies the continental shelf directly offshore from Vancouver Island. These measurements also continue to aid geophysicists in understanding the general behaviour of crustal plates, and the processes that generate earthquakes.

Geodesy in the Provinces

The following is a general overview of provincial geodetic activities. Although most first-order control has been established in Canada by Geodetic Survey, at least three provinces have, over the years, established some on their own to satisfy urgent needs. Since the early 1960s Ontario has done first-order levelling along many provincial highways. Similarly, in Saskatchewan, first-order levelling has been done intermittently since the late 1960s, mainly along northern highways. Both first-order horizontal control and levelling operations have been conducted in Québec for many years. In addition useful geodetic research and development has been undertaken.

First-order control work has, however, constituted very little of the total provincial geodetic activity over the past twenty years. Provincial geodetic field activities have been concentrated very strongly on the densification of control, mainly to second- and third-order standards. This has been dictated largely by the need to facilitate urban development – Canada is still largely a nation of city dwellers – and also to explore and develop natural resources. Although in some provinces the work of densifying control has been driven by the demands of mapping, there has always been an awareness of the virtues of multipurpose integrated control. In some provinces this control has been established in an ad hoc manner to meet immediate needs. In others, however, it has been introduced in accordance with a long-range plan to develop an ultimate and comprehensive land management system. An early example of the latter is the Maritime provinces' LRIS, which is discussed in chapters 4 and 7.

To process the data from their field operations, most provinces developed or adopted sophisticated computer programs such as MANOR (Ontario) and GALS and GHOST (Geodetic Survey) for adjustments, and, for databases, programs such as COSINE (Ontario) and GEODEQ (Québec). Later, as the flood of data and computer power increased, the advantages of total database management systems became apparent, leading to the creation of programmes such as MASCOT (Alberta). These developments were spurred from about the mid-1980s by the need for the provinces to prepare their data for the secondary integration stage of the NAD83 project.

A provincial trend during the process of control densification was the salvaging and upgrading of the pre-existing cadastral survey framework. This was done by making systematic ties to property monuments. Attention was also paid to integrating what appeared to be good, but scattered and unrelated, control surveys done by other provincial agencies or utilities, again by making ties. In Québec, for example, a good deal of effort was expended in locating and tying in the earlier control work of Hydro-Québec.

Another general trend was for provinces to encourage their municipalities to utilize existing control, and to establish more if needed, by offering them various provincial cost-sharing or work-sharing inducements. This was particularly evident in Alberta, Ontario, and Québec. Yet another tack taken is exemplified by the procedure used in British Columbia of officially declaring certain areas well supplied with control as Integrated Survey Areas (ISAS). After declaration the province required that local cadastral and engineering surveys be referenced to the control.

There has been a tendency among the provinces to centralize organization of government surveying and mapping activities. For example in Saskatchewan there was the emergence of the Central Survey and Mapping Agency (CSMA) in 1976 after a long period of gestation. In 1978 a Manitoba government task force recommended the establishment of one central surveying and mapping office for the province, reinforcing the mandate of the well-known Surveys and Mapping Branch (which would celebrate its fiftieth anniversary two years later). In late 1979 a new act was passed in Québec merging the lands, forests, mines, and energy sectors together in the Department of Energy and Resources. Featured in this new department was a Bureau of Surveying and Mapping, reporting directly to a deputy minister. The Alberta Bureau of Surveying and Mapping was created in 1981 and given responsibility for a geographical positioning framework for the province, and for coordinating all provincial surveying, mapping, and geopositioning data bank activities. It was Ontario's turn in 1983 when the Surveys and Mapping Branch in the Ministry of Natural Resources (formed in 1972) was reorganized, and given official blessing to administer the provincial survey system.

Federal government cooperation and assistance helped many provinces. This help was in three forms. First, there was a special programme conducted by Geodetic Survey to provide first-order control in cities and municipalities with populations of 50 000 or more. Between the early 1970s and 1980 some ten urban areas were completed. Examples are the cities of Edmonton and Saskatoon, and the Ontario regional municipalities of Kitchener-Waterloo and Hamilton-Wentworth. Second, some provinces benefitted from cost-sharing or work-sharing when their control needs could be dovetailed conveniently with those of EMR's Surveys and Mapping Branch. The prime example is the previously mentioned ISS programme on the prairies.

The provinces have had to assume much more responsibility over the past ten years or so for processing and managing control data. This has been the result of rapid expansion of their control networks, the transfer to them of large amounts of federal control data, the general provincial trend towards the centralization of surveying and mapping activities, and the growth of geographic information systems (of which control survey data is a fundamental component).

All of this has been spurred on by the NAD83 project, particularly the secondary integration stage. This stage called for a major effort by most provinces to automate, evaluate, and "clean" their data. Following the completion of secondary integration they are now responsible for integrating a multitude of older lower-order control points, as well as the new control that is continually being established. NAD83 has been given birth by the Geodetic Survey, it must now be reared by the provinces.

Geodesy in the Private Sector

Prior to the mid-1960s there were few Canadian firms with special skills in geodesy, other than in providing control for mapping and charting. Most were engaged in mapping, cadastral surveying, or engineering surveys. Today the picture is very different. Virtually any specialized geodetic skill can be found somewhere in the industry, and there are at least six firms capable of carrying out large geodetic contracts anywhere in the world. However hardly any firms do geodetic work exclusively; in most it is one specialty among others such as engineering, mapping, or cadastral surveying.

One of the earliest significant geodetic accomplishments by Canadian firms since the Second World War occurred in 1952 when Canadian Aero Surveys and Spartan Air Services, under contract to the then Army Survey Establishment, were engaged in part of the Canadian Shoran operation described earlier in this chapter. Another early accomplishment was the establishment of ground control in connection with the Mekong River project as described in chapter 6. Other notable accomplishments were the Aerodist operations conducted by Terra Surveys in Guyana in 1966, and in Tanzania in the early 1970s as outlined in chapter 18. In both cases the objectives were to establish a primary horizontal control network and photo control for 1:50 000 mapping.

Much of the success of Canadian satellite Doppler work in Canada and overseas stems from the pioneering work in the late 1960s of Shell Canada of Calgary, then engaged in positioning offshore drilling platforms and in ship navigation.

The industry's satellite Doppler and other skills were much in evidence in northern Nigeria in 1974 and 1975, when Terra Surveys and Marshall Macklin Monaghan Limited completed an improvement of local geodetic horizontal and vertical networks, and provided control for 1:50 000 mapping. Further detail is given in chapter 18. Another example of these skills was the completion of a first-order net of some 238 satellite Doppler stations in Indonesia, in 1978, by McElhanney Surveying and Engineering Ltd. In 1980 this firm produced the MSEL Integrated Navigation System, which integrated observational data from satellite Doppler, Loran-C, ARGO and Mini-Ranger navigational systems, and from gyro compasses.

Significant achievements have not been limited to fieldwork. For example it was J.D. Barnes and Associates that in 1977 produced under contract to the Ontario Ministry of Natural Resources a sophisticated all-purpose adjustment program called MANOR. This saw widespread use in Canada. This firm followed up in 1981 with COSINE, a comprehensive database program subsequently put to good use by the same ministry.

Each year since 1976 the industry has carried out contracts for Geodetic Survey. Most of this work has been precise levelling, with over 80 percent of its levelling having been done under contract since the early 1980s. The balance has been second-order mapping or multipurpose control, GPS positioning on benchmarks, and research and development. The general level of contracting has been about one million dollars per year. Over the past twenty years the industry has also benefitted from the rapid growth of provincial and municipal surveying activities, for which most of the fieldwork has been contracted.

The industry has been quick to respond to new technical advances in geodesy. Soon after ISS arrived on the Canadian scene in the mid-1970s three of the leading firms were capable of providing this type of control. Sheltech of Calgary was bold enough to purchase a number of Ferranti aircraft-type inertial platforms, and started adapting them to surveying needs. This included the intricate task of designing the controlling software. The unit developed became known as the Ferranti Inertial Survey System (FILS) and saw widespread service, both in Canada and overseas. There was a novel application of inertial surveying technology by McElhanney Engineering in 1984. This firm mounted an inertial unit in a vehicle adapted to run on rails, which then followed the CNR railway from Jasper to Prince Rupert, acquiring "as-built" data on the line every 20 m as it rolled along.

Private industry was in the forefront in the development of GPS for surveying in Canada. As early as 1980 Sheltech started testing the STI 5010 receiver made by Stanford Telecommunications Inc. of California, and conducted field experiments jointly with the U.S. Naval Surface Weapons Centre.

Since the early 1980s there has been a proliferation of uses by private industry of GPS and inertial systems, in combination, on land and sea, and in the air. Often in development work there has been joint participation by industry, universities, and government. One of the most successful of these joint efforts has been the combination of Nortech, the University of New Brunswick, the Canadian Hydrographic Service, and the Bedford Institute of Oceanography in developing solutions to marine navigation problems. Another is the joint involvement by Usher Canada Ltd. and the University of New Brunswick in continuing studies of GPS-based methods for monitoring ground movements in New Brunswick and in the oilfields of Venezuela (see also in chapter 16).

A novel event occurred in 1987 when Nortech Surveys produced the first Canadian GPS receiver, the Norstar 1000. A small number of these units were produced and sold, including two to Geodetic Survey.

Clearly, Canadian geodetic surveying firms possess professional knowledge, skills, techniques, and equipment at least the equal of any other nation in the world, but there are clouds on the domestic and foreign horizons. The amount of new domestic business may be more limited now that many basic federal, provincial, and municipal control survey needs have been met. This problem is compounded by GPS, which, by becoming all-pervadingly efficient, calls into question not only the need for more multipurpose control, but also the future need for much of the control already established.

Conclusion

In retrospect the period of some forty-five years following the Second World War may become known as the golden age of Canadian geodesy. During this period the fundamental national networks of gravity determination, horizontal positioning, and levelling were virtually completed. Massive amounts of associated data were refurbished and referred to modernized datums for maximum public utility. In the course of this work the control needs of Canada's national mapping programmes were met. Through the efforts of provincial surveying and mapping agencies, with some federal assistance, considerable progress was made in establishing supplementary control in southern Canada. This control is essential for a host of practical endeavours, including computerized geographic information systems, vital for the efficient management of our complicated urban infrastructures, our environment, and our natural resources.

Advances were made in methods of positioning from satellites and in physical geodesy such that positions and height differences can now be determined very economically anywhere in Canada with a speed and accuracy undreamed of by earlier geodesists. This forty-five-year period also featured impressive development of geodetic skills in virtually all provinces and in private industry. Expertise also developed in private industry: today many of Canada's leading private firms rank with the best in the world.

These achievements came about for a number of reasons: effective organization and management; an aptitude for improvisation and for taking measured risks; good transportation and communication facilities; excellent cooperation between federal, provincial, and private agencies; a good supply of skilled personnel provided by the universities and community colleges; and the readiness to embrace "galloping" technology and apply it rapidly to the tasks at hand.

The future of Canadian geodesy is not assured; some impending concerns have been mentioned in the preceding section. We can be confident, however, on the basis of past performance and present skills, that the Canadian geodetic community is indeed capable of responding well to the continuing challenge of change.

PART 2   INTERNATIONAL AND INTERPROVINCIAL
BOUNDARIES*

The International Boundary

The international boundary between Canada and the United States is the world's longest undefended border. The 8891 km of boundary includes 3830 km of water boundary and

---

* Part 2 of the chapter was contributed by Allen C. Roberts.

5061 km of land boundary,[17] extending from the Atlantic Ocean to the Pacific Ocean and north along the Alaska panhandle and the 141st meridian to the Beaufort Sea.

The boundary is defined by a series of lines connecting more than 11 000 deflection points that have precise geographical positions. Each land boundary turning point is identified by a permanent monument, while the nearly 6000 deflection points along the water boundary sections are referenced by monuments on land.[18] The precise geographical positions along water boundaries do not change with the meandering of boundary streams, even if a deflection point should end up on dry land.[19]

Two locations along the boundary have been established as a symbol of the unbroken harmony between our two nations.

1 The International Peace Arch, which straddles the boundary between Washington and British Columbia at its western end. This arch was dedicated on 6 September 1921, and is surrounded by the British Columbia Peace Arch Provincial Park and the Washington Peace Arch State Park.[20]

2 The International Peace Garden, which straddles the boundary between Manitoba and North Dakota, was dedicated on 14 July 1932. It embraces 947 ha of tended floral gardens, lakes, picnic and camp grounds, and an international music camp.[21]

THE INTERNATIONAL BOUNDARY COMMISSION

During the period 1783–1925 statesmen of both countries laid the diplomatic foundation, by numerous treaties and arbitrations, for the later practical work of establishing and maintaining the International Boundary. The responsibility for conducting surveys to implement the various agreements fell to the International Boundary Commission (IBC) and the International Joint Commission (IJC) for the St Lawrence River and the Great Lakes.

The first commission was created under the 1794 Jay Treaty. Over the years the United States and Canada appointed a series of temporary commissions to oversee surveys of specific sections of the boundary. This work was largely completed by 1874. Then recognizing that the first phase of the work was finished, the United States and Canada established the IBC under the Treaty of 1908 to supervise the re-establishment of border demarcation from the Atlantic to Pacific Oceans. In 1925 it was realized that boundary maintenance was a continuing need, so another treaty was signed establishing the IBC in its permanent form to inspect the boundary and make the necessary repair or replacement of damaged markers. It also charged the IBC with the task of maintaining a clear boundary "vista" (see figure 2-12) and, when necessary, the resurvey of any portion of the boundary to confirm the accuracy of its location, in order to settle any question that might arise between the two governments.[22]

In order to control any construction adjacent to the boundary and to preserve the identity of the boundary line through built-up areas, the International Boundary Commission Act was passed in 1960.[23] Since 6 June 1960 this act regulates any work within three metres of the boundary. The prime consideration is that the work does not obstruct the boundary or cause disturbance to monuments.

The work of the IBC is a joint treaty obligation and is recorded in annual joint reports. The canadian commissioner is appointed by order in council and reports to the secretary of state for External Affairs; the U.S. commissioner is appointed by the president and reports to the secretary of state. Each commissioner has a permanent staff that supervises annual field operations guided by a long-range plan outlining the commission's priorities.

Figure 2-12
Monument 90 on the British Columbia–Alaska Boundary.
The Taku River is in the foreground.
Photo: Canadian Boundary Commission

Each of the Canadian and U.S. field parties is assigned specific segments of the boundary in a given year, and each party carries out its work on both sides of the international line.[24] The cost of this work, apart from the salaries and expenses of the commissioners and their staff, is shared equally by the two governments. The total expenditures jointly incurred by the commissioners from 1925 to 31 March 1992 are for the U.S. section $6,371,943, and for the Canadian section $6,377,095. This is a very frugal amount for sixty-seven years of boundary maintenance!

HIGHLIGHTS OF THE WORK
The terrain covered by the boundary is extremely varied, from the eastern coastal sea through the rough and almost inaccessible highlands region of New Brunswick and Québec (see figure 2-13), over the inland lakes, rivers, rocks, and swamps of Ontario, across a vast prairie, and over the Rocky Mountains to the western coastal sea. Then it runs north over a series of mountain peaks with treacherous glaciers and snowfields (the Alaska panhandle) and on up the 141st meridian to the Beaufort Sea.

Figure 2-13
The winding boundary separating Maine and Québec
in the highland district.
Photo: Canadian Boundary Commission

In order to maintain a well-defined boundary line, three distinct operations are essential:
(a) the maintenance of a clear 6 m vista, (b) the maintenance of precise geographic
positions from which the exact location of the boundary can be determined, and (c) the
physical maintenance of a system of monuments and reference monuments to mark the
boundary.[25]

The planning, organizing, and conducting of surveys and vista clearing along the boundary requires experience, dedication, and ingenuity. The chief of each field party prepares
for the field operations in the early spring, gathering data for the planned work locations
and arranging for instruments and other equipment to be available at the first site. If
camping is required arrangements are made for supplies and camp equipment to be
transported to the road or rail point nearest to the work. Transportation for the season's
operation, by air or ground, must also be arranged.

Once the chief is in the field he or she must hire a temporary crew and give them safety
instruction and training as to equipment use. Before beginning field operations, the party
chief must visit pertinent government agencies on both sides of the border, including both

U.S. and Canadian Customs, the U.S. Border Patrol, the RCMP, and the U.S. and Canadian Forestry Services, to apprise them of the proposed field activities.

There were many interesting experiences on these surveys, some quite different from normal survey operations. As an example of difficult terrain, a field party in 1947 was working on the boundary crossings of the fast flowing Klehini River in the Alaska panhandle where an aerial tramway was built for the men to cross the Klehini River on their way to and from work. A cable was stretched across the river, on which ran a pulley with a rope sling attached, together with a draw line made fast to each shore. A man could then sit in the sling and pull himself across to either shore with the draw line.[26]

Wildlife could be a hazard, as was found out during the 1949 field season by the party working in the Kelsall River area of the Alaska panhandle. Bears are a constant menace in that region. While the party was working on the survey a large grizzly broke into the cook tent at the base camp and devoured some of the supplies. As it was a continuing menace it had to be shot. It took the efforts of four men to drag the carcass to the side of the trail, but a week later it was found that wolves had left nothing but its bare bones.[27]

Many different modes of transportation were used throughout the years, with the surveyor's two feet being the principal means, particularly over rough, steep terrain. In dry, relatively flat accessible areas trucks and vans were used, while in wet and rough terrain four-wheel drive vehicles and tracked vehicles were used. In remote and mountainous areas fixed-wing aircraft to transport crew and equipment into base camps were supplemented with helicopters to ease access and speed operations on the boundary work. Canoes, skiffs, motor boats, and other vessels were a necessity along most waterways.

There are as many as twenty different types of monuments used by the IBC. They vary from a 7.5 cm rock tablet to the 6 m cut-granite monument at the Pacific Coast. Over time boundary monuments deteriorate due to rain, salt spray, and temperature extremes, and are damaged due to natural hazards such as erosion, rock falls, and animal activities. Human activities such as vandalism, construction activity, and vehicle damage also take their toll. Each seasonal operation includes the inspection of existing monuments resulting in the repair or replacement of some. In 1987, a typical season, 709 monuments were inspected, 72 were repaired or rebuilt, and 13 new monuments were set.

New technology and new equipment have greatly helped in both expediting the fieldwork and increasing the accuracy of measurements. In 1965 the Geodimeter was introduced to IBC surveys and used for the first time on the Québec-Vermont boundary. In 1971 the Lambert Observation Tower was developed by a former Canadian commissioner and used in subsequent years, allowing for more accurate measurements over difficult terrain. In the readjustment leading up to the NAD83, the IBC staff was involved in the recomputation of some 24 000 points. In 1980 the gyro-theodolite was put into use, as well as the Doppler positioning system, both being first employed on the New York–Vermont-Québec boundary. In 1988 USNGS made measurements using the GPS on 66 boundary monuments along the 49th parallel, working in cooperation with the IBC field crew, who assisted them with monument selection and with IBC vehicle and helicopter support.[28] In 1990 the survey work was streamlined by the acquisition of a total station (the Geodimeter 440).[29]

The term "vista" was first applied to the International Boundary during the implementation of the provisions of the Treaty of 1908. The commissioners appointed under the treaty formally agreed that "the boundary through timbered areas should be further marked by a vista of sufficient width to give a cleared 20-foot sky line along the boundary."[30]

Figure 2-14
The Haskell Opera House, which straddles the border.
Note the boundary monument in the foreground.
Photo: Canadian Boundary Commission

When reviewing the varied terrain traversed by the boundary it can be seen that the maintenance of such a vista becomes a major task, not only because of the steepness of some terrain, but also because of heavy tree growth and the continuing nature of the task. Axes and chain-saws were the principal means of clearing the vista. In 1972, on the British Columbia–Washington border, a three-mile stretch of boundary vista was groomed by bulldozers and seeded with grass to try grooming and mowing as an alternative to vista maintenance in settled areas.[31] This grooming was successful and is in use in appropriate areas. In 1977 some vista clearing was put out to contract to local firms, with the balance done by staff employed by IBC. This is now a continuing practice.

In the eastern part of the border area there exist a number of line houses that straddle the boundary or lie within 3 m of it. One well-known example is the Haskell Opera House (see figure 2-14), opened in 1904. It lies across the 45th parallel boundary between Rock Island, Québec, and Derby Line, Vermont, in such a way that the audience sits in the United States and watches a performance on a stage in Canada.[32]

In 1935 the commission found that there were more than 100 line buildings. Some have survived and new ones have been erected, such as the first joint border and customs facility between Danville, Washington, and Carson, British Columbia. The proposed design of this building would obstruct the boundary line, so the customs authorities sought and eventually obtained IBC permission for construction. The IBC required that removable window panels be incorporated into the design so that a line of sight through the building could be obtained.[33]

Over the years there have been disputes over the boundary, both between landowners and the IBC and between the two governments. An example of this is the boundary in Lake Ontario between turning points 106 and 107. The boundary is defined in the Report of the International Waterways Commission, 1916, between turning points 106 and 107 as "due West 501,388 feet," both terminal points lying in the same parallel of latitude. At issue was the interpretation of the words "due West." The United States took the position that since both the 1908 treaty and the general wording in the 1916 report speak of straight lines, due west must be interpreted as the straight (geodesic) line between each point. Canada argued that a line running due west between two points in the same latitude can only lie along that parallel of latitude, which is a curved line. The two commissioners could not reach agreement and the dispute was referred to the two governments. They said that if the two commissioners could come to an agreement, then their joint decision would bind both governments. "Eventually the U.S. Commissioner saw it our way, we documented this (in December 1980) and it was the end of the matter," said Alex McEwen, the Canadian commissioner at that time.[34]

Provincial and Territorial Boundaries

The principal reason for the survey of statutory boundaries is the need to define on the ground the limits of jurisdiction for the administration of natural resources and features such as highways, and to aid in their location on accurate maps. The following is a description of the six provincial and territorial boundaries that were surveyed entirely or in part after the Second World War.[35] A total of 3329 km (2069 miles) of boundary line were cut out, measured, and monumented by land surveyors and their crews, who challenged some of the most rugged terrain and extreme weather in Canada.

In order to provide the demarcation of provincial and territorial boundaries as described by statutes, the governments concerned must first agree to the need for the boundary survey and the sharing of costs. Each government appoints a boundary commissioner by an order in council, which order also includes the need and the agreed cost sharing. A federal Privy Council order appoints the surveyor general as commissioner and chairman of the commission. This order gives the commission the authority to issue instructions and to direct the execution of the boundary survey. When completed the boundary commission issues an official report of each survey, which is submitted to the governments concerned. In this report the commission recommends:

a) the acceptance of the survey as the true boundary;

b) that the Provincial Legislature consent to the Parliament of Canada declaring the boundary as the true boundary; and

c) that the Parliament of Canada so declare.

Boundary Commission Instructions   The instructions issued by each of the boundary commissions were similar in regard to the following:

Azimuth   Observations on Polaris to be made at six-mile intervals with an approved theodolite with a striding level.

Alignment	To be maintained with a Wild T2 Theodolite, or equivalent, using the process of double centring. (This is the system for prolonging a line with a theodolite by placing foresight marks, once with the telescope in its normal position and once with it reversed. The prolonged line passes through the point midway between the foresight marks.)
Chaining	All distances to be measured twice, in chains and in feet. Where triangulation is necessary, distances are to be obtained by double triangulation. (Although the last of the surveys listed below was completed in 1962, about four years after the introduction of EDM in Canada, chaining was still considered the only legal method of measuring boundary distances. EDM equipment was used in 1965 for random checking of boundary measurements. In 1969 survey instructions included the use of EDM in lieu of the foot tape-measure.)
Monuments	Permanent monuments are to be erected on the boundary at intervisible points and at deflection points. Monuments are to consist of a special boundary post, stamped with consecutive numbers and the year, and referenced by a pyramidal mound and pits or a stone mound, with bearing trees where available.
Levelling	Continuous spirit levels are to be run, with check levels, along the boundary. Elevations are to be recorded on all monuments, on a benchmark adjacent to each monument, and on other benchmarks at intervals along the boundary. In mountainous terrain, trigonometric levels are to be run by establishing elevations from reciprocal vertical angles.
Line Clearing	The boundary is to be cleared to a six-foot skyline (see figure 2-15).
Accuracy	Specifications are to be provided for the testing of all field measurements.

INTERPROVINCIAL BOUNDARIES

Alberta–British Columbia Boundary   This boundary survey was begun in 1913 and by 1924 had been surveyed from the International Boundary north to latitude 57°26′40″.25. This portion of the boundary was confirmed by Act of Parliament, 1932, 22–3 Geo. 5, c. 17, passed on 4 April 1932. In 1949 there was an expressed need for the remainder of the boundary to be surveyed. A boundary commission was established by order in council dated 14 February 1950.[36]

Postwar field operations began on 10 June 1950, and after three winter operations the boundary was completed to the 60th parallel on 23 January 1953, a total of 177 miles. The terrain covered by these surveys is generally undulating. Winter weather conditions were mixed, with temperatures ranging from 0° to −45°C and snow fall amounts varying each season. Transportation was a problem due to a scarcity of lakes for the regular use of fixed-wing aircraft. This resulted in considerable lost time in moving the crew, supplies, and equipment into the survey. In the three winter surveys it took an average of seventeen days for this operation, using horses, dog sleighs, and motor toboggans, supplemented occasionally by aircraft where this was possible.

A loss of time was experienced in early August 1950, when a sickness spread through many of the crew causing soreness and stiffness, swelling behind the ears, and some vomiting. However, the sickness disappeared when the camp was moved from a stagnant water stream, named Poison Creek by the crew. It is now officially named Foulwater Creek.[37]

Figure 2-15
Manitoba-Saskatchewan boundary. Mounders are ready to move
forward to the next monument.
Photo: Canadian Boundary Commission

Manitoba-Saskatchewan Boundary   The centre of the road allowance between ranges 29
and 30, west of the principal meridian, was selected by the legislators as the western
boundary of Manitoba in 1881. By 1930 this range line had been surveyed from the
International Boundary north to township 40, and at intervals to township 68.

The postwar survey was begun in 1961 and completed in 1972, a total of 602 miles.
Between 1967 and 1972 a comprehensive retracement survey was made of this original
range line in order to preserve the ground position of the statutory boundary. The terrain
for the majority of the boundary line is rolling farmland in the south and rolling forested
land, with scattered lakes, in the north. The weather during the winter seasons was fairly
seasonal, with heavy snow in some areas up to four and five feet.

Transportation for four of the winter surveys was an Otter aircraft based in camp. Two
motor toboggans were used to gather camp firewood and to assist the monumenting party.

On the 1965–66 winter survey a diesel tractor was used to pull two trailers, to clear the line, and to build a road off line where needed, together with a snowmobile and a motor toboggan. Transportation for the southern portion of the boundary was normal road vehicles.

In order to establish a trial line through the southern townships a theodolite was placed at the south limit of a township and sighted on a projectile fired vertically from a mortar on the north limit. The sighted line was then cut through.[38]

Monumentation, where the boundary is the centre of the road allowance, differs from other boundary monuments. One-foot concrete obelisks are placed at 1.5 mile intervals with two-foot concrete obelisks placed near township corners on the statutory boundary. Neither of these monuments are placed on constructed roads; in their place witness monuments consisting of concrete reference marks are placed 46.2 feet east and west of the established point on the boundary.

Two official ceremonies were held pertaining to this boundary survey, one at the north limit and one at the south limit. On 15 August 1963 a ceremony was held at the 60th parallel, where a special aluminum obelisk monument had been placed on 6 April 1962, representing the completion, not only of the current survey, but also of the survey of the more than 1500 miles of the 60th parallel boundary from the mountains of the Alaska panhandle to Hudson Bay. Representatives of the governments of Canada, Manitoba, and Saskatchewan deposited various objects and letters in the obelisk, addressed to government officers in the year 2063.[39]

On 25 June 1970, a special ceremony was held at the southern limit of the boundary to dedicate monument 670 A, placed at this point on the International Boundary. In attendance were representatives of the governments of Canada, Manitoba, and Saskatchewan, the two International Boundary commissioners, and the three Manitoba-Saskatchewan boundary commissioners.[40]

PROVINCIAL-TERRITORIAL BOUNDARIES:

British Columbia–Yukon–Northwest Territories Boundary The part of this boundary between Teslin Lake and Tatshenshini River was surveyed between 1899 and 1908, and retraced between 1950 and 1959. In 1943 with the construction of the Alaska Highway the need for further boundary surveys resulted in the establishment of a boundary commission. Nineteen sets of astronomic observations, to determine the location of the 60th parallel, were made by the Geodetic Survey between 1943 and 1951 at the request of the commission.

Field surveys to demarcate the boundary began on 9 June 1945 and continued for eight summer seasons and two winter seasons, finishing on 22 August 1958 for a total of 453 miles. The only portion of the boundary not surveyed is the final 38 miles between Alsek River and the boundary of the Alaska panhandle, described as heavily glaciated and very rugged.[41]

The terrain along the rest of this boundary is level and gently undulating in the east, hilly and rough in the Cassiar Mountains, and with rugged alpine ridges with steep valleys and glaciers in the west. The weather is very unpredictable; generally subarctic in the mountainous regions with rain, snow, low clouds, and morning fog a serious hindrance to survey operations. In 1958 "the remainder of the season was a sad story of foul weather when it took a month to do a week's work."[42]

Transportation on summer surveys was a combination of horses, packers, boats, and aircraft with a helicopter used in the later seasons. Two boats were built in 1952 before the summer work was started, and these were also used on the 1953 and 1954 surveys. To obviate the risk of having the horses swim across the swift and treacherous Liard River, a corral was built in 1953 on top of a pole platform resting on the two boats lashed together, sufficient to hold six horses. It proved a success.[43] On winter surveys transportation was provided by dog teams and aircraft.

In conducting surveys along the 60th parallel, commission instructions were to survey a series of 486 chain trial chords[44] to the parallel, with a fractional closing chord, between points on the parallel adjacent to each astrofix. The true chords were then run and monumented from these trial chords. An interesting technique on the 1949 summer survey between astrofixes R5 and N6, forty miles apart east of the Alaska Highway, involved the use of a high bare-topped ridge about midway, close to line and visible from both astrofix locations. An elongated form of triangulation was constructed pivoting on this central ridge, which enabled the computed true line to be run and monumented in record time[45].

Alberta–Northwest Territories Boundary   Nearly thirty-six miles of this boundary between Slave River and Little Buffalo River were surveyed between May and August 1925. It was surveyed under the direction of the surveyor general of Dominion Lands, being prior to the 1930 transfer of natural resources to the province.[46]

The boundary commission, established in 1950, requested the Geodetic Survey to put in astronomic control. Twelve astrofix stations were located along the 60th parallel between 1950 and 1952.

Demarcation surveys began on 3 December 1950, and continued for two more winter seasons and one summer season, finishing on 28 August 1954, marking a distance of 310 miles. The terrain along this boundary is fairly flat and swampy with numerous bodies of water. The main physical feature is the Cameron Hills, west of the Mackenzie Highway. The winter seasons produced low temperatures with strong winds and drifting snow.

Winter transportation was provided by horses, a dog team, a motor toboggan, and tractors with sleighs. Tractors in winter proved advantageous in this terrain as one tractor cleared nine miles of line in one day and averaged four miles a day. During the 1954 summer season, camp moves were by man packing and a canoe across water, with aircraft for occasional supply trips. A helicopter was used for camp moves later in the survey. The surveyor's diary reports that on two days the party had no food and could catch no fish.[47]

Saskatchewan–Northwest Territories Boundary   This boundary survey began on 27 December 1954, and after three more winter seasons was completed on 31 March 1958, a distance of 277 miles. A further check measurement was done in 1959.[48]

Thirteen sets of astronomic observations were made between 1953 and 1957 to determine the location of the 60th parallel. Selwyn Lake is the largest feature on the boundary. To the west of Selwyn Lake the terrain is generally low rolling hills with steep rocky ridges and boulder-strewn shallow lakes and creeks. To the east the land is flat and swampy with gently rolling hills and shallow lakes. The weather was generally seasonal with low temperatures in the range of −45°C. Transportation consisted of a fixed-wing aircraft, dog teams, and motor toboggans.

An incident during the 1955–56 season illustrates one winter hazard. A motor toboggan broke down on the trail between camps and was left on the trail overnight. When the driver returned in the morning to effect repairs, he found a nearby creek had overflowed, freezing

Figure 2-16
A tractor swing working on the Manitoba–Northwest Territories boundary.
Photo: Canadian Boundary Commission

the toboggan into six inches of solid ice. It took several days to chop it out, jack it up, erect a tent over it, and keep a tent heater fired in order to thaw out the tracks and skis.

On 31 March 1958, election day, a polling station was granted for the survey camp in the Saskatchewan constituency of Meadow Lake. There was a 100 percent poll,[49] a unique final day for any boundary survey.

Manitoba–Northwest Territories Boundary   This boundary survey began on 8 January 1959 and was completed on 6 April 1960, with a short return trip to obtain additional measurements in September 1961.[59] The boundary length is 249 miles. Three sets of astronomic observations were made along the 60th parallel, one at each end and one near the middle of the boundary.

The terrain in the first winter was rolling, treed country and in the second winter flat, treeless barren land. The weather was typically cold and windy with temperatures down to −55°C. One extreme blizzard on the barren lands persisted for three days. Transportation in 1958–59 was by an aircraft based in camp for the season and two motor toboggans to maintain a firewood supply and assist the monumenting party. In 1959–60, across the barrens, two diesel tractors were used to pull freight sleighs and sleeping cabooses (see figure 2-16). On the survey the tractor train moved each day, which was a safety factor in this blizzard-prone region. It also reduced the daily walk into camp at day's end. The daily production across the barrens averaged 4.4 miles.

This boundary was run as theoretical 486 chain chords to the 60th parallel controlled by astronomic observations on Polaris. No trial lines were run and monuments were erected as the line progressed.[51] Ties were made to the astrofixes at Baralzon Lake and at Hudson Bay, but no adjustments were made to the surveyed boundary. The deduced position of the two boundary monuments N 100 and N 171 adjacent to these two astrofixes are 60°00′00″.21 and 59°59′58″.00 respectively.

The journey from Churchill, up the Hudson Bay coast and along the 60th parallel to the start of the survey, took twenty-eight days. The return to Churchill, including 140 miles of boundary survey, took thirty-three working days.[52]

NOTES

1 Epstein, E.F. 1984. *The Use and Value of a Geodetic Reference System*. Orono, ME: University of Maine at Orono.

2 Thomson, D.W. 1966. *Men and Meridians*, volume 2. Ottawa: Queen's Printer.

3 Thomson, D.W. 1969. *Men and Meridians*, volume 3. Ottawa: Queen's Printer.

4 Hamilton, A.C. 1959. Geodetic Survey of Northern Canada by Shoran Trilateration. *Polar Record*, 9, 61, 320–30.

5 Babbage, G. 1983. A Decade of Doppler at the Geodetic Survey of Canada. *Proceedings of the Conference of Commonwealth Surveyors*. Paper B3. London: Ministry of Overseas Development.

6 Geodetic Survey Division. 1993. *GPS Positioning Guide*. Ottawa: Energy, Mines and Resources.

7 Wells, David, et al. 1986. *Guide to GPS Positioning*. Fredericton, NB: Canadian GPS Associates.

8 Schmidt, M. 1992. An Expedition to Measure the Height of Canada's Tallest Mountain. *CISM Journal*, 46, 3, 247–54.

9 Webb, J.D., and R.C. Penny. 1981. Six Years of Inertial Surveying at the Geodetic Survey of Canada. 1981. *Proceedings of the Second International Symposium on Inertial Technology for Surveying and Geodesy*, 325–41.

10 Babbage, G. 1981. Inertial Surveying: A Study in Accuracy and Reliability. *Proceedings of the Second International Symposium on Inertial Technology for Surveying and Geodesy*.

11 Gibb, R.A., and M.D. Thomas. 1976. Gravity Mapping in Canada. *Proceedings of the Geophysics in America Conference*, Ottawa. Publications of the Earth Physics Branch, 46, 3, 49–56.

12 Thomson, *Men and Meridians*, vol. 3.

13 Young, F.W., and J. Murakami. 1989. The North American Vertical Datum of 1988 (NAVD 88). *CISM Journal*, 43, 4, 387–93.

14 1978. *Specifications and Recommendations for Control Surveys and Survey Markers*. Ottawa: Surveys and Mapping Branch.

15 Young and Murakami, The North American Vertical Datum of 1988.

16 Hearty, D.B., and R.A. Gibb. 1989–90, 1990–91, 1991–92, 1992–93, 1993–94. *National Gravity Survey Program of the Geological Survey of Canada*. Ottawa: Geological Survey of Canada, (separate report for each year).

17 IBC Long Range Forecast, December 1989, 1.

18 *IBC Annual Joint Report*, 1979. Ottawa: NRCan, 26.

19 Ibid., and report of the IBC contained in the 1951 *Annual Report of the Dept of Mines and Technical Surveys*.

20 *IBC Annual Joint Report*, 1986. Ottawa: NRCan, 29–31.

21 Ibid., 1980, 16.

22 Ibid., 1985, 1–2.

23 *The International Boundary Commission Act*, 1960, Eliz. 2, c. 31, sec. 4(1).

24 *IBC Annual Joint Report*, 1985. Ottawa, NRCan, 2.

25 IBC Long Range Forecast, December 1985, 37.

26 IBC report contained in the 1947 *Annual Report of the Department of Mines and Resources, Canada*, 183.

27 Ibid., 1949, 16.

28 *IBC Annual Joint Report*, 1988. Ottawa: NRCan, 15–17.

29 Ibid., 1990, 22

30 Ibid., 1982, 5.

31 IBC report contained in the 1972 *Annual Report of the Department of Energy, Mines and Resources, Canada*, 31.

32 1986. *The Canadian Surveyor*, 40, 3, 279.

33 *IBC Annual Joint Report*, 1987. Ottawa: NRCan, 29–30.

34 1986. *The Canadian Surveyor*, 40 ,3, 287, and *IBC Annual Joint Report*, 1990, 45–6.

35 The boundaries surveyed before the Second World War are described in the following publications:
Ontario-Manitoba:
Thomson, Don. W. 1966. *Men and Meridians*, vol 2. Ottawa: Queen's Printer, chap. 16.
Ontario-Quebec:
Thomson, Don W. 1969. *Men and Meridians*, vol. 3. Ottawa: Queen's Printer, chap. 3.
Ladell, John. 1993. *They Left Their Mark*, Toronto: Association of Ontario Land Surveyors, 177, 178, 221, and 247.
Quebec–New Brunswick:
Pounder, John. 1932. The Southern Boundary of Québec. *The Canadian Surveyor*, 4, 6, 6.
Cote, Georges. 1954. Québec–New Brunswick Boundary. *The Canadian Surveyor*, 12, 1, 21.
Nova Scotia–New Brunswick:
March, J.R. 1954. Nova Scotia–New Brunswick Boundary. *The Canadian Surveyor*, 12, 1, 21.
The Québec-Labrador and Yukon–Northwest Territories boundaries have not been surveyed.

36 *Alberta–British Columbia Boundary Report*, 1955. Alberta–British Columbia Boundary Commission, 5.

37 Ibid., 23.

38 *Manitoba-Saskatchewan Boundary Report*, 1976. Manitoba–Saskatchewan Boundary Commission, 53.

39 Ibid., 1965, 38.

40 Ibid., 1976, 82.

41 *British Columbia–Yukon-NWT Boundary Report*, 1966. British Columbia–Yukon–Northwest Territories Boundary Commission, 7, 62, 93.

42 Ibid., 57.

43 Ibid., 46.

44 The "six-mile township" is actually 486 chains across: $6 \times 80 = 480$ chains, plus 6 road allowances $= 486$ chains. *Manuel of Instructions for the Survey of Dominion Land*, 8th ed. 1913.

45 *British Columbia–Yukon–NWT Boundary Report*, 37.

46 *Alberta-NWT Boundary Report*, 1956. Alberta–Northwest Territories Boundary Commission, 2.

47 Ibid.

48 *Saskatchewan–NWT Boundary Report*, 1956. Saskatchewan–Northwest Boundary Commission, 37.

49 Ibid., 1963, 61.

50 *Manitoba–NWT Boundary Report*, 1963. Manitoba–Northwest Territories Boundary Commission, 52.

51 Ibid., 1964, 11.

52 Ibid., 8.

General Reading

Babbage, G. 1982. The Role of Geodetic Survey in Canadian Geodesy. *Proceedings of the Centennial Convention of the Canadian Institute of Surveying*, vol. 1. 490–517. Available from the Canadian Institute of Geomatics, Ottawa.

Bomford, G. 1980. *Geodesy*, 4th ed. Oxford: Clarendon Press.

Burnside, C.D. 1991. *Electromagnetic Distance Measurement*, 3d ed. Oxford: BSP Professional Books.

Canadian Council on Surveying and Mapping. *Proceedings of Annual Meetings, 1972–1993*. Unpublished. Held in the Library, Geomatics Canada, NRCanada.

Canadian Geophysical Bulletin, volumes 25 to 41. NRCanada.

Canadian National Report to the International Union of Geodesy and Geophysics for 1979–82 (1983), 1983–86 (1987), 1987–90 (1991). Copies held in the library, Geomatics Sector, NRCanada.

Gibb, R.A., D. Nagy, R.K. McConnell, and D.B. Hearty. 1987. *Evolution of the Gravity Map of Canada*. Manuscript held in the library of the Geological Survey of Canada.

Hodgson, J.H. 1989–94. *The Heavens Above and the Earth Below: A History of the Dominion Observatories*. 2 vols. Ottawa: Geological Survey of Canada, Publication Distribution Office.

1974. *Proceedings, Geodesy for Canada Conference*. Ottawa: Surveys and Mapping Branch, Energy, Mines and Resources.

CHAPTER THREE

Photogrammetry and Federal Topographic Mapping

Leslie J. O'Brien and Louis M. Sebert

By the end of the Second World War photogrammetry had become an established component of topographic mapping, and its use was fundamental to the postwar acceleration of Canadian mapping. The advances in photogrammetry over the past fifty years can hardly be understood without some knowledge of the basic elements of the science. This chapter will therefore be divided into two parts. The first will cover the fundamentals of photogrammetry, and the second will follow with an outline history of the federal topographic mapping programme as it evolved over the years.

PHOTOGRAMMETRIC SYSTEMS AND INSTRUMENTS

The science of photogrammetry is based on measurements and related information derived from photographs and electronic images. Its aim is to reconstruct the dimensions, form, and relative positions of selected image features. For this purpose it is essential that the cameras, measuring instruments, and photographic materials be of the highest quality, and that their geometrical characteristics be known.

Air Photography

The most common imagery employed in photogrammetry for topographic mapping is stereoscopic, formed by viewing a pair of overlapping vertical aerial photographs. In this case the camera is mounted in the bay of an aircraft with the camera axis pointed straight down through a viewing port. The mounting is gimballed to keep the camera pointing at or near vertical in flight, regardless of random movements of the aircraft. Each photo flight proceeds at a specified altitude along pre-planned lines and spacing between lines. Photographs are exposed successively along each flight line at intervals that give a nominal 60 percent overlap between them, and the spacing between adjacent flight lines is chosen to give a nominal side overlap of 20 percent. By this procedure an area to be mapped is completely covered by overlapping photos. The amount of ground area covered by each image depends on the photo scale, and this in turn depends on the flight altitude.

As the photographs are spaced to achieve an overlap of about 60 percent along the flight line, when one photo is viewed with one eye while its neighbour is viewed with the other eye, the overlapping images result in the observer seeing the scene in three dimensions. Most people have observed this phenomenon while using a parlour stereoscope or at a three-dimensional motion picture. In photogrammetry the three-dimensional image formed by viewing the common overlap of a pair of aerial photos is called a "model" of the terrain.

A single vertical aerial photo resembles a map, but for accurate map work it has several flaws. To begin with it is a central perspective image, which means that the objects that are closer to the camera are radially more distant from the photo centre than are images that are farther from the camera. That is why the buildings in a low-level air photo of a city all appear to be leaning away from the centre of the picture. This of course also happens to hills and mountains in high-level photography, and is referred to as relief displacement. The displacement is actually radial from the plumb point of the photo, which is the image of the point on the ground vertically beneath the camera. The geometrical centre of the photo is called the principal point (PP). If the camera is absolutely level when the photo is exposed, the plumb point and the PP coincide. If the flight crew taking the photographs are well trained, and if the weather conditions are favourable, the two points will always be very close together.

A second type of image distortion is caused by the camera being slightly tilted at the moment of exposure. Here again the displacement is radial but this time from the isocentre, a point also very close to the PP in near-vertical photography. If the plumb point and isocentre could easily be found they would be used in mapping to correct these distortions, but as they are not easily found the PP must be used in their stead. The PP is located by using the collimation marks at the midpoints of the sides of each photo. By lining a ruler up with these marks a small cross can be drawn at the PP. Experience has shown that a substitution of the PP for the more correct centre points is acceptable for topographic mapping if the flying has been well done. These PPs are important points in the mapping system described in the next section, where they are used to find the true position of selected points around the edge of each photograph. These in turn will be used as points to "control" the plotting of the map detail.

Radial Line Plotting

In 1927 Lt (later Brig.) Martin Hotine, Royal Engineers, published a British army manual titled Simple Methods of Surveying from Air Photographs.[1] In it he describes a simple, inexpensive system for plotting map detail that became known as radial line plotting. It was adopted in Canada in the early 1930s by both military and civil service mapping agencies, and became the mainstay of map compilation from about 1930 to 1947. It will be described here in some detail, both because it is easily understood and because it illustrates graphically the fundamentals behind all the newer air survey systems.

The first step in radial line plotting is to mark the positions of all PPs on the photos to be used in the plot. Because the photos overlap by 60 percent, the position of the PP of the second photo will appear on the right edge of the first photo. The second and all subsequent photos will show three PPs, all of which must be marked carefully on each photo.

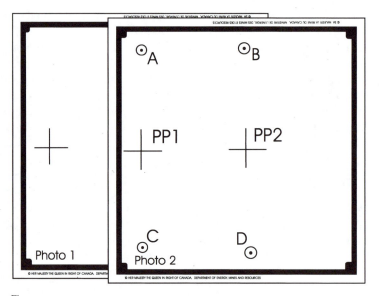

Figure 3-1
The photogrammetric model. The pass points are lettered A to D.
Source: MCE

In radial line plotting the object is to find the correct (i.e., undistorted) position of four points in the corners of each model. In figure 3-1 these points are lettered A to D. They are called "pass points" because, as will be seen, they pass the map detail from one model to the next. (They are also referred to as "minor control" because they control the plotting of the map detail. The "major control" are the ground survey points that, in effect, tie the mapping to the ground.)

Figure 3-2 shows the mechanics of a radial line plot. Figure 3-2A shows the pass points on the first three photos with the radial lines drawn to them from the PPs. It is known that the correct positions of the pass points lie somewhere along these radial lines. The lines between the PPs are called the PP baselines. Note the small triangle on the first two photos. This is a ground survey point, and it is rayed in as though it were a pass point.

Figure 3-2B shows a piece of tracing paper that has been placed over photo 1, and the baseline and the radials have been traced off. Then the second photo is placed under the tracing paper. It is lined up along the first baseline with the image of PP1 under its mark on the paper. Again the radials and the second baseline are traced off. The intersections of the radials give the true position of the pass points above and below PP1. The position of the survey point has also been fixed.

Figure 3-2C shows the plot as far as the seventh photo. Note the three-way intersections at the pass points. These intersections are used to position the third and subsequent photos in their correct positions on the baselines. This makes the whole plot uniform in scale.

The scale of the above demonstration was taken arbitrarily as the scale of the second photo because in lining it up on the baseline, the image of PP1 was placed under its mark on the tracing. The correct ground scale can only be found by raying in at least two ground

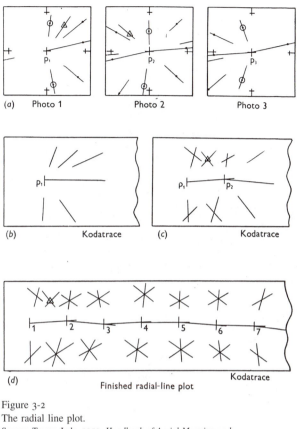

(a)   Photo 1   Photo 2   Photo 3

(b)   Kodatrace   (c)   Kodatrace

(d)   Kodatrace
            Finished radial-line plot

Figure 3-2
The radial line plot.
Source: Trorey, Lyle. 1950. *Handbook of Aerial Mapping and Photogrammetry.* Cambridge: Cambridge University Press

survey points. In actual mapping operations an effort is made to have two survey points in the first model.

When the plot is finished it is placed on the map manuscript, which up to this point contains nothing but the positions of the ground survey points. The ground survey points on the plot are fitted carefully to the ground survey points on the manuscript, and the positions of the pass points are pricked through. The map detail is then plotted using the pass points and a tracing instrument called a Sketchmaster (see figure 3-3). This is a camera lucida device employing a semi-transparent mirror in which both the photo and the manuscript can be seen. The Sketchmaster is adjusted so the pass points on the manuscript fit the pass points on the photo, and then the map detail is traced off.

In the days when radial line plotting was used (1930 to 1947) the drawing of contours was a separate operation. Level lines were run along roads through the area being mapped, and topographers with plane tables used these to obtain their plane table elevations. The air photo of the area was mounted on the plane table, and spot heights were obtained by taking clinometer (i.e., vertical) angles to various features in the landscape. The elevations of these features were calculated by using the vertical angles together with the distances

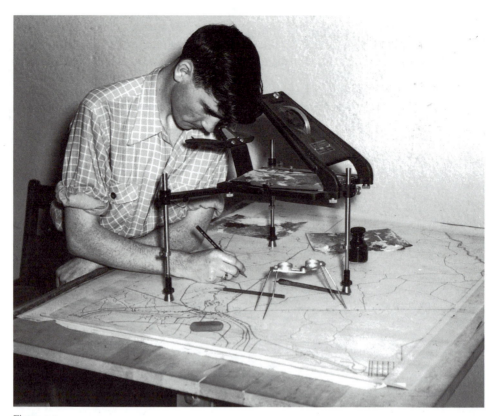

Figure 3-3
The vertical Sketchmaster.
Photo: SMB

to the features scaled from the photographs. Back in the office the spot heights were used
to guide the drawing of contours right on the photo while viewing the model under a mirror
stereoscope.

In essence this is radial line plotting, the first photogrammetric system employing vertical
air photographs to be used in Canada.

The Slotted Template Assembly

As can be imagined, radial line plotting was meticulous but tedious work. While this type
of mapping was going on in Canada, the Americans had started the Tennessee Valley
Authority project. This was an enormous flood-control and hydro-generating project covering thousands of square miles. Because dams were being built that would flood great
areas, good up-to-date topographic maps were needed. Much of the mapping work was put
out to contract, and one of the main contractors was the Fairchild Aviation Corporation.
One of Fairchild's employees, a Mr Collier, invented a mechanical method to replace the
tedious tracing of the radial lines. The principle was exactly the same as the radial line

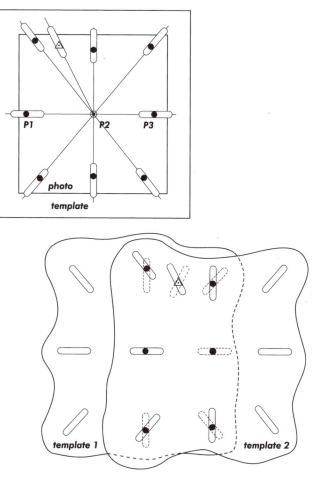

P1 P2 P3

photo

template

template 1   template 2

Figure 3-4
Radial line triangulation with slotted templates.
Source: MCE

plot, but in place of a tracing Collier substituted a fibre-board template, one for each air photo. A hole was punched in the centre of the template to represent the PP, and slots radial from the hole were cut in the template to represent the rays to the pass points. Studs were then inserted in the holes and slots, and the templates were fitted together as shown in figure 3-4. Naturally slots were also cut to the position of the ground control to give the assembly scale and direction. The beauty of this system was that if the first few templates were laid to the wrong scale, this could easily be adjusted as soon as the assembly encountered the ground control.

When the First Corps Field Survey Company of the Canadian army was sent to England in January 1940,[2] the air survey personnel found the British army using the familiar radial line method. But when the American army arrived in 1942 the topographic battalions brought their slotted template equipment with them.[3] It was adopted quickly by the British and Canadian armies, and radial line plotting was abandoned.

THE TRIMETROGON MAPPING SYSTEM

Although vertical aerial photography has been the mainstay of photogrammetric input to Canadian mapping since the 1930s, earlier use was made of oblique aerial photography for production of Canada's first aeronautical charts. In oblique photography the camera is mounted in the aircraft with the axis of the lens intentionally pointed out of the vertical. When the resulting photography shows the horizon it is called a high oblique; otherwise it is called a low oblique. Oblique photography is most suited to small-scale mapping of large areas of relatively flat terrain. Its advantages are that each flight covers a much wider swath of terrain, the need for ground control is reduced, and flying requirements are relaxed.

In the 1930s the Geographical Section of the General Staff (GSGS, the army's mapping agency) and the Topographical Survey cooperated on the production of a small number of aeronautical charts using oblique photography (as described in chapter 9). Late in 1940 American military planners became concerned by the lack of air charts between the United States and Alaska. In March 1941 the U.S. military attaché approached the Canadian government with a suggested cooperative project to map a wide corridor between Montana and Alaska. The Americans had developed a method for small-scale topographic mapping called the Trimetrogon System. As this American suggestion would eventually be responsible for the first complete topographic coverage of Canada, it will be described here in some detail.

Naturally the system required some ground control, but much less than required for mapping with vertical photography. The Canadian contribution to the joint project was the furnishing of this ground control. In some places this control was in place, but where it was not it was provided by astrofixes. The Americans flew the photography and plotted the map detail.

In Trimetrogon mapping three cameras, each fitted with the then modern Metrogon lens, were fixed in a rigid frame bolted to the fuselage of the plane. One camera was pointed straight down while the other two were pointed out to the left and right of the plane. All three cameras were exposed at exactly the same instant, thus providing a panorama from horizon to horizon at right angles to the flight line. The cameras were timed to provide the vertical photos with the usual 60 percent forward overlap. Only the lower half of the obliques were used for plotting, so a sixteen-mile spacing of the flight lines gave a convenient side overlap.

The theory of Trimetrogon plotting is similar to the slotted template assembly, but of course radial lines could not be drawn from the vertical photo onto the obliques without unacceptable distortion. To remove this distortion the ingenious "rectoblique plotter" had been invented by the Americans. The working of this plotter has been described elsewhere,[4] so it is sufficient to say here that it allows true radial lines to be drawn from the PP of the vertical photo to pass points and ground survey points on the obliques. The radial lines were drawn on good quality chart paper. In theory large fibre-board templates could have been made from these paper drawings, but they would have been over a metre wide. Instead a "spider template" was constructed with slotted metal strips radiating outward from a bolt representing the PP. The paper diagram drawn by the rectoblique plotter was used to get the correct angles for the arms of the spider. These spider templates were assembled in the same way as the slotted templates. Very large laydowns were often assembled as shown in figure 3-5. Once the pass points were marked on the manuscript they were used to control the plotting, which was done with a special Oblique Sketchmaster.

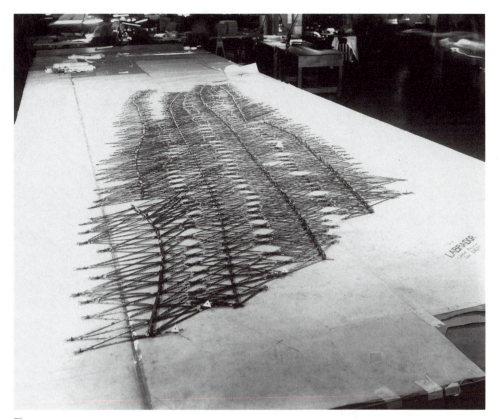

Figure 3-5
A spider template laydown. The work shown is the U.S. Air Force mapping of Labrador.
Photo: ASPRS, by permission

The inventors of the Trimetrogon System claimed that height information could be obtained from the obliques, but the Canadian experience was that such elevations were not reliable. After the Americans joined the war the Trimetrogon work was extended to the whole of the Canadian north, and most of the Eight-Mile aeronautical charts of that region were published without contours and with only a minimum of height information. After the war this serious deficiency was corrected by using the Air Profile Recorder (APR) or barometers transported by helicopters. But during the war pilots used the preliminary air charts to fly much-needed war supplies to Britain and the USSR. It was dangerous living, and it is to their credit that they did so without complaint.

PHOTOGRAMMETRIC PLOTTERS

The Multiplex Aeroprojector

The first photogrammetric plotting instrument to be used in Canada was the Zeiss Multiplex Aeroprojector. As can be seen in figure 3-6 the instrument consists of two or more

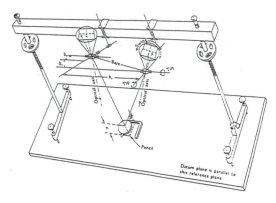

Figure 3-6
The Multiplex Aeroprojector.
Source: MCE

projectors, similar in operation to the common 35 mm slide projector, suspended from a bar and focused downward onto a drafting table. In place of a 35 mm slide the Multiplex used 54 × 54 mm glass diapositives, each of which was reduced from a 9 × 9 inch (230 × 230 mm) air photo. The diapositives in adjacent projectors show adjacent overlapping air photos, so that when their lights are turned on a stereoscopic model is projected down on the drafting table. Red and cyan (blue-green) filters are placed in adjacent projectors to allow the operator, who is equipped with eyeglasses having red and cyan lenses, to see the model. The working of this instrument will be explained in the next section.

The first Multiplex arrived in Canada in 1936. At that time Lieutenant-Colonel (later Lieutenant-General) E.L.M. Burns was in command of the GSGS. In 1934 an article appeared in the German technical journal *Bildmessung und Luftbildwesen* announcing a new device for mapping from air photography. Although more elaborate instruments for such work had been available for some fifteen years, this new device promised simplicity in operation, accuracy in plotting, and a relatively inexpensive price. Burns noted the article, and heard that the Tennessee Valley people were purchasing a number of them. He thought the Canadian army should test the instrument.

In the spring of 1935 Burns wrote to the Zeiss officials suggesting that his unit would provide a strip of air photography and ground control if Zeiss would plot a test map. This was agreed to, and Burns had the RCAF fly a strip from Templeton (now part of Gatineau) north to Perkins, a distance of about eleven miles. Burns took the photographs and ground control to Germany in July 1935. There he watched the map being plotted on a Multiplex. The map was drawn at a scale of four inches to one mile (1:15 840) on drawing paper in coloured inks. The map was then taken back to Canada where it was tested rigorously by field survey. The results were so encouraging that a seven-projector unit was purchased in 1936. It was used only for training and special projects before the war. However when the American army arrived in England in 1942 their topographic battalion was fully equipped with Multiplex equipment. By this time the Bausch and Lomb Company of Rochester, New York, was producing its version of the Multiplex. Thus very soon both the Canadian and British mapping units were also using the Bausch and Lomb equipment.

After the war, when the GSGS was being converted to the Army Survey Establishment (ASE), the new unit was furnished with Multiplex equipment that was used in conjunction with slotted template assemblies. In 1947 the Topographical Survey also adopted the instrument and the slotted template method. Radial line plotting was abandoned in Canada forever.

THE USE OF PHOTOGRAMMETRIC PLOTTERS IN CANADA

Over the years a number of different stereo plotting instruments have been used in Canada. These instruments can be divided generally into four categories: (1) those employing double projection direct viewing, (2) those employing mechanical viewing, (3) the analytical plotters, and (4) the digital plotters. The federal topographic mapping programme has made use of instruments in all categories.

Double Projection Direct Viewing Instruments

The Multiplex (see figure 3-6) was the original member of this category. As has been mentioned it uses small diapositives, which was a design consideration to achieve a practical projection distance and to allow a number of projectors to be mounted on the bar at one time. The diapositives are mounted in optical projectors whose light beams are filtered alternately in red and cyan. The operator wears eyeglasses that have one lens in each of the complementary colours. This "anaglyphic" viewing system separates the view seen by one of the operator's eyes from that seen by the other. Thus when an overlapping pair of diapositives is viewed, a stereoscopic model is seen.

The projectors are mounted on a bar pointing downward onto a working table as shown in figure 3-6. Each projector can be given six possible movements. It can be moved in the x, y, and z directions (i.e., along the bar, moved at right angles to the bar, or up and down). Each projector can also be tipped, tilted, and rotated. In operation the model is viewed on a small (8 cm diameter) platen mounted on a small tracing table. The platen can be raised or lowered by a thumbscrew, which also actuates a scale that shows the platen height. Centred in the platen is a small point of light that provides a floating mark. Directly below the mark is a pencil that can be lowered onto the map manuscript to record the movement of the mark as the map detail is traced off.

The model is set up in the following manner. Diapositives of overlapping photos are set up in two of the projectors. In each projector the diapositive is centred carefully in its holder. This is called interior orientation. Then the left projector is levelled by eye and its light is switched on. The direction of the PP baseline (from PP1 to PP2) is noted and the projector is rotated until the baseline is parallel to the bar. The second projector is then switched on, and by moving the platen to the corners of the model the want of correspondence between the two images is noted. It is removed methodically by using the adjustment screws of the right projector, starting at the PPs and then moving to the model corners. This action is called relative orientation. When it is completed the model has been formed, but its scale is not known and it probably is not level.

To achieve absolute orientation ground control is needed. The minimum is two horizontal control points and three vertical control points. These must be plotted on the map manuscript, which is placed on the table under the projectors. The floating mark is then placed on one of the horizontal control points, and the manuscript is shifted so the pencil under the platen is on the corresponding point on the manuscript. The floating mark is then moved to the second horizontal point and the manuscript is rotated until the platen pencil is on or near the second horizontal point. If a fit is not possible the model scale is adjusted so the two manuscript horizontal points can be placed under their model counterparts. The scale adjustment is made by moving the right projector to the right or left along the bar.

The model is now levelled by taking floating mark readings at each of the vertical control points. At each point the floating mark is placed on the model surface and the scale reading is taken. As the true elevation of each point is known, the correct platen reading for each can be computed by proportion. The model can be levelled by adjusting the projectors or by tipping the model as a whole by adjusting the foot screws on the end supports of the bar. When the model has been levelled and brought to scale, absolute orientation has been achieved. It should be noted that the three orientations (interior, relative, and absolute) are common to all photogrammetric plotters.

It would be prohibitively expensive to require ground control in every model. As has been seen earlier the slotted template assembly provides horizontal control at the corners of each model, but it does not provide vertical control. Because of the small size of the Multiplex projectors, as many as seven can be mounted on the bar at one time. If ground control is available in the first model it can be set up, and then the first projector is switched off and the third switched on. As the second projector is already scaled and levelled, the absolute orientation of the third projector is quite easy. In this way the remaining projectors are brought into correspondence, and in effect a long model is formed. When ground control is eventually met down the strip, the whole strip can be adjusted as required. This operation is called "bridging," a subject that will be discussed in more detail later in this chapter.

The first use of Multiplex in Canada was in fact a bridging operation. In the strip of photography that Burns took to Germany in 1935 he provided the Zeiss personnel with full ground control in the first model at Templeton, in the fifth model, and in the last (tenth) model at Perkins. This was sufficient for accurate plotting, which was checked extensively, and satisfactorily, by field survey in the autumn of 1935.

Improvements to Projection Plotters

As has been mentioned the Multiplex served valiantly during the war and in the immediate postwar period. But in the early 1950s North American photogrammetrists began looking for a more accurate plotting instrument. The small diapositives used in the Multiplex, and the rather primitive lighting system, made it difficult for operators to do precise work. As an answer to this problem two American projection plotters appeared in the 1950s, both following the basic Multiplex design but incorporating significant improvements.

The first of these was the Kelsh Plotter invented by H. Kelsh while he was with the U.S. Geological Survey. At first glance the Kelsh appears to be an oversized two-projector

Multiplex. It has its two projectors suspended about 120 cm above a large plotting table. The projectors hold diapositives that are the same size as the air photos (i.e., 230×230 mm). The illumination of the diapositives, however, employs a system that is completely different from the Multiplex. Instead of having a light-bulb illuminating the whole diapositive, the Kelsh employs a spotlight that is swung above the diapositive focused directly on the small part of the diapositive that is being viewed on the platen below. The two spotlights are aligned by rods joining them to the platen so that as the platen is moved the spotlight illumination follows. The use of large diapositives, and this greatly improved illumination, means that much more accurate plotting can be done, especially in contouring and height measurement. It has been estimated that with a given pair of air photos, if a trained operator could draw 20 m contours on a Multiplex he or she could draw 10 m contours on a Kelsh.

The Kelsh Plotter played a significant role in Canadian mapping from 1953 to about 1975. In 1969 the Canadian army purchased four K200 Kelsh Plotters. These are oversize instruments with a focal length of 200 cm and were used for plotting from very-high-altitude photography. This programme was phased out in 1976.

The second Multiplex replacement was the Balplex (Bausch And Lomb multiplex). This instrument uses 5×5 inch (110×110 mm) diapositives and, like the Kelsh, has greatly improved model illumination. This is provided by using an ellipsoidal mirror over each diapositive, with the light-bulb at one of the foci of the ellipse and the PP of the diapositive at the other. By this rather sophisticated system the inventors have provided illumination at least the equivalent of the Kelsh.

With both the Kelsh and the Balplex the steps of interior, relative, and absolute orientation are the same as with the Multiplex. The Kelsh was never used for bridging; its large projectors made this impossible. There was a limited use of bridging on the Balplex, but this involved a double-length bar, six projectors, and two plotting tables. But this was a short-lived experiment because instrument bridging was being replaced by the much more efficient mathematical bridging that will be described later in this chapter. With the Balplex, however, it was often found convenient to add a third projector on the standard table so an additional model could be added to the model already scaled and levelled.

With both the Kelsh and the Balplex, use is made of pantographs to reduce the model scale to the desired manuscript scale. Generally speaking the red and cyan filters are used with both, but some operators prefer the flicker system in which mechanical shutters on both projectors and above the tracing table are synchronized to provide left-eye and right-eye viewing of the appropriate projection. The white light gives better illumination.

A third projection plotter appeared in 1962. This was the Gamble Plotter, invented by Samuel G. Gamble during his tenure as director of the Surveys and Mapping Branch. It uses two Multiplex-type projectors to form a stereo model, but instead of viewing a tiny part of this model on a platen the whole model is viewed on a plotting table that can be raised or lowered through the model. A closely spaced pattern of luminous dots is projected down onto the plotting table to give the operator the sense of a level plane. The usual moves of interior, relative, and absolute orientation are carried out, and then the terrain is drawn as seen on the table. The plane of the table is kept in touch with the portion of the model being drawn. Contours are sketched by raising the table to the desired height as shown on a scale attached to the table.

The Gamble Plotter was designed mainly for reconnaissance mapping of wilderness areas at medium scales. Unfortunately there was, at the time of its appearance, a diminishing requirement for this type of mapping. Consequently it has gone out of production.

In recalling these production plotters, which in their day were the workhorses of Canadian mapping, a small incident comes to mind. In the Surveys and Mapping Branch there was a constant stream of visitors who were interested in the mapping processes. In the Kelsh room there was one operator who was particularly good at explaining his work to non-technical visitors, and consequently the tour guide generally steered the visitor in his direction. One day a gentleman was being shown through the room, and as usual this operator started his explanation of his work. "I think you can abbreviate your talk, young man" said the visitor. "I'm Harry Kelsh. I invented the instrument."

Mechanical Projection Plotters

The category of stereoplotters based on mechanical projection includes the line of instruments produced by the Wild company (now Leica) of Heerbrugg, Switzerland, a line used extensively in postwar federal mapping.

The term mechanical projection refers to the use of metal rods called space rods, rather than light, to define the intersection of rays in the stereo model from the images of the same point on overlapping photographs. Glass or film diapositives of the two photographs are mounted in holders, and directly below each is an optical objective lens that can be moved to view any point in the imagery. Movement of the two scanning lenses is controlled by movement of the two space rods. Effectively each space rod is pivoted at the perspective centre of its corresponding photograph, and its top end contains the scanning lens. Thus the angle of intersection between the two rods when viewing a point in the oriented diapositives is the same as the angle between light rays from the point to the camera when the photos were exposed. In essence the pivot point of each space rod replaces the camera lens, and the rod replaces the light ray from the point on the ground to its image on the diapositive. The viewing system is binocular through two optical trains, each one beginning at the diapositive scanner and ending at one eye of the operator. A floating mark is provided by using two finely etched lines on glass (referred to as "half marks"). One is inserted into each of the optical trains and together they form the required floating mark. Figure 3-7 illustrates this arrangement.

Once the diapositives are mounted in their holders the usual procedures for relative and absolute orientation are undertaken. Mechanical plotters are generally high-precision devices. Certain ones, such as the Wild A5 and A7 models, were used primarily for bridging in the federal mapping programme because of their high precision. In these models the movements of the space rods and optical scanners are controlled by lead screws driven by handwheels, one for each movement in each of the x and y directions. The apparent height of the floating mark is adjusted by a rotating foot disc. Operators must have considerable skill to coordinate the hand and foot motions needed to keep the floating mark in contact with the stereo-model detail being plotted or measured. For plotting, the x and y movements are transmitted to a coordinatograph through couplings to the handwheels. As can be imagined, the following of an irregular line such as a contour by turning x and y handwheels is infinitely more complicated than moving a platen over the model. For this reason instruments like the A5 and A7 were, in the federal service, almost entirely restricted to bridging, the measurements being recorded on tape rather than plotted.

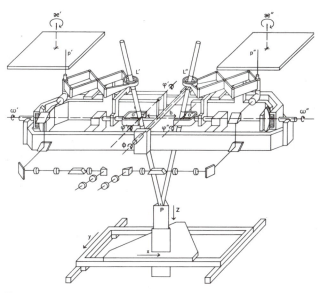

Figure 3-7A
The Wild A8 Autograph – diagram showing the optical and
mechanical trains.
Source: L.H. Systems

Figure 3-7B
The Wild A8 Autograph.
Photo: Terra Surveys Ltd

Bridging with these instruments is possible because the optical trains allow for the "base in" and "base out" methods of viewing a model. For example the first model is set up with the first diapositive mounted in the left holder and the second in the right holder. The first model of a strip is then set up in the usual manner, which is termed the base in mode because the optics are looking inwards, so to speak. After the coordinates of the pass points have been measured, the right optics are moved to the right half of the right-hand diapositive. The third diapositive is mounted in place of the first, and then the second model is formed by viewing the left half of the third diapositive and the right half of the second. This is the base out mode. This action is continued along the strip using alternately the base in and base out modes. (This capability of alternating bases made the A5 and A7 very stable instruments for aerotriangulation.)

Other mechanical projection plotters, such as the Wild B8, were used mainly for map compilation. Instead of X and Y handwheels the B8 uses a freehand movement of a handgrip located at the intersection of the space rods for X and Y plotting, and a foot disc for vertical control. This instrument was found to be well suited to production requirements for compilation of the 1:50 000 sheets of the National Topographic System (NTS).

The Analytical Stereoplotter

This is a high-precision plotting system developed in the 1950s at the National Research Council in Ottawa. The project, led by U.V. Helava, gave rise to a family of instruments referred to as analytical stereoplotters, which were revolutionary at the time. Essentially this type of plotter consists of a stereoscopic coordinate-measuring device, an electronic computer, and an electrically driven coordinatograph, all interconnected (see figure 12-5).

In operation two overlapping air photographs, printed on glass or film, are positioned in horizontal holders on the top of the instrument. The operator places the floating mark on each of the collimation marks of each photo in turn to establish the origin for photo coordinates. This constitutes the interior orientation. Relative orientation is done by the operator removing the parallax (i.e., the lack of focus) at the PPs and the pass points by a simple y motion at each point. The computer uses these y translations as input to a least squares solution of the relative orientation equations. The resulting coefficients are applied to remove parallax at any point being observed in the model. This occurs as an instantaneous movement of one photo relative to the other as the model is scanned by the operator. Absolute orientation is done by placing the floating mark on the ground control points in turn, and introducing the coordinates of each into the computer. By carrying out this step on a number of control points (on more than is absolutely necessary) a least squares solution is computed to achieve absolute orientation.

The coordinatograph, containing the plotting medium (paper, plastic scribe sheet, etc.), is driven by electronic impulses produced by the computer corresponding to the x and y coordinates of the floating mark as it is moved in the stereo model.

An important advantage in this system is the flexibility resulting from the mathematical rather than the mechanical processing. The geometry for any type of stereoscopic imagery can be programmed, and corrections for lens distortion, film shrinkage, earth curvature, refraction, and any other systematic anomaly can be entered numerically into the instrument.

Digital Photogrammetric Workstations

This most recent development in the field of stereoplotting, sometimes referred to as softcopy photogrammetry, makes use of electronic data processing combined with digital images.[5] Satellite images are broadcast back to earth in the form of fine lines of closely spaced pixels, and in the processing of such images the fact that each pixel has a coordinate value gives them certain advantages over normal photography. Air photos are now being digitized to give them these advantages.

As in the case of analytical stereoplotters, the digital plotter uses numerical computations to form and orient the model. But in the video stereoplotter the model is displayed on a computer graphics terminal. Since the coordinates of each pixel are known, the geometry of the system is very stable. This permits such basic manipulations as pan and zoom, and enhancements such as filtering and contrast adjustments.

There are two main sources of input to the system. The first is the imagery from a digital sensor such as the SPOT satellite. The second is from conventional photography that has been scanned to digitize the image. Once the digital imagery is put into the system, ground control points and pass points can be identified so that the parameters of the geometric model can be computed.

Several methods are used to display the digital stereoscopic image. These include a split screen, two video screens, and a flicker screen. The split screen is the simplest but it reduces the field of view by half. The dual screen avoids this reduction but adds to the system's cost. Both of these use a fixed viewing head with lenses similar to those of conventional stereoplotters. The flicker screen system displays each image of the stereo pair alternately on the screen at the rate at which the monitor repeats the image on the cathode ray tube. The operator views the screen using special glasses that are synchronized with the screen display. To avoid visible flickering the refresh rate of the monitor is set at twice that of a conventional monitor. Figure 3-8 shows a typical digital plotter.

The operator controls an electronic floating mark for orienting the model and plotting detail. The output, consisting of coordinates that have been coded to indicate the type of feature, is stored in a database for many uses including map plotting by automated cartography.

Digital Elevation Models (DEMs) can be created with the system. A DEM is a dense grid of spot heights covering the area of the stereo model. The digital plotter can be programmed to go over the model in predetermined gridded steps, and at each location record the x, y, and z coordinates; or the operator can select specific points whose heights are required. Software exists to convert the grid into contours, perspective drawings of the terrain, or many other forms.

Having DEM data adds a further advantage. It can be used to generate orthophotographs, which are photos that have been rectified to present the same accuracy as a map. For certain areas and types of terrain this imagery can serve as a map substitute, or be useful in map compilation or revision by relatively inexpensive means.

Bridging and Aerotriangulation

Bridging, which has already been referred to, consists of joining photogrammetric models together along a strip with the first and last models having sufficient ground control to

Figure 3-8
Zeiss P3 Planicomp – A digital photogrammetric workstation.
Photo: Terra Surveys Ltd

anchor the bridge. The Multiplex bridge, described previously, is an example of such an arrangement. Aerotriangulation extends this concept to the joining together of strips of photography to form a unified cover of a whole area. The slotted template assembly is an example of aerotriangulation, as it ties many strips together and the whole to ground control, but it does so only in the x and y dimensions. Vertical data must be supplied before compilation plotters can be set based on slotted template coordinates.

With the gradually growing availability of electronic computers in the 1950s, activities began in various countries to develop computer programs for numerical aerotriangulation. One such program was developed at the National Research Council of Canada about 1956 as a project headed by G.H. Schut. It was adopted for use in federal mapping in the early 1960s. The Schut method involves, initially, the measurement of x and y coordinates of the pass points and any ground control points in each photograph, referred to a grid with the PP as its origin. Radial corrections are applied for lens distortion, refraction, and earth curvature. Relative orientation of one photograph to another is done numerically based on a vector solution of the geometrical property, explained earlier, that rays from the PPs of overlapping photos to the same point must intersect. In the Schut solution the scale of all models is made the same. The solution includes the third dimension derived from parallax differences based on measured coordinates. When the strip triangulation (i.e., the measurement of the x, y, and z coordinates) is completed, the coordinates of all points are adjusted to ground control by a conformal transformation to the ground coordinate system. Individual strips are then joined, one to the next, to provide model coordinates for the whole area being mapped. These coordinates could then be plotted on the map manuscript, and a compilation plotter (for example a Multiplex, Kelsh, or B8) could then be set up and map plotting carried out.

Even though the electronic computers of the time lacked the power and speed of modern machines, the adoption of the Schut method greatly improved the quality of aerotriangulation compared to previous analogue methods, and it marked the beginning of complete reliance on analytical methods.

A further development, carried out at the University of Stuttgart in Germany in a project led by F. Ackermann, became available in the late 1960s and was obtained for use in the federal mapping programme. This method, referred to as PAT-M, operates on blocks of stereo models rather than strips and was therefore more productive.

A development project conducted by the Surveys and Mapping Branch, under the leadership of R. Blais, produced another version of the block adjustment specially designed for Canadian mapping conditions. This method, referred to as SPACE-M, was adopted in the early 1970s for federal topographic mapping. It was also made available to the Canadian mapping industry, giving it an advantage in international competition for projects under contract.

Both PAT-M and SPACE-M can adjust blocks containing thousands of overlapping photographs. Ground control is surveyed around the perimeter of the block, and additional vertical control within the block is advantageous. Lake elevation information can be used to enhance this aspect, a fact of considerable importance as Canada is a land of lakes.[6]

The program evaluates a spatial similarity for each stereo model in a direct and simultaneous least square adjustment using all available aerotriangulation and ground control data. In fitting the models together, each model has seven "degrees of freedom." Just like the Multiplex projector it can be moved in x, y, and z, and it can be tipped, tilted, and rotated. In addition it can be adjusted in scale. The overall block computation provides transformed coordinate values of model pass points along with residual differences that indicate the need for further iterations. The final output gives the x, y, and z coordinates of all pass points as required for the scaling and levelling of the stereo models in the map compilation operations.

In the early 1960s some limited use of super-wide-angle photography was commenced. Cameras of this class have a shorter focal length lens (88 mm as compared to the wide-angle 152.4 mm) and a wider angular field of view. The photography, therefore, has a smaller scale and covers more ground area at a given flying height. The wider viewing angle results in enhanced depth perception. These characteristics are most advantageous to aerotriangulation, and the photography was obtained mainly for that purpose. An efficient combination of the strengths of both types of photography was to carry out aerotriangulation of model control points using super-wide-angle, and then transfer the points to wide-angle photography for compilation. However there were practical disadvantages in this theoretically perfect solution. The problem of getting two complete sets of acceptable photographs was great, especially in the more distant reaches of northern Canada. Also, during the 1960s there was a marked increase in haze in the atmosphere, particularly in the North where forest fires added to the problem. With super-wide-angle photography the rays of light forming the edges of the photograph have passed a long way through the haze giving poor images at the photo edges. This defeated the advantages of the system and as a result, in 1979, the Surveys and Mapping Branch adopted wide-angle photography for all its work.

Stereocompilation

The transfer of information from aerial photographs to a map manuscript using a stereo-plotter is referred to as stereocompilation. In the federal mapping programme the work on a sheet of the NTS starts with the preparation of the manuscript. A sheet of plastic drawing medium is placed in a coordinatograph, and the sheet lines of the new NTS map are drawn in. The dimensions of these have been calculated from Universal Transverse Mercator (UTM) projection values as this is the projection used for all federal topographic mapping.

The next step is the coordinatograph plotting of all control points from values obtained from the block adjustment. The prepared compilation base is then positioned on the plotting surface of the stereoplotter being used, either directly below the projectors in some cases or on a separate table connected by a pantograph in others. The stereo model is then formed and oriented to the appropriate control points on the manuscript.

Specifications for the map content are followed in deciding the planimetric features to be plotted. In each case, while keeping the floating mark in contact with the feature on the model, the operator traces its shape or linear course. For contouring, the floating mark is set at a specific elevation above the datum of mean sea level, and is brought into contact with the model surface. By moving the mark horizontally while keeping it in contact with the model, a contour line is plotted. The topography and the map contour interval decide the number of contours to be plotted, and they are supplemented by spot elevations to enhance the overall relief portrayal. Contouring is generally the most tedious and demand-ing procedure in compilation. It requires strong stereo vision and concentration to portray the character of the terrain by an accurate blending of contours and planimetry.

When the plotting of a stereo model has been completed and checked, the next model is then oriented to the common pass points for plotting. This model-by-model process is continued until the whole manuscript has been compiled. As a rule a field operation referred to as field completion is carried out to resolve uncertainties in the compilation, and ensure its correctness. Data concerning administrative boundaries, road classifications, types of buildings, names, and so on must be determined to complete the manuscript.

The accuracy of stereocompilation depends ultimately on the quality of the air photog-raphy, the adequacy of the survey data, the precision of the instrument, and the skill of the operator. Allowing for these factors, in 1:50 000 mapping from photography at the same scale it is reasonable to expect the accuracy of compilation to be about 3 m in ground position and 5 m in elevation relative to the datum. Although stereocompilation pertains primarily to the production of new maps, it is also used in the revision of existing maps when the extent of changes from the previous edition make recompilation necessary.

Digital Compilation

In the mid-1960s a project was initiated in the Surveys and Mapping Branch by S.G. Gamble to develop an automated cartography system. The resulting system used a plotting table with *x* and *y* movements driven by step motors, and a plotting head electronically coded to etch lines, map symbols, and words on a coated plastic sheet. The system was operated by commands from a computer whose input came from tape files of map data. The tape files were prepared by manual digitizing of the content of plotted map manuscripts. This reduced the workload of cartographic drafting, and it made possible the selected retrieval of separate categories of map information at any desired scale. Subsidiary data such as profiles, slopes, and areas could also be derived from it. At that time automated cartography technology was undergoing development worldwide because of the flexibility it provided in the storage, manipulation, and management of terrain information. The development has continued, and today a number of sophisticated cartographic output systems are in use. In the 1960s, however, the main disadvantage was the need to prepare the digital input files by the slow and work-intensive process of manually digitizing existing map manuscripts.

In the mid-1970s a follow-up project was initiated by R.E. Moore, who had succeeded Gamble, to develop a digitizing process at map compilation stage and thus eliminate the bottleneck of manual digitization. The digital compilation project was led by J.M. Zarzycki, director of the Topographical Survey Division at that time. The outcome was a system using conventional stereoplotters whose plotting motions are fitted with digital encoders that feed data to computer files. Thus as the plotter operator traces features from the stereo model, the coordinates are transmitted electronically to a computer tape rather than a graphic manuscript. The operator can monitor his work on a video screen and changes, if needed, can be made interactively. The output files contain map data that have photogrammetric accuracy some three to five times better than the printed map, but it lacks some of the quality of cartographic portrayal. For example a road is digitized along its centreline in its correct position. But on the 1:50 000 printed map its width is exaggerated so it can be seen clearly and printed in colour to show its classification. This means that buildings close to the road, if shown in their correct positions, would fall on the widened road symbol. Therefore such buildings must be moved back. This in turn means that two map files must be prepared: (a) a position file with all features digitized in their correct positions, and (b) a representation file with all features digitized as they will appear on the 1:50 000 map.

The representation files provided the digital input needed to operate the automated cartography system, but it became obvious that the position files had other important values. At scales larger than 1:50 000 it is generally not necessary to move features for cartographic clarity, and there are many users who want positional accuracy. Organizations concerned with various categories of geographically related information (as described in chapter 15) began to request the accurate position files to serve as a medium for their particular data bases. This demand has spread as Geographic Information System (GIS) technology has spread. Today digital compilation is the normal method for mapping and, as well, the normal method for supporting GIS.

Because the stereocompilation of contours tends to be time consuming and therefore costly, a system called the Gestalt Photomapper was acquired by the Surveys and Mapping Branch in 1976. The Gestalt, developed in Canada by Gilbert L. Hobrough, is an electronically controlled stereocompiler that, by automatic correlation of matching imagery in overlapping photographs, derives elevation data and orthophoto imagery data in digital form on tape. This instrument was used for the production of contoured orthophotos of Arctic areas where the landscape was not obscured by vegetation. (Further information on the Gestalt Photomapper is given in chapter 12.)

Tables 3-1 and 3-2 on photogrammetry and federal topographic mapping show the acquisition and use of photogrammetric equipment by the federal government from the first purchase in 1946 to the present.

The Aerial Survey Data Base

The production of a map begins with the acquisition of aerial photography and ground control survey data as inputs. They are combined first in the process of aerotriangulation to obtain stereo model calibration data for the plotting of map detail. In the early postwar years an operational balance was established between the productivities of the separate processes based on the technologies employed at that time. Map production was carried out from beginning to end on the basis of individual map sheets. But with the advent of electronic and airborne methods of surveying and ground control, coupled with the adoption of computer methods of aerotriangulation of large blocks of photography for many map sheets, an operational imbalance arose between the map control and map compilation phases of production. Accordingly a two-part approach to production was adopted in the early 1970s. Control extension became a separate sub-activity with operational objectives not being paced by map compilation objectives. An entity was established, referred to initially as the Northern Mapping Data Base (because unmapped areas at the time were mainly in the North). It was subsequently retitled the Aerial Survey Data Base (ASDB). It consists of an accumulation of aerotriangulation data for blocks of maps, and matching aerial photography on which the pass points have been marked. Any map within a block of the database can be routinely scheduled for follow-on compilation at any time.

The advantages gained by this approach are optimum efficiency through handling data in large blocks, and flexibility in scheduling map production to suit user demands as they arise. The ASDB was completed for all unmapped areas of Canada in 1990–91.

The National Topographic Data Base

In 1977 the Department of Energy, Mines and Resources established the Task Force on National Surveying and Mapping under the leadership of P.A. Lapp, a private consultant, to investigate current and future needs of Canada for surveying and mapping. One of the findings of the task force concerning topographical mapping was the existence of a significant and growing need for topographical data in digital form to support geographic information management.[7] But in-house digital mapping operations at that time could sustain a production rate of just twenty-five 1:50 000 maps and files per year. To increase the rate of digital-map production, an optical scanning system was procured that would convert already-published maps into files of digital data. The colour negatives for an existing map are separately digitized by raster scanning, which, after subsequent stages of data processing, results in a digital map file in vector format.

The production rate of the scanning system proved to be about 200 digitized maps per year, and in order to create a base of digital data covering the whole of Canada in a five-year period, its first project was to digitize all 918 maps of the 1:250 000 Series. This was completed successfully, and on schedule, in 1990.

Table 3-1
Federal Topographic Instruments.

INSTRUMENTS	No. of instruments	
	SMB	MCE
Multiplex	26	28
Wild A5	1	1
Wild A6		1
Wild A7	3	3
Wild A8	2	4
Kelsh	10	4
Gamble Plotter	3	
Wild A9		1
Wild A10	1	
Wild B8	36	9
Kern PG2	14	
Baplex	34	
Wild STT 1	2	1
TA3P1 3 Stage Comparator		1
Kelsh 200		4
Zeiss Planimat	1	
Gestalt Photomapper GPM2	1	
Marconi Anaplot	1	3
Intergraph Analytical Plotter IMA	1	4
Intergraph Intermap Workstation		24
Helava Digital Photogrammetric Workstation DPW 770	2	
Helava Digital Scanning Workstation	1	

Timeline (1940–1996) annotations:

- Multiplex: 1:50 000
- Wild A5: 1:50 000 — End of 1" mapping
- Wild A6: 1:50 000
- Wild A8: Start of 1:25 000 mapping in ASE
- Kelsh: 1:25 000, 1:50 000
- Gamble Plotter: 1:50 000
- Wild A9: superwide Angle photos
- Wild A10 / Wild B8: 1:25 000, 1:50 000 — 1:50 000
- Kern PG2: 1:25 000, 1:50 000 — 1:50 000
- Baplex: 1:25 000, 1:50 000 — End of 1:25 000
- Wild STT 1: very-high-altitude photos, 1:250 000
- Zeiss Planimat: 1:50 000
- Gestalt Photomapper GPM2: 1:50 000

Legend:

Bridging
Compilation
Bridging and compilation

SMB – Surveys and Mapping Branch, EMR
MCE – Mapping and Charting Establishment, DND (formerly Army Survey Establishement, ASE)

Source: Bruce Hynes, MCE and J.C. Macdonald, SMRSS

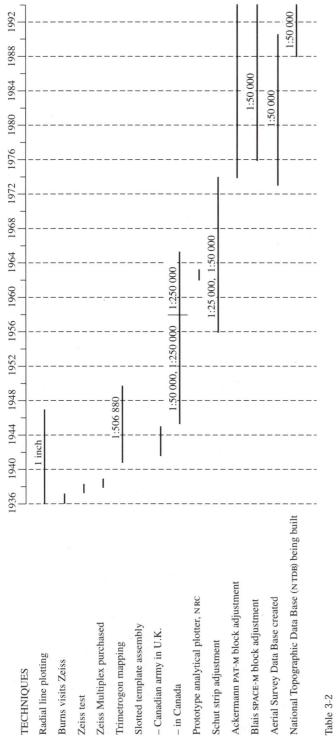

Table 3-2
Federal Mapping Techniques.
Source: Bruce Hynes, MCE and J.C. Macdonald, SMRSS

During the same period the digital technologies for map compilation and digital scanning were transferred to Canadian industry so that it could compete for federal contracts in digital mapping. In addition the long-delayed government decentralization plan for surveys and mapping was finalized in 1983. This resulted in the establishment of a small unit of 30 people in Sherbrooke, Québec. In 1988 this unit was enlarged to 100 positions and became the Canada Centre for Geomatics. This organization was originally equipped with the most modern digital mapping equipment, but in 1992 was converted to the monitoring of digital mapping contracts by private mapping firms.

The overall build-up of digital capability made it feasible in 1988 to develop and adopt a plan for the creation of a National Topographic Data Base (NTDB) containing three levels of map data. The more populated southern regions are to be digitized photogrammetrically as obsolete 1:50 000 maps are replaced by recompilation, or as cooperative arrangements with provincial governments produce digital mapping at larger scales. Those areas lying between the populated south and the northern territories, together with economically and socially important areas of the territories, will be digitized by scanning existing 1:50 000 maps. The remaining regions will be covered by the files from the scanning of the 1:250 000 Series, which has already been completed. In time, areas and sub-areas can be upgraded from one level of digital data to a higher one if needed. Until the overall objective is reached, the 1:250 000 files give some degree of backup. Obviously the NTDB files must be updated periodically and, as with map revision, this is based on new aerial photography or in some cases on remote sensing imagery.

THE FEDERAL TOPOGRAPHIC MAPPING PROGRAMME

The Programme from 1904 to 1946

As Canada entered the twentieth century it was one of the few industrialized countries without a topographic survey. Of course Canada was not entirely without maps in 1900. In eastern Canada most of the counties had been mapped at one or two miles to the inch, and Three-Mile maps of the Prairies were being drawn in the Department of the Interior from the field notes of the Dominion Land Surveyors. But these were superficial maps showing little more than the township survey patterns and the major topographical features. None showed the slightest indication of relief. If answers were required to simple geographic questions such as the distance from Toronto to Sudbury to the nearest quarter of a mile, or the area of the Ottawa River watershed, these facts would not be found on existing Canadian maps.

In 1903 there was the first sign that this situation was about to change. In that year a British mapping authority, Major E.H. Hills who was head of the Topographical Section of the War Office, was invited to come to Canada and report on the Dominion's mapping situation.[8] Hills's first action was to examine the existing mapping of the country. In a word, he was unimpressed. Not only was topographical mapping almost completely lacking, but there was no geodetic surveying taking place on which to base topographical mapping. After several months of study he recommended the establishing of a fifty-four-man unit that could at least get the most essential topographic mapping under way.

Although the report was taken very seriously the establishment recommended was more than the army budget could afford. In late 1903 a twenty-five-man mapping unit was authorized. Work started in 1904 and, for the first few years, progress was understandably slow. The various technicians had to be trained, and despite the assistance of experienced topographers who came from the Ordnance Survey of Great Britain (OSGB) each spring to work through the summer with the men of this new unit, production remained at about five One-Mile sheets per year for the first twenty-five years.

In 1908 the Geological Survey of Canada (GSC) organized its Topographical Survey Division. Most of the work of this unit was planimetric, and none showed the vegetation cover because these features tended to obscure the geological presentation. Contours and forest cover were considered essential topographic features by the military, but where GSC maps were contoured they were welcomed into the slowly growing body of Canadian topography. The military philosophy of the time was evidently "better a map without forest cover than no map at all."

In 1921 the Department of the Interior started to convert its Three-Mile Series to true topographic maps by adding contours and additional topographic detail such as buildings, bridges, and place-names. Roads were classified, and where the vegetation cover existed it was shown. At the same time a modest amount of One-Mile and Two-Mile mapping was also done. The army specifications were followed, and it is almost impossible to tell an army sheet from an Interior version without consulting the imprint.

The first major change in the Canadian mapping establishment occurred in 1936. The Department of the Interior was disbanded, and the two civilian mapping agencies were joined in an enlarged Topographical Survey. Unfortunately the two styles of mapping, geologic and military, were continued within this single unit. By 1936 the army had published 133 One-Mile sheets, and from these had been derived 14 Two-Mile sheets and 3 Four-Mile sheets. The One-Mile production was concentrated in three provinces: 79 in Ontario, 44 in Québec, and 10 in Nova Scotia.[9]

Before its disbandment Interior had converted 51 of its 134 planimetric Three-Mile sheets to true topographic maps, and had published 21 One-Mile sheets and 26 Two-Mile sheets. The latter were not derived from the larger scale, but were surveyed originally at the two-mile scale. The work done by Interior was mainly in Nova Scotia and British Columbia[10].

The Topographic Division of the GSC, as has been mentioned, did not conform to the specifications set out and agreed to by the other two agencies for Canada's NTS. Eleven more years would pass before this would happen, but in the meantime the GSC topographers in the Topographical Survey followed their own (i.e., GSC) specifications. By 1936 they had completed 12 half-sheets that were considered close enough to NTS standards to be included in the 1936 count of 161 One-Mile published sheets. This was a beginning, but not a large one considering that coverage of the whole Dominion would eventually require 12 992 sheets.

The Postwar Federal Mapping Programme

One more government reorganization took place in 1947. Among other changes, the government mapping agencies were grouped in the newly formed Surveys and Mapping Bureau. These agencies were Topographical Survey, Geodetic Survey, the Hydrographic Service, Legal Surveys and Air Charts, the Map Compilation and Reproduction Division, and the International Boundary Commission. Prior to this grouping the above-mentioned two styles of topographic mapping were being produced by the Topographical Survey. With the formation of the bureau all topographic mapping would follow the NTS specifications strictly. To compensate the GSC for the loss of its special mapping style, it was given its own cartographic unit that would use the work of the Topographical Survey but would adapt it to accommodate the needs of a special geological presentation.

The Four-Mile and 1:250 000 Mapping Programme

A major landmark in the progress of Canadian topographic mapping was the 1947 approval by the cabinet of a plan to complete all 918 sheets of the Four-Mile Series within twenty years. The boldness of this plan can be indicated by the fact that in 1947 there were only three contoured sheets of the series in existence. These were Kitchener (40P), Ottawa (31G), and Toronto (30M), all derived by the GSGS from its One-Mile coverage.

The twenty-year programme did not originate with the cabinet. It was very much the initiative of the Canada-U.S. Permanent Joint Board on Defence (PJBD), which included both Canadian and American chiefs of staff. The PJBD formulated the Canada-U.S. Basic Security Plan in 1946. As written this plan had ten appendices, one of which (appendix C)[11] was the Mapping Charting and Air Photography Plan (MCAPP). It is in the original version of this plan that the timetable for the completion of the 1:250 000 mapping of Canada in twenty years is found. The need for good medium-scale mapping of the Canadian Arctic was stressed. The Eight-Mile Series, completed during the war, was in no way adequate for postwar defence purposes. Most of the northern sheets were uncontoured, and on many even the planimetric detail was sketchy.

So vital did the U.S. military consider northern Canada that in the period between 1945 and 1953 the U.S. Aeronautical Chart Service was instructed to produce a 127-sheet series of 1:250 000 maps covering all of Canada north of the 74th parallel. An examination of this series shows quickly that these are low-quality maps drawn without any fieldwork beyond that done for the Canadian Eight-Mile Series. Form lines at 1000-foot intervals give some indication of the relief, but in no way do they depict the ruggedness of the land. Horizontal control for the series was taken from existing maps. As a consequence, position checks reveal errors of up to 15 km. These were obviously stop-gap maps, but the very fact that they were drawn indicates the U.S. strategic interest in the region[12].

Such peacetime assistance in domestic mapping had sovereignty implications, and of course the Canadian government was anxious to replace this American initiative with NTS mapping. The answer was the twenty-year programme, developed by the Topographical Survey and the ASE, and sent to the cabinet committee for approval. It must be noted that the approval, which was soon given, was not based solely on the military merits of the plan. All those involved knew that the proper civilian development of northern Canada required this mapping.

Nevertheless it was an audacious undertaking that could never have been contemplated had it not been for the wartime advances in photogrammetry. Vertical photography of all of Canada was now feasible due to aircraft that could fly higher, thus greatly reducing the number of photos needed. Better cameras were available, which made this small-scale photography perfectly suitable for mapping. The slotted template assembly provided the answer to the horizontal control requirement. It could provide adequate horizontal control for all models based on a framework of ground survey points.

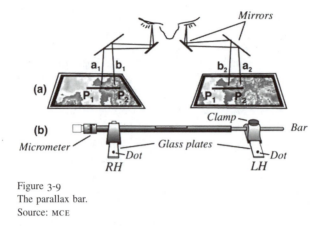

Figure 3-9
The parallax bar.
Source: MCE

Vertical control was more of a problem, but here ingenious solutions, both old and new, were put to work. In the western mountains photo-topography, developed sixty years previously by Surveyor General Edouard Deville, provided elevations of peaks and many other points that could be identified on both the vertical and horizontal photographs. These spot heights were transferred to prints of the vertical photos, which were then contoured under desk stereoscopes. The map detail, including the contours, was later transferred to the map manuscript by Sketchmaster.

Other methods and devices were employed in the plains. The drainage pattern was studied, and by observing barometer elevations of lakes it was possible to interpret river elevations along the drainage flow. Parallax bar readings (see figure 3-9) provided additional spot elevations to assist the staff responsible for the contouring. In especially difficult areas Multiplex bridges were run to provide the elevations required, but this assistance was kept to a minimum because it took these instruments away from their proper tasks on the larger-scale work.

It is difficult to know how much the 1947 planners were relying on technical developments during the course of this project to bring it in on time. From the beginning new techniques were employed, almost before they were tested thoroughly. In 1947 work was started establishing the Shoran net across northern Canada (see chapter 2). These Shoran stations provided the starting and closing points for later Electromagnetic Distance Measurement (EDM) traverses that were run using newly purchased Tellurometers. The traverses then provided the control for the slotted template laydowns of the Arctic areas.

The APR was used from 1947 onwards to give elevation data for contouring. With the coming of helicopters in 1953, barometer traverses gave an alternative to APR heighting. On the whole, barometer heights were preferred because they could be placed at strategic points whereas the APR heights had to be along the flight line. Both systems gave heights of about the same accuracy, though this point was argued vigorously by the proponents of each system.

In brief the whole twenty-year project was treated almost like a laboratory experiment conducted in the open air at full scale. Figure 3-10 is an interesting status map drawn in 1957 by the Surveys and Mapping Branch. In essence this is the "1947 game plan" for completing the project, as seen at the halfway point. The black areas are those that would

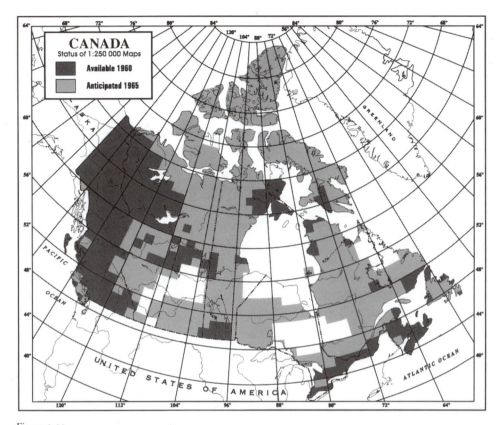

Figure 3-10
A forecast of 1:250 000 production made in 1957.
Source: MCE

be completed in 1960. Note that the mountain sheets, where photo-topography elevations were available, constitute the main progress. Also well advanced are those sheets in settled areas that could be derived from Three-Mile and 1:50 000 contoured mapping. By 1957 helicopters had become the normal means of transportation in northern areas and, as mentioned above, the Tellurometer was ready to go into service. Practical methods for providing both horizontal and vertical control in any part of Canada were now available. This explains the optimistic view of being able to produce the Arctic sheets on time. Northern Ontario and Labrador were obviously expected to present difficulties. Why certain prairie sheets were left to the last cannot be explained today. Possibly 1:50 000 work was in progress that would provide better basic data.

By employing all these new instruments, methods, and vehicles the project was finally completed in the autumn of 1970 with the printing of the last sheet, Coats Island (45 J and I). Since then many checks have been made on the accuracy of this admittedly hurried work. As soon as 1:50 000 coverage becomes available for the area of a 1:250 000 sheet a comparison is made to reveal errors or omissions. The results of these tests have been surprisingly encouraging.[13] Admittedly the rather large contour interval of this medium-scale mapping (100, 200, and 500 feet or 20, 50, 100, and 200 m) gave the contourers appreciable leeway. Nevertheless the successful results of this major project point to the good training of the early postwar topographers.

The Three-Mile, Two-Mile, and 1:125 000 Series

The concentration on the Four-Mile and 1:250 000 Series had an adverse but understandable effect on those scales falling between the Four-Mile and One-Mile. The 1950s were also years of new demands for mapping services, both in the topographic field and in air charting. It was inevitable that less important mapping had to be terminated. One such series was the Three-Mile Sectional Maps of the prairies. Revision of sheets of this series was stopped as soon as Four-Mile coverage of their areas was available.

The Two-Mile and its metric equivalent, 1:125 000, were not stopped immediately, but production was slowed down. These maps were popular in tourist areas, and many were published with shaded relief so that amateur map readers could grasp the lay of the land. But eventually the dead hand was placed on the series. The last new sheet, Goudreau (42C/SE), was published in 1957. Revision was stopped in 1972.

The One-Mile and the 1:50 000 Series

The One-Mile Series, and its successor the 1:50 000, were never in danger because they have always been considered the basic mapping of the country. These were the largest scales at which complete coverage of the country to one set of specifications could be foreseen, and as such they have always had a special status. Production suffered a slowdown during the height of the drive to complete the 1:250 000 coverage, but in 1970 when the drive was over, production was resumed with top priority.

The metric conversion affected the 1:50 000 Series much more than the other scales. The 1:50 000 sheets were almost a fifth larger than the One-Mile, whereas with the other scales the change was almost imperceptible. The increased size of the 1:50 000 sheet forced the publication of all sheets south of the 61st parallel as half-sheets. As will be explained shortly, this caused a number of style changes.

Metrication in mapping began in 1949 with the adoption of the 1:250 000 scale, and was followed in 1950 by the 1:50 000 and 1:125 000 Series. This was long before the official government programme of general metrication. In 1950 there were 437 One-Mile sheets published, distributed across Canada as shown in figure 3-11. As can be seen in this graphic, the greater part of the One-Mile work had been done in the Windsor–Québec City corridor and in the Maritimes. The strong showing in British Columbia was due to provincial mapping, not the federal effort. By 1950 British Columbia had surveyed and drafted 48 One-Mile sheets to the NTS specifications. The provincial mapping agency then turned the colour separation manuscripts over to the Surveys and Mapping Bureau for printing.

Although the ASE was a major contributor to both the 1:250 000 and 1:50 000 programmes it had constant and urgent requests for special military mapping. The first of these appeared in 1954 when a demand was received for the 1:50 000 mapping of a band of country about 25 km wide from the Atlantic to the Rocky Mountains. It ran roughly along the 56th parallel as shown on Figure 5-4 in chapter 5. This was to be the site of the Mid Canada Line, an extensive radar system that would augment the Distant Early Warning (DEW) Line installed previously.

As the Mid Canada Line work is described in chapter 5 it is sufficient to say here that it passed through country where the only existing maps were the uncontoured Eight-Mile sheets. Once again the newest mapping techniques were employed to produce urgently needed maps in difficult country, but this time at 1:50 000 for engineering purposes. With this mapping the contouring had to be accurate because intervisibility between radar towers was a firm requirement. The project was completed within the two-year deadline, but the work required the total commitment of ASE's production for the two years. In many ways this project can be blamed for the three-year delay in completing the 1:250 000 project.

An examination of the status maps for the 1:50 000 Series (figures 3-12A-C) does not reveal the workings of a long-range plan to map Canada methodically from south to north, or in any other planned direction. This is because there have always been several strong influences on mapping priorities, and these priorities have had a habit of changing from year to year. With the 1:250 000 plan all sheets had a high priority, and those for which ground survey and photography were available were mapped first. With the 1:50 000 Series the demands for priority were many, and generally competing. The GSC had, and continues to have, a strong influence on which areas would be mapped first. But their requests were sometime thwarted by nature. The Pine Point mineral area south of Great Slave Lake is a case in point. Starting in 1968 there was a strong demand for 1:50 000 coverage of the area, but year after year it was found impossible to obtain photography. One year it was because of continual rain or fog. The next year was dry and clear, but raging forest fires obscured the terrain. Finally in 1985 the long-awaited maps were published but by that time mineral extraction in the area was in decline, and the maps were not needed. Other mineral areas were more fortunate. The iron-ore deposits of Québec were mapped in good form and on time during the late 1950s.

Political considerations have had their influences. One of the promises made to Newfoundland at the time of union was that the 1:50 000 mapping of the island would receive top priority. Other less urgent work was set aside, and the island mapping was completed in 1960.

It is true that every square inch of Canada has had its advocate for early mapping. In the Arctic islands there are interesting mineral deposits where base maps are needed for detailed geological exploration. The Hydrographic Service wants 1:50 000 mapping of the shores of all navigable channels. The glaciers of Ellesmere Island are of great interest to glaciologists who need contoured maps for their ice-budget studies. No region or area is completely without a champion.

Figures 3-11 and 3-12A-C show the progressive coverage provided by 1:50 000 maps between 1950 and 1995. As shown by these progress maps, by 1995 all provinces and the Yukon had been mapped. In the Northwest Territories the mainland had been covered, and as shown in figure 3-12C so had many areas in the Arctic islands. For the mapping of the remainder of the Arctic islands, the photography, ground survey, and aerotriangulation had been completed, and it only remained for there to be a good economic reason for the remaining maps to be put into work. The cumulative coverage of One-Mile and 1:50 000 mapping of Canada is summarized in figure 3-13.

Progress of the mapping of Canada, 1950–95.

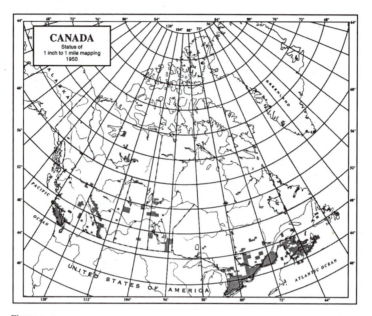

Figure 3-11
Distribution of One-Mile Sheets in 1950. All these sheets were converted to
1:50 000 by 1953.
Source: MCE

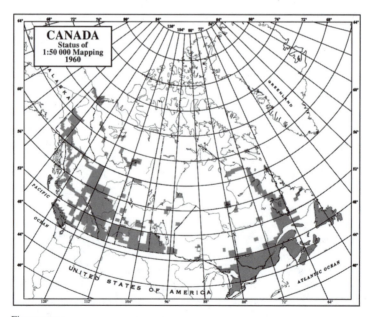

Figure 3-12A
Status of 1:50 000 mapping in 1960.
Source: MCE

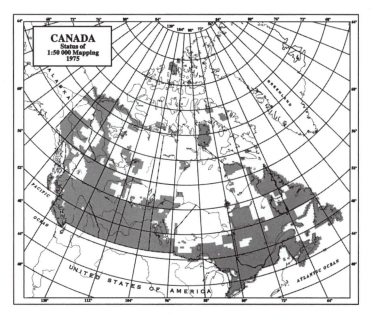

Figure 3-12B
Status of 1:50 000 mapping in 1975.
Source: MCE

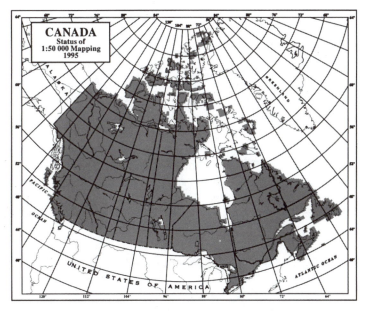

Figure 3-12D
Status of 1:50 000 mapping in 1995.
Source: MCE

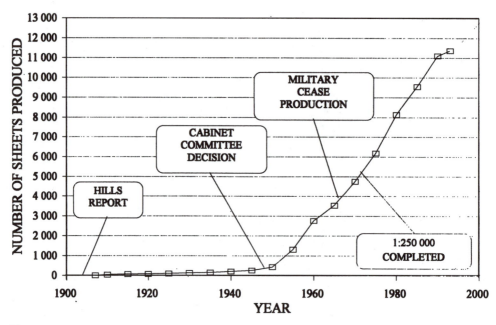

Figure 3-13
Canada Production of One-Mile and 1:50 000 Maps.
Source: Natural Resources Canada

The 1:25 000 Series

The 1:25 000 Series was added to the NTS family of scales in 1953. This scale had been the British army's tactical scale since the 1920s, and had been adopted by the Canadian army for the mapping of army camps and training areas. In 1952 a major decision was made at army headquarters regarding the training facilities to be provided at major training areas. In particular, certain training areas had to be large enough for the full deployment of an infantry brigade with armour support. Two such areas, Gagetown in New Brunswick and Wainwright in Alberta, were the first of these super-large camps. ASE was given the task of producing the necessary 1:25 000 maps. Both areas were much too large to be mapped on one or even two sheets, and thus it was decided that a 1:25 000 NTS Series would be introduced so that these camps could be mapped in orderly fashion. Each sheet would be one-eighth of a 1:50 000 quadrangle.[14] Production started in 1954 using specifications drawn up by ASE and agreed to by Topographical Survey.

In 1959 yet one more new commitment arrived to take priority in the ASE workload. In that year Cold War tensions had reached such a height that a nuclear attack on Canadian cities was considered a distinct possibility. As no large-scale military maps of Canadian cities existed it was decided that the ASE should produce such a set of maps. These were the Military Town Plans (MTPs) described in chapter 5, and thus it is sufficient to point out here that this new work tended to reduce, once again, the ASE's production of 1:250 000 sheets, and delay still further the completion date of that programme. All these new commitments did show, quite strongly, that ASE needed outside help. This was the beginning of the contracting out by ASE of all phases of domestic map production from field survey to map printing. This involvement of the Canadian mapping industry had been resisted strongly in previous times, but with these urgent demands, and funds to pay for them, the involvement of outside assistance could no longer be denied. The growth of this involvement of the private sector in NTS mapping is covered in chapter 6.

As much of the work on the MTPs could easily be used to produce standard NTS 1:25 000 sheets of the same areas, and as the MTPs were classified as confidential, it was decided that the production of urban NTS 1:25 000 should be started to make this mapping available to the general public. In the beginning this was strictly an ASE initiative, but in 1962 Topographical Survey joined the project. The work flourished for a time, and considerable areas quite far removed from major cities were mapped in the Québec City–Windsor corridor. Figure 3-14 shows the extent covered.

The federal 1:25 000 work was stopped in 1978 after 690 sheets had been published. The reasons for abandoning the series are threefold. First, the loss of the ASE assistance on NTS mapping in 1965 placed an additional burden on Topographical Survey to meet urgent demands at the 1:50 000 scale. Second, the 1:25 000 mapping was of rapidly changing areas of Canada, which meant constant and expensive revision. But a third and most important reason was the new interest in provincial mapping at this or larger scales (see chapter 4). The provincial mapping was, in most cases, monochrome, which is much less expensive to produce and to be kept up to date. Generally speaking, large-scale monochrome maps are just as useful as their full-colour brethren. As most of the provinces wanted to enter this field, it was obviously the time for the federal agency to bow out.

Map revision

Publication of a topographic map by government carries with it the responsibility of keeping that map up to date. As the coverage provided by the 1:50 000 Series increases, the revision load increases, but not at a proportional rate. The new maps are entirely of wilderness areas where the rate of change in the topography is slow.

For convenience in planning 1:50 000 revision, Canada has been divided into four areas in each of which the rate of obsolescence of maps is approximately the same. These areas are as follows:

5-Year Review Cycle Maps of cities and their suburbs where development is dense and continuing. There are approximately 250 sheets in this category.

10-Year Review Cycle Approximately 1500 maps of rural areas experiencing moderate development.

15-Year Review Cycle The remaining sheets south of the Wilderness Line, and those sheets to the north covering settlements and northern communication routes. There are approximately 2500 sheets in this category.

30-Year Review Cycle The remaining 8500 sheets north of the Wilderness Line where there is little or no settlement or development activity.

There are two distinct approaches to revision. If the dimensional accuracy of the old sheet is questionable, or if the changes to be made are extensive, the map is recompiled. But if the framework of the old map is sound, the required changes are made on the draftings of the printing colours or on the monochrome manuscripts.

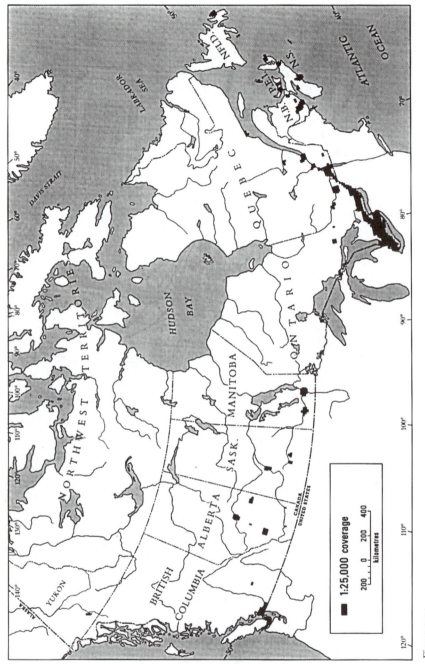

Figure 3-14

1:25 000 NTS mapping at the end of production.

Source: Nicholson, N.L., and L.M. Sebert. 1981. *The Maps of Canada. A Guide to Official Canadian Maps, Charts, Atlases and Gazetteers*. Folkestone, U.K.: Wm Dawson and Sons Ltd, 118

In the early years the need for revision of the maps of a given area was determined by examining provincial road maps, railway plans, city utility plans, forestry leases, and similar documents. This system worked well in settled areas but was unreliable north of the Wilderness Line. Since about 1975 increasing use has been made of satellite imagery both to locate where revision is necessary and, more recently, to provide metric data for the correction of the reproduction material. In almost all cases the revision is first made on the 1:50 000 sheets, and then by derivation on the 1:250 000 sheets.

THE STYLE OF NATIONAL TOPOGRAPHIC MAPS[15]

The Original Style

As has been mentioned, the original 1904 style of Canadian One-Mile topographic maps was similar to the OSGB maps at the same scale. Naturally certain adaptations were made to show correctly the Canadian landscape and use Canadian terminology. None of the OSGB maps showed glaciers or displayed symbols for grain elevators or pingos. British terms appeared in the Canadian map legends for a while, but gradually such expressions as "metalled road" and "tavern" disappeared (the latter possibly due to social pressure), and a distinctive Canadian appearance emerged. As has been explained, the GSC finally gave up their geological version of a topographic map in 1947, and one standard form remained.

The Military Influence

Military requirements have always had an influence on Canadian topographic map design, and this became very evident in 1950 when the change to metric scales was made. The change in dimensions from the One-Mile (1:63 360) scale to 1:50 000 was not great, but it was enough to make the standard 1:50 000 quadrangle too wide to fit on paper of the standard military size. Neither could the ASE's printing presses of the time handle the proposed larger maps. It was necessary, therefore, to publish all sheets south of 61° latitude as half-sheets, East and West. Due to the convergence of meridians the full quadrangle could be printed on military regulation paper north of 61°. The half-sheet solution turned out to have many drawbacks. It increased the drafting and printing load, it caused confusion in the sales offices, and it was unpopular with the users who found the increased number of maps to cover a given area very annoying. A particular difficulty was caused by the fact that both halves of an NTS quadrangle had the same sheet name, though in 1950 and for some years there were geological topographic half-sheets each of which had a different name. The confusion was endless. This unfortunate situation continued until 1967 when the military standard was relaxed, and thereafter half-sheets were joined when they came up for revision.

Another military requirement was the addition of a 1000 m and 10 000 m UTM reference grid to all 1:50 000 and 1:250 000 sheets respectively. Due to American urging the UTM projection had been adopted in 1947 for all federal topographic mapping, though initially Topographical Survey did not print the UTM grid on its maps. This meant that all maps had to be published in two versions, one gridded for military use and one not. However it was agreed in 1964 that to obviate this double printing all maps would be published with the reference grid. This move was not universally popular, and it was particularly resented in the Prairie provinces. In this region the grid lines, although printed in blue, were sometimes confused with the lines of the Dominion Land Survey System. The confusion became more pronounced when photo-copying of maps became common practice. This removed the colour distinction, and blended the grid with the north-south and east-west DLS lot lines. Nevertheless the gridding of the maps continued, and in the present era of digital databases is much appreciated.

Design Changes

The division of most of the 1:50 000 quadrangles into half-sheets in 1950 was such a radical move that it spawned a series of changes in map design. The old familiar design had been abandoned, and it now seemed that anything was possible. The changes in design were made by a joint military-civilian map design committee. There has been much criticism of the frequent changes in design, but it must be remembered that there were pressures on the committee to simplify the presentation in order to speed production. At the same time there were pressures to maintain a dignified appearance suitable for national mapping.

The first design of the 1:50 000 half-sheet was very plain. To compensate for the additional drafting needed, the work to draw the border and set out the margin information was reduced to a minimum. The neat line was made to serve as the map border, and five-minute ticks served as latitude and longitude references. A standard legend was carried in the right margin, and the usual sheet identification (NTS number, sheet name, province, and country) was placed in the top and bottom margins.

In 1953 it was decided that this "military" appearance was too sombre for a national map series, and thus a design similar to the pre-war appearance was restored. The five-line border, and the other detail found on the former One-Inch design, were reinstated.

Provisional Mapping

In order to speed production the first of a number of provisional designs appeared in 1950. At first these were used for Arctic areas only, and were called " Arctic Provisionals" to give the indication that better maps were following. On these sheets all detail was shown in black with a light-blue fill for open water. A more elaborate five-colour provisional was developed in 1966 for use in rural areas of southern Canada. The standard five colours were used in the normal manner (cultural detail in black, drainage in blue, contours in brown, vegetation in green, and road classification in red), but later further shortcuts were introduced. Road casings were dropped to speed production and facilitate revision, but this created a need for a sixth colour (orange) to be use for gravelled roads. The real saving in work was a very simple margin layout that had a plain border and a legend showing only the road classification.

Almost simultaneous with this provisional design was the lifting of the sheet size restriction, which meant that these sheets could be published as full quadrangles. The popularity of the 1966 provisionals at full quadrangle width led to the obvious next step, a design for standard maps of the same size. The design chosen was in many respects the same as the One-Mile sheets of 1949. The exceptions were the road classification that was carried on the face of the map, and a full legend printed in light grey on the back of the sheet.

The 1:50 000 Monochrome Series

There has always been a lapse of time between the completion of the map manuscript and the printing of the full-colour map. In order to meet the demand for new maps the Topographical Survey adopted the practice, early in the postwar years, of making single colour photocopies of the map manuscript available to the public. These were called "advance prints" and were very popular with resource development personnel. The advance prints often appeared as much as three years before the printed version, and during that period they often absorbed potential sales of the finished product. It was decided in 1972 to study this situation to see whether it could be handled in a more formal way. The National Advisory Committee on Control Surveys and Mapping (NACCSM) arranged a conference of major map users in the North during that year. The conference was chaired by Tuzo Wilson, a member of the committee. The committee noted that in northern Canada most maps were used by people trained in map reading (including geologists, prospectors, foresters, and soldiers) who could use a simplified map, similar to the advance print, without difficulty. Thus a simplified monochrome map was produced, with all detail in black and grey on white. To show where these maps would be the normal style, at least for the foreseeable future, an irregular line called the Wilderness Line was drawn across the map of Canada (see figure 3-15). In an arbitrary way this line separated the undeveloped North from the developed and settled South. The production of monochrome maps north of the Wilderness Line resolved a serious backlog in map production and removed the often ambiguous advance print from the mapping scene.

Experience has also shown that in certain parts of Canada the most useful type of map is the photomap. In regions such as the Hudson Bay lowlands there are very few if any man-made features, and the pattern and texture of the swamps and marshes are far more recognizable on a photograph than on the most detailed cartographic presentation. In these areas contoured photomaps are now considered the normal map presentation, and are shown as such on the current indexes.

The government policies on bilingualism and metrication have each made an impact on map design. Legends and other information printed on the map margins, as well as the names and labels inside the margins, have been translated into both official languages. Metrication certainly affected sheet sizes and appearances, but it also affected the contour intervals used. In 1950 the intervals on 1:50 000 maps had a range from 25 to 200 feet depending on the terrain relief, and this was changed to a range from 10 to 40 m. However, given the prohibitive cost to re-contour all maps published with foot intervals, conversion to metric contours on existing maps is being done progressively as they undergo major revision. The new technology of Digital Elevation Modelling will certainly accelerate this process.

CONCLUSION

From this brief description of the topographic mapping of a country as large and geographically diverse as Canada, it is evident that flexibility and innovation were required to satisfy the dynamic needs this country has for map information. Photogrammetry has been applied to topographic mapping for much of this century, and it has played a fundamental role in the federal mapping programme. During the life of the programme the

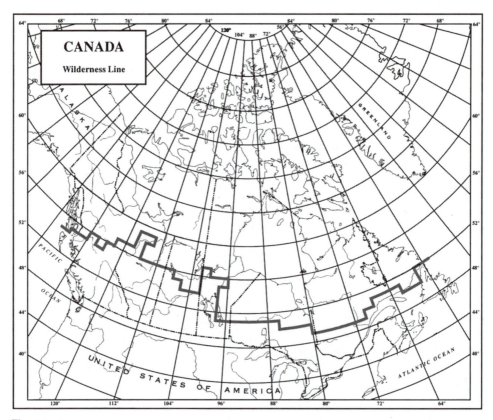

Figure 3-15
The Wilderness Line.
Source: MCE

science of photogrammetry evolved from reliance on optical and analogue processing to one based on electronic technology. As this evolution occurred, which is depicted in tables 3-1 and 3-2, the pace and quality of mapping increased, programme objectives were met and surpassed, and new objectives for digital data production were made possible.

NOTES

1 Hotine, M., 1927. *Simple Methods of Surveying from Air Photographs*. London: War Office.

2 See Thomson, D.W. 1969. *Men and Meridians*, vol. 3, Ottawa: Queen's Printer, 164, for mention of First Corps Field Survey Company's move to England.

3 The U.S. army's use of the slotted template assembly in England in 1942 is mentioned in Burnside, C.D. 1994. The Photogrammetric Society Analogue Instrument Project: second extract. *The Photogrammetric Record*, April 1994, 14, 83, 772.

4 Sebert, L.M. 1992. The Trimetrogon Mapping System. *Geomatica*, 46, 4, 479.

5 Information in this section has been taken, with permission, from O'Brien, D.J. 1994. *Digital Video Stereoplotters*. Geomatics Canada. Unpublished manuscript.

6 Blais, J.A.R., and M.A. Chapman. 1991. *Users Guide Program SPACE-M*, rev. ed. Calgary: University of Calgary, Dept of Surveying Engineering.

7 For convenience the map scales for all non-metric mapping are given by quoting the number of miles represented by one inch on the map. Thus "Three-Mile" indicates three miles to one inch, "One-Mile" indicates one mile to one inch, etcetera.

8 Hills, E.H, 1904. *Report on the Survey of Canada*. National Archives, Rare Books section, 1904–63.

9 Figures on map production are taken from GSGS Index Maps and map catalogues published by Topographical Survey. These are held in the National Archives of Canada, map reading room.

10 Ibid.

11 See DND file HQS-1062–5 (D Engineers), various folios in 1946 and 1947, for the development of the MCAPP.

12 These U.S. maps are held in the National Archives, RG 85M accession number 934022, series A 1948–53.

13 Sebert, L.M. 1986. 94L Revisited. *The Canadian Surveyor*, 40, 3, 363–6.

14 For more detail on NTS map styles, see Nicholson, N.L. and L.M. Sebert. 1981. *The Maps of Canada. A Guide to Official Canadian Maps, Charts, Atlases and Gazetteers*. Folkestone, U.K.: Wm Dawson and Sons Ltd.

15 Ibid.

CHAPTER FOUR

Provincial Topographic Mapping

Louis M. Sebert

Before 1950 British Columbia, due to its mountainous nature, was the only Canadian province publishing topographic maps. A map showing any extent of the British Columbia terrain that did not indicate the existence of mountains and valleys could be very misleading indeed. The other provinces are sufficiently flat that for many years planimetric maps were quite adequate for administrative purposes and the development of natural resources

But by 1990 all provinces had topographic mapping programmes under way. This rather abrupt change in provincial government policy had several causes. In the first place the exploration for natural resources and their development has become increasingly scientific since the Second World War. This is particularly true in the fields of mining and forestry where large-scale accurate maps have become essential for proper management. A second reason is the advent of Geographic Information Systems (GIS). These are powerful research tools that are based on extensive terrain databanks that require good topographic base maps. A third and rather negative reason was the indication in the mid-1970s that the federal government wanted to vacate the large-scale mapping business. In the mid-1950s Ottawa had started mapping at 1:25 000 scale to fill requirements put forward by emergency measures organizations, but as the fear of nuclear attack receded the need for this elegant five-coloured series came into question. It was never the intention to extend the series into the rugged natural resource areas of the provinces, and because there were few who really needed this type of mapping, the series was discontinued in 1978. The obvious conclusion was that if the provinces wanted large-scale mapping of their hinterlands they would have to do it themselves.

Certain patterns appear when the history of provincial mapping is examined. Both the geography and the economic conditions in the various regions of Canada had an influence on the way the provinces developed their mapping programmes. These regions, for the purposes of this study, are:

The Atlantic Provinces
The Central Provinces of Ontario and Québec
The Prairie Provinces

British Columbia

The Territories

In each region the original need for topographic mapping will be examined, the action taken by the federal government to answer this need will be outlined, and then the steps taken by each province to provide modern mapping will be described.[1] But before examining the mapping in each province individually, it will be more expeditious to note certain fundamental aspects of the work that are common to all provinces.

All provinces are now undertaking their topographic mapping digitally. This digital mapping is being done in two ranges of map scales: resource mapping at 1:5000, 1:10 000 and 1:20 000 (which provides coverage of the whole province or at least large areas of it), and 1:1000, 1:2000, 1:2500, and 1:5000 scales for the mapping of populated places. Generally speaking the province selects one scale in each range for the digitizing. If other scales are required they are obtained by digital enlargement or reduction from the appropriate database. In addition it is now common practice to use Digital Elevation Models (DEMS), as described in chapter 3, for the capture of relief data. Contours at any desired interval, to suit the scale of the map being produced, may be derived from the DEMS.

In all provinces topographic data are being layered, or coded, so that data classes (contours, drainage, vegetation, man-made features, etc.) can be printed separately if that is required. With the advent of colour printers, coloured base maps with coloured thematic overprints can be produced as needed. The practice of keeping mylar originals in map sales offices so that monochrome maps could be run off by ozalid printers is gradually being replaced by the use of colour printers that can produce a much more useful and varied product. This can include the production of a map in classical design with all the usual margin information or an austere printout showing only the data needed by the client.

THE ATLANTIC PROVINCES

By the 1960s it was obvious to interested and knowledgeable officials in the Atlantic provinces that economic development in the region was being seriously hampered by an antiquated land registration system, and by the almost complete lack of maps suitable for modern resource development. It was equally obvious that these shortcomings could not be rectified by provincial funding alone. The fact that federal funds were eventually made available was to a large extent the result of the enthusiasm and personal drive of one man, Willis Roberts, the director of surveys of New Brunswick. In 1966 Roberts made a proposal to the Atlantic Development Board to fund a project that would modernize surveying and mapping in the Atlantic region. If approved and put into action the project would proceed in four phases.

Phase 1 would see the placing of survey monuments throughout the Atlantic provinces. They would be placed at a density consistent with the density of population, which could range from 15 km spacing in wilderness areas to 200 m spacing in cities. As much as possible they would be positioned suitable for both mapping and the registration of cadastral surveys. Phase 2 would consist of programmes of resource mapping at 1:5000 and 1:10 000 scales, and municipal mapping at 1:1200, 1:2400, and 1:4800, and later at their metric equivalents of 1:1000, 1:2000, 1:2500, and 1:5000. Phase 3 would involve the design and implementation of an improved land titles registration system based on the phase 2 mapping. Phase 4 would be the implementation of a comprehensive database of land information including the ownership, market value, geographical characteristics, etcetera, of all registered land parcels and all Crown lands. Roberts estimated that without federal assistance this programme would take seventy years to complete. With federal funding the time could be cut in half.

APSAMP 1969 to 1972

In 1968 Roberts's plan was approved in principle by the Atlantic Development Board, and the Atlantic Provinces Surveying and Mapping Program (APSAMP) came into being. But funding had to wait for approval by the newly formed federal Department of Regional Economic Expansion (DREE). Throughout the following four years DREE contributed 90 percent of the cost of the programme. This was set out in two grants: $7,369,000 for 1969–70, and $4,915,000 for 1971–72.[2]

During the first two-year period work proceeded well in the establishing of survey monuments (phase 1), and some work was done on the phase 2 mapping. But there was some dissatisfaction, especially in Newfoundland, concerning the administration of the programme. Consequently Newfoundland decided in 1972 to withdraw from the programme and negotiate a separate mapping arrangement with DREE. This necessitated a new agreement with Ottawa for the Maritime provinces. With Newfoundland out of the picture Roberts proposed that the Council of Maritime Premiers (CMP) take over the administration of a new programme called the Land Registration and Information Service (LRIS). This was approved.

LRIS 1973 to 1994

LRIS would have the same four phases as APSAMP and would also be funded through DREE. The two-year funding periods of APSAMP were considered too short, and Roberts was able to negotiate a five-year plan for LRIS. He would have liked a much longer commitment, but five years was a limit for DREE funding. It was of course presumed that additional five-year plans would follow until, in approximately thirty years, the programme would be completed.

Unfortunately at the end of the first five-year programme DREE notified the CMP that federal funds would not be available for a further five years. This was devastating news, and despite many petitions only one year's additional funding was forthcoming. The cut-off was made in 1978. During the APSAMP period and LRIS until 1978, DREE had contributed approximately $34,000,000 to the two programmes.[3] LRIS continued to operate (mostly on phase 1 and 2 projects, but only with provincial funding) until it was closed on 31 March 1994.

Newfoundland and Labrador[4]

Since joining Canadian confederation and prior to the advent of APSAMP, Newfoundland had relied entirely on the federal government for its topographic mapping. By 1969 all of the province had been covered by 1:250 000 maps and the 1:50 000 mapping programme was well under way. The latter was completed in 1979. The thematic mapping needs of the resource industries were met by using the federal mapping, enlarged if necessary, as bases for provincially produced overprints. This was done mainly in support of the forestry and mining industries. Little cadastral mapping existed outside the cities and larger towns. In the country cartographic evidence of property ownership was rare indeed. As can be imagined the APSAMP and DREE grants came as rays of sunshine on an otherwise bleak landscape.

From the beginning the phase 1 work of survey monumentation went ahead in good form. It was over mapping that a slight difference in opinion arose. A.C. McEwen, the provincial director of Lands and Surveys, decided that the resource mapping should be line mapping at the scale of 1:12 500 rather than the 1:10 000 orthophotomapping chosen by Nova Scotia and New Brunswick. (Prince Edward Island had opted for 1:5000 ortho-photomapping because of its small size.)

The Newfoundland 1:12 500 Series is drawn on the 3° Transverse Mercator (TM) projection with grid lines spaced at 1500 m in eastings and 2000 m in northings. The conventional signs used on the series resemble those employed on the federal 1:50 000 monochrome series. Three classes of roads are shown: paved highways, paved secondary roads, and gravel roads. Divided highways are shown by parallel paved highway symbols. Although all railways in the province have been abandoned, in places where the tracks still are in place they are shown by a broken line with cross-ticks. Forest edges are drawn in a scalloped line. The bulrush symbol is used to depict marshes. Relief is shown by contours at 5 and 10 m intervals depending on the ruggedness of the terrain. Spot heights are used to indicate the highest elevations of hills. All elevations are in metres. In this series labels and notations are used extensively to give information about the countryside and the use of buildings and other structures. The information in the margin is in English only.

The sheet format is based on subdivisions of the National Topographic System (NTS) 1:50 000 quadrangles. Each sheet is 1 minute and 30 seconds in longitude and 45 seconds in latitude. There are, therefore, 400 sheets (20 by 20) in a 1:50 000 quadrangle. It is a handsome and useful series, and it was with considerable regret that work on it had to be discontinued in 1984. By that year 52 sheets had been published. Although the maps are not being revised they are still being widely used.

URBAN MAPPING

The reason for discontinuing the 1:12 500 Series was the more urgent need for municipal mapping at scales of 1:2500 and 1:5000. The new "Community Mapping Program" is being actively advanced with 3767 sheets published by June 1993. Only 740 additional sheets are needed (about four years of work) to complete the initial coverage of all communities on the island and the principal settlements in Labrador. By mid-1993 80 sheets had been drawn for settlements in Labrador. Since 1992 all work has been in digital form.

CURRENT FEDERAL ASSISTANCE

The Newfoundland government has entered into a cost-sharing agreement with the Canada Centre for Geomatics (CCG) for the provision of the digitized version of all 1:250 000 and 1:50 000 NTS maps covering the province. By the end of 1997 all 1:250 000 coverage has been received as has the 1:50 000 coverage of the island. Work is progressing on the Labrador 1:50 000 maps. This means that resource mapping is available at any desired scale in the completed areas in a form in which additional data can easily be added. In some ways this compensates for the lack of greater coverage at 1:12 500.

Note: On the closing of APSAMP in 1973 and the beginning of LRIS under the CMP, a fresh look was taken at the mapping needs of the Maritimes together with a fresh examination made of the resources available to fulfil these needs. The following is a province-by-province description of the various map series that resulted from this study, and the historic factors that governed the decisions and choices made.

In the early days of Confederation, Nova Scotia had been well served by mapping agencies outside the province. During the second half of the nineteenth century the Hydrographic Service of the Royal Navy had carefully charted Nova Scotia's coast. As no part of the province is more than 50 km from the sea, the navy's work served as control for the early medium-scale mapping of the province. The Geological Survey of Canada (GSC) was active there beginning in the 1880s, and by 1910 had completed a ninety-one-sheet series of One-Inch maps covering all of the province except the south-west tip. These geological maps showed only the major topographic features, but they were sufficiently accurate to provide a base for the 20 Chain and 40 Chain (1:15 840 and 1:31 680) provincial resource development maps.

True topographic mapping at the one-inch scale was started in 1922 by a federal programme involving the Geographical Section of the General Staff (GSGS) and the Topographical Survey, Department of the Interior. This activity saw the complete coverage of the province at one-inch scale by 1956, and removed the need for provincial topographic work until the requirement for larger scale resource mapping began to be felt in the mid-1960s. At that time the first plans that eventually resulted in APSAMP were being made. APSAMP started operations in 1968 and passed on the work to LRIS on 1 April 1973. The mapping done in Nova Scotia under this new initiative was designed first to give the province complete coverage with 1:10 000 contoured orthophotomaps, and coverage of its urbanized areas with modern large-scale line maps. With the advent of automated cartography and GIS operations, the Maritime provinces decided to extend their programmes to include 1:10 000 digital line maps.

The following is a description of these LRIS mapping programmes in Nova Scotia. But because the mapping programmes of all three provinces were under the overall supervision of the CMP during their planning stages, their mapping styles are almost identical. To avoid duplication only Nova Scotia's mapping styles will be described here in detail, while those of the other two provinces will be covered only where they differ from Nova Scotia's.

ORTHOPHOTOMAPPING

The designers of the *LRIS* orthophotomaps at 1:10 000 scale used the quadrangles of the NTS 1:50 000 Series for the basic sheet line system. Initially each quadrangle had been divided into thirty-six smaller quads (6 by 6), and this format was used for about three-quarters of the province (1569 map sheets). In an effort to reduce costs and keep the programme on schedule, the layout was changed from thirty-six to twenty-five quads (5 by 5) per NTS sheet, and the remainder of the orthophoto coverage of the province, 442 sheets, was done using this design. The programme in Nova Scotia and New Brunswick involved the publication of three orthophoto series: the basic Planimetric Series, the Topographic Map Series with contours, and the Property Map Series with accentuated property lines. An orthophoto base was first prepared for each sheet. For the Topographic Series the base is overprinted by white contour lines at a 5 m interval. Rivers, streams, and lake shores are accentuated by black lines. Wet ground is outlined by a broken black line with the bulrush symbol, or a label defining the feature. Roads are not cased or accentuated in any way and are not classified. For grid referencing on the newer (5 by 5) format, a 1000 m 3° TM grid is printed in fine black lines over the sheet. For geographic referencing the sheet corners are given their latitude and longitude values in degrees and thousandths of a degree, and the neat line is marked with latitude and longitude dashes. On the earlier 6-by-6 formatted sheets the Transverse Mercator (TM) grid is defined only by ticks in the margin with the tick values given in the north and west margins. The latitude and longitude values of the corners of the sheet are in degrees, minutes, and seconds. (There are no minute marks in the margin so, evidently, the reading of geographical coordinates from these sheets is not anticipated.). On both formats, place-names and labels are in English but the margin information is bilingual.

The sheets of the Property Map Series have no contours but parcel outlines are drawn prominently in black, and roads, by virtue of being property boundaries, are cased. Each parcel is given an identifying number. The sheets are not gridded but 1000 m grid ticks are placed on the neat line. Place-names, labels, and margin information are the same as on the Topographic Map Series.

When planimetric, topographic, and property orthophoto coverage was completed for Nova Scotia in 1986 there were 2010 sheets in each series. In that year, for the first time, the province had accurate mapping at a uniform and large enough scale for resource planning and the definition of rural land ownership. However as the equivalent digital mapping became available the use of these earlier photomap series has declined. They are not being revised.

DIGITAL RESOURCE MAPS

Even before the orthophoto series were completed it was apparent that digital mapping was needed. While photomaps are excellent for showing field limits and boundaries, they are difficult to revise and are particularly unsuitable as a base on which to plot thematic information. They are therefore not suitable for displaying the output of GIS programs. Consequently in 1984 the LRIS mapping agency in Summerside was instructed to start work on 1:10 000 digital mapping. Again the three versions (planimetric, property, and topographic) were required, but this time the NTS quadrangle was divided into twenty-five quads for the 1:10 000 sheet lines of all three series.

On the Topographic Series contours are again shown at 5 m intervals. Five classes of roads are identified: hard surface primary, hard surface secondary, loose surface all-weather, loose surface seasonal, and track. Divided highways are shown by parallel hard-surface symbols. Railways are shown by the usual symbol of a line with cross-ticks. Power lines are indicated by a broken line with dots (representing the pylons) filling the breaks. Rivers, streams, ponds, and lakes are shown by solid lines. Open water is filled by a screened grey, and lake and river names are clearly shown. Forest edges are drawn using the usual scalloped line. Wet ground is outlined by a broken line with the bulrush symbol indicating the content. Fences and walls are shown only if they are important features, but if so they are drawn as fine broken lines with an X (fence) or a W (wall) filling the breaks. A good selection of point symbols is available to show churches, schools, bridges, air strips, and the like. Line symbols are provided for international, interprovincial, county, and park/

reserve boundaries. The grid and geographic referencing lines and values are the same as have been described for photomaps.

By 1997 both the digital planimetric and property map series had been completed. The topographic maps are being produced as required. This is usually when some large-scale engineering project is being planned such as highway construction or hydroelectric power development.

The reason for this lack of emphasis on the topographic series is because the province now has a valuable alternative. In 1993 an agreement was entered into with the CCG for a shared cost digitizing of all the NTS 1:50 000 maps covering the province. The last of these was received in 1994. With this data in hand valuable digital maps are being constructed by enlarging the 1:50 000 coverage and adding the 1:10 000 property and road classification data. Some editing is of course required to eliminate superfluous or unwanted symbols.

URBAN LINE MAPS

Urban line maps existed for Nova Scotia towns and cities long before the coming of APSAMP. These were at a variety of imperial scales, and of course none was digital. In many cases they were seriously out of date. Beginning in 1983 Nova Scotia began compiling digital maps of urban areas through LRIS. When that agency stopped operating, the responsibility for the production of digital urban maps was given to the Nova Scotia Geomatics Centre at Amherst. Good progress has been made in producing this database. By 1997 twenty-two of Nova Scotia's largest cities and towns had been mapped and two areas of major highway construction (the Wentworth Bypass and the Truro Interchange) had been covered. The metro area of Halifax-Dartmouth has been published at 1:1000 because of the closely packed small parcels in this old urban area. The other towns have mostly been mapped at 1:2000 but the 1:5000 scale was used where the required data can be clearly shown at this scale. For the highway work 1:5000 mapping was more than adequate.

For this large-scale work, a digital planimetric base map was drawn first. For the Property Map Series, property lines and property identifiers were added. If topographic mapping was needed, contours and spot elevations were added to the base. Contours are at 2 m intervals on the 1:1000 and 2000 maps and at 5 m for the 1:5000 mapping. On the base maps, street allowances are shown to scale and the streets are named. Buildings are shown to scale, wooded areas are depicted by the scalloped line symbol, and landmark trees are shown in plan view. Wet ground is outlined by a broken line with the bulrush symbol indicating the nature of the ground. Railways and streetcar lines are shown by the railway symbol. Fences, hedges, and walls are important cadastral indicators, and are shown by broken lines with an X, H, or W filling the breaks. Labels are used extensively to indicate land use (cemetery, park, soccer field, etc.) and building use (fire station, school, curling rink, etc.). Screened black is not used to fill open water but lakes and ponds are named. Power lines, which are important easement features, are depicted with the pylons in their true positions. Contours are shown only on the topographic maps and property lines and identifiers only on the Property Map Series. UTM grid lines are drawn at 100 m intervals on the 1:1000 maps, 200 m on the 1:2000 maps, and 500 m on the 1:5000 mapping. Latitude and longitude bars are drawn on the neat line and their values in degrees and decimals are shown in the map corners. The sheet line system uses the NTS 1:50 000 quads divided into 2500 smaller quads (50 by 50) for the 1:1000 scale,

625 smaller quads (25 by 25) for the 1:2000 scale, and 100 smaller quads (10 by 10) for the 1:5000 scale.

New Brunswick

New Brunswick was not of much interest to the federal mapping agencies before the Second World War. Little prospecting and mining had been done in the province, and consequently the GSC had turned its attention to more promising regions. The province was also low on the priority list for military mapping. Therefore little topographic mapping had been done there before 1939. Of the more than eighty sheets of the NTS One-Inch Series that would cover the province, only twelve had been published before war was declared.

The war changed all this. Suddenly topographic maps of New Brunswick were needed as the cartographic bases for aeronautical charts. The lead-zinc-copper deposits in the Bathurst-Newcastle area were at once of prime importance. Federal funds for mapping became available to help meet these needs. Although the One-Inch Series was not completed during the war, the wartime impetus continued after 1945. Following conversion to 1:50 000 scale the series was completed for the whole of the province in 1957.

As in Nova Scotia, New Brunswick elected to use the contoured 1:10 000 orthophotomap for its initial topographic coverage. The work was started in 1968, and the 2718 sheets were completed in 1985. The same three planimetric, topographic, and property series were developed, and were drawn with virtually the same specifications as those of Nova Scotia. The principal exception was the drawing of the New Brunswick sheets on the New Brunswick Stereographic Projection rather than the 3° TM used in Nova Scotia.

New Brunswick started its 1:10 000 digital mapping in 1984. The specifications were nearly identical to those of Nova Scotia. The principal difference was that as usual the New Brunswick maps were plotted on the New Brunswick Stereographic Projection. Originally only the planimetric and property series were produced, and these series were completed in 1994 in 1888 sheets. Digital terrain model data has been gathered since about 1985 so that the planimetric sheets can be contoured as required.

In 1993 New Brunswick, like Nova Scotia, arranged with the CCG for the digitizing of all NTS New Brunswick 1:50 000 sheets. This project was completed in 1996 and, as with Nova Scotia, the availability of this adaptable topographic data has lessened the urgency for 1:10 000 contouring.

The New Brunswick digital urban mapping programme also resembles that of Nova Scotia. Only the 1:1000 and 1:2000 scales are used, again with specifications identical to those of their Nova Scotia counterparts except for the different projection.

Prince Edward Island

Prince Edward Island has a long history of cadastral mapping. It was first surveyed by Samuel Holland and his men in 1765–66. At that time it was divided into sixty-seven "lots" of about 20 000 acres each, each lot being similar in size to a small township in the other provinces. These lots were gradually subdivided and settled, and the settlement pattern of roads and fences remains to this day.

As with New Brunswick, federal mapping agencies showed little interest in the island before the Second World War, only two of the eleven NTS One-Inch Series having been published before 1939. This was all changed by the war when the whole province was considered of strategic importance. All eleven sheets were in print by 1948.

The APSAMP initiatives of 1968 came at a most convenient time for PEI. In that year the province commenced a complete restructuring of its property tax system, and a new system of land information was needed. The planning authorities welcomed the APSAMP resources being offered, and immediately embarked on an orthophotomapping programme.

Because of the small size and open terrain of PEI the 1:5000 orthophoto coverage was chosen. Since the lack of marked relief made contouring unnecessary, only the Property Map Series was needed. Once again the NTS 1:50 000 quadrangle was used for the basic sheet line system. This time it is divided into forty-eight smaller quads, six north-south by eight east-west. The photomap is overprinted with property lines and identifying numbers in black. Place-names and labels are in black or white depending on the photo background. A white 1000 m grid covers each sheet, based on the PEI Stereographic Projection. Grid values are given in the margin and geographic values, in degrees, minutes, and seconds, are shown at the sheet corners. Roads are cased only if they form parcel boundaries, and if they are not classified. The drainage is not accentuated. The series was started in 1969 and completed in 1256 sheets by 1973. Revision of the series was stopped in 1988.

As with the other Maritime provinces a large-scale contoured urban series was also needed. The 1:2500 scale was chosen with two styles being published: an uncontoured property series with all properties clearly outlined and numbered, and a second series with contours but without property lines. This work was started in 1975, and was completed in 1980 for all PEI places with a population over 300, a total of 243 sheets. It was not digitized and is not being revised, but it is still in active use.

To replace the aging 1:2500 Series, a digital series at 1:1000 covering Summerside in twenty-four sheets was started in 1986 and finished in 1988. A similar series was started in 1991 to cover Charlottetown in thirty-eight sheets. It was completed in 1992. As resources become available similar digitized coverage will be put into work for the other PEI towns.

In 1986, about two years after the two larger provinces started their 1:10 000 digital mapping, PEI followed their lead. The specifications for the PEI 1:10 000 Series are much the same as for those of New Brunswick. They have a 1000 m grid based on the PEI Stereographic Projection. Built-up areas are shown in a screened grey, but open water is left clear. Geographic values of the sheet corners are in degrees and decimals, not in minutes and seconds as on the photomap series. The information given in the margin is in English and French. Coverage of the province in 212 sheets was completed in 1990.

THE CENTRAL PROVINCES: ONTARIO AND QUÉBEC

Although Ontario and Québec are quite different culturally, the history of their surveying and mapping before the Second World War is remarkably similar. The first extensive surveys of both provinces were made to lay out townships for immigrant settlers. The township pattern used in both provinces was designed by Governor Haldimand and his chief surveyor, Holland. These township surveys started in what is now Ontario, in 1783, to accommodate the first large influx of Loyalists. The Québec surveys were started in 1792 immediately after the separation of Upper and Lower Canada, and helped provide homesteads in the region between the St Lawrence River and the American border. For the first few years surveyors could work in either the Eastern Townships of Lower Canada or the Western Townships of Upper Canada. The term "Eastern Townships," or its modern equivalent "Estrie," lives on in Québec, but the area named "Western Townships" has disappeared from Ontario.

In 1904 the Canadian army started to map the southern part of both provinces at the one-inch scale. The work was, generally speaking, evenly divided between the two provinces. The maps produced became the first entries in the NTS, and in fact were the bulk of the system for many years. These maps provided for the major topographic needs of the two provinces until after the war.

In the years immediately following the war the resource development ministries of both provinces used medium-scale planimetric maps that were produced cheaply, by provincial mapping agencies, from aerial photographs and a minimum of ground control. But in the early 1970s both provinces decided independently that they needed large-scale accurate topographic maps of at least the southern half of their provinces. Both provinces developed their own, rather similar, mapping systems, which are described below.

Québec

Québec launched a number of major engineering projects in the 1950s that required topographic maps of high accuracy. The former were mainly for the production of hydro-electric power, and maps of large areas were needed. At first this mapping was implemented project by project, but in 1972 it was decided that all such mapping should be organized into a province-wide system of maps at scales of 1:20 000 and larger. The system was called the System Québécois de reference cartographique (SQRC).

The maps of the SQRC are drawn on the 3° TM projection. The sheet line system of the whole SQRC is based on the NTS 1:50 000 quadrangles. Each 1:50 000 quad is quartered to give the sheet lines of the 1:20 000 maps. This quartering and enlarging continues to the 1:10 000 and 1:5000 scales. The 1:2000 scale is used rather than 1:2500, and the quartering and enlarging continues to 1:1000.

THE 1:20 000 SERIES

The major effort of the SQRC is focused on the 1:20 000 Series. The sheets of the series are very large, measuring 69 cm by 93 cm within the neat lines (at latitude 47°). They are drawn on the 3° TM projection and are the largest topographic maps being published by the provinces or by the federal government. They are monochrome, but by a skilful use of screens they give a clear picture of the terrain. Five classes of rural roads are identified: principal, secondary, tertiary, unpaved, and local road. Within towns and cities a wide screened line is sometimes used for streets. Autoroutes are shown by a double principal road symbol. Railways are indicated by a fine black line with cross-ticks. Power lines are shown with their pylons in their true positions. If the pylons are steel they are drawn as small squares; if they are wood they are shown as small circles.

Wooded areas are depicted by a dappled area symbol printed in a 10 percent screen. This is very effective as it shows at a glance the areas on the map that are forested. The same impression is not given by simply showing forest outlines, as is done in most other provinces. The bulrush symbol indicates wet ground. Open water areas (lakes, ponds, wide rivers) are shown by a black shoreline and a 30 percent screened black infill.

Relief is represented by 10 m contours and numerous spot heights. A good selection of point symbols is available to show churches, schools, ruins, bridges, etcetera. Fences, hedges, and walls are shown by a broken line with an X in the breaks for a fence, an H for a hedge (haie), or an M for a wall (mur). Boundary symbols are used for international and interprovincial boundaries.

Eighteen of the sheets of the SQRC 1:20 000 Series are also published as five-colour lithographed maps. Nine of these cover the Montreal area. The other nine are of Québec City and its suburbs. The five colours are used as follows:

Red	Roads, railways, road and railway names and numbers
Blue	Water features and their names
Green	Forests, landmark trees, orchards, etcetera.
Brown	Contours, spot elevations, dunes, and eskers
Black	Man-made features, land names, boundaries

In many ways these maps resemble the sheets of the NTS 1:25 000 Series. The most obvious difference is the lack of the pink built-up area symbol. This means that thousands of house symbols have had to be used to show the extent of construction. This is certainly an elegant set of maps, but they will be difficult and expensive to keep revised. Figure 4-1 shows (in black and white) the symbols used on these coloured maps.

PRODUCTION OF THE 1:20 000 SERIES

To get the true picture of the status of this mapping, two indexes must be used. The first is La couverture cartographique à l'échelle 1:20 000 1997. This shows the layout of the 1842 sheets that are available in lithograph, diazo, or electrostatic printing. The second index is La couverture numérique à l'échelle 1:20 000 1997. This shows the digital mapping coverage available on diskette, tape, or CD-ROM. Of course a large percentage of the mapping is available in both forms and appears on both indexes.

As one would expect, the majority of the mapping at this scale is in southern Québec. According to both indexes 2426 sheets have been published of which 1979 are digital. On the digital index, the programme planners of this work have drawn a dashed red line across the province. It is an irregular line but it runs generally between the 51° and 52° lines of north latitude. The plan is to complete the digitization of the series up to this line by March 2000. This will mean the production of about 700 sheets in the three-year period, but many of these sheets are already published in non-digital form and can easily be digitized from existing reproduction material.

In addition to this impressive workload there will still be a demand for sheets north of the red line in support of resource development projects. At the time of the publication of the indexes 674 sheets had been published north of the line. All new work in this region will of course be digital. However for many years there will be area where 1:20 000 mapping does not exist. In such areas the NTS 1:50 000 sheets will be made available to map users.

QUÉBEC MUNICIPAL MAPPING

Most of the municipal mapping of the SQRC is at the 1:1000 scale, but there is some mapping at 1:2000 for special purposes. In general appearance they resemble the municipal maps of the Atlantic provinces described previously. Streets are indicated by the boundaries of the street allowances and all streets are named. Buildings are shown in plan view at scale. Fences, hedges, and walls show property lines and are indicated by the usual broken

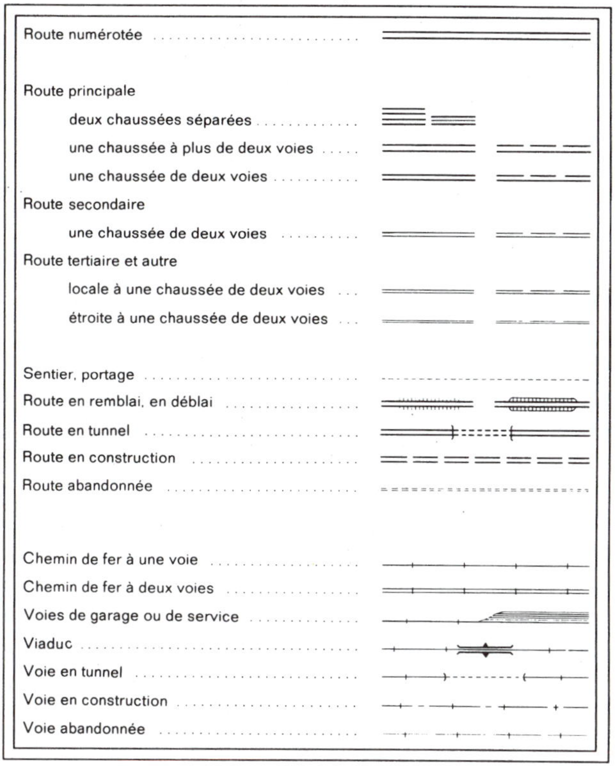

Route numérotée	=====
Route principale	
deux chaussées séparées	== ==
une chaussée à plus de deux voies	==== == — ==
une chaussée de deux voies	==== == — ==
Route secondaire	
une chaussée de deux voies	== — —
Route tertiaire et autre	
locale à une chaussée de deux voies ...	== —
étroite à une chaussée de deux voies ...	== — —
Sentier, portage	— — — —
Route en remblai, en déblai	
Route en tunnel	===: : : : :=
Route en construction	== == == == ==
Route abandonnée	= = = = = = = =
Chemin de fer à une voie	— + — + —
Chemin de fer à deux voies	— + — + —
Voies de garage ou de service	— + —
Viaduc	— + —
Voie en tunnel	— + — — - - - + — + —
Voie en construction	— + — + — + —
Voie abandonnée	— + — + — + — + —

Figure 4-1
Symbols for transportation facilities used on Québec coloured maps.
Note: All symbols are printed in red.
Source: CIG *Geomatica*

line with identifiers (X, H, or M) in the breaks. Wooded areas are shown by a scalloped line rather than the dappled grey area symbol used on the 1:20 000 maps. The 1:2000 maps are published in two styles: a topographic version with contours and spot heights, and a cadastral version without contours but with property lines and property numbers shown.

As in the other provinces many maps from the days of imperial measure still exist and are in constant use. Although these are being retained, and in some cases are being updated by the municipalities, they will eventually be replaced by sheets of the SQRC.

Ontario

Before 1977 the Ontario government relied on NTS maps for its topographic needs. Because the progress of federal surveys into Northern Ontario was expected to be slow, the Ministry of Lands and Forests had organized a series of planimetric maps at the scale of two miles to the inch immediately after the Second World War. These maps covered large areas of Ontario to the north of the NTS coverage, and were most useful for the administration of lumbering and mining activity in the regions they covered.

By 1974 it was most apparent that accurate large-scale topographic maps were necessary for the proper development of the province's natural resources. Québec and the Atlantic provinces had already launched mapping programmes of this sort, and it was now time for Ontario to get going. The initial planning was under the personal direction of Robert Code, the director of surveys for the province. During the early planning sessions several fundamental decisions were made. The scales to be used in the new Ontario Basic Mapping (OBM) programme were 1:2000 for municipal mapping, 1:10 000 for Southern Ontario, and 1:20 000 for most of Northern Ontario. The Hudson Bay lowlands, which are almost entirely flat swamplands, would be depicted cartographically by orthophotomaps. The 1:2000 mapping would be used for cities, towns, and villages; but metro Toronto and other large cities with their own surveying and mapping departments would be excluded from the programme, at least for the first few years.

Once the OBM programme was launched in 1977, it was important to get an appreciable area mapped so the public could see some progress in this new initiative. To accomplish this some troubling decisions had to be made. First it was decided to produce the maps by traditional cartographic methods rather than by digital systems, which, even in 1977, were recognized as the techniques of the future. The reason for this decision was simple. At the time the Ontario mapping companies had little or no experience in structured digital mapping, and consequently were not ready to take on such a large project. In addition manually drawn maps were then cheaper and faster to produce. Another expediency was to publish the maps of south-eastern Ontario, that is, east of the 78th meridian, without contours. Again this was to produce more maps with the funds available, and to produce them quickly. Steps have been taken to redress these deficiencies: since 1986 all production has been in digital format, and contours will be added to the planimetric maps when they come up for revision.

OBM SPECIFICATIONS

The UTM projection and grid is used for all OBM mapping. The UTM 10 000 m grid-lines provide the sheet lines for the 1:20 000 Series, the 5000 m for the 1:10 000 Series, and the 1000 m grid for the 1:2000 Series. Grid-lines are at 1000 m spacing on the 1:20 000 and 1:10 000 sheets and at 100 m spacing on the 1:2000 sheets. This use of the appropriate UTM grid for the sheet lines at each scale ensures that all OBM sheets measure 50 cm between opposite neat lines.

At present all OBM maps are reproduced in monochrome from chronaflex masters by diazo printing or large-format photocopying. Plans are under way, however, to eliminate chronaflex storage and produce copies directly from disc files by electrostatic printing. Initially the product will be monochrome similar to the chronaflex reproduction, but it is intended to take advantage of the fact that the topographic and thematic data in the files are coded according to type, for example contours, drainage, and vegetation. Customized colour printing will therefore be available if the map user wants a product that is more explicit and easier to read.

On OBM sheets roads are shown by the road-casing lines spaced 0.7 mm apart without a distinguishing infill. No distinction is made between paved and all-weather gravel roads. The only road classification is between all-weather and seasonal, the latter being shown by broken casing lines. A dashed line is used for bush roads and tracks. Divided highways are shown by two parallel road symbols. Railways are depicted by the usual line with cross-ticks. Abandoned lines are indicated by a broken symbol. Power lines are shown by a line between small squares if the pylons are steel, or between dots if timber poles are used.

Wooded areas are outlined by the familiar scalloped line symbol. This is quite effective for copses and small forests, but if large areas are tree covered it is difficult to tell if the area is heavily forested or mostly clear. On the 1:2000 sheets a plan-view tree symbol is used for landmark trees. Marshes are shown by the usual bulrush symbol. A swamp (i.e., wet ground with trees) is shown by the bulrush symbol within the treed outline. Streams and single-line rivers are shown by a heavy solid line to distinguish them from the contours that are in screened grey. Open water in the form of lakes, ponds, and wide streams is shown only by the solid line representing the shore or bank. No screened infill is used. Beaver dams and their ponds are an important drainage feature in Ontario, and are indicated by a heavy line across the stream with the letters BD or the label "Beaver Dam" close by.

A good selection of point symbols is available to indicate such features as buildings, survey points, culverts, and towers. The township fabric of township lines, lots, and concessions is shown clearly by screened lines if these boundaries are not easily distinguished from the road or cut line on which they fall. Cut lines are shown by parallel forest-edge symbols. Symbols are also available for international, interprovincial, park, and other boundaries.

Relief is indicated on the 1:2000 sheets by fine solid lines showing 1 m or 2 m contours, depending on the ruggedness of the terrain, by 5 m contours on the 1:10 000 sheets, and by 10 m contours on the 1:20 000 sheets. Spot heights are used liberally to indicate the tops of hills, the heights of road intersections, and other locations. All heights and contour values are in metres.

The text of all OBM maps was only in English before 1989, but after that year new maps are bilingual both in the margin information and on the face of the maps. Figure 4-2 is a section from the OBM Timmins sheet.

THE PRODUCTION OF OBM MAPS

Coverage of the whole province at 1:10 000 for the south and 1:20 000 for the north will require 14 000 sheets. An interim objective was set to map the province to the 51st parallel by 1997, and this target was achieved in March of that year. This is a remarkable achievement but was only possible by giving priority to new mapping over revision. From March 1997 on, much more attention has been given to revision.

It should be noted that from 1977 to 1986 the emphasis was on creating a cartographic product that was cost effective. In 1986 the emphasis was changed to give a higher level of importance to the completeness and up-to-dateness of the digital file. The hard-copy map is now considered, in many ways, as simply a portable "current report" on the status of the digital file.

THE PRAIRIE PROVINCES

The Prairie provinces are divided into two distinct landscapes: the flat and open grassland to the south and the rolling forested region to the north. In 1870 the federal government decided to settle the southern plains, and the first step was to divide the land into square farm lots within almost-square townships. The Dominion Land Surveyors who did this work recorded field notes that were suitable and sufficient for drafting the Three-Mile (to one inch) maps of the prairies.

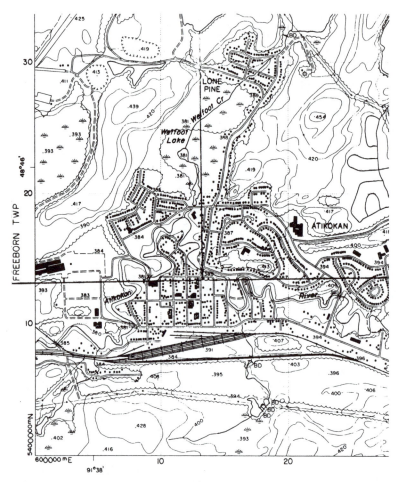

Figure 4-2
Section from an Ontario Base Mapping 1:20 000 map.
Source: CIG *Geomatica*

The Three-Mile maps were in place when Manitoba was just a small "postage stamp" rectangle, and Saskatchewan and Alberta were still part of the Northwest Territories. The first sheet, Edmonton, was published in 1891 and was followed by a steady production of about six sheets per year. Up to 1920 these maps were planimetric and of rather coarse appearance, but in that year a start was made to turn each sheet into a true topographic map of very attractive design. This, coupled with an impressive updating programme, gave the Prairie provinces useful medium-scale topographic map coverage. In time the Three-Mile mapping was replaced by the NTS 1:50 000 Series, but this early federal mapping was the main reason for the rather late entry of the Prairie provinces into topographic mapping. A second and equally important reason was the simple fact that except for the mountainous area of west Alberta, all three provinces are remarkably flat. As a consequence it was not until the 1970s, when large-scale mapping was needed for resource development and GIS applications, that topographic maps were found to be necessary. The following is a province-by-province description of the entry of each into this type of mapping.

Manitoba

Until the late 1970s there was no provincial topographic mapping done in Manitoba. The federal NTS 1:50 000 Series covered the southern part of the province by 1960, and this answered the majority of the local map needs. The engineering departments of the cities provided their own large-scale plans as required for urban development and administration. There was, however, a growing need for detailed knowledge of the smaller settlements and the areas surrounding them. This was particularly noticeable in the north, and in 1979 a monochrome series at the 1:20 000 scale was put into work for settlements of that region.

The 1980s saw an unprecedented growth of topographic mapping in all provinces due mainly to the need for detailed knowledge of the terrain required for GIS applications (see chapter 15). Manitoba was a little late in joining this wave, but in 1988 the Manitoba Surveys and Mapping Branch conducted a detailed study of the matter that led to the decision to map the southern half of the province at the 1:10 000 scale, and the northern settlements at the same scale. In this programme all sheets would be compiled digitally with contours drawn at 5 m intervals. Before any sheets were published it was decided further that although all data were to be captured suitable for 1:10 000 mapping, hard-copy maps would be printed at the 1:20 000 scale and only for the more populated areas of the province. The remaining sheets would be kept on file, and printed on demand to the users' specifications.

In many respects the Manitoba 1:20 000 Series resembles the mapping at the same scale in Northern Ontario. The UTM 10 000 m grid square is used for sheet lines. The Manitoba sheets have a 5 m contour interval compared with the Ontario 10 m, but that is consistent with the flatter terrain. The symbols used are virtually the same in both provinces. One outstanding difference in the two programmes is that Manitoba Natural Resources decided to publish the eighty sheets around Winnipeg as five-colour lithographed maps. The following colours are used:

Red	Roads, screened red for built-up areas
Blue	Drainage features and their names
Green	Vegetation
Brown	Contours
Black	Man-made features including railways, landmark buildings, labels, land names, and spot elevations

These sheets resemble the Québec coloured sheets covering Montreal and Québec City except for their much smaller size and the use of screened red for built-up areas. The remaining sheets of the programme, and all future production at this scale, will be kept on tape and, as has been mentioned, will only be printed when requested by a client. The printing will be done in colour or black and white at the client's request and expense.

Unlike with the other provinces the Manitoba mapping is being done in-house. The January 1993 index shows that in addition to the 80 printed sheets mentioned above there are 58 sheets that have been digitized but not printed. An additional 150 sheets are either in progress or are waiting to be started. When the series is completed, in about ten years, the coverage north to the 52nd parallel will embrace about 1100 sheets.

Saskatchewan

In Saskatchewan the provincial mapping unit is the Central Survey and Mapping Agency (CSMA). When the need arose for large-scale map coverage, this agency approached the problem in a somewhat different way from the other provinces. Instead of embarking on a mapping programme in the 1:10 000–1:20 000 range it contracted with the CCG for complete digital coverage at the 1:50 000 scale. This work, which was started in 1992, was completed three years later, giving the CSMA a digital database. To augment this with a property database, the CSMA has produced township photomaps at a scale of 1:20 000. Each township is covered by a single photograph, and due to the flatness of the terrain it is in essence an orthophoto. The familiar DLS survey pattern makes the identification of property boundaries quite easy. All 3700 surveyed townships have been mapped which means complete coverage up to the 54th parallel. This gives Saskatchewan a suitable cartographic base for resource development and rural land registration.

In the field of urban cartography, 725 populated places have been mapped at 1:2000. These are digital planimetric maps showing roads, drainage, buildings, and the necessary other detail needed for town and city administration. The symbolization used is similar to that on the mapping of equivalent scales in the other provinces.

Alberta

Alberta's first entry into topographic mapping was in 1975 when the then provincial Surveys and Mapping Branch published maps at 1:25 000 of the provincial oil-sands area. These maps covered most of the NTS quadrangles 74D and 84A. This series was not continued because in 1979 the province reconsidered its whole mapping philosophy to address the needs of, and take advantage of, the new and powerful GIS. The responsibility for mapping was given to the newly formed Alberta Bureau of Surveying and Mapping, which was placed in a new ministry, namely Alberta Energy and Natural Resources. However in the 1990 government reorganization the mapping agency was moved to the Information Resource Mapping Services in the Ministry of Environmental Protection.

In the 1960s Alberta developed a series of thematic maps (forestry, transportation, etc.) at the 1:250 000 scale, and information fromn these, suitably updated, has been digitized into a provincial medium-scale series. Data from this work have been transferred to the CCG in Sherbrooke.

In the 1970s it had been decided that Alberta's large-scale mapping needs would be best served by a range of metric scales based on the 3° TM projection. The scales chosen were 1:20 000 for resource development, 1:5000 for rural property mapping, and 1:1000 for municipal mapping. A programme for complete digital coverage of the province at 1:20 000 was put into work in 1983 and was completed in 1997 in 2775 sheets. The following is a description of this work.

THE 1:20 000 SERIES
This series is called the Provincial Digital Base Mapping (PDBM) programme. The sheet lines for the maps of the PDBM are obtained by quartering the NTS 1:50 000 quads of the same area. This method produces large sheets (as it did in Québec) with the same 69.5 cm

north-south dimension as in Québec but, due to the higher latitude, a slightly smaller east-west measurement. At 51° north latitude it is 80.5 cm. For sheet designation the PDBM used the NTS quad number followed by NW, NE, SE, or SW, as appropriate.

Relief is shown by 10 m contours in the plains, and 20 m in the mountains. It is interesting to note that since 1 April 1984 the contouring for this series has been derived from DEMs. Alberta was the first to put this innovative technique into production. It has since been followed by all provinces and the federal government. Seven classes of roads are identified: divided highway, paved road four lanes, paved road two lanes, gravel road two lanes, gravel road one lane, unimproved road, and truck trail. Railways are shown by the usual cross-ticked line. Abandoned lines are labelled and the line is broken. Power lines are not shown. Forest areas are indicated by a very light (10 percent screen) forest area symbol. Streams are shown by a solid line and rivers, if sufficiently wide, are shown by both banks. Lakes and ponds have a solid shoreline but are not filled.

The survey pattern is a prominent feature in this series. Line symbols are available for the following: road allowance surveyed, road allowance unsurveyed, blind line surveyed, and blind line unsurveyed. Other line symbols are provided for county boundaries (including municipal and improvement districts) and the boundaries of various parks and reserves. Point symbols show bridges and tunnels but do not show buildings. Figure 4-3 is a section from an Alberta 1:20 000 sheet. Copies of the sheets of this series are not kept in stock but are run off from disc storage as required.

URBAN AND PARCEL MAPPING
Two cadastral mapping programmes are in operation in Alberta: the Municipal Integrated Surveying and Mapping (MISAM) programme and the Parcel Mapping (PM) programme. The former covers the province's larger populated places, while the latter takes care of the smaller villages and hamlets in the countryside. In addition to the standard cadastral features the MISAM programme also provides 1:1000 mapping with 1 m contours and orthophotos at 1:5000 as well as line maps at the same scale. The contours are derived from DEM data. The MISAM work now covers seventy-two centres and has a portfolio of 438 sheets at 1:5000 scale. As these sheets are only printed on demand they may be obtained with 1 m contours, with the cadastral base, or with both as the client requests. In addition the MISAM programme has produced over 9000 planimetric cadastral sheets at 1:1000. The PM programme was completed in 1996.

British Columbia

British Columbia has a long tradition in topographic mapping because such maps were needed to show the rugged nature of the province. Between 1938 and 1968 the provincial mapping agency cooperated with the federal government in the production of the One-Inch and 1:50 000 British Columbia sheets of the federal series. Of the total of 1140 sheets covering the province, 221 were surveyed, plotted, and carried through the fair drawing stage by the provincial mapping agency before being shipped to Ottawa for printing. This was almost 20 percent of the provincial coverage, truly a remarkable contribution to the federal programme.

The province has always been noted in cartographic circles for its beautifully contoured maps, particularly the old Two-Mile Series (later published at 1:125 000 and 1:100 000)

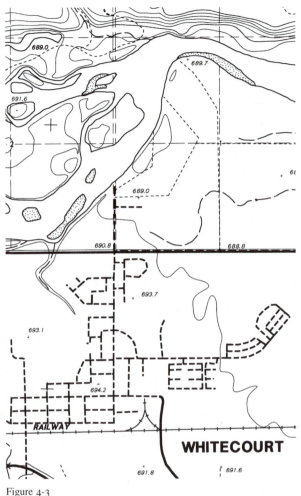

Figure 4-3
Section from an Alberta 1:20 000 Digital Base Mapping map.
Source: Alberta Environmental Protection Ministry

that have been used as standard medium-scale topographic maps and also as recreational maps for hikers and mountaineers.

A completely new look at British Columbia's mapping requirements was taken in 1986. This was the time when it was agreed across Canada that digital mapping was the way of the future. In British Columbia a new concept called the Provincial Baseline Digital Atlas was conceived in which three basic scales would serve the province's needs. The 1:20 000 coverage was organized under the Terrain Resources Information Management (TRIM) programme. Complete provincial coverage at this scale was achieved in 1997 in approximately 7000 sheets. The next smaller scale is at 1:250 000 and embraces 84 sheets, all of which are published. This is a digital version of the NTS Series at the same scale.

The smallest scale is a one-sheet digital map of the province at 1:2 000 000. As with the other provincial digital mapping, all data are coded. The first layer shows the planimetry which, in short, is that usually found on maps at this scale. A second layer consists of a grid of DEM values that can be used for contours or spot heights as required. The third layer can produce, if needed, sheet lines for either the provincial 1:20 000 or the NTS 1:50 000 Series. The fourth layer is a place-names layer in which are stored all the officially named features on the planimetry layer.

In 1988 the British Columbia government underwent a reorganization that saw the Surveys and Resource Mapping Branch relocated from the Ministry of the Environment to the newly created Ministry of Crown Lands. Since then this ministry has had its name changed to Lands and Parks, and most recently to Environment, Lands and Parks. At the beginning of these changes an inter-ministry study group produced the Corporate Land Information Strategic Plan (CLISP). This document has been used to steer the concept of the digital atlas, and has fostered the continuing development of LandData BC, a province-wide automated system that will allow users to share and exchange land information.

THE 1:20 000 SERIES

The 1:20 000 Series is drawn on the UTM projection. The sheet line system uses the NTS 1:250 000 quadrangle, which is divided into 100 smaller quads (10 by 10). If 1:10 000 mapping is required, the 1:20 000 quads are quartered and enlarged.

A very comprehensive transportation classification is provided for this series. Ten classes of roads are digitized. These include four- and six-lane divided highways; one-, two-, four-, and six-lane paved roads; one- and two-lane gravel roads; one-way streets; and truck roads. Railways are classified according to the number of tracks. Transmission lines and pipelines are shown.

Relief is shown by 20 m contours obtained from DEMs. Spot heights are used to show the highest points of hills and other points where elevations would be useful. Rivers and streams are shown by single lines unless the feature is over 1.5 mm wide at map scale, in which case both banks are shown. Lake shores and the sea coast are shown as solid lines, but an open-water fill is not used. Forest areas are enclosed by the usual scalloped line.

Line symbols are provided for administrative boundaries, township and section lines, outlines of mineral claims, and timber leases. Point symbols are available for a wide variety of features including schools, hospitals, and lighthouses. Figure 4-4 shows some of the conventional signs used in this series.

The Territories

Yukon is making very efficient use of digitized files purchased from CCG under the cost-sharing arrangement that is available to the provinces and territories. Forty-five quadrangles covering the Whitehorse area at 1:50 000, and complete coverage of the whole of Yukon at 1:250 000, were obtained in 1989. Additional layers are being added to these files from locally gathered geographic information. The files are in constant use for administration and resource development planning. Municipal mapping at 1:2000 or 1:5000 is available for most communities.

In the Northwest Territories the Department of Renewable Resources makes use of the digital 1:250 000 federal map files for resource-related studies using satellite imagery for GIS applications. The Department of Municipal and Community Affairs has embarked on a programme to develop 1:5000 and 1:2000 digital line maps of all communities. These

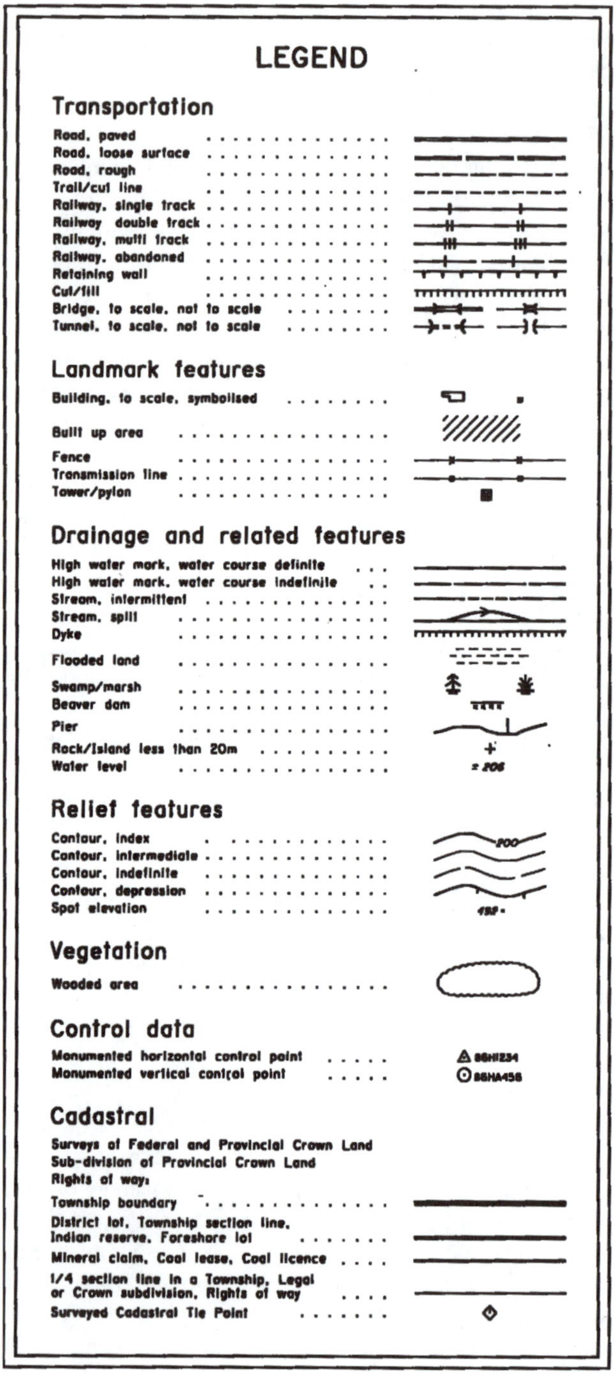

LEGEND

Transportation

Road, paved	....
Road, loose surface	....
Road, rough	....
Trail/cut line	....
Railway, single track	....
Railway, double track	....
Railway, multi track	....
Railway, abandoned	....
Retaining wall	....
Cut/fill	....
Bridge, to scale, not to scale	....
Tunnel, to scale, not to scale	....

Landmark features

Building, to scale, symbolised	....
Built up area	....
Fence	....
Transmission line	....
Tower/pylon	....

Drainage and related features

High water mark, water course definite	...
High water mark, water course indefinite	..
Stream, intermittent	....
Stream, spill	....
Dyke	....
Flooded land	....
Swamp/marsh	....
Beaver dam	....
Pier	....
Rock/Island less than 20m	....
Water level	....

Relief features

Contour, index	....
Contour, intermediate	....
Contour, indefinite	....
Contour, depression	....
Spot elevation	....

Vegetation

Wooded area	....

Control data

Monumented horizontal control point	.....
Monumented vertical control point	.....

Cadastral

Surveys of Federal and Provincial Crown Land
Sub-division of Provincial Crown Land
Rights of way:

Township boundary	....
District lot, Township section line, Indian reserve, Foreshore lot	....
Mineral claim, Coal lease, Coal licence	....
1/4 section line in a Township, Legal or Crown subdivision, Rights of way	....
Surveyed Cadastral Tie Point	....

Figure 4-4
British Columbia Legend of Conventional Signs.
Source: CIG *Geomatica*

maps include topographic and cadastral information, and are available in digital and hard-copy form.

SOME GENERAL THOUGHTS
ON PROVINCIAL TOPOGRAPHIC MAPPING

All provinces are now using digital topographic mapping. There are two scale ranges in general use for this work: 1:10 000 and 1:20 000 for overall provincial coverage, and 1:1000, 1:2000, and 1:2500 for municipal and engineering mapping. An intermediate scale, 1:5000, is being used by some provinces for areas with mostly large parcels such as farms, orchards, timber leases, and mining claims. Table 4-1 shows the principal specifications used by the provinces for their mapping, including their choice of scales.

All provinces are now using the Global Positioning System (GPS) for ground control for photogrammetric mapping at the 1:10 000 and 1:20 000 scales. It is also being used for municipal mapping in the rare cases where additional control is needed.

In all provinces except Manitoba the digitization is now being done by private companies on contract. (The LRIS at Summerside was active in this type of work, but it was closed on 31 March 1994.) The drawing of contours photogrammetrically is rapidly giving way to the compilation of DEMs from which contours at any desired vertical interval can be derived automatically. Modern photogrammetric plotters can record DEMs automatically, but older equipment requires manual intervention.

None of the provinces, with the exception of Newfoundland, conduct field completion surveys with the rigour of the federal mapping agencies. The provinces rely on users, especially land surveyors, to report deficiencies.

Several provinces started with photomap series, some of them with contours, but all have augmented such coverage with digital line mapping. Photomaps have many advantages in identifying parcel boundaries and types of land use, but they are harder to keep up to date and they do not lend themselves to digitization. Both types of mapping have contributed to the modernization of land registration, but digital line mapping is definitely the product of the future.

In many provincial map sales offices monochrome maps are run off on demand from chronaflex originals kept on file. This practice is giving way to map production by colour electrostatic printers. As digital mapping is layered by feature type, such as contours and drainage, the client can be given a choice of a monochrome map or a map with colours. This system is even more important in sales offices where thematic maps are sold, because of the ease with which certain themes can be plotted on the topographic base. An additional advantage is that the compact discs are much easier to store than the chronaflex originals.

Cadastral data are not included in the specifications of the NTDB. As this information is of vital importance to the provinces, and is important to many GIS operations, methods of merging this data with the NTDB have been developed by most provinces.

Unfortunately the expected easy and economic exchange of data between provincial and federal digital databases has not yet materialized. At the present time all provinces are concentrating on improving their provincial digital coverage. Soon the provinces will be able to put more of their resources into revision, and closer cooperation with the NTDB will no doubt be possible. It would seem easier to set up exchanges of new road files, for

Table 4-1
Outline Specifications for Provincial Mapping

Province or Territory	Projection	Datum	Resource Scales and Contours	Urban Scales and Contours	Language	Road Classes	Sheet Lines	Forest Area Symbol	Open Water Fill	Status of Digital Resource Mapping	Year NTS 1:50 000 Completed
Newfoundland	3° TM	ATS77	NTS: 1:50 000 enlarged 10 m	1:2500 / 1:5000 1 and 2 m	English	4	NTS graticule	No	No	NA	1985
Nova Scotia	3° TM	ATS77	1:10 000 10 m	1:1000 / 1:2000 1 and 2 m	Bilingual	5	NTS graticule	No	No	100% completed	1959
New Brunswick	Stereographic	ATS77	1:10 000 uncontoured	1:1000 / 1:2000 1 and 2 m	Bilingual	5	NTS graticule	No	No	100% completed	1959
Prince Edward Island	Stereographic	ATS77	1:10 000 uncontoured	1:1000 / 1:2000 1 and 2 m	Bilingual	5	NTS graticule	No	No	100% completed	1948
Québec	3° TM	NAD83 NAD27	1:20 000 10 m	1:1000 spot heights	French	8	NTS and SQRC	Yes	Yes	80% completed to 51° N. Lat	1985
Ontario	UTM	NAD28 NAD83	1:20 000 1:10 000 5 and 10 m	1:2000 1 and 2 m	Bilingual	2	UTM grid	No	No	100% completed to 51° N. Lat	1990
Manitoba	UTM	NAD83	1:20 000 5 m	1:1000 / 1:2000 1 and 2 m	Bilingual	7	NTS graticule	Yes	Yes	20% completed	1988
Saskatchewan	UTM	NAD83	NTS: 1:50 000 enlarged	1:1000 / 1:2000 1 and 2 m	Bilingual	6	UTM grid	Yes	Yes	NA	1988
Alberta	3° TM	NAD83	1:20 000 10 m	1:1500 / 1:1000 1 and 2 m	Bilingual	7	NTS graticule	Yes	No	100% completed	1986
British Columbia	UTM	NAD83	1:20 000 20 m	1:1000 / 1:2000 2 m	Bilingual	6	UTM grid	No	No	100% completed	1988
Yukon	UTM	NAD83	NTS: 1:50 000 enlarged	1:2000 2 m / 1:5000 5 m	Bilingual	6	NTS graticule	Yes	Yes	NA	1988
Northwest Territories	UTM	NAD83	NTS: 1:50 000 enlarged	1:2000 / 1:5000 5 m	Bilingual	6	NTS graticule	Yes	Yes	NA	Not complete

example, than to exchange complete topographic data sets that have been captured according to different specifications.

The impetus for the recent advances in provincial mapping has been the coming into play of the computer, satellite geodesy, and GIS operations. At every step of the way the cost-benefit ratio of the various inventions has been kept in mind. Already many of the provinces use the new digital maps as bases for a wide variety of thematic maps. For example in Nova Scotia thematic maps are being produced in the ministries of Natural Resources, Transport, Agriculture, Municipal Affairs, Environment, Attorney General, Fisheries, Housing, Tourism, Economic Development, and Supply and Services. This development is of course not unique to Nova Scotia; it is taking place in every province in Canada.

NOTES

1 Information for this chapter was assembled during personal visits to the mapping establishments in each province, and by studying sample sheets and map indexes of their production. Additional data were obtained by correspondence with the following:

Newfoundland: Neil MacNaughton, Surveys and Mapping Division, Department of Environment and Lands, St John's

Nova Scotia: Murray Banks, Surveys Division, Department of Natural Resources, Halifax; Robert Doirn, Nova Scotia Geomatics Centre, Amherst

New Brunswick: Mary Ogilvie, New Brunswick Geographic Information Corporation, Fredericton

Prince Edward Island: James Ramsay, Taxation and Property Records, Charlottetown

Québec: Claude de Saint Riquier, Département des Relevés Techniques, Ministère de l'Énergie et des Ressources Naturelles, Charlesbourg

Ontario: Barry Costello, Provincial Mapping Office, Ministry of Natural Resources, Peterborough

Manitoba: Hartley Pokrant, Surveys and Mapping Branch, Department of Natural Resources, Winnipeg

Saskatchewan: David Arthur, Central Surveys and Mapping Agency, Saskatchewan Property Management Corporation, Regina

Alberta: M.R. Weiss, Surveying and Mapping Division, Department of Environmental Protection, Edmonton

British Columbia: Elaine Ellison, Surveys and Resource Mapping Branch, Ministry of Environment, Lands and Parks, Victoria

Yukon: Lyle Henderson, Lands Branch, Community and Transport Services, Whitehorse

Northwest Territories: Wayne Barraclough, Department of Municipal Affairs, Yellowknife

2 Doig, James, and Barbara Patton. 1994. *The LRIS Story: A Legacy for the Maritimes*. Halifax: The Coucnil of Maritime Premiers, secs. 1.5 and 1.20.

3 *Ibid.*, plus 75 percent of $27,872,000 in sect. 4.09.

4 For an outline of provincial mapping specifications, see table 4-1.

CHAPTER FIVE

Military Surveys

Louis M. Sebert

PART I   WORK ON THE NATIONAL TOPOGRAPHIC SYSTEM

The Early Years

Military mapping in Canada dates from the mid-nineteenth century when units of the Royal Engineers stationed in Canada produced a series of large-scale topographic maps covering the immediate vicinity of the forts along the St Lawrence River. These were fine maps, and today the copies held in the National Archives are of considerable interest to historians. When the British garrisons were withdrawn in 1868 the work lapsed, but it was revived again in 1903 when the Department of Militia set up a small mapping unit called the Mapping Branch of the Intelligence Department.

Topographic work by this fledgling unit was started in 1904 in the Niagara peninsula. For the first few years the sheets mapped were along the U.S.-Canada border. The mapping consisted of one-inch-to-one-mile plane table compilations based on control provided by traverses and spirit level lines run along the roads of the area.

In 1909 the Mapping Branch became the Survey Division of the Department of Militia and Defence, and in 1924 its name was changed once again to the Geographical Section of the General Staff (GSGS). Throughout these years the unit continued to turn out five or six one-inch sheets per year, as well as maps of military camps and training areas. In the 1920s the establishment consisted of two officers, four sergeants-major, four quartermaster sergeants, four sergeants, and twenty-three civilians.[1] By 1939 a total of 147 sheets had been published (Manitoba 2, New Brunswick 2, Nova Scotia 11, Ontario 85, and Québec 47).[2] This may seem a substantial body of work, but it is really insignificant considering the almost 13 000 sheets needed to cover the whole of Canada.

When the Second World War broke out Canadian mapping agencies, both military and civilian, were using the mapping methods of the nineteenth century. It is true that in the 1930s vertical air photographs were being used, but only by plane-tablers who used them to help in sketching the topography. Oblique air photographs were being used to produce medium-scale planimetric maps, but the system was really an airborne version of Edouard Deville's photo-topographic method of the 1880s. Certainly Canadian topographers knew of the European development of advanced photogrammetric plotters, but they were considered too expensive and not particularly applicable to the broad expanses of the Canadian terrain.

The exception to this rather backward view was Lt Col (later Ltd Gen.) E.L.M. Burns. In 1936 Burns was commanding the GSGS, and in that year he acquired a Zeiss Multiplex Aeroprojector. This was Canada's only photogrammetric plotter until after the war.

At the outbreak of the war the First Corps Field Survey Company, a militia unit stationed in Ottawa, was mobilized. It proceeded overseas in December 1939. Later it was joined by two additional companies and a field survey depot. As the activities of these units has been described in volume 3 of *Men and Meridians*, it is sufficient to say here that while overseas the men of these units became fully trained in modern British and American mapping methods. When they returned to Canada many wanted to continue in this line of work. In fact they formed a cadre of trained personnel that filled both the postwar military mapping unit and a number of civilian mapping firms. At this point Canada was ready to take on the huge task of mapping the remaining 12 700 sheets of the basic One-Inch Series, regardless of the difficulties caused by ruggedness of terrain or remoteness of region.

The Postwar Reorganization

The first significant postwar event in the military survey service was the change of the GSGS to the Army Survey Establishment (ASE). This took place on 1 October 1946, and was much more than a simple change of name. The new unit, commanded by Maj. C.H. Smith, had an enlarged strength of five officers, ninety-three other ranks, and thirteen civilians. This was almost a threefold increase over the pre-war GSGS. To a large extent this new establishment was inspired by the officers of the survey service overseas. They knew that Canada was woefully lacking in topographic mapping, and that this lack would seriously impede national development. They also knew from personal experience that wartime developments in air photography and photogrammetry could provide the means by which Canada could correct this national deficiency.

Canada's postwar defence planning strongly emphasized the defence of North America. The defence strategy was, of course, closely coordinated with the plans of the U.S. armed services. At the highest level this coordination was undertaken by the Canada-U.S. Permanent Joint Board on Defence, which produced the Basic Security Plan for North America. The Sub-Committee on Mapping and Charting was required to determine the mapping needs for defence, and to devise a workable plan to meet these needs. This sub-committee had a Canadian and an American section each with members of the army, navy and air force, and civilian representatives from the geodetic topographic and hydrographic agencies of both countries. One of the first actions of the sub-committee was to write the first edition (1947) of the Mapping, Charting and Air Photography Plan (MCAPP). This document reported on the current mapping and charting situation, showed by index maps the maps and charts needed, and set out realistic requests for their production by the country concerned. (The annual reports of the MCAPP, with its coloured index maps, give a graphic picture of the gradual mapping and charting of North America.) In 1976 the MCAPP became simply the Mapping and Charting Plan (MCP) as was mentioned in chapter 3.

Both countries used the MCAPP to write their Defence Mapping Plan. In Canada the plan was used by the minister of National Defence to obtain funding for mapping and charting purposes. For example it was in this way that in 1947 Canada's cabinet approved Canada's first long-range mapping programme, namely to map the entire country at the scale of four miles to the inch within twenty years. The programme was completed, with all maps in print, in 1971. The slippage was caused mainly by the mapping needed for the Mid-Canada Line, which will be discussed later.

Because of the importance of maps to the defence of Canada, the ASE (and its successor the Mapping and Charting Establishment) – MCE has always been equipped with a well-trained staff, the most modern equipment, and sufficient funds for contracts when urgent demands required outside help to augment in-house production. In fact the ability of the military to obtain the most efficient surveying and mapping equipment has been a source of considerable envy in the government's civilian mapping agencies.

Mapping Operations for NTS Maps

The production of a topographic map involves four phases. Phase 1 is the acquisition of the air photography or the satellite imagery of the area to be mapped. Phase 2 is the surveying of the field control. This consists of finding the latitude, longitude, and elevation of a number of points on the ground that can be identified on air photographs. These act as "peg points" to ensure that the maps to be plotted will be correct in position, orientation, and scale. Phase 3 is the plotting of the map from the air photographs. Finally Phase 4 is the reproduction of the map by lithographic printing, electrostatic printing, or any other means. All four phases are described in detail in chapters 2 and 3.

In all phases of mapping the advancement in equipment and techniques since the Second World War has been phenomenal. Indeed it is not an exaggeration to say that none of the mapping methods in use in 1993 was even thought of in 1945. It is against this background of rapid and continual change that the rest of this chapter must be read.

PHASE 1   AIR PHOTOGRAPHY

From its inception the MCAPP had a requirement for the complete coverage of Canada with vertical air photography of "cartographic quality." As it was known by the planners that this would take time, planning maps were drafted for the proceedings of the annual meetings showing the priorities to be given to various areas. To some this seemed like a never-ending commitment. No sooner had the planners' demands been satisfied than better cameras came on the market with greatly improved optics that offered much better image definition and an improved photogrammetric geometry.

Many of these advantages were economic. By using smaller-scale photography the plotting time could be reduced considerably, but this was acceptable only if the accuracy and completeness of the mapping was not diminished. Better cameras with much-improved super-wide-angle lenses made this possible at the same time as jet aircraft made higher flying altitudes and steadier flight lines available. Many areas on the planning maps, previously flown with older cameras and at lower altitudes, were put back on the priority list.

Satellite imagery has been used for locating areas where revision was needed ever since its appearance in the early 1970s. In certain cases, such as providing the necessary detail for plotting a new road through forested areas, it was able to provide sufficient positional data to plot the road. But it was not until SPOT imagery (see chapter 3) became available in 1985 that contoured maps at scales as large as 1:50 000 could be drawn from satellite imagery. This was a significant breakthrough of international importance because from that date detailed maps could be drawn anywhere in the world without violating national air space. The very steady and predictable orbits of the satellites means that ground control points obtained by satellite geodesy are very reliable. Fewer control points are needed than was the case with traditional surveys.

PHASE 2 FIELDWORK

The Packhorse Era   Fieldwork is the most physically demanding phase of mapping. It is also the phase that has seen the most dramatic changes since the Second World War. The first meeting of the MCAPP targeted the Yukon as an area of top mapping priority. Consequently ASE's first summer field season in 1947 saw two survey parties deployed in that region, one under Capt. Walter Johnston and the other under Sgt-Maj. Lou McAdam. Fortunately the ASE had two members with pre-war experience with horse parties. These were Major Smith and Henry West, a civilian engineer on the staff of ASE. Both were able to spend some time with Johnston and McAdam to show them the ropes. This was indeed a new experience for all concerned, and as it is an interesting part of the history of military surveying in Canada, a short description of the system is in order.

In 1947, and for many years before that, a typical survey party consisted of the chief-of-party, one or two survey assistants, a cook, and a packer who looked after the horses. There were from ten to twelve horses provided for transport – five riding horses and the rest packhorses. The supplier of the horses was responsible for providing the harness, pack and riding saddles, and the variety of ropes, canvasses, pack boxes, and the gear and rigging of a pack train. The Canadian army provided the survey equipment, tents, kitchen utensils, and provisions.

Packhorse transport has a long tradition in North America. The method of loading a packhorse is as stylized and as complicated to the uninitiated as a square dance. The diamond hitch that pulls all the load on the horse together into a solid structure must date back to the old west before the American Civil War. It was obvious from the beginning that the loading of the pack train could not be left to the packer. Packing a horse is a two-man job, one man on each side of the horse, and unless two teams work together it takes at least an hour to get the survey party on the trail. Generally speaking, after about two weeks of experience a good party could break camp and get the packing done in about thirty minutes.

There is something quite satisfying in watching a good party pack up. It is poetry in motion; the ropes fly over and under the horse, the boxes are hoisted, the loads are balanced, the top hamper is put up on top, and the diamond hitch is thrown. The last move is a strong pull on the loose end of the diamond, and the whole load comes together at the same time as a loud grunt from the horse indicates that he (or she) thinks the load is tight enough.

On the trail the chief-of-party leads the parade. In 1947 the only aid to pathfinding was an eight-Mile aeronautical chart that had been drawn from Trimetrogon photos as described in chapter 3. Needless to say there were few hints for the land traveller on these charts. The survey pack train would normally cover from ten to fifteen miles in a day's march if

Figure 5-1
Survey pack train fording a small river.
Photo: National Archives of Canada

there was a trail to follow. In proceeding "cross country," where from time to time trees had to be cut to get the packhorses through, the progress was considerably slower. The slowest going of all was through burn areas where some forgotten forest fire had charred the trees and left them to fall into a criss-crossed maze that had to be cut through all the way. A burned pine or spruce is as hard as stone, and even a well-sharpened axe bounces off such wood. When this terrain was met all hands bent to the Swede saw, but it was slow, tedious work. Figure 5-1 shows a pack train fording a small river.

The survey work in the mountains was third- and fourth-order triangulation. For the more accurate work two parties would work as a team. One would go ahead and build cairns (columns of rock) on peaks of designated mountains. The second party would follow, read the angles formed by the cairns, and take a 360° panorama of photos using a special glass-plate survey camera. The allowable error in the triangulation was ten seconds, and, as can be imagined, it was a tense moment each time the three angles of a triangle were added up. If the sum did not come within 10 seconds of 180° it meant a long ride back to one or both of the first two angles.

In the fourth-order triangulation one party operated alone. This meant that it was necessary to "shoot ahead" to the exact spot on the forward mountain where the cairn would be built when the surveyors got there. This required a close examination of the peak through the telescope, and in some cases the drawing of a sketch of the distant peak illustrating the proposed station position in relation to rock outcrops, patches of snow, and the like. In such work the triangulation closure was one minute of arc, but on occasion this limit was exceeded.

The map compilation used in the office during the following winter was to a large extent developed by Deville in the 1880s. The major difference was that in 1947 vertical air photography was available to be used in the map compilation. In Deville's day the surveyor would have to map the linear features of the terrain (such as roads, rivers, and railways) by plane table, but in 1947 the fieldwork was used only to support photogrammetric compilation. The triangulation stations provided the horizontal control for a slotted template block adjustment (as described in chapter 3) while the horizontal photos taken with the survey camera supplied elevations of mountain tops and other identifiable points that were needed for the contouring.[3]

In recent years the region has been mapped at much larger scales, and an assessment has been made of the accuracy of the work done in the horse-party days. A comparison of positions and elevations on the new mapping with that on the old shows that the rather primitive methods used in the decade following the Second World War were surprisingly accurate.[4]

The Helicopter Era   In the 1950s there were two major innovations in field surveying techniques that completely changed the face of topographic surveying. These were the use of the helicopter for transport, and the introduction of electronic systems for measuring distance. The first military use of helicopters for surveying in Canada was in 1949 in the Fort Smith area. As Smith, commanding officer of the ASE, wanted to test for himself the efficiency of this new form of transportation, he and Milne Floyd from the Topographical Survey shared the work on this first airborne survey party. The report of that summer's work stated that the production of a survey party could at least be doubled if there was helicopter support. Further experience over the years has shown that this was a very conservative estimate. The other innovation was the introduction of Electromagnetic Distance Measurement instruments (EDMs). Since the development of these instruments is covered in chapter 2, only their use by ASE will be covered here.

In the 1950s the difficulty of mapping the flatter areas of the Canadian north were of considerable concern to the military planners in Ottawa. The Korean War had broken out and the Cold War had intensified. Yet the field survey methods seemed bound to the nineteenth century. Certainly the Shoran net was in place, but the Shoran stations were some 150 miles apart and at that spacing were of no use for mapping. In an attempt to find some practical method for spreading mapping control into the sub-arctic, the ASE even tried an ingenious system called flare triangulation. In this method parachute flares were dropped from an aeroplane. At a given signal from the aircraft the position of a flare was determined by three observers taking bearings on it from three known locations. Other survey stations, off in the wilderness where horizontal positions were needed, would at the same instant take bearings to the flare. All six theodolites were equipped with small cameras that recorded the horizontal circle reading on a signal from the aircraft. The positions of the wilderness stations would eventually be determined by resection using the bearings to a number of flares. The ASE test that was carried out in 1953 started out at Pilot Mound, Manitoba, on the Canada-U.S. border, and carried the survey north to Pine River, a distance of about 200 miles. Flare triangulation is a system yielding accuracies (in the ASE test) in the range of ±3 m, but it is slow, expensive, and heavily dependent on good weather. In any event the Pine River survey was carried out during the same summer that the Geodimeter, Canada's first EDM instrument, was shown to senior Canadian mapping officials. This new survey instrument was quickly seen as the answer to Canada's field survey problems, and flare triangulation was forgotten.[5]

The Geodimeter, which measured distance by timing the passage of a pulse of light over the distance being measured, was quickly followed by the Tellurometer, which made its measurement by timing the propagation of radio waves over the distance. In 1957 the ASE acquired both a Geodimeter and a Tellurometer for testing. The Tellurometer was judged the better instrument for ASE work. Later in 1957 two sets were purchased, each with a master and a remote. This was just the beginning: over the next twenty years more than sixty instruments were purchased, though many of these were replacements for out-of-date models. At any one time the ASE had about ten pairs of Tellurometers in service.

The use of helicopters and EDMs completely changed field routines. With experience ASE personnel became experts at exploiting the inherent strengths of these new facilities. To illustrate this the following extracts are taken from the report written by Capt. D.M. Matheson on the 1959 field season of his party working on Victoria Island, Northwest Territories.

Because of the extreme isolation of the area and the extreme changes of weather that might be encountered, it was decided that no person would be left on the ground without a survival kit sufficient to last him several days. This kit was kept as a standard pack and was dropped off every time a person was left at a station. The total weight of surveyors, survey equipment, survival packs and magnesium tripod signals exceeded a thousand pounds. The extreme range of operation, the heavy load commitment and the need for special navigation aids led to the choice of two s-55 helicopters for the survey aircraft. [The s-58 was chosen as the support helicopter.] A conventional aircraft of good load-carrying capacity, range and performance was required to keep pace with the high fuel consumption of the survey helicopters, to move camp frequently and to maintain a supply link with Cambridge Bay. An Otter was selected for this role.

The final size of the party came to fifteen men and included the six surveyors, three helicopter pilots, two helicopter engineers, one Otter pilot, one Otter engineer and two cooks. The food requirement came to about five tons and the fuel to 95 tons. The advance party began the job of moving the entire fuel requirement [from Cambridge Bay] into the second camp [Camp B] 300 miles to the north.

Because of the range and the weather, fly camps had to be used. The first two such camps had shown that the mobility of a helicopter-borne Tellurometer traverse rapidly out-distanced fixed camps. When the logistic plan was prepared fly camps had not been anticipated, so no fuel was allotted for this purpose. To overcome these disadvantages a task system was adopted. At the start, two days on the line or a maximum of ten flying hours including the ferry, was considered a task. The ten hours was an aircraft maintenance restriction and was strictly adhered to. The s-55 was used for shelter and sleeping, but the meals were prepared in the open. While on a task the survey team operated whenever the weather was suitable with no regard to time of day. Periods of activity between storms or fog varied greatly from one hour to twenty hours. Periods of inactivity lasted as long as three days. Using this task system the two survey teams traversed 475 miles in eight days to complete the survey planned for Camp B.

In the days of transit and tape traverses along country roads in southern Canada, progress of five miles a day was considered very good going. Matheson's surveyors, with the support of EDMs and helicopters, were averaging sixty miles a day. Obviously surveying had entered a new era. Certainly the open Arctic tundra provided ideal survey terrain, but even in forested country the ASE surveyors were able to maintain very good progress by using helicopter-portable survey towers. But the future would see even more exotic survey systems come into practice.

Risks and Hazards   Survey work in wilderness terrain has always carried with it certain dangers. Even in Samuel Holland's day during the first surveys of the townships of southern Ontario and Québec, the surveyors' journals of the day are replete with accounts of axe injuries and other misfortunes. In the horse-party days of ASE operations in the north-west, the survey parties often operated long distances from the nearest settlements. The possibility of accidents or illnesses was always in the mind of the chief-of-party. It is true that a good first-aid kit was in the baggage of each party, and that very sensible book *The Ship Captain's Medical Guide*[6] was supplied as rather sombre reading material. Serious accidents did occur and they always tested the endurance of both the injured and the rescuers. For example in 1948 a young assistant surveyor who was unused to riding was thrown from his mount and broke his arm. In 1952 Sgt-Maj. Tom Poeltzer was killed in a mountaineering accident.

The arrival of helicopters certainly removed the feeling of isolation but, especially in the early days, they increased the number of accidents. The light helicopters of the 1950s were unstable when attempting landings above about 4000 feet, and in fact the RCAF would not permit their pilots to attempt a landing above 3000 feet. But despite precautions accidents did occur. In 1951 a helicopter chartered from Kenting Aviation crashed while attempting a landing to pick up S.Sgt Bob Denis and Cpl Norman Jeeves. The pilot, Stanley Fraser, was killed. In 1952 Capt. Percy Davis was landing to drop off Capt. Les O'Brien and Sapper Richard Doyle at a mountain station when the wind changed, causing the helicopter to descend rapidly, hit the ground, and roll over. Doyle was injured and had to be evacuated. In 1953 an army helicopter piloted by Capt.Rene Jalbert of the Royal Twenty-second Regiment rolled over on take-off from a mountain in the Nahanni River area. The machine was badly damaged, but neither Jalbert nor the surveyor on board, Sgt Bob Tuttle, was injured. (Captain Jalbert was later to gain fame when, acting as Sergeant-at-Arms to the Québec National Assembly, he successfully disarmed a machine-gun-wielding deranged soldier. For this action he was subsequently awarded the Cross of Valour of the Order of Canada.)

The unfortunate helicopter accidents diminished in frequency as the capabilities of the aircraft improved, but they never ended entirely. In 1970 Sapper W. Scherle was killed on a mountain in British Columbia when the jet helicopter from which he had just alighted rolled over on him. The mountain was subsequently given his name by the Canadian Permanent Committee on Geographical Names. In total there were thirteen serious helicopter and fixed-wing aircraft accidents involving ASE personnel between 1950 and 1970.

Perhaps it might be well to close this section with a wry description of a medical evacuation that had unfortunate consequences for the chief-of-party. In 1949 Sgt-Maj. Jim Barber was operating with his party in the wild country between the Alaska Highway and the Pacific coast. He was several hundred miles from the highway when his packer developed a badly ulcerated tooth. The poor fellow was in agony so Barber saddled two horses. They rode night and day to the Alaska Highway. There they stabled their horses at a telephone repeater station and hitchhiked into Whitehorse where the tooth was removed. Back to the survey they rode, and the work was resumed. Barber of course recorded the incident in his journal where, unfortunately, it was observed by the departmental accountant. Barber had seven days' pay deducted because he had not subtracted this amount from the packer's pay while the packer was off duty. (Whenever a surveyor prepared his field accounts he always had the feeling that the accountant was looking over his shoulder. It is probably true to this day.)

The Beauty of Electronic Surveying   In the 1950s the U.S. navy was faced with a problem. It had to devise a navigation system for its nuclear submarines, which, in their operational role, spent many days at a time submerged below periscope depth. Obviously the standard form of marine navigation could not be employed. Two answers to this problem were produced, and both quickly found their way into civilian survey practice. These were the Inertial Survey System (ISS) and the Doppler Satellite Positioning System. Since both of these systems have been described in chapter 2, it is sufficient to say here that they were adopted with enthusiasm by the MCE field personnel.

PHASE 3   MAP COMPILATION
In the days before the Second World War the GSGS relied almost entirely on mapping by plane table surveys. Such surveys are practicable only in open country such as existed in southern Ontario and Québec where there was a convenient network of roads along which the control surveys could be run. But the postwar military planners saw the major threat to North America coming from the north-west. It was obvious even to the most inexperienced strategist that the mapping of the Canadian Arctic and subarctic could never be done by antiquated mapping methods. Fortunately there was a cadre of Canadians who had been trained in England during the war in the use of modern mapping equipment. It was with these thoughts in mind that the establishment and role of the ASE were planned. The first purchases of equipment for the new ASE were in accordance with this planning.

For the first several years the Multiplex Aeroprojector was the plotting instrument of choice. It had been the workhorse in the compilation of maps for the assault on continental Europe, and it was the instrument with which the men of the Canadian field survey companies were most familiar. In 1946 five Multiplex were purchased and put into operation in the ASE quarters in the Militia Stores Building in Ottawa. These were followed by twelve more in 1948. Additional instruments were purchased in 1950 and 1953 bringing the total to twenty-three.

As has been explained in chapter 3 the basic principle of photogrammetric mapping is to set up an optical model of a portion of the earth's surface and to draw the map from this model. The role of the field surveyor in a photogrammetric mapping organization has always been to provide the necessary points on the ground of known position (latitude and longitude) and elevation needed by the photogrammetrist to level and scale the model. As field surveying can be both difficult and expensive, the most important advances in photogrammetry have been to reduce the amount of field surveying required without reducing the accuracy of the mapping.

Table 3-2 in chapter 3 lists the more important photogrammetric instruments acquired by ASE/MCE over the years. These give an indication of the unit's progress through the various photogrammetric developments described in chapter 3. Figure 5-2 shows Sergeant-

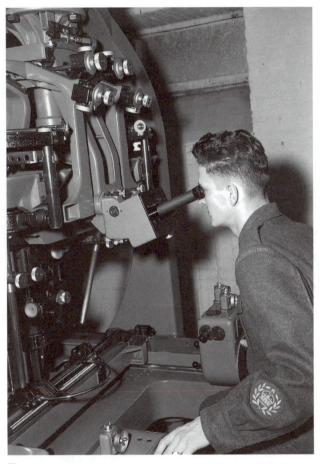

Figure 5-2
A Wild A5 Autograph, the army's first precision plotter.
Photo: MCE

Major Clarkson using a Wild A5, Canada's first precision photogrammetric plotter. Figure 5-3 shows two members of ASE working on a slotted template laydown (as described in chapter 3).

PHASE 4   MAP DRAFTING AND PRINTING

In 1946 the ASE inherited the drafting and printing sections of GSGS. The staff of these sections included well-trained but elderly tradesmen, many of whom had learned their skills in the 1920s. This group was augmented by personnel returning from the field survey companies who wanted to continue their military service in Canada's peacetime army. Naturally the younger people were used to a much faster pace of operations, but the two groups quickly fitted together into an efficient operation. One of the "old timers," George Davidson, used to offer a comparison. He pointed out that in the days of hand lettering the writing of 25 to 30 place-names a day was considered very good going, but the "young

Figure 5-3
An ASE slotted template laydown (see chapter 3 for description).
Photo: MCE

fellows" think nothing of sticking down 200 names. Davidson recalled that on several occasions in the days of GSGS when a place-name or symbol was found to be wrong while the map was being printed, he was called down to the press room to correct the mistake on the printing plate while it was still on the press. "I don't think the new fellows could do that," he said.

In the print shop the pre-war presses were augmented by the purchase of war-surplus AFT Chief presses. This turned out to be false economy because in 1950, when the newly metricated 1:50 000 sheets were ready for printing, it was found that they were too broad for these presses. This was the reason for the 1:50 000 half-sheets. Each quadrangle was printed as an east and west half although both halves carried the same sheet name. This caused much confusion when a client ordered a sheet but did not specify which half was wanted. Other confusions were to follow. In 1957 the whole structure of the NTS sheet-line system was altered to make more 1:50 000 quadrangles narrow enough for printing as a single sheet, but in 1960 this unfortunate move was revoked. By that time larger presses were available and all the original NTS quadrangles could be printed as single sheets. Over the years many of the half-sheets have been joined, but in 1993 there are still well over 1000 half-sheets waiting to be reunited.

In 1952 the Surveys and Mapping Branch introduced negative scribing, a technique in which the image of a map manuscript is photographically printed on a transparent plastic sheet that had previously been coated with an orange emulsion. Using sharp tools the lines and symbols of the image are cut away leaving an artificial negative. This action is done

Figure 5-4
An AFT Chief Press being used at ASE.
Photo: MCE

for each colour of the map thus producing the negatives needed for making the printing plates.[7] ASE took a somewhat different approach. In the ASE method the plastic was coated with white emulsion rather than orange. Again the lines and symbols were scribed by cutting away the emulsion, but here a positive image was formed by putting a sheet of black paper behind the plastic to give a sharp image of the line work in black. This could then be photographed to produce the negative required for making the plate. Both ASE and GSGS had always drafted their maps at one-quarter larger than publication scale. This made the drafting easier and produced a sharp image when the drafting was photographically reduced to scale. It also permitted place-names and mechanically prepared area symbols, such as the bulrush marsh symbol, to be stuck down on the scribed sheet. Despite these advantages ASE joined the rest of the cartographic world by changing to negative scribing in 1960.

Over the years more efficient printing presses were developed by the printing industry, and from time to time ASE/MCE would upgrade its printing plant. Figure 5-4 shows an ATF Chief printing press, the type used by ASE immediately after the war.

Military Survey Staff Organization

When the ASE was established in 1946 the commanding officer (CO), Maj. C.H. Smith, was also the deputy director of Military Survey on the staff of the chief engineer. This joint title was important because it showed that the CO of the ASE was responsible for formulating the programmes for his units, and was also closely in touch with military planning at army headquarters. Before the war the CO of the GSGS was a lieutenant colonel, and in 1947 Major Smith was promoted to that rank.

By 1952 the responsibilities of the military mapping programme had increased to such an extent that it was thought advisable to separate the general staff functions from that of CO of the ASE. Therefore in December of that year the position of Director of Military Survey was established with the rank of colonel. Lieutenant-Colonel Smith was promoted and Lt Col James Lang was posted to the ASE as CO.

In 1964 the initial steps were taken to integrate the Canadian army, navy, and air force into a single entity. The ASE received new tasks to fill requirements for aeronautical and hydrographic charts, and its establishment was increased by a major and a captain for air operations and a lieutenant commander for naval operations. In addition four civilian positions were opened to handle the additional staff work.

On 13 October 1966 the Canadian Forces Operation Order 1:33 came into effect re-designating the ASE as the Canadian Forces Mapping and Charting Establishment (MCE). The title of Director of Military Survey was changed to Director of Operational Services and Survey (DOSS) to reflect better the additional responsibilities of the position. A year later the title was again changed, to Director General of Environmental and Operational Service (DGEOS). (The word "environmental" in this context refers to the terms land, sea, and air environments that replaced the terms army, navy, and air in the Unified Services.) Once again, in 1969, the name of the directorate was changed, this time to the Directorate of Cartographic Operations (D Carto). This name lasted a record of twenty-one years before it was changed in 1990 to Director of Geographic Operations (D Geo Ops). Fortunately during all the above name changing the ASE underwent only one change, to the MCE. Table 5-1 lists the names and tenure of the directors, commanding officers, and sergeants-major of the directorates and units mentioned above.

PART 2   SPECIAL MILITARY MAPPING
DURING THE NTS ERA

Military Training Areas

Although the main function of GSGS before the war was the production of maps of the National Topographic System (NTS), an important subsidiary role was the mapping of military bases and training camps. The ASE inherited this responsibility and its first task of this nature came in the winter of 1946–47 when it deployed a survey party in the Fort Churchill area. The following summer saw survey parties working at Suffield, Alberta, and Rivers, Manitoba. This type of work became a continuing commitment, and almost every summer an ASE field party visited one or more of Canada's many training camps to update existing maps or survey new areas.

In the early postwar days the mapping policy of both the Canadian and British armies considered the 1:25 000 scale best for major military operations. Consequently this scale was prescribed for Canada's training-area maps.

In 1953 there was a major change in military training procedures in Canada. This change involved the use of training areas large enough for a realistic deployment of a complete infantry brigade, including artillery and tank support. The first such area purchased by

Table 5-1
Title

Directors 1946–1993		
Col C.H. Smith	D Mil Svy	1946–62
Col M.C. Sutherland-Brown	D Mil Svy/DOSS	1962–66
Col D.F. Aitkins	DGEOS	1966–69
Col L.J. O'Brien	D Carto	1969–74
Col J.F. Preston	D Carto	1974–79
Col E.V. Schaubel	D Carto	1979–81
Col R. Grainger	D Carto	1981–86
Col D.T. Carney	D Carto/D Geo Ops	1986–91
Lt Col G. Simpson	D Geo Ops (Acting)	1991–91
Col F.W. Noseworthy	D Geo Ops	1991–94
Col E.S. Fitch	D Geo Ops	1995–96
Commanding Officers ASE/MCE		
Lt Col C.H. Smith	OC ASE/DD Mil Svy/CO ASE	1946–52
Lt Col J. Lang		1952–53
Lt Col J.I. Thompson		1953–59
Lt Col E.A Ballantyne		1959–62
Lt Col D.F. Aitkins		1962–66
Lt Col C.T. Osborne		1966–68
Lt Col L.J. O'Brien		1968–69
Maj. M.E. Young		1969–70
Lt Col C.A. Leech		1970–72
Lt Col E.V. Schaubel		1972–74
Lt Col J.C. Sinclair		1974–78
Lt Col R.A. Grainger		1978–81
Maj. L.E. Ott		1981–82
Lt Col D.T. Carney		1982–86
Lt Col G. Focsaneanu		1986–89
Lt Col L.E. Ott		1989–92
Lt Col G.W. Simpson		1992–94
Lt Col J.W. Dawson		1994–96
Regimental Sergeants-Major ASE/MCE		
WOI John McArthur		1959–61
WOI Bruce Coldham		1961–62
WOI Les Perkins		1962–66
CWO Rod Snow		1966–70
CWO Earl McCullough		1970–71
CWO Bob Dennis		1971–71
CWO Luke Williamson		1971–73
CWO Mel Ullett		1973–76
CWO Paul Baryla		1976–78
CWO Jack Houldsworth		1978–83
CWO Bernard Connelly		1983–85
CWO Roger Messier		1985–87
CWO Paul Svetloff		1987–88
CWO Gary Hodgkinson		1988–92
CWO Fred Mandoli		1992–93
CWO Ole Olson		1993–

National Defence was in the Gagetown area of New Brunswick. As soon as the land was purchased ASE began planning the 1:25 000 coverage of the area. This could not be done on one or two sheets, as was the custom for other training areas. Because a number of sheets would be required, Lieutenant Colonel Smith proposed the introduction of a 1:25 000 NTS scale. Maps of the new scale would conform to the general NTS policy regarding sheet lines and symbolization, but would have detailed specifications consistent with the larger scale. William Miller, director of the Surveys and Mapping Branch in the Department of Mines and Technical Surveys, agreed with this plan. A small group of experts in ASE headed by Gerry Desrivieres, its head draftsman, worked out the specifications for this new scale. The contour interval would be ten feet. More detail would be shown such as shorter streams, smaller ponds, and smaller wooded areas or clearings. For sheet lines the 1:50 000 quadrangle would be divided into eight smaller quads (2 rows of 4), and thus for the first time an NTS sheet would be longer in the north-south dimension than in the east-west. The sheet numbering would begin with the 1:50 000 quad number, followed by the lower-case letters *a* to *h* as appropriate. Camp Wainwright was the next large training area purchased, and it was mapped in the same way. Thus was the NTS 1:25 000 Series born.

The Mid Canada Line

A major non-NTS mapping project descended on the ASE in 1953. By that year the Cold War had become a very serious matter and, among other defence measures, it was decided to build two aircraft detection lines across northern Canada. One of these, called the Distant Early Warning (DEW) Line, was built by the U.S. government along the mainland Arctic coast; the second line, called the Mid Canada Line, was built by Canada across the country from Labrador to the Rocky Mountains, roughly speaking between the 51st and 53rd parallels, as shown in figure 5-5. The survey commitment was to produce a strip map, at a scale of 1:50 000, fifteen miles wide along the selected path of the line. Both the DEW and the Mid Canada Lines employed the most modern radar equipment and a microwave communication system. The contour interval of the ASE mapping was twenty-five feet, and as the microwave signals required intervisibility between towers, accurate contouring was vital.

As ASE had fortunately acquired considerable experience of Arctic mapping during the Fort Churchill project, fieldwork was started during the winter of 1953–54. A tractor train, dog teams, snowmobiles, helicopters, and ski aircraft were all employed for transportation (figure 5-6). Following the winter operations the entire map compilation facilities of ASE were devoted to the project. Shoran-controlled photography (described in chapter 3) was used over Québec where there was a lack of horizontal control, and Air Profile Recorder (APR) equipment was installed in the RCAF photo aircraft whenever vertical control was insufficient. The first Mid Canada Line sheet came off the press on 19 July 1954. The last of 125 sheets was printed on 22 November 1954. A total of 201 000 km² had been mapped in twelve months, or nineteen months counting the time spent on fieldwork and survey computations.[8]

Military Town Plans

By 1959 the Cold War had reached such an intensity that nuclear attack on major North American cities was considered a distinct possibility. The senior officers in both the Armed

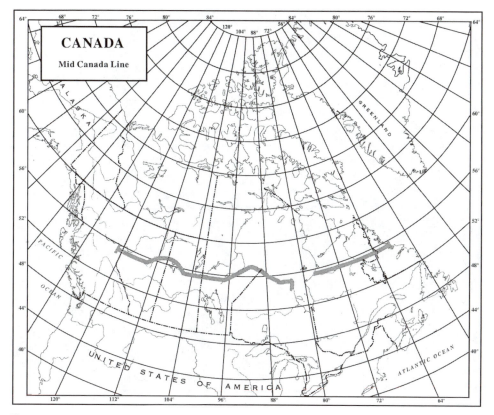

Figure 5-5
The Mid Canada Line.
Source: MCE

Forces and Emergency Measures became concerned at the lack of standard up-to-date maps of Canadian cities. In the case of an attack such maps would be needed for the evacuation of the citizens and eventual re-entry.

Without much warning the Operations and Planning staff at army headquarters gave ASE the task of producing a standard military map of the cities considered at risk. There were sixteen of these, as listed in table 5-2. The required scale was 1:25 000, and the maps were to cover the entire built-up area of each city and include the airport. The maps were originally called Military Town Plans (MTPs), following the NATO designation for similar maps in Europe.

Although the threat of nuclear strikes waned in the 1960s, unrest in Québec increased and was perceived as a threat to law and order. The MTP specifications were modified to change the series to one more suited to combating civil disturbances. In 1970 the series name was changed to Military City Maps (MCM), and the coverage was expanded to cover all Canadian cities with a population over 50 000. Subsequently the reduction of civil disturbances, and economic factors, resulted in a reduction of the maps in the series, as shown in table 5-2. In 1983 the name of the series was changed back to MTPs.

Figure 5-6
Vertol helicopter on supply duty on Mid Canada Line.
Photo: Spartan Archives

Almost from the beginning of this project it was seen that the field survey, air photography, and photogrammetric compilation done for these plans could also be used for the production of standard 1:25 000 maps for civilian use. Thus the production of 1:25 000 sheets began for places across Canada. These sheets covered areas farther from the centres of the cities, and eventually began to cover rural areas. Topographical Survey joined in the work in 1961 and published its first 1:25 000 sheet (21G/1g Ludgate Lake, NB) later that year. In 1962 Topographical Survey was into 1:25 000 mapping in earnest, publishing 28 sheets. But this elegant five-colour NTS series of mainly urban and suburban areas was expensive to keep up to date. As it did not show street names, it was not much used by the public or for city planning. It was discontinued in 1978 after 688 sheets had been published.

The MTP/MCM is still in production. The initial thrust of sixteen cities was completed in two years, but by that time other cities had been added to the list. Eventually, as has been mentioned, all Canadian cities with populations over 50 000 (forty-four cities involving 51 sheets) were mapped as shown in table 5-2. At first these maps were classified "restricted," not because of any secret military installations shown on them but because the whole of the vital functions of the city (e.g., hydro terminals, pumping stations, and

Table 5-2
Military Town Plans/City Maps

	*	**		*	**
Brantford			Québec	*	**
Calgary	*	**	Regina	*	**
Cambridge			Richmond Hill		
Charlottetown	*	**	Sarnia		
Chicoutimi			Saskatoon		
Cornwall			Shawinigan		
Edmonton	*	**	Sherbrooke		
Fredericton	*	**	Saint John, NB	*	**
Guelph			St John's, NFLD	*	**
Halifax	*	**	Thunder Bay		
Hamilton			Toronto East	*	**
Kingston		**	Toronto West	*	**
Kitchener-Waterloo			Trenton-Belleville		
London	*	**	Trois Rivières		
Montréal Nord		**	Vancouver East		**
Montréal Sud		**	Vancouver West	*	**
Montréal Ouest	*	**	Vancouver Delta		**
Montréal Est	*	**	Vancouver Coquitlam		**
Niagara Falls			Victoria		**
North Bay			Whitehorse		
Oakville			Windsor	*	**
Oshawa			Winnipeg East	*	**
Ottawa-Hull	*	**	Winnipeg West		
Peterborough			Yellowknife		

Note: Cities marked thus * were the first sixteen to be mapped. Eighteen maps were required because of the size of Toronto and Montréal. Cities marked thus ** are those with maps now available in the programme.

sewage treatment plants) were displayed on them. If some underground organization wanted to disrupt the life of a city these maps were almost a blueprint for their planning. Since this restriction removed valuable maps from public use, a civilian version was produced with some of the more sensitive information deleted.

Although it was a popular series, the city map was also an expensive series to keep in revision. As the Cold War scaled down, and the threat of civil disorder decreased, it made sense to keep the maps of only the most important cities in revision.

Maps in Aid of the Civil Power

During the period of civil unrest in Québec between 1969 and 1971, beginning with the so-called October Revolution, it was found that many of the 1:50 000 sheets of southern Québec were seriously out of date. A rapid revision of seventy-five of these sheets was undertaken in 1971. The method used was to overprint in purple new roads, new buildings, and other landmark features that had appeared since the last printing. The Surveys and Mapping Branch assisted in this work by taking on twenty of the seventy-five sheets. Also, in 1971, there were a number of disturbances in federal prisons. MCE was called upon to produce large-scale maps of the areas surrounding the prisons to be used in case of riots or mass escapes.

Rapid Mapping Exercises

One function of a military mapping agency is to produce maps quickly. In Lieutenant Colonel Burns's day a rapid mapping exercise was carried out each year. The object was to survey and print a map of considerable size, usually of an area about six to eight miles square, within twenty-four hours. To do this an area was selected near Ottawa, vehicles were requisitioned, and on the appointed day the control traverse surveyors and about ten plane-tablers would take to the field and start to work. By evening they would have finished their work, and throughout the night the draftsmen and reproduction staff would complete the map. At the end of the exercise, the following morning, copies of the map were handed out for inspection, and Burns would disclose a table loaded with sandwiches and a keg of beer. On the last of Burns's exercises, in 1936, the newly purchased Multiplex replaced the plane-tablers.

In the 1950s these expedient mapping exercises were resumed – for a time they were called Burnsway Exercises – to keep alive the skills needed for such work. Difficult terrain was often chosen to encourage ingenuity, and unexpected complications were introduced into the exercises. For example the Petit Mecatina Exercise involved the mapping of an area on the north shore of the Gulf of St Lawrence, including in the map the hydrographic data for the water area of the map. It was, supposedly, a map for a small military landing on a hostile shore. In more recent times photomaps have been produced to cut down on the drafting time. Field printing equipment has also been added to the MCE equipment list to allow defence overprints to be made during large-scale training exercises.

The End of Military NTS Mapping

In 1963 a Treasury Board efficiency expert, R.J. Caldwell, was assigned the task of examining the production of Canadian topographic maps. He immediately "discovered" that two agencies in different departments were doing essentially the same work. He probably never realized how close was the cooperation between ASE and Topographical Survey, and how insignificant was the duplication or waste in having two units producing maps of the same series. In fact if he had looked more closely he might have seen that friendly competition may have been a spur to increased production.

Be that as it may, Caldwell's investigation culminated in a Treasury Board minute,[9] dated 24 October 1965, ordering ASE to stop routine work on NTS maps "except for those that might be needed for operational training, and in such cases the work will be closely coordinated with EMR programs." Fieldwork for NTS mapping was permitted because it was excellent experience in surveying map control, but here the work was always in support of EMR programmes. Map printing in ASE was to be reduced to a small training establishment. (This last restriction is somewhat ironic in that, as will be explained shortly, twenty-five years later MCE was called upon urgently to print large orders for military maps for the Gulf War.)

The ending of sixty years of GSGS/ASE work certainly came as a blow to the pride of the unit. Nevertheless from a strictly strategic point of view the essential military mapping of Canada was virtually completed. The complete coverage of the country at the 1:250 000 scale was within months of happening, and the settled regions were mapped at 1:50 000. Non-NTS city mapping and training-area maps would continue to be a military responsibility. Indeed it could well be argued that the restrictions of the Caldwell report were a blessing in disguise, because very demanding military mapping programmes were just beyond the horizon.

PART 3   MAPPING IN SUPPORT OF NATO AND THE UN

Field Survey During Peace-keeping Operations

Over the years Canada's military surveyors have joined other Canadian units in support of the peace-keeping operations of the United Nations. In 1956 General Burns, the former commander of the GSGS, was in charge of the UN force in the Middle East. One of the contentious diplomatic disputes between the Egyptians and the Israelis was the exact location of the boundary between the Gaza Strip and Egypt. Burns asked for two military surveyors to come out and clear up this matter. Capt. K.R. Gillespie and Sgt K.G. Nethercott were sent to join Burns's staff. This was no easy task. Even before any surveying could be started, trips to Haifa and Jerusalem had to be made to examine and copy old boundary records. After considerable work Gillespie and Nethercott were replaced by Capt. R.E. Coldham and Sgt J.L. Stewart in 1958. The fieldwork by both teams was at times interrupted by rifle fire that prolonged the task more than anticipated. Despite these hazards, and the continual presence of snakes, scorpions, and land mines, the task was completed in 1959 to the satisfaction of both sides.

In 1960 Sgt D.F. Falls was sent to the Congo for survey duty there. As it was thought that his work would be boundary surveying similar to that done in Gaza, he was given a refresher course in astrofix observing. However when on the ground the work consisted of lining up radio antennae on a given true bearing, a much less demanding task.

In 1960 Capt. Joe Reichart, WO John McArthur, and Sgt Ken Munroe were sent to the Israel-Syria border to determine whether or not a patrol track built by the Israelis was entirely in Israeli territory. Here again old boundary records had to be examined before any surveying could be done. Finally it was established clearly that the track was entirely in Israeli territory. Figure 5-7 shows work being done on this project.

In 1974–75 Sgts J.M. Mokken and J.C. Dirksen were sent to the Golan Heights to provide survey support for the construction of a UN field camp. Support for the UN continues to the present time. Operations during the Gulf War required literally millions of maps, and they were needed immediately. The MCE was called upon to help out, which it did on an "around the clock" schedule. Similar UN tasks have been accepted to assist the work in Somalia and Bosnia.

The Joint Operation Graphics Programme

The first of these new military mapping programmes was the production of Joint Operation Graphics (JOG). The JOG is a 1:250 000 map intended for joint land-air operations. It shows all the detail normally found on topographic maps of that scale, together with some additional features needed by pilots of low-flying aircraft. The military reasoning behind the JOG is that it is the largest practical scale that can be kept in readiness for military operations anywhere in the world. On such maps all airports, railways, and highways would be shown, as would all drainage features that would be considered military obstacles. The nature of the terrain would be indicated by symbols, such as forests, wet ground, tundra,

Figure 5-7
RMS John McArthur takes a reading on the Israeli-Syria boundary while an Israeli soldier waits to check the measurement.
Photo: MCE

and deserts. All populated places larger than hamlets would be shown. Contours at 25 m or 50 m (depending on the relief) would indicate the lay of the land.

The special military features shown on JOGs include two reference systems: a 10 000 m Universal Transverse Mercator projection (UTM) grid, and a 15-minute geographical graticule. Notes in the margin give the elevation of the highest point on each sheet, and warnings regarding deficiencies in the accuracies of the contours or positions of features. The sheet lines and numbering system of JOG maps are derived from the quadrangles of the International Map of the World (IMW). Each IMW quadrangle is divided into JOG sheet lines that are 1° in latitude and from 1.5° to 3° in longitude, depending on the latitude of the sheet.

The JOG mapping programme was an American initiative in NATO. All countries were encouraged to publish JOG maps of their territory and, if possible, assist in the mapping of other countries where military operations might take place. Canada supported this programme from its inception. Work on domestic JOGs was started in 1965, with the first sheet being published in 1966. By the end of 1993, 326 domestic sheets had been published.

Canada also supported the mapping of foreign territory where UN peace-keeping operations might be carried out. In a cooperative programme with the U.S. and the U.K., Canada started the production of foreign JOGs in 1967. Many countries permitted air photography over their territory, but when such permission was not forthcoming the U.S. flew very-high photo missions (about 80 000 feet above sea level) for the required photography. The use of such high-level photography was stopped when SPOT imagery became available (see chapters 3 and 14). To engage efficiently in such work the Director of Military Survey, Col M.C. Sutherland-Brown, requested and received state-of-the-art photogrammetric and computer equipment at an expense of several million dollars.

The following is a short description of a foreign JOG sheet:

Sheet number, name, and country: NJ48–5 Minqin, China.

This sheet extends from latitude 38° to 39°, and from longitude 102° to 103° 30″. The country shown lies at the south edge of the Alashan Desert of Inner Mongolia. The contour interval is 50 m with a 25 m interval being used in places. The place-names are romanized in two systems: the more modern Hanyu-Pinyin are printed in red-brown, the older Wade-Giles are in black. The following colours are used:

Red-brown	Roads, red-brown screen town fill, Pinyin names
Blue	Drainage, UTM grid, blue screen airdrome fill
Purple	Airdrome outline, flight information, power lines
Green	Vegetation
Brown	Contours, sand dunes
Black	Buildings, graticule, black names, spot heights

A portion of the Great Wall is shown on this sheet.

Automated Mapping and Military Geographic Information Systems

In automated mapping the horizontal positions of all map detail has been coordinated and stored in data banks, and the vertical information has been recorded in Digital Elevation Models (DEMS). From this data contoured maps can be plotted at any desired scale, but in addition profiles of the land can be drawn, perspective views can be constructed, and many other useful tasks can be performed (e.g., measurement of ranges, areas, volumes, and bearings). The military was quick to appreciate this advanced "map reading" capability. They were also quick to appreciate the relative ease with which digital mapping can be kept up to date and on file to be printed when needed.

Military planners were also quick to develop a military form of Geographic Information Systems (GIS). As explained in chapter 15, a GIS is a computer-based system for analyzing spatially referenced data. When digital mapping is available many military problems can be solved, such as the location of dominating ground, intervisibility from given locations, etcetera. But with the storage of terrain data, the military geography of the land can also be made clear. Such items as the type of vegetation cover, the depths of rivers, obstacles to tank movement, and many other terrain features can be stored for future use.

Recent history has shown that no part of the world is immune to hostile military action. This is why the present NATO work in GIS is worldwide in scope. The JOG programme is certainly valuable as an interim measure, but a great deal of cartographic effort must be spent in keeping the JOGs up to date. There is also the undeniable fact that for many operations the JOGs are at too small a scale. The answer is provided by the almost infinite capacity of modern computers to absorb data and then produce it, when needed, in the most useful form for solving the problems at hand. The scope of the NATO GIS is worldwide. Data are obtained from many sources including published maps, air photography, and satellite imagery. It was obvious that if Canada wanted to be a useful partner in this enterprise the most efficient equipment must be made available for use in the MCE.

Since 1993 the MCE has been equipped with some of the most modern photogrammetric plotters available. With this equipment the formerly tedious tasks of setting up the photogrammetric model is done automatically. The collection of DEM data is also done automatically. Map detail can be from air photography, satellite imagery, or existing maps. Other sophisticated operations, such as the above-mentioned drawing of perspective views, can be done with very little human intervention. These instruments are supported by the necessary computer hardware and digital printing equipment.

CONCLUSION

It is quite true that none of the instruments used today by the MCE in the field or in the office was even dreamed of at the end of the Second World War. The equipment purchases needed to keep Canada's military mapping and charting unit at the front of the mapping art have been expensive. But the fact that the MCE has this equipment and can use it efficiently has won the respect of our allies in NATO. The Canadian Armed Forces mapping unit can be counted on for the rapid production of maps in an emergency, and the continued participation in major operations when maps or survey operations are needed. The MCE motto *Ostendamus Viam* (We Lead the Way) is as true today as it was fifty years ago when it was first used.

NOTES

1 Legal Surveys and Map Service. 1939. *Catalogue of Maps, Plans and Publications*. 7th ed. Ottawa: Department of Mines and Resources.

2 All events dated after 1945 in this chapter are taken from the ASE/MCE Historical Record. CWO Bruce Hynes, custodian, Ottawa.

3 Thompson, J.I. 1948. Application of Terrestrial Photogrammetry to Multiplex Heighting. *The Canadian Surveyor*, 9, 10, 4–10.

4 Sebert, L.M. 1986. 94L Revisited. *The Canadian Surveyor*, 40, 3, 363–6.

5 Sebert, L.M. 1955. Flare Triangulation. *The Canadian Surveyor*, 12, 6, 364–73.

6 Leach, H., and F. MacIntyre. 1946. *The Ship Captain's Medical Guide*. London: His Majesty's Stationery Office, 2.

7 See Thomson, D.W. 1969. *Men and Meridians*, vol. 3. Ottawa: Queen's Printer, 62–4.

8 Smith, C.H. 1956. *Mapping for the Mid Canada Line*. Paper given at the 1956 meeting of the American Society of Photogrammetry, Washington, March 1956.

9 TB 582565, 24 October 1965 to DND. There was a second Treasury Board minute of 2 July 1965, TB 640941, to Mines and Technical Surveys in which Topographical Survey was given responsibility for all NTS mapping.

CHAPTER SIX

Canada's Private Sector Air Survey Industry

Donald W. McLarty

INTRODUCTION

Wars, horrific as they are, spawn advances in technology driven by the need to be as good or preferably better than the other side. The Second World War was no exception. Accurate information on the disposition of troops, the locations of gun and missile sites, and the topography of the land opposite was essential to the conduct of battle. Aerial photography was the tool of choice with which to develop this information. Techniques in photo interpretation were honed, aerial cameras were improved, and aircraft, as suitable platforms for the cameras, became available in many configurations. Rapid mapping of land features and topography from aerial photography was much in demand. As a result by the end of the war great strides had been made in the development of photogrammetry.

The Canadian air survey industry was an important beneficiary of these developments. While aerial surveys were first performed in Canada as early as 1920, and were used fairly extensively in forest inventory and mapping projects throughout the following two decades, it was not until the termination of the Second World War that the Canadian air survey industry really came into its own. At that point war-surplus aircraft and, more important, flying crews who had been well trained by the Royal Canadian Air Force (RCAF) and other air forces, became available in abundance.

While the terms "air survey" or "aerial survey" adequately described the services of early postwar companies, they expanded their range of capabilities rapidly. They began with aerial photography, added the production of various types of photo mosaics (the joining of many photographs to cover one large area), expanded into planimetric and topographic mapping, undertook the establishment of suitable ground control for mapping purposes, and in 1960–61 commenced preliminary work on GIS (Geographic Information Systems). This growth in the range of services led in 1988 to the change of name from the Canadian Association of Aerial Surveyors (CAAS) to the Geomatics Industry Association of Canada (GIAC) – a name that more accurately describes the scope of activities performed by its member firms today.

The industry has always been extremely innovative and aggressive in marketing its services outside Canada. At one time it was said to be performing more than 75 percent of all new mapping in the world. Some have also maintained that this was largely because of the government of Canada's generous assistance programmes to developing nations. However studies of all the work performed overseas by the Canadian industry show that a considerably higher percentage of dollars earned were generated from sources other than the Canadian government. The fact is that the industry has earned an enviable reputation, second to none in the world, for quality of work, resourceful solutions to difficult problems, and delivery of work on time.

AN EVOLVING INDUSTRY

Canada's vast wealth of timber and pulpwood had long been recognized by the time hostilities terminated in 1945. The use of aerial photographs to delineate forest limits, and to aid in species identification and board-foot measurements, was already a recognized methodology. It was this activity that had driven the creation of Canada's early air survey companies, and some of these had survived the war period.

Don W. Thomson has described very fully and accurately the beginnings and fortunes of most of these companies.[1] Suffice it to say here that following a period of restrictions and material shortages imposed by the war, those companies still in business at the cessation of hostilities were more than delighted to welcome and offer employment to the returning pilots, navigators, and aircraft engineers. In turn these young men were glad to find employment readily available, although many had to face the choice of accepting what could be a lucrative employment opportunity or returning to school or university to complete an education that had been interrupted by the war.

One of the most aggressive employers during that period was Frank T. Jenkins, who was running the air survey section of Canadian Pacific Airways (CPA). Also active at that time was Albert E. Simpson, operating under the name A.E. Simpson Limited at a location near Montréal. "Simmie" Simpson purchased his flying from other aviation companies, but offered specialized services in mapping and the production of mosaics for various uses.

In Western Canada, Aero Surveys Limited was operating out of Vancouver, and Arctic Air Lines, under Leigh Britnell, conducted most of its activities in the Prairies. Other companies existed at the time, but all were shortly to be overwhelmed by a rash of new companies, amalgamations, and buy-outs. This was to result in serious overcapacity causing fierce competition, which was to plague the industry for many years to come. The upside of the problem was that competition was the engine for innovation, an expansion of services, and a drive for new markets.

Two new companies were incorporated in 1946 that were to play major roles in the development and growth of the Canadian air survey industry. The Photographic Survey Corporation Limited (PSC) came into being early in the year with its head office in Toronto. It was headed by Douglas Kendall, who had been educated at Oxford, worked for an air survey company in South Africa before the war, ran the photo interpretation unit of the Royal Air Force during the hostilities, and had been decorated by the British and U.S. governments for his distinguished services. He had been sent to Canada by Percy (later Sir Percy) Hunting as head of the Hunting Group, a large and diversified U.K.-based company heavily involved in the oil industry, to bid on a large forestry project for the province of Ontario.

Around the time that Kendall was getting PSC started in Toronto, the idea of forming another air survey company was germinating in the minds of a number of RCAF war veterans still flying with the photographic squadrons stationed at Rockliffe Air Base, Ottawa. John A. Roberts, a pilot from western Canada with a background in geology, was joined by Russell L. Hall and Joe Kohut, both navigators with extensive experience in air photography. Together they incorporated Spartan Air Services Limited (Spartan) in August 1946, although actual flying operations did not commence until the following January. Roberts, who had acquired the nickname "Patch" because of his insistence on flying and attempting photography on any occasion when a sliver of blue sky could be seen among the cumulus, was the first to obtain his discharge from the RCAF so that he could devote himself full time to getting the fledgling company airborne. Hall joined him shortly after, while Joe Kohut flew for some months with CPA before moving to Spartan. Other important players in the early days of Spartan were Jimmy Wells, a lawyer with excellent connections in the government, and Barnett MacLaren of the pulp and paper family from Buckingham, Québec, who helped with the financing of the new enterprise. Both PSC and Spartan grew at an impressive rate, and were to become world leaders in air survey related activities.

In Québec La Compagnie Photo-Air Laurentides and Aéro Photo Inc. were incorporated in 1947. In 1949 the air survey activities of CPA were sold to Photographic Surveys (Québec) Limited, a subsidiary of PSC in Toronto. A.E. Simpson Limited was acquired by Aéro Photo Inc. in 1965, which in turn was sold by its founder, André Cassista, to Maurice Gaudreault and his partner, Romeo Pigeon, in 1973. Gaudreault was to become an active participant for many years in Québec and Canadian survey and mapping activities.[2] Over the months and years ahead many new companies came into being, and all regions of the country could boast at least one air survey practitioner.

A new major company appeared on the scene in May 1950, not in the traditional role of an air survey firm, but rather to perform an airborne magnetometer survey of the Peace River area for a group of oil companies. This was Canadian Aero Service Ltd, a subsidiary of Aero Service Corporation of Philadelphia, which expanded rapidly into photogrammetric mapping, cartography, and geodetic and engineering surveys. Flying for the new company was provided initially by Spartan. Later in 1950 Aero Service brought to Canada an entrepreneur, Thomas M. O'Malley, who was named president of Canadian Aero Service Ltd and who was to become a pioneer, leader, and major player in Canadian air survey history. In 1953 O'Malley was joined by J.M. (George) Zarzycki, who had come to Canada from his native Poland via Switzerland where he had received his D.Sc. from the Swiss Federal Institute of Technology. Zarzycki was named chief engineer of Canadian Aero, and later was appointed executive vice-president. The team of O'Malley and Zarzycki was to pioneer many innovative solutions to complex air survey problems. Zarzycki became director of the Topographical Survey Division of Energy, Mines and Resources Canada in 1974; and in 1985 he was named Director of Surveys, Mapping and Remote Sensing in the Ontario Ministry of Natural Resources. O'Malley met with an untimely death from cancer in 1976.

Fortunately for the firms starting up after the war, many types of aircraft were decommissioned from the services and sold as surplus at bargain prices. The Avro Anson Mk V had been one of the workhorses of the RCAF photographic squadrons based at Rockliffe, and soon assumed a similar role under civilian colours. The Anson was an excellent and reasonably economical aircraft for large- to medium-scale aerial photography (1:2000 to

1:30 000). It was a twin-engine aircraft constructed mainly of fabric-covered plywood, and it lent itself readily to the necessary modifications for installing a camera. When demand grew for small-scale photography (1:40 000 to 1:60 000), mainly in the Arctic islands and northern regions of Canada, the search began for suitable aircraft capable of flying at 30 000 feet or more above the ground. This need was filled by a variety of complex aircraft with designed lifespans geared to wartime expectations. This led to costly, and often dangerous, air survey operations in Canada and elsewhere in the world requiring high-level flying. In this category of aircraft were the Lockheed P-38 and the de Havilland Mosquito. Both types, for example, had a bad habit of overheating if delayed on take-off. The P-38 often required a change of spark plugs before it could take to the air. The Rolls Royce Merlin engines powering the Mosquito had a designed engine life of 400 hours between major overhauls. It was cause for celebration when they exceeded 200 hours. A major Merlin engine overhaul cost $20,000, an amount to make a bank manager shudder at that time.

A more benign aircraft of that period was the Lockheed Hudson purchased from Trans-Canada Airlines, now Air Canada, as they were replaced by more modern passenger aircraft. The most worthy aircraft of the period, and still in operation today in many parts of the world, was the Douglas DC3, known as the Dakota by the military. Shortly after the war a Dakota could be purchased for $20,000, but over the years the price increased to $120,000. The DC3 was always known as the real workhorse of the skies and was never replaced adequately. Also in use for a time, mostly on Shoran control flights, was the Lancaster, the renowned four-engine British bomber on which many young Canadians crewed during the war.

The companies gradually replaced their war-surplus aircraft with more efficient modern machines. These were mainly in the light twin-engine category, mostly turbo-charged for high-altitude photography. In this group were the Piper Apache, the Cessna 320, and the Aero Commander, although one single-engine Cessna 180 did Trojan service for a while until it was realized that the going was too tough for one engine. These aircraft were later augmented by turbo-jet and pure jet aircraft.

The first jet aircraft to be used for aerial photography in Canada was a Lear Jet 24B, leased by Spartan in 1968. Spartan's Argentina subsidiary used the same aircraft to obtain high-level photography over the Andes in 1968–69. During the next ten years Lockwood Survey Corporation Limited (later renamed Northway Survey Corporation Limited), Capital Air Surveys Limited, as well as Spartan operated different models of Lear Jet aircraft at various times on photography for Surveys and Mapping Branch, EMR. Some 350 000 line miles of high-level photography were obtained at an average cost of $13.89 per line mile. The operation was considered a complete success, and substantial savings were achieved relative to those experienced using conventional aircraft.[3]

In 1979 North West Surveys Corporation (Yukon) Ltd evaluated pressurized turbine aircraft for aerial photography. The Cessna Conquest 441 propjet had been introduced recently, and was selected because of its range, speed, and service ceiling. Dual camera hatches were designed and installed. This was the first Conquest put into photographic configuration in the world, and proved to be an excellent performer in Canada and internationally. The Conquest was particularly productive at altitudes of 30 000 to 35 000 feet above sea level on federal and provincial small-scale programmes. From 1980 to 1987 the Conquest performed the majority of this work in Canada. In 1987 the Conquest was used in the inauguration of the United States Geological Survey National Aerial Photography Program (NAPP),

Figure 6-1
The Anson Mark V Aircraft. It was used for taking mapping photography in the early postwar period.
Photo: Spartan Archives

Figure 6-2
Crew of a de Havilland Mosquito in the early postwar period.
Photo: Spartan Archives

Figure 6-3
The Lancaster (background) and the Mosquito 35, two survey aircraft used in high-level photographic and Shoran control flight operations carried out by the Canadian air survey industry.
Photo: Spartan Archives

and quickly proved to be the best aircraft on that programme. The Conquest was sold to North West Geomatics Ltd in 1988, and continues to be used in national and international photographic contracts. Since the introduction of the Conquest into Canada in 1979, another six aircraft have been configured for aerial photography.

The cameras most in use in the early postwar years were the British Williamson Eagle IX and the U.S. Fairchild K17B. The Williamson camera in particular was infamous for its electrical troubles. It also had an interesting static problem. Instead of the film being held flat against the platen by vacuum, the film in the Williamson camera passed between two glass plates. This worked fairly well in most situations, but at high altitudes where the air is extremely cold and dry the film would be induced to discharge a burst of static electricity that would render anything from one negative to the whole film useless. These problems were eliminated, and a much improved definition was achieved, with the advent of the Swiss Wild RC series and the German Zeiss cameras.

Most flying operations were undertaken by a crew of pilot, navigator, and camera operator. In some cases the functions of navigation and camera operation were combined in one individual. Accurate navigation was of course critical. Most flying operations were

Figure 6-4
An air survey industry plotter being used on a provincial mapping project.
Source: Spartan Archives

laid out in blocks of parallel lines on the best maps available, though sometimes there were none. Standard overlap conditions were applied. Depending on the scale of the photography, as little as one-quarter mile of deviation from a given position on the ground could result in a gap in the photography. On a map with sparse detail or an inaccurate map a good navigator would draw in features of his next line as he progressed along the active line of photography or other sensor operation. Doppler receivers, and more recently airborne Global Positioning System (GPS) navigation aids, are now used to keep aircraft on position.

There is much talk these days of the information age and Geographic as well as Land Information Systems (GIS and LIS), but there seemed to be a pent-up demand for geographic and resource information following a period of stagnation imposed by the war. Not only in Canada but also in foreign lands, particularly in what are now called "developing countries," there existed a thirst for knowledge of the extent and location of resources. Forests have already been mentioned as a natural resource that lent itself to evaluation from the air. But forests are only one of many resource studies that benefitted from the application of air survey technology. Water resources, soil types, crops, and land use could all be identified by studying aerial photographs. The potential for mineral deposits and oil-bearing strata were first established by a geological study of aerial photographs, often supplemented by airborne geophysical surveys.

Basic mapping was a prerequisite to the delineation of resources. This was often in the form of mosaics or a simple planimetric map produced by early photogrammetric techniques. Basic mapping quickly grew into the production of topographic map sheets requiring height measurements usually expressed in the form of elevation contours. Specialized photogrammetric mapping was required for highway, railway, and power line location. Line-of-sight communications, dams, floods, and watersheds all required their own specific mapping treatment.

Some Early Contracts and Activities of the Period

When Kendall came to Canada in February 1946 to bid on the Government of Ontario Forest Resources Inventory Project, little did he know that his parent company would be successful and that he would be returning to Canada in April of the same year to establish the new company, PSC. The project was one of the largest of its kind ever undertaken in any country, and was to take over five years to complete. The contract required photographic coverage and planimetric mapping of most of Ontario, as well as the photographic interpretation and groundwork necessary to complete an inventory of all forested areas of the province. As soon as the snow had disappeared each spring, four Anson aircraft would start on the job and, given a high enough sun angle and sufficiently clear weather, would stay on the job until the snow returned in the fall. Operating bases moved from Toronto to North Bay, Kapuskasing, and Armstrong, generally along the Canadian National Railway route in Northern Ontario. In all, the work was to cover some 128 000 square miles of the province. In 1949 PSC was awarded another large contract, this time by the Alberta Department of Lands and Forests. Small-scale photography was to be obtained of most of the province, some 250 000 square miles, to be followed by planimetric mapping of the entire area. A new contract followed for larger-scale aerial photography of all of the forested areas of the province.

In the meantime Spartan had started flying operations, the majority of the early contracts being for forestry companies. The RCAF was still providing most of the aerial photography required by federal government departments, but a break came in 1948 when nearly $300,000 worth of federal photography was negotiated, on a trial basis, with the five firms then in business. It was not until 1951, when the RCAF was required to curtail its aerial photography activities severely because of the diversion of personnel to meet the demands of the Korean War, that the federal photography was contracted to private industry. The annual value of aerial photography for federal departments was to fluctuate between approximately $1.25 million and $2.8 million for a number of years to come. Much of this work called for small-scale photography (1:60 000) of the high Arctic, requiring flying heights of up to 35 000 feet above sea level. Such an operation taxed the ingenuity of the two or three companies then able to provide these services. Landing strips suitable to accommodate high-performance aircraft had to be carved out of the tundra; living, eating, and maintenance facilities had to be constructed or erected; and gasoline and provision caches had to be sustained. Shipments were usually brought in by air, or moved by vehicle over the snow and ice during the winter months.

At the same time competition and overcapacity were rapidly becoming serious problems. As a partial response PSC, which had an excellent mapping capability from the start, extended its services to include a broad range of natural resource studies. Kendall had found that it was easier to sell a fully integrated project worth $5 million involving aerial photography, mapping, and natural resource studies than it was to sell a $1 million stand-alone aerial photography contract. The corporation was also quick to enter the airborne geophysical field, being the first Canadian company to offer airborne magnetometer exploration services.

One of Canadian Aero's first major projects was the Québec Cartier Mining Company contract, which involved engineering surveys for a 320 km railway, a town site, a hydro-electric site, and a harbour. Another interesting undertaking was the production of radar response simulation terrain models for the military.

THE CANADIAN ASSOCIATION OF AERIAL SURVEYORS

As the industry grew through the 1950s it became evident that there was a need for a forum where matters of common interest could be discussed, and where a degree of discipline could be imposed on the somewhat unruly young enterprise known as the air survey industry. At the same time there was a requirement to address both federal and provincial authorities with one voice. This problem was also recognized by S.G. (Sam) Gamble, then director of the Topographical Survey. He was to play a pivotal role in the growing relationship between the industry and the federal government, and at the time urged the industry to name one spokesman to negotiate with his department.

It was with this background that in January 1961 a number of petitioners (named in table 6-1) requested the secretary of state to issue Letters Patent incorporating the CAAS. They were issued on 20 April 1961. The named petitioners represented the founding firms, and were the first directors of the association.

The purposes and objects of the association were the usual for such a body.
- To promote the science of aerial surveying and the knowledge of the members in connection with the practice of aerial surveying
- To encourage the establishing of high standards of workmanship with respect to aerial surveying
- To promote an ethical approach in business relationships in the field of aerial surveying
- To promote the adoption by government of policies favourable to aerial surveying in Canada
- To establish and support or aid in the establishment and support of funds or trusts calculated to benefit aerial surveying in Canada
- To adopt such means for making known the objects and purposes of the corporation to the general public as may seem expedient
- To promote and engage in research and development of the science of aerial surveying
- To do all such other things as are incidental or conducive to the attainment of the above objects

As table 6-2 shows, the presidency rotated on an annual basis, usually among the chief executive officers of the member firms. This continued until 1968 when, again largely at the urging of Gamble, and also because the members had concluded that a more aggressive stand was required if the association's aims were to be achieved, a permanent president was named. This relieved the company representatives of the day-to-day responsibilities for the management of the association, and allowed for a more confrontational style of lobbying when that was deemed advisable. The member firms continued to appoint chair-men for annual terms until 1974 when the term, with a few exceptions, was increased to two years. The first involvement of industry in the production of National Topographic System (NTS) maps occurred in 1953. The Army Survey Establishment (ASE) under the

Table 6-1
Canadian Association of Aerial Surveyors: Founding Firms

Founding Firms	Petitioners
Canadian Aero Service Limited	J.W. Strath, Ottawa
Hunting Survey Corporation Limited	E.W.I. Keenleyside, Ottawa
Shaw Photogrammetric Services Limited	R.P. Shaw, Ottawa
Canadian Air Surveys Limited	J.F. Fleming, Ottawa
Spartan Air Services Limited	W.U. Hardy, Ottawa
A.E. Simpson Limited	A.E. Simpson, Montréal
La Compagnie Photo-Air Laurentides	C.W. Garrard, Québec
Aero Surveys Limited	F.J. Churko, Vancouver

Table 6-2
Officers, Canadian Association of Aerial Surveyors

PRESIDENTS

1961–62	Richard P. Shaw	Ottawa
1962–63	John W. Strath	Ottawa
1963–64	Col Cyril H. Smith	Ottawa
1964–65	Thomas E. Rowlands	Ottawa
1965–66	William H. Morton	Ottawa
1966–67	Douglas N. Kendall	Toronto
1967–68	André Cassista	Québec
1968–69	Douglas G. MacKay	Ottawa

CHAIRMEN

1969–70	Philippe Amyot	Québec
1970–71	Dr J. M. Zarzycki	Ottawa
1971–72	William H. Morton	Ottawa
1972–73	Thomas M. O'Malley	Ottawa
1973–74	Robert A. Brocklebank	Vancouver
1974–76	Maurice Gaudreault	Québec
1976–78	William H. Morton	Ottawa
1978–79	William A. Dymond	Toronto
1979–80	John D. Barnes	Toronto
1980–81	A. Denis Hosford	Edmonton
1981–83	Jacques Bureau	Montréal
1983–85	John E. Macartney	Ottawa
1985–87	Phillip J. Boase	Vancouver
1987–89	Guy Béliveau	Québec
Name Change to Geomatics Industry Association of Canada		
1989–91	John D. Barber	Toronto
1991–93	Douglas K. MacDonald	Dartmouth

PERMANENT PRESIDENTS

1968–88	Donald W. McLarty	Ottawa
1988–	Edward A. Kennedy	Ottawa

direction of Col C.H. Smith had found it neccessary to have industry assist in the urgent mapping of major Canadian army training areas. The first two such areas to be mapped were Gagetown, New Brunswick and Wainwright, Alberta. Contract mapping of 1:25 000 scale NTS Series sheets covering military training areas was extended in 1959 to include Canadian cities with populations over 50 000. The entire 1:25 000 ASE mapping programme at that time was driven by Cold War tensions, as it was thought that Canadian cities might become targets for nuclear bombs. The contract mapping included aerial photography, ground control, aerotriangulation, and compilation. The city maps were published in two forms: as standard topographic maps and as military specials called Military Town Plans (MTPS). The ASE contract mapping programme continued until 1965 when ASE assistance to the 1:25 000 NTS Series was discontinued. Although industry's involvement was terminated in 1965, the 1:25 000 scale mapping was continued until 1978 as an in-house activity of the Topographical Survey, adding fuel to the tension that was already building between that agency and the private sector firms.

Early in the 1960s the Geological Survey of Canada (GSC), as part of the joint "Roads to Resources" programme with the provinces, began to contract with industry for aeromagnetic surveys of the Precambrian Shield. These contracts were to be of considerable importance to the growth and improvement of the industry's capability in this field. Unfortunately the bidding process was so competitive that immediate profitability soon turned to losses for the companies, and deliveries and quality suffered accordingly. Through the good offices of L.W. Morley, who was in charge of the programme for the GSC, and the CAAS, the companies were formed into consortia in 1968. The outcome was the restoration of profitability, as well as timely deliveries and acceptable quality.

The GSC airborne geophysical and ASE mapping programmes could be held up as excellent examples of collaboration between government and industry that resulted in important benefits to both parties. The same could not be said of the industry's attempts to have mapping activities diverted from the Topographical Survey to the private sector. Such a move had long been opposed by the then Department of Mines and Technical Surveys, and EMR as its successor. It was, therefore, a top priority in the mandate given to the first permanent president to resolve this problem. This proved to be a long and arduous task that resulted initially in only piecemeal successes.

The industry had never sought government handouts. It fought aggressively, however, for what it always considered its most effective role in the mapping of Canada. It contended in the strongest terms possible that the flexibility and profit motive inherent in the private sector would result invariably in better production performance than is possible in the public sector. Furthermore participation in the basic mapping programme for Canada was essential to provide a base from which to establish credibility when seeking contracts abroad and the export of services.

This position led to serious confrontation over a long period of time between industry and the federal Surveys and Mapping Branch (SMB), an unfortunate situation that was noted by a task force on surveying amd mapping.[4] This was resolved only with the intervention of the Treasury Board, and the support of the Ministry of State for Science and Technology, the Ministry of State for Small Business, and Industry, Trade and Commerce Canada. It resulted in an agreement of December 1977 to reduce the establishment of the Surveys and Mapping Branch by attrition, the total being 240 person-years over the following ten-year period at the rate of 24 person-years per annum. This was to provide $30,000 for contract mapping per person-year lost to attrition, or total annual increments of $720,000. While the objectives of the programme were never met fully, funding of contract mapping did reach $3,385,000 in the fiscal year 1984–85. The mapping programme executed by the private sector was acknowledged to have been highly successful, producing excellent quality work, on time, on budget, and achieving significant savings in inspection and other costs to the SMB. At the same time there had been a dramatic improvement in the relationship between the industry and the SMB, particularly with the Topographical Survey Division.

Mapping Consortia

At the time the SMB contract mapping started in earnest, the federal government had issued a policy statement requiring that contracts be shared geographically across the country, and fairly between small and large companies. By 1977 the CAAS membership had grown to fifteen companies, and there were two or three other mapping firms on the Department of Supply and Services (DSS) approved list that had not yet applied for membership in the association. This situation, of too many foxes chasing the same hen, had already resulted in prices on early aerotriangulation contracts being depressed to levels that could only lead to the eventual demise of the firms involved. Furthermore, because aerotriangulation was assigned the lowest level of priority in company production schedules, deliveries and quality suffered. This led naturally to a high level of tension between the companies and the client.

The CAAS had long argued that surveying and mapping should be recognized as the professional service that it was, and be treated in the same manner as other professional services in the government procurement process. This argument had never met with much success, and it appeared that the newly established contract mapping programme might be destined to the same end as the earlier aerotriangulation contracts. Fortunately good sense prevailed. With the understanding of A.D. Costello of DSS, and the cooperation of EMR, a proposal submitted by the association was accepted.

This proposal was based on the model first adopted for GSC aeromagnetic contracts in 1968, and also used in the case of a number of External Aid Office (later Canadian International Development Agency, CIDA) projects. Replacing the usual lowest price tender call would be a Request For Proposals (RFP) asking for responses in two sections: one on the technical and management issues and solutions, and the other providing cost estimates. A certain level of points had to be achieved on the first before the costs would be taken into account. This system was already in use for the procurement of other professional services. In addition it was necessary to ensure that work was spread across the country and the smaller firms were given a chance to participate in the mapping contracts. Thus CAAS organized all the DSS-approved companies into three consortia, each with a prime contractor experienced in the mapping programme. In turn EMR grouped the work to be contracted into three large parcels, each of which could be undertaken by one consortium. It was the intention that each consortium, although in fact bidding against the other two, would win one parcel of mapping. This was because the consortia were assembled in such a way that there was a logical geographic distribution of the work. The intention was often realized in practice. Sometimes, however, one consortium would win two or even all three contracts. In this case the consortium would have to prove that it had the capacity to complete the work by the specified delivery date. Individual firms were not precluded from responding on their own, but they would be subjected to the same delivery requirements. Most firms found it to their advantage to be part of a consortium.

The system worked extremely well, and was also carried into provincial mapping programmes. Individual company pricing errors and desperation bids were avoided. The price submitted by the prime contractor was the average of all prices submitted by the consortium members. The prime contractor also took responsibility for quality control and assisted the less experienced firms in achieving national standards. Inspection costs were reduced dramatically for the client, excellent quality was assured, and delivery schedules were met. The consortia approach was an ideal solution to what could have become a very difficult situation for both government and industry, further aggravating relations between the two. Instead it achieved excellent results for all parties.

Each year representatives of EMR, DSS, CAAS, and the industry met (and still do meet) to discuss the results of the previous year's contracts and the forthcoming projects for the current fiscal year. The sixth annual meeting held on 4 February 1982 illustrates the achievements of the mapping consortia. The meeting was told that the previous year's mapping programme had amounted to a little over $3 million. It had consisted of 261 sheets of new 1:50 000 mapping, processing the surrounds (or marginal information) for 539 sheets, and various large-scale mapping projects for other government departments. The quality of the work had been good and delivery schedules had been met. It was also announced that the forthcoming programme would include "digital mapping" for the first time. When asked, three companies stated that they were equipped to undertake such work. Thus was a new phase of consortia mapping opened.

The LIFT Project

Another interesting cooperative programme in which the association played an important role was the Lower Inventory for Tomorrow (LIFT) project. In 1970 the government of Canada, faced with excess production of wheat, created a novel programme that would compensate farmers for leaving their wheat fields fallow or converting them into grassland. This offer resulted in over 100 000 claims from farmers, for which some form of verification was required. It was decided that this could best be accomplished by obtaining aerial photography of the entire wheat-growing area of the three Prairie provinces. A small area in British Columbia was also included, making the total area to be covered a little over 300 000 square miles. What made the project unique was that the aerial photography had to be accomplished between 10 July and 15 August 1970, a period of five weeks in the middle of the busiest period of the year for air photographers.

It was estimated that given reasonable weather, seven aircraft would be required to obtain the photography in the stipulated period. Four firms were willing to assign the necessary aircraft to the project. A consortium was formed under the leadership of Spartan-Aero Limited of Ottawa and the work was completed on time, a feat that astounded all concerned. The entire project was a complete success and the final interpretation of the photographs, which required about a year, proved that western farmers were honest men and women.

Relationship with Land Surveyor Organizations

As the air survey industry matured and the level of mapping activity increased, some land surveyors appeared to feel threatened by what they perceived to be an encroachment on their traditional role as legal surveyors. The context was the discussion taking place in

Canada on the use of photogrammetry for the mapping of cadastral boundaries, and a series of practical tests that were made in the late 1950s and thereafter.[5] Initially efforts were made to discredit aerial surveyors. Claims for the accuracy that could be obtained from photogrammetric mapping were contested vigorously at every opportunity. However as it became evident that the "new boy on the block" was here to stay, other strategies were developed. Three provincial land survey associations attempted to legislate photogrammetric mapping as an activity that could only be carried out under the act governing their profession. Had they succeeded, this would have effectively put the existing photogrammetric firms in those provinces out of business.

In one case a member firm of CAAS was taken to court by a provincial land survey association on the grounds that the firm was showing property limits illegally on a photogrammetrically compiled plan. The land survey association claimed that only its members had the legal right to establish property boundaries. The case was contested strongly, and subsequently was thrown out of court. In another case a provincial land survey association was on the verge of having legislation enacted that would have embraced photogrammetry as an activity that could only be performed by its members. Fortunately the CAAS was alerted to the ploy. It sent a strong letter to the minister concerned, which was followed by the president of CAAS and the government member on the council of the land survey association meeting with the minister in his office. This put an abrupt end to the matter.

In the meantime many of the more progressive legal survey firms were acquiring photogrammetric capabilities, and eventually became valuable and supportive members of the CAAS. As the lines of separation between surveying and mapping activities became blurred, relationships between all parties have become much more cordial.

The Thomas M. O'Malley Award

In 1980 the association struck an award in honour of Thomas M. O'Malley, who had been its strong supporter. The award is given in recognition of a person's "outstanding contribution in furthering the ideals and objectives of the Association and in promoting conditions conducive to the continued growth and leadership of the Canadian aerial survey industry." The first recipients were Kendall, whose contributions to the association and the industry have already been recorded, and Bill Morton. The latter was chosen to receive the award in recognition of his outstanding work on behalf of the industry during his three terms of office in the association. The third recipient of the award was Donald McLarty in 1988 on the occasion of his retirement as president of the association, then the GIAC, following twenty years in that position. The fourth and most recent recipient was George Zarzycki, acknowledging his many valuable contributions to aerial surveying and mapping technology, both in the private and public sectors.

The CAAS in Repose

The name of the Canadian Association of Aerial Surveyors was changed by Supplementary Letters Patent in December 1987 to the Geomatics Industry Association of Canada. By then membership in the association had increased to thirty firms. Shortly before the change of name, the Department of Energy, Mines and Resources and CAAS agreed on a Memorandum of Understanding (MOU). This was signed on 30 November 1987 by the Minister of State for Forestry and Mines, Honourable Gerald A. Merrithew, on behalf of the department and by Donald McLarty for the association. The MOU covered cooperation between the two parties in such matters as technology development, international marketing of geomatics services, and education. This was one of the first of a number of MOUS entered into by the Surveys, Mapping and Remote Sensing Sector of EMR with various national and international bodies.

During the twenty-eight years the association carried on business as the CAAS, a primary aim had been to promote contracting out to the private sector the needs of the public sector surveying and mapping agencies. A secondary objective had been to contain growth within these organizations. These were not easy tasks since surveying and mapping activities had become firmly entrenched in federal and some provincial government departments. At the same time the association had a mandate to improve relations between the industry and these same government agencies, a sometimes contradictory assignment. Over the years, however, both objectives could be said to have been attained. Evidence is available in the signing of the MOU at the federal level and in the numerous excellent provincial government mapping programmes being carried out by industry. The association also dealt with numerous other federal and provincial departments on behalf of the industry, and engaged in marketing of Canadian capability at international events.

The work of the Canadian Association of Aerial Surveyors, a name that became well recognized in Canada and abroad, continues now under its new banner – the Geomatics Industry Association of Canada.

THE INDUSTRY OVERSEAS

The Canadian air survey industry has left its mark in 110 countries of the world. In doing so it has achieved an enviable international reputation for innovative solutions and successful completion of contracts, on time and on or under budget. A number of factors played a role in the early growth of overseas activities. Foremost was the Canadian climate, permitting only six months each year of flying or field operations, even much less if aerial photography was required under "leaf-free, snow-free" conditions for mapping purposes. This meant idle air crews and field personnel for the six winter months of the year. Efforts were made to integrate these personnel into office activities, albeit with considerable reluctance on all sides. Notable exceptions did occur, but a better solution was to find projects in countries that enjoy a more benign climate during Canada's winter. This seasonal limitation combined with a growing thirst for geographic and resource knowledge in many developing countries, and Canada's rapidly acquired expertise in servicing these needs, led to a host of successful forays overseas.

Kendall was one of the first to realize that if an air survey firm was to be economically viable in Canada, it must obtain work employing aircraft and crews elsewhere during the winter months. Even as the Ontario forestry project got underway, Kendall was in Colombia selling an aerial photography contract to the Royal Dutch Shell Group. This initial contract in 1946 was to escalate into the formation of a Colombian company that was to employ a number of PSC crews and aircraft over many Canadian winters. Another important source of international business during the early years was the United Nations Development Programme (UNDP) in New York, and its agriculture, irrigation, forestry, and hydrology arm in Rome, the Food and Agriculture Organisation (FAO). Major infrastructure projects were handled by the World Bank, as continues to be the case today. FAO was to award Kendall's company two contracts in the early years. The first was a three-year project to study the Schebeli River in Somalia with the aim of opening up the irrigation area that had once been run by the Italians when they were in control of the country. This was followed by another contract in Malawi, again an irrigation project including a marketing and experimentation study of the Elephant Marsh to see what vegetation would grow and sell best. PSC also became active in Venezuela, Ecuador, Brazil, and later in Argentina, all excellent winter alternatives! However experience in cold-weather operations led to another interesting PSC project in the Falkland Islands.

The Falkland Islands and Dependencies

Under this two-year contract, 1955–57, PSC was to provide two amphibious PBY-5A Cansos equipped with precision cameras and airborne magnetometers. All of the Falkland Islands territory was to be photographed. The story may best be told in Kendall's own words as recorded in his memoirs, written for his children and future family generations.

During the summer we moved from the Falkland Islands to certain territories which came under the administration of the Falkland Dependencies. One of these was Deception Island which was also claimed by Chile and Argentina. This island contained a large volcano which was open to the sea on one side. It was quite active. The entrance makes the whole bay a good anchorage and a suitable place from which we could operate amphibious aircraft.

The shoreline had a number of hot water spouts which kept Deception Bay free of ice and populated with an unusually large number of penguins. They live on shrimp. And it was the shrimp that would get caught by the hot water spouts and thrown up on the beaches already cooked.

The mapping of Deception Island was carried out using the air photographs. And in the process they named one mountain ridge after me – Kendall Ridge.

Another pleasant surprise was a visit by the Duke of Edinburgh to Deception Island. He arrived on the royal yacht Britannia and presented one of our managers with a medal for his contribution to aviation.

Our Hunting Associates in the United Kingdom secured the contract. The reason that they turned to us to provide the amphibious aircraft was that such equipment was unavailable in the U.K. Moreover, we had a vast amount of experience operating aircraft under very cold conditions in the Arctic.

Under the contract, Hunting was to supply a ship equipped with a helicopter landing pad, two helicopters, a number of survey crews, plus all logistic and camp maintenance personnel. The survey parties were to be landed by helicopter and to set up a geodetic network to use in the mapping of Graham Land. The data was to be photographed by the two Cansos which were also to carry airborne magnetometers for securing the geophysical data.

The operation went well and 45,000 square miles of Graham Land was successfully photographed and tied down geodetically. The base on Deception Island had to be created from scratch with quarters for 45 men and a ramp so that the Cansos could be beached.[6]

The technical and logistical aspects of this unusual and interesting project have also been described by Peter Mott of Hunting Surveys, U.K.[7] Some of the maps and aerial photographs were to be put to good use later by the U.K. forces during the Falkland Islands war with Argentina.

Other Early Overseas Projects

In the meantime Spartan had not been idle in overseas markets. One of Spartan's first sallies into foreign skies was also in Colombia. In 1955 a contract was acquired to photograph much of the Magdalena River valley at a scale of 1:40 000 on behalf of the Tropical Oil Company. This required a flying height of 20 000 feet above mean ground level, which was accomplished by using three Mosquito aircraft over a number of "dry weather" seasons. The high-level capability of the Mosquito was required because of the two mountain ranges that constitute the spine of Colombia. Unfortunately the dry weather season of December to February was also favoured by the farmers as the best time of the year to burn brush, causing a pall of smoke to lie over the entire valley floor. This resulted in many frustrating attempts to obtain suitable photography, and necessitated numerous re-flights.

Spartan went on to obtain major contracts in the Dominican Republic and Argentina, as well as a helicopter contract in Peru. The Argentine contract was interesting in that it required the development of a cadastre of the entire cultivated area – mostly vineyards – of the province of Mendoza and parts of the province of San Juan. Landowners in Mendoza had reported and paid taxes on 800 000 ha of vineyards, and a corresponding number of kilometers of irrigation. However in flying the area Spartan aircraft extended flight lines beyond the expected limits to capture unreported cultivation and irrigation. The total area turned out to be 1 200 000 ha, 50 percent more than originally reported. Since the project had been covered extensively in the news media, the landowners had no option but to report voluntarily cultivation that had not been reported previously. The resulting tax assessments paid for the entire project many times over. Incidentally, Mendoza-produced red wines compare favourably with some of the best red wines of the world.

The Mendoza and San Juan projects led to numerous other contracts in Argentina and bordering countries. The locally incorporated company, Spartan Air Surveys Argentina Ltda., survived successfully for many years under the excellent management of Jorge Glenny, and only gave up its charter when Glenny died prematurely in 1970.

Spartan was also awarded a number of contracts by the U.K. Directorate of Overseas Surveys, including aerial photography projects in the Bahamas, Trinidad and Tobago, and the Seychelles off the east coast of Africa. The Seychelles project called for a seaplane operation, and for this a Norseman was specially equipped in Canada and shipped to the job. Unfortunately it was found that when the weather was clear enough for aerial photography, the wind blew so hard that the resulting seas made it impossible for the Norseman to take off. Many hair-raising attempts were made until the very real threat to life made it necessary to purchase and refit a Grumman Goose, a sturdy amphibious flying boat, as a substitute for the Norseman. The Goose was able to handle the heavy seas and completed the job successfully.

Development Assistance Projects

All of the overseas projects discussed so far in this chapter were financed by sources other than government of Canada international assistance programmes. They are just a small sample of the many projects of this nature carried out in South and Central America, the United States, and Europe, and more recently in the Arab countries, particularly in the Gulf

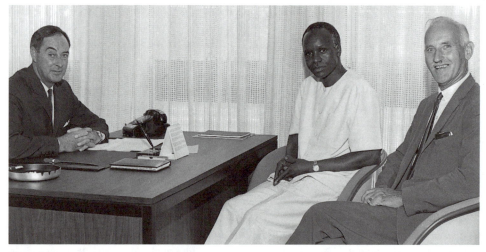

Figure 6-5
A meeting at the office of Spartan Air Service to negotiate a Canadian International Development Agency
project. Left to right: Don McLarty, President of Spartan; His Excellency Gospar Rutabanzebwa, High
Commissioner of Tanzania; Colonel C.H. Smith, Executive Vice-President of Spartan.
Photo: Spartan Archives

states. This has been reported purposely so that the reader may gain a proper perspective
of the many varied and interesting projects undertaken by the Canadian air survey industry
in foreign lands, not necessarily financed by Canadian foreign aid as has been suggested
elsewhere.[8]

There is no question that the foreign assistance projects undertaken by the industry on
behalf of CIDA, and its predecessor organizations, have been of immense value to the
industry in terms of experience gained and utilization of human and other resources. In
many cases it provided firms with a first opportunity to gain overseas experience, which
in turn led to other foreign opportunities. Furthermore most of these contracts have been
in the multimillion-dollar, multi-year category, making them of significant economic importance to the industry.

International development projects in which the Canadian air survey industry participated
in a major way are discussed in chapter 18. It should be noted here, however, that while
such aerial surveys – which were understood to include aerial photography, mapping,
ground control and other surveying, airborne geophysical surveying, and natural resource
studies, singly or in any combination – were of great benefit to the industry, they also were
and are of immense value to the recipient countries. Much of the information generated
by these projects continues to be in daily use on an ongoing basis. Many of these projects
included a training and technology transfer element, and in this way left behind expertise
capable of managing and updating the data.

Unfortunately, current policy rethinking by the government and at senior management
levels of CIDA, coupled with major technological changes occurring within the geomatics
community itself, have brought assistance programmes in this field to a virtual halt. It is
to be hoped that emerging technology can soon be brought to bear to provide even more
valuable data to the developing world.

Figure 6-6
An Aerodist tower in Guyana on a CIDA project.
Photo: Terra Surveys Ltd

Finally it is interesting to note that the aerial surveying firms were the first Canadian service industry to pursue overseas opportunities actively. For many years in the early postwar period it outpaced the engineering community, for example, in terms of foreign exchange earned. Not surprisingly, engineering projects eventually surpassed aerial surveying in terms of sheer size and total dollar volume.

INDUSTRY PROLIFERATION

One problem that had long plagued the industry was the ease with which individuals or non-industry-related companies could claim, and did in fact provide, aerial photography and mapping services. This may best be illustrated by the fact that at a time when only seven professional and experienced aerial photography firms were offering vertical photography for resource study and mapping purposes, 125 aircraft operators had been issued Class 7, Aerial Photography and Survey (APS) licenses by the Air Transport Committee of the Air Transport Board. Furthermore any Class 4 charter operator could convert an aircraft and offer it to anyone owning or leasing a suitable camera.

When it came to mapping, any ambitious individual could purchase expensive mapping equipment on excellent financing terms from the manufacturer, and set up and operate a mapping facility in the basement of his or her home. Political considerations made it difficult to restrict source listing to the well-financed, experienced firms. Indeed some clients were notorious for expanding their source lists as much as possible in order to drive down prices, knowing full well that the operators just starting in business were likely to bid low prices in order to win a job. This difficult situation was exacerbated by most government departments and commissions, which insisted on awarding contracts on the lowest bid price basis.

The end result of these procurement practices and the consequent industry proliferation was a serious overcapacity of aerial photography and mapping services, thereby driving prices ever lower, to the point where the industry was in fact subsidizing government departments. Fortunately over the years some sense did prevail, but not before a number of the industry firms, large and small, suffered serious financial setbacks. Improvements came with the realization that quality work could not be delivered on time under the existing conditions, nor could the industry maintain its competitive edge internationally without generating the funding necessary to embrace emerging technology. Changes came with a new generation of government departmental and procurement managers, some with industry backgrounds, and with more enlightened policies and procedures for contracting out.

Competition

As a result of proliferation and overcapacity, competition for both domestic and overseas work financed by CIDA and its predecessor agencies was fierce. Competition had a habit of feeding on itself. When a firm did secure a major multimillion-dollar overseas project, invariably it required a build-up of equipment and personnel. On completion of the project this additional capacity had to be utilized, resulting in an even lower round of prices the next time a similar project came up for tender.

It was not until the companies came together in consortia, so that existing facilities and human resources could meet the demands of major projects, that some sense was brought to bear on the problem. Strangely, work for foreign governments and some international funding agencies was often won, not on the basis of price alone, but on the merits of the technical proposal and the reputation of the Canadian firm or firms involved.

While originally competition came from within the industry itself, as the information age took hold and computers played a more important role in data processing, others began to make inroads into the traditional roles of aerial surveyors. GIS/LIS, remote sensing, and other related activities have combined to create a geomatics community that now extends far beyond the composition of the early aerial survey industry. Internationally other donor countries have become more active in the developing world. To survive today requires a sympathetic bank manager, an unbridled faith in and understanding of the evolving technology, a commitment to technical ingenuity, and increasingly a willingness to form alliances with others in bidding on projects.

INDUSTRY AND PROVINCIAL MAPPING PROGRAMMES

Provincial topographic mapping is discussed by Lou Sebert in chapter 4. Some of the provincial mapping programmes were and are, however, of particular interest and of considerable benefit to the industry firms. In most cases industry participation in the programmes has been limited to the companies domiciled in the contracting province, although this is changing under pressure of current attempts to bring about interprovincial free trade.

In the early postwar years, Newfoundland, Prince Edward Island, New Brunswick, and Nova Scotia contracted their aerial photography and mapping needs on an ad hoc basis to the lowest bidding firm anywhere in Canada. Much of this work was for highway planning and improvement.

After the formation of the Maritimes Land Registration and Information Service (LRIS) in the early 1960s, most of its work was performed in-house. The related surveying was, however, undertaken by local land surveying firms, and the orthophotograph production was contracted to mapping firms. The first such contract was awarded to Survair Ltd of Ottawa, which had acquired the first commercially operated orthophotoscope in Canada. Later, when Atlantic Air Survey Company Limited procured a Gestalt Photomapper, much of the LRIS orthophoto needs were contracted to that company. LRIS International Corp. was created at a later date in an attempt to capitalize on the organization's experience and sell similar services overseas. This venture did not meet with success, and LRIS International Corp. was subsequently dissolved. Overall there has been no sustained mapping programme involving industry in the Atlantic provinces.

Contract mapping in Québec has been variable over the years. Hydro-Québec has long been a good source of business to the Québec-based industry firms, as has the provincial Department of Energy and Resources and the Ministry of Transport. All was not always honey and roses, however, between the industry firms and the government of Québec. In the mid-1970s the government made an incursion into the commercial field by purchasing the firm Photo-Air Laurentide, subsequently renaming it La Société de Cartographie du Québec. The company competed with industry for all work originating in the province of Québec. Furthermore the company managed to have its name placed on the source list for federal government contracts, including those originating with CIDA. This drew an immediate and strong response from the CAAS which convinced the Minister of Supply and Services that this constituted unfair competition. The company was consequently de-listed. After accumulating many millions of dollars of losses for the provincial government the company was eventually dissolved. Relationships between the industry and the province rapidly improved after this unfortunate event. Starting in 1985 the Québec firms entered into sustained long-term contracts with the provincial government under a ten-year cadastral reform programme. The contracts call for the production of 1:1000 scale digital maps.

Commencing with the major forestry contract awarded to PSC in 1946, Ontario has always been a fertile source of work for the companies based in the province. While some in-house capability existed, for example in the Department of Highways, most provincial aerial photography and mapping needs have been contracted to industry. In the early years each department of the provincial government produced or contracted its mapping requirements to the private sector, virtually uncoordinated insofar as scale, geographic referencing, and duplication were concerned. In the early 1970s the Ontario Ministry of Natural Resources was given the mandate to create a comprehensive geographic referencing system, and to assume responsibility for coordinating provincial mapping standards and needs.

A very important outcome was the Ontario Basic Mapping (OBM) programme initiated in 1978 by then surveyor general and director of Surveying and Mapping, R.G. (Robert)

Code. This was designed to provide map cover of the province at 1:20 000 scale in the sparsely populated areas of Northern Ontario, 1:10 000 in Southern Ontario, and, in partnership with municipalities, 1:2000 of towns and cities. Mapping is now compiled almost wholly in digital format. An extraordinary level of rapport and mutual respect evolved rapidly between those in the government responsible for the programme and the industry firms in three consortia that competed for contracts to expose aerial photography, undertake aerial triangulation, and compile maps photogrammetrically. The programme has been of great benefit to the companies, not only in terms of the business it has generated, but also in assisting them to make the transition to digital technology and, ultimately, GIS/LIS.

The provinces of Manitoba and Saskatchewan have long satisfied their mapping needs by in-house production with the result that a significant private mapping industry has been inhibited in those provinces. Some departments in Alberta contracted their aerial photography and mapping requirements to industry, although much work was accomplished in-house. In 1981 the Alberta Bureau of Surveying and Mapping was created under Alberta Energy and Natural Resources, and this included the mapping functions of Alberta Transportation. At that time contracting-out rules were adopted that required procurement of mapping services on the basis of a proposal rather than the lowest bid. Under this arrangement points were awarded for the management and technical proposal, with the price component valued at approximately 40 percent. Projects contracted to industry included the orthophotomapping of seventy-three communities under the Municipal Integrated Surveying and Mapping (MISAM) programme. The mapping scale was 1:5 000 with 1 m or 0.5 m contours, the contours being derived in later years from photogrammetric digital elevation models. A dense network of survey control markers in each town was also accomplished by contract. In 1983 a 1:20 000 scale digital mapping programme was tested in a pilot project, and contracted to industry fully in the following year. The project, which also required contours interpolated from photogrammetrically derived digital elevation models, was intended to cover Alberta's 650 000 km² in ten years. Coverage of 85 percent of the province had been completed when the programme was suspended in 1993. These various programmes enabled the Alberta industry firms to acquire high quality orthophoto and analytical stereoplotting equipment, as well as the experience necessary to compete in world markets.

The situation was much the same in British Columbia, except that for many years virtually all of the province's aerial photography and mapping requirements were satisfied by in-house provincial facilities. From the early postwar years well into the 1970s, the province owned and operated a fleet of survey-equipped aircraft, crewed and maintained by provincially employed pilots, navigators, camera operators, and engineers. It was not until cost and productivity comparisons were made with the private sector that this practice was discontinued. Significant mapping contracts were let to the industry firms around the same time. The first sustained mapping programme contracted to industry was a ten-year, $20 million project announced by the minister on 13 August 1979. A later initiative involved the ten industry firms located in British Columbia, functioning together under the banner of the provincial chapter of the CAAS led by P.J. (Phil) Boase of the McElhanney Group, and the Surveys and Resource Management Branch of the Ministry of Environment. This resulted in the Terrain Resource Information Management (TRIM) programme, which began in 1986 and is a very sophisticated 1:20 000 scale digital base mapping programme to be undertaken entirely by the British Columbia industry firms. Some 7 000 sheets will be required to complete the project, and the cost has been estimated at between $60 and $70 million. This sustained mapping programme has been of considerable value to the British Columbia segment of the industry.

Some provinces, for example Ontario, required little or no convincing that there would be benefits in having private industry provide the aerial photography, ground control, mapping, and related services needed, rather than have them performed in-house. Other provinces, with long-entrenched in-house facilities, took longer to be convinced. Some have yet to be convinced. However, great strides have been accomplished during the period, to the ultimate benefit by all.

A WORLD-CLASS INDUSTRY

Considering its relatively small size, Canada's air survey industry has enjoyed a number of remarkable achievements over the years. Internationally the mapping of West Pakistan by PSC was a world first. The project required air photography of the entire country, which was then used to create maps at 1:100 000 scale. Land use and soil surveys were recorded on these base maps, as well as geological data of some 330 000 square miles. The entire project required seven years to complete and employed a total staff of about sixty, including twelve geologists. Field parties were moved by helicopter, jeep, and camel. In all it was a remarkable accomplishment.

The first cooperative effort by the industry overseas entailed preparatory surveys and base mapping for the Mekong River project of flood control, irrigation, and hydroelectric power generation on the lower portions of the river. This project involved the six major Canadian air survey companies of that time, and was started in 1959 and lasted until 1964. The Hunting Survey Corporation Limited (formerly PSC) was the lead company, and the project was managed by R.A. (Bob) Brocklebank, Hunting's chief engineer and now president of the McElhanney Group in Vancouver. The Mekong extends from the highlands of Tibet some 4500 kilometers to its low delta flood plain in Vietnam. Along the way this great water highway forms the border between Laos and Thailand, and flows through Cambodia and Vietnam. This was a project of many parts requiring ground control surveys, aerial photography, Airborne Profile Recorder (APR) control at various scales, and the production of 800 topographic map sheets, also at various scales. Included in the ground surveys were 970 km of primary and 2700 km of third-order levelling. The logistics involved in getting a project of this magnitude started and sustained over a lengthy period, as well as the problems to be overcome in running surveys over four countries in South-East Asia, taxe the imagination. It was largely because of the fertile mind of Kendall, who conceived the Canadian involvement in the project, and Brocklebank's superb project management that the venture met with total success.[9]

Of the many hundreds of projects undertaken by the industry all over the world, some stand out. One other such notable project was the contract awarded to Canadian Aero Service Limited by the Canadian government in 1961 under the Special Commonwealth African Assistance Plan. The original contract required aerial photography, ground control surveys, and photogrammetric compilation of ninety-six topographic maps at 1:50 000 scale with fifty feet contours covering 73 000 km^2 of Nigeria. The contract was later extended to include an additional 78 000 km^2 of aerial photography, and 22 000 km^2 of topographical mapping. Some regions of the world have been virtually impossible to photograph from the air because of coverage by constant cloud, haze, or smoke. The region of Nigeria selected for mapping fell into this category. Many attempts had been made to photograph this area over the previous ten years, but all had failed. The problem was that on days when the constant cloud cover was driven out to sea by northern winds, the clouds were immediately replaced by harmattan haze, which consisted of moisture droplets and fine Sahara sand, impossible to penetrate using standard aerial photography procedures. The heaviest layer of haze lay between 12 000 and 20 000 feet. To be forced to use conventional wide-angle aerial photography exposed below the base of the harmattan haze would have made the ground control and mapping phases of the project exorbitantly expensive. Zarzycki, then chief engineer of Canadian Aero, evolved a unique solution to the problem by combining the use of a Wild RC 9 aerial camera equipped with a super-wide-angle 3.5 inch Super-Infragon lens and black-and-white infrared film, with a Wild Horizon Camera and a Wild Statoscope. Radan-Doppler was used for navigation. This integrated system permitted aerial photography to be obtained from 11 600 feet at an economic mapping scale of 1:40 000. The Horizon Camera helped to establish differential tilt and tip of the aerial photography camera at the moment of exposure, whilst the Statoscope registered the difference in elevation at each exposure station with respect to a reference barometric altitude, thus reducing the amount of costly ground control required for the mapping process.[10]

These overseas projects are mentioned here to emphasize the stature and recognition Canada's air survey industry earned worldwide. Also acclaimed internationally and at home were a number of other typically Canadian solutions to difficult operational problems owing to Canadian climatic conditions, vast distances, and accessibility.

Shoran Surveys in Northern Canada

A consortium of Spartan Air Services Limited and Canadian Aero Service Limited was awarded a contract by the ASE for geodetic control by Shoran trilateration, described in chapter 2, and a grid of Shoran-controlled photography combined with airborne profile recorder control. This method provided all control required for photogrammetric mapping and compilation of topographical maps at a scale of 1:250 000. All the data reduction, geodetic computations, and adjustments were performed by the companies' engineers. A total of 1 300 000 km² of northern Canada was covered by Shoran control between 1952 and 1955. The experience and know-how gained on this project were to become important Canadian exports.

The Airborne Profile Recorder (APR)

The APR is a typical example of a private company taking an experimental instrument developed in a government laboratory at NRC, improving it, and bringing it to a stage where it can be put to practical applications commercially. The APR consists of a three-centimetre radar from which the signal is transmitted by a parabolic reflector under the aircraft. The signal is sent from the aircraft, reflected by the ground, and received by the reflector. By measuring the time of the signal's journey, the height of the aircraft can be calculated. By running a series of measurements the profile of land can be determined along the flight track.

PSC of Toronto experimented with APR for some time, introduced important improvements, particularly to the height corrector component of the instrument, and developed data-reduction techniques. The company manufactured several instruments that have been employed in APR surveys, not only in Canada but also in the U.S., Africa, Australia, and South and Central America.

The Gestalt Photomapper (GPM)

Canada's air survey industry proved to be innovative not only in employing and improving existing technology, but also in developing new technology. The prime example is the Gestalt Photomapper. As early as 1959, G.L. (Gil) Hobrough, then associated with PSC of Toronto, developed an automatic image correlator and installed it on a Kelsh stereoplotter, thus introducing the world's first automatic photogrammetric instrument. This plotter was capable of drawing contour lines automatically. It was the beginning of Gestalt.

In 1967 Hobrough formed Hobrough Limited in Vancouver, and began developing the GPM for commercial applications. In September 1970 the first orthophotographs were produced fully automatically by electronic means based on a digital terrain model. This technological breakthrough had profound influence on future developments in photogrammetry, and was the forerunner of today's digital photogrammetric workstations. Amongst the GPM instruments shipped overseas was one purchased by the Instituto Geografico Agustin Codazzi, the national mapping organization of Colombia. This was used in the cadastral pilot project in Bogota for which Dr Blachut of NRC was the advisor. For his invention of the GPM, the International Society for Photogrammetry and Remote Sensing awarded Hobrough the prestigious Brock medal in 1980.

There have been many other notable achievements unique to Canada's air survey industry including, for example, Zarzycki's development of a survey system employing Aerodist technology to establish first-order geodetic networks. Unfortunately space does not permit all industry achievements being discussed here. However there is one other series of events that originated with the early days of the industry and resulted in a major Canadian technology success story, which is not generally known and deserves to be told.

From PSC Applied Research Limited to Spar Aerospace Limited

Realizing the rapidly growing importance of electronics to the business, the Photographic Survey Corporation Limited formed a research and development company named PSC Applied Research Limited in 1948. This company was responsible for the development of a number of airborne geophysical instruments, as well as the improvements to the APR. From these early beginnings the company grew very rapidly into developing and producing several sophisticated items for the Canadian Armed Forces. These included the R-Theta Navigator, a truly state-of-the-art breakthrough in analog computerization. The R-Theta Navigator was to become the highly advanced navigation system for the Canadian CF-100 fighter aircraft. By 1956 the company had 300 professionals on staff, almost equally divided between research and production personnel. It had also become a training ground for many successful future executives.

It was the success of the R-Theta Navigator that eventually caused the company to be sold. New orders for the Navigator would have required the company not only to increase staff from 300 to 650, but also acquire new premises and other facilities. PSC was reluctant to take these steps; at the same time, A.V. Roe was eager to move into space technology. A convenient sale of PSC Applied Research Limited to A.V. Roe was therefore negotiated, and the company was renamed Canadian Applied Research Limited (CARL). Unfortunately A.V. Roe ran into trouble when production of the Arrow aircraft was cancelled. As a result CARL was sold to De Havilland Canada. De Havilland had a small division known as the Special Products Division into which CARL was merged to form the SPAR (Special Projects Applied Research) division, under the able management of Larry Clark. This was eventually spun off into a public company. Thus was born SPAR Aerospace Limited, which has grown from strength to strength and never looked back. One of SPAR's most notable achievements is the manipulator arm, highly visible on the U.S. space shuttles. SPAR Aerospace Limited is just one of a number of success stories originating with Canada's air survey industry, a business that over the years, has "done Canada proud."

GIAC AND THE FUTURE

When the CAAS changed its name in 1987 to the GIAC, it did so in recognition of the need for one association to embrace all sectors of the spatial information business. The term "geomatics" is defined as "the field of scientific and engineering activities involved in the application of computer and communication technologies to the capture, storage, analysis, presentation, distribution and management of spatial information to support decision making"[11] – quite a mouthful, and a quantum leap from "aerial surveying." New and evolving technologies such as remote sensing from space, digital image processing, GPS, land/ geographic information systems, and software development have radically changed the nature and future of the industry. While the scope of activities has grown in leaps and bounds, and new opportunities seem limitless, at the same time new challenges and difficult decisions face the surviving firms of the air survey industry. Many new players have entered the data acquisition phase of the business, and others are involved in data processing and presentation. Jet-prop and pure jet aircraft, forward motion compensation cameras, and GPS navigation systems have changed aerial photography activities dramatically. Digital data acquisition and presentation in tape, orthophoto, and other forms, including GIS/LIS, have similarly added exciting new dimensions to the mapping process.

However the new and evolving technologies may blur the history of Canada's air survey industry, its important influence on the development of Canada and the world will never be diminished. And the people, unfortunately not all named here, who had the imagination, the far-sightedness and the courage to guide the many firms that have made up the industry over the years deserve the recognition of those who follow. Much can be learned from their many achievements.

The integration of disciplines and the move towards globalization of activities means the adoption of new and forceful strategies if Canada is to maintain a leading international role in the total field of geomatics. Governments and industry must work closely together and be prepared to form alliances when appropriate to capitalize on opportunities abroad. Given good will and cooperation, Canada's richly deserved international reputation in the field, both old and new, can be continued.

ACKNOWLEDGMENTS

In writing this chapter I accept full responsibility for errors of fact, real or perceived bias, and omissions of important events. I have shamelessly refreshed my memory from readings of Don W. Thomson's previous publications, particularly "Skyview Canada" and "Window on the Third World." I thank Joan Kendall for allowing me to quote from Douglas Kendall's memoirs. I have had numerous communications from many individuals who have made important contributions to various sections of the chapter. Risking the omission of some, I particularly want to thank the following: George Zarzycki for his help with a number of sections; Bob Brocklebank for background on the Mekong River survey; Harry Godfrey for details of the early days of PSC; Mike Toomey and Bob Batterham for information on Alberta's mapping programmes; Gary Sawayama and Brian Foley for details of British Columbia's TRIM programme; Al Daykin for background on Maritimes matters; Fred Welter for information on aircraft; Robert Fowler for an insightful look into the future; and Doug MacKay and Roy Depper for a look into the past. Special thanks are due to Ed Kennedy for the use of an office and access to CAAS and GIAC files; and last but not least, to Melanie Hudson for corrections to my spelling and for a first edit and production of the manuscript.

NOTES

1 Thomson, D.W. 1975. *Skyview Canada. A Story of Aerial Photography in Canada.* Ottawa: Department of Energy, Mines and Resources Canada.

2 Stretton, W.D. 1982. From Compass to Satellite. *The Canadian Surveyor*, 36, 4, 183–203.

3 Zarzycki, J.M. 1981. History of Jet Photographic Operations for Mapping in Canada. *The Canadian Surveyor*, 35, 4, 387–94.

4 Lapp, P.A., A.A. Marsan, and L.J. O'Brien. 1978. *Report of the Task Force on National Surveying and Mapping.* Ottawa: SMB, EMR, 95–99.

5 Blachut, T.J. 1959. Use of Photogrammetry in the Legal Survey Project at Alnwick. *The Canadian Surveyor*, 14, 8, 336–49; Andrews, G.S. 1960. Some Statutory Aspects in Cadastral Use of Photogrammetry. *The Canadian Surveyor*, 15, 5, 309–16; Moore, R.E. 1962. The Cornwall Island Project – Photogrammetric Methods Used: Accuracies Attained. *The Canadian Surveyor*, 16, 5, 243–47.

6 Kendall, Douglas. *From My Memory.* Toronto: private publication. By kind permission of his widow, Joan.

7 Mott, P.G. 1958. Airborne Surveying in the Antarctic. *Geographical Journal*, 124, 1; Mott, P.G. 1958. Falkland Islands Dependencies Survey Expedition. *Photogrammetric Record*, 2, 11, 309–29; Mott, P.G. 1959. The Modern Approach to Mapping in Cold Climates. *Proceedings, Commonwealth Survey Officers Conference.* Paper 23. London: Directorate of Overseas Surveys.

8 McLaughlin, J., S. Nichols, A. Wood, and T. Bezanson. 1993. A Review of the Canadian Geomatics Industry. *Geomatica*, 47, 2, 106.

9 Brocklebank, R.A. 1961. Mekong River Survey. *The Canadian Surveyor*, 15, 7, 402–10.

10 Zarzycki, J.M. 1963. Super-infragon Photography and Auxiliary Data on a Mapping Program for Nigeria. *The Canadian Surveyor*, 17, 1, 13–26; Zarzycki, J.M. 1963. Experience with a New Mapping System Employed on a Topographical Survey in Nigeria. *Proceedings, Conference of Commonwealth Survey Officers.* Paper 50. London: Directorate of Overseas Surveys.

11 Kennedy, E.A. President, Geomatics Industry Association of Canada. December, 1997. Personal communication.

CHAPTER SEVEN

Cadastral Surveys in Canada

Alec McEwen

CADASTRAL SURVEYING

What Is a Cadastral Survey?

Cadastral is an adjective that is not familiar to most Canadians, and even within the land surveying profession in this country the word was little used outside Québec until about thirty years ago. Of Greek origin, *cadastre* originally meant a tax register, arranged according to individual land parcels. Nowadays a cadastre is capable of serving a variety of purposes for society, but its two basic elements remain the same: the accurate identification of the location of each land parcel, and a recording or registration system by which the ownership and other legal rights affecting the parcel can be determined readily. Since the law declares that there is no land in Canada that does not have an owner, it follows that every land parcel, whether owned by a private person or by a public authority, must also have boundaries that are legally defined. In practice, however, both ownership and boundaries may be difficult to ascertain at times. Boundary uncertainties can usually be removed by the skilled services of cadastral surveyors, acting in cooperation with the legal profession, but in the final analysis boundary disputes can be settled only by the courts or by special statutory procedures where they exist. There is no single cadastral system in Canada, with respect to either the mathematical survey framework or the registration of land rights. Each of the provinces and territories, as well as the federal government, makes provision in its laws for the cadastral surveying and the availability of land ownership information for all the real property (or real estate) within its jurisdiction.

Cadastral Applications

Because the cadastral structure is based on the individual land parcel, it lends itself very well to the superimposition of all types of land-related information. A multi-purpose cadastre can now be regarded as part of a Land Information System (LIS), in which the land parcel units form the building blocks for the identification, storage, manipulation, and retrieval of computerized data. Historically a cadastre can be divided into three main categories: fiscal, legal, and economic.

A fiscal cadastre is a system by which the economic value of each land parcel is assessed and recorded for land taxation by the municipal or other taxing authority. Each parcel is identified by its street address, subdivision lot or quarter-section number, or by some other appropriate method, so that its size, shape, and dimensions can be calculated or estimated. Changes of ownership that result from dealings in land are entered to ensure that the record is kept continuously up to date. Buildings on the land parcel, and other improvements, may also be taxed. Because of the close relationship between fiscal land records and the registration of land title, the two cadastral structures could be combined to serve both functions. In Canada, however, they are usually kept separate and administered by different levels or departments of government.

A legal cadastre is a public record of individual land parcels that contains a reliable description of the location and boundaries of each parcel and identifies its owner. It also lists all legal claims against the property, such as mortgages and easements, together with the name of the respective claimant. In Canada there are two types of legal cadastre: deeds recording and title registration. Deeds recording exists exclusively in Newfoundland, Nova Scotia, Prince Edward Island, and Québec, and partially in New Brunswick, Ontario, and Manitoba. Land titles registration, or the Torrens system as it is often called, exists exclusively in Saskatchewan, Alberta, British Columbia, Yukon, and the Northwest Territories, and partially in New Brunswick, Ontario, and Manitoba. Deeds recording provides evidence, but not necessarily proof, of land ownership or other legal right. Any competing claims to the same land are given priority according to their recorded date. Title searching under a deeds recording system can be laborious, inefficient, and costly, and in some Canadian provinces it relies solely on an index of owners' names rather than on a geographical index of uniquely numbered land parcels. Land title registration provides an assurance or warranty by the government that a registered owner is in fact the true proprietor of the land described in the certificate of title, subject to such mortgage or other legal claims, if any, as are specified in the register. Searching under a land titles system is relatively simple because virtually all the required information appears on the register, and all land parcels are indexed by unique identifiers, not by the names of owners.

An economic cadastre is essentially an inventory that includes such information as land utilization, soil classification, agricultural or other potential, population density, and environmental factors. This information may be displayed textually or graphically, as attributes of the cadastral base for a particular region, parcel, or group of parcels. Economic cadastre is an expression not commonly used in Canada, for in this country it is normally regarded as an adjunct to the legal or the fiscal cadastre, or as a component of an LIS. This may be contrasted, for example, with the situation in the independent countries that formed part of the Soviet Union where, in the absence of private land ownership or land taxation, no legal or fiscal cadastre existed, yet economic information was recorded at the provincial and county levels for all local land occupancies, enclosures, and open spaces.

Cadastral Detail

Cadastral detail may be shown on either a plan or a map. A cadastral plan is a graphic representation of the extent of title, either by the creation of new parcels, as in a registered subdivision, or by the identification and description of existing individual parcels and their boundaries. It has a legal or a quasi-legal status. A cadastral plan necessarily covers a small geographical extent, and although it is sometimes required to be integrated with the provincial or national control survey network, its primary purpose is to show the correct relationship between one parcel of land and its neighbours. The cadastral plan is the principal form of representing individual parcels in Canada. In contrast a cadastral map provides a graphical index of many parcels. It is normally integrated with survey control, and covers an area that is limited in extent only by the chosen map scale and the size of the map sheet. It is commonly in planimetric form, that is it does not show topographical information such as rivers and streams, except where they form a parcel boundary. Since the 1970s the cadastral map has become an important element in modernizing and automating land registration, and many thousands have been produced. This began in the Maritimes and gradually spread to other provinces. Since cadastral maps in Canada are designed and used mainly for indexing and identifying land parcels, they do not have the same legal status as cadastral plans. The exception is Québec where the new civil code gives them a special evidentiary recognition with respect to the parcel boundaries they portray. Another distinguishing feature of the cadastral map is that its use is not confined to parcel indexing for land titles, as it also serves a variety of purposes that include property assessment, land use planning, the design of municipal services, and real estate. The importance of the cadastral map is illustrated by sales in New Brunswick during 1992–93. Hard-copy cadastral (or property) maps comprised half of the sales of provincial and federal National Topographic System (NTS) hard-copy maps by the five regional Registry and Mapping offices in the province. If the sales of digital data are included, the hard-copy and digital cadastral maps represented 45 percent of total sales.

A cadastre may be classified as graphical or numerical, according to the type of detail it displays. A graphical cadastre portrays each parcel in its correct geographical relationship to adjacent parcels, but does not show the numerical dimensions, bearings, or surface area of the parcel. This information can be scaled from the cadastral map to an accuracy that is sufficient for many purposes. A graphical cadastral map is easy to read and comparatively inexpensive to produce. It normally depicts parcel limits as general boundaries, that is to say, boundaries that are defined on the ground by physical features such as fences, walls, hedges, or ditches. Under the general boundaries system the exact position of a boundary line is not precisely defined, but it can be established by adjoining owners if they wish, at their own expense. Although graphical cadastres are common in England and in some other parts of the world, their principal application in Canada is in the province of Québec.

A numerical cadastre displays the dimensions, bearings, and surface area of each parcel. It may also show the coordinates of each boundary corner or provide grid lines from which those coordinates can be scaled approximately. Some cadastral maps do not contain this coordinate information, but it is available from a separate record. A numerical map must be presented at a fairly large scale to permit the measurements to be read clearly. Because of its greater detail the numerical map is more complicated and more costly to produce than the graphical map. The mathematical information is obtained from actual field measurements, which adds to the time and expense needed to complete a numerical cadastre. Numerical cadastres are found in many countries where precise mathematical boundary information is usually required, and they are by far the most common type of cadastre in Canada. A numerical cadastre portrays parcel limits as fixed boundaries. This means that the parcel boundaries are mathematically established to a specified accuracy at the time of the field survey. But the boundaries are not fixed permanently, for they can be changed after the survey as a result of land transfer or other legal process.

Cadastral Survey Systems

The historical and geographical patterns of land surveys to support property rights in Canada can be divided into four main groups:
• Irregular-shaped parcels
• Seigneuries and river lots
• Concession and lot townships
• Rectangular sectional townships
It is tempting, but not quite accurate, to say that the progress in Canada from an early patchwork of sometimes crudely surveyed, frequently unconnected, individual parcels toward a more scientific, orderly layout of rectangular township sections lay entirely in an east-west direction; and that surveying and land subdivision techniques tended to improve as settlement advanced westward across the country. One need only look, however, at the extreme ends of Canada, Newfoundland and British Columbia, to discover examples of isolated surveys as well as rectangular townships. In both provinces the rugged topography restricted the widespread employment of regular geometric designs to carve up land for Crown grant and private conveyance. Nonetheless it is generally the case in Canada that the older, necessarily more primitive, surveys of the late eighteenth and early nineteenth centuries took place in areas of the country that are, or were, subject to deeds recording only. Even where both systems of land ownership records exist, as they still do in Ontario, for example, the surveying methods used to provide plans and descriptions for title registration were for many years virtually the same as those supporting the identification and location of parcel boundaries in the less illustrious deeds registries. Yet the common but erroneous belief that title registration carries assurances of the accuracy of boundaries and acreages no doubt contributes to the view held by many people that the greater the certainty of a parcel's registered title, the more precisely defined must be its boundaries.

IRREGULAR-SHAPED PARCELS
There is no inherent superiority in the design of land parcels that have a rectangular or other regular shape. Where land is open for alienation there may be a clear advantage in using natural features such as rivers or watersheds as title boundaries. But even where no obvious natural boundary features occur, the preference of a prospective purchaser may rest upon other considerations, for example drainage, soil characteristics, vegetation, and tree cover. The main problem with irregular-shaped parcels is not their irregularity, but their historical tendency to be isolated pieces of land that have been alienated and surveyed sporadically. Newfoundland offers innumerable instances of land grants and conveyances that are separated physically from their neighbours, and have never been mathematically connected to one another by field surveys. The mountainous terrain did not readily adapt itself to systematic land allocation or to coordinated surveys, and the rectangular township system introduced in the late 1800s was abandoned after a few years of operation.[1] Similarly in British Columbia, where rectangular townships have only a limited application, the prescribed layout is the district lot system in which the individual lots, though normally

required by the Land Act to be rectangular with boundaries running true north, south, east, and west, are permitted to have variations in shape and orientation where the topography makes the normal layout impracticable.

SEIGNEURIES AND RIVER LOTS
Although the seigneuries in Québec and the river lots in Manitoba were laid out as geometrical figures, they had no uniform size and were originally surveyed as long, narrow parcels fronting on a major river. No new seigneuries were created after 1854, by which time the quadrilateral township, divided into concessions, or tiers, of lots, had become well established in Québec, as it had in southern Ontario.

CONCESSION AND LOT TOWNSHIPS
The early years saw a variety of these township systems, each with its own mathematical peculiarities and imperfections. Roads, theoretically placed along parallel reservations at preordained intervals, disregarded topographical suitability and frequently proved impossible to construct in their legally assigned locations. In some townships the interior lot lines were not run during the original survey, and it is often unclear whether they were eventually established on the ground by qualified land surveyors or by the owners of adjoining lots.

RECTANGULAR SECTIONAL TOWNSHIPS
Although rectangular townships are found in other parts of Canada, they are primarily associated with the three Prairie provinces. Strictly speaking it is incorrect to describe them as rectangular for, except where fractional layouts occur, each township forms a trapezoid enclosed by two converging meridians of longitude and two chords to parallels of latitude. Of the three township systems adopted for the surveys of Dominion (now Canada) Lands, the third is by far the most important. It is the most recent, though now seldom-used, method of subdividing unsurveyed territory within federal and much provincial and territorial jurisdiction. It also covers more geographical area than all the other Dominion Lands Survey systems combined. Although the pressure to accommodate settlers forced the pace of many township surveys, they provided a very reliable framework for the allocation of land parcels, and boundary disputes and litigation are less frequent under the township system than in the older parts of the country.

Resurveys

The object of the Dominion Lands Survey systems, like that of the earlier township layouts of eastern Canada, was to provide a simple, rapid, and relatively inexpensive method of placing settlers on parcels of land. These should be identified readily and unmistakably, both on the ground for individual occupation and in public offices for deeds recording or title registration. This initial object having been achieved, an ensuing problem was the retracement of original survey lines and the restoration of original survey monuments in situations where there was uncertainty or dispute concerning the true location of a particular boundary. For this purpose statutes under which townships were laid out contain provisions, supplemented by regulations and official manuals of instruction, to guide the surveyor in undertaking resurveys. Where no specific statutory direction exists for the resurveying of old boundaries, recourse must be had to the principles of the common law or the Québec civil codes, and also to the by-laws or rules of practice of the appropriate land surveyors' association.

One of the greatest challenges facing the surveyor during resurvey work is the problem of reconciling the facts of physical occupation with official plans and title or deed records. The imperfections of early surveys and boundary descriptions in the deeds-recording areas of Canada tend to become cured as boundaries stabilize through the beneficial effects of adverse possession, or acquisitive prescription in Québec. Provided all the elements of such possession are proved, this allows fences or other evidence of occupation to become the accepted limits of ownership. Even for land held under title registration, where adverse possession is normally inapplicable, a surveyor may not be safe in disregarding fences or other occupational limits that do not closely coincide with theoretical measurements. A distinction must be drawn between a fence, for example, that was never intended to define a boundary and one that provides the most reliable evidence of an original monument's position. Herein lies the key to cadastral resurveys, the object of which is to re-establish boundaries as they were actually run during the original survey, not to locate boundaries where they would have been placed had the original survey been mathematically perfect. Despite the differences of boundary legislation and surveying practice that prevail throughout Canada, the fundamental principle that original lines and monuments, or their exact positional replacements, control the location of the boundaries they were intended to mark is of nationwide application.

Technical Standards

Although the employment of current sophisticated technology for the surveying of new land parcels significantly lessens the possibility of boundary discrepancies, even the application of such technology cannot by itself solve problems of re-establishing older work. In cadastral boundary resurveys it is knowing where to place the boundary that is to be measured, not the actual technique of measuring it, that imposes the greatest demand on the land surveyor's professional training and judgement.

Yet the improvement of surveying techniques since the end of the Second World War has changed dramatically the manner in which cadastral surveys are undertaken, both in the field and in the office. The traditional method of surveying property boundaries used a theodolite and steel tape, and this continued for more than twenty years after the war. This has been replaced almost entirely by the use of electronic equipment that is suitable for the measurement of short lines in cadastral surveys. Versions of the Geodimeter and Tellurometer instruments, which operated in the visible and microwave portions of the spectrum respectively and were suitable for the measurement of short lines, were introduced in the mid-1960s. A further important development was the introduction of electromagnetic distance measurement in the infrared part of the spectrum, a technique that was adopted quickly by Canadian cadastral surveyors.[2] Electronic equipment is now represented by the Total Station, which was introduced in the early 1980s and allows both angles and distances to be measured electronically by a single instrument. This modern technology permits the design and layout of subdivisions, for example, to be pre-computed and executed to a degree of accuracy that meets or exceeds all realistic standards for the mathematical positioning of parcel boundaries. It has also helped increase productivity, thereby helping moderate the rising costs of cadastral surveys.

For about twenty-five years after the war the computation and adjustment of survey traverses and other field observations was undertaken laboriously with the assistance of trigonometric tables and mechanical, later electrical, desk calculators. Cadastral surveyors took early advantage of the power of hand calculators, and several manufacturers developed survey programs for the programmable hand calculators that were introduced during the early 1970s and were in vogue for a number of years.[3] So also were desktop computers pressed into use in cadastral surveying from about 1970. Larger surveying firms began to utilize minicomputers during the late 1970s, but more significant was the availability of microcomputers in the early 1980s. Software has been developed in Canada for use on microcomputers in computing and adjusting survey traverses, and computing and plotting radiations, coordinate transformations, setting out, and other aspects of cadastral surveys, for example the software packages COGO85, GEM, Geopan, and Smart COGO. Similar advances have occurred in the preparation of cadastral plans. The older practices relied on freehand drawing with mechanical aids, and the use of laborious mechanical lettering sets until preprinted, self-adhesive lettering became available. The major transformation came in the 1980s with computer-aided drafting (CAD) software packages operating on micro-computers. These have led to a more rapidly produced and higher quality representation of parcel boundaries, in either digital or hard-copy form, than was ever possible using the older practices. Of increasing importance is the applicability of the Global Positioning System (GPS) to cadastral surveys. While the employment of this satellite technology to determine boundary location is not yet widespread in Canada, its potential is already demonstrated for the surveys of large areas such as national parks or aboriginal land claims. As this equipment becomes more familiar to land surveyors and less expensive to purchase, its use for even small surveys can be expected to increase. Some Canadian jurisdictions already permit the use of GPS for cadastral surveys in certain circumstances. For example section 16 of the Alberta Survey Regulation states that if the ordinary method of survey is impractical, the provincial director of surveys may direct that public land be surveyed by fixing the corners of parcels by reference to survey control markers of the geographical positioning system.

SERVING THE PUBLIC

Role of the Cadastral Surveyor

The cadastral surveyor's principal role is to contribute to the identification and stability of real property ownership by providing professional services and informed opinions regarding boundary location. Even when called upon to establish a new boundary on the ground, the surveyor cannot do so by measurements and monuments alone. There must be a valid land transaction, a statutory process, or some other act that the law recognizes as sufficient to create a boundary before it can come into legal existence. In the retracement of a boundary that is already legally established, the surveyor's responsibility is to undertake a thorough investigation and assessment of all the available field and office evidence that will enable the surveyor to give an opinion as to the boundary's correct location. Whether surveying new or old boundaries, the cadastral surveyor is obligated to act honestly and impartially, without favour to employer or client, as part of the professional duty to serve and protect the public's interest in knowing the limits of individual land holdings.

Cadastral services for legal purposes include:

- Subdivision surveys, which may involve the planning and designing of lots, streets, parks, and other open spaces, the submission of proposed subdivision plans for municipal and other official approval, the registration of the final plan, and the surveying and monumenting of lot boundaries
- Lot or parcel surveys, in which the boundaries of an individual property are measured, and a monument is placed at each corner
- Surveyor's Real Property Report, sometimes referred to as a Building Location Certificate, which is required by a purchaser, or by a person to whom a lot or parcel is mortgaged, to obtain assurance that buildings and other structures are within the property boundaries. It indicates on a plan the extent of any encroachments or easements affecting the property, the boundary measurements and bearings, the legal description of the land, the municipal address where applicable, and the designation of adjacent properties, streets, lanes, etcetera
- Right of way surveys, for easements, transmission lines, and other utility services, that show on a plan the dimensions of the right of way and its relationship to the boundaries of the properties through which it passes
- Boundary descriptions, in textual or graphical form, to show clearly and unambiguously for title registration or deeds recording the identity and geographical location of the land described
- Boundary litigation, in which the cadastral surveyor may be called as an expert witness to give testimony in cases involving disputed property boundaries

Why Consumers Need Cadastral Surveys

The employment of a cadastral surveyor may arise from an owner's desire to subdivide and sell land, or to know the exact location of property boundaries. For many individual consumers, however, a cadastral survey represents not a desire but a requirement that must be satisfied to obtain, for example, the approval of a mortgage by a lending institution or a building permit from a municipal government. A cadastral survey contributes to the security of land ownership by indicating the actual physical location and extent of the legal title under which it is held. Not only does the survey provide assurance to owners, lending institutions, and other interested parties, it also facilitates conveyancing or transfers of ownership and legal interests in land. From a societal point of view integrated cadastral surveys create a parcel-based framework to which other types of land-related data can be attached to create an LIS from which governments, corporations, and individual members of the public derive ultimate benefit.

CADASTRAL REFORM

As noted briefly in chapter 1, Canada's post–Second World War expansion was characterized by massive immigration and a burgeoning economy as it moved from being a predominantly rural society to become a major industrial competitor in world markets. Expansion also led to increased land values and to corresponding demands for improved cadastral services. Among the more striking developments across the nation was the survey and subdivision of large areas of vacant land for residential, commercial, industrial, and recreational purposes, and the replacement of rectangular residential street patterns by more imaginative designs. The latter were not only aesthetically pleasing, but also produced safer communities and savings in road construction costs.

At the same time, shortcomings were revealed in metes and bounds descriptions where the boundaries of a parcel were defined by words, frequently without the existence of or any requirement for an accompanying plan that illustrated the parcel. This applied particularly to the severance of parcels from tracts of land where no new official subdivision plan was created to give each new unit an identifying lot number. A number of jurisdictions introduced the requirement for the registration of a reference plan. This was based on actual survey, and identified clearly the boundaries of the new land units. It helped to avoid gaps and overlaps between adjacent titles, and to obviate the need to plot the boundaries of a number of severances from, for example, an original quarter-section in order to discover the location and extent of the remaining land. In deeds-recording provinces especially, where the deposit of a survey plan to accompany a land transaction is not always required, the increasing availability of large-scale property mapping, constructed from air photography, facilitates the processes of conveyancing and registration. Three outstanding examples of the reform of title registration/deeds recording are the pioneering work of the Land Registration and Information Service (LRIS) in the three Maritime provinces, the ongoing Province of Ontario Land Registration and Information Service (POLARIS) project, and the current renovation of the Québec cadastre. These three will be described in more detail.

Progress toward replacing the local deeds-recording system by land title registration received impetus in Ontario as a result of Law Reform Commission recommendations in 1971, and also in New Brunswick where a pilot land titles project was completed in 1987. Yukon and the Northwest Territories have each enacted a Land Titles Act to replace the previous federal statute. Recommendations for a simplified Model Land Titles Act that could be introduced by any interested jurisdiction were presented in 1990[4] by a committee consisting of representatives from the two territories and all provinces except Québec and Newfoundland. Additional recommendations are contained in the committee's final revisions in 1993.[5] The Alberta Law Reform Institute has proposed provincial legislation along the lines recommended by the joint committee, and some other western provinces are considering similar proposals. The first practical implementation of model land titles legislation is an Alberta regulation that established the Metis Settlements Land Registry in 1991.

Despite the very real progress that has been made in some jurisdictions, cadastral reform is proving to be a slow process. This is especially the case with the conversion of deeds recording to land titles registration. As a consequence no reliable completion dates can be given at present. In Ontario, for example, it took almost eight years for the Ministry of Consumer and Commercial Relations to move from the Law Reform Commission's recommendations to the development of an improved land registration system for Ontario.[6] This established the architectural plan for POLARIS and set the province on the road to the concurrent modernization of the deeds-recording and land titles systems. In western Canada, where the land titles system operates well, the need for improvement may seem to be less obvious. Neverthless cadastral reform there includes parcel mapping, the automation of records, the development of a cadastral spatial database, and, in Alberta, the partial privatization of the Land Titles Office by the creation of local registries. At present these registries offer only searching and copying services, but may eventually be given additional powers and responsibilities.

Aboriginal land claims, both in the form of comprehensive claims based on aboriginal title and special claims based on treaty obligations, are a fertile field for cadastral survey, especially in the two territories where vast areas of land are now recognized as the property of First Nations. The management of these lands, as well as of the more than 2500 reserves within the jurisdiction of the Indian Act, presents challenges and opportunities for instituting new methods of boundary survey and title registration that are appropriate for traditional societies. One example is the establishment of a special land registry system in 1986 to serve Cree and Naskapi communities in northern Québec.

CADASTRAL SURVEYING INSTITUTIONS

Both the nature and role of federal and provincial cadastral surveying agencies have undergone dramatic changes since the Second World War. The laying out of townships and other large tracts of land for settlement has virtually disappeared. This has given way to such activities as maintaining the boundaries of Crown lands and performing or examining surveys and plans prepared for or by other users. Perhaps the most significant development has been the expansion of cadastral surveying organizations into non-traditional areas such as control surveys, topographic mapping, remote sensing, and Geographic Information Systems (GIS). In many jurisdictions there is a movement away from the performance of all government cadastral surveys by in-house staff to contracting such work to industry. Increasingly the role of the institution is one of regulating, setting technical standards, undertaking research and development, and examining or approving surveys and plans made by private surveyors. Indeed even the routine examination of all survey plans for title purposes has tended to be replaced, in some instances, by a system of random plan checking and field inspection that is symptomatic of a greater government reliance on the professional competence and integrity of the private practitioner. Also noteworthy is the decentralization during the 1970s of the cadastral surveying organizations of Natural Resources Canada and Public Works Canada, leading to the establishment of regional survey offices across the country. This allows departmental services to be more responsive to local needs, and gives regional surveyors a certain measure of autonomy in deciding work priorities and allocating resources.

Most cadastral surveying institutions in Canada are administered by a director of surveys or an officer with a similar designation. The old and honourable title of Surveyor General survives only in the Legal Surveys Division of Natural Resources Canada, in Ontario, and in British Columbia. It is a statutory appointment, and the incumbent may have an additional title for administrative purposes.

National and Regional Organizations

LEGAL SURVEYS DIVISION, NATURAL RESOURCES CANADA
This division, a component of Geomatics Canada, is administered by the surveyor general of Canada Lands and traces its origin to the year 1871. Its principal function is to perform, regulate, examine, and approve surveys and plans of lands defined by the Canada Lands

Surveys Act, and to maintain official records of them. It also undertakes similar duties relating to some other lands over which the federal or a territorial government exerts jurisdiction. One of the division's most important services is that provided to the Department of Indian Affairs and Northern Development, to satisfy survey and boundary description requirements concerning both Indian reserves and aboriginal land claims. Another major client is Parks Canada, with respect to surveys of national parks and national historic sites.

A significant organizational change took place in 1972 when the division decentralized its field operations to provide an improved service to local clientele. Regional surveyor offices were established in nine locations: Vancouver, Edmonton, Regina, Winnipeg, Toronto, Sherbrooke, Amherst, Yellowknife, Whitehorse. Regional surveyors were given certain delegated powers but the surveyor general remained responsible for their work. Most survey work initiated by the division is performed by private industry under contract. All surveys of Canada Lands, as well as surveys of mineral claims in the two territories, must be undertaken in accordance with instructions issued by the surveyor general.[7] The surveyor general also chairs the board of examiners for Canada Lands Surveyors, an appointed body responsible for examining candidates for admission to practice, for issuing a commission to each candidate who completes the requirements, and for dealing with instances of professional misconduct. As a result of recent legislation the board will disappear and its functions transferred to the Association of Canada Lands Surveyors in its new self-regulating capacity.

LAND REGISTRATION AND INFORMATION SERVICE

In the three Maritime provinces of Nova Scotia, New Brunswick, and Prince Edward Island the predominant system of land registration is, and has always been, deeds recording. Under this system, documents providing evidence of ownership and other interests may be deposited in the appropriate local office where they are available for public inspection. The system is self-supporting through the imposition of registration fees, and in fact it yields a profit for the provincial governments. All three provinces have passed Torrens-type land titles legislation, but the Nova Scotia (1978) and the Prince Edward Island (1971) acts have never been proclaimed, while the New Brunswick Land Titles Act of 1981 has so far been given a very limited geographical application.

Largely as a result of initiatives taken by the then director of surveys for New Brunswick, Willis F. Roberts, the Atlantic Provinces Surveying and Mapping Program (APSAMP) came into being on 22 March 1968. This two-year programme, funded initially by the Atlantic Development Board and later by the federal Department of Regional Economic Expansion (DREE), consisted of four distinct but related phases:

Phase 1   Control surveys
Phase 2   Large-scale mapping (which is discussed in chapter 4)
Phase 3   A land titles system using the large-scale map as a foundation
Phase 4   A land data bank

Shared-cost agreements were made with each of the three provinces under which the federal government contributed 90 percent of the funding, as it also did under a separate agreement with Newfoundland. A second APSAMP agreement took the programme to 31 March 1972, with the DREE contribution restricted to phases 1 and 2 only.

The creation of the Council of Maritime Premiers (CMP) in 1971 led to the early establishment of three regional agencies, one of which was LRIS. Henceforth LRIS would be a central organization serving the Maritime provinces only, Newfoundland having declined to participate. The LRIS objectives were essentially the same as those of the four phases of APSAMP, and although the programme was administered centrally from Fredericton, a number of the agency's technical and other operational arms were distributed among the three provinces for political and economic reasons. Both the land titles and the property mapping divisions of LRIS were located in Halifax. The DREE contribution of 75 percent (or $20.9 million) under the LRIS agreement for the five-year period 1 April 1973 to 31 March 1978 applied to phase 3 only to the extent of making a new land titles system technically operational. After this the provinces themselves would be required to bear the related costs. Phase 4, the purpose and details of which were never developed to DREE's satisfaction, was to receive no federal funding under the agreement until joint feasibility and planning studies had been undertaken.

Although the LRIS agreement contemplated an eventual conversion of deeds recording to a land titles system, there were serious differences of opinion concerning the LRIS desire to administer the new system and to include guaranteed boundaries as part of a guaranteed title. Opinions also varied on the reluctance of the provincial governments to relinquish their present control over land registration to an agency that might not even exist after March 1978.

An attempt by LRIS to extend the DREE agreement for a further five years initially proposed a budget of $110,970,800. This figure was later cut almost in half to $58,308,000, of which $14,379,000 was earmarked for phase 3. Even this reduced sum was too rich for DREE, which under a final one-year extension of the agreement provided only $7.1 million as its 75 percent contribution, none of which was to be applied to phase 4.

The withdrawal of federal funding for LRIS after March 1979 compelled the CMP to determine the agency's future. Phase 4 was eliminated, and the phase 3 objective changed from the specific introduction of a land titles system to broader assistance in the implementation of an improved system of land registration. On the other hand a continuation of the phase 2 property mapping, which identified land parcels and portrayed them on base maps, was regarded by the council as essential. LRIS survived under regional agreements until March 1990, when it was terminated and its functions returned to the provinces. Its most notable success in the implementation of the phase 3 objective was the proclamation of the New Brunswick Land Titles Act with respect to Albert County, for the purpose of undertaking a pilot land registration project. During the project period from 9 July 1984 to 31 March 1987, certificates of title were issued for 2045 land parcels, or about 14 percent of the 14 192 parcels in the county, as compared with the approximate total of 916 000 parcels in all three provinces.[8] The project tested not only the new act, but also the system of parcel identification. In a marked departure from an early LRIS desire for guaranteed boundaries, a regulation made under the New Brunswick statute follows other Canadian jurisdictions, such as Ontario, in providing that the "description of registered land is not conclusive as to the boundaries or extent of the land."[9]

The innovative LRIS, well-intentioned but overly ambitious in some of its goals, proved to be a noble if costly experiment that has left, among other useful legacies, the valuable resource of province-wide property mapping. It has also provided the impetus for the pursuit of similar, more realistic, cadastral-related programmes by the individual Maritime provinces to suit their own particular needs and abilities.

ALBERTA

Land Survey Division, Alberta Environmental Protection   As head of the Land Surveys Division the director of surveys is responsible under the Surveys Act for supervising surveys of public lands in unsurveyed territory, confirming plans of such surveys to give them official status, and undertaking resurveys of other lands, under direction from the minister, following a request by a municipal council. The director also administers the performance of integrated surveys, from which the horizontal coordinate values of property boundary corners are obtained.

Alberta legislation now permits the registration in land titles offices of plans of surveys where no monuments were placed to mark parcel boundaries. This policy of deferred monumentation avoids the frequent loss of monuments incurred, for example, during road construction or utilities installation in new subdivisions. A surveyor wishing to take advantage of deferred monumentation must place the required monuments within one year of the plan's registration, except where the director authorizes a longer period of time.

Another important change, which took effect on 1 January 1992, is that the director of surveys no longer routinely examines all plans submitted for registration under the Land Titles Act. Pre-registration plan examination is still undertaken in some instances, however, and it may be requested by the Registrar of Titles where discrepancies occur or explanations are needed. The director maintains a monitor standards program, under which random checks are made on work performed by private surveyors. This activity is complementary to the field and office inspections carried out by the Practice Review Board of the Alberta Land Surveyors Asociation.

BRITISH COLUMBIA

In 1945 the Surveys Branch of what was at that time the Department of Lands and Forests contained three divisions: Surveys, Topographic, and Geographic. The Surveys Division, later called Legal Surveys Division, was responsible for Crown cadastral surveys, survey records, and land reference maps. After the addition of the Air Surveys Division in 1946 the organization remained essentially unchanged for thirty years.

Legal Surveys Division saw a period of rapid growth throughout the postwar period, as the provincial resource boom, combined with a policy of doing most government survey work in-house, placed heavy demands on divisional capabilities. By 1960, however, the staff numbers had become stabilized. A major reorganization in 1976 led to the administrative separation of Legal Surveys from the mapping agency, and for more than a decade the two organizations were in different government departments. In 1987 Legal Surveys was renamed the Surveyor General Branch, and in 1991 it became once again closely associated with Surveys and Resource Mapping Branch when both branches were placed in the new Ministry of Environment, Lands and Parks.

A gradual movement of the cadastral field programme to the private sector began in 1976. Currently all such work except for inspections and unusual special projects is contracted out, mostly by Lands Operations regional offices with audit, advisory, and quality control functions exercised by the Surveyor General Branch.

An important development took place in 1963 with the establishment of British Columbia's first Integrated Survey Area. Since that time approximately forty-six such areas have been officially designated, with the requirement that all cadastral surveys performed in those areas be tied to the horizontal control monuments that are distributed throughout the area. Although Integrated Survey Areas cover only urban and suburban parts of the province, they include over 85 percent of all parcels.

British Columbia's basic cadastral and land title systems appear to support provincial requirements adequately, and there are no present plans for their reform. A major concern of the Surveyor General Branch is to build a complete cadastral information system, covering the entire province and incorporating, either directly or by means of index pointers, all information about each parcel, including dimensions, content, location, history, and boundary evidence.[10]

MANITOBA

Land Titles Office   Until about thirty years after the Second World War, many thousands of certificates of title were issued by Manitoba land titles offices without a proper survey of the land being made or a plan of it registered. This practice contributed to a situation where Manitoba still has the fewest land surveyors per capita of all the provinces, and it also led to a grave deterioration of the local survey fabric. By the late 1970s provincial land surveyors were experiencing costly retracement and restoration because many of the original township section corners had become lost or obliterated. In addition the land titles offices themselves were finding it increasingly difficult to determine the exact location of existing titles described textually by metes and bounds. In some instances as many as thirty registered parcels in a single quarter-section had such descriptions. This frequently meant the time-consuming plotting of a plan showing all neighbouring parcels, in order to determine the location of the parcel in question. Largely as a result of representations made by the Association of Manitoba Land Surveyors, the provincial government granted funds for township resurveys under the Special Survey Act. The work was undertaken partly by private surveyors under contract to the Examiner of Surveys in the Winnipeg land titles office, and partly through the director of surveys.

Consequent changes to the land titles system included the requirement that in future no more than two easily described parcels would be permitted to be transferred from any one quarter-section, and that any subsequent parcel transfer must be supported by a survey and plan of the land. In addition a programme was established under the Real Property Act to simplify existing title descriptions by showing parcels as lots on compiled plans known as special plots, and to require a survey and plan for any subdivision of a lot. Seventy-five percent of titles in Winnipeg have been graphically portrayed under this programme, and the land titles office in that city is now almost completely computerized.[11]

Department of Natural Resources   The Surveys and Mapping Branch of Manitoba Natural Resources was first created in 1930. It has grown from an organization that was primarily concerned with legal surveys of provincial Crown land to a multifaceted agency that also provides digital mapping, map and air photography distribution, and remote sensing products and services. Among its notable postwar projects was the completion of the surveys of Manitoba's boundaries with Ontario, the Northwest Territories, and

Saskatchewan, all of which were undertaken in cooperation with the respective provincial and federal counterparts.[12] These interprovincial boundary surveys have been described in chapter 2.

Department of Highways and Transportation Since its formation in 1901 as part of the Department of Public Works, the Highways legal surveys section has made a significant contribution, not only with respect to the many surveys and plans it has produced but also to the number of land surveyors it has employed and trained. Two years after the establishment of Highways as a separate department in 1965, its land surveys operation took a first step toward decentralization with the opening of a district office in Brandon. A second office followed at Dauphin in 1971. After the 1969 transfer to Natural Resources of its responsibility for undertaking surveys on behalf of the Water Control and Conservation Branch, the land survey office's principal role remained the making of surveys and plans of provincial roads and northern airports.[13] As the result of a reorganization that took place on 1 April 1994, the surveying functions of the Surveys and Mapping Branch and those of the Highways' land surveys unit were absorbed within a new provincial land information centre.

NEW BRUNSWICK

Geographic Information Corporation Legislation came into force on 31 March 1990 that created the New Brunswick Geographic Information Corporation as the successor of the former Maritime LRIS and its activities carried out within the province. The new Crown corporation's statutory mandate includes, among other responsibilities, the coordination of geographic information services and the provision of a system of registration for real and personal property. The headquarters is in Fredericton, there are land information centres at Bathurst, Edmundston, Moncton, and Saint John, and there are nine local sub-offices. Registry and Mapping is one of the corporation's six administrative divisions. It is responsible for registry and mapping offices, the maintenance of registration and searching services at each of the fifteen counties in the province, and regional survey control and sales. It is currently ugrading the existing, largely manual, records to a fully automated record management system. During the fiscal year 1992–93 a total of 91 799 real property documents were registered, and 51 698 property searches were undertaken. The corporation's cadastral maps have also been converted to digital format that is linked to the databases in the registry system, and to the valuation and taxation system. Modernization of the real property registration system is seen by the corporation as a long-term goal. But the legislative machinery is already in place in the form of the Land Titles Act, and valuable experience has been gained as a result of the pilot land titles project carried out in Albert County.

NEWFOUNDLAND AND LABRADOR

Lands Branch, Department of Environment and Lands The establishment of individual land ownership in the province is reflected in the pattern of its cadastral surveys, which, with some exceptions such as official subdivisions, often relate to irregular-shaped, sometimes isolated parcels. Many land holdings have no traceable documentary title, and present-day claims of ownership frequently depend on assertions of peaceful, long-continued possession.[14] Even today there are instances of unlawful encroachment upon undeveloped Crown lands and, in the absence of adequate cadastral maps and title records, it is difficult for the provincial government to state with assurance what land it owns and where the boundaries are.

It was partly recognition of the uncertain condition of local land titles that prompted Newfoundland's participation in the APSAMP initiative of 1968, which later enabled it to secure a separate agreement with DREE during the period 1972–78. Under the latter the federal government provided full reimbursable funding for control survey (phase 1) and large-scale mapping (phase 2), in a total amount of $3,965,000. No funds were made available, or promised, for the implementation of an improved land registration system (phase 3) or for the development of a computerized land data bank (phase 4). The Registry of Deeds has since automated its records, but its fundamental character as a deeds recording, as distinct from a title registration, system remains unaltered.

The Crown Lands Division of the Lands Branch of the department undertakes field inspections in connection with applications for leases and grants of public lands, and it examines survey plans relating to the issue of new Crown titles. The Registry of Deeds neither exercises nor requires plan examination with respect to surveys of land for private transactions.

NORTHWEST TERRITORIES

Surveys and Mapping Division, Department of Municipal and Community Affairs The division was established as recently as 1986, although a land surveyor and survey technicians had been employed by the department's predecessor organization for a few years before that date. The division's technical support to the territorial and community governments includes cadastral surveys. A major problem in many communities, other than the larger centres of Yellowknife, Fort Smith, and Hay River, is the frequent discordance between official subdivisions laid out during the thirty years after the Second World War and the actual occupation. This has resulted in such anomalies as buildings that straddle lot boundaries or that encroach on road allowances, and roads that have been constructed outside their allowances. A significant amount of the division's cadastral survey activities is directed toward the reconciliation of these discrepancies.

An important step in the Northwest Territories' progress toward greater powers of self-government was taken on 19 July 1993 when the federal Land Titles Act, almost 100 years old, was repealed and replaced by a territorial enactment of the same name. Effective from the same date are the Land Titles Plans Regulations. A local Condominium Act has existed since 1974.

An interesting firsthand account of cadastral surveys during the years 1944–82, especially in connection with the mining industry, is given in the unpublished memoirs of John Anderson-Thomson.[15]

NOVA SCOTIA

Surveys Division, Department of Natural Resources The provincial government's major surveying and mapping agency traces its origin to 1934 when the need arose to survey and monument the boundaries of Crown land, 200 years after the first land grants were issued. From modest beginnings the division grew to twelve regional survey parties by 1970, and it now maintains ten district field offices. Until about the year 1990 most Crown land surveys were performed by in-house staff. Since that time some of its work has been contracted to private surveyors, much of which has been related to boundary maintenance. In addition to other duties, such as undertaking surveys for expropriation or for land title clarification, departmental staff become involved in problems and negotiations concerning ungranted Crown land. This applies particularly to Cape Breton and the three eastern counties of the mainland, where individual land ownership claims based on settled possession affect or challenge the Crown's title.

About 99 percent of the division's cadastral projects are mathematically connected to the Nova Scotia horizontal coordinate system, which is also widely used by private surveyors. No reforms to the province's cadastral survey or land registration systems are contemplated at present, but it is proposed to computerize the information in the province's deeds recording offices.[16]

ONTARIO

Survey and Title Services, Ministry of Consumer and Commercial Relations   Among the most important of Ontario's cadastral developments since the Second World War is the implementation of various measures to improve the deeds recording and the land titles systems, particularly with regard to the quality of survey plans and parcel boundary descriptions. In addition to amending the Registry Act and the Land Titles Act, which originated respectively in 1795 and 1885, Ontario introduced three significant new statutes: the Certification of Titles Act in 1958, the Boundaries Act in 1959, and the Condominium Act in 1967. The Certification of Titles Act enables the title to land recorded under the Registry Act to be certified by the director of titles, and it also requires such certification before subdivision plans or condominium plans may be registered. The certificate is declared by statute to be indefeasible, and the Certification of Titles Assurance Fund provides monetary compensation to claimants who are subsequently found to be wrongly deprived of their interest in the land to which the certificate relates. The Boundaries Act provides for the official confirmation of the true location on the ground of lost monuments, without recourse to the courts. Its purpose is to re-establish old boundaries, not to create new ones.

The year 1958 also saw the appointment of the first examiner of surveys in the Land Titles Office, David W. Lambden (later to be a professor in the Department of Survey Science at the University of Toronto). The current examiner of surveys holds the additional title of Deputy Director of Land Registration, and there are six assistant examiners, who also occupy the position of regional surveyor, in Toronto, London, Ottawa, Sudbury, Kitchener, and Peterborough. Separate codes of standards for surveys, plans, and descriptions, first introduced for the land titles sytem in 1958 and for the deeds recording system in 1964, were combined into one uniform code in 1978. One of the principal innovations was the replacement of textual metes and bounds descriptions by the preparation and deposit of reference plans, on which each new part of an existing parcel is portrayed with its boundary dimensions and given a distinct identifier or parcel (part) number.

Recent years have brought a drastic lessening of plan examination by the examiner of surveys and deeds registry staff, and a corresponding acceptance of that responsibility by the Association of Ontario Land Surveyors. In January 1986 the association established its Survey Review Department, which was assisted by an initial government grant. Currently it is funded by the sale of stickers, one of which must be attached to a form accompanying every plan to be registered or deposited in any of the province's fifty-five land registry/land titles offices. The examiner of surveys' examination of survey plans is now mainly confined to those prepared under the Boundaries Act.

As part of its ongoing reform of the dual land registration system, prompted to a large degree by recommendations of the Ontario Law Reform Commission,[17] the province is implementing automated information recording and retrieval, and digital property mapping. Under the POLARIS programme, facilitated by the Land Registration Reform Act of 1984, a pilot project for the conversion of manual deeds records to an automated system was completed at Woodstock. Similar projects are now being undertaken in Toronto, Ottawa, London, Sudbury, and Chatham. Another important development was the test undertaken in London during 1990 of converting a sample of deeds to qualified titles in the automated system after a full forty-year search of the registry records. In 1991 the POLARIS activity was taken over by Teranet Land Information Services Inc., under a strategic alliance between the Ontario government and the private sector.[18]

Both the surveying profession and the general public have benefited significantly from the legislative and administrative changes resulting from the ministry's activities. Regulation by government and, increasingly, by the land surveying profession itself have combined to ensure the provision of surveys and survey plans of a quality and quantity not always available in earlier years. This has led to an improvement in property boundary stability, and to a corresponding reduction of uncertainty and dispute regarding the ownership and physical extent of land parcels.

Surveys and Design Office, Ministry of Transportation Cadastral surveys are made in support of the ministry's transportation facilities, which evolved from the sole provision of highways during the 1940s to a multi-modal focus in the 1980s. Depending on the demand and the availability of resources, surveys have historically been undertaken by in-house staff and by contract to the private sector. This work, which includes determining the boundaries of land required for new or widened highways, may also involve boundary retracement or monument restoration as the need arises.

PRINCE EDWARD ISLAND

Properties and Surveys Section, Department of Transportation and Public Works In 1942 the government of Prince Edward Island established a survey organization under the Department of the Provincial Secretary. The provincial secretary at that time, William Wade Hughes, was also a land surveyor. Because of the anticipated need for new subdivisions during the postwar period, a new system for accurately locating and recording the subdivided parcels was considered essential. This led to a cooperative project undertaken by the provincial government and the Geodetic Survey of Canada that resulted in the establishment of the Prince Edward Island Lambert Conformal Projection System. The system was replaced during the 1960s by the Prince Edward Island Stereographic Projection System, which is still in use.

Most of the survey work undertaken by the surveys section is performed by in-house staff, but there has been some recent movement towards contracting survey services to private industry, especially with respect to surveys for road or highway design. Carl MacDonald was appointed chief surveyor in 1986 after having acted in that position for several years.

Although the mathematical connection of cadastral surveys to the horizontal control network is not required by legislation, it has been a common practice since the late 1960s. Since 1975 all cadastral surveys in the province have been coordinated.[19]

QUÉBEC

Direction du Cadastre, Ministère de l'Énergie et des Ressources   Historically the Québec cadastre derives from two legal sources: the Cadastre Act originating in 1860, and the Civil Code of Lower Canada, adopted in 1866, each of which has been amended over the years. Prior to 1 October 1985 the cadastral system consisted of two separate elements, namely cadastral plans and books of reference. The cadastral plan provided an index to lots by showing their boundaries and their geographic relationship to each other in graphical form only, and by assigning to each lot an identifying number that was unique within the particular parish or other cadastral area. The accompanying book of reference contained a description of each lot shown on the cadastral plan, the name of the owner, and other explanatory remarks. The cadastral plan itself did not confer ownership rights, nor did it necessarily represent the true size and shape of the lots it portrayed. Its main purpose was to identify a lot by its geographic location and by a serial number that formed the link between the lot and all future transactions affecting it. An important advantage of the cadastral system is that it was designed to facilitate both the legal description of land parcels and the examination of land title. In 1989 the inhabited part of the province, comprising 10 percent of the total area, was covered by 1230 official cadastres.[20]

In the course of time the cadastral plans became badly outdated, and in many instances they failed to show the manner in which the original lots had been divided into smaller parcels. While the Civil Code of Lower Canada provided for the deposit with the provincial government of a subdivision plan showing distinct numbers for the new lots, it also permitted owners to describe and convey land as part of an original lot. These latter transactions had the effect of creating new parcels that could not always be reliably identified on the cadastral plan, and did not represent official amendments to it. Other problems arose from the gradual deterioration of original documents, the frequent discordance between recorded and occupational boundaries, and even the portrayal of some lots on two different cadastral plans. To remedy this situation An Act to Promote the Reform of the Cadastre in Québec (which also amended the Cadastre Act and the Civil Code) was passed in 1985. It provides for the establishment of a cadastre reform fund that will be maintained by fees levied on users of the cadastral and land registration system. The fund will permit the preparation of a cadastral renewal plan for any area where the parcelling of original lots makes such plans necessary, the appropriate redesignation of parcel identifiers, the holding of public hearings at which affected owners can be heard, and the filing of the final plan in the registry office.

In 1985 it had been estimated that the cadastral reform programme would involve ten years of work and cost $83.8 million. After six years of operation only 168 000 lots had been renewed, representing about 5 percent of the total parcels. To provide additional funding from increased registration fees, the cadastral reform act was amended in 1992.

Cadastral reform is now expected to be completed in 2006, at a cost of $508 million in 1991 dollars over the fourteen-year period.[21]

It must be emphasized that the Québec cadastre is a means of illustrating land parcellation; it does not purport to delimit parcel boundaries. Proprietors who wish to determine the exact limits of ownership have recourse to the *bornage* procedures available under provincial law. The new cadastral plans depict the dimensions and area of each parcel, but neither bearings nor monuments are shown. Coordinates of parcel corners do not appear on the plan but their values, computed on NAD83, are available upon request. Each cadastral plan takes effect on the day that a corresponding land file is opened in the applicable registry office. Article 3027 of the new Civil Code of Québec, which came into force on 1 January 1994, gives evidentiary status to cadastral plan boundaries by providing that, "In the case of discrepancy between the boundaries, measurements and area shown on the plan and those mentioned in the documents presented, those on the plan are presumed accurate." The most sweeping change to the Québec cadastre, apart from its improved reliability, is that it is becoming a more comprehensive record of land ownership, with numerical, instead of merely graphical, parcel information.

SASKATCHEWAN

Central Survey and Mapping Agency   A most important development in Saskatchewan occurred in 1982 when the provincial surveying, mapping, and land database activities were consolidated into a new Central Survey and Mapping Agency (CSMA), which is now a legislated entity of the Saskatchewan Property Management Corporation. CSMA is responsible for developing, managing, and distributing Saskatchewan's basic survey, mapping, and geographic information systems. Among its five operational components is the Legal Survey Branch, responsible for the administration of cadastral surveys performed under the Land Surveys Act. The present general manager of CSMA is also the controller of surveys appointed under that act, an office that requires the holder to be a Saskatchewan Land Surveyor. The Department of Highways and Transportation, which no longer maintains its own legal survey expertise, relies on CSMA for advice and plan examination, and for the approval of departmental road and other plans intended for filing in the land titles offices.

Chief Surveyor's Office, Property Registration Branch, Department of Justice   Although the eight land titles offices in Saskatchewan have a close working relationship with CSMA, they continue to maintain their own separate Chief Surveyor's Office in Regina for the routine examination of survey plans filed under the Land Titles Act. The chief surveyor is required by statute to be a Saskatchewan Land Surveyor, and has a staff of eleven. An interesting example of cooperation between government and the land surveying profession was the initiation in 1992 of a survey inspection programme. This was undertaken by a committee of the Saskatchewan Land Surveyors' Association in consultation with the chief surveyor, and involves the random field inspection of surveys, especially those relating to the re-establishment of primary (township) corners.

LAND SURVEYORS' ASSOCIATIONS

The years since the Second World War have seen remarkable progress in the institutional organization of land surveyors in Canada. During the period 1953–68 new self-regulating licensing associations were incorporated in Newfoundland, New Brunswick, Nova Scotia, and Prince Edward Island. Other new institutions are the Canadian Council of Land Surveyors and the Association of Canada Lands Surveyors. Each of the six older provincial associations has made statutory and other changes to provide an improved service to its members and the public. Among these changes may be noted:

- Establishment of permanent offices for association headquarters
- Publication of journals, newsletters, and manuals of professional practice
- Appointment of public members to serve on councils of management and boards of examiners
- Programmes of continuing education for professional development
- Closer links with the legal and real estate professions
- Better communication with government and the public

Other changes that have been introduced or are contemplated by some associations allow the incorporation of survey firms and the enlargement of registered membership. The latter is intended to accommodate as non-cadastral surveyors those practitioners in other branches of the wider surveying profession who seek the professional environment offered by a recognized and well-established institution.

Despite their long history and statutory recognition, land surveyors in Canada are few in number compared with many other professions. The total membership of cadastral surveyors in self-regulating associations is at present about 3000, though the figure may be somewhat inflated because it includes surveyors who are licensed to practise in more than one jurisdiction.

National Associations

CANADIAN INSTITUTE OF GEOMATICS (CIG)

The institute, which started life in 1882 as the Association of Dominion Land Surveyors, changed its name to the Canadian Institute of Surveying in 1934. Minor variations in the organization's official title took place in 1950 when the words "and Photogrammetry" were added, in 1957 when those same words were dropped, and in 1986 when the words "and Mapping" were added. In 1992 a major change occurred with the adoption of a completely new name: the Canadian Institute of Geomatics/l'Association canadienne des sciences géomatiques.

There are two main differences between the institute and the provincial land surveyors' associations. First, CIG is a professional society, not a licensing body, and its membership is open to any person involved or interested in the practice or development of geomatics and associated sciences. Second, it embraces all those disciplines or fields of activity that are subsumed under the name geomatics, including land surveying, cartography, control surveying, engineering surveying, geodesy, hydrography, land information management, mining surveying, photogrammetry, and remote sensing.

Although the institute is much less focused on cadastral surveying than it was in past years, it attracts membership and support from practising land surveyors in both their individual and their corporate capacities. Its land surveying committee is one of seven technical standing committees and, together with the Canadian Council of Land Surveyors, the institute sponsored the important textbook *Survey Law in Canada*, 1989. *Geomatica*, its quarterly journal (formerly *The Canadian Surveyor*), is among the most respected publications serving the national and international surveying communities.

CANADIAN COUNCIL OF LAND SURVEYORS

An umbrella organization, the Canadian Council of Land Surveyors was formed in 1976 to bring together the provincial land surveying associations for common purposes. It is an association of associations, made up of directors and representatives from nine of the ten autonomous provincial organizations. The Québec Order of Land Surveyors, an original member of the council, withdrew from membership in January 1993. The Association of Canada Lands Surveyors, though not yet a full member, enjoys observer status at the council's meetings. Among the activities of the council are accrediting baccalaureate degree programmes in surveying at Canadian universities, arranging or recommending liability insurance packages for practising land surveyors, developing common standards for land surveyors' real property reports, and sponsoring or supporting professional development.

The council has its headquarters in Toronto, and is funded by a per capita membership levy collected from each participating provincial association. It produces a periodical, *Focus,* for distribution to individual land surveyors, and it has also produced several issues of a successful journal, *Terravue.*

ASSOCIATION OF CANADA LANDS SURVEYORS

The association was formed in 1985, and is the youngest of its kind in Canada. It can, however, lay some claim to being among the oldest, for its pedigree can be traced to 1882 when the Association of Dominion Land Surveyors was established in Winnipeg. Despite their professional title, however, the exclusive jurisdiction of Canada Lands Surveyors does not extend to every part of the country but only to statutory Canada Lands. These include all Indian reserves, national parks, and offshore oil and gas lands, as well as certain other lands belonging to the Sechelt and the Cree-Naskapi aboriginal nations.

The association also differs from its provincial counterparts in that it is not a licensing body, merely a voluntary society. Canada Lands Surveyors receive their commission to practise after meeting the examination and other requirements of a board appointed under the federal Canada Lands Surveys Act, and they are not required to belong to the association. Under a proposed new Canada Lands Surveyors Act the association would attain considerable powers of self-regulation, including the duties and responsibilities now exercised by the government-appointed board of examiners. If this legislation comes into force in the form that is now envisaged, all Canada Lands Surveyors will have to be registered under the act and be members of the association if they wish to continue practising cadastral surveying within the applicable jurisdiction.

Provincial Associations

ALBERTA

On 19 March 1910 The Alberta Land Surveyors' Act was passed to incorporate the newly formed association. As a result of concerns expressed by the federal surveyor general, the act was changed a mere nine months after its introduction to give resident Dominion Land Surveyors the right to practise throughout Alberta without further service or examination, and to allow their non-resident colleagues the same privilege upon passing a test in certain local laws. No other significant changes occurred until the enactment of The Alberta Land Surveyors Act, 1965. This replaced the previous legislation and dealt mainly with the management and functions of the association and the qualifications and professional conduct of its members. It also conferred on association members the exclusive right, with a few specified exceptions, to practise land surveying in Alberta.

The Land Surveyors Act, a completely new statute that came into force in 1981, provides that at least one member of the public shall be appointed by the provincial government to the association's council of management. It also permits the registration of land surveying firms that are incorporated under the Companies Act.

As part of its movement toward the establishment of an expanded surveying profession in Alberta, the association has proposed a draft Surveying Professions Act. Among other matters, this would accommodate non-cadastral surveyors by enabling them to apply for a permit to engage in the practice of surveying, except with respect to the practice of cadastral surveying, which would still have to be undertaken only by those licensed under the act for that purpose.

BRITISH COLUMBIA

Until almost the end of the nineteenth century, authorization to practise land surveying in British Columbia derived from the chief commissioner of Lands and Works and from the surveyor general. This arrangement was formalized in 1891 by The Provincial Land Surveyors' Act, which established a board of examiners consisting of the surveyor general and five land surveyors appointed by the government.[22] The legislation was prompted by pressure exerted the previous year by the newly formed Association of Professional Land Surveyors of British Columbia, although the association itself did not receive statutory recognition for more than fourteen years after its formation. Incorporation came as a result of the British Columbia Land Surveyors' Act, which came into force on 1 June 1905 and repealed the 1891 act.

A new Land Surveyors Act to replace the previous legislation was passed on 1 April 1936. It has received remarkably little amendment since that time, although its current 1979 manifestation was amended in 1992 to permit the registration of private land surveying corporations. The association still carries the somewhat unwieldy official title, the Corporation of Land Surveyors of the Province of British Columbia, that it was given in 1905. Like the corresponding Ontario association, it counts its age and numbers its annual meetings from the date of incorporation, not from the year of its organization.

A statutory failure to define the expressions *land surveyor* and *land surveying* led to the dismissal of actions initiated by the corporation against a firm of persons not registered under the Land Surveyors Act who were in the business of preparing building location certificates for mortgage lenders. In *Attorney-General for British Columbia et al. v Infomap Services Inc. et al. (1990)*, 69 D.L.R. (4th) 1, the British Columbia Court of Appeal adopted a position similar to that taken by the court in the Manitoba *Carefoot* case (*Association of Manitoba Land Surveyors v Carefoot* (1986), 42 Man. R. (2d) 255. It held that since the act must be construed strictly, and since the defendants had not themselves established or defined property boundaries but had merely used cadastral plans prepared by British Columbia Land Surveyors to show the location of structures within the boundaries, they did not act as land surveyors and the plaintiffs' application for an injunction must be denied. The corporation has since sought amendments to the act that would secure it the desired protection.

MANITOBA

The Association of Manitoba Land Surveyors enjoys the distinction of being the oldest provincial land surveyors' association in Canada. Its formation can be dated as far back as

1874, but the attempt at that time to obtain statutory incorporation proved unsuccessful and the association appears to have lain dormant until its reorganization in 1880.[23] An act to incorporate the Association of Provincial Land Surveyors was passed in 1881, and two years later it was re-enacted with amendments as The Land Surveyors' Act, 1883. On 31 January 1905 the association's name was altered to its present form by a new act that took effect on that date. Very few changes to the act have occurred since that time. Recent judicial examination of the legislation has exposed certain weaknesses, with respect to the definition of land surveying and the association's ability to prevent unauthorized practice, that even a 1990 amendment to the current 1987 act has not yet removed to the satisfaction of the profession.

The association has suffered two serious setbacks relating to the unauthorized practice of land surveying. In 1986 the Manitoba Court of Queen's Bench dismissed an action in the *Carefoot* case, on the grounds that the Land Surveyors Act, while it prohibited anyone other than a Manitoba Land Surveyor from acting as "surveyor of lands," failed to define that expression, and that the defendant's actions could not therefore be described as illegal. At the association's request the act was amended in 1990 to define both surveyor of lands and the practice of land surveying. Three years later a different issue arose in *Association of Manitoba Land Surveyors et al. v Manitoba Telephone System et al.* (1993), 100 D.L.R. (4th) 420, which turned on the award by the telephone company of a land surveying contract to the second defendant, a firm of professional engineers. In dismissing the plaintiffs' application for permanent injunctions against both defendants, the court pointed out that no such civil remedy or private right is conferred by the Land Surveyors Act, that the telephone company had committed no statutory offence by engaging the surveying services of a company not authorized by law to practise land surveying, and that the only legal remedy available to the association, had it chosen to pursue it, would have been against the second defendant under section 54. This section had been amended following the *Carefoot* decision, and provided for a fine upon summary conviction for anyone found guilty of unlawfully engaging in the practice of land surveying.

NEW BRUNSWICK

The Association of New Brunswick Land Surveyors was incorporated by The New Brunswick Land Surveyors Act, 1954, passed on 12 April 1954. Under this legislation the new association became a self-regulating body, with the exclusive right for its members to practise land surveying anywhere in the province, except that the act did not apply "to the laying out of a highway or in any way restrict the powers given the Minister of Public Works by the Highway Act and the Public Works Act to determine the location of the right of way of any highway or bridge" (section 44). The statute repealed the Land Surveyors Act, first enacted in 1874, which had provided for the admission of land surveyors to practice by a provincially appointed board of examiners.

A complete statutory monopoly was secured by The New Brunswick Land Surveyors Act, 1986, which came into force on 1 February 1987 and replaced the previous legislation. Subsection 16(1) states that "No person shall practice in New Brunswick as a land surveyor unless registered to practice under the provisions of this Act." The current statute strengthens the definition of land surveying and gives additional powers to the association including, for example, the issue of a certificate of authorisation that allows a partnership or corporation of land surveyors to practise their profession.

Before the Second World War and for a few years afterwards, persons wishing to practise land surveying in Newfoundland applied to the government for the privilege of performing such work. "In a great many cases these applications were accepted either on a political or friendly basis."[24] A significant change occurred on 1 July 1953 with the passage of the first Land Surveyors Act. This legislation incorporated the Association of Newfoundland Land Surveyors, and established rules governing membership and professional practice. Ten years later the act was amended to transfer from the government the power to examine prospective land surveyors, and to authorize the association to constitute and appoint members of a board of examiners that henceforth would be responsible for examining candidates for admission as Newfoundland Land Surveyors.

The land surveying profession in Newfoundland is now regulated by the Land Surveyors Act, 1991, which preserves and enlarges the principal features of the previous statute. The association is governed by a council of management consisting of not more than twelve elected persons, all of whom must be members, except that a maximum of two of the councillors may be elected from outside the membership where the by-laws permit this to be done. At present there are no public members of the council. The act, which came into force on 1 May 1992, authorizes the council to appoint a four-person board of examiners, one of whom may but need not be a member of the association. Employees of the provincial government who practise land surveying in the course of that employment need not be registered as Newfoundland Land Surveyors, but most of them are.

NOVA SCOTIA
Despite early attempts by provincial land surveyors to obtain formal organization and statutory recognition, a bill that would have incorporated their professional association did not pass the legislature when it was presented in 1928.[25] An inhibiting factor at that time may been the existence of the Nova Scotia Provincial Land Surveyors' Act, passed in 1910. This provided for the establishment of a government-appointed board of examiners to admit to practice those candidates who had passed the prescribed examinations, and also to six other classes of applicant. These ranged from Dominion Land Surveyors to holders of a technical college diploma in land surveying who had served as a theodolite operator on a railway survey for an aggregate period of not less than two years.

It took another thirty-one years before the Association of Nova Scotia Land Surveyors was able to achieve statutory incorporation and the privilege of self-regulation. The Provincial Land Surveyors Act, which came into force on 1 October 1959, repealed the 1910 legislation and survived until its replacement by the Nova Scotia Land Surveyors Act of 1977. The current statute, the Land Surveyors Act, as revised to 1989, is substantially unchanged from its 1977 predecessor. Of particular interest is the composition of the seven-person board of examiners. Four are elected annually by the association's council, while each of the remaining three is appointed respectively by the provincial government, the Association of Professional Engineers of Nova Scotia, and the Nova Scotia Barristers' Society.

The Land Surveyors Act does not apply to persons entitled to practise engineering under the Engineering Act. The overlapping of land surveying and engineering with respect to road design and layout was considered by the Appeal Division of the Nova Scotia Supreme Court in *R. v Robb (K.W.) & Associates Ltd* (1991), 101 N.S.R. (2d) 216, where the court stated that the two acts will support an interpretation that both land surveyors and engineers are involved in road design – surveyors in a rudimentary, preliminary way for the surveying purpose of locating road allowances, and engineers in a much more complex and specific way for the engineering purpose of road construction. In allowing an appeal brought by the surveyor, and setting aside his conviction, the court also remarked that the "demarcation line should long since have been determined between the two professions by negotiation, fixed by regulation or statutory amendment, and settled by practice."

ONTARIO

Although the land surveyors in Ontario formed an association as early as 1886, the profession dates the organization from 1892, the year of its statutory incorporation. Minor changes to The Land Surveyors Act occurred over the years until the passing of a new statute, The Surveyors Act, which came into force in 1970. This legislation allowed land surveyors in private practice to incorporate their business, thus removing their previous restriction to sole proprietorship or partnership. The current statute, passed in 1987, made significant alterations to the power and responsibility of the association. For example its council of management of fourteen members is now required to include three persons from outside the profession, appointed by the provincial government, one of whom must be a barrister or solicitor of at least ten years' standing. Another major change is the statutory distinction drawn between the "practice of cadastral surveying" and the "practice of professional land surveying." Only a member of the association who holds a licence for that purpose may undertake cadastral surveys. A non-cadastral member may receive a certificate of registration that entitles the holder to practise professional land surveying in such areas as the determination of natural and artificial features of the earth's surface and their representation in cartographic or other form, provided such work is not related to land parcel boundaries.

As befits a successful and comparatively wealthy professional organization, the association actively promotes the education and development of its members and it maintains high standards of practice. In January 1986 it established a survey review department to undertake a systematic review of at least one plan each year from every private land surveying firm or government cadastral survey organization, and a comprehensive review of each firm or organization every five years. Although the department was not created to replace the routine government examination of plans submitted to land registry/land titles offices, that examination has since been reduced progressively and is now virtually eliminated, except for certain special requirements.

Among the association's publications is the quarterly journal *The Ontario Land Surveyor*. On the occasion of its corporate centenary the association published a commemorative volume containing an illustrated history of land surveying in Ontario.[26]

PRINCE EDWARD ISLAND

With the passage of the Prince Edward Island Land Surveyors Act on 25 April 1968, the establishment of a professional land surveyors' association in each of Canada's ten provinces became complete. Immediately prior to the statutory incorporation of the Association of Prince Edward Island Land Surveyors, there were fifteen resident land surveyors qualified to practise in the province and a further six who resided in other parts of Canada.

The first provincial statute governing the admission of land surveyors was the Land Surveyors' Act, 1884, which established a three-person, government-appointed board to examine candidates and authorize them to practise. A new act of the same name appeared in 1939, but it was replaced only six years later by the Survey Act, which made the licensing of land surveyors the responsibility of the provincial secretary, assisted by a board of examiners appointed by that minister. An interesting amendment to the 1939 act, made in 1944, required a surveyor wishing to enter upon any land for the purpose of making a survey to notify the owner of the land in advance of the entry, by means of a notice published in a local newspaper. Fortunately this restriction survived for only one year before its repeal by the 1945 Survey Act.

The Land Surveyors Act, as the 1968 legislation is now known, has received little amendment since its introduction. The current 1988 version requires any person practising land surveying in the province to be a member of the association. Admission is governed by a five-person board of examiners, three of whom are appointed by the provincial government, and two of those three need not be association members.

QUÉBEC

An ordinance concerning the appointment of land surveyors in the old province of Québec, which then included much of what is now Ontario, was passed by the legislature as long ago as 1785. It was almost a century later before the profession itself became fully organized as a self-regulating association. On 27 May 1882 the land surveyors of Québec were incorporated by statute, and their first general meeting was held the following July. Seven years later the association was renamed Land Surveyors and Geometers of the Province of Québec, and in 1973 a new act continued the corporation as l'Ordre des arpenteurs-géomètres du Québec.

The 1973 act, which substantially repealed the previous legislation, has been updated to show periodic revisions. Of particular interest is section 34, which begins by stating that a "land surveyor is a public officer" and continues with a detailed definition of the "practice of the profession of a land surveyor." Although the principal application of section 34 is to surveys "for boundary purposes," it is sufficiently broad to embrace all geodetic, photogrammetric, cartographic, and electronic activities that serve or are undertaken for those purposes. No operations described in section 34 are legally valid unless performed by a Québec Land Surveyor, but that restriction does not apply to geodesy students in training, persons merely gathering information for their own use, or to engineers, forestry engineers, and appraisers in those fields recognized by law to be within their own special competence.

SASKATCHEWAN

Although the title of Saskatchewan Land Surveyor was first created by statute in 1909, a provincial society of professional surveyors was not formed until the following year.[27] On 19 December 1913 the Saskatchewan Land Surveyors Association became incorporated under the Saskatchewan Land Surveyors Act, with powers that included the examination of candidates for admission to practice and the management of professional activities. The sole right of Saskatchewan Land Surveyors to perform land surveys in the province was not yet completely exclusive, for the act did not apply to "restoration surveys or resurveys of land in the province made by Dominion land surveyors under the authority of any department of the government of Canada" (section 52). This restriction was lifted on 15 April 1935 by a statutory amendment that made the Dominion Lands Surveys Act no longer applicable to Saskatchewan, as a result of the 1930 transfer to the province of responsibility for certain natural resources that were previously under federal ownership and jurisdiction.

A new Saskatchewan Land Surveyors Act that came into force on 1 July 1962 gave the association more control over its internal affairs by transferring a number of administrative provisions from the statute to the association by-laws. Among other matters the current Land Surveyors and Professional Surveyors Act accommodates and gives a class of membership to non-cadastral surveyors, as part of its move toward an expanded surveying profession.

CONCLUSION

The years since 1947 have seen a marked change in the practice of cadastral surveying in Canada. Among the more obvious examples is the introduction and utilization of highly sophisticated technology that allows parcel boundary positioning to be undertaken more rapidly and to a higher degree of accuracy than was ever before attainable. But perhaps more striking is the change in public attitude toward surveying. No doubt, in the minds of some members of the public, a survey such as a Real Property Report remains an unfortunate extra expense, made necessary only by the imposed conditions of a lending institution. Yet there appears to be a growing public awareness of the need for reliable information concerning property boundaries and ownership, and an appreciation that such information is valuable for purposes beyond the requirements of an individual land owner. Since the earliest times cadastral surveyors have been concerned with the gathering of land-related information, though this part of their work was not always recognized. Today it can be fairly stated that the cadastral survey system continues to represent the geographical framework of a modern LIS.

Also noteworthy is the strength of the cadastral surveying profession in Canada, as represented by the ten provincial and one federal land surveyors' associations, several of which came into existence only after the end of the Second World War. Few professional organizations in this country are allowed to operate so quietly and unobtrusively, and with such a degree of self-regulation, as the associations, all of which enjoy a statutory monopoly with respect to the right to perform cadastral surveys. This considerable privilege is a measure of the trust that the public has in the accountability of the surveying profession. The associations' own commendable achievements in ensuring professional ethics and high technical standards, in exerting disciplinary measures over the membership where appropriate, in promoting continuing professional education, and in maintaining good relations with the public provide assurance to modern society that its cadastral surveying requirements are being fully met.

NOTES

1 McEwen, Alec. 1983. The Township System of Surveys in Newfoundland. *The Canadian Surveyor*, 37, 2, 39–50.

2 Monaghan, J.W.L. 1971. The DI10 Distomat in a Canadian Land Survey Practice. *Papers, Commonwealth Survey Officers Conference.* Paper B4. Southampton, U.K.: Ordnance Survey.

3 Stretton, W.D. 1982. The Age of Electronic Surveying. In *From Compass to Satellite. The Canadian Surveyor*, 36, 4, 286.

4 Joint Land Titles Committee. 1990. *Renovating the Foundation: Proposals for a Model Land Recording and Registration Act for the Provinces and Territories of Canada.* Edmonton: Alberta Law Reform Institute.

5 Joint Land Titles Committee. 1993. *Final Revisions: Renovating the Foundation: Proposals for a Model Land Recording and Registration Act for the Provinces and Territories of Canada.* Edmonton: Alberta Law Reform Institute.

6 Ontario Law Reform Institute. 1979. *An Improved Land Registration System for Ontario.* Toronto: Ministry of Consumer and Commercial Relations. Vol. 1, *An Executive Summary of the Design Concepts and Recommendations.* Volume 2, *Design Concepts and Recommendations.*

7 Legal Surveys Division. 1994. *Manual of Instructions for the Survey of Canada Lands*, 3d ed. Ottawa: Queen's Printer.

8 Doig, J.F. 1987. *Albert County Land Titles Pilot Project.* Fredericton: Land Registration and Information Service, 14, 41, annex Q.

9 Land Titles Act, RSO 1990, c. L-5, s. 140(2).

10 Duffy, D.A. 1993. Letter to author.

11 Boutilier, L. 1993. Letter to author.

12 Surveys and Mapping Branch. 1990. *Surveys and Mapping Branch, 1930–1990: Its First Sixty Years.* Winnipeg: Department of Natural Resources.

13 Gauer, G. 1980. *A History of the Department of Highways and Transportation's Legal Survey Office.* Winnipeg: Association of Manitoba Land Surveyors (unpublished), 7.

14 McEwen, Alec. 1977. Land Titles in Newfoundland. *The Canadian Surveyor*, 31, 2, 151–8.

15 Anderson-Thomson, J. N.d. *Memoirs, 1944–1982.* Yellowknife: Territorial Archives (typescript).

16 Aucoin, K. and Doig, J.F. 1993. Letters to author.

17 Ontario Law Reform Commission. 1971. *Report on Land Registration.* Toronto: Department of Justice, 80–4.

18 Madan, R. Paul. 1993. Letter to author.
Lambden, David W., and Ronald A. Logan. 1991. Land Information Management by Strategic Alliance. In *Report of Proceedings, Conference of Commonwealth Surveyors.*Part 1, paper F4. Southampton, U.K.: Ordnance Survey.

19 MacDonald, C. 1994. Letter to author.

20 Girard, Grégoire, J. André Laferrière, and Gérard Raymond. 1989. The Law in Québec. In *Survey Law in Canada.* Toronto: Carswell, 403.

21 1992. *Pour une relance de la réforme du cadastre québécois.* Ministère de l'Énergie et des Ressources, Direction générale du cadastre, 6, 27.

22 Andrews, G.S. 1956. The Land Surveying Profession in British Columbia. *Report of Proceedings of the Fiftieth Annual General Meeting.* Victoria: Corporation of Land Surveyors of the Province of British Columbia, 62–3.

23 Thomson, D.W. 1967. *Men and Meridians*, vol. 2. Ottawa: Queen's Printer, 60–2.

24 Newfoundland. 1953. *House of Assembly Proceedings*, Thirteenth General Assembly, 30 April 1953, 711, per the Minister of Public Works.

25 Thomson, D.W. 1969. *Men and Meridians*, vol. 3. Ottawa: Queen's Printer, 332–33.

26 Ladell, J.L. 1993. *They Left Their Mark: Surveyors and Their Role in the Settlement of Ontario.* Toronto: Dundurn Press.

27 Thomson, *Men and Meridians*, vol. 2, 75–8.

CHAPTER EIGHT

Hydrographic Surveying and Charting

David H. Gray

INTRODUCTION

In the second and third quarter of the present century we have seen two major explosions in hydrographic technology and are at present experiencing a third. The first resulted from the invention of echo-sounding, the second from the development of electromagnetic and other electronic methods of ship-fixing, whilst the third, possibly the most difficult for the surveyor to cope with, has been brought about by the advent of the computer and results from efforts to combine echo-sounding and electronic fixing data within a logging system capable of reproducing on-line or off-line plots and bathymetry, with the hope that this will lead to more rapid and more accurate compilation of sea surveys.[1]

Although Admiral Ritchie of the United Kingdom said these words in 1973, little did he realize the future impact of the computer revolution on hydrography. Survey methods have changed totally, and presentation of the results is in the throes of changing from the paper chart to a total system in which the navigational situation and the chart are displayed on a video screen. How these and other changes in hydrographic surveying and charting came about will be described in this chapter.

SITUATION AT THE END OF THE SECOND WORLD WAR

Six years of wartime expediencies left the Canadian Hydrographic Service (CHS) in a sorry state. Hard-pressed CHS staff had surveyed harbours and bays for the war effort using only launches, including highly secret bathymetric, temperature, and current surveys in preparation for the construction of the atomic energy plant at Deep River, Ontario. The service had also supported the war effort by printing vast quantities of charts of the Atlantic seaboard. The Royal Canadian Navy (RCN) had commandeered the hydrographic vessels *Acadia* and *Cartier* for the duration of the war, whilst the *Wm. J. Stewart* was used in special surveys for the RCN on the Pacific coast. She ran aground on Ripple Rock in June 1944, was beached, and later raised, repaired, and returned to CHS in 1945.[2] The *Cartier* was scrapped. This left the CHS with only the thirty-four-year-old *Acadia* and the thirteen-year-old *Stewart*. *Acadia* now resides at the Maritime Museum of the Atlantic in Halifax. The *Wm. J. Stewart*, renamed *Canadian Princess*, became a floating fishing resort at Ucluelet, British Columbia.

Before and during the war the CHS field staff had offices in the Labelle Building in the market area of Ottawa, while the headquarters personnel were in the Confederation Building just west of Parliament Hill. Both offices were brought together after the construction of #8 Temporary Building west of Dows Lake in Ottawa. At the end of the war the CHS was part of the federal Department of Mines and Resources. Its Pacific region office in Victoria, British Columbia, had been established in 1907, and in 1945 was under the direction of H.D. Parizeau. He retired in 1946 and was succeeded by W.K. Willis, to be followed later by R.B. Young, M. (Mike) Bolton, and, most recently, A.D. (Tony) O'Connor.

The mandate of the CHS in 1947 was very much as it is today, namely to provide nautical information to mariners for Canadian waters. The word "mariner" simply meant a ship's officer. Little concern was given to the commercial fisherman, and none at all to the recreational boater. "Canadian waters" did not include those of Newfoundland, nor did they extend too far offshore or go into the Arctic.

1947–52: R.J. FRASER AS DOMINION HYDROGRAPHER

The Organization

F.H. Peters held the post of surveyor general and chief of the Hydrographic and Map Service from 1936. He was thus in charge of what are now considered to be four major units of the federal government's surveying, mapping, and charting programme: Legal Surveys, Hydrographic Surveys, Aeronautical Charts, and Geographical Services. Although Peters was the administrative head of the CHS, he left much of its day-to-day operation to R.J. Fraser who from 1940 was assistant chief of the Hydrographic Service. Due to government reorganization Peters was promoted to chief of the Surveying and Mapping Bureau in January 1948, and Fraser succeeded him as head of CHS. This appointment was accompanied by a change in the name of the position to dominion hydrographer. Fraser had started working for CHS in 1909 on Lake Superior and rose through the ranks. He was a man of genial disposition, a reformed drinker, and a gifted writer.

There had been criticism in the House of Commons much earlier over Wm J. Stewart's appointment as the first Canadian to be chief hydrographer since he had not been a mariner first.[3] In contrast the Second World War brought to CHS a wealth of naval officers with sea experience: Colin Angus, Harvey Blandford, D'Arcy Charles, Derek Cooper, and Ralph Wills, to name but a few. Mike Eaton and "Sandy" Sandilands came to CHS as hydrographers from the Royal Navy. Civilian mariners such as Stan Huggett, Tony Mortimer, and Sam Weller have also come over time. Some hydrographers have followed Stewart's example by getting their mariners "tickets" while in CHS, including Jim Bruce, Julian Goodyear, and Barry Lusk. Russ Melanson and Gerry Wade were amongst the small number of land survey school graduates, whilst "Dusty" DeGrasse was one of the topographic survey engineers. This diversity was to prove successful.

The immediate postwar period also brought to CHS some very interesting people, each with unique expertise. Hans Pulkkinen was a Finnish surveyor who loved working in the

Table 8-1
Canadian Hydrographic Service

Time	Dominion Hydrographers	Regional Hydrographers				
		Pacific	Atlantic	Central	Québec	Nfld Sub-region
— 1945	F.H. Peters R.J. Fraser	H.D. Parizeau W.K. Willis				
— 1950	F.C.G. Smith					
— 1955	N.G. Gray	R.B. Young				
— 1960			G.W. LaCroix			
— 1965			R.C. Melanson	M. Bolton		
— 1970	A.E. Collin G.N. Ewing	M. Bolton		T.D.W. McCulloch		
— 1975				A.J. Kerr	H. Furuya	
— 1980	S.B. MacPhee		A.J. Kerr	G.R. Douglas	J. O'Shea R.K. Williams	
— 1985	G.R. Douglas	A.D. O'Connor	P. Bellemare	E. Brown	P. Bellemare D. Hains	J.E. Goodyear
— 1990						

North, "Gerry" Dohler had served in the German Navy, and Frank Strachan had been a Scottish Spitfire pilot. Paul Brunavs was a former geodesy instructor at the University of Riga in Latvia, who thrived on meticulous mathematical investigations, yet was always patient in understanding problems and advising on solutions.

Vessels Converted for Hydrography

The saying "it's an ill wind that blows no good" applied well to CHS as the Second World War did bring its benefits. A new, wooden *Cartier*, which was originally destined as a coastal minesweeper for the Soviet navy, arrived in 1948. Then HMCS *Kapuskasing* and *Fort Frances* were converted from Algerine class minesweepers to full-fledged hydrographic ships and commissioned in September 1949. *Kapuskasing* met an ignominious end when it was sunk as a target by the navy. The eighty-seven foot coastal patrol vessel *Parry* (ex-USS *Talapus*) joined the CHS Pacific fleet in 1946. The *Ehkoli* was a sister ship. Both are still afloat as charter fishing vessels.

The End of Copper Engraved Charts

The year 1947 saw the retirement of the last chart that was produced using the technique of copper engraving. The 200 or so copper plates, each weighing 25 kg, were stored in one room at #8 Temporary Building. Unfortunately the building had not been designed for such a heavy static load, and the floor began to sag. Eventually the plates were no longer needed. Some found a new life, surreptitiously, as coffee tables but most were, equally illegally, trucked away for the scrap-metal content.

Canada's International Role

It was not until 1951 that Canada, represented by the CHS, joined the International Hydrographic Bureau as the forerunner of the International Hydrographic Organization (IHO). The bureau had been established in 1921 to foster the international exchange of hydrographic data, to establish quality assurance, and to standardize chart presentation. Canada's membership has been both active and distinguished, and recently has included the election of a Canadian as a director of the organization.

1952–57: F.C.G. SMITH

The Organization

The new dominion hydrographer, F.C. Goulding Smith, rose through the ranks of the CHS as a hydrographer, and was head of chart production during the war when so many demands for large quantities of charts and limited resources made the job difficult. He has been regarded as the dominion hydrographer who knew so much about each job within CHS that he could demonstrate the correct procedure to any member on staff. Each hydrographic office represented at IHO has its own crest. Under the watchful eye of Smith, Gordon Croll designed and ornamentally illustrated the CHS crest about 1953. Through unknown channels the Canadian High Commission presented the crest to Queen Elizabeth II for approval, much to the chagrin of the heraldic bodies in London. The signed original still hangs in the dominion hydrographer's office as a much-coveted artifact.

Sealers and Other Vessels

The *Marabell* had been a U.S. navy minesweeper, and later a private yacht, before being bought by CHS in 1953. *Arctic Sealer, Algerine, Theron, Theta,* and *North Star IV* were used in seal hunting off Newfoundland and Labrador in the spring, and were often chartered for surveys along those coasts in the summer. Through interdepartmental cooperation, hydrographers started to travel on Department of Transport icebreakers serving in the Arctic (e.g., *C.D. Howe*) as early as 1951 to carry out surveys whenever an opportunity arose.[4]

New Requirements for Surveys

The iron ore development along the Labrador-Québec border opened up the ports of Sept Îles and Port Cartier, whilst aluminium smelting at Kitimat required surveys of Douglas Channel and Caamaño Sound. Construction on the St Lawrence Seaway started in 1954. It became operational in 1959, thereby providing a twenty-seven-foot depth from Montreal to Lake Superior instead of the previous fourteen-foot controlling depth in the section from Montreal to Prescott. The CHS surveyed the new channels and locks, including the whole of a new man-made lake. Topographic plots of areas to be flooded were converted to depths below a sloping sounding datum. The twelve charts were published repeatedly as new editions as conditions changed.

Charting: The Introduction of Scribing

The office work of preparing a chart for publication was divided between compilers and draftspersons. Compilers assembled the field sheets at the desired chart scale, selected the soundings to be shown, drew the contours, and added the aids to navigation and other required information. The draftspersons then used the newly introduced technique of scribing coated plastic scribe-coats with the line work. From the scribe-coats the photo-mechanical section could make peel-coats so that sections between lines could be removed to form temporary negatives for the colour separations. The soundings and light character-istics were all scribed by hand so that the chart would look like a copper plate engraving, but with colours! Ells Walsh designed a small, pen-like drill in order to make dots in the scribe-coat for the smallest intervals in the border, the centres of light symbols, and other point features. In 1953 the cartographers started to use type set on plastic strips that were stuck down with wax. Lead-type typesetting, which had never been popular with the typesetters, was then abandoned. Chart 4368 of St Ann's Harbour, Nova Scotia, was the first in the world to be produced by engraving on plastic. The St Lawrence Seaway charting indirectly brought about the systematic inspection of chart dealers when it was found that some were selling outdated charts. Bill Covey was assigned the task of inspection and removal of obsolete stock.

1957–67: N.G. GRAY

The Organization Expands

Norm Gray, an hydrographer who had surveyed from sailing gigs in the 1930s, succeeded F.C.G. Smith as dominion hydrographer in 1957, and several years later led CHS into its new quarters. The Surveys and Mapping Building at 615 Booth Street in Ottawa was constructed in 1960 with the requirements of mapping in mind: the press room in the basement, extra-heavy floor loadings for photogrammetric equipment, no vibration, and constant atmospheric conditions – but not air conditioning, which came later with computers. The Atlantic Region field staff moved to Halifax in 1959, and then to the newly formed Bedford Institute of Oceanography in Dartmouth, Nova Scotia, in 1962 under the leadership of G.W. LaCroix. He was succeeded by Russ Melanson, and later by Adam Kerr and Paul Bellemare. In the same year CHS left Surveys and Mapping Branch to become part of the newly formed Marine Sciences Branch of Energy, Mines and Resources. A Central Region of CHS was created in 1964 under the direction of Mike Bolton, and was housed in separate offices in Ottawa. The end of Gray's tenure as dominion hydrographer coincided with Canada's centennial year and an IHO conference, both in 1967. They were marked by *Baffin* visiting the conference as a centennial project and to demonstrate how Canada undertook hydrographic surveys. Renaud Pilote was on board as a bilingual host/hydrographer, and he succeeded where many others fail – at the gambling tables.

New Hydrographic Vessels

Gone were the days of make-do ships or chartering unemployed sealers. Time could be spent in designing ships to meet particular needs, and there was money enough to build them. *Baffin* was built in 1956 as a large hydrographic ship capable of penetrating northern waters, the offshore oceanographic vessel *Hudson* was added in 1962, and the two inshore hydrographic ships *Maxwell* and *Richardson* in 1961 and 1962 respectively. *Vector, Parizeau,* and *Dawson* (1967), and *Limnos* in 1968, were designed towards the end of the period and built for offshore multi-disciplinary surveys, which emerged as a new and significant commitment. Because of technologies developed during the war, radar and radio navigation equipment were acquired for ships. Loran-A had become available to civilians in 1946 with stations in Nova Scotia, Newfoundland, and British Columbia. Four Decca Navigator chains were installed in Atlantic Canada in 1957, one of which was re-configured in 1961 and another in 1964.

Requirements for Surveys in the North

Planning began in 1954 for the construction of the Distant Early Warning (DEW) Line radar stations along the 69th parallel of latitude, extending from western Alaska to the east coast of Greenland at fifty-mile intervals. Since the only through navigation in the Canadian Arctic up to 1950 had been by Roald Amundsen in *Gjoa* and Henry A. Larsen in *St Roch*, the Arctic was essentially unsurveyed territory. Deeply laden ships would transport the construction and technical materials to the DEW Line sites. Routes, landing sites, and wintering havens were surveyed in 1954 by HMCS *Labrador* and USS *Burton Island* in Prince of Wales Strait, and in 1955 by USS *Requisite* and *Storis* from Dolphin and Union Strait to Shepherd Bay. *Labrador* sailed through the north-west passage in 1954, thus becoming the first large ship and first naval vessel to make such a voyage. *Labrador* surveyed Bellot Strait in 1957, and then led USS *Storis, Spar,* and *Bramble* through this escape route so that they became the first American ships to transit the north-west passage.[5]

Captain R.M. Southern was contracted during 1957–58 to write the three volumes of the *Arctic Pilot*. The books were welcomed by mariners and others as they provided the sole source for information on climate, ice conditions, and villages. Sid van Dyck predicted the tides for the coming few days at beach landing sites of the DEW Line stations by taking the observed tidal regime for the period prior to full moon and applying it as a mirror image to the period after. Tidal predictions are normally far more extensive, but van Dyck's method satisfied the extemporaneous nature of working in the Arctic.

Tidal currents are not familiar to east-coast captains. When the *Algerine* proceeded into Lac aux Feuilles (Leaf Basin), Ungava Bay, just overcoming the ten-knot current with full speed ahead, the captain dropped anchor and automatically reversed engines to take the way off the ship. But he forgot about the strong tidal current and in moments the anchor chain was jumping out of the chain locker with sparks flying. As the crew looked back down what is now Algerine Passage, a pyramid-shaped rock rose out of the centre of the channel. It is now called Whaleback Reef and is known to be 5.8 m above low tide in a tidal range of 16.6 m.

In the late 1950s George Hobson said that the Americans "came to us and asked if we [the Canadian government] could supply the data on gravity in the Arctic, or if not, they

Figure 8-1
Sid van Dyck and Stu Dunbrack (seated on left) were two CHS hydrographers from HMCS *Labrador* when, in 1957, their pilot crashed while landing on an island in Frobisher Bay. A second helicopter from the ship broke a tail rotor in the rescue attempt. The four men were picked up the next day by a military helicopter, an example of interservice cooperation.
Photo: S. van Dyck

would go there and get it themselves. We decided it would be better if we supplied it ourselves."[6] The need for surveys of many types having been recognized, the logistical support for these Arctic surveys was provided through the coordinating body known as the Polar Continental Shelf Project (PCSP), which was established on 4 April 1958. The PCSP has fulfilled its mandate admirably since inception.

Extensive survey work has been carried out within the Arctic archipelago and offshore, with the logistical support of PCSP, by sounding through the ice at a regular grid of data points in late winter. About 1959, holes were drilled or blasted through the ice and a lead-line was lowered to take each sounding. Transportation was by snowmobile. The helicopter was first used in Canadian hydrographic surveying from HMCS *Labrador* during surveys of the water approaches to many of the DEW Line sites in the eastern Arctic in 1954 (see figure 8-1). Helicopters were used directly for hydrography in the 1962 PCSP survey of Penny Strait, and of Hell Gate in the following year. The transducer was mounted in a fish towed by the helicopter flying at low altitude. Although the method was successful, it was nerve-racking because one false move could put the helicopter in the drink.[7] The *Baffin* and *Hudson* were designed with a helicopter deck and hangar at the stern, whilst the *Parizeau* (1967) had a helicopter landing deck added to its focsle – not an entirely suitable location. The much later design of the *John P. Tully* (1984) placed the helicopter deck just forward of the wheelhouse, and *Matthew* (1991) has its helicopter deck high above the midship section.

Positioning in Hydrographic Surveys

The advent of the Tellurometer for electromagnetic distance measurement has been described in chapter 2. The instrument was acquired by the hydrographers shortly after it was released, and allowed them to traverse rather than triangulate. Thus the amount of time needed to establish the land-based horizontal control needed for hydrographic surveys was reduced. The first field operation with the Tellurometer in CHS was during 1957 in Frobisher Bay under Chuck Leadman. Always suspicious of a new toy, the hydrographers measured the length of a baseline along the airstrip by both invar tape and Tellurometer. The difference in length was 0.1 feet in 7600 feet. Whilst the invar tape measurement took two days, the Tellurometer measurement was completed in one half-hour.[8] Later in the year two long Tellurometer traverses were run successfully, one of them along the eastern shore of Nova Scotia. Since then later models of Tellurometers and, more recently, infrared distance measuring instruments have helped hydrographers to establish control and to position important features.

The marine version of the Tellurometer was Hydrodist, which had an extra-wide beam width to overcome the pitch, roll, and yaw of the ship so that it could be located by two distances, or by distance and angle. Nevertheless the requirement to orient the antennae correctly was always a disadvantage. Other radio positioning systems came on the market that were much simpler and had omni-directional antennae (see figure 8-2 of a typical survey launch). Some allowed several survey launches to work in the same area simultaneously. The multiple-user systems often had transmitters on shore that worked together to establish a set of two overlapping hyperbolic navigation patterns so that only passive receivers were needed in the launches.

Survey-quality distance measuring systems cover the electromagnetic spectrum from low frequency to visible light. Their accuracy depends on knowledge of the velocity of electromagnetic waves. In the low and medium frequencies velocity is a non-linear function of frequency, distance, conductivity, and permittivity, which together create different effective velocities for seawater, fresh water, land, and ice. The CHS has spent considerable time and effort in verifying the empirical formulae with observed data.[9]

Most of the systems had their idiosyncracies. CHS purchased its first Decca 6-*f* chain in 1955, and deployed the master unit on *Kapuskasing* and the slave units on shore for a survey of the south-western portion of the Gulf of St Lawrence. Decca and other positioning systems counted lanes on an odometer-like meter but could easily lose one or more lanes, particularly at night. This necessitated revisiting known positions such as anchored buoys or positioning the ship accurately from shore. Undetected "lane jumps" caused discontinuity in the surveying of underwater canyons and ridges that could only be resolved by experienced researchers moving Decca fixes by an integral number of lanes to make the canyons and ridges line up on the plot. The grounding of the *Baffin* on Black Rock in 1957 was caused by undetected lane jumps, and the resulting inquiry recommended that the captain had the final authority for the safety of the ship.[10] The grounding also led to the establishment of a navigation group at the Bedford Institute under Mike Eaton to establish independent assessments of the accuracy of survey systems. The Decca-Lambda system

Figure 8-2

A CHS launch sounding. The view shows: the winch (on the side of the cockpit) and pulley (side of cabin) for lowering the acoustically reflective cone used to verify the sounder; the microwave distance measuring transceiver (white box on mast) for positioning; radio antenna for communications (port side of cabin); radar and a radar reflector for navigation and safety; the number on the bow for easy identification; the high percentage of enclosed cabin for inclement days; tarpaulin over hatchway that would be open if sextant resection angles were being used for positioning; buoys (on cabin roof) that would be anchored as a reference point in a shoal examination; anchor on bow; and coxswain dressed for the weather.

had a lane-identification feature that, although not foolproof, at least allowed some external knowledge of the lane counts without having to revisit a known location.

Improvements in Sounding

The advances made to acoustic equipment during the Second World War were applied to sounders. Higher operating frequencies became more typical for shallow water where a very distinct profile could be obtained because the energy was projected downwards in a narrow cone. Lower frequencies, with their correspondingly higher output of energy, were used for greater depths. In the case of the latter, however, the energy was more dispersed and therefore a smoother profile of the sea bottom was developed. To quantify the zero and velocity errors, an acoustically reflective cone or bar is lowered from the ship or launch to various depths, and the errors are noted on the sounder record. Adjustments to depths indicated by the sounder can then be made based on the corrections derived. Before these physical facts were too well-known, Colin Martin described the accepted CHS practice of correcting the launch soundings, done with one type of sounder, so that they agreed with the cross-check soundings done by the ship using a different sounder.

By the early 1960s commercial fishing vessels had the tools needed for accurate positioning and determining the depths of water. Starting in 1964 CHS catered to the needs of

Figure 8-3
Measuring a 14-knot current at Sechelt Rapids on the British Columbia coast. The boat's speed is adjusted so that it is stationary (relative to shore) and a current meter is lowered over the side.
Photo: Mike Woodward

the fishermen with special-purpose charts that provided extra hyperbolic lattices, more depth information, more information on the type and roughness of the sea bottom, and the locations of wrecks – as both a hazard and a desirable place to fish. The scale of the fishing charts was made larger than that needed for safe passage. The development of aquaculture (or fish farming) has also required showing these navigational hazards.

Even for a government's inventory of resources, knowledge of the continental shelf requires information on bathymetry and geology. Seismic, magnetic, and gravity techniques are used to detect the rock layers and identify their types. The obvious solution was to load all the necessary equipment onto one ship and perform a multi-disciplinary survey. Such surveys were begun in 1964 and the results were published by CHS and Geological Survey of Canada.[11] On the basis of these surveys oil companies established areas that required further investigation, including drilling at some selected sites. At the cost of several million dollars a drill site, the importance of proper surveys offshore was not lost to Energy, Mines and Resources, which convened government and industry workshops on surveying Canada's offshore lands for mineral resource development. Three editions of the report summarized current technology.[12,13,14]

On the Pacific coast it is necessary to provide the times for slack water (or zero velocity) for some channels in which, at other times of the day, the velocity can be up to sixteen knots, causing rapids, overfalls, and eddies (see figure 8-3). Seymour Narrows was particularly dangerous. The middle of the channel was obstructed by Ripple Rock with a least depth of only 2.7 m, which had claimed 114 lives and sunk or severely damaged twenty large ships, including the CHS's own *Wm J. Stewart*. The demolition of the two peaks on 5 April 1958 by the largest non-nuclear explosion detonated worldwide to that date flattened the tops and reduced the eddies. Although the maximum current remained, the least depth is now 13.7 m. The explosion was scheduled near extreme low water so that the rock fragments would be dispersed as far as possible. With an eleven-knot current flowing northwards the concussion from the explosion would be reduced towards the south, and the rock fragments would be dispersed in the water column. Finally, the event was planned for the spring when the fish population was minimal.[15]

Innovations in Charting

Most charts are hand corrected up to the time they leave the depot. Where the corrections are numerous and complicated, gluing a correction patch to the chart is the only practical solution. An ingenious innovation was implemented about 1958 after Gerry Jasky, who moonlighted wrapping meat in heat-seal paper, suggested using the heat-seal paper for correction patches. The production of patches then increased rapidly from an average of four to sixty patches per year at CHS, because of heat-seal paper.

The survey of the eastern side of Georgian Bay (1959–63) was one of the first devoted to the recreational boater. Strip charts were first produced in 1964 with an orientation along the direction of the route, and folded like an accordion so they could be used in small craft. Barkley Sound, the Gulf Islands, and the Strait of Georgia have also been surveyed for the boater. The popular *Atlas of the Gulf Islands*, which presents charts, sailing directions, and photographs in a single volume, was the inspiration of Sev Crowther, the chief of chart production for the Pacific Region. CHS representation at boat shows in major cities started in 1958 in Toronto. They were, and still are, popular booths.

Chart production increased not only because of recreational charting, but also due to the take-over of U.S. charts for the DEW Line sites and the assumption of responsibility for the British Admiralty charts of Canadian waters, principally in Newfoundland (see figure 8-4). At one time CHS carried as many as ninety-four former British Admiralty charts. In 1994 thirty-eight still remain as reproductions.

Training

The CHS established a training programme for incoming hydrographers because there were no Canadian post-secondary education facilities in hydrography. Since ships and personnel could not be devoted to such a project during the normal field season, in-class instruction was held in the fall after which the class boarded the *Baffin* for practical work in the Caribbean. The location was determined by agreement with the British Admiralty or local governments. Rumour had it that some people joined CHS just for the Caribbean exposure in winter. There were two levels of hydrographic training, the "how-to" as the first level and the "why" as the second. When the IHO developed international standards for training courses in hydrography, CHS training was credited with the highest standard.

It was during this period that the Civil Service Commission established a drafting school in Ottawa. Candidates for cartographic jobs were given formal training to qualify them for

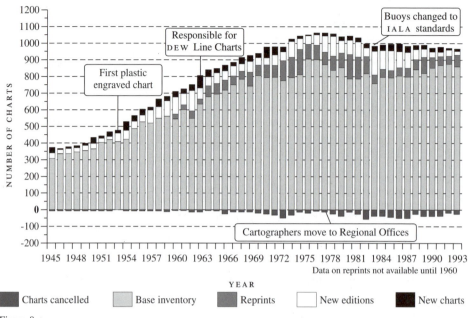

Figure 8-4

CHS chart production over the years. The top line gives the number of charts on inventory at the end of each calendar year. The space between successive lines is the number of charts printed during the year as new charts, new editions, or reprints. At the bottom is the number of charts cancelled during each year.
Source: CHS

positions in hydrographic, topographic, and agricultural cartography. Each office provided a staff member to act as instructor, with Norman Veitch representing CHS.

1968–72: DR A.E. COLLIN

Changes in the Organization

The choice of Art Collin, an oceanographer, as the next dominion hydrographer reflected the multi-disciplinary nature of offshore surveying. During his tenure CHS was transferred from Energy, Mines and Resources to the Department of the Environment in June 1971. The latter department experienced several minor name changes until, finally, the CHS became part of the Department of Fisheries and Oceans in 1979. The Central Region office was moved to the Canada Centre for Inland Waters at Burlington, Ontario, in 1970. When Mike Bolton, as Central Region director, was posted to the Pacific Region, he was replaced by Tom McCulloch, and in turn by Adam Kerr, Ross Douglas, and Earl Brown. The University Training Programme was introduced in Art Collin's time as a major effort to strengthen professionalism by educating rather than training. The sharp increase in technology meant that in-house training was no longer sufficient for the senior field or management positions. Thus staff were encouraged to study for a first university degree or to pursue further education at the postgraduate level.

The Arctic is not noted for being hospitable, and much that is done is at the whim of Mother Nature. *Richardson,* CCGS *Camsell,* and USS *Northwind* were caught fast in ice off Point Barrow in 1967. *Parizeau* was damaged by ice in 1976. Nevertheless the CHS surveying and charting programmes continued to be driven by the economic needs of Canada. The lead-zinc mines at Nanisivik, oil exploitation on Cameron Island, and exploration in the Beaufort Sea near Tuktoyaktuk are examples of charting requirements for resource development. The American demonstration of transporting oil from Prudhoe Bay, Alaska, by the very large crude carrier *Manhattan* in 1969 spurred hydrographic surveys in Canadian waters. During that mission the CCGS *Sir John A. Macdonald* discovered the first pingo-like feature (PLF), now known as The Admiral's Finger, which would be a hazard to such deep draught ships. The whole area was too large to survey at sufficiently close line spacing to detect all PLFs, and consequently only a ten-mile-wide corridor was surveyed. The work was done by launches from both *Hudson* and *Baffin* working four four-hour shifts per day for several field seasons.

Procedures for sounding through the ice were modified by attaching the transducers to the ice acoustically with a smear of oil. Helicopter transport quickened the pace of surveying. For intensive surveys such as proposed pipeline crossing points, it was expedient to use a tracked vehicle with a spike transducer hydraulically rammed into the ice. The spike transducer is now mounted on helicopters as well. Between 1968 and 1970 CHS tried using hovercraft in the near-shore area, but the towed transducer kept breaking the surface when at speeds greater than twenty knots. The transducer was moved to a strut fixed to the hovercraft, and speeds of twenty-five knots were then achieved. Unfortunately the rubber skirt of the craft kept freezing to the beach at night and had to be chopped free in the morning, thus losing its ability to hold a cushion of air under itself.[16]

1972–78: G.N. EWING

The Organization: Further Decentralization

In 1972 Collin was succeeded by a geologist, Gerry Ewing, as dominion hydrographer. From time to time senior managers have sought to locate their departments in one building. Following the 1971 transfer to the Department of the Environment the headquarters office was able to deflect such attempts by demonstrating how the special requirements of CHS were met by the Surveys and Mapping building, and by being physically near other government mapping agencies in EMR and DND. Cyril Champ, the long-time assistant to the dominion hydrographer, was instrumental in averting the moves. But by 1975 the chart storage space at headquarters had become too limited, and better warehouse facilities were found on Russell Road in Ottawa's east end. The chart hand correctors followed, and the Sailing Directions group also moved there for several years. Except for the Reprints and Notice to Mariners staff, many of the cartographers departed from Ottawa in 1976 on assignment to each regional office except St John's. The increase in computer graphics equipment required more space, which became available as the cartographers moved to the regional offices. A Québec Region was formed in 1976 at the Gare Maritime in Québec City under two temporary regional directors, Hiro Furuya and John O'Shea, before Ken

Williams, Paul Bellemare, and later Denis Hains were appointed on a permanent basis. In 1986 the Québec Region office was moved to the Institut Maurice LaMontagne at Mont Joli, Québec. During Ewing's tenure as dominion hydrographer the *Advent* was designed and built, and CHS's fourth *Bayfield* was purchased and modified for hydrography.

Developments in Navigation and Positioning

The digital recording of survey data was recognized as a means of eliminating errors and reducing the personnel on the survey launch. The use of sextants for positioning had been replaced earlier by range-range or hyperbolic measurements, which could be recorded digitally, relieving the second hydrographer of this task. A digitizer on the sounder replaced the seaman standing watch at that instrument. The many teething troubles with digitizers have been overcome. The recording equipment has also been a major source of problems since the launch environment is very hostile, being wet, either too hot or too cold, and subject to vibrations and power fluctuations. Fortunately these have been overcome by degrees.[17] When sextants were used the coxswain navigated along compass bearings, with corrections supplied by the hydrographers after each resection fix. With range-range, range-bearing, or hyperbolic type surveys, the launch was navigated along arcs of circles or hyperbolas using a left-right sensor to determine the deviation from a single position line. But with the computer equipment on board today, the coxswain now steers a series of parallel courses in the form of a grid based on the real-time positions derived from the electronic positioning system.

There are no checks on the individual determination of position save for the change in relative position since the last fix. In earlier days launches were positioned by two resection angles measured with sextants on the vessel. The electromagnetic distance measuring era followed similar principles – two ranges, two hyperbolic range differences, or shore angle and distance were measured. Only when it was realized that the Trisponder and Mini-Ranger positioning systems suffered from interference, caused by the rays reflected from the water surface weakening or cancelling the direct signal (a situation known as "range holes"), was corrective action taken. Signal-strength indicators, measuring three or more ranges, and analysing the rate of change in the ranges were all adopted as normal working practices.[18] When CHS purchased the Syledis system in 1983 it was the first time that positioning could benefit from the measurement of multiple ranges and a least squares solution for the position of the vessel.

With the launching of the Sputnik satellite in 1957 it was realised that the Doppler effect on its radio signals could be used to determine the orbital characteristics of the satellite. By 1968 civilians could use the Doppler effect of signals from TRANSIT satellites to position points on land. If the ship's velocity was known accurately, its position could be determined to ±150 m based on a single pass of the TRANSIT satellite. Dave Wells and Steve Grant at the Bedford Institute developed a navigation system called BIONAV. This used TRANSIT satellite fixes at about three-hour intervals coupled with rho-rho Loran-C range measurements. The Loran provided the velocity input during the satellite pass, and the satellite fixes provided information on the relative clock drift between the cesium frequency standard controlling the Loran transmitters and the one on board the ship. This method of positioning was used to survey much of the Grand Banks, Labrador Shelf, and Davis Strait.[19] The system was modified later by adding a sonar log, which also used the

Doppler effect, for monitoring the velocity of the ship with respect to the sea bottom. The central part of Hudson Bay was surveyed using this log coupled to the satellite receiver since no Loran signals were available, and the bay was shallow enough to provide the reflections from the bottom needed for the Doppler sonar.

Navigation by Deep- and Shallow-Draught Vessels

It was necessary to find new ports that could accommodate the very large crude-oil carriers that entered service during this period. Port Hawkesbury, Nova Scotia, and Come By Chance, Newfoundland, were two such Canadian sites. Admiral (later Sir) David Haslam commented on the survey requirement: "An indication of the rapid development in the draughts of merchant shipping recently is given by the use of the 'Dangerous Wreck' symbol on British charts. Until 1960, this represented a depth of less than 14.6 m (48 feet); from 1960 to 1963 this was lowered to less than 18.3 m (60 feet), and until 1968 to less than 20.1 m (66 feet). It is now [in 1979] 28 metres (92 feet) or less."[20] The CHS standard followed suit and, in 1994 was 20 m.

Shallow-draught tugs and barges transport goods along the Mackenzie River system from the railhead at Hay River to Tuktoyaktuk without the need for locks, a journey that is equivalent in distance and change in elevation to that from Sault Ste Marie to Québec City. Much of the hydrographic survey was done using jet-powered boats that could skim over the shallows. The charts produced by CHS are ozalid prints of the National Topographic System (NTS) 1:50 000 sheets annotated with the soundings, range markers, and other navigational information. The oil companies progressed northwards along the Mackenzie River valley in which Esso had had wells at Norman Wells since the 1930s. The companies moved into the shallow waters off the delta, building artificial islands or berms with caissons. The oil companies chartered Coast Guard ice-breakers and even built their own. A remarkably fine grade of oil from Rae Point on Cameron Island is being shipped out through a specially designed tanker, MV *Arctic*.

Further Changes in Charting

The emergence of the French language as equal to English in all government publications caused CHS to publish charts in a bilingual format, and *Sailing Directions* and *Tide Tables* in both official languages. The increased use of symbols required that they conform with the charts of other nations. Only 56 percent of CHS charts are bilingual even after almost twenty years.

The CHS decision to convert to metric units followed some experience with special metric charts and preceded, by a few months, the government's White Paper on Metric Conversion in January 1970.[21] Metrication meant conforming with the international community of chart makers: even the British Admiralty, the patriarch of chart makers, was converting. It was foreseen that a user might think the water was deeper than it actually was because the wrong units were assumed. A survey of mariners indicated that depths should be portrayed by contours rather than a dense display of soundings. This provided CHS with a means of differentiating imperial and metric charts, the former being characterized by dense soundings in fathoms or feet and the latter emphasizing metric contours. In 1994 there were 387 metric CHS charts, or 40 percent of the total Canadian charts.

Imperial-unit charts were based on a scale in which 1 inch on the chart represents one or more nautical miles on the earth's surface, e.g., Chart 4385, Osborne Head to Betty Island (or the approaches to Halifax), scale 1:36 480 (or 2 inches represent 1 nautical mile) with depths in fathoms and feet, first published in 1952. The scale of metric charts is typically one unit on the chart representing several thousand units on the earth's surface, e.g., Chart 4237, Approaches to/Approches au Halifax Harbour, scale 1:40 000 with 5, 10, 20, 30, 50, and 100 m contours, first published in 1988. In addition to metrication of the information and the change of scale, charts were also converted to metric size paper, most often AO size of 1189 × 841 mm. These changes have prompted CHS to redefine the limits of the individual metric chart, a process known as re-scheming. CHS has been able to combine these requirements into one charting programme of re-scheming, metrication, and making the charts bilingual. The first bilingual, metric charts were printed in 1976, but as of 1993 only 14 percent were metric, bilingual, and on the North American Datum of 1983 (NAD83) – yet another requirement in modernizing the charts.

The IHO has promoted the establishment of an international series of charts (or INT charts) for which one nation gathers the surveyed information and produces the chart (the "producer nation"). Other nations request the reproduction material, alter the notes and language to meet their needs, and print the resulting chart ("printer nation"). Canada produced three of the 1:3 500 000 scale INT charts of the Atlantic Coast in the period 1972–74, and then four charts for Halifax Harbour and approaches in 1986–87.

The use of Loran-C west of Nova Scotia started in 1972. Coverage became available on the British Columbia coast (1977), in Atlantic Canada (1980 and 1984), and within the Great Lakes (1980). Five transmitters are now located on Canadian soil. Charts with hyperbolic lines of positions were necessary to be able to plot observations made with Loran-C.

Until 1969 Decca and Loran-A hyperbolic lattices were drawn manually. Points had to be calculated along each hyperbola, plotted manually, and joined by long splines held down by "ducks." The challenge was to lay the spline down along points of the same hyperbola, and not cross from one hyperbola to the next. Manual scribing of one set of hyperbolas for a single chart took two people two to three weeks. After 1969 the drafting of lattices became part of computer-assisted cartography. Consequently more elaborate routines could be used in the computations, e.g., a non-linear velocity model, a polynomial, or a grid of data to express over-land signal delays (Additional Secondary Factor, or ASF)[22]. The ASF corrections are supplied through *Radio Aids to Marine Navigation* for users of coordinate converters. CHS lattice drafting techniques are held in high regard internationally.

The plotting of borders, grid lines, and lattices was only the beginning of computer-assisted cartography. The flatbed plotter with its focused light drawing on a large sheet of photographic negative could draw complex chart symbols, straight lines, mathematical curves, or complex curves such as contours or shoreline. In 1978 Chart 8015 (Northeast Newfoundland) was the first assembled through interactive graphics for which all line work and features were drawn by the computer. Charts were also assembled from digital, rather than graphic, field sheets. Thus it became possible to reposition chart information in order to match the current geodetic coordinates of the control survey points; convert from one map projection to another accurately; change the vertical datum; contour automatically; select spot soundings to improve the depiction of the depth between contours; and make the colour separations for any closed polygon on the chart. All this work is now done interactively by the modern cartographer (see figure 8-5). The computer can just as easily send the digital file via satellite to a regional office or, theoretically, to the ship. The digital chart file is used to print single copies of charts on a multicolour printer in cases where there will be a low volume of sales, e.g., Arctic communities.

Although most cartographers had acquired drafting skills at technical schools or technical colleges, the changes that have been described necessitated additional cartographic training. In-house courses were started in the 1970s.

Tidal and Water-Level Information

The Liverpool Observatory and Tidal Institute in the U.K. calculated tidal predictions for Canada using analogue computational methods, and then sent them to Ottawa for printing. Canada assumed responsibility for the 1975 edition, and since then the most modern computers have speeded up the process to a mere fraction of the time taken previously.

The tidal regime at any point is a summation of defined sine wave functions of different periods, amplitudes, and offsets, constituents that can be isolated. The CHS and Marine Environmental Data Service (MEDS) initiated in 1977, and thereafter have maintained, a library of the tidal constituents of all tidal stations in the member states of the IHO. CHS accepted full responsibility for the database in 1993.

Water-level gauges have been installed at various inland ports, not to record the tide but to provide instantaneous water levels. Ships' masters leaving foreign ports want to know the water level that can be expected in Montreal two weeks hence, for example, so that the vessels can be loaded for that expected depth, and costly partial unloading at Québec City or elsewhere can be avoided. Today synthesized voice messages respond automatically to phone requests from ships' masters and provide information needed to load the ship to the maximum available draught.

The Law of the Sea

At the end of the war the limit of a country's sovereignty was still considered to be three nautical miles. But that too has changed over the half-century. There have been three United Nations Conferences on the Law of the Sea. The first was in 1958, which resulted in conventions on the territorial sea and the continental shelf. The second conference in 1960 was unproductive. The third went through many sessions from 1974 until the signing of the convention in 1982. Countries may now claim a territorial sea 12 nautical miles (n.m.) wide, an exclusive economic zone 200 n.m. wide, and the possibility of a continental shelf for considerably greater distance given the appropriate geological and bathymetric conditions.[23] With Canada's increased interest in claiming these zones it was necessary to define the points of land that control their definition. Parts of Canada's coast were, and still are, poorly charted so that the locations of islands and rocks are not well-known. Betty Fleming of Topographic Survey, EMR searched satellite imagery to locate possible rocks along the Labrador coast. Dick LeLievre and Ken Williams as hydrographers-in-charge on *Baffin* in separate years were required to substantiate her findings. Some islands previously charted were proven not to exist, and new islands found in the imagery were verified.[24]

Figure 8-5
At the left is a copy of the field sheet of Belleville, Ontario, reduced to chart scale. Note the density of the surveyed soundings. At right is a copy of the resulting chart contoured and with selected soundings.

1979–87: S.B. MACPHEE

The Organization

Steve MacPhee, an acoustic engineer who had specialized in sonar equipment, was appointed dominion hydrographer in 1979 when Gerry Ewing became an assistant deputy minister. The

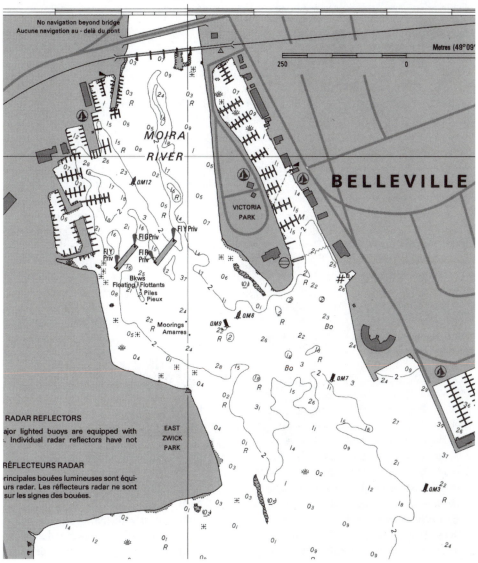

requirement for qualified surveyors to delineate property rights offshore prompted the surveying community to develop standards for hydrographic surveying. This was done under the auspices of the Canada Lands Surveyor (CLS) accreditation, the successor to the Dominion Land Surveyor. Several CHS hydrographers obtained their CLS qualifications during the period 1980–82 through a "grandfathering" arrangement. This recognized their lengthy experience and relieved them of the necessity to write most of the examination papers. The offshore property rights surveying function created the need for hydrographic surveyors in private practice, and there are now companies notable in that field.

Detailed Sounding in Shallow Waters

Shipowners maximize their profits by loading their ships to the maximum possible draught, thus reducing the clearance under the keel of the ship. As ships now tend to have much smaller keel clearance, sweeping navigation channels with a wire or bar, or obtaining total coverage of the channel bottom with acoustic sounders, has become necessary. Since the former is a very slow operation, CHS opted for the latter. CHS tried side scan sonar first, but that provided only an impression of the bottom roughness. Nevertheless knowing that something needs further investigation is better than not knowing at all. An array of sounders pointed in radial directions sideways from the ship was better, but due to the non-uniform velocity of sound the oblique rays travelled a curved path to and from the bottom. The third method was to spread a series of transducers along a boom extending from either side of the ship. The concept was proven by using a boom made from a television tower supported by two Laser sailboats, the whole being pushed by a launch. The production version was the *F.C.G. Smith*, a catamaran with wing booms that allows thirty-five transducers to survey a swath 46 m wide (see figure 8-6). The handling of the 42 000 soundings per minute from such surveys has also been addressed.[25] Other ships designed and built in this period were *John P. Tully* in 1984 and the barge *Pender* in 1980 as support for inshore field operations.

When the concept of continuous three-dimensional positioning using the proposed Global Positioning System (GPS) was first mentioned in the mid-1970s it sounded like a fairy tale coming true. It was implemented slowly throughout the 1980s, and finally was approved for use in 1993. During the period 1979–85 CHS proved the usefulness of a LIDAR laser sounder to measure the depth of water from an aircraft positioned first by microwave distance measuring equipment, and then by differential GPS.

In the Arctic, ships' masters change their plans unexpectedly because ice blocks their intended routes. In some years channels are wide open, and in other years totally blocked. The wind can change the situation in hours. Any open water within range could be surveyed by LIDAR with a DC-3 aircraft positioned with differential GPS. Selection of the survey area was made daily as the ice reports were received. Chart 7750 of Cambridge Bay, published in 1988, is the first CHS chart incorporating LIDAR laser depth measurements and GPS positioning.

Measuring depths of water using photogrammetry from normal air photos was found to be ineffective. The use of a rigid frame for mounting two vertical cameras that were triggered simultaneously proved to be better, but was still not acceptable for everyday use. Both suffered from lack of contrast in the image of the bottom. The shoals that are within the surf at the east and west ends of Sable Island were surveyed with the novel technique of air photo interpretation based on colour tones, supported by a few lines of soundings. The low-water line for charts could be extracted quite confidently from infrared colour photography taken at extreme low water.

Further Developments and Challenges in Charting

Acceptance of the International Association of Lighthouse Authority's (IALA) system for buoyage presented a new challenge to the cartographers. The change of left-hand buoys

Figure 8-6

F.C.G. *Smith* with booms deployed and performing a 100% bottom coverage survey.
Photo: CHS

from black to green was relatively minor, but the introduction of cardinal buoys (i.e., showing the cardinal direction to the hazard) was new. As a result many charts were reissued as new editions during 1983.

During the period 1975–82 CHS prepared and published the nineteen maps of the fifth edition of the General Bathymetric Chart of the Oceans (GEBCO) for the IHO and the International Oceanographic Commission. Previous editions had suffered from lack of financial support, but the Canadian government agreed to scribe, print, and provide sales outlets subject only to receiving the income from the sales. Work was carried out under the direction of David Monahan, with Sev Crowther and Rolly Hamilton as production supervisors. George Medynski had the hard task of preparing the single sheet of the world at 1:35 million.

This group of cartographers had originally started to produce Natural Resource Maps (NRMs) of the continental shelf in 1969. These maps were an extension of the NTS 1:250 000 maps, and there were bathymetric, free air gravity anomaly, and magnetic versions of each sheet. The data for these maps came from the offshore multi-disciplinary surveys started in 1964. The National Earth Science Series (NESS), at a scale of 1:1 000 000, were compiled from the NRMs.

The preparation of these detailed maps led to official recognition of the geographical names of undersea features by the Canadian Permanent Committee on Geographical Names (CPCGN, see appendix B) through the Advisory Committee on Names for Undersea and Maritime Features. The results were published in the *Gazetteer of Undersea Feature Names*.[26]

Digitization of Charts

For over 200 years chart production has been the responsibility of a single organization. Today chart making is becoming complex. There is the need for continual development through university research, by the computer hardware manufacturer who wishes to sell units in the marine navigation market, by the government survey agency that holds much of the original data, and by the software developer who manipulates the data in the computer and displays them on the screen.

The creation of a digital chart file was developed within CHS in a system called GOMADS (Graphical On-line Manipulation and Display System). The expertise was passed to Universal Systems Limited of Fredericton for further development, maintenance, and sales. The acronym for their interactive cartographic system is CARIS (Computer Assisted Resource Information System). CARIS is used by all CHS offices and has been sold to several hydrographic offices overseas.

The printing of a digital chart file on the ship is unlikely. It is more probable that the mariner will use an electronic chart, sometimes known by its full name Electronic Chart Display and Information System (or ECDIS). In 1983 the CHS Centennial Conference heard a futuristic presentation of a ship approaching Newfoundland using an electronic chart system with the following features:

- *Notices to Mariners* radioed from St John's
- Offshore shoals and collision with fishing boats avoided
- Precise positioning achieved with a GPS/Loran-C integrated system
- Sun's true bearing at sunrise calculated
- Next day's route planned and entered given certain horizontal and vertical clearances, including tidal considerations
- Reporting procedures checked in the computerized *Sailing Directions*
- Vessel's position adjusted to match the radar coastline
- Shore-based radar imagery added
- Plotting of both the horizontal track and the sounder's depth compared with the charted depth
- Use of the electronic chart at its largest scale to assist in docking[27]

Ten years later it is becoming a reality. Offshore Systems Ltd of Vancouver is in the forefront of marketing electronic chart systems. The company first installed systems on the Tsawwassen to Swartz Bay, British Columbia, ferries. Later they proved to be essential in docking the large CN Marine Atlantic ferries in Port aux Basques, Newfoundland. The change from proof of the concept to reality came when Canada Steamship Lines ordered eleven systems in the spring of 1993.

Sailing Directions describe what mariners will encounter. They used to be typeset, but the process has evolved into desktop publishing where the layout for a camera-ready copy is undertaken in a personal computer. Although the updating of the master text is possible as the information is received, the books are only reprinted every few years with updates being provided through *Notices to Mariners*. Hard-bound books have been replaced by soft-covered editions, and now three-ring binders of smaller booklets have been introduced for the waters of the St Lawrence Gulf, estuary, and River.

Legal Liability for Chart Information

The CHS has found itself in court on many occasions in the last half-century. Fortunately it has emerged relatively unscathed. The first major case was the collision between two ships in Lac St Pierre, Québec, in 1965. One ship, following the range line provided by two horizontally separated lights, suddenly veered across the channel into the path of an oncoming ship. It was found that the ice had moved the front light, thus moving the range line nearer the edge of the dredged channel. The hydrodynamics of the ship passing too close to the side of the channel had forced the ship to sheer away. Colin Martin endured two days of gruelling cross-examination in the Exchequer Court defending CHS charts and survey procedures. CHS and the Coast Guard agreed in 1968 that it was the responsibility of CHS to survey the position of navigational aids. The *Arrow* grounding on Cerberus Rock in Chedabucto Bay, Nova Scotia, prompted issue of the *Charts and Publications Regulations* which require all vessels to carry approved charts and publications. The grounding of the *Golden Robin* at Dalhousie, New Brunswick, caused a thorough tidying of the procedures in publishing *Notices to Mariners*, and highlighted the need to survey more frequently channels that silt.[28] A ship touched bottom in the Miramichi River, which had been surveyed with close spacing of sounding lines. This resulted in 100 percent bottom coverage being recognized as paramount for dredged channels, hence the commissioning of the *F.C.G. Smith* in 1985.

Not all court actions involved CHS as the respondent. The rate of erosion at Port Burwell, Ontario, was addressed in one court action in which the shoreline at various epochs was required, starting with the 1890s surveys of W.J. Stewart. Fishing violation trials sometimes require an expert witness to testify on the location of the violation, and the accuracy expected from the navigation equipment. A final illustration is taxation litigation concerning the locations of gas wells near Sable Island. Their positions with respect to the territorial sea limit necessitated examining the maps and surveys of the island over a period of 200 years.[29]

The collision of the tug *Ocean Service* with the oil tank barge *Nestucca* off Juan de Fuca Strait in December 1988, followed by the grounding of the *Exxon Valdez* on Bligh Reef in Prince William Sound, Alaska, in March 1989, led to a public review panel on marine safety chaired by David Brander-Smith. His report recommended that the upgrading of hydrographic charts along tanker routes, and the development of the electronic chart, should be accelerated.[30] The presentation of the latter to the review panel was under the guidance of Neil Anderson. The resulting development of the electronic chart within CHS was led by David Monahan.

The CHS was represented by John Cooper during the Third United Nations Conference on the Law of the Sea. He assisted the Canadian delegation at the International Court of Justice in the case of the Gulf of Maine maritime boundary. Both he and David Gray were Canadian team members in the boundary arbitration between Newfoundland and St Pierre and Miquelon.

Assistance to Other Countries

Mention has been made of Caribbean nations benefiting from hydrographic surveys performed in the CHS training programme under the supervision of qualified hydrographers.

Foreign hydrographic staff have been trained by Canadians in Malaysia, Jamaica, Indonesia, and India. Canadians have also assisted several countries in the form of special projects. Bob Marshall was in charge of the offshore survey of Senegal and The Gambia in 1976. Graeme Richardson helped in a survey of the Nile in Egypt, whilst Warren Forrester and Renaud Pilote visited Mali to advise on the water level gauging of the Niger River. David Gray provided advice on maritime boundaries to Namibia, and P.K. Mukherjee wrote Trinidad's Shipping Act. Lung Ku undertook tidal gauging in Pakistan, and Burt Smith assisted Guyana with hydrographic surveys. Gerry Dohler chaired a United Nations coordinating group on tsunami warning systems in the Pacific from 1974 to 1984, and was the associate director of the International Tsunami Information Center in Hawaii during the years 1982–83.

There were also many foreign nationals who came to Canadian universities for education in hydrography, and to benefit from practical experience at CHS. The former included visitors to Erindale College in the University of Toronto for Law of the Sea courses offered by the International Centre for Ocean Development (ICOD), and instructed by Rear Admiral D.C. Kapoor, formerly of the Indian navy.

1987–95: G.R. DOUGLAS

The Organization

When Steve MacPhee accepted a position at the Bedford Institute in 1987, Ross Douglas became the eleventh head of the CHS. A Newfoundland sub-regional office was opened during the same year in the offices of the Northwest Atlantic Fisheries Organization in St John's, Newfoundland, under Julian Goodyear. Also of note in 1987 was the election of Adam Kerr as the first Canadian, and first non-naval officer, to be a director of the International Hydrographic Bureau (the administrative wing of the IHO). He was re-elected in 1992 for a second term.

Professional Associations

As much as the IHO provided a forum for standardizing charting worldwide, and an outlet for professional papers through its *International Hydrographic Review,* it did not provide a forum for professionals to meet. This was better carried out through the Canadian Hydrographic Association (CHA) and the Canadian Institute of Geomatics (CIG). The former started in the 1950s as a staff association within CHS, but later sponsored annual conferences and a semi-annual magazine, *Lighthouse.* Many CHS staff members held positions of office in CHA. The CIG and its forerunners has been more elusive to the majority of hydrographers, who failed to see the need to join another professional association. Several did and made their mark as senior officers of the CIG. Others wrote papers for its journal, *The Canadian Surveyor,* later renamed *Geomatica.*

New Vessels for New Tasks

To determine the outer limit of the continental shelf, particularly according to the 1982 Law of the Sea Convention, many sounding profiles are required to locate the foot of the slope and the 2500 m isobath. A diesel-powered, semi-submersible called DOLPHIN was proposed and tested. The concept had major benefits: it was more stable than a launch of the same size, it was faster (indeed it could outrun its mother ship), and it was unmanned. Data were transmitted to the mother ship via radio link.[31] Once the problem of retrieving the vessel from the sea was conquered, and multibeam sonar and differential GPS were installed, three DOLPHINs were transferred to Geo-Resources Inc. in Newfoundland for marketing worldwide.

Both the *R.B. Young* (1990) and *Matthew* (1991) were designed and built for inshore hydrography. The *Frederick G. Creed* was purchased by CHS in 1989, and tested by the United States/Canada Hydrographic Commission. The *Creed* is a Small Waterplane Area Twin Hull (SWATH) vessel of 20 m length. It is exceptionally stable because of its design and is capable of twenty-two knots. It is equipped with a multibeam sounder and thus can provide total coverage of the sea bottom.

Other Recent Developments

The landing sites at some Arctic communities have only recently been surveyed. Since re-supply vessels are the only visitors, the charts will be printed by computer when needed. This practice is known as Print on Demand (POD), of which Charts 7134, 7135, and 7195 of Baffin Island were the first products in 1993.

One of the most significant events during Douglas's tenure is the establishment of a chair in ocean mapping at the University of New Brunswick. Universities, hardware manufacturers, software developers, and government have to work together for the data gathering and presentation of the future. The creation of a professorship at a university is just one sign of the new interrelationship. An outstanding achievement was the IHO award in 1992 of the Prince Albert (of Monaco) Medal to T.V. (Tim) Evangelatos. He and others have been instrumental in international standardization for electronic chart systems, which will be built by manufacturers using chart data provided by hydrographic offices.

CONCLUSION

Canada's economic well-being depends on shipping grains, ores, and fuels through the Great Lakes, St Lawrence Seaway, Gulf of St Lawrence, and several major ports. These waters have been hydrographically surveyed several times to meet increasing needs and physical changes. But parts of Canada's submerged land mass, which equals about half of the land mass above sea level, have not been surveyed even once as priorities were put elsewhere. Whereas photogrammetric techniques can be used easily to map great expanses of terrain, hydrography means the laborious profiling of the bottom from a ship or launch.

The CHS has endeavoured to survey and chart Canadian waters using the most efficient means at its disposal, and is a recognized leader internationally in the development of those means. But the real glory belongs to the hydrographers and cartographers who have used "tried and true" equipment and methods to achieve results. What is innovative one year becomes the production method shortly thereafter, and is tried and true within a decade. This is why the CHS record of achievements is outstanding, even if the work is not complete.

Nautical Magazine welcomed Rear Admiral D.W. Haslam to his post as the new U.K. hydrographer of the navy with these words: "Hydrography is a never-ending battle of too few resources against too many tasks. The situation has been like that since Alexander Dalrymple became the first Hydrographer in 1795. And it will never be any different in the future. Never."[32]

NOTES

1 Ritchie, G.S. 1974. Technological Advances and the Sea Surveyor. *International Hydrographic Review*, 51, 1, 7–15.

2 Fillmore, Stanley, and R.W. Sandilands. 1983. *The Chartmakers*. Toronto, Canada: NC Press Ltd, 169–74.

3 Sandilands, R.W. 1983. Hydrographic Surveying in the Great Lakes During the Nineteenth Century. *International Hydrographic Review*, 60, 2, 55–81.

4 Meehan, O.M. ca. 1967. The Canadian Hydrographic Service – From the Time of Its Inception in 1883 to the End of the Second World War. Ottawa: Marine Sciences Branch, Dept Energy, Mines and Resources.

5 Treadwell, T.K. 1958. Hydrographic Surveys in the Arctic. *International Hydrographic Review*, 35, 2, 33–41.

6 Foster, Michael, and Carol Marino. 1986. *The Polar Shelf: The Saga of Canada's Arctic Scientists*. Toronto: NC Press Ltd, 11.

7 Eaton, R.M. 1963. Airborne Hydrographic Surveys in the Canadian Arctic. *International Hydrographic Review*, 40, 2, 45–51.

8 Leadman, C.M. et al. 1957. The Tellurometer in Field Survey Operations. *The Canadian Surveyor*, 13, 10, 668–75.

9 Brunavs, P. and D.E. Wells. 1971. *Accurate Phase Lag Measurements over Sea Water Using Decca-Lambda*. Report AOL 1971–2. Dartmouth, NS: Bedford Institute of Oceanography.

10 Fillmore and Sandilands. 1983. *The Chartmakers*, 212.

11 Haworth, R.T. 1974. Gravity and Magnetic Natural Resource Maps (1972), Offshore Eastern Canada. *International Hydrographic Review*, 51, 1, 131–55.

12 *Surveying Offshore Canada Lands for Mineral Resource Development*. Ottawa: Energy, Mines and Resources.

13 1975. *Surveying Offshore Canada Lands for Mineral Resources Development*, 2d ed. Ottawa: Surveys and Mapping Branch, Energy, Mines and Resources.

14 1982. *Surveying Offshore Canada Lands for Mineral Resource Development*, 3d ed. Ottawa: Surveys and Mapping Branch, Energy, Mines and Resources.

15 Rutley, J.I.A. 1959. The Demolition of Ripple Rock. *International Hydrographic Review*. 36, 1, 19–28.

16 Douglas, G.R. 1979. Hydrographic Research in the Canadian Arctic. *The Canadian Surveyor*, 33, 4, 373–82.

17 Bryant, R.S., C. Doekes, and R.L.K. Tripe. 1976. INDAPS – Integrated Navigation, Data Acquisition and Processing system. *International Hydrographic Review*, 53, 2, 65–85.

18 Casey, M.J. 1982. Multiranging – An Expensive Solution to a Simple Problem. *Lighthouse*, 25, 41.

19 Grant, S.T. 1973. Rho-Rho Loran-C Combined with Satellite Navigation for Offshore Surveys. *International Hydrographic Review*, 50, 2, 35–54.

20 Haslam, Rear-Admiral D.W. 1979. The Surveying Requirements for Deep-Draught Routes. *The Canadian Surveyor*, 33, 4, 363–71.

21 Collin, A.E. 1971. The Metric System in Hydrography. *The Canadian Surveyor*, 25, 4, 440–6.

22 Gray, David H. 1980. The Preparation of Loran-C Lattices for Canadian Charts. *The Canadian Surveyor*, 34, 3, 277–95.

23 1983. *The Law of the Sea – United Nations Convention on the Law of the Sea*. New York: United Nations.

24 LeLievre, D.D., and E.A. Fleming. 1977. The Use of LANDSAT Imagery to Locate Uncharted Coastal Features. *Proceedings of the 16th Annual Canadian Hydrographic Conference*. Burlington, ON, 99–101.

25 Burke, R.G., S. Forbes, and K. White. 1988. Processing 'Large' Data Sets from 100% Bottom Coverage 'Shallow' Water Sweep Surveys. *International Hydrographic Review*, 65, 2, 75–89.

26 1983. *Gazetteer of Undersea Feature Names 1983*. Ottawa: Department of Fisheries and Oceans.

27 Eaton, R.M., N.M. Anderson, and T.V. Evangelatos. 1983. The Electronic Chart. *Proceedings Centennial Conference Canadian Hydrographic Service*. Ottawa: Fisheries and Oceans, 188–95.

28 Troop, Peter M. 1983. The Legal Liability of the Chartmaker. *Proceedings Centennial Conference Canadian Hydrographic Service*. Ottawa: Fisheries and Oceans, 46–50.

29 Gray, David H. 1992. Where Has Sable Island Been for the Past 200 Years? *CISM Journal*, 46, 3, 265–75.

30 Brander-Smith, David. 1990. *Public Review Panel on Tanker Safety and Marine Spills Response Capability – Protecting Our Waters*. Ottawa: Supply and Services.

31 Malone, A.K., R.G. Burke, and R. Vine. 1984. Dolphin: A Proven Hydrographic Vehicle. *Lighthouse*, 30, 38–41.

32 1975. *Nautical Magazine*, 214, 6, 323.

CHAPTER NINE

Canadian Aeronautical Charts

Louis M. Sebert

CANADA'S FIRST AERONAUTICAL CHART SERIES

Early Flying in Canada

There is little doubt that the single most important factor in the exploration of the Canadian north was the invention of the aeroplane. Before the arrival of the bush pilot travel in the north was painfully slow; but with the arrival of float- or ski-equipped planes immediate access to thousands of square miles became available. Distances that earlier meant a season's strenuous canoeing became a mere afternoon's flight.

Prior to 1931 the pilots flying to the north of the settled areas of Canada did so without aeronautical charts. They were ingenious in providing themselves with navigation aids. Some used maps torn from school atlases, others used maps derived from the sketches of the early explorers. Still others made their own sketch maps as they penetrated farther and farther into the unknown. But by 1930 the Department of the Interior realized that something had to be done to improve the safety of northern flying.

After some consultation by representatives from Interior and the Department of National Defence, a joint project was started to produce strip air charts of the more important transportation routes of northern Canada. The RCAF provided a Vickers Vedette flying boat that was equipped to take oblique air photographs suitable for mapping. The RCAF also provided the flying crew and the photographer (see figure 9-1). Interior made a surveyor available to take astrofixes throughout the country being photographed. These were necessary to act as "peg-points" to tie the photography to the ground so that the maps to be drawn would be true to scale. The actual drawing of the maps and the printing was done in Ottawa by the Geographical Section of the General Staff (GSGS). The charts produced between 1931 and 1939 are listed in table 1.

Other developments in the air charting field were taking place in 1931. In that year the US Coast and Geodetic Survey published the first two charts of an eighty-seven-chart series that would cover, by 1940, the whole of the United States and parts of southern Canada.[1]

Figure 9-1
Vickers Vedette flying boat with crew and camp equipment.
Photo: MCE

These charts were drawn at 1:500 000, and were the result of an American study of the style and content of European air charts. They were, in short, the most up-to-date design in the air charting field. As the Detroit sheet of the series covered all of Ontario south of the 44th parallel, pilots flying out of airports at Toronto, Hamilton, Windsor, and other southern Ontario places obtained their first experience of using a true aeronautical chart with this 1931 American example. Demands for similar Canadian charts soon reached Ottawa.

There was another important development that would greatly affect the production of air charts in Canada: in 1932 work was started on the Trans-Canada Airway. This was to be a chain of airfields at intervals of about 400 miles stretching right across Canada. Obviously charts would be needed to fly along this route.

The Eight-Mile Base Map[2]

By 1932 there was no doubt that Canada had to produce its own aeronautical chart series. At that time there were two individuals intimately concerned with this development: F.H. Peters, the surveyor general and director of the Topographical Survey of Canada, and Maj.

Table 9-1
Arctic and Subarctic Strip Maps (published between 1931 and 1939)

Name	NTS Location	Scale
Churchill River–Fidler Lake	54E and 54L	4 miles to the inch
Stoney Rapids–Wholdaia Lake	74P and 75A	4 miles to the inch
Wholdaia Lake–Barrow Lake	75A and 65E	4 miles to the inch
Barrow Lake–Dubawnt Lake	65L and 65N	4 miles to the inch
Dubawnt Lake–Beverly Lake	65N and 66C	4 miles to the inch
Beverly Lake–Lower Thelon River	66C, 66B, 66A	4 miles to the inch
Sifton Lake–Thelon River	66D and 75P	4 miles to the inch
Fort Reliance–Sifton Lake	75J and 75K	4 miles to the inch
Mcleod Bay–MacKay Lake	75L, 75M, 76D	4 miles to the inch
Lake Aylmer–Lake Beechey	76C and 76G	4 miles to the inch
Lake Beechey–Bathurst Inlet	76G, 76J, 76O	4 miles to the inch
Lac de Gras–Bathurst Inlet West	76D and 76E	4 miles to the inch
Lac de Gras–Bathurst Inlet East	76L and 76K	4 miles to the inch
Yellowknife River–Reindeer Lake	85J, 85O, 86A	4 miles to the inch
Reindeer Lake–Point Lake	86A and 86H	4 miles to the inch
Point Lake–Big Bend	86H and 86J	4 miles to the inch
Hunter Bay–Coppermine	86J and 86K	4 miles to the inch
Hunter Bay–Dease Bay	86F, 86L, 86J	4 miles to the inch
Dease Bay–Coppermine	86L, 86N, 86O	4 miles to the inch
Rae–Hardisty Lake	85K, O, N, 86C	4 miles to the inch
Hardisty Lake–Hunter Bay	86C and 86E	4 miles to the inch
Waterways–Fitzgerald	74D to 74M	8 miles to the inch
Fitzgerald–Providence	74M to 85F	8 miles to the inch
Providence–Camsell Bend	85F to 95J	8 miles to the inch
Camsell Bend–Norman	95J to 96C	8 miles to the inch
Norman–Thunder River	96C to 106O	8 miles to the inch
Thunder River–Mackenzie Delta	106O to 107C	8 miles to the inch

Source: CIG

(later Lt Gen.) E.L.M. Burns, commanding officer of the GSGS. Neither man was a flyer, but both had associates with flying experience: Peters with the surveyors who had worked on the Arctic Strip Chart Programme, and Burns with several RCAF flyers who had a special interest in air charts. A meeting of great importance to the air chart work was held in Ottawa on 2 September 1932. In addition to Burns and Peters there were in attendance senior officials of the Departments of Interior, Transport, and Defence who had a concern for air charting. The subjects discussed were the ways and means for producing an up-to-date series of Canadian aeronautical charts.

At subsequent meetings Burns and Peters made major decisions on the specifications for this first air chart series. The scale of eight miles to the inch was agreed to quickly. This scale of 1:506 880 was virtually the same as the very successful American 1:500 000 Series. As the Eight-Mile scale was part of the National Topographic System, the NTS grid would be used for the sheet-lines of the series. Elevations would be shown by contours and layer tints, again following the American example. Since this would be new medium-scale mapping for large areas of Canada, Peters was adamant that it should be dual-purpose mapping suitable for use both in the air and on the ground. This meant the inclusion of extra place-names and symbols that Burns considered clutter. When he was informed that Peters was insisting that the location of post offices be shown, he is reported to have said that they might be of some use to flyers. If they were forced down they could at least write home.

An aeronautical chart without good elevation data is almost a contradiction in terms. Unfortunately in 1932 there were very few places in Canada covered by contoured topographic maps. As mentioned in chapter 3, these were in southern Ontario and Québec, where the GSGS One-Inch maps had been drawn, a few areas in Nova Scotia where both Interior surveyors and the GSGS had been at work, and on the prairies where the Interior contoured Three-Mile Series existed. When approval was given to go ahead with the Eight-Mile Series it was stipulated clearly that, because of financial restrictions caused by the Depression, this would have to be a compiled series. This meant that data for the sheets would have to be obtained from existing maps, and if additional surveys were needed they would have to be requested from Topographical Survey. As this agency had its own restricted budget and its own programme of work, the acquisition of data for air charts would have to be fitted in as convenient.

As can be imagined these restrictions slowed progress during the first years of the air chart programme. An examination of the NTS sheet-line grid for the Eight-Mile Series showed that it would take 221 sheets to cover all of Canada. After seven years of work on what was supposedly a priority programme, only seven full sheets and one half-sheet had been published by 1939[3] (see figure 9-2).

The War Years

War was declared against Germany in September 1939. From that month Peters lived in a world of constant pressure. Previous priorities were set aside and a new list of demands was presented. The RCAF were the first to react. Air Marshal George M. Croil, chief of the Canadian Air Staff, pointed out that flying operations against the German navy would certainly be conducted from the Canadian east coast and Newfoundland. Therefore the production of Eight-Mile charts of the area must be given the highest priority. It is fortunate that in wartime almost unlimited funds become available, and Peters was quick to react. Staff was hired, new and larger accommodation was obtained, and before the end of 1939 six new sheets (Halifax-Louisburg, Charlottetown-Sydney, Magdalen Islands–Charlottetown, Mingan–Cape Whittle, Yarmouth-Windsor, and Clarke City–Mingan) were published. Six others in the area were in progress. Compared with the former peacetime production this was a breathtaking pace but in stepping up production, standards of quality were not maintained. In particular Clarke City–Mingan and Mingan–Cape Whittle were drawn without air photography and with virtually no terrain elevation information. Only when second editions were compiled from air photography in 1943 was it seen how poor the first editions really were.

Nevertheless Peters's Air Chart Section did the best they could, and the pressure never let up. In 1939 the Commonwealth Air Training Plan was founded. This massive organization was responsible for training air crew and ground personnel for the air war in Europe, and obviously charts of the best quality were needed. Schools were set up in the Maritimes, central Ontario, and the southern Prairies, and these became new areas of top priority for charting. Fortunately they were situated where contour information was available.

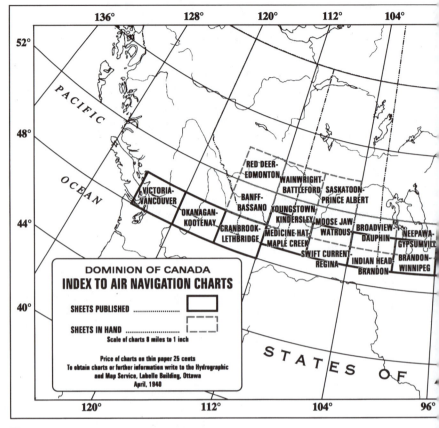

Figure 9-2
Index to eight-mile air navigation charts, 1940.
Source: MCE

The first indication that charts were needed for the Canadian north came on 27 February
1941. On that day the American military attaché in Ottawa presented both a request and
a plan to the Department of National Defence. The request was for the charting of a broad
corridor running from Montana to Alaska. The plan was for a joint U.S.-Canadian operation
to produce the necessary charts. As this was nine months before Pearl Harbor it was obvious
that American military strategic planning was behind the request.

The essence of the American plan was that if the Canadians would put in the required
ground control (i.e., astrofixes), the Americans would use their newly developed Trimetrogon Mapping System to plot the charts. The charts would then be published by both
countries at the scales being used in the two countries: eight miles to the inch in Canada
and 1:1 000 000 in the U.S. The Trimetrogon system (which is described in more detail in
chapter 3) was much more efficient for mapping wilderness areas than the Canadian
Oblique System. This was a generous offer and was quickly accepted.

The programme was under way and working well when, on 7 December 1941, the
Japanese bombed Pearl Harbor, and the U.S. was in the war. Almost immediately air routes

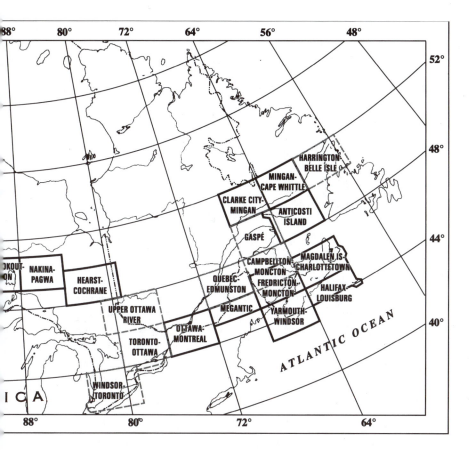

were set up to supply Russia and Britain from the mid-western United States where much of the American aviation industry was located. These routes went across areas of northern Canada where no maps suitable for air navigation existed. It was decided almost immediately that strip charts were not acceptable in this region of few landmarks where planes could be forced off course by adverse weather conditions. Coverage of the whole region by the Eight-Mile Series was the order of the day.

The result of this "full ahead" effort by the Canadian and American teams was that in July 1944 the final Eight-Mile map came off the press. But this statement can be misleading; few of these maps could be described as good, and many were barely adequate. When Peters and Burns were setting out the specifications for these charts, one of the first decisions was that the charts would be layer tinted. This was the usual practice on charts of other countries, and such depiction presented no problem when contoured base maps were available. But in the Canadian Arctic and subarctic few maps existed and none of them was contoured. The drawing of contours using the Trimetrogon system was theoretically possible, but the process was slow and inaccurate. The only answer for the wartime production was the one adopted: publish the charts without contours or layer tints, but where mountains could be seen on the air photos they would be sketched in as hachured hills to give a rough indication of the terrain. Such symbolic representation was usually accompanied by notations such as "Mountains 3000 to 4000 feet." It is certainly to the credit of the pilots who used these charts that they did so with skill and bravery, and without complaint.

As well as lacking height information, many of charts the more northern regions had blank areas marked "unsurveyed area" or "unexplored." These breaks in the topography were caused by a lack of photography. The Trimetrogon plotting teams, both in Canada and in the U.S., were being pushed to the limit, and if photography was not available on schedule, due to bad weather or other causes, a decision had to be made whether to publish or wait for the data. If the gaps were not large the order to publish was usually given. The pilots were expected to fly over the blank area and pick up their check points on the other side.

Postwar Improvements

It was known as early as 1943 that the Americans had developed a radar device that would measure very accurately the distance a plane was flying above the ground. It was essentially a safety device that would activate an alarm in the cockpit whenever the plane flew below a pre-set distance to the ground. It was called, rather succinctly, Terrain Avoidance Radar. In 1944 two of the men in the Department of Mines and Resources, John Carroll of the Topographical Survey and Charles Taggart from Peters's staff, reasoned that this form of radar could be used to obtain terrain elevation data. The suggestion was turned over to the National Research Council in Ottawa, and within a year a new device called the Airborne Profile Recorder (APR) was being tested. When this device was in operation two figures were continually recorded on a graph: the vertical distance from the plane to the ground, and the flying height of the plane above sea level. The latter distance was obtained from a very accurate altimeter that was part of the system. When height information was needed for a chart, parallel lines of APR recordings, spaced at about ten miles, were flown over the area being charted. From the information gathered contours could be drawn and used as binding lines for layer tints. The APR revolutionized the acquisition of vertical control in wilderness areas, and it has been used by many countries for their small-scale topographic mapping. In Canada APR was used extensively for the second editions of the northern sheets of the Eight-Mile Series.

In 1947 the cabinet approved a programme to complete the Four-Mile mapping of Canada within twenty years, as described in chapter 3. To accomplish this goal both the Topographical Survey and the Army Survey Establishment (ASE, the successor to the GSGS) gave high priority to work at this scale. This had its effect on the Eight-Mile sheets because the larger-scale work was of course superior to the Eight-Mile plotting. All of the Four-Mile (and the succeeding 1:250 000) sheets were compiled from vertical photography controlled by an array of horizontal and vertical survey points. When the four Four-Mile sheets covering an Eight-Mile sheet were published, a close examination of the Eight-Mile sheet was made. In most cases it was surprising how well the Trimetrogon work held up planimetrically. It was in the relief depiction that the Eight-Mile, and some of the subsequent 1:500 000, were sometimes found wanting. When errors were found they were corrected immediately using data from the Four-Mile mapping.

In 1958 it was decided to convert the Eight-Mile Series to 1:500 000, eight years after commencing metrication of the NTS maps. This delay was caused by flyers, both civil and military, wanting to stay with altitudes expressed in feet above sea level and distances in nautical miles per inch. After much consideration it was decided to keep elevations in feet, but to change the scale to 1:500 000. The change in scale took fourteen years to complete, but with the publication of Wolf Lake–Watson Lake (105 SE) in 1972,[4] all sheets of the series were in print at 1:500 000.

Changes in Format and Design

During the 1960s there was an almost explosive growth in air travel and in the air transportation industry. Canadian pilots were flying to all countries of the world, and the number of air miles being flown each year was growing exponentially. Canadian pilots were also becoming familiar with the charts produced by many other countries, and this was a cause of growing dissatisfaction with the format of the 1:500 000 Canadian air chart. This style was essentially the same as that designed by Peters and Burns in 1932, but since then the jet plane had come into operation. Flying speeds and flight ranges had at least tripled during the intervening years.

Once again the Americans were the catalysts for change. Many of the U.S. charts being produced covered large areas of Canadian territory, and these were printed on both sides of large sheets of paper. Thus an American chart would cover four times the area of a Canadian chart, and would sell at about the same price. In 1978 it was decided that the Canadian chart should use the same format. The first chart, Toronto, was published in 1979. Each side of the sheet covers two degrees of latitude and eight degrees of longitude, thus covering a four-by-eight degree quadrangle. Fifty-one sheets cover all of Canada, as shown in figure 9-3. The last sheet to be published (Frobisher Bay) appeared in 1990.

The new series has many other modifications besides the enlarged format and back-to-back printing. As green is no longer used as an altitude tint, the increasing elevation is depicted entirely by increasing tints of buff and brown. Hill shading is used to emphasize abrupt changes in elevation. Although yellow continues to be used for cities and towns, it is now used also to fill small circles for villages. Roads, railways, and power lines are shown, but they are given a somewhat subdued presentation by being printed in grey. Two colours are used for air information: blue for radio aids to navigation (including flight paths) and magenta for airport information, critical elevations, and obstructions. It is interesting to note the prominence given to radio navigation, and the relegation to the background of such features as railways and power lines that were considered vital fifty years ago. Post offices are not shown.

CHARTS FOR INSTRUMENT NAVIGATION

Flying operations are carried out under either of two different types of conditions. Visual flying operations are conducted under Visual Flight Rules (VFR), and in these circumstances the pilot must keep track of his position by visual observation of the ground. The development of Canada's 1:500 000 aeronautical charts, which have been described, was done to provide charts for visual flying. Instrument flying operations are conducted under Instrument Flight Rules (IFR). During such flights the pilot navigates the plane by reference

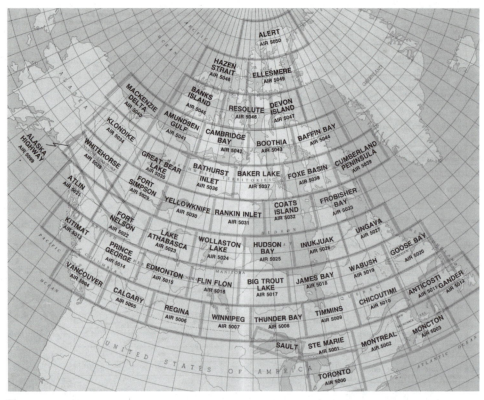

Figure 9-3
1990 index to VFR navigation charts (1:500 000 scale).
Source: Aeronautical Charts Information Service, NRCan

to instruments, with few if any references to ground features. IFR charts are designed for use on such flights. To understand the lines and symbols on IFR charts, one must have some knowledge of the functioning of the more important radio aids to air navigation. The following is a brief description of such aids.

Air Navigation Instruments

RADIO RANGE
The first system for instrument air navigation in Canada was the radio range. In a talk given at the 1938 annual meeting of the Canadian Institute of Surveying, D.R. MacLaren, assistant to the vice-president of Trans-Canada Air Lines, described the radio range in the following manner:

Considering the various methods of radio navigation, the simplest is that provided by the radio range system as is now being installed on the Trans-Canada Airway. Radio range facilities have been or are now being installed at intervals approximating one hundred miles along the route and are located with consideration to terrain and proximity to landing fields. Each radio range provides four courses or equi-distant zones which normally are separated in a 90° pattern, although this spacing may be varied to coincide with established airways. Normally, two of the courses are directed over the airway with the other two courses directed on important off-line geographical points. The four courses from each station are obtained by the transmission of the letter "N" (dash dot) in code in two opposite quadrants and the letter "A" (dot dash) being transmitted in the two remaining opposite quadrants. Each quadrant slightly overlaps the adjacent quadrant so that in a narrow wedge formed by the overlap the two signals are heard with equal intensity – the dots and dashes of the two signals interlocking to produce long dashes, known as the "T" signal. This is explained in this way to correct the general impression that the "T" signal is a beam. By this process, a pilot flying a plane equipped with the proper receiver will hear a series of long dashes while he is on course, but if he deviates to one side or the other he will hear the dot-dash or dash-dot signal.[5]

The radio range was a low and medium frequency (LF/MF) system that became obsolete and was shut down in the United States about 1959, and to a large extent was phased out in Canada between 1960 and 1970. A few radio ranges lingered on after 1970 in isolated regions. In fact to some extent the radio range has entered the folklore of Canadian flying. There are pilots who, as late as 1980, claimed that they heard a mysterious "A" or "N" signal coming from somewhere in northern British Columbia (or some other unlikely place). Of course such rumours are not to be taken seriously.

The main disadvantage of radio range was that it provided only four courses to fly. If the pilot was not flying the range, he could not get an unambiguous position line to the sending station. It had other disadvantages. It was difficult to use when thunderstorms created static, or in areas where there were other forms of radio interference. In the 1950s it began to be replaced by two direction-finding systems that are described below.

AUTOMATIC DIRECTION FINDER (ADF)
ADF was the first of the systems that replaced the radio range. It works on the principle of the direction-finding antenna. Long before the Second World War it was known that if a radio had a loop antenna it could be used to find the direction of a low or medium frequency broadcasting station by rotating the loop. When the loop was at right angles to the direction of the station the signal was loudest, but when the loop was in line with the station the signal was cut out.

In the first airborne use of such equipment the loop antenna was rotated by hand, and an indicator inside the plane showed the direction to the station broadcasting the signal. Before long this was automated so that the ADF equipment would search for and lock onto the direction of the broadcasting signal to which the set was tuned. In the first design of the ADF the indicator needle turned over a card that was fixed with 0° pointing toward the nose of the plane, and 180° toward the tail. The needle therefore gave the bearing to the beacon relative to the course that the plane was flying. For example if the beacon was 30° to port (i.e., 30° left of the plane's nose), the needle on the indicator would point to 330°. If the pilot wanted to fly a course to the beacon he would simply turn the plane until the needle pointed to zero.

A later development allowed the pilot to rotate the indicator card until it showed the magnetic heading of the plane opposite the index mark. The needle then pointed to the magnetic bearing to the beacon. The beacon for ADF equipment is called a Non-Directional Beacon (NDB) and it operates on low or medium frequencies. The position of NDBs are shown on charts by a small (1 cm) dotted circle, as illustrated in figure 9-5 and on the chart section at figure 9-7. As NDBS are also shown on VFR charts, the dotted circle symbol can also be seen in figures 9-4 and 9-6.

VERY-HIGH FREQUENCY OMNI-DIRECTIONAL RANGE (VOR)

The second common direction-finding system is the VOR. With this system the ground beacon sends out signals on magnetic bearings called radials. To understand the principle of the VOR a searchlight analogy is useful. Imagine a searchlight mounted on a high tower. The light is mechanized so that it sweeps around the horizon once every 100 seconds, or a sweep of 3.6° per second. Every time the beam passes magnetic north, a short dash is broadcast from a radio on the tower. A person within sight of the tower could then determine his magnetic bearing from the tower by measuring the lapse of time between the dash signal and the arrival of the beam. If the time lapse was 10 seconds the observer would know he was on a 36° magnetic bearing from the tower. In actual practice all this is done electronically by the VOR equipment, but the principle is the same.

VOR bearings are called radials as they radiate from the VOR beacons. There is a radial for each degree of the circle. In the aircraft a VOR set detects the radial it is on, and turns a needle so that it points to the magnetic bearing of the radial (i.e., the bearing "from" the beacon), but only if a switch on the indicator is set at "from." If the switch is set to "to," the bearing shown is that "to" the beacon, i.e., the reciprocal of the radial. Thus a VOR "to" bearing can be used to give the pilot the course to fly to a VOR beacon, and the "from" bearing if a course away from the beacon is wanted.

A VOR beacon is shown on air charts by a small (3.2 cm) compass rose orientated to magnetic north. The exception to this is in the far north (Canada's Northern Domestic Airspace) where the proximity of the north magnetic pole makes compass readings unreliable. In this region the VOR compass rose is oriented to true north. At the centre of the rose is a small hexagon that is the symbol for the VOR beacon (see figures 9-4 and 9-5, and chart sections at figures 9-6 and 9-7).

It should be noted that while the NDB beacon is non-directional (i.e., it does not send out a bearing), the VOR beacon is omni-directional in that it sends out a radial bearing on each degree of the circle. Both of these systems can provide the pilot with a direction to a beacon, but without a distance to the beacon he is still without a position fix. Distances can be provided by a system that measures the distance to a beacon.

DISTANCE MEASURING EQUIPMENT (DME)

In essence the DME is a radio transmitter/receiver system that gives the pilot a continuous reading of the distance from the plane to the DME broadcaster on the ground. This is accomplished by the set in the plane sending out a distinctive signal (i.e., a signal specially coded to that particular set), which is picked up by the ground station and immediately rebroadcast to the plane. As the rate of propagation of radio waves is known, the lapsed time taken by the signal on its round trip can be translated into a distance. This is displayed for the pilot, in nautical miles and tenths, on a read-out similar to the mileage indicator in a car. The distance is continually changing, increasing or decreasing, unless the plane is flying a circular course around the DME beacon.

The DME was developed in the U.S. in the late 1960s and came into Canada in 1978. It is normally set up with the VOR installations. The DME symbol is a small (4 mm) square, as shown in figures 9-4, 9-5, 9-6, and 9-7.

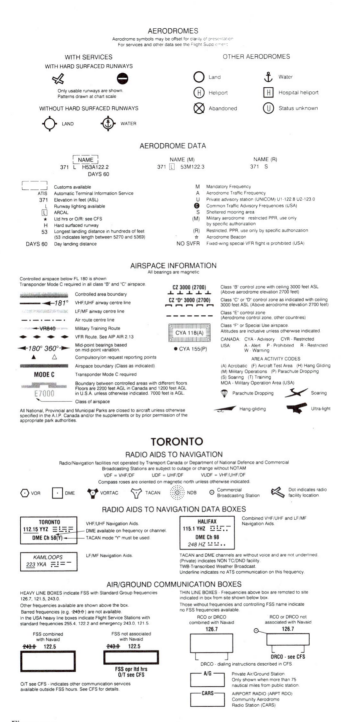

Figure 9-4
VFR chart symbols.
Source: Aeronautical Charts Information Service, NRCan

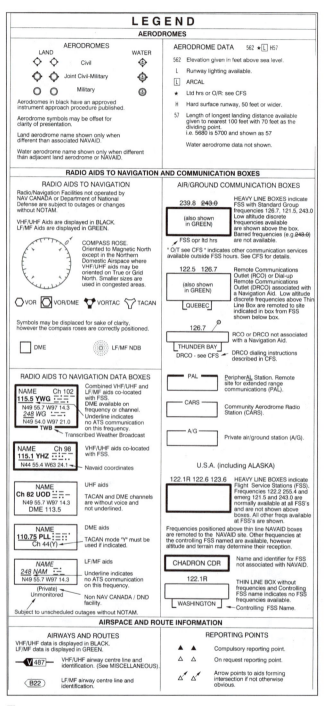

Figure 9-5

IFR chart symbols.

Source: Aeronautical Charts Information Service, NRCan

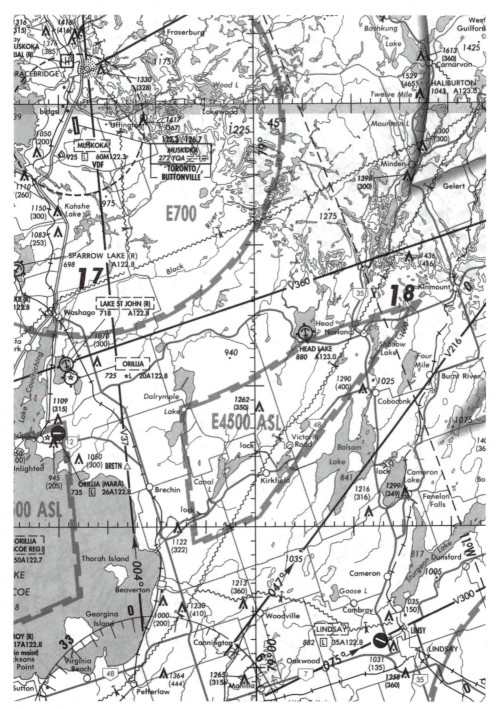

Figure 9-6
Section from a VFR chart.
Source: Aeronautical Charts Information Service, NRCan

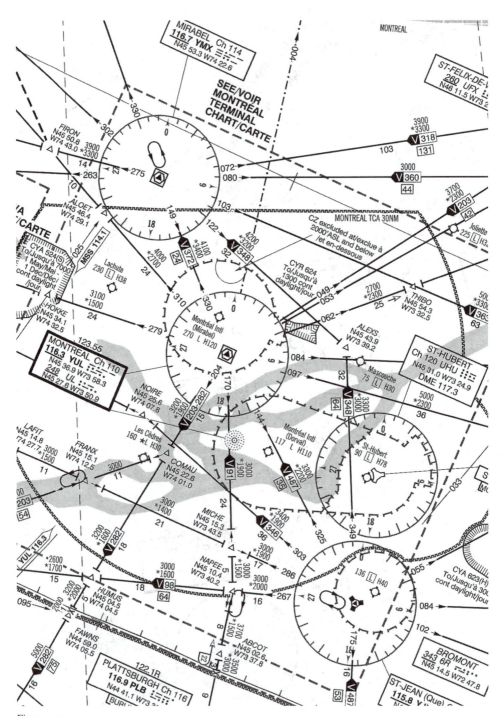

Figure 9-7

Section from an ifr low-altitude chart.

Source: Aeronautical Charts Information Service, nrcan

TACTICAL AIR NAVIGATION (TACAN)

This is a military navigational aid that works in much the same manner as VOR and DME, but uses ultra-high frequencies (UHF) instead of very-high frequencies (VHF).

VORTAC

This is also a military aid, and in it VOR and TACAN are combined so that use can be made of both VHF and UHF installations. All the above systems rely on ground stations that are shown on the charts by symbols shown in figures 9-4 and 9-5.

LORAN (LONG RANGE AID TO NAVIGATION)

During the Second World War the Loran system was developed for precision bombing. Each Loran establishment involves three broadcast stations – one master and two slaves. Signals from such an array allow a receiver in the aircraft to give the aircrew data on the position of the aircraft, either in a form for plotting on special Loran charts or in latitude and longitude for plotting on standard charts. This system has been used until recently for operations such as search and rescue, during which a plane must fly to a given point on land. Since the Global Positioning System (GPS) can now perform the same operation and is much more accurate than Loran, the latter is being phased out.

NAVIGATION AIDS NOT BASED ON GROUND INSTALLATIONS

At the same time as the systems described above were being developed, the U.S. navy was experimenting with methods for navigating its nuclear submarines. Two of these systems have entered the fields of geodetic surveying and air navigation. These are the INS (Inertial Navigation System) and the GPS.

The systems are described in detail in chapter 2, but for convenience are outlined briefly here. In the INS very sensitive accelerometers continually measure the movement of the INS set in the three dimensions. If the readings on the INS had been set at the airport before take-off, the continual change in the position of the set will be noted by the set to give an up-to-date position, again in the three dimensions. This will provide the pilot with the plane's position at all times. (Note that in chapter 2 the INS is called Inertial Survey System or ISS.)

Global positioning is also covered in chapter 2, but some of its navigational characteristics need some amplification. On the ground, where a GPS receiver can be left stationary for some time, four satellites are needed to get a reliable position with sub-metre accuracy using differential positioning techniques. In the air in a moving plane, six satellites are considered the minimum for a reliable fix. However as the aircraft is above ground obstructions this is not a serious disadvantage. While *en route* the pilot is quite happy with a position with a possible error of several hundred metres, but when landing a much better fix is needed. Therefore differential GPS is employed in this navigational equipment. This requires a GPS receiver situated at a point of known position and elevation at the airport. This "slave" set is kept operating at all times, and furnishes the set in the plane with the corrections needed for an exact position. This gives the pilot data, furnished in the form of cross-hairs, sufficient to stay on course to within five metres and at an altitude of one or two metres. To accommodate GPS equipment, charts have been printed since 1981 with the latitude and longitude of airports in the radio aids data box.

Other systems have been developed, such as the use of the Doppler effect for obtaining precise air speed, and ring laser gyroscopes for obtaining a more precise heading, but as these do not effect the data on charts they will not be covered here.

AERONAUTICAL CHARTS AND FLIGHT PUBLICATIONS

Aeronautical Charts

When radio aids came into general use all air navigation was divided into two classes: VFR, in which the pilot navigates by visual reference to the ground, and IFR, in which the pilot navigates by radio signals broadcast for air navigation. The following is a listing of the types of charts currently being produced by Canada's Aeronautical Chart Service:

1 VFR *Charts*

VFR Navigation Charts (VNC)	1:500 000
World Aeronautical Charts (WAC)	1:1 000 000
VFR Terminal Area Charts (VTA)	1:250 000

2 IFR *Charts*

Low Enroute Charts (LE and LO)	12 to 45 nautical miles to 1″
High Enroute Charts (HE)	45 to 65 nautical miles to 1″
Instrument Terminal Area Charts	About 8 nautical miles to 1″

3 *Plotting Charts*

Aeronautical Plotting Chart	1:5 000 000
Polar Plotting Chart	1:3 000 000
Canada-North-west Europe Plotting Chart	1:6 000 000
Canada-North-west Europe Strip Plotting Chart	1:6 000 000
North Atlantic Plotting Chart	1:5 000 000
Canada Plotting Chart	1:3 000 000
Sheet 1G (Eastern Canada)	1:3 000 000
Sheet 2G (Western Canada)	1:3 000 000
Sheet 3G (Northern Canada)	1:3 000 000

4 *Special Military Charts*

Low Level Pilotage Charts

Joint Operations Graphics

Several general observations must be made that pertain to all Canadian charts for sale to the public before the charts of the individual series are described. All charts except VTA charts have a bilingual legend and information panel. All heights are in feet, and when distances are given they are in nautical miles per inch. Bearings are magnetic except in the Northern Domestic Airspace where they are true due to the unreliability of the compass close to the North Magnetic Pole. All charts have a distance bar scale in one or more of the margins.

VFR Charts

CANADIAN VNC

These charts are drawn at 1:500 000, and are the true descendants of the original charts designed by Burns and Peters in 1932. Over the years the style and sheet lines of the series have been changed to keep up with the requirements of visual air navigation. Today there are fifty-two charts in the series, which has already been described. Although these charts are specifically designed for visual navigation, they contain sufficient data for instrument flying in the area depicted on each chart. An example is shown in figure 9-6.

WAC

This is an international series drawn at 1:1 000 000 to specifications established by the International Civil Aviation Organization (ICAO) in Montreal. Coverage of the world requires 262 sheets, of which 19 are Canadian. The topography is similar to that shown on the VNC charts mentioned above, except for the normal generalization that occurs when reducing the scale from 1:500 000 to 1:1 000 000. The symbols for both topographic features and aids to navigation are much the same as on the VNC Series. As with the VNC charts both layer tinting and shaded relief are used to depict the lay of the land, but on the WAC charts only three layer tints are used: green for any level terrain regardless of altitude, buff for hilly terrain between 3000 and 5000 feet above sea level, and yellow for mountainous terrain above 5000 feet. Prominent blue numerals on the face of the map give the maximum altitude in feet in each of the graticule quadrants. Airways are shown by vignetted blue boundary lines, with the VOR magnetic bearing centre lines depicted by solid blue lines with arrows showing the radial direction. NDB lines are shown as a thick screened blue line with the magnetic bearings to the beacon.

All WAC sheets are printed on both sides, and generally cover four degrees of latitude (two degrees on each side) and six degrees of longitude. There are special sheets drawn for congested flying areas that do not follow the standard sheet lines. The sheets are folded with an accordion fold first, then a single north-south fold giving a packet 5.25 by 10.25 inches. A bar scale giving distances in statute miles, nautical miles, and kilometres is placed in the left margin.

VTA CHARTS

These charts are drawn at 1:250 000 for six of Canada's major airports, namely Vancouver, Toronto, Montreal, Winnipeg, Edmonton, and Calgary. The last two are printed back-to-back on one sheet. The chart uses layer tinting, hill shading, and contours to show the relief in detail. The instrument flying symbols are standard for Canadian VFR charts. Low-level hazards such as power lines and significant obstructions are symbolized clearly. Visual flying routes are shown by a line of blue diamonds if two-way, and by a line of small solid-blue triangles if one-way. A section from a VTA chart is shown in figure 9-8. These six charts should not be confused with the IFR Terminal Area Charts, published for instrument flying, which are described in the next section.

Instrument Navigation Charts

Charts used for *en route* flying under IFR are published in two forms, Enroute Low Altitude (figure 9-7) and Enroute High Altitude. The former is for use up to and including 18 000 feet above sea level, the latter for flying above that altitude.

The charts of both series are similar in appearance. They have been stripped of almost all topographical features normally used for visual reference. Only major rivers and lakes remain, and these are printed in an unobtrusive light grey. None of these features is named. Obviously no change in this sparse topographic background will be made during the periodic

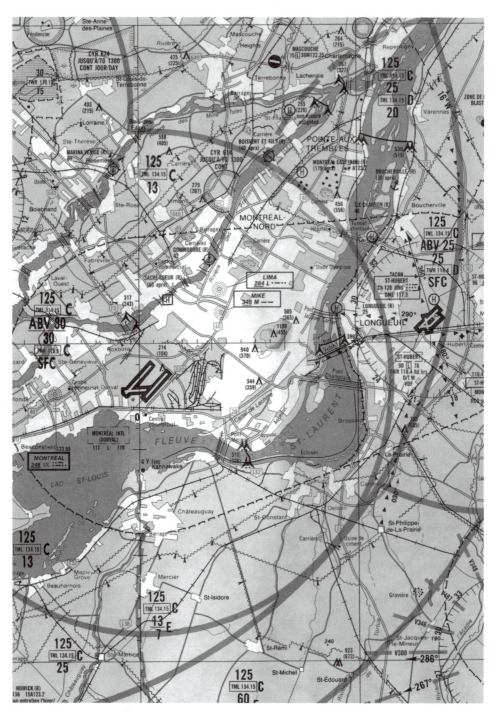

Figure 9-8

Section from a VTA chart.

Source: Aeronautical Charts Information Service, NRCan

revision of these charts. But this does not hold for the main message of these charts, which is data concerning the electronic aids to navigation throughout the area shown on the chart. Important changes to frequencies and beacons occur often, and therefore regular revision of each chart is imperative. As a consequence all IFR charts are revised every fifty-six days.

The main difference between the high- and low-level charts is their scale. High-altitude charts run from fifty to sixty nautical miles to the inch compared to twelve to forty-five nautical miles to the inch for the low-altitude charts. On both high- and low-level charts the two main types of instrument navigation are shown, using heavy black lines for VOR and thick screened green lines for NDB. The "communication boxes" that are placed beside each airfield showing the station call sign and the frequency are coloured the same way. Mileages between VOR beacons are given in black, while those between NDBs are in green.

Airports are identified on the Enroute charts by a small compass rose centred on the airport location. Existing beacons and holding patterns are shown, but the actual hard-surface runways are not. Their absence from the Enroute charts is compensated by the runway sketches and much other information on the airport contained in the *Canada Air Pilot* described below.

On all IFR charts there is so much useful information that only a brief outline of the more important symbols has been mentioned in the above brief description. Good legends are included on all charts (see figure 9-5), and the handbooks described below give all additional explanations that might be required by a pilot.

An additional chart publication for the instrument flyer is the single-sheet publication entitled Terminal Area Charts that shows the information for an instrument approach to fifteen Canadian airports[6] and the islands of Bermuda, Iceland, and the Azores. The scales for the airports vary from about seven to ten nautical miles to the inch, while those for the islands are much smaller (twenty to fifty nautical miles to the inch).

Plotting Charts

In 1944 the Legal Surveys and Map Service published Canada's first plotting chart. It was entitled Airways Facilities Planning Chart and Peters was proud to point out how quickly and inexpensively it was produced. The 100 Mile Railway Map of Canada was used as a base. On this black and light-blue base the outlines and names of the Eight-Mile Aeronautical Editions were shown in green. Airways, aerodromes, and radio range facilities were printed in red. It was not too different from the current planning chart.

Today the chart service also publishes small-scale plotting charts for flight planning. As these charts are revised annually, radio frequencies and other ephemeral information are not shown. The locations of airports and the more important beacons are shown so that the pilot can obtain the information he or she needs from up-to-date Enroute charts. Compass variation is an important item on plotting charts, as are restricted areas and zones such as the ADIZ (Air Defence Identification Zone), where identification is required from the aircraft.

Special Military Charts

LOW-LEVEL PILOTAGE CHARTS
These are charts specially designed for training military pilots in low-level military operations. The sheet lines used are those of the NTS 1:500 000 Series. A thirty-minute

graticule is printed on each sheet, and the maximum elevation in each quadrangle is shown prominently in hundreds of feet. As lakes and ponds are useful for visual reference, they are printed in dark blue. Isogonic lines for each degree of variation change are printed across the chart. No radio aid information is given, but obstructions such as high towers are plotted and their heights above ground and above sea level are shown.

JOINT OPERATIONS GRAPHIC (AIR)
These map/charts are described in chapter 5, Military Surveys.

Flight Publications

The Aeronautical Chart Service is responsible for producing the publications needed by pilots to augment the information printed on the charts. The more important of these booklets are described below.

CANADA AIR PILOT
This is a loose-leaf publication in three volumes, East (English only), East (bilingual), and West (English only), with amendments published every fifty-six days. It has separate pages for the various runways and navigation systems for each airport. Runway sketches and dimensions are given, as are all radio aids and frequencies. Any Canadian airport that has at least one instrument approach is included. A special military version is published for the Armed Forces as *GPH 200 Instrument Procedures*.

CANADA FLIGHT SUPPLEMENT
This book is a civil publication issued every fifty-six days. It contains information on aerodromes and is used for the planning and safe conduct of flying operations. The data enclosed are truly vast, and include abbreviations used in flight publications, symbols used on charts, an airport directory with airport sketches and other vital airport information, flight-planning instructions, and much more. The January 1994 issue contains 1072 pages in English, and a French section of 232 pages.

WATER AERODROME SUPPLEMENT
This booklet contains a directory of all water aerodromes. Sketches show the landing area, docks, and radio aids where they exist. Remarks are included giving data such as ice-free months and the heights of surrounding hills.

DESIGNATED AIRSPACE HANDBOOK
This handbook, issued every fifty-six days, gives the area control centres, flight service stations, location of control towers, holding patterns, compulsory reporting points, and a wealth of other data. Maps show domestic air spaces, control areas, and designated mountain regions.

FLIGHT PLANNING AND PROCEDURES
This publication is a military flight information publication published twice yearly. It provides a ready reference to planning and procedural information used in IFR operations.

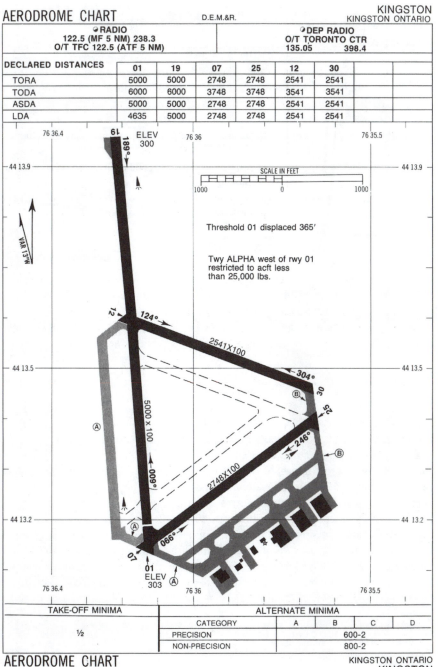

AERODROME CHART   D.E.M.&R.   **KINGSTON**
KINGSTON ONTARIO

⦿ RADIO 122.5 (MF 5 NM) 238.3 O/T TFC 122.5 (ATF 5 NM)	⦿ DEP RADIO O/T TORONTO CTR 135.05 398.4

DECLARED DISTANCES	01	19	07	25	12	30		
TORA	5000	5000	2748	2748	2541	2541		
TODA	6000	6000	3748	3748	3541	3541		
ASDA	5000	5000	2748	2748	2541	2541		
LDA	4635	5000	2748	2748	2541	2541		

Threshold 01 displaced 365'

Twy ALPHA west of rwy 01
restricted to acft less
than 25,000 lbs.

SCALE IN FEET

TAKE-OFF MINIMA	ALTERNATE MINIMA				
½	CATEGORY	A	B	C	D
	PRECISION	600-2			
	NON-PRECISION	800-2			

AERODROME CHART   KINGSTON ONTARIO
EFF 6 JAN 94   CHANGE: Comm boxes   **KINGSTON**

Figure 9-9
Page from the *Canada Air Pilot* showing Kingston Airport.
Source: Aeronautical Charts Information Service, NRcan

The ICAO

There are few if any operations in the world today that are more international than air traffic. With the ending of the Second World War and the rapid increase in international travel, the need for coordination and standardization resulted in the creation of ICAO in 1946. Since 1948 it has had its headquarters in Montreal.

The major concern of ICAO has been the production and standardization of air charts and flight publications to common specifications worldwide. As a signatory to the ICAO Convention, Canada has published civil charts and flight publications to ICAO specifications developed in conference by member countries. A major initiative by ICAO in this regard was the achievement of worldwide VFR coverage by the WAC at 1:1 000 000. Canada completed the nineteen charts covering Canadian territory in 1973.

North Atlantic Treaty Organization (NATO) Agreements

On the military side, special standardization agreements were entered into by NATO countries to facilitate military air operations in Europe and the North Atlantic. Here the standardization was in special military charts and military flying procedures.

A second group included the U.S., U.K., Canada, Australia, and New Zealand. Its function was much the same as the NATO Working Party, but with the South Pacific as its area of concern.

National Coordination

Three federal departments in Canada have an interest in aeronautical charting: Transport Canada, the Department of National Defence, and Natural Resources Canada. The single production agency is the Aeronautical Chart Service in Natural Resources Canada. The production of charts and flight publications is controlled by the Interdepartmental Committee on Aeronautical Charting. This committee is responsible for policy, the design and specifications of new products, and approval of all issues. The membership of the committee is drawn from the three departments, and the director general, Civil Aviation, in Transport Canada is the chairman. A working group within the interdepartmental committee is made up of members from the three departments who are at the operational level, and is chaired by the chief of Aeronautical Charts Service in Natural Resources Canada. The working group meets monthly to review the progress in chart production, to consider new requirements, and to make recommendations to the main committee on how to schedule the workload.

CONCLUSION

Canada started to produce aeronautical charts relatively late. In the 1930s the depressed economic conditions made it difficult to embark on a comprehensive charting programme, and short-term solutions, such as strip maps, left most of the country without charts of any kind. The Second World War thrust Canada into the forefront of air charting, and even though the wartime production was far from perfect it showed that the whole of the country could, and should, be covered. Canadian charts have kept abreast of developments in air navigation. The country's good record in air safety is, in no small measure, due to its high standard of air charting.

NOTES

1 Ross, R.L. 1933. The United States Sectional Airways Maps. *The Canadian Surveyor*, 4, 9, 10–13.
2 For more details on this subject see Sebert, L.M. 1986. Canada's First Aeronautical Chart and the 8-Mile Series. *Cartographica*, 23, 4, 79–119.
3 1939. *Catalogue of Maps, Plans and Publications*, 7th ed. Ottawa: Legal Surveys and Map Service , Department of Mines and Resources.
4 Letter Groot to Kihl. 19 December 1972. File 23/262.8.122.3.
5 1938. Proceedings of the CIS Annual Meeting. Supplement to *The Canadian Surveyor*, 6, 3, 17.
6 The fifteen airports are Calgary, Edmonton, Gander, Halifax, Moncton, Montreal, Ottawa, Québec, Regina, Saskatoon, Thunder Bay, Toronto, Vancouver, Windsor, and Winnipeg.

CHAPTER TEN

Canadian Atlases: National, Provincial, Educational, and Thematic

George Falconer, Lillian J. Wonders, and Iain C. Taylor

INTRODUCTION

When Gerardus Mercator adopted the more convenient title *Atlas* for his compendium of maps that he called alternatively and impressively *Cosmographical Meditations upon the Creation of the Universe, and the Universe as Created*, he began a practice that has multiplied beyond count. It now encompasses virtually all branches of knowledge, extending even into the realms of apparently non-geographical information. If any information can be portrayed or spatially located according to some definable system or purpose, then today the result stands a good chance of being called an atlas.

This chapter deals with the development of atlases in postwar Canada. Perhaps more than any other mode of cartographic communication, the many varieties of Canada's atlases are being affected dramatically by the revolution in information technology. Geographical Information Systems (GIS) can and will displace many of the common applications and uses of atlases as reference works. Indeed it can be argued that many atlases will be only one of a number of products from a GIS and electronic databases. However although the intellectual requirement to define and select geographical information for portrayal in atlases may be assisted by artificial intelligence and similar computer-based techniques, it seems likely it will require a human mind for the foreseeable future.

The first part of this chapter deals with the last three editions of *The National Atlas of Canada* in its federal government context. It is followed by a section on the impressive array of atlases sponsored by provincial governments. Finally the chapter reviews the salient features of the many and diverse thematic atlases that have appeared in Canada since 1946. Taken together these accounts indicate the Canadian attraction to the atlas as an indispensable means of understanding the nature and reality of Canada in all its splendid vastness.

Five editions of the national atlas of Canada have been published by the federal government of Canada since 1906, three of them since 1949[1]. The production of these more recent editions was greatly influenced by the changing administrative and financial environment of government, and the emerging technological revolution in map making and computerization of geographical information. As a result both the fourth and fifth editions in their final forms were significantly different from the first conceptions.

The Third Edition

Canada's involvement with national atlases dates from the beginning of this century when the first and second editions appeared. Although wars and depressions intervened, interest was rekindled in 1937 when the National Committee for Geography, chaired by Lt Col G.L.P. Grant-Suttie, suggested that a new edition be considered.[2] Benoit Brouillette's later report on a possible atlas of Canada was another valuable contribution.[3] In 1947 the Cabinet approved the formation of a Geographical Bureau (later Branch) in the Department of Mines and Technical Surveys, to make geographical information on Canada and other countries available for government purposes. During its existence from 1947 to 1966 it carried out a diverse range of geographical research across Canada. From the outset the production of a national atlas was its responsibility, and by August 1948 Cabinet had approved work on a third edition of the atlas.

An atlas committee was set up in 1949 to decide the overall content and size of the national atlas. It was chaired by Norman L. Nicholson, editor-in-chief and assistant director (and later director) of the Geographical Branch. Once the basic decisions on the contents of the third edition had been made, the committee and its subcommittees were disbanded. The work of research, design, and compilation was then undertaken wholly by the Geographical Branch. Base maps, drafting, and map production were the responsibility of the Surveys and Mapping Branch. Equal importance was placed on the categories of physical environment, human geography, and economic geography, and it was decided that while the atlas should be mainly thematic, there should also be a reference section with regional maps of populated places. The atlas was intended as "a coherent story in maps of Canada in all its aspects,"[4] to be published in separate English and French editions.

The Geographical Branch had a well-defined mission to provide the type of information the new atlas was intended to contain, but the help of others was needed. It was estimated that about 150 geographers, in the federal government, universities, and elsewhere, made contributions to the third edition. About 25 cartographers and drafting staff were also involved.

DESIGN OF THE THIRD EDITION
The atlas was planned and executed as a set of loose-leaf maps fitted into a specially designed binder. Each map measured 52 by 70 cm, and had a punched linen strip pasted onto a central fold so that the map could be detached and replaced. The basic scale of

---

* Part I was contributed by George Falconer, who acknowledges the help of John J.S. Thompson and Iain C. Taylor in reducing and improving a much longer original text.

1:10 000 000 allowed a map of Canada on a double-page spread, compiled on a Lambert conformal projection with two standard parallels at latitudes 49° N and 77° N. For the small area of the land mass north of latitude 80° N, a modified polyconic projection was used.[5] The 110 sheets contained some 450 maps that were printed between 1955 and 1958. Although the English version bore the imprint 1957, it was released in 1958 about ten years after the start of the project. The French edition appeared in 1959, also with the imprint 1957.[6]

SALES OF THE THIRD EDITION
By 1962 some 7000 copies of the English version and about 1900 of the French version had been sold at twenty-five dollars per copy out of a press run of about 10 000 English and 5000 French copies, apart from the sale of separate maps at fifty cents each. Two years later the edition was out of print, a grand total of 12 000 copies having been sold at prices ranging from twenty-five to thirty-two dollars. Thereafter maps were reprinted for sale separately and made available as sets in a cardboard container. Thus the third edition was published in all three modes of publication: separate maps, boxed set, and bound version.

EARLY WORK ON THE FOURTH EDITION
A comprehensive strategy for the future of the atlas or map revision is not on record. Gerald Fremlin, later to become the editor-in-chief of the fourth edition, had responsibility for developing a possible future update of the atlas. He made a study of the third edition in preparation for planning the contents and possible design of a fourth edition.[7] Fremlin was a geographer with a strong background in cartography and his ability, experience, and wide-ranging interests were put to good use in the next phases of The National Atlas of Canada.

THE DESK OR CENTENNIAL ATLAS OF CANADA
The Geographical Branch proposed in 1961 that a small desk version of The National Atlas of Canada should be produced as a contribution to the centenary of Canada in 1967.[8] This also responded to interest in a more portable version of the third edition that would reduce its significant weight and size. It was definitely not considered to be the next edition of the national atlas proper. An outline proposal for the desk atlas was produced by Fremlin in 1963 based on his work on The National Atlas of Canada. The desk atlas was planned as a bound volume of forty to fifty maps, each measuring about 46 × 23 cm, at the scale of 1:15 000 000. The high-school population was regarded as the prime market. In spite of the enthusiasm that the desk-atlas project generated, the resources needed to ensure its completion in time for the Centennial were never applied in sufficient strength.

PLANNING THE FOURTH EDITION
The long-range planning for the fourth edition was left almost solely to Fremlin,[9] who reviewed the contents and design with a number of internationally known geographers and specialists. A small atlas team worked on the information for both The National Atlas of Canada and the desk atlas. Brooke Cornwall and George Falconer coordinated the research and initial editing under Fremlin's direction as editor-in-chief. Cartographic design was the responsibility of Henry Mindak, who was a versatile cartographer with experience in virtually all aspects of map design and production, ranging from topographic mapping to special maps for books and scientific journals.

At about this time the government of Canada began to seek ways to reduce costs and to avoid overlaps of responsibility. The Geographical Branch came under scrutiny, culminating in 1966 with its dissolution[10] and the transfer of the atlas project and staff to the Surveys and Mapping Branch. This interruption had a lasting impact on the continuity and nature of national-atlas work. A decision was made to concentrate efforts on a fourth edition of the national atlas, and any work done on the desk atlas was adapted to save the existing investment. This meant that the relatively compact format and scales of the desk atlas became the de facto format of the fourth edition of *The National Atlas of Canada*.

The Fourth Edition

Published in its final bound version in 1974, the fourth edition also became a starting point for early work on the contents of the fifth edition. The fourth edition consisted of some 307 maps contained in 127 double-paged spreads dealing with the geography of Canada. An innovative comprehensive source list was included. The atlas built on the precedent of the third edition, expanding some areas and omitting subjects in others.

In the research phase of production, base maps at the scale of 1:7 500 000 were used before creating the smaller-scale maps at 1:15 000 000. A separate Special Interim Map Series was also started in order to publish information in greater detail at the scale of 1:7 500 000.[11] The interim plan at that stage, pending a complete review of the whole programme, was to produce groups of maps at intervals and eventually to release a boxed set. The plan allowed for republication of all the maps later as a bound version.

Enough work had been completed to publish a few sheets by 1968. By 1969 it had become the practice to issue groups of maps in folios at intervals. For orderly collection of the maps a special box was eventually manufactured and made available.

FIRST ADVISORY COMMITTEE ON *THE NATIONAL ATLAS OF CANADA*
An advisory committee on *The National Atlas of Canada* was established in 1971 and was chaired by Lt Col L.J. O'Brien, then head of the Army Survey Establishment (ASE). The committee was a mix of geographers and other specialists.[12] It met in May 1971 and largely supported the programme being developed.

CONTINUING NATIONAL ATLAS PROGRAMME APPROVED
In 1972 a cabinet committee agreed that a continuing programme for the publication of *The National Atlas of Canada* and *l'Atlas National du Canada* in each census decade should be approved. In addition it was decided that Treasury Board should establish an adequate level of funding to permit a viable programme for the fifth and ensuing, editions of the national atlases of Canada. These decisions were duly confirmed by the full cabinet on 11 May 1972.

ORIGINAL PLAN FOR THE FIFTH EDITION
The successful submissions to the cabinet on the national atlas programme defined the future fifth edition as a comprehensive three-volume atlas. Volume 1 was to consist of socio-economic subjects, volume 2 of physical and historical topics, and volume 3 of general reference maps and a gazetteer. The proposal called for 480 maps. By separating the socio-economic maps in a separate volume it was intended that the more time-sensitive

information it would contain could be updated without having to reissue the physical and historical maps. The third volume of reference maps and gazetteer had its antecedents in the populated-places map section of the third edition, and also in a reference work, *Atlas and Gazetteer of Canada*, which the Surveys and Mapping Branch had produced independently for the Centennial.[13]

PUBLICATION OF THE BOUND VERSION OF THE FOURTH EDITION
Publication of loose maps of the fourth edition started in 1968, and by February 1974 the boxed set of maps comprising the national atlas was complete. Preparations started in 1973 for publication of a bound edition, and the possibility of a co-publishing venture with the private sector emerged from discussions with Information Canada. A contract was awarded to the Macmillan Company of Canada in April 1974. Because changes had been made to a few map sheets, the bound atlas was identified as the "Fourth Edition (Revised)." The volume was graced with a dedication signed, and personally edited to some degree, by Prime Minister Pierre Elliott Trudeau.

After leading this project to fruition in difficult circumstances from the mid-1950s, Fremlin left the public service in 1974. The success of the fourth edition was largely due to his intelligence, ability, and persistence. He was supported by an excellent professional and technical staff, which shared the achievement recognized by the Royal Canadian Geographical Society with the award of its Gold Medal. Following the departure of Fremlin, Falconer was asked to provide continuity of leadership and later was appointed editor-in-chief.

REVIEWS AND SALES OF THE FOURTH EDITION
The fourth edition received mainly good reviews. The popular media's superlatives included the judgment that "it is a triumph of organisation which becomes that rare thing, a collective masterpiece."[14] The academic reviewers found things to commend but noted an overabundance of economic maps and the problem of outdated census information. In the Report of the Committee on Canadian Studies,[15] entitled "To Know Ourselves," prepared by Thomas Symons for the Association of Canadian Universities and Colleges, the atlas was commended and said to "demonstrate superbly the vital contribution the study of geography can make to our perception and understanding of this country." This report also urged that the continuity of the atlas programme be supported properly by government. Macmillan of Canada, and later Gage Ltd, retailed the atlas at fifty-six dollars through booksellers across the country. By 1983 the 12 800 English and 2400 French bound editions were virtually exhausted.

The Fifth Edition

Following cabinet approval in 1972 of a three-volume national atlas and a continuing national atlas programme, work commenced on developing the contents. The need to expand subject matter was stated in the submission, and between 1972 and 1974 considerable work was done on investigating possible contents. A comprehensive series of base maps was also designed. From the outset the contents adopted largely echoed the approach taken in the fourth edition, but with gaps and omissions resolved. Preliminary work also commenced on the reference map and gazetteer volume.

Seeking further confirmation of the direction that the programme should take, Surveys and Mapping Branch sought advice through a second advisory committee. This committee was chaired by Lewis J. Robinson of the University of British Columbia and included a number of prominent professional geographers. When the committee met in October 1974 it became evident that the classical multi-volume atlas was not favoured, and thus other approaches were discussed, the chief of which was a significantly smaller atlas. This would be geared to a wider public interest, incorporate dynamic themes, and diverge from the traditional structure of subject matter followed hitherto. The production of a gazetteer atlas was supported.

The report of the second advisory committee was received by the Department of Energy, Mines and Resources in June 1975,[16] articulating many of the committee's preferences. This implied a marked divergence from the policy under which the project had been authorized originally. As a result it took until October 1976 for a formal departmental decision to be made on the long-term nature of the national atlas. A major re-examination of all projects in the department was under way at the same time, aimed at making economies by eliminating programmes. The atlas project was affected significantly, suffering a significant reduction in resources as a result.

The Surveys and Mapping Branch management committee eventually approved the advisory committee's main recommendations. The objective then became to produce a popular, compact national atlas of some forty thematic maps, which would incorporate the dynamic synthesizing themes that the committee had urged. The themes would deal with geographical changes and spatial movements over time, focusing on associations of subjects rather than presenting detailed database information on separate phenomena. A gazetteer-atlas component, also supported by the advisory committee, was to contain fifty location maps, and thirty pages of place-names and names of physical features. A separate geographical map series was also envisaged to allow publication of larger individual thematic maps of key subjects in more detail.[17]

Approval of the plan was received from the departmental executive committee by March 1977, with the added stipulation that the completion date be advanced to tap the Christmas book-buying market in 1979. This necessitated a further reduction in the proposed contents.

Proposals for co-publication with the private sector were then reviewed with the Canadian Government Publishing Centre, and this led to meetings with representatives of major publishers interested in atlases. Unfortunately it became apparent that the proposed joint venture was economically unattractive to the industry unless the project was subsidized, and made more popular to the extent that it would cease to represent a national atlas in any accepted sense.

DEVELOPMENTS TOWARDS THE NATIONAL ATLAS INFORMATION SYSTEM

As a result of these developments the popular approach had to be rethought completely. The outcome was a strategy in which the national atlas would take the form of a separately packaged series of large maps, similar to the Geographical Map Series. Timeliness and flexibility of use were cornerstones of this strategy. The *Canada Gazetteer Atlas* was targeted for completion as a separate publication in 1979; and in addition the concept of the national atlas as a GIS, rather than a publication, began to be explored.

A reorganization occurred at about this time in which the atlas group became the core of a new National Geographical Mapping Division, with a number of other mapping responsibilities. In 1978 another round of staff reductions forced the diversion of all resources to the speedy completion of the *Canada Gazetteer Atlas*.

A new philosophy for the national atlas emerged in the light of these realities. The overall nature of the national atlas was changed radically from that of being solely a printed publication to that of a multi-purpose system. In time this would embrace the developing possibilities of handling and disseminating geographical information in digital form. An earlier executive decision to exclude thematic mapping from the development of automated cartography systems within the Surveys and Mapping Branch had slowed the entry of the national atlas into this field, but adoption of computerized methods now became a guiding principle. Gathering and compiling information after 1978 was done bearing in mind its possible future use in digital form. By providing geographical information in a uniform coordinated manner at a sufficiently detailed level it was believed that products could be created by others to satisfy many different needs. Information was to be provided in maps of uniform design at scales of 1:7 500 000 and 1:5 000 000.

The report of a major review of surveys and mapping activities prepared for the Department of Energy, Mines and Resources in 1978 by a committee chaired by Philip Lapp supported the decisions already made. It recommended that by 1983 the Geographical Services Directorate, in which the atlas was situated, should "shift to a new program based on new concepts, ideas and formats, using digital technology to treat data and produce thematic maps that could be delivered at user's request or be assembled in folio or book form."[18] In the following year the new policy on the future digital path of the national atlas was publicized in a key paper given by Richard Groot to an international seminar sponsored by the Pan-American Institute of Geography and History.[19] However, given the changing nature of the technology and systems available, the size of the task made it unlikely that the time frame stated in the Lapp report could be met. The task force report also asked for completion of all work on the conventional paper atlas by 1984.

Organizational changes took place. The atlas staff were split into two groups, one responsible for geographical research under Ruth Jay, and the other for cartography and toponymy under John Thompson. Later the two groups were to be recombined under Thompson's direction. The editor-in-chief, Falconer, then functioned in an advisory capacity to Groot, the director of Geographical Services, to whom the separate divisions producing the atlas now reported directly.

The Canada Gazetteer Atlas

The year 1980 saw successful release of the *Canada Gazetteer Atlas* in both English and French, with Macmillan of Canada and Guérin éditeur as co-publishers with Energy, Mines and Resources.[20] Work on this atlas had been started by Fremlin in the 1970s. However its earlier connection with the national atlas was severed when it became a separate publication with a completely different design. As it was not intended to replace the existing gazetteers of the provinces, it provided a distillation of essential information on geographical names in ninety-six pages of maps. The names of 22 000 populated places were mapped and recorded in an indexed list that also gave extra census information on population, status, and geographical coordinates. A selection of 13 000 key physical features was included. Lack of resources to complete research meant that the atlas was based solely on the 1976 census data and designations of populated places.

For the most part the atlas was received favourably. Both language versions were sold initially for $39.95 – 8000 English and 5000 French. The cartographic design by Mindak and his staff employed a subtle background of shaded relief, with symbols for populated places graduated and varied according to the size of the population. The atlas received unexpected attention from the media, was the subject of unsolicited interviews, and revealed a lively public interest in place-names and their origins.

Fifth Edition after 1980 – National Atlas Information System

With successful completion of the *Canada Gazetteer Atlas*, attention again returned to the fifth edition and the reorientation required to move towards a digital future. The concept of an electronic atlas arose, and cartographic and research staff were reassigned periodically to support this experimental work. This project was discontinued in 1993 because of the increasing availability of commercial systems.

As the database approach to national-atlas information was developed, three components emerged involving different map scales. The scale of 1:2 000 000 was adopted for detailed research and compilation of thematic subjects, infrastructure, and topographic information. These maps were to be available for open-file consultation by users, and eventually in digital form. An irregular series based on these maps was given the title of National Atlas Database Map Series.[21] Base maps used for plotting national atlas information were made available later as a printed series,[22] and by 1993 as digital files. The second level of atlas work was to be at the scale of 1:5 000 000 in order to satisfy a demand for wall maps. Finally, the basic atlas scale for publishing remained 1:7 500 000.

It was hoped that the national atlas could progress effectively along these lines. Unfortunately another serious delay was imposed in 1982, when two large mandatory mapping obligations forced the wholesale diversion of resources to non-atlas work. Two Surveys and Mapping Branch priorities involving a nationwide series of maps for the chief electoral officer, and official language revisions to topographic maps, overrode all other considerations. Many of the atlas staff were diverted to this work.

The only practical option to keep the national-atlas project alive was to treat it as an open series of maps in serial form. This would be representative of key aspects of the geography of Canada, and would be published whenever resources became available. A priority rating for map production was devised, responsive to issues and concerns of the day and particularly the priorities of the Department of Energy, Mines and Resources. These events reinforced the belief that a computerized atlas database was the best way in which the diversity of interests and needs for timely information could be satisfied. Steady progress was made in the introduction of computerized methods in the years following, especially in cartographic operations.

MARKETING THE FIFTH EDITION
When the impact of diversions lessened, the output of maps began to recover and the need for a rational marketing plan returned. During the early 1980s the matter had been studied

with the Canadian Government Publishing Centre and in consultation with private sector marketing specialists. In 1985 the Communications Branch of EMR and a private sector consultant firm carried out a review of the marketing options available in conjunction with the Canadian Government Publishing Centre and the Surveys and Mapping Branch. This took account of the loose-sheet nature of the atlas, the accumulated sheets, their size, and the low probability of a bound version of the atlas being developed. The objective was to devise a manageable method of presenting the growing set of atlas maps in an orderly way, capable of expansion and in a form that could be distributed, preferably through the private sector. A comprehensive marketing survey was undertaken by the consultants. In addition views were sought from publishers with potential interest in marketing atlas maps.[23]

It was decided finally to launch the national atlas as a consolidated entity by the publication of a special selection of thirty maps already in print. A stout and visually attractive container was produced for permanent storage of the maps, incorporating a design that reflected the prestige associated with a major national publication. Marketing remained the responsibility of the Canada Map Office, EMR.

While this was happening a third National Advisory Committee for the National Atlas of Canada (NACNAC) was being planned. T.H.B. Symons, the Vanier Professor of Trent University, who had followed the progress of the national atlas with deep interest, accepted an invitation to chair the committee. It held its first meeting in the Centre Block of Parliament in January 1986.

REVIEWS OF THE FIFTH EDITION

Some generally supportive reviews of individual maps had already been received, but release of the boxed selection stimulated comment on the fifth edition and the policy towards geographical information that it represented. Some reviewers had high praise for the atlas, usually with reservations about particular features. Others were strongly opposed to the box format and the use of standardized maps. One reviewer said that the separate boxed sheet approach "made it possible to produce maps large enough to deal with Canada's immensity without resorting to a small scale for the whole nation."[24] The same reviewer said it was "a national atlas for now and for the future." A markedly contrasting view described the atlas as the "National Box of Maps of Canada" and called it "a great awkward behemoth frustrating to use," containing maps that were called "useless at the concrete level of map use."[25] This view represents in a forceful manner the difficulty encountered by some users who wanted a convenient, bound volume with maps at a variety of scales. Yet another reviewer praised the open-ended format because it would allow revision and updates. Scientific content and high scholarly and cartographic standards received praise, justifying the care taken to ensure them. It was called "a superb example of a national atlas, produced to the highest cartographic standards which need never be out of date and capable of infinite expansion."[26] This praise was qualified, however, by the further comment that while it would be essential to every learned planning and research institute, it would prove a disappointment to "those schools, households and individuals who had hoped to replace their now sadly outdated 1976 bound edition."

In general the reviews demonstrated the seemingly insoluble problem of trying to satisfy all audiences, from schoolchild to university scholar, with a single vehicle. The diversity of user requirements calls for a programme and system that allows many ways in which to analyse, display, and transmit geographical information. This justified the route finally taken in the development of the national-atlas programme for database development, and its output into several different formats.

By 1994, 1573 boxed sets of the fifth edition (1220 English and 353 French) and about 30 500 separate maps had been distributed. In 1995 the fifth edition was priced at $185 for a complete boxed set of 92 maps. Individual maps retailed at $9.75. Overhead colour transparencies, microfiche, and computerized products based on atlas information have also been made available through commercial vendors. In addition special groupings of atlas maps on matters of national interest have been published as "map packs" with accompanying explanatory commentaries. The interest in such "spin-offs" encouraged belief in the systems approach as a means of rendering information dynamic.

NACNAC

Whereas two previous advisory committees had provided timely advice, their existence was transitory and they met as bodies only on single occasions. The third advisory committee, chaired by Symons, was intended to be a continuing source of advice and guidance as the atlas moved into the world of digital information systems.

By 1988 the committee had formulated a number of important policy recommendations concerning the National Atlas Information System. These were submitted to the minister of state (Forestry and Mines) in a special report, and later supplemented by a proposed action plan. The recommendations called for completion of the boxed national atlas by 1992 through the production of sufficient maps to ensure a comprehensive balanced coverage. A second edition of the Canada *Gazetteer Atlas* was also supported, to be published with the private sector. The development of the electronic digital component of the National Atlas Information System required acceleration and, in the committee's view, a compact bound version of *The National Atlas of Canada* was also required. The committee emphasized the pressing need to publicize both the potential and existing products of the National Atlas Information Service,[27] and to encourage their exploitation by the private sector.[28]

The secretary of the committee up to 1989 was Falconer, who had been editor-in-chief since the departure of Fremlin. At this point he left the government service. Following his departure the function of editor-in-chief lapsed, but overall scientific editing of the national atlas was ably continued by Diane M. Chapman, an experienced geographer who had held senior editorial and research management responsibilities since the 1970s. Iain C. Taylor, formerly associate professor of geography at Athabasca University, was appointed chief geographer and head of research in 1991.

COMPLETION OF THE FIFTH EDITION

At a special ceremony in 1993 the Department of Energy, Mines and Resources announced completion of the fifth edition. This event was said to close the official record concerning the fifth edition. That this final effort to complete the atlas had again taxed the available resources may be deduced from the list of contents. This reveals the absence of maps on a number of major subjects including geology, soils, zoogeography, settlement, languages, health and welfare, law, religion, education, finance, commerce, tourism, and leisure.[29] In order to meet the deadline for completion accepted earlier, work was cut off on several map sheets under development.

Since then the National Atlas Information Service has moved into an innovative period of diversifying its products, services, and capabilities in a variety of media in cooperation with the private sector and other departments. This was demonstrated magnificently during the federal elections in 1993. The National Atlas Information Service created computerized real-time maps for television broadcast, even as election results were coming in. Immediately afterwards it was able to supply, by digital transmission, all the information needed to print a very fine and detailed colour map of election results in national newspapers.[30] Interactive, electronic map displays, based on the fifth edition, have been available at the World Wide Web site since 1994. Users now create about 200 000 interactive maps annually and an impressive eight million document accesses per year are recorded at this site.

The existence and record of five editions of the national atlas of Canada, a score of provincial atlases, and countless others shows clearly that geographical information has special significance to this vast nation, and that it will always be a special Canadian need and challenge. The National Atlas Information Service now seems well positioned to meet that challenge, utilizing new methods and technologies, but carrying forward what is now an almost century-old responsibility in ways undreamed by its precursors.

PART 2 PROVINCIAL, SCHOOL, AND COMMERCIAL ATLASES*

Provincial Atlases

The history of atlas production in Canada has been remarkable. For such a large country with such a small population, the output of all types of atlases is second to none. Only Finland had a national atlas before Canada. As described in the previous section, the *Atlas of Canada* was first published in 1906 and has gone through many editions to the present. Its high standards have spurred the production of quality provincial, junior, and commercial atlases in ever-increasing numbers. No other nation can compare with Canada in the scope of this accomplishment.

At a cartographic workshop held in Alberta in 1970 on the themes of education and regional atlases, Professor Weir of the Department of Geography at the University of Manitoba noted that "the highest expression of thematic mapping finds itself in the regional atlas which embodies all the most recent and up-to-date ideas of cartographers and people who envision what should be put on maps. When the story of cartography in Canada is fully written, one of the most interesting chapters will be that on regional atlases.[31] He used the term "regional atlas," but this is often used interchangeably with "provincial atlas," which will be used in this part of the chapter.

Each Canadian province and territory has its own atlas. These volumes have appeared for the most part since the mid-1950s, with the greatest numbers in the 1970s. The latest is the *Atlas of Newfoundland and Labrador*, which did not appear until 1991. Because of the cost of printing and the short press runs of provincial atlases in Canada, it is impossible to recover costs. Therefore most of these atlases have been funded by government. The five "pioneers," the first provincial atlases, are described in the following paragraphs. The more recent provincial atlases are listed in table 10-1.

The development of provincial atlases in Canada originated with the Fourth British Columbia Resources Conference of 1951. It was at this conference that two professors

---

* Part 2 was contributed by Lillian J. Wonders.

Table 10-1
Provincial Atlases

Year	Title	Editor/Cartographic Editor	Publisher
1956	British Columbia: Atlas of Resources	J.D. Chapman, D.B. Turner/ A.L. Farley, R.I. Ruggles	British Columbia Natural Resources Conference
1960	Economic Atlas of Manitoba	T.R. Weir/G.J. Matthews	Dept of Industry and Commerce, Manitoba
1969	Economic Atlas of Ontario	W.G. Dean/G.J. Matthews	University of Toronto Press for Govt of Ontario
1969	Atlas of Alberta	J.J. Klawe	Govt of Alberta and U of Alberta Press in association with of Toronto Press
1969	Atlas of Saskatchewan	J.H. Richards/K.I. Fung	U of Saskatchewan
1969	Nova Scotia Resource Atlas		Dept of Development, NS
1971	Atlas of the Prairie Provinces	T.R. Weir/G.J. Matthews	Oxford University Press, Toronto
1977	Atlas du Québec		Cartex Inc.
1978	Perly's Detailed Provincial Atlas of Ontario		Perly's Variprint Ltd
1979	Prince Edward Island: Urban and Resource Mapping		Govt of Prince Edward Island
1979	Atlas of British Columbia	A.L. Farley	U of British Columbia Press
1980	New Brunswick: Urban and Resource Mapping		Govt of New Brunswick
1980	Alberta in Maps		Alberta Bureau of Surveying and Mapping
1983	Atlas of Alberta	T. Byfield	Interwest Publishers
1983	Atlas of Manitoba	T.R. Weir	Surveying and Mapping Branch, Natural Resources, Manitoba
1985	North of 50°: An Atlas of Far Northern Ontario	J.E.J. Fahlgren, Royal Commission on the Northern Environment/G.J. Matthews	Govt of Ontario and U of Toronto Press
1989	British Columbia Recreation Atlas		Govt of British Columbia/ Infomap
1991	The Maritime Provinces Atlas	R.J. McCalla/D. Allen and P. McCalla	Maritex
1991	Atlas of Newfoundland and Labrador	C. Wood and G.E. McManus	Breakwater

from the Department of Geography at the University of British Columbia, J.D. Chapman and R.I. Ruggles, along with their colleague A.L. Farley and D.B. Turner, director of conservation in the province, decided that the proceedings should be presented in the form of a regional atlas. The result was the *British Columbia Atlas of Resources*, published in 1956. Because of the shape of British Columbia, the atlas was designed with a very large format (56.5 × 44 cm or 22.25″ × 17.5″). Single-page maps presented the province at a scale of about 1:3 500 000. It was introduced with coloured end-papers showing British Columbia from all directions. The large, thin (95 pages), dark-red, soft-bound atlas contains some twenty-five large-scale maps, setting an example of style and content for the provincial atlases to follow. A complete explanation of each map, together with black-and-white photographs, contributed to the success of the atlas. The work was largely carried out in the Department of Geography at the University of British Columbia under the guidance of Ruggles and Farley.

Thus began the publication of provincial atlases in Canada. It is not possible to describe all the atlases in detail, but it is worth commenting briefly on the following four provincial atlases that appeared in the late 1960s and early 1970s. These varied enormously in size, format, cartographic design (such as colour, type, and folios), and subject matter.

The *Economic Atlas of Manitoba* appeared in 1960. This was prepared under the direction of Professor Weir at the University of Manitoba. The cartographic design and production was the work of Geoff Matthews, who had arrived recently from Australia and was working on the Manitoba floodway cost-benefit study in Winnipeg. This atlas was similar in size to the British Columbia resources atlas, having to be large enough to accommodate the shape of the entire province of Manitoba on single sheets.

Even though the *Economic Atlas of Ontario* was completed twenty-five years ago, it is still prestigious among Canadian atlases. It was designed by Matthews and William Dean from the Department of Geography at the University of Toronto. It is highly unlikely that such a volume will ever be produced again. Today we can appreciate it not so much for its statistics, which in most cases are no longer pertinent, but for its art and cartographic design. The artistic use of colour in the *Economic Atlas of Ontario* is memorable. Even after twenty-five years one is struck by the hues of pumpkin, brick-red, chartreuse, yellow, olive, and gold that grace its 226 pages. These colours have a remarkable effect on the perceptions and subjective reactions of the map reader. In addition the end-papers of the atlas deserve special mention. Matthews explained that the "colour" was composed of the lines of drainage from the base map of Ontario unreduced, stepped every half-inch, and "bled" off on all sides. This repetition was printed in sand, orange, brown, and olive over and over again making the texture for the design.[32] This is the only known case of an atlas winning a prize for excellence at the Leipzig Art Book Fair in Germany.[33]

Canada celebrated its Centennial year in 1967, and across the country projects were initiated to pay tribute to this special landmark in Canadian history. The conception of a provincial atlas for Alberta had long been contemplated within the Department of Geography at the University of Alberta. However funding was a problem and a catalyst was needed to bring the conception to reality. The Centennial provided this. The atlas was approved as the Centennial project of the University of Alberta and as one of those of the government of Alberta, with both bodies providing financial and technical support. The purpose of the atlas was to provide the widest possible range of information about the province. It was to appeal to government agencies, educational institutions, and professionals, as well as to citizens at large. The project also played an important role in providing training for graduate students in the Department of Geography.[34]

An executive committee was formed under the chairmanship of W.C. Wonders, with members from both the university and government. The chief cartographer was Professor Klawe, who had a large staff of cartographers, technicians, and research students. The maps were prepared by the students and then sent to the technical staffs of the Department of Lands and Forest and the Department of Highways who transformed the worksheets into final copy. Although the project was begun in 1965 it was not completed until 1969.

The *Atlas of Alberta* had the largest dimensions of the early atlases, though it contained fewer pages than the Ontario atlas. It displayed bright and strong colours and employed many innovative statistical methods. In addition to the usual economic maps, there was a very attractive section of historical maps and unusual settlement pattern maps.

The last atlas to be produced in this period was the *Atlas of Saskatchewan*. It came off the presses in record time, and also distinguished itself with a remarkably low budget. It is a tribute to the cartographic staff that such an attractive and professional production could be accomplished so economically. The editor was J. Howard Richards and the cartographic editor was K.I. Fung, a protégé of Klawe. It has been referred to as an omnibus atlas – with something in it for almost everyone. Unlike the *Atlas of Alberta* and the *Economic Atlas of Ontario*, coloured photographs were incorporated within text material among the maps in the main body of the atlas. The colours chosen for the atlas were close to the standard "process colours" in order to provide separation negatives for the coloured photographs. However adjunct colours of grey, green, and brown were added. Unlike with the other atlases, all work such as scribing, photo-mechanical separations, typesetting, colour proofing, and that on final negatives was carried out in the Department of Geography at the University of Saskatchewan. This was a remarkable feat for a small department.

These original five, along with ten subsequent "provincial type" atlases, have provided the material for study and analysis by scholars, as it is important for future researchers to understand who created them and how they were produced. One of the first to compare the provincial atlases was Norman Nicholson from the University of Western Ontario.[35] A recent study by Diana Hocking and other cartographers at the University of Victoria has attempted to analyse Canadian provincial atlases.[36] The results appeared in a paper with comparative tables on the number of pages, types of maps, dates of printing, and other information. These careful comparisons are commendable. It is questionable, however, whether atlases can be compared scientifically if they are also works of art. It is the individual design of each atlas that will be best remembered. Moreover it is difficult to visualize the aesthetic qualities of these atlases from statistical data alone. The doyen of American cartographers, Arthur Robinson, has stated that "lettering, structure and colour encompass most of the aspects of a map capable of evaluation from the visual point of view."[37] Through the centuries a gap has occurred between art and science in map making. This gap has expanded with the increase in scientific accuracy, to the detriment of aesthetic qualities.[38] In a later paper Hocking and Keller have analysed not only the provincial atlases of Canada, but also some of the state atlases of the United States.[39]

Canada has been endowed with many provincial type atlases since 1987, as table 10-1 shows. The list is not definitive, however, as the very term "provincial" can be ambiguous. Some provincial atlases are thematic in organization, for example *Atlas of Alberta Lakes*, and some commercial atlases are provincial in scope, for example *Alberta Report Atlas of Alberta*. Both the *British Columbia Atlas of Resources* of 1956 and the *Economic Atlas of Manitoba* of 1960 have been succeeded by new atlases, though they are much more modest in format. This is a reflection of the difficult financial times, and an indication that the necessary large sums of money and manpower of past years are no longer available.

Glancing through the various provincial atlases, some pages are truly memorable in the use of colour. In the *Economic Atlas of Ontario* the map of southern Ontario (plate 8) is unforgettable with its shades of midnight blue and black, and the white dots of urban centres that coalesce into white patterns. The maps of soils in the *Atlas of Alberta* uses soft blue-greys; the *British Columbia Atlas of Resources* uses vivid colours of pink and electric blues for the map of precipitation; the *Economic Atlas of Ontario* even employs purple for death rates and green for money values. Colour makes a lasting impression.

To appreciate the complexity and magnitude of the provincial atlases, each must be examined on its own merit.

School or Junior Atlases

Some twenty years ago a curator of maps at the American Geographical Society bemoaned the ever-increasing flood of national, regional, topical, special, and even junior atlases that kept arriving at the map library from all over the world.[40] Though this "problem" increased for a decade or more, it has now subsided. Depressed economic times have seen few new atlases.

School-book publishers existed from the early days of public education in Canada, and provided school atlases as well as other books for students. Sometimes these "atlases" were really more geographies than atlases as we think of them today, for example *Ontario Public School Geography* published by W.J. Gage & Co. Ltd of Toronto in about 1936. However, the major publishers were all active in atlas production.

Some school atlases now used in Canada have little Canadian content, as they are orientated to the U.S., for example *The National Geographic Picture Atlas of Our Fifty States*, the *National Geographic Picture Atlas of the World*, or the *Rand McNally Junior Atlas*. Nevertheless even these have a Canadian section (see table 10-2). This is important for Canadians, as a general atlas does not provide a separate gazetteer with detail of Canadian place-names and Canadian content.

Some publishers have invested large sums of money to provide school atlases for Canadians, for example Thomas Nelson & Sons, George Philip and Son, J.M. Dent Ltd, Oxford University Press, Gage Education Publishing, Ginn & Co., Guinness Publications, Hammond University Press, and Methuen Publishers. These publishers have a high degree of interest in providing an atlas that is suitable for the social studies curriculum of each province where it is sold.

To ensure the suitability of the contents the provincial Department of Education may have been consulted as well as university expertise. As an example, in preparing *Thinking About Ontario* the publisher had the services of Henry Castner, who was a geographer and cartographer from Queen's University well-known for his innovative techniques, T. Dickson Mansfield (Ontario education consultant), and two professors of education, Gary deLeeuw and Ronald Carswell, as education and series research editor respectively.

The publishers mentioned above target the Canadian market as is illustrated by such titles as *The Canadian Oxford Atlas, Nelson's Canadian School Atlas*, and *Gage's Junior Atlas of Canada*. Most of these school atlases are commercial enterprises and are sold to school boards across Canada at prices that have met the approval of the provincial Departments of Education. This is a very different situation from the provincial atlases that were mainly government subsidized. The *Junior Atlas of Alberta* differs from other school atlases. It was funded by the Alberta Heritage Learning Project, is the property of the Alberta Department of Education and is not available commercially.

A recent development has been the emergence of junior atlases at the provincial level. Examples of this are *L'InterAtlas – les ressources du Québec et du Canada*; *Atlas CEC, Monde, Canada, Québec*; and *Thinking About Ontario*. These provincial atlases have been

Table 10-2
Junior and School Atlases

Year	Title	Editor/Cartographic Editor	Publisher
1953	Canadian Social Studies Atlas	L. Wonders	J.M. Dent and Sons (Canada) Ltd
1956	Moyer's School Atlas for Canada	G. Goodall	Moyer School Supplies with George Philip
1958	Nelson's Canadian School Atlas	J. Wreford Watson	Thomas Nelson and Sons (Canada)
1960	Looking at Maps	W.C. Wonders and L.J. Wonders/G. Weber	J.M. Dent and Sons (Canada) Ltd
1962	Nelson's Canadian Junior Atlas	J. Wreford Watson	Thomas Nelson and Sons (Canada)
1963	Canadian Oxford School Atlas	E.G. Pleva	Oxford University Press, Toronto
1966	Senior Atlas for Canada	Harold Fullard	George Philip and Son
1967	Atlas du Monde Contemporain	Pierre Gourou	Renouveau Pedagogique
1967	The United States and Canada	John Chapman, John Sherman	Clarendon Press, Oxford
1968	Guide to Understanding Canada	James Peters	Guinness Publishing, Ltd
1970	Le Canada: Géographie Contemporaine	Louis Hamelin, Colette Hamelin	Renouveau Pédagogique
1971	Atlas Larousse Canadien	B. Brouillette, Maurice Saint-Yves	Librairie Larousse, les Éditions Françaises
1973	Atlas of Canada and the World	A.M. Willett	George Philip Raintree
1975	Dent's Canadian Metric Atlas	H.E. Mindak	J.M. Dent and Sons (Canada)
1977	The New Oxford School Atlas	Quentin Stanford	Oxford University Press, Toronto
1979	Junior Atlas of Alberta	J.-C. Muller, L.J. Wonders	Heritage Learning Resources Project
1979	Gage Junior Atlas of Canada	G. Cluett and others	Gage Educational Publication (Canada)
1980	Nelson Atlas of Canada	G.J. Matthews	Nelson Canada
1981	The World Book Atlas of the United States and Canada	William Nault	World Book, Childcraft
1981	Canada. Its Land and People	Don Massey	Reidmore Books
1981	Thinking About Ontario	Henry Castner, T. Dickson Mansfield, Gary J.A. deLeeuw, Ronald J.B. Carswell, Shelley Laskin	Hosford Publishing
1981	Atlas CEC	Jean Carriere	Centre Éducatif et Culturel
1983	The Methuen Atlas	B.M. Willett	Methuen Publishers
1985	Atlas des Jeunes Québécois	Jean Carriere	Centre Éducatif et Culturel
1985	Thinking About Our Heritage	Gary J.A. deLeeuw, John Money, Stephen Murphy, Rick Checkland	Hosford Publishing
1986	L'InterAtlas	Pierre Paradis, Yves Tessier, Louise Marcotte	Centre Éducatif et Culturel
1992	Macmillan School Atlas	R.C. Daly	The Macmillan Company of Canada Ltd

designed exclusively for younger students. This specialization is another first in Canada's history of atlas production.

The term "junior" or "school" has different meanings from atlas to atlas with regard to the grade level of the student. Some atlases are definitely elementary, for example *Looking at Maps*, some are intermediate, for example *Canada, Its Land and People*; and others are much more sophisticated for the senior high school, for example *The Canadian Oxford School Atlas.*

The elements of cartographic design, that is the organization of content, layout, colour, typography, symbolization, and scale, vary greatly for each educational level. The more elementary the level, that is first atlases for children up to grade three, the more simplified are the maps. Strong colour, photography, and stories are used to add interest to the atlas. At the intermediate level some thematic maps are introduced together with gazetteers. Finally, for the senior high school students, atlases provide more geographical concepts in addition to increasing the number of maps.

The organization of the atlas contents is similar in most of the atlases listed in table 10-2. Usually there is an introduction to "the beginnings of the earth," as in *Nelson's Canadian School Atlas* plate "The Makings of the Earth," in which an airbrush technique is used with blue shadings, or the plate "Our Solar System" in *Atlas C E C*. Other examples of pages in this introductory section are "scale," as in *Thinking About Ontario* and *Atlas des Jeunes Québécois*, which combine cartoons of little creatures from outer space; and "latitude/longitude and time zones" interpreted by colour and diagrams in the *Junior Atlas of Alberta*. The next section in the atlases continues with an historical section, socio-economic maps, and regional maps. The last pages include the index, gazetteer, and special information. The arrangement may vary somewhat, but this is a typical approach.

Almost all the school and junior atlases in Canada have been designed to fit a format of 8 1/2″ × 11″ (22 cm × 28 cm). This is a standard size that can be stored easily, and which is not too cumbersome in size for young students.

The layout of a page is as essential in good map design in these atlases as in any other atlas. Several of the junior atlases have utilized the double-page spread to increase the map space and create more interesting design possibilities. This is the case with *Atlas des Jeunes Québécois*, *L'InterAtlas*, and the *Junior Atlas of Alberta*. Together with the layout other important considerations include borders or no borders, floating maps, bleeds, and folios. Some of these elements are illustrated in the following examples. Double-page spreads are used in the *Junior Atlas of Alberta* to provide a large space for the map elements to flow freely across the gutter, whilst in the *Atlas des Jeunes Québécois* double-page spreads (or flats) are used with no borders. The folio (page number) is displayed effectively in small outline maps of Québec. Compared to the provincial atlases of Canada, the junior atlases are much more dramatic in design.

As noted previously type is an integral part of designing every map. It is especially important when designing maps for the junior levels, and this has necessitated serious examination of this subject. In recent years there have been several studies in the field of map typography, including some exclusively for children's atlases.[41,42]

When the type styles to be used in the *Junior Atlas of Alberta* were being considered, specialists in early childhood education stated that the young child identifies the lower-case letters sooner than capital letters. The design of lower-case letters has far more individual differences than capital letters. The *Junior Atlas of Alberta* utilized this concept, and thus the lower-case letter has been featured throughout the atlas. Many of the junior atlases use the seriffed letters of Century School Book or Times New Roman. The former was specially designed for children's textbooks. It should also be noted that school atlases have much more text material accompanying each map, which further supports the importance of careful type selection.

Colour played a dominant role in the junior atlases, setting them apart from their counterparts, the provincial and world atlases. The profuse use of colour created a strong interest that set the scene for the incorporation of map information by the student. Almost without exception the pages of this group of atlases were filled with colour to make a vivid impression on the young readers. Colour reproduction is complicated and expensive, however, thereby imposing an additional responsibility on the cartographic staff.[43]

Map symbols must be designed carefully for use in school atlases. It is a challenge for cartographers to create a symbol that is both simple and clear. Pictorial symbols are nearly universal in maps for children, who enjoy looking at them, and it is an excellent way to demonstrate that all marks on a map are, in fact, symbols. Some illustrations of the use of pictorial symbols in junior atlases include "Ecotours" in the *Junior Atlas of Alberta*, and "Atlantic Canada" in the *Gage Junior Atlas of Canada*. Complicated patterns such as occur in the portrayal of geology and agricultural products can be simplified by showing one geological formation or product per map. This is far easier to interpret than superimposing tones or patterns one on top of the other. An example is "Agriculture" in the the *Junior Atlas of Alberta*. Landsat satellite images were used effectively to illustrate land patterns in the *Methuen Atlas of Canada and the World*.

An outstanding atlas in the use of symbols, diagrams, and other innovative techniques is the *L'InterAtlas*. The graphics on the page showing water use ("L'eau de tous les jours") is just one example of artistic talent combined with imagination that is demonstrated throughout this exciting atlas.

In conclusion junior and school atlases are not just scaled-down versions of existing atlases, they are independent cartographic designs demanding special approaches and techniques. They have been given special attention in Canada since the Second World War, and add greatly to the many facets of Canadian atlas achievements.

Commercial Atlases

Commercial atlases can be placed in three groups according to the intended map user, that is (1) reference, (2) travel, recreation, and transportation, and (3) aesthetic attraction. Table 10-3 lists a group of atlases produced commercially for the Canadian market. The atlases included are mostly Canadian in content, or have a substantial section devoted exclusively to Canada. The category is difficult to define as many school atlases and even some provincial atlases are produced commercially. One of the great difficulties for publishers in Canada is the small market. It is more economic to add a Canadian section to an American atlas than to try to design an atlas solely for sale in Canada. This has raised the problem in the past of assigning a suitable atlas for first-year university students in geography. The main choice is usually between *Goode's World Atlas*, which has excellent economic maps of the world, detailed maps of the U.S. and other parts of the world, but only partial Canadian coverage, and the *Canadian Oxford Atlas*. The latter has a strong Canadian section, but provides weaker coverage in other areas.

Other atlases stress the physical and economic differences of regions within Canada. One atlas to do this very effectively and with imagination is *Nelson's Atlas of Canada and the World*. The unusual approach in this atlas is to provide coverage of six major regions

Table 10-3
Commercial Atlases (relating to Canada)

Year	Title	Editor/Cartographic Editor	Publisher
1962	Rand McNally Atlas of Canada		Rand McNally
1970	Western Canada		Sunset Travel Guide
1970	Travel Guide to Western Canada		Lane Books, Menlo Park, CA
1972	Canadian Road Atlas from Coast to Coast		Rand McNally
1975	Oxford Regional Economic Atlas of the United States and Canada	John Chapman, John Sherman	Oxford University Press, Toronto
1976	Canadian World Atlas	Harold Fullard	Philip Nelson, Canada
1977	New Canadian Oxford Atlas	Quentin Stanford	Oxford University Press
1980	Nelson Atlas of Canada	G.J. Matthews	Nelson Canada
1982	Atlas du Canada	G.J. Matthews	Nelson Canada
1983	Atlas of Canada and the World	B.M. Willett	Methuen
1983	Drive North America	Winchester	Gousha Co.
1984	Canada and the World	G.J. Matthews, Robert Morrow Jr	Prentice Hall (Canada) Ltd
1985	Shaping of Ontario	Nick and Helma Mika	Mika Publishing Co.
1986	Philip's New Canadian World Atlas	B.M. Willett	George Philip
1986	Canada from the Air	Clive Friend	Coome Books (Colour Library Books, Ltd.)
1993	AAA Road Atlas of Canada and the United States		American Automobile Association National Travel
1993	Reader's Digest Atlas of Canada		Reader's Digest
1993	Rand McNally Road Atlas		Rand McNally

of Canada: the Far North, the Near North, the Western Mountains, the Prairies, the Great Lakes–St Lawrence, and the Atlantic. For each of these regions three double-page spreads are provided. For example in the section on the Near North a sample of a topographic map is reproduced together with photographs, satellite images, and socio-economic maps with statistical diagrams. It is an informative and excellent atlas available in book stores for the general public.

There are several types of tourist and travel atlases available. Some of them cover both the United States and Canada, for example *The AAA Road Atlas of Canada and the United States*, whilst some are restricted to a smaller area such as *Western Canada: A Sunset Travel Guide*. This group of atlases is limited in coverage to highway maps and tourist information, and provide no physical or economic information. The most useful road atlas is *The Rand McNally Road Atlas*, which covers all of the United States, Canada, and Mexico. The maps show in great detail highways, (from interstates to unpaved roads), urban areas, towns, villages, hydrography, airports, parks, and recreation areas. This type of atlas is especially important today with the disappearance of free provincial and state road maps from automobile service stations. Within this one atlas all provinces and states are shown, so it is not only useful for travel but also for reference information.

Many of the commercial atlases are attractive as graphic presentations in themselves, and this aesthetic aspect appeals to the general public. As an example, the unique *Canada from the Air* provides an approach different from the ordinary collection of maps found in most atlases. Many of the atlases listed in table 10-3 have been successful because of the imagination of the editor and cartographers.

PART 3   THEMATIC ATLASES OF CANADA*

Introduction

The last half-century has seen a flourishing output in Canada of specialized atlases, however narrowly they may be defined, which have served a wide variety of purposes and have been produced by a broad range of agencies. As pointed out earlier in this chapter, geographical information does seem to have special attraction to Canadians. The vastness of the country, the diversity of people, and the varied uses of its land and water resources all contribute to the special interest that Canadians have in atlases.

After an examination of the titles and bibliographic descriptions of more than 500 works defined by the National Archives as Canadian "atlases,"[44] the sheer economic investment made in producing specialized atlases is readily apparent. A rough calculation suggests that perhaps $30 to $50 million has been spent on producing thematic atlases during the last fifty years. Given the size of this investment it is hardly surprising that atlases have generally needed government (or public) sponsorship.

It follows that the history and nature of thematic-atlas production is to some considerable degree a reflection of those issues that have concerned governments or the public. For some issues the questions and answers presented in atlas form have related to the findings of research on pressing public or scientific needs. In other cases there was a need to communicate these findings to the public, or to provide a vehicle for the publication of geographic information that would contribute to a broader or more generalized public good.

The Issues Behind Thematic Atlases

Broadly speaking the issues reflected in thematic atlases can be seen as part of the wider socio-economic agendas faced by governments and the public in Canada since the Second World War. An emphasis on resource mapping was most evident in the 1950s and 1960s when the strategically and economically important northern areas stimulated increased military preparedness and investment in resources. This persisted to some degree later in western Canada than in the East. Other issues, more environmental and cultural in nature, prevailed during the 1970s and 1980s.

Occasionally the approach to resource mapping could itself create a form of provincial atlas, for example in British Columbia,[45] so focused were the agendas of the time. The terms "environment" or "ecology" do not appear in such an atlas, but there is much said about the potential for power sites (dams) and timber yield (clear cutting). The cartographic portrayal and analysis of the exploitation of natural resources also lay behind a number of other atlases, this time in a more socially adapted form. Depicting employment, economic growth, regional economic development and government plans to stimulate it generated several atlases, particularly in the provinces or regions in Atlantic Canada and eastern Québec. Concern for the country's marginal farmers led to an extensive programme of

---

* Part 3 was contributed by Iain C. Taylor.

study, research, and financial assistance under the Agricultural Rehabilitation and Development Act (ARDA), which in turn helped set in place the Canada Land Inventory (CLI) (see chapter 11). These programmes also provided the financial resources for making economic and thematic atlases, especially in eastern Canada.

By the late 1970s and beyond, the concerns expressed by public and government about environmental degradation resulted in a series of atlases on aspects of this question. Land-based pollution and misuse, the loss of land to urban development, and holistic views of the entire human-environmental ecosystem were the subjects of atlases or studies incorporating geographic databases expressed in map form. There were also special regional examinations of the Great Lakes and the St Lawrence.

The Centennial celebrations in 1967 saw a quickening of national pride in Canadian achievements. Later this was expressed in various "nation-building" policies of government such as official bilingualism and multiculturalism, as well as programmes aiding the development of educational materials on Canada for use by Canadians and others. Enrichment of self-knowledge about our cultural and regional diversity, our history, and our geography lay behind a series of magnificent historical atlases. Although some were supported heavily by national funding agencies, there was a variety of more modest local atlas products.

In addition to these underlying social and political trends affecting the sponsorship and production of atlases, there have been fundamental changes in technology and research approaches since the end of the 1960s. This has meant that the very process of collecting, analysing, and displaying cartographic data has resulted in a veritable revolution in what we can see and how we can see atlas maps portrayed. The quantitative revolution in geography as a spatial science developed techniques of analysis that depended for results on the ability of new computing power to handle and manipulate large data sets of variables.

These same computers could also begin to display this spatial information and the resultant analyses. The first computer maps were crude and primitive by today's standards, and thus it is easy to overlook the profound nature of the revolution that was under way. However the arrival of more easily accessible and spatially flexible databases was not long in coming. Atlases may now be seen as but one special output from such databases, with the power of the computer being used to produce the linework, symbolization, and labelling needed for thematic atlas maps.

Where once the cartographer suffered from a dearth of data, it is now argued there is excess.* This increased accessibility to contemporary data has underlined the continued importance of sharpening research design. In this way the proper questions will be asked by people who understand the inherent limitations of the data, and who know how to overcome then in communicating effectively with an audience.[46]

Thematic Atlases by Topical Group

The thematic atlases selected for closer examination have been grouped into six types: historical and cultural; physical (climatic, hydrographic, and geological); economic and resources; environmental; medical and electoral; and urban (table 10-4 lists the selected atlases).

---

* See chapter 15 for reference to the surveys of federal digital data sets in 1983 and 1990.

Table 10-4
Canadian Thematic Atlases, 1951–93*
(short form titles of major works and those referred to in the text in order of reference)

Title	Date	Author(s)	Publisher	# Maps, Plates
1. HISTORICAL AND CULTURAL ATLASES				
1.1 Historical Atlas of Canada (3 vols.)	1987–93	Matthews, Harris, Holdsworth, Kerr and Gentilcore	U of Toronto Press	69; 58; 63
1.2 Manitoba Historical Atlas	1970	Warkentin & Ruggles	Historical Society of Manitoba	312
1.3 A Country So Interesting	1991	Ruggles	McGill-Queen's	66
1.4 Ontario History in Maps	1984	Gentilcore and Head	U of Toronto Press	268
1.5 Atlas of New France	1968	Trudel	Presses de l'U Laval	95
1.6 The North Part of America	1979	Verner & Stuart-Stubbs	Academic Press	46
1.7 Ottawa in Maps	1974	Nagy	National Map Collection	32
1.8 Winnipeg in Maps	1975	Artibise & Dahl	Nat. Map Collection	31
1.9 From Sea Unto Sea	1982	Armstrong	Fleet/Lester & Orpen Denis	38
1.10 Peterborough County Atlas	1975	Peterborough Historical Atlas Foundation	The Foundation	127pp
1.11 Original Mennonite Villages, Manitoba	1988	Rempel & Harmes	private	25
1.12 Vancouver Visual History	1992	Macdonald	Talonbooks	52
1.13 Creating a Landscape	1989	Luciuk & Kordan	U of Toronto Press	70 pp
1.14 Nunavut Atlas	1992	Riewe	Canadian Circumpolar Institute & T.F.N.	259 pp
1.15 Nunavik. Inuit Place Name Map Series	1981	Muller-Wille	Avataq Cultural Institute	12
1.16 British Columbia Ghost Towns	1982	Basque	Sunfire Publs	41
1.17 Ontario Ghost Towns and Scenic Back Roads	1985	Brown	Cannonbooks	64 pp
2. PHYSICAL ATLASES				
2.1 Climatological Atlas of Canada	1953	Thomas	Canada, Transport, & NRC	84
2.2 Atlas of Climatic Maps (10 series)	1967–70	Thomas & Anderson	Canada, Transport, Met. Branch	30
2.3 Climate Atlas Climatique-Canada (5 vols.)	1984	Canada, Environmental Service	The Service	ca. 400
2.4 Atlas Climatologique	1978	Houde	Québec, Min. des Rich. nat.	42
2.5 Great Lakes Surface Water Temperature	1992	Irbe	Environment Canada	108
2.6 Ice Atlas of Arctic Canada	1960	Swithinbank	Scott Polar Res. Instit.	67 pp
2.7 Canadian Arctic Waterways	1981	Markham	Environment Canada	198 pp
2.8 Canadian Sea Ice Atlas	1992	LeBrew, Barber & Agnew	Environment Canada	36 images
2.9 Hydrological Atlas of Canada	1978	Canadian National Committee on the International Hydrological Decade	Canada, Fisheries & Oceans	68 pp

Table 10-4 *(cont'd)*
Canadian Thematic Atlases, 1951–93*
(short form titles of major works and those referred to in the text in order of reference)

	Title	Date	Author(s)	Publisher	# Maps, Plates
2.10	*Water Resource Atlas of Newfoundland*	1992	Ullah	Newfoundland, Water Res.	79pp
2.11	*Atlas of Alberta Lakes*	1990	Prepas	U. of Alberta Press	675pp
2.12	*Canadian Geophysical Atlas*	1987–92	Canada, Geological Survey	The Survey	15

3. ECONOMIC AND RESOURCE ATLASES

	Title	Date	Author(s)	Publisher	# Maps, Plates
3.1	*Canada Descriptive Atlas*	1951	Canada, Citizenship & Immigration	The Department	13
3.2	*British Columbia Resource Atlas*	1956	Chapman et al.	B.C. Natural Resources Conf.	48
3.3	*Economic Atlas of Ontario*	1969	Dean & Matthews	U of Toronto Press	234
3.4	*Ontario Resource Atlas*	1958, 1963	Ontario, Lands & Forests	The Department	34
3.5	*Alberta Resource Maps*	1972,80, 86	Alberta, Highways & Transp.	The Department	55; 82; 81
3.6	*Quebec Economic Atlas*	1976	Quebec, Industry & Commerce	The Department	14
3.7	*Resource Atlas of Newfoundland*	1974	Newfoundland, Forestry	The Department	17
3.8	*Ontario Arctic Watershed*	1975	Hutton & Black	Canada, Lands Directorate	23
3.9	*North of 50°*	1985	Matthews	U of Toronto Press	119 pp
3.10	*Atlas Regional du Saguenay–Lac Saint-Jean*	1981	Morin, Gauthier & Bouchard	Gaëtan Morin & Ass.	97

4. ENVIRONMENTAL ATLASES

	Title	Date	Author(s)	Publisher	# Maps, Plates
4.1	*Canada's Special Resource Lands*	1979	Simpson-Lewis	Canada, Lands Directorate	232 pp
4.2	*Rural-Urban Land Conversion*	1980	Gierman	Canada, Lands Directorate	71 pp
4.3	*Stress on the Land*	1983	Simpson-Lewis	Canada, Lands Directorate	323 pp
4.4	*Atlas Régional du Bas-St-Laurent, Gaspésie*	1966	Bureau d'aménagement de l'est du Québec	le Bureau & ARDA	80
4.5	*Lancaster Lakes Environmental Atlas*	1982	Dirschl & Dobbin Ass.	Canada, Indian Affairs	84
4.6	*Great Lakes Environmental Atlas*	1988	Betts, Krushelnicki & Hughes	Canada, Environment & U.S., EPA	44 pp
4.7	*St Lawrence Environmental Atlas*	1990–	U Laval, Dept Geography	Canada, Environment, St Lawrence Centre	14

5. HEALTH & ELECTORAL ATLASES

	Title	Date	Author(s)	Publisher	# Maps, Plates
5.1	*Atlas Médical des Cantons de l'Est*	1980	Castonguay, Fortin & Thouez	Éditions Naaman	125 pp
5.2	*Mortality Atlas of Canada* (4 vols.)	1980–91	Canada, Health & Welfare	Statistics Canada	30; 36; 45; 47
5.3	*Geographical Distribution of Cancer, Ontario*	1991	Marett	Ontario Cancer Center and Research Foundation	49

Table 10-4 *(cont'd)*
Canadian Thematic Atlases, 1951–93*
(short form titles of major works and those referred to in the text in order of reference)

	Title	Date	Author(s)	Publisher	# Maps, Plates
5.4	Geography of Death, Mortality Atlas of B.C.	1992	Foster & Edgell	Western Geog. Series	52
5.5	Atlas électoral du Québec, 1970–6 (6 vols.)	1979	Beaudry	Québec, Éditeur Officiel	
5.6	Atlas des élections féderales au Québec	1989	Drouilly	U du Québec à Montréal	22
6. URBAN ATLASES					
6.1	Computer Atlas of Ottawa-Hull	1970	Taylor & Douglas	Carleton Geography Dept	48
6.2	Employment Atlas of Montreal	1972	Marois	Presses de l'U du Québec	92
6.3	Atlas Urbain, Sherbrooke	1976	Castonguay	Éditions Naarman	45
6.4	Canadian Urban Trends	1976	Ray, et al.	Statistics Canada	138
6.5	Census Atlas of Newfoundland	1977	Inst. Social & Economic Research	The Institute, Memorial U	175 pp
6.6	Atlas of Winnipeg	1978	Weir	U of Toronto Press	67
6.7	Metropolitan Atlas [series of 12]	1989	Statistics Canada	Statistics Canada	26
6.8	Atlas of Residential Concentration [series of 3]	1986	Kralt	Statistics Canda	71 (each)
6.9	Atlas of Alberta	1984	Byfield, Alberta Report	Interwest Publications	160 pp

* These tables were derived from a longer listing of Canadian atlases. A list of 170 atlases (40 historical and cultural, 30 physical, 35 economic, 3 electoral, 15 environmental, 7 health, and 40 urban) has been provided on a National Atlas www site, http://cgdi.ga.ca.

Only one published listing of Canadian Atlases (95 in total) has come to our attention. This is contained within a world survey and is now badly outdated though still useful. It was published by the International Cartographic Association as part of an international survey by Stams, W. [1980?] *National and Regional Atlases: A Bibliographic Survey*. Paris: International Cartographic Association.

HISTORICAL AND CULTURAL

The three-volume set of the *Historical Atlas of Canada* published between 1987 and 1993 by the University of Toronto Press was created by a nationwide consortium of scholars under a complex set of editorial arrangements.[47] In terms of its size, expense of production, and impact on the general reading public and the world of Canadian scholarship it certainly deserves pride of place in any analysis of Canadian thematic atlases. In many ways it was itself a national atlas, and indeed represented more intellectual and financial investment than many of that title. Most striking was its integrity of conception, covering in a broad sweep the human occupancy of the country from its first peopling to 1961. Its innovative visual design broke new ground in the integration of graphics with novel and pleasing cartographic depictions.

There was some continuity of guiding forces behind the inception of the *Historical Atlas of Canada* and those central to the influential *Economic Atlas of Ontario* in the 1960s. Like its predecessor it relied heavily on large-scale sponsorship from public bodies, a fact wryly acknowledged in William Dean's foreword to volume 1. "No good atlas exists that did not cost more than was expected and take longer than was projected. [These] ... are however part of the cost of being Canadian."[48] The calculated costs ($7.5 million) were indeed large, but were in line with other contemporary publication mega-products such as the *Dictionary of Canadian Biography* ($15 million) or the Canadian Encyclopedia ($12–13 million).[49]

Historical atlases have also included the reproduction of historical maps. John Warkentin and Richard Ruggles's pioneer work, *The Manitoba Historical Atlas,* published in 1970, was the most notable early example utilizing contemporary maps and commentary to depict elements of past geographies. Also a noteworthy work, though not strictly speaking an atlas, was Ruggles's later *A Country So Interesting* with its facsimile manuscript maps and a descriptive list of 220 maps in the Hudsons Bay Co. archives. The University of Toronto Press published *Ontario's History in Maps* in 1984 at the time of the bicentenary of the province. This work by R. Louis Gentilcore and Grant Head presented a wide variety of map facsimiles of different types of all periods, the text indicating the role of maps as valuable source documents.

Indeed there were a large number of facsimile atlases and collections of maps published in the period, indicating the growing interest in the history of mapping[50] as well as the popularity of genealogical research. The wholesale reproduction of nineteenth-century county atlases, particularly of Ontario and notably by Mika Press, bears witness to this.[51] The names of landowners on the maps and the charming illustrations of contemporary people and farms added to their desirability for family historians. A fine example of the work a local society might do to further knowledge of its own area can be seen in the *Illustrated Atlas of Peterborough County.* Despite its nineteenth-century style and format this was not a reprint, but a faithful re-creation of the maps of landowners style for a county that had not been originally mapped "because of sparseness of settlement."[52]

A recent and significant hybrid publication in terms of its style, audience, and manner of production is the *Vancouver Visual Atlas*, which shows what is possible with the new power of the desktop computer and a high degree of enthusiasm from the author, B. MacDonald. Neither a reproduction atlas nor chiefly a quantitative atlas, it depicts at ten-year intervals the emerging form of the city of Vancouver from forest clearing to Pacific metropolis.

The historical atlas of Ukrainians in Canada, *Creating a Landscape*, by L. Luciuk and B. Kordan, with cartographer Geoffrey Matthews, provides a systematic treatment of one of Canada's leading ethno-cultural communities since 1891. The style may be characterized as "Matthews graphical" in that this leading cartographer has experimented with approaches utilizing the best modern colours, forms and typography of the commercial world of graphic design.

More research-oriented and in large non-commercial format is the *Nunavut Atlas* – a highly significant project in many ways. Under an agreement with the federal government the Tungavik Federation of Nunavut gathered information in 1986–87 from their own communities' hunters and elders. The large-format maps at a scale of 1:2 000 000 for each community show wildlife, areas of archaeological interest, campsites, and travel routes. They provided an essential component in the successful completion of land claims and treaty negotiations.[53]

Amateur enthusiasm for the production of special atlases may have reached its peak in *British Columbia's Ghost Towns*. The author, Garnet Basque, wrote "I am not a cartographer by trade, nor am I a professional writer. I prefer to call myself a publisher, though there may be those who would dispute even that."[54]

PHYSICAL ATLASES

Portraying the earth's physical processes in atlas form is a well-established style. Those elements that had particular importance to the economic growth and well-being of Canada had their origins in the nineteenth-century geology and agricultural climate maps of the early national atlases. Pioneering efforts by physical scientists to employ the atlas format to portray their extensive observational data commenced with Morley Thomas's *Climatological Atlas of Canada*, first published in 1953.[55] The work was a joint project with the Building Research Division of the National Research Council, which needed to define the requirements for outside work in the North in the 1940s. It relied on data held in 100 000 punch cards – an early indication of mechanical data storage and manipulation.

The atlas format for climate data was also utilized in a series of later, more specialized, and more localized publications. These were characterized by ever-increasing volume of data and statistical sophistication for such topics as upper winds, rainfall intensity and frequency, and agroclimate, and for regional studies of Québec, Great Lakes water temperatures, the Prairies, and the Arctic. Most were strictly scientific studies, though often with economic, engineering, or even broader underpinnings. Evidence of this rationale lies in the *Atlas Climatologique* of the Québec Ministère des Richesses Naturelles (1976): "à des besoins de connaissance ordinaires de la collectivité québécoise et aussi à des besoins plus spécifiques face à l'état de changement apparent du régime climatique global."[56]

In glancing at the smooth isolines curving in easily understandable patterns across vast distances, it is easy to overlook the immense labour expended in gathering and interpreting the millions of observations required to produce these maps. The *Great Lakes Surface Water Temperature Climatology* of 1992, however, hints at the drama behind the cold science. It acknowledges those "... who endured through hundreds of hours of low-level flight, sometimes pushing themselves and the crew to the limits, in order to complete a survey in weather conditions when sensible ducks would not venture forth ..."[57]

Perhaps in no other area have the technological advances of remote (including satellite) sensing played a greater role in revolutionizing our knowledge of Canada than in the earth sciences. This has led to the creation of a series of atlases portraying these phenomena in ways that would have been inconceivable a few decades ago. A series of sea-ice atlases for the observation periods 1961–68, 1969–74, and 1975–78 were based on aerial photography, initially from twin-engined aircraft. W.E. Markham's *Canadian Arctic Waterways* of 1981 and the *Canadian Sea-Ice Atlas* of 1992 were derived from data taken from the polar-orbiting Landsat and Seasat satellites.

The wider interests lying behind the support given to this work are referred to by Markham in his introduction. As noted in chapter 1 the economic need was for resource exploration and exploitation, especially for oil after 1974, and to reinforce sovereignty against surface and sub-surface marine intrusions. By 1992 and the International Space Year, however, the warming of the Earth's atmosphere was cited as a principal reason to extend Arctic ice studies.

Similarly international cooperation during the International Hydrological Decade saw the federal Department of Fisheries and Environment produce the *Hydrological Atlas of Canada* (1978) with a large number of maps at 1:10 000 000, and 1:20 000 000 scales.

Water resources at the provincial level were also the subject of atlases in Alberta (1990) and Newfoundland (1992).

In the former, the *Atlas of Alberta Lakes*, science apparently mixes with tourism as revealed in the foreword by the then Minister of the Environment, Ralph Klein. "Collected in a single volume is a wealth of interesting and useful information about 100 Alberta lakes, everything from water quality and biological characteristics to the best spots for landing a northern pike. Scientist and student alike will find the atlas valuable and so will any family looking for a recreation site."[58] The finished atlas is an impressive and even lavish work using "only data that are consistent with the best modern techniques in the field." The *Water Resource Atlas of Newfoundland* is more general, and is intended for education and the general public to reflect the "acute awareness of our environmental responsibilities."[59]

The *Canadian Geophysical Atlas* (1987, ongoing) is a loose-leaf production that to date consists of fifteen sheets of impressive technical sophistication and striking colour presentation. The data is derived from 600 000 observations expressed in more than sixty subtle colour gradations. Perhaps nowhere is there a more impressive display of the marriage of science and artistic rendering, made possible by recent advances in the manipulation of large data sets and the power of computers in cartography.

ECONOMIC AND RESOURCE ATLASES

Atlases that contain "economic" or "resource" in their titles, but that are sufficiently comprehensive to be considered provincial atlases in their own right, have been discussed earlier in this chapter.[60] Starting with some of the general atlases, the *Descriptive Atlas of Canada*[61] should be singled out as it was probably seen by more people than any other atlas published in the country. As a federal information document it was sent or handed to prospective immigrants, who doubtless formed some of their first impressions from its colourful pages. Originally produced by the Department of the Interior in 1908, the content was probably linked to and generalized from the first edition of the national atlas published two years earlier. It was republished as many as ten times, with the last edition in 1951 just making it part of the period covered by this volume. The text gives rules for aspiring colonists, and lists immigration bureaux in Europe and the U.S. The 1951 edition pronounces that the immense region north of the Saguenay between Labrador and Hudson Bay remained largely unexplored. This presumably was for the aspiring colonist. The maps show the physical landscape with resources highlighted by a somewhat crude overprint in red. There seems in this mild form of state propaganda something of a metaphor for resource atlases in general. They lay out cartographically for all to see, and perhaps to exploit economically, what in Premier Bennett's phrase was a magnificent heritage.

In the same class could be placed the several editions of the *Ontario Resource Atlas* of 1955, 1958, and 1963 (which started its existence as the *Ontario Forest Atlas* in 1945); the *Alberta Resource Maps* series in loose-leaf format from 1972, 1980, and 1986; the *Québec Economic Atlas* (title supplied by the National Archives) of 1976; and the *Resource Atlas of Newfoundland* of 1974 (based on CLI information reduced to a province-wide scale).

A more sophisticated version that could be seen as a regional development atlas or a form of sub-provincial atlas of its own is the *Ontario Arctic Watershed* of 1975. This was produced by the Lands Directorate of Environment Canada for a joint federal-provincial study,[62] itself part of the provincial Royal Commission on the Northern Environment. This commission also published a small atlas on "issues" in 1978.[63] In turn this was reused and popularized by the University of Toronto Press and Geoff Matthews as *North of 50°* in 1985.

Though not strictly a resource atlas, the *Atlas Régional du Saguenay Lac-Saint Jean* of 1981 should be mentioned as a striking example of the application of geographic concepts to an atlas format. Consciously evoking the regional theories of the French human geographers of the uniqueness of place, the geographers Morin, Gauthier, and Bouchard of the Université du Québec à Chicoutimi have mapped "the kingdom of the Saguenay" with as much attention as most Canadian provinces. Detailed textual vignettes accompany each of the nearly 100 maps, of which a quarter are in colour.

ENVIRONMENTAL ATLASES

These atlases and reports based heavily on maps have largely been the product of the federal Department of the Environment and its former Lands Directorate, which in the decade following the mid-1970s were very active in mapping matters of environmental concern.[64] Much of the data used were based on the CLI system described in chapter 11, an early example of which is the atlas of Eastern Québec and the Gaspesie, 1966.

A specialized atlas generated by the need to assess the environmental and human effects of oil and gas exploitation in the Lancaster Sound region of the eastern Arctic was published in three languages in 1982, and signalled a new attention to resource extraction in the North.

Since then publications have been made on less classic atlas lines, with a reduced emphasis on cartography and an increased use of graphically designed tables, charts, and other illustrations. This trend has continued in the reports on the state of the environment, and in the environmental atlases of the Great Lakes and of the St Lawrence.[65] These publications have tended towards simpler cartographic depictions, leaving the analysis to the text. In this sense they can be seen as trends counter to the increased sophistication of modern cartography, which performs the integration in the spatial patterns of the maps themselves.

HEALTH AND ELECTORAL ATLASES

Atlases of diseases and mortality have become a well-developed specialist approach to identifying those environmental factors that have the capability of affecting life and health. The earliest were the *Atlas Medical des Cantons de l'Est* of 1980 and the *Mortality Atlas of Canada*. The latter was initiated in 1978 in a joint project of the Department of Health and Welfare and Statistics Canada. The cartography of these atlases used early versions of computer-mapping software that had been adapted to the prevailing needs.

In addition there have been provincial studies in atlas form. The *Geographical Distribution of Cancer in Ontario* of 1991 used computerized files of the causes of death, which were mapped by SAS/GRAPH software and printed using PostScript files sent to a Linotronic photo-typesetter. The *Geography of Death: Mortality Atlas of B.C.* of 1992 provides a second illustration. This visually striking atlas uses colour-coded maps produced by computer to provide readily understandable community level information to local health care practitioners and planners and the community at large.

Electoral mapping has proved of interest in Québec since 1976. It has resulted in the publication of two detailed and analytically sophisticated atlases, the *Atlas électoral du Québec, 1970–6* in 1979, and the *Atlas des élections fédérales au Québec, 1867–1988* in 1989. The first mapped the results of the elections of 1970, 1973, and 1976 analysed by ecological models of electoral behaviour (but not in mapped form). The second produced twenty-two different electoral base maps used since 1867, with electoral and linguistic distributions since 1945.

URBAN ATLASES

Almost without exception atlases of individual urban areas or inter-urban comparisons have relied heavily on the data generated by Statistics Canada, which, until forced recently to abandon it through cut-backs, produced an urban atlas series of its own. In addition in no other grouping of atlases has the increased role and sophistication of computer databases and computer mapping played such a major role. Much of the pioneer work for these developments came from university geography departments. It began with the influential *Computer Atlas of Ottawa-Hull*[66] of 1970, developed by D.R.F. Taylor and David Douglas to illustrate the potential of the computer in producing maps and draw attention to the growing field of computer graphics [SYMAP]. The line printer combinations of the characters AVNZX1/- formed the thirty-one maps of Ottawa-Hull and the seventeen maps of Ontario, and were to become familiar output formats in the decade that followed. There were several others of this type including the *Employment Atlas of Montreal* in 1972; the *Atlas Urbain, Sherbrooke* in 1976, which reflected a well-developed research design; the *Census Atlas of Newfoundland* of 1977 with prominence given to St John's; and the *Atlas of Winnipeg* in 1978, though this did not use computer-based output directly.

It was the lavish full-colour, three-volume *Canadian Urban Trends* that demonstrated the full potential of a marriage between computer data and cartographic output. It was based on 1971 data, and was co-published in 1976 by Statistics Canada and Copp Clark. Though much of the space was taken by detailed statistical tables, the sweeping conception (with a descending order of scale from the world to the national and thence metropolitan and neighbourhood levels) and innovative cartography (using oblique projections and proportionate circles, columns, and coloured choropleths) make it a *tour de force*. Unfortunately it was not to be repeated. Instead it was succeeded by the more modest *Metropolitan Atlas* series, published using 1986 statistics for the twelve major metropolitan regions, which marked the culmination of this trend. It was designed to appeal to many audiences, although its economy of production with only three colours and lack of place identifiers made it appear less attractive than its conceptualization warranted. The subject matter was extensive, and included measures of demography, family and social, housing, employment, and income variables. With the decision to abandon this series for the 1991 census, an end, at least for a time, appears to have come to Statistics Canada's urban thematic conventional atlas production.[67]

Another government urban atlas series was published in 1986, though it was highly focused on one particular question in the three major urban areas of Toronto, Montréal, and Vancouver. The Atlas of Residential Concentration (three publications) portrayed 1981 census data with a view to seeing the degree of ethnic concentration in those areas. Using an index of concentration, it portrayed for the first time the relative distributions of "visible minorities" in the three largest Canadian centres where between a quarter and a half of the populations reported ethnic origins other than British or French.

The venture by a private publisher in this field of atlas production is noteworthy. Land-use maps of every town and city were included among a large selection of general purpose maps of the province published by the Alberta Report in 1984.

The economic downturn of the past five years has certainly had an effect on the production of new atlases, financed as much as it has been by discretionary government or public spending. At the same time the costs of data acquisition have diminished so considerably, and so many agencies have made the expensive conversion to computer-based, even GIS-based data-gathering structures, that ironically the ability to produce atlas maps has perhaps been enhanced during this time. Building on these capabilities a few experiments in electronic atlases and maps have commenced in the past five years using floppy-disk formats. It remains to be seen what is likely to be the acceptability and long-term market demand for these.[68]

Certain trends are becoming evident. The paper/book format still holds its own for the great majority of users, though this will likely be challenged during the next decade. The rise of the CD-ROM, the interactive access to computer networks, commercially available and user-friendly mapping software, and electronic files in floppy-disk formats have already generated greater demands by users for desktop accessibility to atlas data.[69] How interactive or passive will be the need to engage the data? This is likely to be determined by the user's interests and technical sophistication. How far will this affect the traditional editorial control exercised by the originating agency? This is likely to diminish as user control grows. The challenges for atlas cartography and map making will continue to be ones of attempting to provide accurate and timely answers to relevant spatial questions, and to communicate effectively with appropriate and imaginative cartographic design.

NOTES

1 1906. *Atlas of Canada*. Ottawa: Department of the Interior.

1915. *Atlas of Canada*, rev. and enl. Ottawa: Department of the Interior. French versions of the 1st and 2d editions were not published.

1957. *Atlas of Canada*, 3d ed. Ottawa: Department of Mines and Technical Surveys.

1957. *L'Atlas du Canada*, 3d ed. Ottawa: Ministère des Mines et des Relevés Techniques.

1973. *The National Atlas of Canada*, 4th ed. (boxed maps). Ottawa: Department of Energy, Mines and Resources.

1973. *L'Atlas National du Canada*, 4th ed. (boxed maps). Ottawa: Ministère de l'Énergie, des Mines et des Ressources.

1974. *The National Atlas of Canada*, 4th ed., rev. (bound version). Toronto: Macmillan Company of Canada Ltd in association with the Department of Energy, Mines and Resources and Information Canada.

1974. *L'Atlas National du Canada*, 4th ed., rev. (bound version). Toronto: Macmillan of Canada avec le concours du Ministère de l'Énergie, des Mines et des Ressources et d'Information Canada.

1978–94. *The National Atlas of Canada*, 5th ed. Ottawa: Energy, Mines and Resources Canada. (This English language edition was a serial publication of which the first map was published in 1978 and the last in 1994. A special container for the maps, including front matter, was made available in 1985.)

1978–94. *L'Atlas National du Canada*, 5th ed. Ottawa: Énergie, Mines et Ressources Canada. (This French language edition was a serial publication of which the first map was published in

1978 and the last in 1994. A special container for the maps, including front matter, was made available in 1985.)

2 Grant-Suttie, G.L.P. 1947. New Atlas of Canada. *Industrial Canada*, 47, 12, 63–6.

3 Brouillette, B. 1945. *Atlas of Canada Project: A Preliminary Survey.* Ottawa: Canadian Social Science Research Council.

4 Papers on Atlas of Canada. File SM7245. Surveys, Mapping and Remote Sensing Sector, Natural Reources Canada.

5 A proper mathematical description of the modified polyconic projection used was not made until 1981 when it was needed for computer plotting of data by geophysicists. See Haines, G.V. 1981. The Modified Polyconic Projection. *Cartographica*, 18, 1, 49–58. The Lambert conformal projection was also used in the 4th and 5th editions.

6 Nicholson, N.L. 1961. Some Elements in the Development of the National Atlas of Canada. *Geographical Bulletin*, 16, 45–53.

7 Fremlin, G. 1963. Color and Design in the British Columbia and Manitoba Atlases and the National Atlas of Canada. *Geographical Bulletin*, 20, 130–42.

8 Correspondence, Norman L. Nicholson to Marc Boyer. 6 March 1961. Papers on Atlas of Canada. File SM7245.

9 Papers on Atlas of Canada. File SM7245.

10 Reasons for the dissolution of the organization were offered publicly by the Minister of Energy, Mines and Resources, the Hon. J.-L. Pepin in a speech to the Canadian Association of Geographers annual meeting on 1 June 1967.

11 Fremlin, G., and H.E. Mindak. 1968. Lakes, Rivers and Glaciers/A Map Commentary. *The Canadian Cartographer*, 5, 2, 133–7.

12 Minutes of the First Meeting of the Advisory Committee on the National Atlas of Canada. May 4–5, 1971. Papers on Atlas of Canada. File SM7245.

13 Energy, Mines and Resources Canada, Surveys and Mapping Branch. 1969. *Atlas and Gazetteer of Canada*. Ottawa: Queens Printer.

14 Woodcock, George. 1974. *Books in Canada*, November.

15 Symons, T.H.B. 1975. *To Know Ourselves – The Report of the Commission on Canadian Studies*, vol. 1. Ottawa: Association of Universities and Colleges of Canada, 57.

16 Report of the National Advisory Committee on a National Atlas of Canada. 5th Edition. May 1975. Papers on Atlas of Canada. File SM2745.

17 Only one sheet in this series was ever published: Canada-Relief, 1976. *Geographical Map Series – No. 1 MCR 88*. Ottawa: Surveys and Mapping Branch; Energy, Mines and Resources Canada.

18 Lapp, P.A., A.A. Marsan, and L.J. O'Brien. 1978. *Report of the Task Force on National Surveying and Mapping*. Ottawa: Surveys and Mapping Branch; Energy, Mines and Resources Canada, 113.

19 Groot, R. 1979. Canada's National Atlas Program in the Computer Era. In Barbara Gutsell, ed. 1979. *The Purpose and Use of National and Regional Atlases*. Toronto: B.V. Gutsell. Monograph no. 23, supplement no. 1 to *The Canadian Cartographer*, 16, 41–52.

20 1980. *Canada Gazetteer Atlas*. Toronto: Macmillan of Canada in cooperation with Energy, Mines and Resources Canada and the Canadian Government Publishing Centre.
1980. *Canada Atlas Toponymique*. Montreal: Guérin éditeur conjointement avec Énergie, Mines et Ressources Canada et le Centre d'édition du gouvernement du Canada.

21 For example, see 1984. Canada – Indian and Inuit Communities – Quebec 1:2 000 000 *National Atlas Data Base Map Series, map no. NADM-3, MCR4026*. Ottawa: Energy, Mines and Resources Canada.

22 For example see 1987. 1:12 500 000 *Canada Base Map Series, MCR138*. Ottawa: Energy, Mines and Resources Canada.

23 Falconer, G., and P.J. Lloyd. 1984. Marketing the National Atlas of Canada. In *Papers, Symposium on the Marketing of Cartographic Information*. Kingston: Queen's University, 69–77.

24 Cuff, D.J. 1987. The National Atlas of Canada. *Cartographica*, 24, 3, 101–3.

25 Harding, K. 1987. The National Atlas of Canada Fifth Edition: Format, Scale and Distribution. *Association of Canadian Map Libraries Bulletin*, 65, 13–14.

26 Sandford, H.A. 1987. The National Atlas of Canada (5th edition, English language) and L'Atlas National du Canada (5th edition, French language). *The Cartographic Journal*, 24, 2, 167–8.

27 The National Atlas Information System was now redesignated as a "Service."

28 National Advisory Committee for the National Atlas of Canada. 1988. *The National Atlas Information System, a Report to the Minister of State (Forestry and Mines)*.
National Advisory Committee for the National Atlas of Canada. 1990. *The National Atlas Information System, a Report to the Minister of Energy, Mines and Resources*.

29 National Atlas Information Service. 1994. Table of Contents January 1994 – The National Atlas of Canada – Fifth Edition (list). Ottawa: Dept of Energy, Mines and Resources.

30 1993. *Results of the Thirty-fifth Federal Election October 25, 1993*. National Atlas Special Map Series no. 1. MCR 196. Ottawa: Surveys, Mapping and Remote Sensing Sector; Natural Resources Canada. The results of the constitutional referendum in 1993 were similarly mapped in a very short time period, the production team winning a special departmental merit award. The address of the World Wide Web site of the National Atlas in 1997 is: http://cgdi.gc.ca.

31 Weir, T. 1970. Transcribed discussion in *University of Alberta Studies in Geography, Occasional Papers 1*. Report of the Cartographic Workshop (Janusz J. Klawe, Chairman), 66.

32 Matthews, G. 1970. Transcribed presentation in *University of Alberta Studies in Geography, Occasional Papers 1*. Report of the Cartographic Workshop (Janusz J. Klawe, Chairman), 73.

33 Klawe, Janusz J. 1970. Transcribed discussion in *University of Alberta Studies in Geography, Occasional Papers 1*. Report of the Cartographic Workshop (Janusz J. Klawe, Chairman), 85.

34 Klawe, Janusz, J. 1970. A First in Alberta. *The Alberta Geographer*, 6, 11.

35 Nicholson, N.L. 1970. Canada in Six Atlases. *Canadian Cartographer*, 7, 2, 126–30.

36 Hocking, Diana, Peter C. Keller, and Cheryl Peterson. 1991. Thematic Content of Canadian Provincial Atlases. *Cartographica*, 28, 2, 38–50.

37 Robinson, A.L. 1952. *Look of Maps*. Madison, WI: University of Wisconsin Press.

38 Arvetis, Chris. 1973. The Cartographer-Designer Relationship, A Designer's View. *Surveying and Mapping*, 33, 2, 193–5.

39 Hocking, Diana, and Peter C. Keller. 1993. Analysis of State and Provincial Atlas Reviews. *Professional Geographer*, 45, 1, 73–83.

40 Yonge, Ena L. 1962. Regional Atlases: A Summary Survey. *Geographical Review*, 52, 407–32.

41 Bartz, Barbara. 1971. Designing Maps for Children. In Castner, Henry W., and Gerald McGrath, eds. 1971. *Map Design and the Map User. Cartographica*, monograph no. 2. Toronto: B.V. Gutsell, 35–40.

42 Gerber, R.V. 1982. An International Study of Children's Perceptions and Understanding of Type Used on Atlas Maps. *Cartographic Journal*, 19, 2, 115–21.

43 Wonders, Lillian J. 1980. The Junior Atlas of Alberta: Introducing New Mapping Techniques to Young Students. *Canadian Geographer*, 3, 306–11.

44 The National Archives cartographic accessions computer database is not structured to allow user searched of classes of items of the type reviewed here. A manual search had to be performed of

all entries of atlases in the typewritten card catalogue, current to the year 1992. Considerable assistance in this search was provided by staff at the Map Collection of National Archives.

45 The *British Columbia Atlas of Resources*, 1956, has been discussed in part 2 of this chapter. It is important to note that such thematic resource atlases had been published earlier. For one example see Richard M. Highsmith, *Atlas of the Pacific Northwest Resources and Development*, Oregon State College, Corvallis, OR [not dated, but around 1953]. This was based on an earlier *Economic Atlas of the Pacific Northwest* in editions of 1939 and 1942.

46 Paucity and inconsistency of information remain the usual problems in the design of historical atlases. Advances in knowledge and research concepts have, however, focused the questions and topics in view, while progress in techniques of visual communication have improved standards of cartographic presentation.

47 The background of this complex project has been described by Piternick, Anne. 1993. The Historical Atlas of Canada: The Project behind the Product. *Cartographica*, 30, 4, 21–31.

48 Harris, R. Cole, ed. 1987. *From the Beginning to 1800*. Vol. 1 of *Historical Atlas of Canada*. Toronto: University of Toronto Press, 13.

49 Piternick, Anne. 1993. The Historical Atlas of Canada, 25. It was estimated that a similar multi-volume work for the United States would have cost $6 million in 1970s dollars.

50 Such as Marcel Trudel's *Atlas of New France*; Coolie Verner's *The North Part of America*; Thomas Nagy's *Ottawa in Maps*; Alan F.J. Artibise and Edward Dahl's *Winnipeg in Maps*; as well as the more personal publication of Joe Armstrong's own map collection in *From Sea unto Sea*.

51 The list of counties for which atlases have been re-published is provided in table 2 of Nicholson, N.L. and L.M. Sebert. 1981. *The Maps of Canada*. Folkestone, Kent: Dawson.

52 Of this type also note Rempel, John and William Harms, 1988. *Original Mennonite Villages and Homesteads*. Privately published, in which the editors "travelled many miles and spent unending hours of timeless effort in the process of researching old records" (introduction).

53 In a similar vein the trilingual atlas of northern Québec *Nunavik Inuit Place Name Map Series*, 1991, showed the new interest in mapping the North from the local cultural perspective.

54 Basque, Garnet. 1982. *British Columbia Ghost Towns*. Langley, BC: Sunfire Publications. This publication was mirrored in Ontario by Ron Brown, *Ontario Ghost Towns*, 1985.

55 Subsequently revised and reissued in later editions under different titles in 1967 and 1984.

56 Houde, Angèle. 1978. *Atlas Climatologique*. Québec: Ministère des Richesses naturelles du Québec, introduction.

57 Irbe, G.I. 1992. *Great Lakes Surface Water Temperature*. Ottawa: Department of Supply and Services, 5.

58 Mitchell, Patricia and Ellie Prepas, eds. 1990. *Atlas of Alberta Lakes*. Edmonton: University of Alberta Press, 9.

59 Ullah, Wasi, project manager. 1992. *Water Resources Atlas of Newfoundland*. St John's: Water Resources Division, Department of the Environment and Lands, 3.

60 The *British Columbia Atlas of Resources* and the *Economic Atlas of Ontario* are of this type, though the former is much more unashamedly a display of the province's riches.

61 References have been found to editions of 1908, 1912, 1913 (with Rand McNally), 1915, 1919, 1920, 1923, 1936, and 1951.

62 It had commenced as a work of the Economic Geography Section of the Department of Energy, Mines & Resources, which was transferred to the Lands Directorate in 1971.

63 Published as part of *Issues: A Background Paper on Behalf of the R.C. on the Environment*. This commission was called into being after a proposal by a forest company to establish an

integrated forest products complex at Red Lake, with a licence to exploit 50 000 km² of Crown land.

64 A series of six map folios were published before 1983, the most general of which included *Special Resource Lands* in 1979, *Rural-Urban Land Conversion* in 1980, and *Stress on the Land* in 1983.

65 The latter "atlas" has been published as an unbound occasional series of posters of mixed text and graphics containing a few maps.

66 This is believed to have been the first such computer-generated atlas in the world.

67 Statistics Canada has pioneered, for educational purposes only, a digital data, mapping, and graphics CD-ROM, E-STAT, which makes available selected 1991 census variables at the census sub-district level.

68 After expensive pioneering efforts within the Department of Energy, Mines and Resources since the early 1980s to build an interactive test version of an electronic atlas, it now seems likely that any future such version of *The National Atlas of Canada* will be marketed only in commercially available mapping or GIS software formats.

69 A prototype display of samples of national atlas data and thematic maps (at user-controlled scales) utilizing Mosaic software from a World Wide Web site that commenced in September 1994 points to one way of delivering atlas products in the future.

CHAPTER ELEVEN

Federal, Provincial, and Private Sector Thematic Mapping

George Falconer

All maps can represent only a specific selection of information about the earth and space. In that sense all maps might be regarded as thematic, and much information has geographic significance. The topographic map is a special case that has evolved in response to widespread needs for a reliable set of frequently used and standardized geographical information. It serves also as the foundation for special mapping of other particular themes, features, and concepts.[1] In their fully developed and most sophisticated form, topographic maps display high standards of accuracy and rely on a precise geodetic framework on which to base the topographic information. In contrast thematic maps are made for a wide variety of purposes. Although there are examples of thematic maps having an accuracy comparable with that of topographic maps, there are also thematic maps in which positional accuracy is reduced drastically in order to communicate or emphasize ideas and concepts.

THE USES AND USERS OF THEMATIC MAPS

There is virtually no field of human activity or interest that has not been the subject of a thematic map. The purposes range from the near frivolous, as in some ephemeral maps produced for the media, to the deadly serious such as maps showing the incidence of mortality from disease. They may be used to store detailed scientific information at relatively large scales, as in forest inventory mapping, or they may be intended simply as conjectural illustrations in a text. Some maps contain information that makes them essential operational tools, for example to deploy police forces in a city, or they may be propagandistic in purpose and meant to influence the user's attitude towards an issue.

This chapter traces some highlights of thematic mapping in Canada since 1947. A review of such mapping reveals immediately both the impressive volume of work and the extremely diverse subject matter. Furthermore the cartographic concepts and techniques employed seem unlimited and reflect an enormous variety of purposes and audiences. Subject matter may comprise information on geology, climate, soils, land use, forestry, economy, demography, culture, language, and history. The diverse applications include inventories of natural resources, urban and regional planning, demographic and socio-economic surveys, planning health and welfare services, industrial and retail trade location, tourism and recreation, environmental conservation, disaster and emergency planning, and land claims of aboriginal peoples. The maps may be in the form of a series, the result of large-scale precise surveys, or single, small-scale, generalized, and even exaggerated depictions that provide summary information for the entire country. They may deal with a single theme or combine a number of related themes. Thematic mapping in Canada since 1947 is also an history of the development of classifications to describe geographical phenomena, and the steadily growing awareness and exploitation of the power of maps as a medium for storing and communicating information.

The period since the Second World War has seen national and regional resource inventories undertaken, and the increasing availability of socio-economic information derived from censuses. Since the 1970s these have been combined with the remarkable developments in computer-assisted cartography and Geographical Information Systems (GIS) to foster common spatial referencing of many types of thematic information to the standard topographic base map. The arbitrary distinction between topographic and thematic information is now becoming blurred. It is being replaced by a continuum of geographical information from which the user selects, manipulates, and displays as required. Thematic mapping increasingly involves the direct input of geographically referenced information from fieldwork, remote sensing, or statistical sources into GIS with a variety of options for its graphic representation. The future of thematic mapping is clearly bound up with the evolution of the new position-finding technologies, remote sensing, and GIS which are treated in chapters 2, 14, and 15 respectively. Atlases, which bring together maps according to some organized system, are dealt with in chapter 10.

THE PRODUCERS OF THEMATIC MAPS

Given the diversity of subjects and purposes it is not surprising that there are many producers, publishers, and distributors of thematic maps, though it is difficult to arrive at an estimate of their changing numbers over time. Some information exists in various lists of map sources issued over the last two or three decades, but as these were compiled by different agencies using different methods and criteria it is hazardous to rely on them.[2] Perhaps over 300 Canadian agencies or individuals either are or have been engaged in some form of thematic map making. A great many may have been involved in the production of only a single map and may not regard themselves as map producers, whereas the output of a few large agencies runs into many thousands of maps each year. About 17 federal government agencies have been involved in some type of thematic map creation or publishing in the last several years, and some 50 provincial government agencies. Approximately 200 municipalities across Canada and perhaps 75 private sector enterprises have produced a thematic map or maps. In 1982 the respective rough estimates were 14 federal government agencies, 80 provincial agencies, 190 municipalities, and 50 in the private sector. The grand total was roughly the same as today, although there now may be more private sector producers and fewer provincial. According to the list made in 1973 the federal total was 10 and the provincial 56, or about the same as today.

The major producers of thematic maps today, and probably throughout the period since the Second World War, are the federal and provincial agencies engaged in forest inventory and management, soil mapping, geological mapping, land inventory, conservation, and environmental protection.

MAPPING THE NATURAL ENVIRONMENT AND RESOURCES

During the 1940s making an inventory and mapping the features and characteristics of the environment and natural resources lagged well behind the topographic map coverage of the country. At the same time a return to peacetime life saw explosive economic growth and many changes. These required a visionary attitude to resource management if Canada was to realize its potential in a world economy vastly different from that which prevailed before the upheaval of the Second World War. It was evident that considerable gaps existed in vital scientific knowledge and even basic distributional information on the natural features and potential resources of very large areas of the nation, especially beyond the settled southern fringe. Large parts of the North were virtually unknown apart from their outline topography.

Northern Reconnaissance Mapping

Kenneth Hare, a leading Canadian geographer, summed up the situation by saying that the nation's expansion depended on nothing less than "the re-exploration of Canada, on the re-examination of our natural resources. Hitherto we have barely passed the phase of preliminary reconnaissance. Our 8-mile maps symbolize the situation. They contain a fairly accurate record of our rivers, lakes and coastlines. But beyond the limits of the southern population districts, they remained essentially blank until recent times. Our knowledge of the geology, forest resources and even power potential has remained sketchy, and in many northern areas can barely be said to exist."[3]

Small-scale, rapid surveys of large areas were a first requirement to provide reconnaissance information on geology, forest resources, land use, natural vegetation, and terrain conditions. The interpretation of aerial photographs, backed by carefully chosen ground studies, was one means of meeting this need. Hare himself led pioneering teams of investigators in reconnaissance mapping of the natural vegetation and landforms of virtually the entire Québec-Labrador peninsula, using RCAF Trimetrogon air photography. Stereoscopic photo interpretation could be done on the consecutive vertical photographs, while sideways perspective views gave the interpreter a quick grasp of the regional physiography and features being studied. A similar project, covering an even larger part of northern Canada, was carried out by a small group of geographers led by the geophysicist J. Tuzo Wilson. In this project surface materials, glacial features, and structural lineaments in the Northwest Territories and northern parts of the provinces were mapped. In addition to the national need for more geographical information as the basis for resource development and conservation, there was an important need for such intelligence from the national security viewpoint. With the terrifying threat of trans-polar nuclear war, radar surveillance lines and networks were constructed in the Arctic and subarctic areas – the Pinetree Line, the Mid Canada Line, and the Distant Early Warning Line. Preliminary gathering of information for these major engineering and logistical operations in harsh and unknown environments included reconnaissance mapping of terrain characteristics and trafficability. The Geographical Branch of the federal Department of Mines and Technical Surveys (DMTS) produced a number of such maps, based on air-photo interpretation and fieldwork. Few of these maps were made widely available, but they later contributed to the publication of small-scale maps and scientific reports.[4]

Geological Mapping

The importance of geological information to Canada's growth was amply demonstrated after the war. The discovery of oil and gas in Alberta during 1947 opened up the possibility of Canada being self-sufficient in these fuels. Exciting new and important metal and mineral discoveries, including nickel, gold, and iron, were made and subsequently developed in Manitoba, Ontario, Québec, British Columbia, and the Northwest Territories. The long-recognized iron deposits of Knob Lake in Labrador were brought into production. No less important was the increase in uranium mining, stimulated by demand from the United States.

A major responsibility rested with the Geological Survey of Canada (GSC) to ensure that the geological and geophysical mapping programme kept up with the increasing demand for scientific information from the many resource companies, prospectors, and agencies working in areas with potential for economic mineral development. Geological mapping already had a long and illustrious history in Canada, going back to the foundation of the Geological Survey in 1846 before Confederation. However the pace of postwar development was unprecedented and required new techniques to speed up the traditional field surveys in which geology had been mapped slowly by far-flung field parties working laboriously on the ground.[5]

In the immediate postwar period less than 20 percent of Canada's bedrock geology had been mapped adequately, and that mainly in preliminary form.[6] Twenty years later, following an impressive drive employing a new approach to geological survey operations, over 60 percent of the nation had been mapped at various scales larger than 1:50 000. Undoubtedly the single greatest factor in the record of geological mapping after 1947 was the extensive employment of fixed-wing aircraft and helicopters in support of field survey operations. Entirely new forms of mapping were also required to provide geophysical information, which became increasingly important in the search for minerals and as a means of understanding the complexities of geology. Unravelling the more recent geological history, and mapping materials used for constructing roads, airstrips, and railways, were also given increased priority. Paralleling all this were improvements in cartographic technology and progress towards computer-assisted cartography.

Geological mapping is an involved process. The first requirement is an adequate base map on which to plot occurrences of rock types and locations of samples obtained by fieldwork. The patterns and traces of structural lineaments, faults, outcrops, and many other geological features are also delineated on the base map. As geology is a three-dimensional subject, research involves the detection and measurement of the disposition of rocks and deposits deep under the surface of the earth. Many scientific techniques are utilized in collecting and interpreting the data needed for geological maps. Information on the nature, age, chemical constitution, and qualities of rocks may be gathered using the methods of biology, chemistry, physics, mineralogy, ecology, and paleontology. Sampling is done in the field, and measurements and plots are made using air photographs and topographical base maps. A complete system of cartographic conventions has been built up carefully over many years to allow consistency of representation in the field records and maps that geologists prepare. Similarly the final printed maps conform to careful standards for the representation of geology, using colours and symbols. Although automation of cartographic processes has speeded up geological map production in the last twenty years, such is the demand for timely information that some maps are reproduced and made available to users in their manuscript state along with file material, so as not to delay use of important information while waiting for publication of the final map.

SURFICIAL GEOLOGY

Mapping the unconsolidated material of the earth's surface is an important aspect of geological surveys. It has gained in importance and utility as a key component of environmental impact studies, natural hazard research, work on global climatic change, and tracing minerals to their points of origin. From the 1930s into the 1970s much surficial geological mapping was done, with one of its major objectives to estimate groundwater resources. In the early postwar period the rapidly expanding economy meant that the demand for groundwater-potential studies increased. This was also the case with surficial geological information as the basis for soil surveys and construction projects. Mapping was based on extensive use of air-photo interpretation and field surveys. The conceptual approach to mapping also evolved. Prior to the 1960s surficial geological maps essentially described surface geology in terms of map units defined in geological terms, and also with features shown by symbols.[7] Later a demand for information on surficial geology started to come from a number of new users. Information was needed for land inventories, environmental impact studies, and forest management. Whereas the classification used previously was oriented towards use by other earth scientists, new ways of mapping information and describing surface phenomena had to be found.

"Terrain analysis" best describes the approach that was developed. A number of new classifications were tested and applied, notably in south Labrador and in mapping done for the Mackenzie Valley pipeline corridor studies. In the terrain analysis approach, map units are made up of components with similar types of land-forms and surface materials, each component defined in terms of genesis, land-form, and texture. This is similar to the approach taken in biophysical land classification. Inevitably mapping Canada's surficial geology and terrain will be affected as GIS methods are tested further and put to use. An advantage already foreseen is the possibility of storing detailed point data, which could not be shown easily on a printed map, and the inclusion of ancillary information such as laboratory analyses of geological samples.

GEOPHYSICAL MAPPING

Most people are aware of the typical map of bedrock geology, showing rock types, ages, structures, faults, dips, and strikes, often mapped in bright, well-defined areas of colour. A totally different map of the world is revealed through the instruments of geophysical survey, such as magnetometers and gravimeters that measure the physical state of the earth's surface and near surface.[8] The results of magnetic anomaly surveys in maps reveal a strange and unfamiliar geography of swirling forms and patterns. However the scientific interpretation of these maps has proven very successful both in adding to fundamental geological knowledge and in predicting the existence of hidden ore bodies. This is a science and technology in which Canada has a justified world reputation. From a modest start in 1946, aeromagnetic surveys in Canada have been steadily extended until in 1991 a large part of the country has been mapped. Even the earliest aeromagnetic surveys produced quick benefits. For example aeromagnetic mapping in 1950 showed a prominent magnetic anomaly that soon led to discovery of the rich Marmora iron deposit in Ontario. Since then many other techniques have been developed. A feature of the GSC's advances in these fields has been the transfer of technology to the private sector, which not only carried out a large volume of the survey work in Canada but also put the techniques to good use in other countries. An equally important aspect of this type of survey, and its development since the Second World War, has been the degree of cooperative work undertaken jointly by provincial and federal agencies. In 1960 it was realized that even though aeromagnetic surveys held great promise in adding to geological scientific understanding, and to the discovery of new mineral deposits, the rate of mapping was so slow that it would have taken fifty years to map the Canadian Shield. This was reduced to twelve years when a joint federal-provincial cost-sharing programme was organized in conjunction with industry. In addition to the airborne surveys, shipborne surveys have extended coverage in the important offshore areas.

SEISMOLOGICAL AND GEOMAGNETIC SURVEYS[9]
Mapping geological and geophysical phenomena usually requires mounting regional surveys in which data gathering involves the transport of scientists, equipment, and instruments over great distances using a variety of modes of transport and platforms for instruments and sensors. Since 1949 these have ranged from the packhorse to the earth-orbiting satellite. However there is one type of geophysical survey in which the data travels to the scientist rather than the other way round. Canada now has a well-developed network of seismic observing stations for detecting and recording the characteristics of earthquakes. These sensitive seismographic stations pick up the shockwaves of seismic events, measuring their intensity and allowing their epicentres to be fixed. From the accumulation of these data it has been possible to produce maps of seismic hazard in Canada. These have important applications in siting installations sensitive to hazards, such as nuclear powerplants, and in formulating building codes that allow for possible earthquake damage. These evaluations of hazard potential began in 1945, and a map of Canada was produced by the Dominion Observatory for the 1953 National Building Code that showed four categories of earthquake probability. More data and refined methods made an improved version possible in 1970, said to be the first ever truly probabilistic earthquake hazard map. Even more sophisticated maps were produced by 1985 as observational data on earthquakes increased. Now work is in progress using more advanced techniques, including digital observations and transmission of data by satellite communication. Attention has been given to incorporating the possibility of very large earthquakes in future maps. These would take into account the impressive volume of research done to unravel the tectonic history of south-west British Columbia, where enormous forces build up and produce the probability of very powerful earthquakes as the Pacific plate slides under the North American Continental plate in the Cascadia subduction zone.[10]

GEOMAGNETISM
The North Magnetic Pole wanders in the central Arctic islands, and observations of the resulting changes in magnetic declination date back even to the records of explorers such as Jacques Cartier and Samuel de Champlain. Although the first magnetic charts were

produced by John Henry Lefroy in 1883, it was not until 1922 that magnetic charts produced by the Topographical Survey started to show the magnetic pole, located by James Clark Ross in 1831. Responsibility for producing magnetic charts passed to the Dominion Observatory in 1942, and the charts produced by the observatory then had the benefit of actual magnetic pole surveys. With the adoption of computers for chart production it became apparent by 1965 that a mathematical model of the magnetic field was required. Technical problems were, however, not overcome until 1985 when the Canadian Geomagnetic Reference Field was developed. This permitted the incorporation of data from satellites and aircraft surveys. The model now permits charts of magnetic declination, inclination, and total intensity to be generated by computer. But more importantly users can obtain magnetic data directly through computer links without the need to consult a chart.[11]

NATIONAL GEOSCIENCE MAPPING PROGRAM
The bedrock survey of Canada by the federal and provincial governments was, in a sense, complete by the late 1970s when maps of some form were available for all parts of the country. It is paradoxical that something that appears to be as permanent as geology becomes out of date in twenty-five to thirty years due to the improvement in scientific interpretations of geological data, and to new scientific methods that allow refinement and reinterpretation. Consequently the data acquired in the large mapping operations of previous decades is now increasingly in need of updating and reinterpretation. In response to this need federal and provincial governments have combined with industry and the university scientific community in the National Geoscience Mapping Program (NATMAP). The programme was conceived in 1989 and emphasizes strongly cooperative work in geological and geophysical surveys, mapping, and the storage and retrieval of geoscience information by computer. It also promotes increased training opportunities for geoscientists who will carry on the mapping of Canada's geology in the future.

Soil Mapping

Canada's productive soils may be rated as an equally precious natural resource relative to its substantial mineral and forest-based wealth. Agriculture represented 10 percent of the nation's economic activity in 1992, but the soil's vital importance as the supporter of food production and life gives it a significance beyond the purely economic. The result of countless geological, climatic, biological, and human interactions over vast periods of time, soil is irreplaceable but often misused and always the subject of much scientific scrutiny.[12]

Modern soil surveys began with soil mapping carried out in 1914 by the Ontario Agricultural College at Guelph. Thereafter, apart from limited surveys done in the 1920s for Alberta, Saskatchewan, and Manitoba, usually by university pedologists, it took until 1939 for soil surveys to become established in all provinces. These soil surveys often produced broad reconnaissance mapping to establish a basic inventory, except in small areas of special agricultural significance where detail was required. A turning point came in 1940 when a National Soil Survey Committee (NSSC) was formed with representatives of the provincial and federal governments. The object of the committee was to bring together soil experts who, though knowledgeable about soils in their own regions, had little opportunity to compare classifications, terminology, and methods of survey and analysis with their counterparts in other areas of Canada and North America. Because the war intervened the committee did not actually meet until 1945.

By the end of the war the combination of provincial soil surveys and federal participation had achieved some form of soil mapping coverage of about 50 million hectares. Nevertheless it was apparent that many variations existed throughout the country in the identification of soils and soil-mapping units. Similar differences existed on the concepts of soil formation and methods of soil analysis. The NSSC had the task of achieving a more uniform approach to soil survey and mapping by working towards a taxonomy of soils that would be applicable throughout Canada, and by promoting coordination between the different surveys. The NSSC led to the formation of special subcommittees and regional meetings, all of which improved coordination.

By 1953 systematic reconnaissance soil surveys existed for over seventy-six million hectares. The map scales employed by the provincial agencies varied greatly, depending on the reasons for and the nature of the survey. The actual surveys were often the result of cooperative work by provincial and federal soil experts, geologists, and other specialists contributing to the research and fieldwork required for the maps. Topographical base maps were an important requirement, along with air photographs on which delineations of field observations were made for transfer to the map bases. Federal base maps might be available in some areas, and elsewhere provincial maps were used or specially constructed for the soil survey. Making the soil map required extensive travel in the field using a variety of vehicles. Always there was the requirement to dig pits or to bore holes to reveal the profile of a soil so that the various soil horizons could be examined. Detailed notes were made on the wide variety of soil characteristics that form an essential basis for soil mapping. Laboratory analysis of soil samples would be required later to classify the soils fully, to describe their composition, and to add to knowledge of their fertility and best use.

After 1960 many of the provincial and federal soil surveys, as well as university research groups, were occupied fully with the vast amount of work required to complete the soil capability for the agriculture component of the Canada Land Inventory (CLI). Many existing soil maps and data from new surveys were used to estimate soil capability for the inventory. The NSSC continued to provide a focus for soil scientists to consider the soil-mapping programme on a nationwide basis, and to debate the growing need for a system of soil taxonomy or classification that would meet Canadian requirements. The need for a computerized national soil-related information system was also attracting growing interest, and was proposed by the subcommittee on data handling of the Canada (formerly National) Soil Survey Committee in 1970.[13] Work by the many groups engaged in the CLI already presaged revolutionary advances in the computerized storage and use of geographical information that led to the Canada Geographic Information System (CGIS). The Canadian Soil Information System (CanSIS) was aimed at making soil information available in more efficient and more comparable mapped form. Soil information generated for the CLI, together with an increased demand for mapped information generally, led to a veritable explosion of soil information. This was a general trend in most of the larger thematic mapping agencies in the decades following 1960. At about the same time that the national soil database was being developed, a revised soil taxonomic system was accepted and published[14] that would be crucial to coordinated national soils mapping.

A manifestation of the increasingly cooperative nature of soil surveys in Canada was the expanding role of the federal Soil Research Institute in the correlation of soil surveys across Canada. Federal soils survey units located in the provinces worked closely with their provincial counterparts, but after 1974 were administered from headquarters at Ottawa.

Provincial agencies concentrated on providing the soil input to the CLI, but as this work neared completion the normal soil-mapping programmes resumed. Not all provincial surveys experienced growth. In Ontario soil surveys slowed to a virtual halt in the late 1970s, but resumed as concern over the loss of agricultural land rose. By 1975, because of the impetus given by the work on the CLI, about 35 percent of Canada's land area had been mapped by some form of soil survey

In addition to the publication of a national system of soil classification, other important publications and new types of maps were produced by the Soil Research Institute and by provincial agencies. An overall map of Canada's soils at 1:10 000 000 scale had been published in the *Atlas of Canada* (3d edition) in 1957. By 1964 a start had been made on a new and more detailed national map. In 1977 enough information and agreement on terminology existed to permit the publication of a new *Soil Map of Canada* at the scale of 1:5 000 000. The map and its accompanying soil report and soil inventory represents a milestone in Canadian pedology.[15] The inventory volume of this work provides a large amount of tabular information on each of the 750 separate soil units appearing on the face of the map itself. The same soil information was used for Canada's contribution to the Food and Agriculture Organisation (FAO) world soil map, also at 1:5 000 000.[16] Though the nomenclature for the world map was markedly different, the areal distributions were the same. The *Soil Map of Canada* shows the distribution of the main soil groups using alphanumeric symbols and colours with patterned overprints. Dominant and sub-dominant soils are mapped, and modifications such as soil texture, slope, and moisture are indicated by overprints. Other maps of soil temperature and soil moisture were provided with the main soil map. Miniature versions of all three maps were published a little earlier, in reduced and generalized form, in the fourth edition of *The National Atlas of Canada*.

The availability of data and the demand for interpretation for many different purposes in agriculture and other fields, together with the many opportunities provided by automated cartography and GIS, have led to a significant increase in printed thematic maps on soil and agricultural subjects. They have also created a virtually unlimited capability to create thematic maps on demand. Their volume and variety are beyond the scope of this account. Among them may be mentioned series dealing with soil landscapes, and soil degradation due to salinity, wind erosion, and water erosion. Soil landscape maps are produced at 1:1 000 000 and provide an overview of soils between the broad generalization of the *Soil Map of Canada* and the detailed surveys done by the provinces.[17]

Forestry Mapping

Canada's forests cover about half of the country, or some 453 million hectares, and have always represented a major factor in the nation's life and economy. Debate on their current use and future stirs strong emotions. Forests face growing stress from many quarters such as air pollution, acid rain, and inefficient use. Natural controls such as forest fires, insects, and disease also have serious impacts. Yet forests are the resource base for over 15 percent of Canada's manufacturing industry and 3–4 percent of GDP, and contribute in some way to the existence of one in fifteen jobs. The forests are also the fragile habitat of over 3000 tree and plant species, 200 different mammals, 550 species of bird, 90 amphibians and reptiles, and over 100 000 different insects and invertebrates.

Although a federal forest survey has existed since 1899, organized forest inventories were not widespread at the provincial level until after the Second World War. The Canada Forestry Act of 1949 provided for federal-provincial government cooperation in forest inventory. In the 1950s a number of agreements were reached to fund forest inventory and mapping by the provinces. The existence of these agreements has promoted similarities in the methodology and type of inventory carried out, but it is not possible here to deal with the details of each provincial programme since 1946.

All forest inventory mapping involves the adoption of a system of classification for forest characteristics, and other information on controls that may influence the forestry operations. Generally speaking the following types of information are mapped: ownership and status of the land for forestry operations, descriptive information about the land and its reproductive quality, density of the forest, a description of the forest canopy (hardwood, softwood, or mixed), identification of the tree species, the age and maturity of the forest, and disturbance of the forest by fire and insect damage.

Special base maps are normally produced for forest inventory, and these are often derived from existing federal or provincial topographic maps. Air photos typically are interpreted to define homogeneous forest areas and their characteristics. Field checks by foresters are made to verify the photo interpretation, to identify species, and to measure the height, diameter at breast height, and age of the trees in representative sample areas. These data are utilized in estimating the potential volume of merchantable timber, and as a means of determining the forest management practices to be employed. The maps are often made available in monochrome, and may be printed on demand inexpensively. Scales vary according to the age of the inventory and special needs of each province. Provincial inventory and re-mapping takes place on a ten-year cycle, but the currency of forest inventory mapping is not uniform across the country.

Many other types of mapping are produced related to the management and understanding of the forests. They include maps of slopes, surface materials, and ecological characteristics. Private sector logging companies also carry out very substantial mapping in connection with logging and silvicultural operations.

The need for an overall national inventory and associated summary maps of forest resources has long been recognized. In 1937 W.E. Halliday produced the first modern classification of Canada's forests, accompanied by a map. This was revised later by J.S. Rowe, although the broad characteristics of the map did not alter dramatically. It was the basis for a national vegetation map published in the fourth edition of *The National Atlas of Canada*, also incorporating information from other sources. A provisional Forest Map of Canada at 1:5 000 000 was produced later.[18]

The formation of a national-level forest information system was recommended at a national conference on forestry statistics in 1976.[19] Subsequently it was decided to use existing information available through the provincial surveys, and to produce a national summary based on these sources. The computerization of forest-related information on maps also dates back to the production of land capability for forestry maps as part of the CLI in the 1960s. The Canadian Forestry Service played a major role in the CLI work, and in the early stage the responsibility for it was carried by the Department of Forestry and Rural Development.

The availability of computerized methods for consolidating the mass of provincial maps and data was an important factor in the production of the new Canadian national forest inventory in 1981.[20] Summary thematic maps of aspects of the national inventory were important outputs of this and subsequent inventories. In the late 1970s and 1980s a series of conferences and policy statements reflected growing concern over the forest resource. The need was acknowledged for national-level understanding in addition to the detail available at the operational or inventory level. Thematic maps were recognized as an important means of improving this understanding. The Canadian Forest Resources Data System (CFRDS) has been developed since 1981, becoming an important tool for strategic decision making. It is equipped with automated cartography and GIS technology, capable of producing reports and custom thematic maps at the national level to meet a variety of user needs. Essentially the same type of information is taken from over 40 000 map cells in the provincial inventories. Each cell is usually 100 km² in area. Forestry information contained in the cells can be processed and combined with other data to produce choropleth maps. Naturally all the information from the provincial sources is not always directly comparable, nor are the data cells all of the same size. But sufficient similarity exists to allow the production of national maps at 1:5 000 000 scale and smaller. Not only is automated mapping of forest resources possible, but climatic, biophysical, and phytogeographic subjects can be accommodated.

A completely new approach to mapping vegetation and forests at the national level is represented by some striking maps produced from 1 km resolution data sets obtained from the U.S. National Oceanic and Atmospheric Administration satellites. Using automated means, data with a resolution of 1 km² have been used to create a seamless digital forest data set for all Canada.[21] The forest-related agencies and industries of Canada have always been leaders in the adoption of computerized techniques in handling forest data, and continue to exploit new mapping technologies to aid in managing this important resource.

LAND

Economic growth and resource development were foremost concerns in postwar Canada, but this was accompanied by a growing appreciation of the finite character of natural resources and the fragility of the environment. Although topographic, geological, soil, and forestry surveys had been in progress since the beginning of the century, they were far from complete in all areas. With respect to information on characteristics such as land capability and land use, there was a virtually complete lack of information suitable for regional and national planning.

As Canada transformed itself from a predominantly rural to an urban society, the pressure on first-class farm land caused by relentless urbanization and inadequate planning became a serious concern. This led to perhaps the largest coordinated thematic mapping effort in Canadian, if not world, history. A huge project to construct inventories and undertake mapping was launched, aimed at creating a database and comprehensive map coverage to provide reconnaissance information on the land resources of Canada's settled area, or ecumene, and the associated fringe areas.

The first significant work on land-use mapping on a national basis was commenced in the 1950s by the Geographical Branch of the Department of Mines and Technical Surveys[22] in which Norman Nicholson, Brooke Cornwall, Charles Raymond, and others were involved. Present land use was mapped in a number of representative areas across Canada, which were selected to provide a variety of testing areas for a classification of land use adapted from a system used in the United Kingdom. This series of maps was a precursor to the land-use maps produced as part of the major project known as the CLI.

The Canada Land Inventory

By the late 1950s and early 1960s national concern over the need for an inventory of land resources was evident. In August 1958 a special committee of the Senate on land use in Canada recommended the creation of "a systematic land-use survey based upon appropriate factors, to provide for an economic classification of the land according to its use suitability."[23] Further impetus was given by the findings of a number of groups taking part in the "Resources for Tomorrow" conference in October 1961. This large gathering of experts from many agencies examined the need for a national land-use policy that would cover uses in agriculture, forestry, wildlife, and recreation. They recommended the undertaking of nationwide land-use and land-capability surveys with the concomitant development of standardized classifications of the relevant geographical information.[24]

The CLI began in 1962 and the project was approved by the federal government in 1963 under the Agricultural Rehabilitation and Development Act (ARDA) as a joint federal-provincial venture. Under the leadership of L.E. Pratt, the CLI was a most remarkable feat of coordination and planning. About 100 agencies of federal and provincial governments were involved, together with a large number of participants from the private sector and universities. From the outset it was foreseen that the enormous volume of data that would be gathered could only be handled and used if computerized methods were employed. Innovative equipment and techniques for scanning manuscript maps and using the digital information were invented and developed for the project. A notable achievement associated with the CLI was the creation of the world's first, largest, and still functioning geographical information system, the CGIS, which is described in chapter 15. This world-famous system, initially conceived and developed by the Canadian geographer R.F. Tomlinson, expanded its role and application in subsequent years and is considered the veritable pioneer of the multitude of GIS in operation today. Eventually about 2.6 million km² of settled and fringe areas of Canada were mapped, and the information computerized according to the various categories of use and capability. This represented about one quarter of the total land area of Canada. Taking all factors into account, the planning and successful execution of this epic work ranks as a major achievement in the history of world mapping.

In the early days of the CLI it was estimated that some 1500 map sheets of the various types of land capability at scales of 1:250 000 and 1:50 000 would be involved. However in 1963 Tomlinson's economic and technical feasibility studies of computerizing the procedures revealed that 2500 to 3000 map sheets were required. Later, as the possibilities were explored further, it was even envisaged that between 15 000 and 30 000 map sheets, including scales larger than 1:50 000, could be accommodated. However this potential volume was never attained and small scales were used to speed up input. By the early 1990s the CGIS contained some 10 000 maps, including information not forming part of the original CLI. The Canada Map Office has published 1093 maps of the various types of land capability and land use of the CLI at scales of 1:250 000 and 1:1 000 000.

A crucial factor in the success of the CLI was the requirement to agree upon a set of classification systems for each land and soil capability, and present land use. The capability classifications rated the land in terms of its estimated capability to support its use for agriculture, forestry, wildlife, and recreation. The initial work in devising a capability classification for agriculture was done by the NSSC in 1963, and later that year the federal government approved the undertaking of the inventory.

The CLI classified land capability according to a seven-point scale in which level 1 was assigned to land having the highest capability to support the activity or use in question. Level 7 applied to land with no capability. Thus level 1 in the agricultural capability classification represents land with no significant limitations on use for crops (in the case of this category, developed from a large body of existing research on soils, the capability referred to soil rather than land). Within the major capability classes, a further division into subclasses was employed that expressed physical limitations such as wetness and slope.[25]

The present land-use classification identified fourteen classes based on the current human activities or natural cover. By using existing land-use surveys of the Geographical Branch, and air-photo interpretation, the need for expensive additional fieldwork was reduced. In addition to the information on capability and present use, the CLI also included information on the socio-economic classification of land, based on Statistics Canada's information and also information relating to the climatic requirements for agriculture.

Many striking facts emerged from the CLI, which also brought home the precious nature of the nation's land resources. For example 86 percent of Canada was found to have no capability for agriculture, and only 5 percent was free of physical limitations to crop production.

Northern Land Use Information Series

The establishment of the CLI created a powerful tool and information base for the formulation of national land policy, regional and local planning, land use and environmental regulation, research, and public awareness of national environmental issues for the settled agricultural areas of the country. In the postwar period resource development in northern Canada, particularly the search for oil and gas, began to demand an equivalent information base to ensure orderly development in the fragile northern environment. The Northern Land Use Information Program (NLUIP) was started in 1971 and included a special thematic map series, the Northern Land Use Information Map Series.[26] This 1:250 000 map series was completed during the period 1971–88. About 360 maps covered Canadian areas between 60 and 70 degrees north latitude. The standard 1:250 000 topographic map was overprinted with coloured alphanumeric, linear, and tonal symbols depicting land use and environmental information together with considerable supporting text. Maps were printed and distributed by the Department of Energy, Mines and Resources through the Canada Map Office. Overall initiative, direction, and research was the responsibility of Environment Canada and the Department of Indian Affairs and Northern Development, while cartography of the overprinted information was done by the Land Resource Institute of Agriculture Canada. The series brings together a massive amount of multi-disciplinary information from existing sources, as well as from specially conducted field studies. The list of mapped information is considerable and includes ecological overviews, coastal classification, land-forms, climate, wildlife, fish resources, hunting, trapping, historical and archaeological information, resource development activities, routes, communities, and transportation information. The initial impetus for the mapping programme was the prospect of major hydrocarbon resource development in the Mackenzie valley, but the programme has been extended to cover much of the Arctic and has been used in connection with environmental problems in many areas.

As the North became the focus of attention for private sector resource development companies, a considerable volume of thematic mapping was carried out by independent and non-governmental organizations. Due to the numerous disciplines, varied objectives, and often small areas covered the resulting mapping is beyond the scope of this review. Cumulatively they added significantly to the mapped information sources that provided an important part of the NLUIP map series.

From the land-use surveys of the 1960s and 1970s arose the need to monitor the continuing changes that were taking place. Nowhere was this more important than in the valuable agricultural land adjacent to the main urban centres. The Canada Land Use Monitoring Program (CLUMP) was begun by Environment Canada in 1978 to map changes in the amount, location, and type of land use in different types of national setting.[27]

Four geographical components were identified in which different types of change occurred: urban-centred regions, prime resource lands, rural areas, and wild lands. Canada as a whole was included as a fifth viewpoint so that the various changes could be understood in terms of their overall national significance. Each component of the monitoring programme represented a different set of factors and rates of change. Because a significant portion of the nation's class 1 agricultural land was threatened by urban expansion, mapping land-use change in urban-centred regions was a priority. The results of the CLI had shown that a mere 0.5 percent of Canada's land area contained all the prime agricultural crop land with no limitation to cultivation. About 50 percent of this was located in southern Ontario. An interdepartmental task force on land use made the striking observation that 37 percent of Canada's class 1 agricultural land is located within 160 km of Toronto, and could be seen on a clear day from the top of Toronto's CN Tower.[28]

CLUMP mapping used a classification combining the land cover and land-related activity occurring in an area. Mapping was based on air photographs, satellite imagery, and fieldwork utilizing NTS maps at 1:50 000 and 1:250 000 scales. The data embodying the evidence of changes at five-year intervals was analyzed, and computerized comparisons were made. The results of this work led to a more informed perception of the problem of permanent loss of a food-producing resource through urbanization. It also clarified the similar problems afflicting other prime resource lands, rural communities, and wildlife.

ECOLOGICAL MAPPING

Ecological mapping by its very nature requires careful work to establish agreement on classifications. Mapping wildlife habitats requires agreement between biologists, climatologists, botanists, geomorphologists, and other scientists on common terms and definitions, if their various findings are to be compared safely. As leading ecological expert J.S. Rowe pointed out "we ought not to expect thematic maps of the same area to agree. Separate studies of soils, vegetation, topoclimates, wildlife habitats, and landforms carried out by uni-disciplinary experts who are uninterested in subject matter other than their own will infallibly differ because goals and methods are different."[29]

Early efforts at establishing a national set of standards for coordinated ecological surveys and mapping took place in the late 1960s. The need to establish a classification system for what was called "bio-physical mapping" was recognized in the context of work on the CLI. In 1969 guidelines for ecological (bio-physical) classification were produced by a national subcommittee.[30] This work was the foundation for later developments by various agencies. At one stage some twenty classifications dealing with ecological phenomena were identified.

Ecological land survey is recognized by many agencies as an essential basis for approaching conservation and environmental management in the less populated areas of the country. A considerable amount of work has been done by national committees and working groups, which incorporate federal and provincial government specialists as well as those from universities and the private sector. Indeed there are committees that specialize in classifications and methods for mapping wetlands, wildlife, vegetation eco-regions, ecoclimates, land/water classifications, and climatic change. The results of this work are reflected in various local ecological surveys and mapping projects, as well as in some important national scale maps. An illustration of the former is the 1:50 000 Wetland Mapping series of southern Ontario published by Environment Canada to show current wetlands, wetlands gained and lost between 1967 and 1982, and certain classes of vegetation. Also of note is the mapping of wetlands in the Prairie provinces by Ducks Unlimited, a non-government organization. National maps have been published at 1:7 500 000 scale of wetlands and of ecoclimatic regions.[31]

PARKS, TOURISM, AND RECREATION

Canada's first national park had its origin with the discovery of hot springs near Banff in 1883 during construction of the transcontinental railway. George Stewart, a Dominion Land Surveyor sent to survey the site, pointed out the great scenic and natural attractions of the wider surrounding area and this was included in his survey. Interest in preserving this area led to pioneer legislation, the Rocky Mountain Park Act, and eventually the present-day government policy of preserving large tracts of land as national or provincial parks for future generations. The conservation and management of the many and varied types of parks and related sites relies very much on surveys and maps. These record not only the legal boundaries and topography, but also their ecological, historical, and recreational characteristics. National parks today are designated bearing in mind the preservation of representative examples of all the various eco-zones in Canada. There is thus a direct link between the eco-zone classification and mapping approaches adopted by many agencies working in the environmental field. About a dozen of the more important national parks have been mapped by the former Surveys and Mapping Branch of Energy, Mines and Resources Canada for the Parks Branch of Environment Canada. They are in map series designed specifically for use in parks management, in planning, and by visitors. A number of other parks are covered only by standard topographic map coverage. The extent, type, and degree of use by visitors, and other factors, have influenced the mapping response over time so that available coverage now includes maps dating from 1966 up to the present. In recent decades a re-examination of parks maps has taken place resulting in new designs and formats. In 1969 research on the map needs of Waterton Lakes National Park in Alberta by Gerald McGrath led to later production of a prototype map that demonstrated the opportunity for new approaches.[32] Subsequently McGrath and Henry Castner investigated the potential for using the 1:250 000 topographic maps as a base for a tourist series throughout the settled zone of Canada.[33] An example of recent commercial efforts in the general field of parks mapping oriented towards tourism is a map of Banff/Canmore published in 1990 by Stanley Associates Engineering Ltd. This was undertaken in response to an earlier initiative by the Canada Centre for Mapping of Energy, Mines and Resources aimed at stimulating the further use of topographic maps and digital topographic data to produce value-added cartographic products in the private sector.[34]

All provinces and territories, and a number of private sector agencies, produce a wealth of maps of provincial parks and areas of touristic or recreational value, in addition to their well-known and sometimes free highway maps. The range of type and treatment is extensive and includes maps with long lifetimes and large audiences as well as maps that might well be classified as cartographic ephemera.

CLIMATE

The mapping of climatological information has progressed greatly since 1930 when Canada's dominion climatologist provided climatic maps for an early international compendium on climates of the world, *Handbuch der Klimatologie*. The Meteorological Branch of the Department of Transport, later the Atmospheric Environment Service (AES) of Environment Canada, recognized the importance of maps in operational weather forecasting. In addition maps were useful for summarizing and presenting the salient features of the vast accumulation of climatic data that are being collected continuously. Many thousands of electronic and paper maps are issued each year as an essential part of the weather forecasting operations.

The Meteorological Branch began publication of a series of maps of selected climatic parameters in 1967. The series of black-and-white maps was based on climatic data for the period 1931–60. Some twenty-six sheets at scales of 1:12 500 000 and 1:25 000 000 were produced and published at intervals up to 1970. The set of ten-map series was eventually brought together and presented as the *Atlas of Climatic Maps*.[35]

Constant change is the nature of climate, and the need soon arose to update the series of maps based on new data contained in the Canadian Climate Normals for 1951–80. About 400 bilingual maps grouped into ten sections were produced and published in this map series. The first set became available in 1984 and contained a variety of maps dealing with temperature and degree days. The other two series were released in 1986. The second series was devoted to precipitation whilst the third covered such subjects as pressure, humidity, clouds, thunderstorms, and frost. As with the earlier series in 1967, all the maps eventually constituted a climatic atlas entitled *Climatic Atlas Climatique*.[36] The atlas format was favoured by AES and was used to publish a number of other climatic maps on special subjects. These included the *Rainfall Frequency Atlas of Canada* and the *Great Lakes Climatological Atlas*, as well as atlases of sea-ice distribution and type.

In recent years the subject of pollution by airborne chemicals, often the product of industry distant from the polluted area, has become a subject of intense concern. This has been reflected in maps attempting to portray the sensitivity of terrain to acid precipitation.[37] A number of small-scale maps have appeared that deal with a host of pollutants and other factors, particularly in the publications on the state of the environment by Environment Canada.

It is perhaps in the mass media, printed as well as electronic, that the greatest public awareness of climatic maps exists. The ubiquitous weather map is the thematic map most known to the general public, and it is possible to have almost instant access to weather maps at any time through dedicated television channels.

Climate has an impact beyond the environment of the earth's immediate surface. This is reflected in the existence of permafrost, which may be regarded as a condition of material in the soils and rocks of the earth where the temperature remains below zero degrees Celsius for a number of years. Permafrost was mapped on national maps by the Building Research Institute of the National Research Council in 1967, 1973, and 1978, largely through the efforts of R.J. Brown. An earlier attempt at a national delineation based on limited field observation was that of J.L. Jenness in 1949. The NRC maps were a combination of predicted occurrence, based on climatic information, as well as an increasing number of field observations. The precise delineation of continuous and discontinuous permafrost remains elusive because of the peculiar difficulty of making observations. However the work of the GSC continues in this field.[38]

Although thematic mapping of the oceanic areas around Canada is excluded from this chapter, but mentioned in chapter 8, some reference must be made here to sea- and lake-ice surveys and mapping. This has evolved from limited mapping based on aerial reconnaissance such as the sea-ice surveys of the Geographical Branch, DMTS in the Gulf of St Lawrence and the St Lawrence River from 1956 to 1965. These surveys were intended to produce a better understanding of navigation conditions, were conducted every ten days, and involved manual plotting of sea-ice type, concentration, age, and other parameters. Some of the results of these surveys were published in small-scale maps and monographs. Later much more extensive surveys were done in arctic Canada resulting in atlases of sea-ice conditions by the Polar Continental Shelf Project of EMR and the AES. The advent of satellite-borne sensors has revolutionized this field of thematic survey, as it has many others where repeated surveillance is an essential requirement.

SOCIO-ECONOMIC MAPPING

The last fifty years have seen enormous growth in thematic maps concerning socio-economic, demographic, and similar subjects. Population increase and accelerated economic activity have generated a vast amount of socio-economic information, and this has been accompanied by a parallel demand for such information from many quarters. The mass media has also made a great impact on the ways in which such information is communicated through the medium of maps. The public uses thematic maps in some manner on a daily basis, often consulting maps in newspapers and magazines or through television. The range of map scales, styles, and purposes in the socio-economic field is extremely wide. For operational and planning purposes larger-scale surveys based on census information at the block face or street level may be used for such matters as city planning and siting of commercial businesses. At the other end of the scale a transient television map may briefly illustrate or clarify some news item.[39] In the popular print media tiny thematic maps, only a column wide, may communicate an important geographical fact with an immediacy, and sometimes inaccuracy, beyond words. In fact the map is sometimes used as a symbol, especially in advertising, and has found its way onto an amazing variety of objects – even clothing. This everyday acceptance by the public of the thematic map, formal or informal, is part of a general trend in which the power of visual communication tends to supplant the purely verbal. Given the scope and diversity of the field it is possible here to consider only a few of the salient developments since 1947.

Census and Statistical Mapping

The source for the majority of statistically based thematic maps is the Census of Canada, but other sources such as special surveys by various levels of government and the private sector are very important. Census mapping has two aspects. The first is the provision of suitable maps of the various information collection areas for use in the actual census. The second is the use of the census and other statistical information in maps displaying the information that was collected.

In the 1930s and 1940s census data was available at the county and census division levels. With rapid urban and population growth during the postwar period there has been an increasing demand for a finer-grained census data collection system. Adjustments have been made progressively in the hierarchy of census units, and in particular municipalities and census tracts were adopted for urban-centred areas. As topographic maps became available for southern Canada, the Census of Canada adopted the enumeration area (EA) as a census building block in 1961. By 1971 geocoding of census areal units was begun as a step towards customized selection of census data to fit the user's needs. At that time the census reference maps available totalled some 2200 separate sheets. They included maps of census divisions and subdivisions, census tracts, enumeration areas, and electoral districts, together with supporting documentation. Most of the maps were supplied on demand in the form of special inexpensive prints. Scales varied according to the type and size of census area portrayed, ranging from 1:5 000 000 for a map of Canada showing census divisions and counties to about 1:10 000 for maps of census tracts. Changes in population distribution and density require readjustment in the boundaries of census unit areas, and thus the maps must undergo periodic change. Electoral maps, which delineate the boundaries of parliamentary constituencies, require the same adjustments.[40]

The present system maintained by the Geography Division of Statistics Canada is extensively computerized and makes use of computer-assisted cartography and GIS techniques. Census-related mapping is integrated in the Geographic Frame Data Base (GFRD). This can accommodate the many data-gathering operations of the census, and also respond to the need for thematic maps based on census data as well as non-map information. Not all the information involved is from the census as data from other sources can be accommodated.

A number of computer files make up the GFRD. The Street Network File (SNF) defines street names, address ranges, and block faces. The Geographic Attribute Data Base (GADB) lists each enumeration area as the building block of the census, linked to other levels in the hierarchy of census areal units including the geographical coordinates of the EA's central point, the number of the relevant NTS map, and population counts for the unit. The Digital Boundary File (DBF) provides the boundaries of federal electoral districts, census divisions and subdivisions, census tracts, and enumeration areas. Finally a Postal Code Conversion File (PCCF) links Statistics Canada areal units to about 7 000 000 postal codes.[41]

An organized programme of thematic mapping that mainly uses computerized methods has existed in Statistics Canada since at least 1970, although before then important statistical maps and atlases were produced from time to time using traditional methods. The geographical framework for census data collection, adopted and modified by Statistics Canada, has provided the basis for countless thematic maps created by other agencies and researchers, as well as by Statistics Canada.[42]

The availability of inexpensive means of generating computer maps of census data, for example SYMAP, allowed Statistics Canada to issue a number of thematic maps in the 1970s based on the 1971 census. These small, monochrome choropleth maps showed all of populated Canada or large regions of the country, and dealt with such subjects as population distribution, mother tongue, and ethnic composition. They represented a foretaste of much more sophisticated cartographic capabilities to follow. The rapid growth of computer mapping technology and software for handling geographical information was reflected in the increasing range and variety of cartographic products that became available. They included a series of atlases and thematic maps dealing with the characteristics of metro-politan areas and with aspects of disease mortality in Canada. By 1976 the move to computerization had made available digital files for census base maps.[43]

Increasingly Statistics Canada collaborated with other governmental agencies, both federal and provincial, as well as with various municipalities and private sector companies in the development of new mapping approaches. These were designed to fit the special needs of a host of census data users who were interested in mapping phenomena related to their interests and combining it with census data.

While Statistics Canada produces the reference maps needed to carry out the census and other socio-economic surveys, as well as a variety of thematic maps displaying the results of the census, a large number of thematic maps have been produced by many other agencies and individuals that use census data and data from other sources. The variety of purposes and types of map is such that it is difficult to summarize the overall output of maps of this type during the period. There are, however, some maps and map series that can be noted as representative.

The CLI was undoubtedly the largest single Canadian thematic mapping endeavour in terms of the land area covered and the detailed surveys involved. But ARDA also gave rise to other types of small-scale thematic mapping projects and map series. A map series appeared in 1964 dealing with economic and social disadvantage in Canada. Based on the 1961 census, nine coloured maps revealed the extent and severity of socio-economic disadvantage in Canada at the census division level. Selected indicators included income, employment, education, and infant mortality.[44]

While some maps aimed at relatively straightforward reflection of census data, there were others in which more sophisticated methods were used. An example of this type of mapping, consisting of a set of thirty-four maps grouped under the general title Dimensions of Canadian Regionalism, used factor analysis of demographic and other data to explore the regional structure of Canada. This series was published as a monograph on the subject and exemplifies the thematic map as a research tool.[45]

Some thematic maps were produced that occupied very large sheets of paper. Such large map sheets responded to the challenge that face cartographers in attempting to deal with complex and diverse subject matter that must be presented for the whole of Canada, or for sizeable regions of the country. Sometimes large map sheets were in effect single-sheet atlases, composed of a main map and supporting maps at smaller scales, often with substan-tial texts. Usually this type of map had a general message on some environmental or socio-economic issue of national significance. The maps could also function as permanent wall displays from which understanding could be assimilated by the user. Some maps even func-tioned as a kind of cartographic poster. Environment Canada exploited this technique with success, an example being a map sheet titled "The Windsor-Québec Axis."[46] This large sheet includes a large central map of the region showing population density, with smaller-scale maps showing various factors that affect the urban-rural conflict over land use. Throughout the period cartographic techniques for displaying information became more and more innovative as the impact of thematic maps in support of issue-oriented texts was recognized.

PRIVATE SECTOR THEMATIC MAPPING

While government agencies have been increasingly active, the last two decades have also seen the growth of a private sector thematic mapping capability. Numerous maps of all sizes and subjects have been produced for different purposes ranging from bicycle paths to plots of oilwell locations and large detailed analyses of resources in major regions of the country. Most cities and communities of any significance have commercially produced maps that display varied information for tourists and the general public. A survey in the late 1980s indicated that at least fourteen commercial map producers included thematic mapping in their range of products and services.[47] The maps tended to be concerned principally with tourism and transportation, but a number of companies were also active in the production of thematic maps dealing with natural resources and environmental information.

Some fine examples of cartographic design have come from the private sector. Notable is the work of Canadian Cartographics Ltd., which was formed in 1971 and has long been considered a national leader in Canadian thematic mapping. Some highly successful and informative thematic maps have been produced by this company under contract to various federal and provincial departments. The company has undertaken research for the actual information displayed in maps, as well as being responsible for their design and preparation. An early achievement predating the actual formation of the company was the well-known Isodemographic Map of Canada, in which areal statistical divisions were represented by a scale related to population rather than space.[48] The base map thus produced could also be used to map socio-economic data in an illuminating way. In addition the company has been responsible for a large number of special thematic maps relevant to environmental and resource issues, commerce, development, recreation, and tourism in British Columbia and elsewhere in Canada.[49]

Another thematic mapping company is MapArt, which typifies the private sector's role in producing the multitude of street guides and road maps essential for everyday life and for the functioning of transportation systems, tourism, and traffic organization. From its base in eastern Canada this company produces about sixty different sheet maps or atlases of Canadian cities, as well as a considerable number of maps and atlases of the United States and Europe. From its inception in 1970 and registration as a company in 1978, it now produces thematic maps for government departments, newspapers, car rental firms, urban transit systems, stores, restaurants, real estate companies, and publishers. Other prominent companies active in thematic map production include Allmaps Canada Ltd of Markham, Ontario, Brault and Bouthillier of Montréal, Pathfinder Map Inc. of Carp, Ontario, and Perly's Maps of Toronto.

THE FUTURE

To predict the future of thematic mapping involves the danger of either oversimplification and statement of the obvious, or embarking on a hazardous analysis of the complex issues facing many different disciplines that use thematic mapping. As J.-C. Muller has observed, the word "revolution" is overworked in discussion of recent events in cartography. But perhaps he is correct in stating that revolution may be the normal state of affairs, so far-reaching are the developments in the fields of information handling, computer graphics, and communications.[50] The technology of data collection, and its rapid incorporation into systems and databases for cartographic data management and manipulation in GIS, can be expected to continue at a galloping pace. Continuing advances in chip technology leading to faster, smaller, and more versatile computing systems will inevitably have an impact on thematic mapping. So also will the effects of parallel processing in computer operations. Remote sensing as a technique of data acquisition, together with the widespread use of global positioning systems, can also be expected to open up further the prospect of very rapid mapping of many types of phenomena. As these kinds of technological advance continue to revolutionize mapping, many concepts about the nature of maps will need major revision.[51]

It seems likely that users will require more custom-made maps that are tailored to their particular needs. The emergence of desktop publishing has provided some indication of what may happen to thematic mapping. A user can have easy access to a variety of databases containing quite complex subject matter, but without the intermediary of expert knowledge on the subject that is normally incorporated during the creation of thematic maps produced with current technology. Some see artificial intelligence as the means of preventing cartographic chaos by incorporating expert knowledge into systems so that the innocent or unversed user can be protected from inappropriate cartographic practices or data analysis. More challenging even than this is the need to accelerate the development of common standards for geographical data. No longer can data be regarded as solely usable by the original collector. Some form of universal compatibility will be required of all geographic data if the dream of effortless exchange of information and the creation of meaningful thematic maps on demand is ever to be realized.

ACKNOWLEDGMENTS

The help of the following persons in providing information and advice is gratefully acknowledged: F. Cadieux, L. Cardinal, B. Chen, D.S.C. Mackay, G. McGrath, L.E. Pratt, P. Schut, H. Stevens, J.J.S. Thompson, R.F. Tomlinson, and R. Warne.

NOTES

1 Of a number of definitions of the debatable term "thematic map," that of the International Cartographic Association is useful: "A map designed to demonstrate particular features or concepts. In conventional use this term excludes Topographic maps." International Cartographic Association. 1973. *Multilingual Dictionary of Technical Terms in Cartography*. Wiesbaden, Germany: Franz Steiner Verlag GMBH.

2 *List of Map Sources*. 1972. Ottawa: Department of Energy, Mines and Resources: Departmental Map Library.

Allin, J. 1982. *Map Sources Directory*. Map Library, York University.

See also Inter-Agency Committee on Geomatics. 1991. *Report on Current Status and Trends in Federal Digital Geographic Data in Canada*. Ottawa: Dept of Energy, Mines and Resources.

Information on Canadian map producers in 1994 provided by the National Atlas Information Service, Natural Resources Canada.

3 Hare, F. Kenneth. 1954. The Re-Exploration of Canada. *The Canadian Geographer*, 4, 85–8.

4 For example, 1958 *Glacial Map of Canada*. 1:3 801 600. Waterloo, ON: Geological Association of Canada.

5 Zaslow, M. 1975. *Reading the Rocks*. Ottawa: Macmillan Company of Canada Ltd in association with the Department of Energy, Mines and Resources and Information Canada.

6 Harrison, J.M. 1960. History and Work of the Geological Survey of Canada. *Canada Year Book 1960*. Ottawa: Dominion Bureau of Statistics.

7 An informative review of the history of surficial geology mapping by the Geological Survey is provided by R.J. Fulton, on whose work this note is mainly based. See Fulton, R.J. 1993. Surficial Geology Map Needs. *Canadian Journal of the Earth Sciences*, 30, 2, 232–42.

8 Based on Teskey D.J. et al. 1993. The Aeromagnetic Survey Program of the Geological Survey of Canada: Contribution to Regional Mapping and Mineral Exploration. *Canadian Journal of the Earth Sciences*, 30, 2, 243–60.

9 Based on Basham, P.W., and L.R. Newitt. 1993. A Historical Summary of Geological Survey of Canada's Studies of Earthquake Seismology and Geomagnetism. *Canadian Journal of the Earth Sciences*, 30, 2, 372–90.

10 Ibid.

11 Ibid.

12 Much of this summary is based on a history of soil surveys by McKeague, J.A., and P.C. Stobbe. 1978. *History of Soil Surveys in Canada 1914–1975*. Historical series no. 11. Ottawa: Research Branch, Canada Department of Agriculture.

13 Dumanski, J. et al. 1975. Concepts, Objectives and Structure of the Canada Soil Information System. *Canadian Journal of Soil Science*, 55, 181–7.
MacDonald, K.B., and K.W.G. Valentine. 1992. Can*sis* Manual – Cansis/*NSDB*: *A General Description*. Ottawa: Land Resources Division, Centre for Land and Biological Resources Research, Research Branch, Agriculture Canada.

14 1970. *The System of Soil Classification for Canada*. Publication 1455. Ottawa: Department of Agriculture.

15 Clayton, J.S. et al. 1977. *Soils of Canada*. Ottawa: Research Branch, Department of Agriculture. Vol. 1. *Soil Report*; vol. 2. *Soils Inventory*. Contains maps "Soils of Canada," 1:5 000 000, "Soil Climates of Canada" (two maps), 1:10 000 000.

16 FAO-Unesco. 1975. Vol. 2 of *North America Soil Map of the World*. *1:5 000 000*. Paris: Unesco.

17 1988. *Soil Landscapes and Procedures Manual and User's Handbook*. Contribution no. LRRC 88-29. Ottawa: Research Branch, Agriculture Canada, Land Resources Research Centre.

18 Halliday, W.E.D. 1937. *A Forest Classification for Canada*. Forest Service Bulletin 89. Ottawa: Department of Mines and Resources.
Rowe, J.S. 1959. *Forest Regions of Canada*. Bulletin 123. Ottawa: Forestry Branch, Department of Northern Affairs and National Resources. With map "Forest Classification for Canada," 1:6 336 000, 1957.
Rowe, J.S. 1972. *Forest Regions of Canada*. Publication 1300. Ottawa: Canadian Forestry Service, Department of the Environment. With map "Forest Regions of Canada," 1:6 336 000, 1972.
1974. *Vegetation Map 1:15 Million*. *The National Atlas of Canada*, 4th ed. Ottawa: Macmillan of Canada Ltd in association with Energy, Mines and Resources Canada and Information Canada, 45–6.

Forest Management Institute, Canadian Forestry Service, 1979. *Provisional Forest Map of Canada. 1:5 Million.* Ottawa: Environment Canada.

19 Gray, S.L., and K. Nietmann. 1989. *Canada's Forest Inventory 1986 – Technical Supplement.* Information report PI-X-86. Chalk River, ON: Petawawa National Forestry Institute, Forestry Canada.

20 Bonnor, G.M. 1982. *Canada's Forest Inventory 1981.* Ottawa: Forestry Statistics and Systems Branch, Canadian Forestry Service, Department of the Environment.

21 Palko, S., J.J. Lowe, and H.T. Pokrant. 1993. Canada's New, Seamless Forest Cover Data Base. *Proceedings GIS'93 Symposium.* Hull: Ministry of Supply and Services, 985–90.

22 Nicholson, N.L., I.H.B. Cornwall, and C.W. Raymond. 1961. *Canadian Land-Use Mapping.* Geographic paper no. 31. Ottawa: Geographical Branch, Department of Mines and Technical Surveys.

23 1958. *Proceedings of the Special Committee of the Senate on Land Use in Canada.* No 4, Wednesday, 20 August 1958. Ottawa: Queen's Printer, 74.

24 A summary of recommendations of the conference appears in 1965. *The Canada Land Inventory – Objectives, Scope and Organization.* Report no. 1, January 1965. Ottawa: Dept of Forestry.

25 1978. *Canada Land Inventory – Land Capability for Agriculture – Preliminary Report.* Report no. 10. Lands Directorate. Ottawa: Environment Canada.
Coombs, D.B. and J. Thie. 1979. The Canada Land Inventory System. In *Planning the Uses and Management of Land.* Agronomy series no. 21. Madison, WI: Soil Science Society of America, 909–33.

26 Rump, P.C. N.d. Land Inventories in Canada. In Gentilcore, R. Louis, ed, *China in Canada: A Dialogue on Resources and Development.* Hamilton, ON: McMaster University, 38–51.

27 Ibid.

28 1980. *Land Use in Canada – The Report of the Interdepartmental Task Force on Land-Use Policy.* Lands Directorate. Ottawa: Environment Canada.

29 Rowe, J.S. 1987. Wildlife Habitats and Ecological Classification. *Wildlife Working Group Newsletter,* Canada Committee on Ecological Land Classification, 8, 2–4.

30 Sub-committee on Bio-physical Land Classification. 1969. *Guidelines for Bio-physical Land Classification,* (compiled by D. Lacate). Publication no. 1264. Ottawa: Canadian Forestry Service. Canada Committee on Ecological Land Classification. 1989. *Achievements (1976–1989) and Long Term Plan.* Ottawa: Environment Canada.

31 1989. *Ecoclimatic Regions of Canada.* Ecological Land Classification series no. 23. Ottawa: Canadian Wildlife Service. Contains map "Ecoclimatic Regions of Canada, 1:7 500 000."

32 McGrath, Gerald. 1971. The Mapping of National Parks: A Methodological Approach. In Castner, Henry W. and Gerald McGrath, eds. Map Design and the Map User. Toronto: B.V. Gutsell. *Cartographica,* monograph no. 2, 71–6.
McGrath, Gerald. 1974. Tourist Mapping and the National Cartographic Agency: A Challenge Unfulfilled. *Abstracts of Papers, Seventh International Conference on Cartography.* Madrid: International Cartographic Association, 21.

33 McGrath, G., and H.W. Castner. 1977. *The Design of a Tourist Map Series Based on the National Topographic 1:250 000 Map Series.* Final Report under contract 02SU.23246-5-5596 to Topographical Survey Directorate, Surveys and Mapping Branch, Department of Energy, Mines and Resources, Ottawa.

34 1990. *Banff/Canmore. Map 1:50 000.* Tourist Oriented Planning Series. Calgary: Stanley Associates Ltd.

35 Mackay, G.A., and M.K. Thomas. 1971. Mapping of Climatological Elements. *The Canadian Cartographer*, 8, 1, 27–40.

36 Environment Canada. 1988. *Climatic Atlas Climatique*. Ottawa: Atmospheric Environment Service.

37 Environment Canada. 1987. *The Potential of Soils and Bedrock to Reduce the Acidity of Atmospheric Deposition in Canada. Map 1:7.5 million.* In *Acid rain: A National Sensitivity Assessment.* Environmental fact sheet 88-1. Ottawa: Inland Waters and Lands Directorate.

38 Heginbottom, J.A. 1984. The Mapping of Permafrost. *The Canadian Geographer*, 28, 1, 78–83.

39 Gauthier, M.-J., ed. 1988. *Cartographie dans les médias/Cartography in the Media.* Sillery, Québec: Presses de l'Université du Québec.

40 Winearls, J. 1972. Federal Electoral Maps of Canada 1867–1970. *The Canadian Cartographer*, 9, 1, 1–24.

41 Parenteau, R., and P. White, 1989. Statistics Canada. The Canadian Postal Code System and Census Data. *The Operational Geographer*, 7, 2, 36–7.

42 1973. *Thematic Maps of 1971 Census Data* (fourteen maps at various scales). Ottawa: Statistics Canada.

  1973. *Availability of Reference Maps 1971 Census.* G-71, 1-13. Ottawa: Statistics Canada.

43 Broome, F.R., and S.W. Witiuk. 1980. Census Mapping by Computer. In Taylor, D.R.F., ed. *The Computer in Contemporary Cartography.* Toronto: John Wiley and Sons, 190–217.

44 Hodges, R.C. 1965. The Role of Special Maps in the National Economy. *The Cartographer*, 2, 2, 72–5.

45 Ray, D.M. 1971. *Dimensions of Canadian Regionalism.* Geographical paper no. 49, with thirty-four foldout maps. Ottawa: Policy Research and Coordination Branch: Energy, Mines and Resources Canada.

46 Simpson-Lewis, W. N.d. *The Windsor-Québec Axis.* Nine maps at various scales. Ottawa: Urban Affairs Canada and Environment Canada.

47 McGrath, Gerald. August 1993. Interview.

48 Skoda, L., and J.C. Robertson. 1972. *Isodemograpic Map of Canada* (contains map). Geographical paper no. 50. Ottawa: Lands Directorate, Department of the Environment.

49 Skoda, L. 1991. Map Publishing in Canada. *CISM Journal*, 45, 1, 112–16.

50 Muller, J.-C. 1991. Prospects for and Impediments against a New Cartography in the 1990s. In Muller, J.-C., ed. *Advances in Cartography.* London and New York: International Cartographic Association and Elsevier Applied Science, 1–13.

51 Rhind, D. 1993. Mapping for the New Millenium. In *Proceedings of the Sixteenth International Cartographic Conference.* Bielefeld: Deutschen Gesellschaft fur Kartographie, 3–14.

CHAPTER TWELVE

Research in Canada

Gérard Lachapelle, Teodor J. Blachut, Jerzy M. Zarzycki, and Henry W. Castner

INTRODUCTION

During most of the period covered in this chapter, 1947 to 1994, research in all fields of surveying and mapping was encouraged by most governments in the developed world. In the private sector research was almost mandatory if a designer or manufacturer was to keep up with the competition. Universities specializing in survey engineering found financial encouragement available from both government and industry. Even research in cartography, which had been sadly neglected in pre-war years, was fostered so that the results of mapping efforts could be better displayed. This rallying of support was to a large measure due to the Cold War. The rapid advance in electronics and computer applications, by both sides in this "war," had its peaceful result in a remarkable development of surveying and mapping equipment. As will be seen in this chapter, it was an exciting time to be involved in these fields of research.

PART I   GEODETIC RESEARCH IN CANADA: 1947–94[*]

Overview and Major Thrusts

During the period 1947–94 geodetic and survey research evolved from being a small component of government activities to its present status as major targeted research programmes in academic and industrial sectors as well as government. The reasons for these major changes have been the rapid evolution of related mathematical and physical sciences, the increasing demands of users, and the development of a permanent graduate education and research infrastructure at universities.

The key scientific and technological developments that have affected geodetic research are advances in mathematics (particularly estimation theory), computer technology, and

---

[*] Part I was contributed by Gerard Lachapelle.

inertial and satellite positioning techniques. These enabling technologies have resulted in major research efforts in the fields of geodetic networks, physical geodesy, Doppler satellite positioning, Global Positioning Systems (GPS), Inertial Survey Systems (ISS), and Very Long Baseline Interferometry (VLBI). As a result of these, and of increased user requirements, the Canadian industrial sector became involved in the development of hardware and software products starting in the 1970s.

The level of geodetic research in Canada developed rapidly from the 1960s when Laval University and the University of New Brunswick (UNB) established viable graduate programmes. They were joined in 1979 by the University of Calgary (U of C). In the late 1970s a research programme also evolved at the Erindale campus of the University of Toronto. In the postwar years research skills in Canada were also improved through Canadians seeking advanced degrees at foreign universities, and trained geodesists moving from Europe to Canada. The reputation of Canadian work in this field grew at such a rate that, by the late 1960s, UNB and Laval had become training grounds in postgraduate research for both Canadian and foreign students.

These activities led to technical and commercial successes. The results of research were communicated through international research conferences held both in Canada and abroad, and in technical journals. The first major international conference held in Canada to include geodesy was the general assembly of the International Union of Geodesy and Geophysics (IUGG) that met in Toronto in the 1957 International Geophysical Year. The IUGG, which includes the International Association of Geodesy (IAG), reconvened in Canada at Vancouver in 1987. Several Canadians have served as officers of international associations related to geodesy. Two internationally successful books were written by Canadians as a result of these activities, namely *Geodesy: The Concepts*, by P. Vanicek and E.J. Krakiwsky,[1] and *Guide to GPS Positioning* by a group of eleven authors under the leadership of David Wells.[2] The latter book had sold over 10 000 copies by the end of 1994.

Geodetic Network Related Research

The period under review began with research into the use of Shoran for horizontal ground control and the control of aerial photography. This research was led by the dominion geodesist J.E.R. Ross, assisted by A.C. Hamilton, W.J. MacLean, and R.A. Monaghan. As described in chapter 2 this work resulted in the "Shoran Net" across northern Canada that made possible the completion of the 1:250 000 National Topographic Series (NTS). Shoran was itself replaced by HIRAN (High Accuracy Shoran) and Aerodist (Airborne Distance Measuring System). Research in these last systems was conducted by S.A. Yaskowich and H.E. Jones.

The first Tellurometers and Geodimeters were acquired by Geodetic Survey in the late 1950s. Evaluation of their performance under operational conditions, and related research such as the effect of ground waves (ground swing), were conducted by various Geodetic Survey personnel, notably Jones, C.D. McLellan, and Yaskowich. Similar work was also carried out at the National Research Council (NRC) by A.G. Mungall and J. Saastamoinen. Related fundamental atmospheric refraction research was also done by Saastamoinen. These events led to research by L.F. Gregerson and others into the precise methodology required for the establishment of accurate Electromagnetic Distance Measurement (EDM) baselines across Canada. These are of primary importance for the testing and calibration of EDM equipment by all users. During this same period Gregerson published an essay on the estimation of the most probable value of a set of geodetic observations, a paper that was subsequently hotly debated in the pages of *The Canadian Surveyor*.[3]

In the 1960s the development of computer programs for the adjustment of triangulation chains was initiated at Geodetic Survey under the direction of L.A. Gale. The first program, GROOM (Generalised Reduction of Observed Material), was developed by A.J. Wickens and H. Klinkenberg. The program GALS (Geodetic Adjustment by Least Squares) was developed shortly after by G. Katinas, A.E. Peterson, and C.D. McLellan. This in turn was succeeded by GANET (Geodetic Adjustment of Networks), which resulted from the work of D. Beattie with the assistance of J. Allman, a professor of geodesy on sabbatical leave from the University of New South Wales. These programs were mainly for the adjustment of horizontal control; LEVELOB (Levelling Observations) and other levelling data processing software were developed at Geodetic Survey by Peterson and M.T. Swanson.

Research into network adjustment by computers was one of the first tasks undertaken by the surveying engineering division at UNB. The early efforts at Geodetic Survey and UNB identified large discrepancies and inconsistencies in the horizontal networks due to earlier section-by-section adjustments. By the early 1970s Geodetic Survey and its American counterpart, the U.S. National Geodetic Survey (USNGS), had agreed to redefine all major horizontal networks. The project eventually let to the adoption of the North American Datum of 1983 (NAD83). Technical aspects of the problem were discussed at the International Symposium on Problems Related to the Redefinition of North American Geodetic Networks. This was organized by E.J. Krakiwsky and P. Vanicek and held at UNB in 1974. As can be imagined this tremendous project created much research and adjustment work throughout the Canadian geodetic community. At Geodetic Survey the work was led by C.D. McLellan, P. Henderson, M. Pinch, and R.R. Steeves. G. Blaha, of the Ministère des Terres et Forêts in Québec, made significant contributions to the theory of network adjustments, which was most useful during this period. The mathematical model for NAD83 was developed by Steeves and T. Vincenty of the USNGS. Beattie used this model to formulate the program GHOST (Geodetic Adjustment, Using Helmert Blocking, of Space and Terrestrial Data). This program is now being used by Geodetic Survey and the provincial agencies in adjusting data to NAD83.

NAD83 is based on earth-centred coordinates. The fundamental parameters of this system are the position of the earth's centre of mass and the position of the polar axis, which is known to the scientific community as the Conventional Terrestrial Pole (CTP). The earth tends to wobble slightly, which means that the direction of the pole changes very slightly, over time, with respect to the stars. This change is in a predictable direction and rate. It is recorded and can be predicted with reference to a position known as the Conventional International Origin (CIO).

In helping to find the exact relationship between the pole and the CIO, S. Vamosi of the Geodetic Survey undertook the recalculation of all astronomic observations made by the Geodetic Survey between 1910 and 1977. Also involved in this work was A.J. Robbins, the reader in geodesy at Oxford, who was on leave for one year at Geodetic Survey. He used observations made with the Photographic Zenith Tube (PZT) to add to data regarding the CIO-pole relationship. The PZT is an instrument that uses a camera to photograph the stars in the immediate vicinity of the zenith. From the resulting photographs a very precise value for time and latitude can be obtained. More information on the adoption of NAD83 is given near the end of this chapter.

In the process of adjusting to NAD83 an investigation was made into the distortions of the NAD27 coordinates. This was carried out at Geodetic Survey by L.A.R. Blais and D. Junkins.

While the NAD83 horizontal adjustment was going on, similar work was being done with the vertical network. This again was a joint project by Geodetic Survey and the USNGS. Technical aspects of the project were discussed at the International Symposium on Problems Related to the Redefinition of the North American Vertical Geodetic Networks, organized by G. Lachapelle of Geodetic Survey, and held in Ottawa in 1980.

During the 1970s and 1980s there was considerable geodetic research into precise levelling. This work, under the leadership of R. Gareau at Geodetic Survey and Vaníček at UNB, investigated such matters as the advantages of adding gravity measurements to levelling observations and testing the stability of junction-point benchmarks. The very small movements in the earth's crust have always been of interest to geodesists. Crustal motion in the Great Lakes and other areas has been watched by Geodetic Survey by using repeated levelling data beginning in the 1950s. Two of the key researchers in this endeavour were J.E. Lilly and N.M. Frost. G. Laflamme, originally at Geodetic Survey but later at the Ministère des Terres et Forêts did considerable research in this field. In the 1970s Vaníček at UNB initiated extensive research into crustal motion, including glacial rebound in the Hudson Bay area, in the context of his geodynamic research programme.

Investigation into methods for extending geodetic networks seaward from Canada's coastlines began in the late 1960s when petroleum exploration off the east coast was being considered. This joint effort by the petroleum industry, Geodetic Survey, and the Canadian Hydrographic Service (CHS) is described further in chapter 8. The joint industry–Geodetic Survey effort led to the publication in 1971 of *Surveying Offshore Canada Lands for Mineral Resource Development,* edited by H.E. Jones.[4] The third edition was published in 1982, and was still used in 1994 for offshore survey training and practice.

Physical Geodesy and Geodetic Astronomy

Research into physical geodesy began in Canada in the early 1950s when C.H. Ney of Geodetic Survey began investigating the geoid in parts of eastern Canada using the astro-geodetic deflection observations available at that time. During astronomical observations the height of stars from the horizon is measured, which is a plane at right angles to the vertical (i.e., the plumb-line). But inequalities in the mass of the earth's crust can pull the vertical line a very small angle to one side or the other. This "deflection of the vertical" affects the value of astronomic latitudes because they are obtained by measuring the height of stars above the horizon. If the horizon is tipped slightly by the pull of gravity, the latitude obtained will differ very slightly from the geodetic latitude obtained by triangulation or other survey networks. If a number of deflections can be obtained the results can be used to determine the shape of the geoid in the area. Ney's work was hampered by a lack of data, and it was not until the 1960s that enough deflections were available to begin research in earnest. The first continental astro-geodetic geoid model that covered the United States and the southern part of Canada was calculated by Irene Fischer of the U.S. Army Map Service in 1967. Throughout the 1960s geoid research was pursued at Geodetic Survey by Gregerson, G.A. Corcoran, and others. Investigations into more effective methods of conducting and reducing astronomic observations were conducted by Wickens, Katinas, and Moreau, with contributions by A.R. Robbins. Moreau focused his efforts on automated star tracking for longitude determination while Robbins investigated the use of Black's Method for the simultaneous determination of latitude and longitude in high latitudes. Astronomic positioning in the far north was a problem of much importance until the 1970s when satellite geodesy took over.

In earlier times Wickens and Jones derived one of the first computer programs, APPLAC (Apparent Places), for the computation of precise star coordinates at upper and lower transit of the observer's meridian. This early effort was continued by Katinas and resulted in FORTRAN programs that greatly reduced the drudgery of star computations. These programs have been used by many countries. Precise timing is of course essential in astronomic observing and in this regard Vamosi, working with Guy Gaumont and Gordon Symons, developed the Digital Astro Printer. This instrument combines a highly accurate sidereal rate chronometer, a printing chronograph, and a short-wave receiver in the one instrument.

Research into the use of precise gyro-theodolites was carried out by Gregerson.[5] Gyroscopic compasses of moderate precision have long been used for navigation, but in the 1960s the very precise gyro-theodolites appeared on the market. The thrust of Gregerson's investigation was to determine the accuracy of these instruments to see if they might replace astronomical theodolites to obtain precise azimuths. It was established that they could not equal the precision of the traditional instruments but, as is described in chapter 16, they are most useful in mine surveying.

The Earth Physics Branch made significant contributions to time keeping and polar motion monitoring through operations of its telescopes and PZTs, and its TRANET (Tracking Network) stations. J. Popelar was the first to fully automate a TRANET station. This system was used at Priddis near Calgary, and Shirley's Bay near Ottawa, to contribute to precise star catalogue generation and polar motion monitoring. This work was done in cooperation with the U.S. Defense Mapping Agency (DMA) and the U.S. Naval Surface Weapons Center (NSWC).

In the meanwhile several other data sources that were going to affect geoid research in the 1970s were evolving rapidly, namely gravity observations, digital terrain modelling, and satellite dynamic data. A gravity mapping programme was undertaken by the Earth Physics Branch under the direction of J.G. Tanner and K. McConnell. By 1994 most of Canada was covered at regular, but different, intervals depending on location. (This is described in chapter 2 and shown in figure 2-8.) Starting in the mid-1970s a 10-km-interval digital terrain model for the Western Cordillera was extracted from topographic maps by the Earth Physics Branch assisted by Geodetic Survey. This was used to reduce the gravity anomalies in that area, and to contribute to geoid research generally. With the advent of satellites the large undulations of the geoid were being determined very precisely. In 1972 Dr Nagy of the Earth Physics Branch produced a preliminary gravimetric geoid. At about the same time research into geoid determination using heterogeneous data (gravity, levelling, satellite) was initiated at Geodetic Survey under Lachapelle, at UNB under Vanicek, and at Laval under J.G. Leclerc. This work was of considerable value when the conversion to NAD83 got under way. Valuable information, namely Doppler satellite–derived undulations accurate to about 1 m, had become available for assessing the accuracy of geoid solutions and, in many cases, to contribute to those solutions. Work was undertaken in Geodetic Survey in the late 1970s to estimate the deflection of the vertical using astronomic records and the latest topographic maps. This was done in support of the NAD83 project, but it had practical applications as well. The results of this research were used in precise surveys such as those carried out in the early 1980s for the CPR Mount MacDonald Tunnel described in chapter 16).

During the second part of the 1970s research into the effects of gravity on levelling was undertaken at UNB under Vanicek. During the same period D. Delikaraoglou and Vanicek began research into the determination of the ocean geoid using satellite gravimetry and tidal data.

In the 1980s the need became apparent for the calculation of the geoid over the Canadian land mass, referenced to the GRS80 ellipsoid (Geodetic Reference System of 1980) and accurate to a few centimetres. Satellite geodesy was by this time able to provide heights accurate to within 2 or 3 cm, but these were heights above or below the ellipsoid, and were of little use unless the separation of the geoid and the ellipsoid were known. A Canadian geoid committee was formed by Geodetic Survey to steer the research being conducted: at Calgary by Schwarz and Sideris, at UNB by Vanicek, and in Geodetic Survey by Mainville and Véronneau. The development of efficient methods to combine existing records with the new data became of prime importance. Geoid undulations derived from a combination of GPS ellipsoidal heights and levelling data along first-order level lines became an important data source to verify or contribute to new geoid solutions. New data-acquisition methods, such as airborne gravimetry and high-resolution altimetry, were gaining in importance.

As an example of a practical use of this emerging technique of satellite heighting, let us consider that there is a need to find the difference in height between two points on a river in northern Canada where no levelling has been carried out. If the geoid-ellipsoid separation is known to within 2 or 3 cm, as it is in many parts of Canada, the descent of the river could be ascertained in a few hours to a precision of about 5 cm. If the two points in question were about 10 km apart, this would be a levelling accuracy of 5 ppm.

The Canadian geoid calculated by Geodetic Survey in 1993 is shown in figure 12-1. The knowledge gained in physical geodesy at Canadian institutions from 1970 onward has been noted on the international scene. For instance a strong Canadian presence was seen at the 1984 Beijing International Summer School on Local Gravity Field Approximation, the first IAG-sponsored activity in China.

Doppler Satellite Positioning

The Navy Navigation Satellite System (NNSS), initially developed by the U.S. navy in the late 1950s for the navigation of its Polaris submarines, became available publicly in 1967. By 1968 three Canadian organizations, namely the Bedford Institute of Oceanography (BIO), Shell Canada, and UNB, were in the forefront in investigating its use for geodetic positioning. During that year D.E. Wells of the BIO established the first geodetic station in the Arctic using Doppler positioning. The station was at the northern tip of Greenland and contributed to the precise location of the island's northern shore. Thus the era of satellite positioning in Canada began, an era that would have a tremendous impact on geodesy worldwide.

As has been explained in chapter 2, the Doppler system consisted of several satellites in circular orbits 1100 km above the earth. As the satellites arose above the horizon they were tracked throughout their passes, which typically lasted about twenty minutes. The

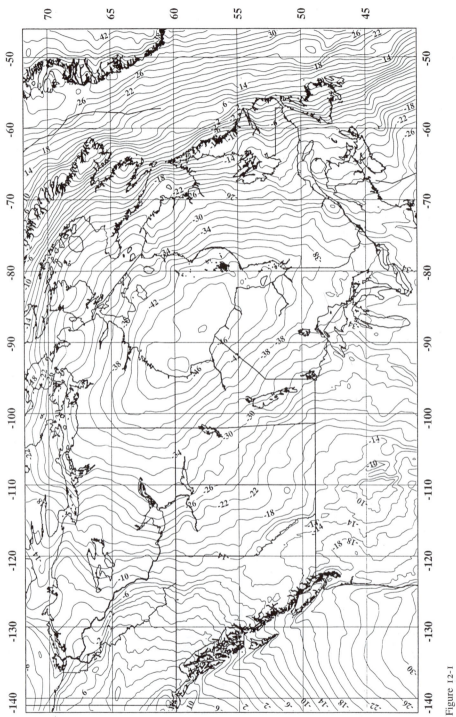

Figure 12-1
The geoid in Canada. The figures are in metres above and below sea level.
Source: Geodetic Survey of Canada

number of observations at a position were at times allowed to accumulate over hours and days, and when this occurred the precision of the position increased. Accurate positions could be obtained using the single point method, but even greater precision could be arrived at by using the translocation method in which the station observations are compared with those at another nearby station of known location. The most accurate Doppler fixes eventually reached a precision of about 50 cm.

While the work at BIO and Shell, spearheaded by Wells and A. Hittel respectively, initially focused on field experiments, the effort at UNB under Krakiwsky and Kouba was on estimation procedures using simulated data. Progress across the country was accelerated by a transfer of personnel, with Kouba joining Shell in 1970 and Wells going to UNB for postgraduate studies. Research into error detection and estimation was pursued vigorously at both Shell and UNB.

A unique and effective sequential adjustment (i.e., adjustment by sections in series) was developed by Kouba for the reduction of Doppler observations. It was implemented in a Shell computer program that was the precursor of GEODOP (Geodetic Doppler) and was developed by Kouba after his transfer to Geodetic Survey in 1973. Starting in 1971 Shell Canada conducted large survey control densification projects, both in Canada and overseas, using the translocation mode. This mode is very effective in detecting and removing errors caused by atmospheric conditions. In the meantime the Canadian Marconi Company (CMC) and J.M.R. Instruments Canada were manufacturing effective Doppler receivers that were being exported worldwide.

Throughout the mid-1970s the field procedures and data-processing methods of Doppler observations were improved by the Geodetic Survey and were implemented in GEODOP. J.D. Boal and others made significant improvements in this area. By the late 1970s accuracies better than 1 m were being obtained after several days of observations. GEODOP by this time had gained worldwide acceptance and was being used in some seventy-five countries. Canadian participation at international symposia on satellite positioning was strong and influential.

Many Canadian private companies used the knowledge gained through the above research efforts to win overseas contracts for positioning services. But in the early 1980s research related to Doppler positioning rapidly gave way to research in the new and more accurate GPS.

Inertial Survey System (ISS)

The concept of using inertial navigation systems for surveying and geodesy emerged simultaneously in Canada and the United States in the mid-1970s. The Geodetic Survey, under the direction of L.J. O'Brien, acquired its first system (a Litton Auto-Surveyor local level platform equipped with floated gyros) in 1975. An active research programme headed by Gregerson and others ensued.

Within two years Shell Canada had purchased two similar systems from Ferranti. Inertial research at both Geodetic Survey and Shell focused on the development of field procedures for the so-called ZUPTs (zero velocity and alignment updates) described in chapter 2. Soon the data-processing methods were available for the handling of large surveys. Geodetic Survey also sponsored research at UNB under Krakiwsky and Schwarz to investigate the use of ISS in determining the deflection of the vertical.

By the late 1970s Shell Canada under Hittel's direction had independently developed its own data-reduction methods, thanks to the considerable efforts of J. Hagglund and his colleagues. Sheltech, the new survey arm of Shell Canada, had by this time obtained six ISS systems and was providing survey control for large geophysical and other survey projects in many parts of the world. In 1977 the first international Symposium on Inertial Technology for Surveying and Geodesy was held in Ottawa.

Upon transferring from UNB to Calgary in 1979 Schwarz and R.V.C. Wong vigorously pursued ISS research. The second and third international symposia on ISS were organized by Schwarz and held in Banff in 1981 and 1985. But it soon became obvious that unaided ISS would be supplanted by the emerging GPS for many applications. However the concept of integrating ISS and GPS remained viable and was first tested on a ship in 1982–83 under a joint project involving the U of C, Shelltech, and its successor, Nortech Surveys. By the late 1980s several ISS research programmes were in place. For example Pulsearch Navigation Systems of Calgary, with the assistance of U of C, developed and successfully commercialized ISS "Pigs." (These are small robot instrument carriers that pass through pipelines to check for leaks, etcetera. The ISS read-out provides a precise location for any faults discovered.)

By the early 1990s research into gravimetry and gradiometry using GPS-ISS techniques was initiated under joint programmes involving the U of C and industrial organizations. The design of multi-sensor systems combining GPS-ISS with a cluster of CCD (Charge Coupled Device) cameras for mobile GIS services is another important development area. The importance of combining GPS and ISS was underscored at the Banff international symposia on kinematic systems in geodesy and related subjects, organized by Schwarz, Lachapelle, and M.E. Cannon in 1990 and 1994.

GPS

GPS was conceived by the U.S. Department of Defense in the early 1970s as a successor to the Doppler system. By 1980 a few satellites provided limited coverage in various parts of the world. This availability was used for research and development, and was employed in some practical applications such as drilling-platform positioning. The system became fully operational in 1994 with at least twenty-four satellites providing worldwide continuous coverage.

GPS research in Canada began at Sheltech in 1979 and was pursued by Nortech Surveys into the 1980s under the leadership of Hittel and Lachapelle. The company's earlier successes with Doppler created a stimulus for this new research. Intense development efforts took place in the early GPS years in developing improved field techniques, software research, and the evaluation of the various receivers that were coming on the market. This programme, headed by Lachapelle until the late 1980s, received considerable support from the CHS. Evaluations at sea were conducted by M. Eaton of the CHS and Wells of UNB.

The first commercially available GPS receiver, built by Stanford Communications in 1979 and used by Sheltech in 1980, was a one-channel, 500 kg unit that consumed 1500 watts of electric power. No built-in computer was available for position calculations, and an absolute accuracy of only about 50 m was possible after several minutes of observation. By 1983 portable multi-channel units capable of delivering accuracies of 1 or 2 m began to appear on the market, namely the T14100 and the Macrometer. Although the cost of

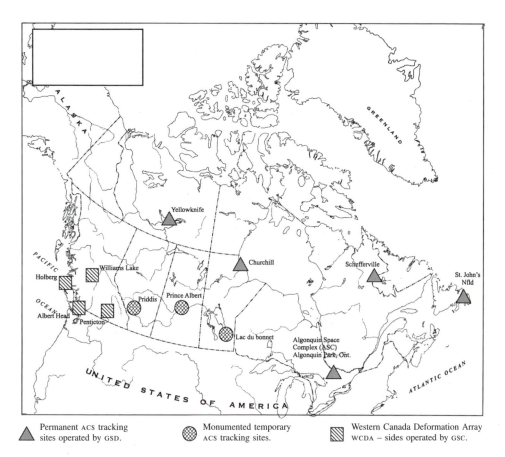

Permanent ACS tracking sites operated by GSD.

Monumented temporary ACS tracking sites.

Western Canada Deformation Array WCDA – sides operated by GSC.

Figure 12-2
Canadian Active Control System (ACS) stations and the Western Canada Deformation Array (WCDA) stations.
Source: Geodetic Survey of Canada

these receivers was still in the order of $100,000, the weight was down to about 50 kg. The T14100 developed by Texas Instruments became the unit preferred for research in Canada. By 1983 Nortech Surveys was developing and testing differential GPS methods and software programs. Static accuracies of about 1 m and mobile accuracies of 5 to 10 m in both the airborne and marine mode were demonstrated for the first time.

In 1984 N. Beck and F. Héroux transferred from Nortech to the Geodetic Survey and, under the direction of G. Babbage and D. Boal, began GPS research on precise differential positioning. This group also included Delikaraoglou and Steeves. In the late 1980s the concept of a Canadian Active Control System (ACS) gradually evolved at Energy, Mines and Resources. This system, which is described in more length in chapter 2, would monitor the orbits of the satellites and furnish Canadian units with more precise data than was being provided from the satellites themselves. A prototype ACS station was developed at UNB by R.B. Langley working under contract for Geodetic Survey. The positions of the ACS stations, which continually track the satellites, are shown in figure 12-2. The ACS measurements are used for a variety of purposes: to provide fiducial (i.e., reference) sites for GPS surveys, to generate post-observation precise orbits for high-accuracy positioning, to monitor and verify the integrity of GPS data, and to facilitate the general positioning of survey nets during the conversion to NAD83. The post-observation orbit and satellite-clock corrections were effective in reducing system errors. The fiducial sites are part of the international network of permanent stations coordinated by the International GPS Service for Geodynamics (IGS). The global data were used for research in geodynamics, crustal movements, and earthquake prediction, and as a contribution to the International Earth Rotation Service's Terrestrial Reference Frame (ITRF), an internationally agreed terrestrial coordinate system accurate and consistent to 10 cm. In early 1994 the Geodetic Survey, at the request of IGS, assumed the responsibility for the coordination of the IGS analysis centres, including the generation of combined ephemerides of the GPS satellites from data submitted by other IGS centres. J. Kouba was one of the key experts in charge of this programme.

GPS research at UNB and U of C began in the early 1980s. Two departments were involved at UNB, namely surveying engineering and electrical engineering. The surveying engineering effort (initially led by Wells but thereafter involving many researchers including Vanicek, Langley, and Kleusberg) grew in importance throughout the 1980s. In 1983–84 G. Beutler, on sabbatical leave from the University of Bern, initiated his GPS studies at UNB and made major contributions to the field. His research into precise static GPS led to the development of DIPOP (Differential Positioning Program), a software package to post-process carrier phase measurements for precise static differential positioning. This program is used internationally. Advances were also made in the area of atmospheric effects on GPS measurements and on carrier phase ambiguity resolution when mobile receivers were being used for centimetre-level accuracies. The work in the Electrical Engineering Department, under J. Tranquilla, focused on antenna development and multi-path analysis. Extensive research was conducted in the area of antenna phase centre stability, an important aspect in precise positioning. The graduate students who worked in these programmes were sought by major international survey companies and antenna manufacturers.

At U of C GPS research was initiated by Krakiwsky and Schwarz. This initially focused on orbit-monitoring improvements, kinematic (i.e., moving) GPS, and GPS-ISS integration, mentioned previously. By the mid-1980s, master's and doctoral degrees were being awarded on the basis of studies relating to GPS and, as with UNB, graduates quickly found employment internationally. Lachapelle transferred from Nortech Surveys to U of C in 1988 and continued actively in GPS development including the calibration of Loran-C by GPS, and the use of multi-receiver systems for the determination of the attitude (i.e., orientation) of moving platforms (e.g., on aircraft, ships, etc.). In 1991 M.E. Cannon, having received her Ph.D. from the U of C, joined the Department of Surveying Engineering as a faculty member where she undertook research into aircraft positioning and altitude determination. This led to the development of SEMIKEN and C3NAV, two kinematic positioning software programs that became known internationally. Research into the use of GPS with digital maps for vehicular navigation was carried out by Krakiwsky, and his work was soon noticed in the private sector with Pulsearch Navigation Systems of Calgary taking the lead. In the late 1980s research was also being carried out at Laval under R. Santerre and J.-G. Leclerc.

By the mid-1980s the level of GPS knowledge among the above groups was second to none in the world. A group of eleven authors, under the leadership of D.E. Wells, formed

Canadian GPS Associates and wrote the previously mentioned *Guide to GPS Positioning*, a book that quickly gained worldwide popularity.

By the late 1980s Nortech Surveys, under the direction of T. Crago, was in a position to offer GPS commercial software programs and other GPS services as a result of their sustained development efforts. In the 1990s many other companies initiated major GPS development programmes in what had become a small but important Canadian industry.

GPS development in Canada has not been confined to methodology and software production; major hardware initiatives were undertaken. Early efforts began at the CMC early in the 1980s. By the 1990s the company had secured a share of the U.S. military GPS receiver market. Civilian navigation receivers were also produced at CMC by 1990. In the mid-1980s Northstar Instruments, a division of Nortech Surveys, began development of a multi-purpose civilian receiver. Unfortunately this effort failed, but the research team transferred to NovAtel Communications Ltd and carried on their work. Under the leadership of B. Timiniski and P. Fenton this led to a totally new product. Patents were awarded to NovAtel for the so-called Narrow Correlator spacing technique. This technology has many advantages including the vital ability to detect and reject measurements affected by reflected signals. These receivers have gained rapid acceptance in both domestic and foreign markets for a variety of precise positioning and navigation applications. It has also become a research tool for further development in this expanding technology.

In the 1990s many development efforts have been directed toward new uses for GPS such as aircraft-to-aircraft positioning, animal tracking, and tidal measurements. These efforts are taking place in both the industrial and academic sectors, and increasingly are being sponsored by foreign agencies, thanks to the success and visibility of Canada in GPS research. The enormous growth of applications witnessed during the period 1990–94 can be attributed partly to the completion of the satellite constellation and to the dramatic drop in receiver prices, illustrated in figure 12-3.

Several national and international meetings pertaining to GPS research were held in Canada from the mid-1980s onward. In 1988 the Canadian GPS User and Supplier Workshop, sponsored by the Canada Centre for Surveying, was held in Ottawa. In 1990 the Second International Symposium on Precise Positioning with GPS was also held in Ottawa.

Very Long Baseline Interferometry

Radio interferometry is the process of reading the fringe frequency observed when the same signals from a quasar, received by two radio telescopes, are combined while the distances of the two telescopes from the quasar are changing, one relative to the other. If the two radio telescopes are too far apart for the signals to be combined by a direct connection in real time, the system is called a VLBI. The procedure is then to record the signals at each station on magnetic tape along with signals from extremely precise Hydrogen Maser clocks. The combining of the signals is done by playing the two tapes together, synchronized by the clock signals.

The fringe frequency is basically dependent on the differences in the geocentric coordinates of the two telescopes, the coordinates of the quasar, the rate of rotation of the earth, the rate of change of the rotational axis (polar motion), and the wavelength of the observed radiation. If many quasars are observed over a period of time, values for all these quantities

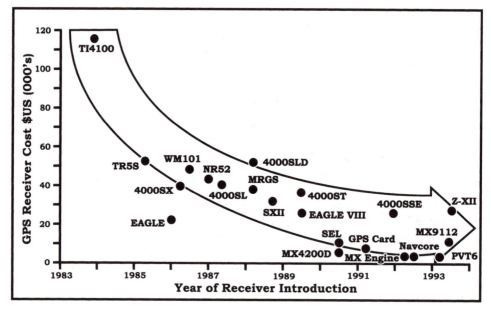

Figure 12-3
GPS receiver price trend, 1980–94.
Source: Gerard Lachapelle

can be obtained in a mathematical adjustment. The length of the baseline (i.e., the distance between the two telescopes) can then be derived.

The first successful playback of baseline tape recording on a radio-interferometer was performed by a team of Canadian scientists at the National Research Council's Herzberg Institute of Astrophysics in 1967, with N. Broten a key member of the team. The potential of this new technique for the study of various geodetic and geophysical phenomena was perceived at once by members of the Geodetic Survey. In 1968 H. Jones of the Geodetic Survey wrote a paper in *The Canadian Surveyor* describing this project.[6] In it he explained the potential value of the technique for extremely accurate geodetic measurements. The results of his calculations on this first measurement by radio-interferometry were most encouraging, even though they were carried out using prototype equipment. The derived length of the line between the Algonquin Radio Telescope in Ontario and the telescope at the Prince Albert Satellite Station in Saskatchewan, had a large standard deviation of about 10 ppm, but the potential for much greater accuracy had been demonstrated.

Interest in VLBI grew rapidly in the United States following the 1967 experiments, but little happened in Canada until 1973 when a York University research group (W.H. Cameron, W.T. Petrachenco, and R.B. Langley) initiated an international observing programme. This involved the cooperation of the National Research Council, the U.K. Science Research Council, and the University of Toronto. The geodetic part of the research included the analysis of the relationship between VLBI and Doppler coordinate systems. This and related work at the Geodetic Survey by J. Kouba was used in the definition of the NAD83.

During the period 1978–91 Canada participated in the NASA Crustal Dynamics Project to investigate the North American Plate deformation. The Canadian team consisted of A. Lambert and H. Dragert from the Earth Physics Branch, R.B. Langley from UNB, J.D. Boal, P. Mathieu, and M. Berubé from the Geodetic Survey, and W.H. Cannon from York University. VLBI observations were carried out at Whitehorse, Yellowknife, Penticton, Albert Head, and Algonquin. During this programme it was noted, as expected, that best results came from the large permanent radio telescopes, but mobile equipment contained in two vans gave quite acceptable measurements.

By 1994, under the guidance of J. Popelar of Geodetic Survey, the VLBI stations at Algonquin and Yellowknife were devoted almost exclusively to geodetic use. They are two of the thirteen worldwide basic stations of the ITRF controlling the reference framework for GPS coordinate computations. Thus VLBI provides the basic datum for the entire GPS surveying system. The accuracy of VLBI measurements is a few parts per billion, or a fraction of a centimetre on lines of over 1000 km in length.

The North American Datum of 1983 (NAD83)

The conversion from NAD27 to NAD83 was one of the momentous events in Canadian geodesy in the period covered in this book. As has been mentioned earlier in this chapter, in the 1960s geodesists began discovering serious discrepancies when they tried to adjust new surveys to older survey nets. Their counterparts in the U.S. were having the same problems. This led in 1972 to an agreement between the geodetic surveys of the U.S. Mexico, and Canada to cooperate in a continent-wide updating of their horizontal control networks, and ultimately to a revised North American Datum. At the same time the people undertaking geoidal research were finding many problems in using the Clarke 1866 ellipsoid as a reference for their work. Col A.R. Clarke, a British army officer, had calculated this ellipsoid using the American survey data available at the time, and while it fitted the forty-eight states very well, when it was extended into northern Canada relatively large separations between the geoid and the ellipsoid were noticed. In parts of Labrador and Baffin Island the combined effect on horizontal geodetic coordinates reached tens of metres. In addition to this problem, which resulted in horizontal position distortions, the yearly adjustment of new triangulation chains by holding to values obtained previously was also contributing to network distortions. The answer to these problems obviously lay in a vigorous readjustment of the first-order surveys based on a new and, at least for Canada, better-fitting ellipsoid.

While these studies were taking place geodetic satellites were establishing precise positions throughout North America, and these of course contributed to the readjustment. They also had an important effect on geoid studies. The flight of a satellite is very much influenced by the earth's gravitational field, and as the field itself shapes the geoid, the tracking of the satellite orbits provided a wealth of geoidal data. As the satellites completely surround the earth they provide worldwide information on the shape and position of the complete geoid. It was obvious, therefore, that the new ellipsoid should be fitted to the entire geoid and not just North America. In 1980, after considerable study, the IAG adopted a new ellipsoid called the GRS80, which in 1983 became the reference ellipsoid for NAD83. The Canadian Doppler stations established in support of this work are shown in figure 12-4.

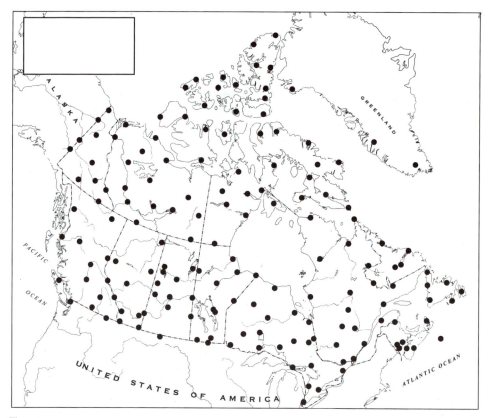

Figure 12-4
Canadian Doppler stations established in support of the move to NAD83.
Source: Geodetic Survey of Canada

The NAD83 is based on earth-centred coordinates. The fundamental parameters of this system are the earth's centre of mass and the position of the polar axis (the CTP). The earth's centre of mass is the origin of the system's axis. The Z axis is on the CTP with the X and Y axis in the plane containing the centre of mass at right angles to the CTP. The x axis is parallel to the zero (Greenwich) meridian (as defined by the Bureau International de l'Heure) and the y axis is at right angles to it. This provides a three-dimensional system that can be translated to earth surface coordinates (latitudes and longitudes) on the NAD83 reference ellipsoid.

The NAD83 ellipsoid has a semi-major axis of 6 378 137 m (69.4 m less than Clarke 1866) and a semi-minor axis of 6 356 752 m (168.5 m more than Clarke 1866).[7] These dimensional changes, together with corrections to old networks, resulted in coordinate changes across Canada. These range from about 120 m westerly on the west coast to 70 m easterly in Labrador, to some 100 m northerly in the Arctic islands. Naturally these fundamental changes have been unsettling, but now that Canada is well on the way to completing the transformation the country is in a strong position to take full advantage of the tremendous power of satellite geodesy.

PART 2 PHOTOGRAMMETRIC RESEARCH
AT THE NATIONAL RESEARCH COUNCIL OF CANADA*

Introductory Events

There have been two periods of original and intensive development in the field of photogrammetry in Canada. The first took place toward the end of the nineteenth century and was the work of Edouard Deville, the surveyor general at the time.[8] The second occurred after the Second World War and lasted until the closing of the Photogrammetric Section at the NRC in 1986. In both periods Canada participated in, and frequently initiated, profound changes in photogrammetric techniques.

Photogrammetry is an indirect measuring technique in which the measuring operations are not performed in the natural space (i.e., on real objects) but on precise models of the natural space. These models are achieved by using appropriate photographic images of the natural space.

The twentieth century's spectacular scientific and technological progress that was stimulated so dramatically by the Second World War had a major impact on the surveying and mapping disciplines. This impact was particularly noticeable in photogrammetry because of its direct military applications. Canada participated in the war effort in many ways that required the presence of Canadian scientists close to the war scene. One of these was Dr. Leslie Howlett, a physicist with a particular interest in optics. During his stay in London he established close connections with the relevant British institutions and met various scientists working in his field. One of them was W. Romer from Poland, who was concerned with the physical phenomena affecting the quality of aerial photographs.

After the war Howlett joined the Division of Physics at NRC. Soon he became associate director of the division, working closely with the director, Gerhard Herzberg (later a Nobel laureate). NRC was then a modest scientific establishment, but of excellent quality, which was rapidly gaining a well-deserved international reputation.

Howlett and Douglas Carman, another scientist interested in optics and photography, established the camera calibration facility at NRC, which was of fundamental importance to serious photogrammetric research. In particular this preoccupation with high-quality photographs, a basic factor in photogrammetric operations, sensitized the professional community of the country to this critical requirement. It also had a profound impact on the general efficiency of photogrammetry. Canada was soon recognized as a leader in the field of aerial photography. Early results of the NRC work forced the manufacturers of aerial cameras to modernize their testing procedures. This research programme grew in stature under the leadership of H. Ziemann until the dissolution of the research in photogrammetry in 1986.

Founding the Photogrammetric Section at NRC

In 1950 two important events occurred in the Ottawa photogrammetric community. Two Wild Autograph A5 stereoplotters were installed, one in the Surveys and Mapping Branch (SMB) of the Department of Mines and Technical Surveys and the other in the Army Survey

---

* Part 2, by Teodor J. Blachut, was reduced from a longer text.

Establishment (ASE). These so-called first-order universal plotters were a far cry from the Multiplexes that at the time were the most up-to-date instruments being used. The Wild Company had sent T.J. Blachut and H. Wey to Ottawa to supervise the installation of the instruments and to train the first operators.

During the installation of the plotters there must have been discussions about bringing a trained photogrammetrist to Canada to work at NRC. As a result, one evening while Blachut was working in Ottawa he received a telephone call from Sam Gamble, who at the time was the head of the air section (i.e. photogrammetric section) at SMB. During the call Gamble invited Blachut to attend an important meeting at the home of Howlett. At the meeting Howlett explained that the Division of Physics at NRC would like to establish a section to be called "Photogrammetric Research." Blachut was offered the position as head of this section. The necessary arrangements were made, and on 5 August 1951 Blachut reported to Herzberg for work.

Building the Photogrammetric Section

Very modest but sufficient space was assigned to the new section at the main NRC building on Sussex Drive in Ottawa. The usual organizational and operational problems were resolved and two plotters, a Wild A7 and a Zeiss Stereoplanigraph, were purchased. At the time they constituted the most advanced plotting instruments in the mainstream of world mapping technology. The first technician and plotter operator, Ralf Latta, was transferred from SMB. One could not find a more suitable person. Intelligent, resourceful, and with a thorough knowledge of the local scene, he was of great help in those early days.

The most difficult problem was the finding of high-quality scientists to work in photo-grammetry. Canada at the time had only one university, Laval, with a department of surveying. A similar situation existed in the United States. In contrast in Russia there were several universities with complete faculties for the various geodetic disciplines, and in Moscow a separate university with five faculties and 4000 students specializing exclusively in the fields of surveying and mapping.

The answer was to attract promising researchers from Europe. Fortunately NRC had at the time an intelligent scheme for this purpose, namely the post-doctoral fellowship programme. A candidate when approved could join the NRC for a period of one year, which could be extended. The salaries of these "post-docs" were meagre, but the scientific reputation of the NRC was such that many young scientists applied for the available posts. Among these early recruits for photogrammetric research were Gerry Schut (Holland), Uki Helava (Finland), Vladimir Kratky (Czechoslovakia), Marius Van Wijk (Holland), Zarko Jaksic (Yugoslavia), Jauko Saastamoinen (Finland), Hartmuth Ziemann (Germany), and George Zarzycki (Poland), all of whom decided eventually to stay in Canada. Others returned to their countries after concluding their term of associateship. Among these were such prominent scholars as A. Bjerhamer (Sweden), J. Inghillery (Italy), Z. Sitek (Poland), and Chester Slama (U.S.).

Broadening the Research in Photogrammetry

It was obvious from the beginning that this new NRC section, modest in size and in finances, had to make judicious decisions in planning its research programme. The improvement and adaptation of existing techniques is an engineer's responsibility but the development of innovative systems can, as a general rule, be done only by a scientist who has a thorough knowledge of a given field and an irrepressible urge to improve it. Among the early candidates for NRC fellowships were two photogrammetrists, Schut and Helava, who both had a particular capability in the research field.

Mapping the vast Canadian territories required the most advanced techniques if the work was to be done quickly, accurately, and inexpensively. The methods described in chapter 3 (slotted templates and multiplex bridging), used by the federal mapping agencies for establishing control nets in the 1950s, were becoming obsolete. In these early days an obvious way for NRC to help to improve this situation was to follow two approaches: to try to control by an independent means the rapid accumulation of errors in the aerial triangulation process, and to develop a new, more efficient and precise technique of aerial triangulation.

In the first approach an important factor was the integration of Airborne Profile Recorder (APR) data into the aerial triangulation process. In the initial work carried out in the SMB on the use of APR data, heights of terrain points extracted from the data were used in mapping operations. However a proper integration of the complete APR data into the aerial triangulation offered significant advantages.

It should be noted that in addition to the elevation of selected terrain points, the APR allows the determination of the scale of each individual photograph. Thus the scale propagation error along the triangulation strip, always difficult to determine, can be found. Moreover both the APR terrain elevations and the scale determinations are affected by significant local errors in contrast to the aerial triangulation values. Therefore the combination of both determinations, from two independent processes, offered superior results. This was confirmed by strictly controlled aerial triangulations covering a distance of over 300 km.

This work attracted the attention of the international photogrammetric community, and several foreign scientists participated in the studies (from Finland, Austria, and the U.S.). Some of this work was carried out in close cooperation with the Photographic Survey Corporation, an intensive user of APR techniques both in Canada and abroad.[9] The British military establishment kindly provided NRC with some of their APR data for further analysis. After electronic computations were more in general use, NRC introduced APR data in one of its aerial triangulation adjustment programs.

However it was the introduction of the analytical block adjustment that was the most important innovation in photogrammetry in this period, and the NRC group was in the forefront of this advance. The analytical adjustment became a practical proposition once the electronic computers achieved an acceptable level, and when the measuring equipment offered an efficiency required by production operations. The block triangulation approach has become recognized as the most efficient method of aerial triangulation. It has been proven that by adjusting, as an entity, a number of parallel triangulation strips or blocks of strips, superior results can be achieved with a minimum of ground control points, usually at the four corners of the block with one at its centre.

The NRC group soon became one of the internationally recognized pioneers in the field of analytical aerial triangulation. With modest means at their disposal the NRC scientists had to tax their minds and ingenuity to maintain meaningful progress. There was no lack of discouraging situations. Once Blachut was invited to the photogrammetric laboratories of one of the U.S. defence mapping agencies. In the first room visited there was an IBM 360 computer that was absolutely beyond the financial reach of the NRC group. As the visitor expressed surprise and delight that such a powerful computer had been provided for their work, the American host replied, "Oh yes, we're using it to organize and feed the entry data to our main computer." It was difficult not to be depressed by such a situation.

However there were some advantages to being relatively poor. The solutions resulting from the NRC work were tailored toward modest facilities. Developing these solutions required a very solid knowledge of the subject, a logical operational approach, clever mathematical formulations of the problem, and very efficient programming. This operational approach was soon recognized by both the Canadian and international community. By 1965 over 200 mapping agencies throughout the world, both government and private, were using the NRC programmes.

Schut was responsible for this work, and his name became, in international circles, a synonym for analytical aerial triangulation.[10] There were other photogrammetrists who formulated programmes based on different concepts, but for the reasons mentioned above the NRC solutions, which were continually updated to reflect the general progress in the field, remained popular. This was particularly true in countries that could not afford the very powerful computers required by some formulations.

The Invention of the Analytical Plotter

The intensive involvement with analytical methods, together with an intimate knowledge of analogue plotters (and their limitations), led the members of the NRC section to think about a completely new approach to photogrammetric plotters. Even though the modern analogue plotters introduced a new level of accuracy, they were not able to overcome their inherent limitations. As a result they were also not able to exploit fully the superb performance of the newest aerial cameras that were producing first-rate images on dimensionally stable film. The traditional seesaw competition between the performance of aerial cameras and plotting instruments was again in play. Also it must be remembered that the precision of the new analogue plotters was paid for by formidable mechanical complexity and a very high cost.

One can find similar situations in other fields. In aviation once the propeller-driven aircraft approached the limit of its performance, the designers had to turn to completely new techniques, which they found in jet engines and rockets. Similarly, to provide a future-oriented solution in photogrammetry the plotters had to be freed from the genetic limitations of analogue instruments. Helava understood this and formulated the concept of an analytical plotter. The section proceeded with the development of a prototype[11] (see figure 12-5). In this revolutionary instrument the enormous complexity of analogue solutions was replaced by straightforward mathematical calculations. As a result the previous heavy plotters were reduced to simple coordinate-measuring devices controlled by computers.

The analytical plotter also resolved, very efficiently, the intricate problems connected with the geometry of aerial photographs and cartographic projections. The rays of light producing a photographic image are bent by atmospheric refraction, and the reference surface in mapping is not a plane. In certain applications complex map-projection systems are involved. Rigid analogue systems could not cope adequately with the resulting geometries, even when using the simplest conventional photographs.

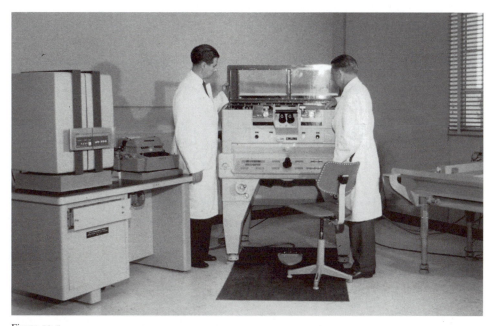

Figure 12-5
Prototype of the analytical plotter. Dr T.J. Blanchut is on the right, Dr U.V. Helava is on the left.
Photo: Teodor Blachut

No less important were the operational advantages of an analytical plotter. The previous laborious interior, relative, and absolute orientations of stereo pairs became a matter of a few minutes rather than hours. Additional observations were incorporated into the operation using mathematical adjustment procedures. Through the transfer of pertinent parameters, the subsequent orientations during the plotting operation could be carried out without losing time or accuracy. As a result complex processes were drastically shortened and the quality of work significantly improved. There was no longer a place for the operator's "guesswork" often necessary in analogue plotting.

As an example of improved efficiency a typical situation in aerial triangulation can be quoted. An experienced operator could bridge on the Wild A7 up to seven overlaps in a working day. With the NRC Anaplot up to forty-five overlaps were triangulated in the same time. Moreover, the result of bridging on the A7 was nothing more than raw strip coordinates while those from the analytical plotter were rigorously adjusted to ground control as a matter of routine production.

The development of the prototype encountered all sorts of difficulties, the most serious of which were caused by the inadequacies of the early electronic computers. At one point the section even decided to develop, in cooperation with the NRC Division of Electrical Engineering, its own hybrid computer. Fortunately just at this time Packard Bell introduced its miniaturized computer, which could be used for the section's prototype plotter. All the projects came together as planned, and the prototype was completed in time to be unveiled at the Second International Photogrammetric Conference on the Analytical Plotter held in Ottawa in 1963.[12]

Figure 12-6
The Anaplot as exhibited in Helsinki in 1976.
Photo: Teodor Blachut

When the invention of the analytical plotter was announced at the Ottawa conference the reaction of leading manufacturers of photogrammetric equipment was discouraging. K. Schwidefsky from Zeiss told Blachut, "You have sufficient experience in the manufacture of photogrammetric equipment to realize that this wonderful dream of yours can never come true." Hugo Kasper from Wild was even more blunt: "I do not think Wild would be interested in this kind of a plotting table." It is no wonder that Canadian manufacturers, to whom photogrammetry was totally unknown, did not show any interest at all. Thus this revolutionary invention was in danger of fading away. Fortunately powerful allies were found in the U.S. air force and the unforgettable Dr Umberto Nistri, a pioneer in photogrammetry and the owner of a small photogrammetric equipment factory in Rome. Nistri acquired the patent rights from NRC and sold a large number of analytical plotters to the U.S. air force.

This new commercial interest in the analytical plotter permitted NRC to continue development with the help of Instronics Ltd of Stittsville, near Ottawa. The substantial progress in the development of electronic components and computers greatly facilitated the design of an improved analytical plotter. After Helava left NRC, first to join Nistri in Italy and eventually to form his own company in California, the key roles in the advancement of the analytic plotter, in addition to Blachut, were played by Z. Jaksic (internal architecture of the system), R. Real (electronic systems), V. Kratky (application programs), J. Pekelsky (optical systems), and B. Moeller (position verifier that displayed the plotting results). Eventually a very impressive instrument was created. Under the name of Anaplot (see figure 12-6) it was displayed to enthusiastic acclaim at the International Congress of Photogrammetry held in Helsinki in 1976.[13]

But the euphoria of a very positive reception in Finland was short-lived. As a result of the cancellation of two large unrelated contracts, Instronics Ltd went bankrupt. Richard Payne, of the Instronics design team, was able to convince an Ottawa firm, Systemhouse, to embark on another analytical plotter of his own design. Regrettably this project was plagued with many development problems and, after the expenditure of hundreds of thousands of dollars, it too was cancelled.

Prior to this unfortunate incident Marconi of Canada entered into an industry-oriented agreement with NRC aimed at a commercially viable production of the analytical plotter concept. Supported by NRC, and with orders from the ASE, Marconi and NRC designed and built yet another analytical plotter. The industry's effort was lukewarm, however, and there was no evidence of a long-range policy or strategy. It was, rather, a typical "one-shot effort" of significant interest to industry since it provided paid access to new technologies together with the solutions of related problems. But once again there was little or no interest in this Canadian initiative outside the Canadian government. One must conclude from these unfortunate events that the most useful invention in the field will fail commercially if the proper industrial will and strategy is not in place.

The Invention of the Monocomparator

The intense preoccupation of the section with analytical methods in aerial triangulation raised the question of measuring the coordinates of discrete points. For a variety of reasons analogue plotters were not a suitable, logical, or economic choice for the purpose. The need for a more logical solution had earlier been recognized in Great Britain where the Cambridge Stereocomparator was built. This was intended to be a very precise instrument, an essential point in the development. The British War Office owned this device and, always helpful, was willing to lend it to the NRC for experimenting. On this instrument the recording of each coordinate required the reading and writing down of the coordinates on countless dials, a tiring and lengthy operation that was subject to human error. To improve the recording process a magnifying glass was placed over each dial, and a camera was positioned to photograph all readings. The camera was placed high above the instrument and a microscope was used to read the photographs. Obviously this was not an ideal instrument for production mapping, but for the NRC the experience was very valuable.

Soon modern stereocomparators came on the market and NRC was able to obtain the model produced by Nistri. This had three plate carriers to facilitate point transfers along the triangulation strip. It had another unique capability, namely the automatic recording of coordinates by the use of drum encoders. Despite some very interesting features this instrument was also not ideal for production mapping. In addition it was very expensive.

A curious situation existed at this stage of development of photogrammetric techniques. There was a fast-growing interest in analytical methods, but at the same time the instruments for measuring coordinates were both inefficient and expensive. A possible solution was to mark on the photographs, using stereoscopic observation, the single points to be measured, and then take off the coordinates of these points on each photograph separately. This approach was supported by a study that seemed to indicate that results based on this kind of measurement were, contrary to theoretical considerations, somewhat better than those based on stereo measurements.[14] The section decided to look into this matter, and again Helava came up with an ingenious solution, introducing a "multi-mark measuring plate."[15] With this system a plate is used on which there is an array of precisely coordinated points at a mutual distance of 2 cm. The point on the photograph is then measured using the nearest point on the measuring plate. This reduces the run of the measuring screw

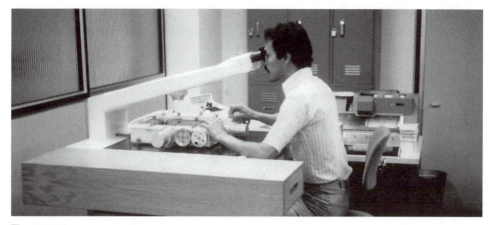

Figure 12-7
The NRC monocomparator.
Photo: Teodor Blachut

assembly to about 2 cm rather than some 23 cm if the whole photo was to be covered, as is necessary in conventional systems.

After some refinements[16] the manufacturing rights to the NRC monocomparator (figure 12-7) were sold to a local company, Leigh Instruments, which manufactured and sold about forty-five of these instruments. Several of them have been noticed by members of the NRC staff in various countries around the world.

Occasionally NRC involvement with domestic and foreign firms had unexpected results. As an example when Ottica Mecanica Italiana (OMI-Nistri) was looking for a suitable company to be its representative in Canada, NRC suggested Computing Devices of Canada, located in Ottawa. Two or three years later a telephone call was received from Charles Hembery, president of CDC, thanking the section at NRC for recommending his company. Whereas CDC had not been able to effect any sales for OMI, the Italian company had placed multimillion dollar contracts in NATO countries for the navigational equipment built by CDC.

Test Areas and Comparative Studies

Assessing the precision of photogrammetric instruments and techniques requires the use of a variety of test areas. For instance if the analysis of the quality of photogrammetric contouring of very flat terrain is to be carried out, a small, well-surveyed area is sufficient. On the other hand establishing the efficiency of aerial triangulation based on radar profile data requires hundreds of kilometres of hilly or mountainous terrain with a dense net of control points. Most developed countries have such test areas, which are used routinely to assess new equipment or procedures. From time to time international tests and experimental projects are organized by scientific societies in various photogrammetric domains.

International experiments generally require one country to provide the test materials. This often involves considerable expense by the host country, such as occurred when France offered hundreds of glass plate high-altitude photographs of the French Massif Central to a number of participating countries. This 100 km square block was a test area of inestimable value.

On Canada's part NRC has provided experimental material for international use. An early test was called the Canadian Controlled Mapping Experiment, and for it a test area was prepared at Renfrew, Ontario.[17] Aerial photography of the area at 1:50 000 scale was provided along with suitable ground control. Participating countries were asked to map the area at 1:25 000. Forty-five submissions were received and when the results were analyzed a number of lessons were learned. Probably the most important was that the main errors in mapping were not caused by defective photographs or instruments, but by erroneous procedures commonly used by operators. In addition the experiment provided unbiased information about the performance of different plotters.

There were some humorous incidents. A famous professor from a foreign country insisted stubbornly that the central control point had the wrong elevation. Eventually, to avoid his embarrassment, he was told (despite the rules of the project) not to forget that the earth is round. The internationally known Professor Finsterwalder from Munich was so taken by the experiment that he published a sophisticated multicolour map of the Renfrew test area.[18] On another occasion a participant from a remote country asked where in Canada Ottawa was located. When told he exclaimed, "Why, it must be close to Renfrew."

Two other projects in this category must at least be mentioned. NRC carried out an experiment at the Gagetown military base in New Brunswick to show the applicability of photogrammetric techniques in legal surveys. This theme was continued at the Alnwick Indian Reserve in Ontario.[19] Although these tests failed at the time to convince the legal surveyors, they provided very valuable operational results that have eventually borne fruit. An extension of this project was an experiment in the use of winter photography for legal survey purposes.[20]

The intense development of analytical photogrammetry made essential the establishment of a test area different from Renfrew. Photogrammetric accuracy was moving into the range of single centimetres, and therefore the targeted control points of the test area had to be established to at least the same accuracy. After extensive investigation the moon-like area adjacent to Sudbury was selected. The International Nickel Company, whose acid fumes had destroyed the vegetation, was pleased to find such a noble use for part of its property. It was surveyed by Saastamoinen, a "classical" geodesist, with an accuracy of the order of ±1.0 cm. While working on various geodetic assignments, Saastamoinen made a major scientific contribution in the field of geodesy. His methods for the correction of electromagnetically measured distances were confirmed, and recommended for use, by the International Geodetic Union.

The Orthophoto and Stereo-orthophoto Concept

The central projection of an aerial photograph taken from a finite distance above the ground, prevents the taking of accurate measurements directly from it. If the distortions caused by the central perspective, the tilts of the camera, and the topography could be removed, the resulting image would have both the geometric accuracy of a very accurate map, and the wealth of detail of a photograph. This is exactly what is accomplished in an orthophotograph.

Although various instruments have been designed to produce orthophotos, they are all based on a simple principle. When two overlapping photos are placed in a photogrammetric plotter, and when the three orientations are carried out (interior, relative, and absolute – see chapter 3), a properly oriented three-dimensional model of the photographed terrain is created. By scanning the model methodically, with the floating mark kept constantly in

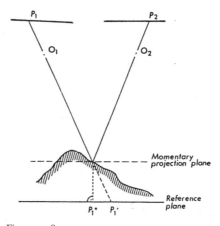

Figure 12-8
The geometric principle of orthophotos.
Source: Teodor Blachut

contact with the "ground," and by recording (photographically) in a continuous fashion the image immediately around the floating mark, an orthophoto results. This is essentially what happens in all processes used in the production of orthophotos (see figure 12-8).

However a pair of adjacent orthophotos cannot be viewed stereoscopically to get a three-dimensional image because the removal of height "parallaxes" also flattens the three-dimensional image. This undesirable effect has been corrected by the invention at NRC of the stereo-orthophoto system. The basic geometry of this system is quite simple: if two orthophotos are made of overlapping air photos, the first is left without change while the second is modified by "artificial horizontal parallaxes." These are obtained by a horizontal shift of each point in the photograph relative to the elevation of that point over an assumed reference plane. This is equivalent to an image obtained from a parallel projection of the second photo, as shown in figure 12-9. When the oblique projection is viewed simultaneously with the orthogonal projection, a correct relief impression is obtained.

The invention of the stereo-orthophoto permitted simple and inexpensive plotters, called stereocompilers, to be built, in which the time-consuming relative and absolute orientations are reduced to the simple alignment of both orthophotos. NRC designed several models of these stereocompilers, from very simple devices to be used by earth scientists, geographers, and the like, to instruments for precise plotting capable of graphical and numerical plotting and recording (see figure 12-10). In addition to the work of Blachut on this project, outstanding contributions were made by S.H. Collins of the University of Guelph, who joined the section as a visiting scientist.[21] Angel Garcia Amaro, a post-doctoral fellow from Mexico, and Manfred Paulen from the section both helped in the design of certain important components of the system. Marius van Wijk and Blachut conducted varied experimental work including international projects in the field. International symposia on the subject were organized in Canada and abroad in Paris, Krakow, Sao Paulo, and Bogota. A prominent photogrammetrist from the U.S. Topographic Command thought the invention and development of the stereo-orthophoto concept to be one of the leading achievements of this century in the field of photogrammetry.

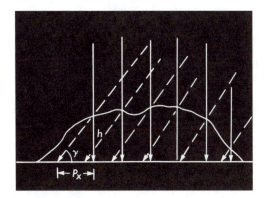

Figure 12-9
The basic geometry of the stereo-orthophoto.
Source: Teodor Blachut

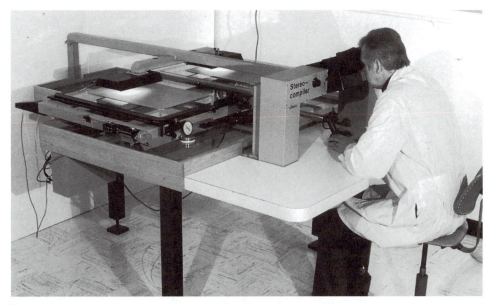

Figure 12-10
The Stereocompiler Mark III.
Photo: Teodor Blachut

Participation in Glaciological Research

McGill University in Montreal developed an impressive glaciological project in conjunction with the Jacobson-McGill Expedition to Axel Heiberg. The determination of the behaviour of glaciers in the high Arctic was an important part of the project. The director was the well-known Swiss geologist and glaciologist Fritz Mueller, at that time a professor at McGill. He was familiar with the exemplary use of photogrammetry in the Swiss Alps and planned to take a similar approach in the Canadian Arctic. Even though the object of glaciological investigation in both countries was similar (i.e., to establish the glacier's rate of flow, direction, and ablation rate), the difference in scope and general working conditions was enormous. The Swiss glacier under similar investigation was a few minutes flight from a major airport, and thus the Swiss researchers could use methods that were out of the question in northern Canada. The Swiss, for example, could spray tonnes of soot on the areas under investigation to make the photogrammetric measurements in critical areas much more precise.

In the Canadian project all technical specifications and pertinent logistical and operational details were prepared in the NRC section. Terrestrial and aerial photogrammetric techniques were involved, in addition to the field survey operations needed to establish an extensive control network for the glaciological determinations. Certain parts of this work were to be repeated in a few years to assess the long-term phenomena, and this had to be considered in the initial planning.

The detailed planning of both the fieldwork and office work, including photogrammetric determinations, was the responsibility of Dieter Hauman, a post-doctoral fellow from Munich. He was also responsible for the extremely delicate plotting of the map manuscripts that were the basic end-products of the operation (figure 12-11 is a typical example of this work). In the work involved in the production of these maps, Haumann was ably supported by Allan Richens and Don Honneggar from the section. The mapping consisted of a series of 1:5000 glaciological maps. In addition to *The Canadian Surveyor* publication on the project,[22] McGill published a most impressive work illustrated by the NRC maps and in Switzerland Mueller published a fine text titled *Hoher Norden* (The High North).[23] This is a popular scientific publication dealing with the Canadian Arctic and its physical makeup and life.

Non-Cartographic Photogrammetry

Although non-cartographic photogrammetry is beyond the scope of this book, a mention of NRC's involvement in this field seems appropriate. There are competent opinions that consider non-cartographic applications of photogrammetry so important that they will eventually constitute the major activity in the field.

Engineering is an obvious area where photogrammetric techniques can be used. For example it is the only reliable technique for the precise determination of wave characteristics and their patterns in harbour zones. It can also be used in wind tunnels in real-time deformation studies of structures under varying loads. In robotic design it has many uses. For example in the development of the now famous Canadarm for NASA, use was made of photogrammetry to guide the grasping movements of the arm. In all such investigations, and in many others, the superiority of photogrammetry can easily be demonstrated.

The recording of architectural heritage and historical monuments is another growing photogrammetric field. Both governments and heritage societies are most interested in

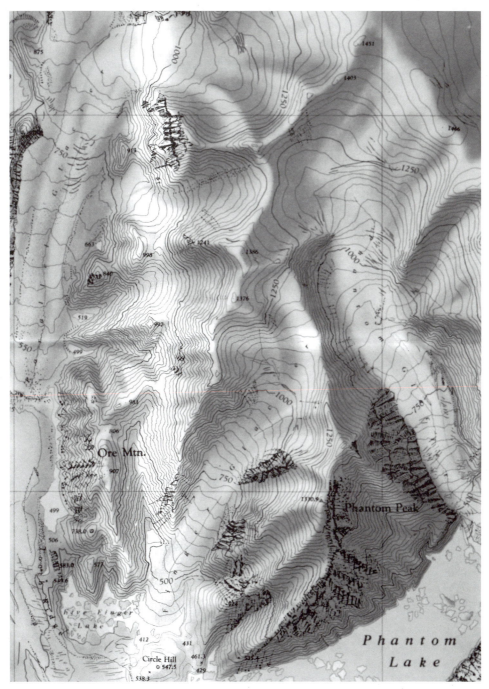

Figure 12-11
Section from the map of the Thompson Glacier Region produced at the Photogrammetric Research Section of
the NRC. An experiment in rock drawing and glacier depiction. (Original in Colour)
Source: Teodor Blachut

obtaining detailed plans and elevations of existing buildings. Photogrammetric techniques provide the only reliable method for preparing such drawings.

The most heart-warming developments are occurring in the medical applications of photogrammetry. Very gratifying results have been achieved at NRC in the investigation of spinal defects. It was also at NRC that the first automated ultrasound brain scanner was developed and submitted to test at the Neurological Institute in Montreal.

Some Concluding Remarks

This necessarily limited presentation provides only a few glimpses into the work of the Photogrammetric Research Section of the NRC. The section has made a valiant effort to serve the country, its surveying profession, and the world community in this field. This effort and activity was formed by the NRC mandate and the excellent climate of the institution, at the time, created by the scientifically competent and idealistic NRC leadership.

The section was aware of the problems facing the surveying profession, the dynamic Canadian mapping industry, the universities and technical schools, and the federal and provincial surveying and mapping departments. If it wanted to create some meaningful impact on all these components, then it had to carry out substantial activities beyond its laboratory walls. No exciting results could be expected from isolated solitary research effort. There was a necessity to keep in touch with foreign development, and there was the NRC obligation to work with the international community. The scientists of the section had to be exposed to and confronted with the whole range of problems, concepts, and approaches. Thus the section, from the start, became involved in and initiated widely diverse activities.

Hundreds of original publications flowed from these involvements, some of them in book form. Two of these were particularly notable: *Urban Surveying and Mapping*, the only text in western literature on the subject, and *Historical Development of Photogrammetric Methods and Instruments*.[24] This last book resulted from Blachut's long association with the International Society for Photogrammetry (see chapter 18).

Regrettably the Photogrammetric Research Section was dissolved in 1986, six years after the retirement of its founder and head for 29 years. This occurred just as the section was preparing to unveil the remarkable next step in development – real-time photogrammetry. There were protests from Canadian and foreign scientists, organizations, and universities, but to no avail. It seems inconceivable that a country with such a wide and diverse geography should not have a national laboratory dedicated to the advancement of photogrammetric methods for exploring and developing this vast domain. Unfortunately that is the case today.

PART 3   RESEARCH IN PHOTOGRAMMETRY
AT CANADIAN UNIVERSITIES*

Introduction

During the last fifty years photogrammetry has undergone a spectacular change in the technology of data acquisition, data handling, and data display. Hand-held cameras in an

---

* Part 3 was contributed by J.M. Zarzycki.

open cockpit were replaced by high-resolution electronically controlled aerial cameras and digital imagery. Slotted template radial triangulation gave way to sophisticated analytical block adjustment, and GPS controlled aerial photography practically eliminated the need for ground-control surveys. Analogue stereoplotting instruments are being replaced by computer-driven analytical stereoplotters and digital photogrammetric workstations. Digital mapping and softcopy photogrammetry makes us think in terms of spatial information systems (SIS) rather than the familiar concepts of mapping.

Canadian universities have taken an active part in this evolution and have made substantial contributions at all stages of its development. The scope of this research covered a broad spectrum and included practically all aspects of photogrammetry. It was carried out in an interaction with the Canadian surveying and mapping community and the photogrammetric centres around the world. It would be impossible in the space provided in this chapter to list and discuss all research work, and to name all who took part in it. Limitations of space permit but a snapshot. It is hoped, however, that a clear picture of the extent of research in photogrammetry at Canadian universities will emerge.

The research work was carried out principally at the surveying engineering or survey science departments of UNB at Fredericton, Laval University at Québec City, Erindale College of the University of Toronto, and the U of C. But even before surveying engineering departments were established, K.B. Jackson, professor of applied physics at the University of Toronto, carried out pioneering research to determine and define factors affecting the interpretation of aerial photographs. He had set up a test area at the Forestry Experimental Station in Maple, Ontario, and constructed different kinds of targets to test and define the qualities of photographs best suited to the needs of the photo interpreter and photogrammetrist. His ultimate purpose was to find methods for extracting the maximum information from aerial photographs. His research was undertaken primarily in response to the needs of the forestry community, which at the time was faced with the enormous task of carrying out a complete forest inventory of Ontario. Jackson reported his findings at the International Congress of ISP in Stockholm in 1956, and in London in 1960.

University of New Brunswick

The formation of the Surveying Engineering Department at UNB signalled the beginning of photogrammetric research there. Initial work was in the field of glacier mapping and ice-movement determination in the Canadian Rockies and Alaska, and on Ellesmere Island, using mainly terrestrial photogrammetry. This work by Konecny provided insight into issues such as contouring of snow-covered areas, motion parallaxes, and refraction. Because of this experience the Surveying Engineering Department was chosen to participate in the photogrammetric mapping of the Kennedy, Hubbard, and Alveston mountains.

When new types of imaging devices became available, Derenyi and Konecny commenced investigations into the geometric aspects of unconventional imaging systems. In the late 1960s Konecny was involved in the NASA lunar mapping programme prior to the landing of a man on the moon. Dr Faig pursued non-metric and close-range photogrammetry. He developed calibration procedures (self-calibration) and different sets of additional parameters to make non-metric (amateur) cameras function as precision tools. This was done by using analytical plotters as well as modified analogue instruments. Other studies dealt with the use of video-based raster stereography in close-range applications.

Two bundle-adjustment programs were developed at UNB (Faig, EL-Hakim, Maniva) with additional parameters. The program GEBAT directly utilizes geodetic measurements in a rigorous spatial adjustment. This was later expanded to a "four-dimensional" photogrammetry for deformation studies, with time being the fourth dimension. As early as 1972 Dr Masry conceived the epipolar correlation principle, which reduced the time and effort of the correlation of stereo pairs. This principle is now widely used in digital photogrammetric workstations (DPW) of different manufactures. A study was carried out by Derenyi, Masry, and MacRitchie on the application of radar imagery for mapping, and an evaluation of Skylab photography.

The Surveying Engineering Department at UNB played a significant role in the development of digital mapping coupled with Geographic Information Systems (GIS). Work by Masry, assisted by Y.C. Lee, resulted in the development of the Computer Aided Resource Information System (CARIS). Masry left the university to form Universal Systems Ltd, which built and further developed CARIS as well as marine digital information systems, selling them on international markets.

Other research at UNB included development of a pseudo-stereo digital mapping system for map revision, raster-vector integration, and seabed mapping techniques using small-format photography. A wide range of research was carried out by Lee in many fundamental problems of SIS, such as interchange standards, special data models, object-oriented data models, and the management of uncertainty in special data.

Laval University

The Faculty of Forestry and Geomatics at Laval University in Québec City is very active in photogrammetric research on a broad front. Dr Brandenberger has done pioneering work in the use of industrial photogrammetry and has developed techniques for a number of industrial applications. He also refined photogrammetric methods for the measurement and monitoring of deformation of large engineering structures such as power dams. This work was stimulated by an extensive programme of hydroelectric dam–construction in Québec. He also carried out investigations into error propagation in aerial triangulation, and later devoted much effort to the economic aspects and the inventory of photogrammetry and cartography around the world.

Studies of image quality versus metric capability were undertaken by S.K. Ghosh. He also investigated the use of an electron microscope for volume determination, and developed methods of photogrammetric calibration of scanning electron microscopes as well as techniques for using stereo x-ray imagery of brains for the introduction of probes in surgery. Photogrammetric techniques for tree height measurements for forest inventories were developed under the direction of P.-A. Gagnon.

The year 1988 marks an important turning point and the beginning of a new period in research at Laval. It saw the emergence of the softcopy photogrammetry concept, which led to the development of the now well-established digital video plotter (DVP). At the same time it saw the emergence of a formidable research team as the basis of this important breakthrough: Jean-Paul Agnard, Paul-Andre Gagnon, and Clement Nolette. Michel Boulianne joined the team several years later. From 1988 on nearly all the research efforts in photogrammetry at Laval have been in relation to microcomputer softcopy photogrammetry. Up to 1994 this line of research had led to more than thirty publications, and provided the subject of numerous technical conferences covering such topics as automatic stereo-pointing, prototype construction of the DVP (1988), aerotriangulation with digital pugging (i.e., digital control point transfer), DVP base-map updating, digital rectification, automated image matching, DVP-SPOT for three-dimensional data collection from SPOT imagery, development of DVP-FOR for forestry applications and tree height measurements, differential rectification, digital orthophoto maps and mosaics, as well as automatic scanner calibration and correction file generation, interactive photogrammetry using COGO, and superimposition functions for terrain analysis and cadastral applications. The basic objective behind the DVP research has been, and continues to be, to increase the accessibility of photogrammetry and to extend its field of applications through optimal use of microcomputer technology.

The Centre for Research and Development in Geomatics at Laval University is also engaged in research in SIS. Current projects concern mainly spatial data modelling and structuring, time management in GIS, and the use of spatial considerations in forestry applications.

University of Toronto, Erindale Campus

At the Centre for Survey Science at Erindale the research in photogrammetry was relatively modest but nevertheless covered a wide spectrum. Gordon Gracie conducted studies on the application of terrestrial photogrammetry to airport zoning and obstruction surveys. This included a review of the mathematical formulation, a theoretical analysis of accuracy under different configurations, preparation of computer programs, and two field tests. Gracie also investigated the application of close-range photogrammetry to the treatment of ulcers at McMaster University Medical Centre. A.M. Wassef investigated photogrammetric methods for constructing digital terrain models, and the fidelity in representing topography by these methods. V.P. Robinson and A.P. Sani undertook research and evaluation of the use of the MEIS II (multispectral electro-optical imaging scanner) for municipal and utility mapping. F. Csillag carried out research on the integration of GIS and remote sensing, as well as the geostatistical analysis of remotely sensed data. Other work included studies on microcomputer-based aerial video mapping and design of SIMEANS: a microcomputer-based system for single-image photogrammetry. With the move of the Centre for Surveying Science to the Department of Geography an expanded research programme in mapping, photogrammetry, remote sensing, and GIS is under way.

University of Calgary

The scope of photogrammetric research in the Department of Geomatics Engineering (formerly Surveying Engineering) at the University of Calgary appears to reflect an influence of a strong geodetic research group in the department. Dr Blais refined and expanded the SPACE-M aerial triangulation adjustment program (developed by him at the Topographical Survey Division of EMR) to include auxiliary information such as lake surfaces that are so prevalent in northern Canada. Later, statoscope and ISS data were incorporated into SPACE-M. Test flights over the Kananaskis Valley, 100 km west of Calgary, provided photography and ISS data as well as statoscope and laser profiler data for a research project undertaken in cooperation with the Canada Centre for Remote Sensing in Ottawa. These research activities tested the incorporation of auxiliary data in

SPACE-M and prepared the way for the combination of airborne sensors that are currently available for multispectral imagery for all types of environmental mapping applications.

The ability of photogrammetric techniques to position many distinct points precisely at a given epoch in time makes it attractive to use close-range photogrammetry to monitor the changes or deformations of structures at periodic intervals. Several projects of this type were undertaken, notably the Frank Slide at Turtle Mountain, and during the construction of the Jubilee Auditorium and the Olympic Speedskating Oval. The concept of machine alignment has provided another application of precise close-range photogrammetry. Using CCD cameras and specially designed targets, shaft centrelines could be positioned precisely employing near-real-time photogrammetric algorithms (Cosandier and Chapman). These subjects are also covered in chapter 16.

The increased use of digital imagery for topographic mapping sparked an interest in the development of digital methods for the transfer of control points (both pass points and ground-control points) from one image to its stereo mate. With digital imagery the coordinates of a point can be as precise as the individual pixel. Therefore by using digital image edge matching of either a ground signal or a pass point with a definite, identifiable image edge, a very precise coordinate transfer can be achieved. Blais and Lam have confirmed that image matching based on the general concept of object-oriented modelling will find many practical applications.

The integration of the airborne GPS with ISS has been researched by M.E. Cannon, and a number of research projects related to georeferencing of remotely sensed data were undertaken by K.-P. Schwarz and others. These integration projects involved the development of a special purpose photogrammetric bundle adjustment program, which is being refined for more extensive applications.

Blais also investigated the possibilities of applying to environmental studies the analytical tools and procedures developed in photogrammetry for terrain reconstruction, deformation simulation, scene rendering, and spatial visualization. Such procedures could be applied in situations ranging from local sites to global-change monitoring using appropriate data-assimilation strategies.

Concluding Remarks

The scope and extent of photogrammetric research at Canadian universities reflects the rapid development and impact of computer science, satellite data, GPS, and general information technology on the professions of surveying and mapping (now the profession of geomatics). It has also secured for Canadian universities a seat in the first row in the international photogrammetric community.

PART 4 CARTOGRAPHIC RESEARCH IN CANADA*

Introduction

Much of this volume recounts the successes of Canadian programmes in surveying and mapping, the invention of new tools for those programmes, and the responsiveness of new

---

* Part 4 was contributed by Henry W. Castner.

systems and technology to changing demands and conditions. Fundamental to these successes was a large body of research in a variety of fields both within and beyond the disciplines described here. Given the connective nature of most scientific research[25] there undoubtedly are exciting stories to be told of technological innovations in the broad field of mapping. But to tell such stories would extend this chapter beyond its stated purpose. Rather, to define its scope, it will be useful to consider the meaning of the two terms "cartographic" and "research."

Cartography

Two technical revolutions in the mapping profession in this half-century have changed the meaning of cartography. At the beginning of the postwar period, cartography referred to the display aspect of the mapping profession. Most maps produced were of an inventory nature, in relatively uniform map designs, for a very limited group of map users. Design was largely concerned with maintaining legibility and with finding the best ways of encoding information in symbols.

But the close of the Second World War saw the ultimate application for plastics and photomechanical processes to the mapping industry. Basic to this first revolution was negative scribing in which instead of inking lines and images on paper, the draftsman cut away portions of specially coated stable-base films to produce those same point, line, and area symbols. The reduction in costs and the increase in quality derived from using these materials and procedures were exceeded only by the flexibility they gave to the design process. The increasing demand to produce maps for particular users with specific needs made it necessary to alter what had been traditional approaches to design.

We are currently in the midst of a second technical revolution with the continuing development of electronic techniques associated with computers, automation, and telecommunications. The display of spatial information is now but one facet of a larger sphere of operation. The traditional boundaries between mapping steps and the disciplines supporting them have now become blurred. A host of new procedures are now possible for manipulating this information and for deriving products from it, not all of which are graphic in nature. As a result we have a host of users each with quite different needs both in the type of information they require and in the form in which it is to be used.

Cartography can now be considered a professional activity with identifiable conceptual bases whose nature and scope are undergoing dramatic changes. Whether we continue to call it cartography or create a new name for it remains to be seen. Of interest here are the underlying concepts and processes of capturing, manipulating, representing, and thinking about spatially arrayed information – the heart of the cartographic process.

Research

When cartography was but the activity of displaying spatial information produced by various surveys and data-gathering methods, research generally focused on specific problems related to production or design. Often it involved developing ways in which general findings from research in other disciplines (such as chemistry, physics, or electronics) could be integrated into existing procedures or production steps. As such, research was conducted with identifiable constraints on cost, technical options, time, or the like. This type of applied research tended to be less systematic in scientific terms, and its most distinctive characteristics were seen in its results: 1) they saw only limited circulation within the organization, 2) they received little or no independent or formal review, and 3) they were rarely related to general solutions or underlying concepts.

In the 1960s and 1970s cartographers became increasingly interested in how their map information was perceived and utilized. This generated inquiries aimed at producing general solutions and principles that could guide design in other mapping activities. For this, research had to become more systematic, utilizing increasingly sophisticated statistical procedures in order to summarize the many variables recognized in the use of maps, whether simulated in a laboratory or observed in the field. The findings of this research were widely circulated and their increasing volume over the years was a major factor in the growth of journals, monograph series, and the formal meetings and discussions that are a part of any intellectual discipline. This growth was also influenced by the development work associated with the integration of electronic technologies and procedures into surveying, data gathering, and mapping. Research supporting this integration concerned not only practical innovations but also the review of general principles.

Cartographic research has been greatly influenced by the growth of academic cartography. Cartographers in university environments were faced with two pressures. One came from the intellectual community, with its bias toward publication, wanting a more systematic model of research in order to gain intellectual acceptance. The other came from the reality that applied research often carried rewards in terms of equipment, students, and money to the university. Finding an appropriate balance between these forces has been a continuing problem for most university cartographers during the past quarter-century. This situation was exacerbated by the fact that there was at the end of the war no tradition for map producers to obtain independent or outside assessments of their traditional customs and practices. Thus academic research often did little to link diverse segments of the profession, yet in many ways it was evolutionary. It grew out of the postwar period as one aspect of a response to technological changes that affected the nature of Canadian surveying and mapping.

We now see the mapping profession as a broad array of scientific endeavours merged into one large spatial information enterprise. In it there are few seams between the gathering, storage, manipulation, and display of that information. As a result the original map-making activities and their associated technologies are often unrecognizable. But, in contrast, one can differentiate between the fundamental concept of mapping and the technological changes that have affected the ways geographic data are treated. Thus research, the second term to be defined, can refer to several things.

First, it could refer to those activities aimed at developing and implementing new technological procedures and systems. Much of the content of this book has already alluded to or described this research. Much of it had to do with the application of systems that were in fact adaptations of pure research from some other fundamental discipline.

Second, there is also research aimed at describing the increasing role that maps, air photographs, and other associated or derived products have played in the continuing development of Canada. This research is largely descriptive of the various ways in which users of spatial information employ it. Implicitly this research is also being covered in this book by the descriptions of the various changes in surveying and mapping that have taken place, largely to meet the increasing needs and demands of Canadians.

Third, research also includes work that looks more broadly at the human interaction with spatial information whether in its gathering, manipulation, or use. This kind of research attempts to define and establish a theoretical basis for how maps work by adding the perspective of how people think about maps and the information they represent, and thus what value they may place upon them. Given the second technical revolution mentioned above, we are striving to understand which mapping concepts remain invariant (and there are many) in this transition to an electronic environment, and what new intellectual (and technical) opportunities have been opened to us.

Each of these three kinds of research has produced important results that tell a distinctive story of Canadian cartography. Each will be considered in this volume. But it is this third type of research, the one corresponding most closely to the more formal, systematic research described above, that will form the strongest but not exclusive focus of this portion of chapter 12.

Agents in Support of Research

PROFESSIONAL SOCIETIES AS AGENTS

In the early postwar period cartographic research was often not reported outside the place it was conducted. Presentations of such research at professional meetings were equally rare. At the time the Canadian Institute of Surveying (CIS) was the only society that tried to represent the interests of practising cartographers as well as those of other disciplines within surveying and mapping. The chair of its cartography committee, T.H. Kihl, stated in his 1968 report "that the needs of the cartographer were being virtually ignored."[26] As a result, a decision was made to develop, in principle, a cartographic group within CIS to "fill the void that has existed for quite some time." In actuality cartographic meetings sponsored by the CIS had been held in 1962 and 1964, as reported by L.J. O'Brien and C.T. Osborne respectively.[27,28]

In 1966 and 1967 the Ontario Institute of Chartered Cartographers (OICC), which had been organized in 1959, also held cartographic meetings. But in a talk given by the cartography chair for 1967, Osborne, it had become evident "that there was no room in this field in Canada for two active cartographic groups." Events were to show quickly how dynamic and diverse the field actually was. In any case the CIS and OICC began a collaboration, which was to last many years, whereby the two societies often met simultaneously to mount technical cartographic sessions.

This led Osborne to state that "the vacuum that existed in this area just after the war when the CIS decided to stimulate interest in cartography now appears to be adequately filled."[29] The level of interest can be seen in the cartography session at the 1969 CIS convention, which was attended by some 200 people. Two technical papers were presented: "The Use of Color Photography in Orthophotography and Photomapping for the Production of Topographical Maps" by Maj. E.B. Schaubel and "Cartographic Problems in Meeting Customer Demands" by J.A. Haddon. There was also a travelogue of one delegate's travels to an international meeting in India and a display of historical maps.

Two technical papers were presented at the CIS convention in Halifax, 1970, and in Ottawa, 1971. October of that year saw the formation of a third cartographic organization, the Society of University Cartographers (SUC) made up of cartographers working in university production offices. In total the CIS now had a list of agencies and some

350 persons in Canada interested in cartographic matters. The year 1971 also saw the first of a series of special events, a cartographic symposium focusing on map use and map design – a topic that will be examined presently.

In the meantime it was becoming increasingly clear that the CIS cartography committee would have difficulty in representing all facets of interest in cartography in Canada as long as the committee remained a dependent branch of one organization. It was also brought to our collective consciousness that there were two other professional organizations in Canada with strong interests in cartography and mapping: the Association of Canadian Map Libraries (ACML), and the Canadian Association of Geographers (CAG). In an effort to include all such groups, the chair of the cartography committee, Robert St Arnaud, proposed a reorganization of the cartography committee into a Canadian (and later National) Commission for Cartography (NCC). In August of 1974 he also invited several dozen individuals, from diverse geographic regions and cartographic interests, to meet for two days at Forêt Montmorency in Québec to discuss how such a commission might operate.[30] As reported by Adam Kerr the commission came into being in June 1975.[31] Its membership included twelve persons selected from CIS members whose prime interest was cartography, all Canadian representatives to the International Cartographic Association (ICA) commissions, and one appointed delegate each from the ACML, CAG, and OICC.

From its creation the prime objective of the commission was to improve communications between cartographers, including information about research. For some years the CIS funded a newsletter, *Chronicle/Chronique*, which appeared up to six times a year. In its communication role the commission was undoubtedly effective. But it failed to win the all-out support of those who felt that a more comprehensive association was required in which all cartographers, and those interested in maps, might find collegial stimulation and greater support for the publication of research. As a result the Canadian Cartographic Association (CCA) was founded in Ottawa in October 1975, and in the following May the first meeting of l'Association Québécoise de Cartographie (or Carto-Québec) took place in Sherbrooke. This brought to seven the number of professional societies promoting, among other things, research pertinent to their memberships. By the 1990s the four organizations with specific cartographic interests claimed a collective membership of more than 3000. Clearly there were far more Canadians interested in mapping than had ever been suspected. It was during this period of growth that Canada reached a critical mass of people interested in the broad area of cartography and conducting research in its various aspects.

One way in which these numbers began to influence the research environment was in fostering cartographic meetings and symposia. The Symposium on the Influence of the Map User on Map Design was held in Kingston in September 1971 with over 100 participants from Canada, Great Britain, and the United States. It was organized by Professors Castner and McGrath of Queen's University and funded in part by the National Advisory Committee on Control Surveys and Mapping (NACCSM), the Canada Council, and Queen's University.[32] Other symposia followed in succeeding years, at different places and with various sponsors. For example the NACCSM organized a conference on urban surveying and mapping that was held the following year. The years 1977 and 1979 each saw a conference on the research and development requirements in surveys and mapping. In May of 1980 a seminar on cartographic technology was held in Edmonton through the cooperation of the CIS Edmonton branch and the CCA. It attempted to meld the use in map production of both traditional and computer technology processes for some 120 participants.

However the role of the computer increasingly became the focus of meetings and conferences. For example the State and Utility of Computer-Assisted Map and Chart Production Conference was held in 1981; the Land Data Base Management and Computer-Assisted Cartography Seminar was organized by the Ottawa branch of CIS; and a national conference on the economic development of the surveying and mapping industry met in 1986.[33] With the decade's end, each year had seen a meeting considering the latest developments and research into GIS (see, for example, GIS'90).[34] The diversity of cartographic interest can be seen in the sponsoring organizations of these and other symposia that have been held in recent years. Besides those named above, Forestry Canada, the National Capital Geographic Information Processing Group, Statistics Canada, and numerous universities have been sponsors.

The CCA and NCC extended the practice of organizations having joint or sequential annual meetings in the same geographic area. This enabled people to make efficient use of their travel funds and time to obtain broad exposure to cartographic research. For example what was to be named the First National Cartographic Day was organized by the NCC in May of 1977 in Ottawa. Two interest groups of the CCA joined with the CIS and OICC to present a variety of workshops and paper sessions. On Thursday of that week the ACML began its meetings in Montreal. Two years later the second National Cartographic Day was organized in Toronto with the participation of the NCC, CIS, CCA, and OICC. Also during this period the CCA began a series of "distributed" meetings, organized around the work of one or two of its constituent interest groups, so that cartographers across Canada could attend, regionally at least, one meeting a year. Thus there was a sharp contrast between the years 1975 and 1976. In the former the three existing organizations (ACML, CIS, and OICC) held annual meetings in three different locations. In the following year the five cartographic organizations held nine different meetings in seven different locations. Three of the six meetings that took place in 1977 were in three new geographic locations. By 1980 meetings had taken place in sixteen different cities in six different provinces. While the number of meetings per year has fallen off, the practice of joint meetings between various combinations of these professional societies has continued to the present. In addition these programmes consistently have taken up two or three days, not just a single half-day session, including not only talks and field trips, but also workshops and focused discussion periods – as one would expect in any lively, intellectual domain.

During all this time, in one way or other, the work of Canadian researchers was being presented in the world context at various meetings of the ICA and other international organizations. These activities will be described in chapter 18.

The growth and development of cartographic research in Canada was also fostered by the publication of results in various professional journals. At first there was only *The Canadian Surveyor*, published by the CIS. But in 1964 the OICC began publishing *The Cartographer*. After four years its editor and founder, Bernard Gutsell, took over its publication and changed the name to *The Canadian Cartographer*. In 1971 a monograph series, *Cartographica*, appeared and in 1980 this became the united series name. During this period an association with the CCA developed.

The numerical publication record of *Cartographica* and its predecessors reveals how the number and productivity of research-oriented cartographers has grown. Over the thirty years of its publication more than 500 articles have appeared. In the first six years there were on average ten articles published each year. With the initiation of *Cartographica* in

1971, the average number of articles doubled. The 1970s saw twenty-four monographs published, but with the merger of the journal and monograph series under this title, only twelve monographs appeared in the next decade. The mix of publications changed but the overall level of production has continued to the present.

Of perhaps greater significance has been the growth in the number of reviews published, a reflection of both the volume of research and the number of people available and interested in examining that work. In the first two decades of publication an average of nine or ten reviews appeared each year. In the early 1980s the number of reviews tripled with an average of some thirty-four reviews per year. Over 60 percent of these reviews have been of scholarly works, that is books and monographs. About one-third examined atlases, while barely 5 percent looked at maps themselves – and half of these reviews were published by 1975. Learned interest clearly has come to be focused more on thinking about the mapping process than on maps themselves.

UNIVERSITIES AND COLLEGES

This ascendance of interest in the nature of mapping rather than in map making itself can be seen in the growth of courses and programmes in cartography in colleges and universities – a topic dealt with in chapter 13. This interest is also manifest in the growth of the number of universities with a faculty conducting cartographic research, the number of such faculties, and the sum of their declared research interests. This growth is shown in table 12-1.

The steady growth in all these regards has only recently levelled off in the numbers of institutions and faculty. Nearly four out of five of all forty-one institutions reporting in 1992 have someone declaring an interest in cartographic research. The number of research interests and activities is still increasing as we continue to explore the ways in which contemporary cartography offers new challenges and opportunities. Growth in the early years of the sample reflects the development of the discipline. In 1966 fifteen (or 79 percent) of the names of faculty with interests in cartography were new; in 1970 twenty (or 87 percent) were new. But the number of new names continues, reflecting the dynamic nature of the discipline, its changing demands for expertise, and the number of other professionals attracted to it, especially with the increased use of GIS. Thus in 1986 there were twenty-three new names representing 52 percent of all geographic cartographers; in 1989 there were twenty-six (or 42 percent) new names; in 1992 another twenty-nine (or 46 percent) new names.

The apparent drop in numbers in 1986 is a reflection of the workload brought on by the *Historical Atlas of Canada* project, which involved many geographers in the preparation of atlas plates. Thus nine of the names reporting research on this project in 1980 did not appear again. The growth in all respects during the decade of the 1970s must not be unrelated to the fact that both the CCA and Carto-Québec were founded during this period. Clearly a critical number of researchers was reached, and the instruments supporting their activities matured.

The influence of a growing cadre of academic researchers can also be seen in the number of graduate degrees awarded. Within departments of geography there was only one year before 1972 when more than one degree was awarded to a cartography student somewhere in Canada; in many years there were none. The 1970s saw a surge in graduates with 1975 and 1977 being peak years with seven master's degrees awarded in each. These numbers fell dramatically early in the next decade with no degrees being awarded in 1984 and 1985.

Table 12-1
The number of declared research topics or cartographic interests by faculty in departments of geography at Canadian colleges and universities. Taken from a sample of the annual *Directory, Canadian Association of Geographers*.

Year	1963	1966	1970	1975	1980	1986	1989	1992
Number of interests	5	24	32	37	72	66	95	104
Number of individuals	5	19	23	25	50	44	62	63
Number of institutions	4	13	17	18	26	33	33	32

By decade's end, however, the numbers were exceeding those of the mid-1970s. Almost exclusively these were master's degrees as Canadians sought the Ph.D. degree elsewhere and few students from abroad came to take that degree here.

In the case of survey engineering departments, mapping programmes have long been in place, with advanced degrees being awarded as early as 1953 in the case of the University of Toronto, 1962 at Laval, and 1963 at UNB. As one would expect, these programmes were involved in many aspects of mapping so that truly cartographic research topics are overshadowed in number by those in surveying, geodesy, photogrammetry, air-photo interpretation, and remote sensing. As with geography departments the number of graduates are few and sporadic before a modest peak around 1970. There is a steady but small flow of graduates during the 1980s, and by decade's end there has been a healthy growth averaging more than ten degrees per year.

GOVERNMENT AGENCIES

The role of government agencies, especially federal, was not particularly strong before 1980. Through the instrument of the NACCSM the Surveys and Mapping Branch of the then Department of Energy, Mines and Resources supported a number of seminars and research contracts. Among the former mention has already been made of the cartographic meeting in 1966 and the Kingston symposium in 1971. Support was also forthcoming for conferences on research and development requirements in surveys and mapping in 1977, and on the state and utility of computer-assisted map and chart production in 1981. The few research contracts included a report on the administration of surveys and mapping in Canada by G.S. Andrews, former surveyor general of British Columbia,[35] and a study on the proposed nationwide adoption of the UTM grid reference system by Gordon Gracie and Brian Allen.[36] There were also conferences on research and development requirements in surveys and mapping in both 1977 and 1979.

The Topographical Survey Directorate sponsored an evaluation of the 1:250 000 map series of the NTS Series, which was carried out in 1975 by Castner and McGrath.[37] Two years later a study of the design of a tourist map series based on that NTS Series was undertaken by the same authors.[38] They also conducted a preliminary study of the design of the Canadian Nautical Chart in relation to the chart user's needs for the Department of Fisheries and Oceans, CHS.[39]

From 1981 to the present the Department of Energy, Mines and Resources entered into a number of research agreements, largely with university personnel. The number of agreements, made with researchers at sixteen different universities, has grown from five in the first year to more than two dozen in recent years. Universities receiving grants in five or more of those years included Carleton, Guelph, Laval, Memorial, New Brunswick, and Ottawa. While they covered a variety of topics, more than three out of every four dealt with automation and the development of various kinds of land or spatial information systems.

The Nature of Canadian Research in Cartography

Perhaps the research work actually performed is the most significant element of this story. There are several sources that shed light on this work: the declared active research interests of Canadian cartographers, the work of their graduate students, and the record of actual publications. The first suggests intent while the last is a measure of accomplishment. But research often necessitates many years of directed labour and thought before a published paper of value appears. In the meantime, however, presentations at meetings of professional organizations and the work of graduate students indicate progress and help to refine research goals into useful products. Canadians have produced an impressive body of research on all aspects of map making and cartography. But it is clear that there have been three areas of particular interest and strength: 1) cartographic communication including map design and map user needs; 2) computer cartography including automation and GIS; and 3) the history of cartography, particularly in the mapping of Canadian territories.

An analysis of the articles published in *Cartographica*, the cartographic journal with the most comprehensive coverage of the subject, shows that one-fifth of the more than 500 articles published since 1963 were in the general area of computer cartography, another 20 percent on the history of cartography, and one-seventh examined topics in cartographic communication. The design, production, and history of atlas making comprised another 7 percent. There are a number of other topics that have been addressed more or less continuously over this thirty-year period, but which individually account for only 2–5 percent of the items. These include (in descending order) education and training, data generalization, symbolization, special-purpose mapping, topographic and reference mapping, image generalization, map projections and coordinate systems, production techniques, and thematic mapping.

The apparently low attention paid to thematic mapping is due to the fact that many cartographic communication studies are addressing questions in thematic map design. During these thirty years if we add the some fifty cartographic articles published in *The Canadian Surveyor*, the number of articles on subjects pertinent to large-scale, thematic, and special-purpose mapping increases somewhat but the percentage of all articles published is hardly changed.

The articles in *Cartographica*, however, are not all written by Canadians because it is a journal with international support in both its contributors and readers. A more comprehensive national picture emerges when one considers the declared research projects by geographic cartographers as in table 12-1 above. A breakdown of those numbers is shown in table 12-2.

It is clear that the production of atlases and maps for particular regions, processes, or phenomena has been and continues as an important focus of short bursts of creative energy. Research interests in the history of cartography appear in the mid-1960s and grow to a modest peak in 1980. This interest appears to have fallen off but it will probably continue at a low but consistent rate. A slow but continuous growth is seen in cartographic communication, map design, and map use. This interest began sometime in the mid-1960s. Later

Table 12-2
The number of declared research projects or cartographic interests by faculty in departments of geography at Canadian colleges and universities arranged by special topics. Taken from a sample of the annual *Directory*, Canadian Association of Geographers.

Year	1963	1966	1970	1975	1980	1986	1989	1992
Mapping and atlases	5	14	14	14	20	9	19	10
History	–	5	6	3	10	3	4	3
Communication, design	–	3	3	4	9	8	12	8
Automation, computer	–	–	6	8	8	20	15	15
GIS	–	–	–	1	2	9	26	44
Education	–	–	–	4	3	4	4	7
Other	1	2	3	2	9	11	13	15

in that decade an unrelated interest in the computer appeared and experienced tremendous growth, peaking in the mid-1980s. In the mid-1970s this interest evolved into one in GIS, experienced a meteoric rise in the late 1980s and early 1990s, and does not appear to be losing momentum. GIS, automation, and computer cartography now account for nearly 60 percent of all expressed research interests in cartographic topics. However a closer look at these expressed and published interests reveals that more than two-thirds of them have to do with broad aspects of cartography and mapping, for example image and data generalization, compilation, and education and training. In other words while the nature of map making has changed, the operation of SIS is bringing research back to problems concerned with the basic cartographic operations of information gathering, manipulation, and use.

With an increased understanding of how maps are used and of the visual process itself, and with concerns about the effects of technology, cartographers in the 1970s developed a more formal interest in education (particularly of young children, the future map users) and the training of future cartographers. Much of this is reported on in chapter 13.

MAP DESIGN, CARTOGRAPHIC COMMUNICATION,
AND MAP-USER NEEDS

Reference was made earlier to the technical revolution at the end of the Second World War involving plastics and photomechanical processes. These improved materials and procedures allowed greater freedom to manipulate the various composite map images, that is the various information-carrying components. During this time there were a number of more general developments. These included the elaboration of black-and-white aerial photography into the great variety of products remotely sensed, the great increase in the availability of specialist information about both physical and human environments, and the arrival of the computer, which made it possible to manipulate all this information for specific display purposes.[40] As well there was the general growth of the social sciences including geography, and the quantitative revolution that made geographers aware of the power of descriptive and inferential statistics. All this gave impetus to the production of thematic maps. In such an environment, where the number of expressive possibilities has been increased technologically, the question arose as to which solution is the best. This led to inquiries into the role of the intended map, that is, what do its potential users want to do with it? What information do they want from it? What designs facilitate these acquisitions? In time we came to the more basic questions of how the map works: how information is acquired visually and thus what is the nature of human visual perception and cognition?

Research of this sort, in various forms, first started appearing in the late 1960s. Of particular interest was how well maps were meeting the needs of those who used them. For commercial map producers this information came from sales. For government agencies, however, various systematic surveys had to be employed.[41] Hence there was, for example, a study of the use requirements and users of a topographic map series at scale 1:12 500.[42] Others examined the information needs of the users of topographic maps,[43] maps of national parks,[44] a provincial highway map,[45] and charts for recreational boaters.[46]

Early master's theses illustrate another approach by trying to establish the communicative effectiveness of various coloured dot symbols,[47] visually equal-stepped grey values,[48] hue contrasts on thematic maps,[49] methods of relief representation on topographic maps,[50] and different designs of isopleth maps.[51] For this research experimental subjects were asked, directly or indirectly, if they could see certain symbol contrasts. The indirect questioning relied on timing visual search tasks to measure the ease or difficulty of extracting information accurately from maps,[52] or studying eye-movement recordings to see how subjects reacted visually to particular map designs while performing specific map-use tasks.[53]

Implicit in all these methodologies is that with the knowledge of the information needs of map users, and the visual tasks required to extract that information from complex graphic images, cartographers would be better able to design maps for those users.[54] As a result more specialized research has been directed at the design and perception of specific map elements, and at designing maps for particular map users. In the first category studies by Grant Head have examined the differentiation of the land/water boundary,[55] and Clifford Wood has studied the role of map design in segregating figural elements from background information.[56] Brian Cromie has examined the perception of contours (see note 52), while others have examined shaded relief[57] and point symbols for tourist maps.[58] The general use of colour in thematic map design is described by Janet Mersey and Ronald Eyton.[59,60]

Arising from this type of research have been attempts to articulate general rules for manipulating the expressive variables in graphic communication. These variables include such things as the size, colour value, texture, colour hue, orientation, and shape of image elements. Some of these attempts summarized large areas of research,[61] while Jean-Claude Muller interpreted the work of the French semiologist Jacques Bertin for North American cartographers[62] and Louise Marcotte did the same for children.[63]

The second category has included studies of blind users,[64] the use of maps by children,[65] maps employed in engineering planning,[66] and the use of maps in the media.[67] Map use by those who study cities and urban systems is covered by Jean Raveneau and D.C Symons,[68] whilst Philip Sooke investigated the use of maps by astronomers.[69]

Cartographic research has also been concerned with a wide range of problems associated with generalization, both of image components[70] and numerical information. Some fundamental problems in mapping such data by point and line symbols were investigated by Ross Mackay.[71] His work was elaborated by Jenks and Coulson,[72] who developed rules for classing data in statistical maps. The close connection between these concerns, the development of thematic cartography, and the general research of geographers was pointed out by Raveneau.[73] The perception of statistical maps, and the visual tasks undertaken with them, have also been studied.[74] However the fullest elaboration and application of statistical procedures has been with the development of GIS and the numerical analysis that has accompanied them.

The theory of map communication has attracted the attention of those who have simply posed the question "What is a map?"[75] to those who have argued that a true map must have a meaningful context, without which it is simply a supplier of isolated information.[76] There have also been attempts to develop the idea of cartography as language by reference to the theories of sign systems[77] and artificial intelligence and expert systems[78] Implications for education of these theoretical approaches to cartography have also been explored.[79]

One other outgrowth of the interest in map users has been in the value placed upon spatial information. In these times of fiscal restraint, when map makers increasingly must recoup their costs, a new research interest has been considering how spatial information should be marketed – the topic of chapter 17.

COMPUTER CARTOGRAPHY, AUTOMATION, AND GIS

The second technical revolution, referred to at the outset of this section, involves the computer. The introduction of the computer into the mapping process made it possible to handle larger amounts of information, to perform other operations upon it, and to relieve humans of many repetitive production tasks. As a result the first attempts to use the computer were in the automation of basic steps in the map-making process. As well concurrent developments in photogrammetry and remote sensing, reported in chapters 3 and 14, made possible the automatic gathering of vast quantities of data and the positioning of this information on useful spatial frameworks that is on theoretical geodetic surfaces for storage and manipulation, and on various map projections for presentation and use.

The early solutions to these problems utilized computer hardware and software designed for uses other than map making. As a result much cartographic research focused on how they might be usefully adapted to map making. Fundamental solutions were sought using information in digital form in which values are represented by a number code. Digital mapping rests on the proposition that map features are symbolized by points, lines, and area symbols whose position and extent are described by x, y coordinates. These coordinates, suitably coded, can be transmitted, transformed, selected, and processed in a computer in order to change their datum, projection, scale, and level of generalization. The coordinates can then be used to control the drafting and revision of a display within some computer environment. The accuracy of the resultant image is directly limited by the density of x, y coordinates and indirectly influenced by other factors such as the quality of the technology, source materials, the procedures utilized, and the operational personnel. All of these operations and factors are the subjects of research, many of which are also reported elsewhere in this volume. The overall record of research in this important area is difficult to describe and characterize because of two factors: the dynamic nature of developments and the sometimes unique characteristics of the contexts in which they took place.

The dynamic growth of computer cartography, as suggested by table 2, was a reflection of the challenge of so many unprecedented technical problems in map making, problems whose solutions held so much promise. With few guides to show the way, the place and timing of the reporting of research were probably more significant than where ultimately it was published. The importance of exchanges at conferences and personal communications are acknowledged by many. One observer asserts that "we did not publish our results … We worked on specific grants and contracts and, as soon as one was complete, busily hurried off to the next one."[80] Another declares that "we were far too busy to write papers in the early days and there was no compelling need to do so. But there were personal contacts."[81] The fact that much research was carried out by groups of people also makes it difficult to track the progress of ideas and developments. One of the most striking features of developments in the 1960s was that initiatives were occurring independently in many places, often without reference to, and even in ignorance of, related work.[82] Added to this is the international (both locational and participatory) and cross-disciplinary nature of this research. For example since the early 1970s Canadians from many different disciplines have been active in a number of international venues that will be reported in chapter 18. All this is not to diminish the significance of the published reports. But for the reader of this volume, the research cited herein provides primarily historic records and general surveys of the problems being addressed.

Many of the reports of research include considerable discussion of the particular system in or for which the research was conducted. Why this is so is not clear. But given the great variety of hardware and software, limited in the early years by the narrow vision of the non-cartographers who developed it, it is not surprising that much of the computer cartography research is specific to particular technological settings and to the practical concerns with map making, rather than to concerns with map using.[83]

Efforts to move to partially automated map making began in the late 1960s and early 1970s. Harris pointed out that the tasks suitable for automation had long since been identified.[84] There were many occasions, as during the Second World War, when special operations required, for example, the compilation onto existing maps of specialist or more recently acquired field information, the reclassification of roads and bridges on medium-scale maps, to be used by army combat vehicles, and recalculations of coordinate positions when changing a projection's central meridian on large-scale maps for tactical use by artillery. Such laborious tasks could, theoretically, be accomplished far more easily with the aid of a computer.

It is therefore not surprising that the drive to automation was led by the national mapping organization, the Surveys and Mapping Branch. The development, reported in part in chapters 3 and 15, involved a number of steps taken sequentially through the decade beginning with 1967. This sequence reflected the evolution of a system philosophy and illuminated the research agendas necessary to support it. Initially there were practical problems in making a pilot system operational, such as in perfecting off-line topographic data capture (e.g., digitizing) and processing in batch mode. It soon became a necessity, however, to make digitizing an on-line procedure for detecting procedural and hardware errors and in reducing turn-around time. For the system to develop in complexity, research had to focus on questions of generalization and system control (i.e., interfacing). In order to meet the information demands of an increasing number of cartographic and land-related information users, ways of integrating thematic information into the topographic database had to be developed. Finally, there was the need to perfect the system to accommodate emerging technologies such as image processing and data sharing through networking. Much of this record of development has been described by Harris,[85] and subsequently by Allam,[86] Gibbons,[87] Linders,[88] and Moore and Simpson.[89]

This general developmental sequence was not exclusive to the Surveys and Mapping Branch, for many Canadians have conducted research or reported on the questions that it implies. These have involved developing such basic system capabilities as digitizing, edge matching, generalizing and editing, polygonization, labelling, plotting, storing, managing and updating information, browsing, and plotting a desired map. The development of these capabilities involves solving many more and sometimes overlapping tasks.[90]

For example digitizing has progressed from labour-intensive manual methods[91] to semi-automated, but largely unsuccessful, line-following systems.[92] Today's truly automated digitizers are raster scanners that replace an operator's movements with a mechanical sensor that subdivides space into a matrix of regular cells or pixels, which are then individually classified.[93] Each type of digitizing produces a distinctive type of data: raster in the case of scanning, and vector where features have both x, y coordinate and directional components. As well there are encoding problems when features have both geographic and useful attribute characteristics.[94] To provide multiple access to such encoded data, and still achieve computational efficiency, special data structures must be created.[95]

Once captured, techniques are developed for conserving valuable computer storage space by reducing the number of points required to accurately represent linear features,[96] or by compressing the raster records.[97] Given the value of both types of data to mapping, and the ease of certain manipulations when information is in a particular form, much effort has been directed toward simulating one with the other and toward ways of converting one to the other.

A related concern has been to develop standards of data storage that are sufficiently flexible so that the information remains accessible even as systems and requirements change.[98] As Evangelatos shows, this is a complex issue that affects many aspects of systems and persons involved with the use of its information.[99] Without solutions further growth of GIS will likely be impeded.

Edge matching, another basic system capability, originally referred to a process of ensuring that digitized details along the edge of two adjacent map sheets or photographs match correctly. In fact there are a number of related problems that have been classified as "spatial adjacency" issues.[100] These include problems of interpolation, error estimation, and building of polygon structures around designated centroids (polygonization). For example the creation of digital terrain models depends on various "linkages" for interpolation between adjacent data points.[101] But procedures are also needed to ensure the matching of boundaries of networks of digitized areas.[102]

Research has also been directed at producing traditional maps in new and more efficient ways and at developing new map products. Among the former have been the development of new machine approaches to contouring[103] and the production of marine charts by automated means.[104] Achieving the requirements of interactive display and edit facilities is critical to the creation of thematic maps for specialist users.[105] Such users may be census takers, as suggested by Yan and Bradley, or novices to map reading, as described by Castonguay and Thouez.[106,107] Such interactive displays are fundamental to new products such as electronic atlases,[108] and the electronic charts mentioned in chapter 8.[109] Interactive displays also demonstrate the new manipulative possibilities provided by computer systems that allow users to interrogate the data and try a number of solutions to problems.

During the 1970s new communications technologies emerged. Videotex systems allow information retrieval and display in graphic or textual form on a video screen or home television set. Fraser Taylor has described the cartographic potential of Telidon, a Canadian system.[110] Videodisc technologies have much higher storage capacities and longer life, and with a microcomputer offer random accessibility of visual imagery, including maps.[111] Such a system has been developed by the Québec government for its integrated information system of natural fauna.[112] Beyond this Tomlinson envisioned the possibility that some GIS may develop the capability, now available in some CAD systems and flight simulators, of scene generation, that is the ability to create and "move around" three-dimensional landscapes and built forms.[113]

In all these situations the spatial information or a database has become the unifying element around which systems of data gathering, processing, and presentation are being developed and cartography itself is being defined. These GIS have come to be valued in all aspects of environmental research, social planning, and municipal and governmental affairs.

HISTORY OF CARTOGRAPHY

As suggested by table 12-2 there has been a continual interest in the history of the discovery, exploration, and settlement of Canadian lands as expressed in maps. In describing the richness of this work Richard Ruggles lists over 180 works, albeit many by non-Canadians, on a dozen different themes.[114] He also presents evidence and expresses the hope that soon there might be a history of the cartography of Canada to take its place alongside Don Thompson's *tour-de-force*, *Men and Meridians*. Given this review by Ruggles, and the great survey works he singles out,[115] the overview here can only be cursory and limited to the works of Canadians.

The mapping of native peoples has attracted some interest as with the work of Spink and Moodie on the Inuit maps of the eastern Arctic, of Moodie on Indian map making of the fur-trade West, and of Pentland on cartographic concepts among the Northern Algonquin.[116,117,118] Beattie has surveyed the Indian maps in the Hudson's Bay Company archives.[119] But the work of native Canadians remains a largely uncultivated field.

The role played by European explorers and cartographers has been an important focus. For example reflections of seventeenth-century European cartographic thought are seen in the maps of Newfoundland as described by Fabian O'Day[120] and of New France as outlined by Heidenreich,[121] and particularly the maps of Samuel de Champlain discussed by Heidenreich and Dahl.[122] The many questions raised about the John Cabot voyages are addressed by T.P. Jost and O'Day.[123] J.S. Pritchard has studied early French hydrographic surveys of the St Lawrence River and their charting of the east coast of Canada.[124] Historical plans, maps, and sketches have been reproduced in facsimile as they relate to New France and to Manitoba.[125,126] Ontario's History in Maps has been very well documented by Gentilcore and Head.[127] Ruggles, in many different works, particularly his monumental volume of 1991, documented the role of traders with the Hudson's Bay Company.[128,129] Verner has studied the English firm of Aaron Arrowsmith and its contributions to the mapping of Canada, and considered the maps of nineteenth-century explorers in the Canadian Arctic.[130,131]

As one would expect, the exploration and mapping of all areas of Canada have been examined. These include Newfoundland,[132] Acadia,[133] New Brunswick and Nova Scotia,[134] and New France, mapped by early cartographers such as Franquelin,[135] Bellin,[136] and Chaussegros de Lery.[137] To the west there are studies of Huronia,[138] southern Ontario,[139] districts of western Upper Canada,[140] and the Great Lakes.[141] The western interior in French maps has been examined,[142] as well as the cartographic documents relating to the Riel Rebellions.[143] Research on perimeter areas of Canada has included British Columbia,[144] the Kootenay,[145] Hearne's route through the North-west,[146] and the Arctic islands.[147] The pioneering map making of the Royal Engineers, 1845–1906, and its influence on the development of British Columbia have been described by Frances Woodward.[148] Even the mapping of urban areas has received attention as with Ottawa,[149] Québec,[150] and Winnipeg.[151] The cartography of the fire insurance industry has been well documented by Hayward,[152] and with Woodward.[153] Many of these and other similar reports can be found in Farrell and Desbarats' collection of essays.[154] The significant contributions of Canadians in the field of national, provincial, and county atlases are considered in chapter 10.

The interest in the history of mapping has not, however, been limited to Canadian lands. Studies of specific areas include East Africa,[155] and Russia from classical times to 1800,[156] and during much of the seventeenth to the nineteenth centuries.[157] Specific mapping activities in foreign lands have focused on the work of the British Directorate of Overseas Surveys,[158] and the mapping associated with Napoleon's invasion of Egypt.[159]

There is also a growing body of work examining the very process of studying the history of cartography and its impact on other disciplines. Joan Winearls has provided an important buttress for all historical research by elaborating the cartobibliographic theory and practice for precisely describing the various cartographic documents.[160] The value of historical maps as sources of historical evidence has been considered both in general terms,[161] and in terms specific to geographers.[162]

Finally, there are a number of studies on technical aspects of cartography. These range from research on the techniques and instruments used in the fifteenth to nineteenth centuries to incorporate tones and shadings on maps,[163] to a mathematical examination of Mercator's famous map projection.[164] Of interest have been David Thompson's instruments and methods used in his work in the north-west, and particularly how he determined longitude.[165,166] Mackay describes the work of Canada's first chief geographer, James White, whose developing office was responsible for a standard base map of Canada, a fifty-sheet map series that was a forerunner of the NTS Series, and for the publication of the first edition of the *Atlas of Canada*.[167]

Conclusion

The research that has been described in this chapter has to a large extent been responsible for the complete change not only in the worldwide practice of surveying and mapping since the Second World War but also in the way we understand how users interact with the information maps contain. In 1945 plane tables were still the principal mapping instrument in Canada; baselines were still being measured by Invar wire; and maps were being drawn by pen and ink for a relatively small number of specialized users. From the results of a broad range of research efforts, Canadians have been at the forefront in the development of modern spatial information systems that are utilized and valued by a great variety of map users. In addition we have created significant methodologies for the study of the spatial information needs of map users, and how, in theory and in practice, this information is manipulated and utilized. These are accomplishments in which Canadians can certainly take great pride.

NOTES

1 Vanicek, Petr, and E.J. Krakiwsky. 1986. *Geodesy, The Concepts*. New York: Elsevier Publishing Co.

2 Wells, David, Ed. 1986. *Guide to GPS Positioning*. Fredericton: Canadian GPS Associates.

3 Gregerson, L.F. 1958. The Most Probable Value of a Set of Observations. *The Canadian Surveyor*, 15, 6, 333–9.

4 Jones, H.E., ed. 1982. *Surveying Offshore Canada Lands for Mineral Development*, 3d ed. Ottawa: Department of Energy, Mines and Resources.

5 Gregerson, L.F. 1970. An Investigation into the MOM Gi B2 Gyroscopic Theodolite. *The Canadian Surveyor*, 24, 1, 117–35.

6 Jones, H.E. 1969. Ties between Continents by Means of Radio Telescopes. *The Canadian Surveyor*, 23, 4, 377–88.

7 Barnes, D. Craig. 1990. *Moving to NAD83*. Ottawa: The Canadian Institute of Surveying and Mapping.

8 Blachut, T.J., and R. Burkhardt. 1988. *Historical Development of Photogrammetric Methods and Instruments*. Washington: American Society of Photogrammetry and Remote Sensing.

9 Blachut, T.J. 1955. Airborne Controlled Method of Aerial Triangulation. *Photogrammetria*, 12.

10 Schut, G.H. 1956. Analytical Aerial Triangulation. *The Canadian Surveyor*, 13, 10, 92–8.
Schut, G.H. 1964. Practical Methods of Analytical Block Adjustments for Strips, Sections and Models. *The Canadian Surveyor*, 18, 5, 352–72.
Schut, G.H. 1980. Block Adjustment of Bundles. *The Canadian Surveyor*, 34, 2, 139–52.

11 Helava, U.V. 1957. New Principles for Photogrammetric Plotters. *The Canadian Surveyor*, 14, 2, 89–96.

12 Blachut, T.J., and U.V. Helava. 1960. Second International Conference on the Analytical Plotter, Opening Remarks (Blachut), The Analytical Plotter (Helava). *The Canadian Surveyor*, 17, 2, 130–48.

13 Jaksic, Z. 1976. The Significance of Analytical Instruments for the Development of Methods and Techniques in Photogrammetric Data Processing. *Archives of the Thirteenth Congress of the International Society for Photogrammetry*, Helsinki, vol. 21.

14 Blachut, T.J. 1963. Monomeasurements in Photogrammetric Operations. *Conference of the Commonwealth Survey Officers*, Cambridge. Paper 49. London: Commonwealth Association of Surveying and Land Economy.

15 Smialowski, A.J. 1963. The NRC Monocomparator. *The Canadian Surveyor*. 17, 2, 224–32.

16 Blachut, T.J., and A.J. Smialowski. Monocomparator. Canadian patent 024 666, 9 July 1968; U.S. patent 839 580, 7 July 1969.

17 Blachut, T.J. 1960. Second International Mapping Experiment – Renfrew Test Area. Results of Experimental Plotting for 1:50 000 Maps. *The Canadian Surveyor*. 15, 3, 137–70.

18 Forstner, R. 1963. Further Results of the Renfrew International Experiment. *The Canadian Surveyor*, 17, 1, 27–35, and 17, 2, 60–7.

19 Blachut, T.J. 1957. Use of Photogrammetry in the Legal Survey Project at Alnwick. *The Canadian Surveyor*, 14, 8, 336–49.

20 Blachut, T.J. 1971. Winter Photographs in Cadastral Surveying. *The Canadian Surveyor*, 25, 5, 603–12.

21 Collins, S.H. 1968. Stereoscopic Orthophoto Maps. *The Canadian Surveyor*, 22, 1, 167–76.

22 Hauman, D. 1963. Surveying Glaciers on Axel Heiberg Island. *The Canadian Surveyor*, 17, 2, 81–95.
Mueller, F. 1963. An Arctic Research Expedition and Its Reliance on Large-Scale Maps. *The Canadian Surveyor*, 17, 2, 96–112.

23 Mueller, F. 1963. Axel Heiberg Island, Preliminary Report, 1961–1962. Montreal: Dept of Geography, McGill University.

24 Blachut, T.J., A. Chrzanowski, and J.H. Saastamoinen. 1979. *Urban Surveying and Mapping.* New York: Springer-Verlag. Blachut and Burkhardt. 1988. *Historical Development.*

25 Burke, James. 1978. *Connections.* Toronto: Little, Brown & Co.

26 Kihl, T.H. 1968. Report of the Cartography Committee. *The Canadian Surveyor,* 22, 3, 316.

27 O'Brien, L.J., ed. 1962. *Canadian Cartography: Proceedings of the Symposium on Cartography.* Ottawa: CIS.

28 Osborne, C.T., ed. 1964. *Canadian Cartography: Proceedings of the Symposium on Cartography.* Ottawa: CIS.

29 Osborne, C.T. 1967. Report of the Cartographic Committee. *The Canadian Surveyor,* 28, 3, 261.

30 St-Arnaud, Robert. 1974. Report of the Cartographic Committee. *The Canadian Surveyor,* 28, 4, 357.
St-Arnaud, Robert. 1975. Report of the Cartographic Committee. *The Canadian Surveyor,* 29, 3, 261.

31 Kerr, Adam J. 1976. Report of the National Commission for Cartography. *The Canadian Surveyor,* 30, 4, 328–9.

32 Castner, Henry W., and Gerald McGrath, eds. 1971. *Map Design and the Map User. Cartographica,* monograph no. 2. Toronto: B.V. Gutsell.

33 Kennedy, E.A., and N. Thyer. 1987. *Proceedings, National Conference on the Economic Development of the Surveys and Mapping Industry.* Ottawa: published jointly by the CISM, NACCSM, and CAAS.

34 See for example GIS'90: *Making it Work.* Proceedings. (An international symposium on geographic information systems.) Co-sponsored by Forestry Canada and Reid, Collins and Associates.

35 Andrews, G.S. 1970. *Administration of Surveys and Mapping in Canada, 1968.* Ottawa: Surveys and Mapping Branch, EMR.

36 Gracie, Gordon, and Brian Allen. 1975. *A Study of the Proposed Nationwide Adoption of the Universal Transverse Mercator Grid Reference System.* Ottawa: Surveys and Mapping Branch, EMR.

37 McGrath, Gerald, and Henry W. Castner. 1975. *An Evaluation of the 1:250 000 Series of the National Topographic System and Possible Modifications to the Series.* Interim report under contract OSU 3–0551. Ottawa: Department of Energy, Mines and Resources, Surveys and Mapping Branch, Topographical Survey Directorate.

38 McGrath, Gerald, and Henry W. Castner. 1977. *The Design of a Tourist Series based on the National Topographic 1:250 000 Map Series.* Final report under contract 02SU.23246–5–5596. Ottawa: Department of Energy, Mines and Resources, Surveys and Mapping Branch, Topographical Survey Directorate.

39 Castner, Henry W., and Gerald McGrath, with the assistance of Sally Rudd. 1992. *Preliminary Study of the Design of the Canadian Nautical Chart in Relation to the Chart User's Needs.* Final report under contract #OSC81–00060. Dartmouth, NS: Department of Fisheries and Oceans, Canadian Hydrographic Service.

40 See Castner, Henry W. 1983. Research Questions and Cartographic Design. In D.R.F. Taylor, ed. *Graphic Communication and Design in Contemporary Cartography.* Toronto: John Wiley, 87–8.

41 For example McGrath, Gerald, and R.P. Kirby. 1969. Survey Methods on the Use of Maps and Atlases. *Canadian Cartographer,* 6, 2, 132–48.

42 McGrath, Gerald. 1967 and 1968. *The Users and Uses of Official Maps of Jamaica.* Report to the Director of Surveys, Jamaica; Parts I and II.

43 St-Arnaud, Robert. 1971. The Role of the User in the Map Communication Process. In Castner and McGrath, eds. *Map Design and the Map User*, 18–22.

Sebert L.M. 1971. Problems in Satisfying the Needs of the Canadian 1:50 000 Map Users. In Castner and McGrath, eds. *Map Design and the Map User*, 54–61.

44 McGrath, Gerald. 1971. The Mapping of National Parks: A Methodological Approach. In Castner and McGrath, eds. *Map Design and the Map User*, 71–6.

45 Anderson, Jacqueline. 1975. A Road Map Study Based on the 1974 Official Alberta Road Map. Master's thesis, University of Alberta.

Anderson, Jacqueline. 1977. Map User Research and Modern Road Map Design. *The Canadian Surveyor*, 31, 1, 62–4.

46 Kerr, Adam J. 1978. Designing Navigational Charts to Meet the Needs of Recreational Boaters on the Great Lakes. *The Canadian Surveyor*, 32, 3, 321–30.

47 Zvankin, I.M. 1968. An Exploratory Study into the Communicative Effectiveness of the Multi-Colored Geographic Dot Symbol and Munsell Color Space. Master's thesis, University of Manitoba.

48 Meinhardt, Aldy. 1970. An Analysis of Visually Equal-Stepped Gray Values for Automated Cartography. Master's thesis, University of Victoria.

49 Campbell, C. 1972. A User-Oriented Approach to Perception of Hue Contrast on Thematic Maps. Master's thesis, University of Alberta.

50 Brandes, Donald. 1975. Relative Effectiveness of Selected Relief Representation Methods for Topographic Maps. Master's thesis, University of Calgary.

51 Underwood, Jean D.M. 1975. Perceiver Variables and the Interpretation of Isopleth Maps. Master's thesis, University of Waterloo.

52 For example Cromie, Brian W. 1978. Contour Design and the Topographic Map User. Master's thesis, Queen's University.

53 Castner, Henry W., and J. Ronald Eastman. 1984. Eye-Movement Parameters and Perceived Map Complexity – Part I. *American Cartographer*, 11, 2, 107–17.

1985. Eye-Movement Parameters and Perceived Map Complexity – Part II. *American Cartographer*, 12, 1, 40.

54 Castner, Henry, and Gerald McGrath. 1984. Educating Map Publishers: Evaluating Changes in Map Design on the Basis of Map Reading Activities and Visual Tasks. *Technical Papers*. Perth: Twelfth Conference of the International Cartographic Association, 680–90.

55 Head, C. Grant. 1972. Land-Water Differentiation in Black and White Cartography. *Canadian Cartographer*, 9, 1, 25–38.

56 Wood, Clifford. 1992. Is Cartographic Design Important? The Example of the Figure-Ground Relationship. *CISM Journal*, 46, 4, 435–48.

57 Castner, Henry W., and Roger Wheate. 1979. Re-assessing the Role Played by Shaded Relief in Topographic Scale Maps. *Cartographic Journal*, 16, 2, 77–85.

58 Forrest, David, and Henry W. Castner. 1985. The Design and Perception of Point Symbols for Tourist Maps. *Cartographic Journal*, 22, 1, 11–19.

59 Mersey, Janet E. 1990. Colour and Thematic Map Design. The Role of Colour Scheme and Map Complexity in Choropleth Map Communication. *Cartographica*, monograph no. 41.

60 Eyton, J. Ronald. 1990. Color Stereoscopic Effect Cartography. *Cartographica*, 27, 1, 20–9.

61 For example, chapter 7 in Castner, Henry. 1990. *Seeking New Horizons: A Perceptual Approach to Geographic Education*. Montreal: McGill-Queen's University Press.

62 Muller, Jean-Claude. 1981. Bertin's Theory of Graphics: A Challenge to North American Thematic Cartography. *Cartographica*, 18, 3, 1–8.

63 Marcotte, Louise. 1984. Et mis en image, par Pierre E. Roy. *La planète du silence: initiation au language silencieux de la graphique.* Montreal: Musée d'art contemporain de Montréal.

64 Squirrell, Ray B. 1983. A New Approach to Tactile Maps. In Joseph W. Wiedel, ed. *Proceedings, First International Symposium on Maps and Graphics for the Visually Handicapped.* Washington, March 10–12. Bethesda, MD: ACSM.

Nagel, Diana, L. Dacen, and Michael Coulson. 1990. Tactual Mobility Maps: A Comparative Study. *Cartographica*, 27, 2, 47–63.

65 Carswell, Ronald J.B. 1971. Children's Abilities in Topographic Map Reading. In Castner and McGrath, eds. *Map Design and the Map User*, 40–5.

Anderson, Jacqueline. 1993. Mapping in the Future: The Needs of Young Children. *Proceedings. Sixteenth International Cartographic Conference.* Cologne, Germany: ICA, 797–804.

66 McLennan, K.A. 1971. Published Map Use in a Consulting Engineering Office. In Castner and McGrath, eds. Map Design and the Map User, 7–12.

Moldofsky, Byron M. 1989. The Use of Geographic Information in Addressing 'Semi-Structured' Problems in the Planning Process. Master's thesis, Queen's University.

67 Gauthier, Majella-J. 1988. *La cartographie dans les médias – Cartography in the Media.* Québec: Les Presses de l'Université du Québec.

68 Raveneau, Jean, ed. 1972. *Les méthodes de la cartographie urbane.* Québec: Association des géographes du Québec. (Edition des Actes d'un colloque organisé par l'auteur.)

Symons, D.C. 1973. Automatic Mapping and Its Relation to Urban Information Systems. In Aubrey LeBlanc, ed. 1973. *Computer Cartography in Canada. Cartographica*, monograph no. 9. Toronto: B.V. Gutsell, 49–61.

69 Stooke, Philip J. 1991. Lunar and Planetary Cartographic Research at the University of Western Ontario. *CISM Journal*, 45, 1, 23–31.

70 For example Rusak Mazur, Ela, and Henry W. Castner. 1990. Horton's Ordering Scheme and the Generalization of River Networks. *Cartographic Journal.*, 27, 2, 104–12.

71 Mackay, J. Ross. 1949. Dotting the Dot Map. *Surveying and Mapping*, 9, 3–10.

Mackay, J. Ross. 1951. Some Problems and Techniques in Isopleth Mapping. *Economic Geography*, 27, 1, 1–9.

Mackay, J. Ross. 1953. The Alternative Choice in Isopleth Interpolation. *Professional Geographer*, 5, 2–4.

72 Jenks, George F., and Michael R.C. Coulson. 1963. Generalization in Statistical Mapping. *Annals, AAG*, 53, 15–26.

73 Raveneau, Jean. 1970. La cartographie thematique: technique auxiliaire ou discipline autonome? *Canadian Cartographer*, 7, 1, 61–6.

74 Muller, Jean-Claude. 1976. Objective and Subjective Comparisons in Choropleth Mapping. *Cartographic Journal*, 13, 156–66.

Muller, Jean-Claude. 1980. Visual Comparison of Continuously Shaded Maps. *Cartographica*, 17, 1, 40–52.

Mak, Katherine, and Michael R.C. Coulson. 1991. Map-User Response to Computer-Generated Choropleth Maps: Comparative Experiments in Classification and Symbolization. *C&GIS*, 18, 2, 109–24.

75 Freundschuh, Scott et al. 1990. What Is a Map? *Cartographic Journal*, 27, 2, 119–23.

76 Guelke, Leonard. 1976. Cartographic Communication and Geographic Understanding. *Canadian Cartographer*, 13, 2, 107–22.

77 Schlichtmann, Hansgeorg. 1985. Characteristic Traits of the Semiotic System 'Map Symbolism.' *Cartographic Journal*, 22, 1, 23–30.

78 Head, C. Grant, ed. 1988. *Report on the First North American Seminar on the Concepts of Cartographic Language*. Waterloo: Wilfred Laurier University.

79 Castner, Henry. 1991. Cartographic Languages and Cartographic Education. *CISM Journal*, 45, 1, 81–88.

80 Chrisman, Nicholas. 1988. The Risks of Software Innovation: A Case Study of the Harvard Lab. *American Cartographer*, 15, 3, 291–300, 296.

81 Tomlinson, Roger. 1988. The Impact of the Transition from Analogue to Digital Cartographic Representation. *American Cartographer*, 15, 3, 249–61, 256.

82 Coppock, J.T. 1988. The Analogue to Digital Revolution: A View From an Unreconstructed Geographer. *American Cartographer*, 15, 3, 263–75, 263.

83 Tomlinson, The Impact of the Transition from Analogue to Digital Cartographic Representation, 249–61.

84 Harris, Lewis J. 1983. *The Canadian Automated Cartography System Development*. Ottawa: Surveys and Mapping Branch, EMR.

85 Harris, Lewis J. 1973. An Approach to Automatic Cartography for Topographic Mapping in Canada. Aubrey LeBlanc, ed. *Computer-Cartography in Canada*. Cartographica, monograph no. 9, 10–21

86 Allam, M. Mossad. 1982. Digital Mapping in a Distributed System. *Proceedings Auto-Carto 5*, Crystal City, VA. Bethesda, MD: ACSM and ASPRS, 13–22.
Allam, M. Mossad. 1986. The Development of a Data Model and National Standards for the Interchange of Digital Topographic Data. *Proceedings, Auto-Carto London*. Cambridge: British Cartographic Society.

87 Gibbons, J.G. 1984. Surveys and Mapping Branch: Digital Mapping 1977–1983. Unpublished manuscript.

88 Linders, James G. N.d. Computing Requirements for Automated Cartography. Unpublished manuscript.

89 Moore, Ray, and R.L. Simpson. 1986. Exchanging Digital Map Data Between National and Local Mapping Agencies. *Proceedings, Auto-Carto London*. Cambridge: British Cartographic Society.

90 Tomlinson, Roger F., and A. Raymond Boyle. 1981. The State of Development of Systems for Handling Natural Resources Inventory Data. *Cartographica*, 18, 4, 65–95, 68–9.

91 Allam, M. Mossad. 1982. Acquisition of Digital Topographic Data and the Need for a Standardized Digital Data Base. *Proceedings, ISPRS Commission 4 Symposium*, Hamburg: ISPRS, 1–11.

92 Boyle, A. Raymond. 1980. Development in Equipment and Techniques. In D.R.F. Taylor, ed. *The Computer in Contemporary Cartography*. Toronto: John Wiley, 39–57.

93 Lee, Y.C. 1991. Cartographic Data Capture and Storage. In D.R.F. Taylor, ed. *Geographic Information Systems: The Microcomputer and Modern Cartography*. Toronto: Pergamon, 21–38.

94 Wood Bruce D, and David H. Douglas. 1984. Cartographic Feature Coding. In David Douglas, ed. *Cartographica*, 21, 62–72.

95 Peucker, Thomas K. 1980. The Impact of Different Mathematical Approaches to Contouring. In Adam J. Kerr. 1980. *The Dynamics of Oceanic Cartography*. Cartographica, Monograph 25, vol. 17, no. 2. Toronto: B.V. Gutsell, 73–95.

96 Douglas, David H., and Thomas K. Peucker. 1973. Algorithms for the Reduction of the Number of Points Required to Represent a Digitized Line or Its Caricature. *Canadian Cartographer*, 10, 2, 112–22.

97 Comeau, M.A., and E. Holbaek-Hanssen. 1984. Compression and Compaction of Binary Raster Images. *Auto-Carto 6, Selected Papers*. Cartographica, monograph nos. 32, 33, vol. 21, nos. 2 and 3, 140–7.

Goodchild, Michael, and Andrew Grandfield. 1983. Optimising Raster Storage: An Examination of Four Alternatives. *Automated Cartography: International Perspectives on Achievements and Challenges.* Proceedings of the Sixth International Symposium on Automated Cartography, 2 volumes, Ottawa, vol. 1, 400–7.

98 Linders, James G. 1972. The Interchange of Computer Data. *Canadian Cartographer*, 9, 1, 61–5.

99 Evangelatos, Timothy V. 1991. Digital Graphic Interchange Standards. In D.R.F. Taylor, ed. *Geographic Information Systems: The Microcomputer and Modern Cartography.* Toronto: Pergamon, 151–66.

100 Gold, Christopher M. 1991. Problems with Handling Spatial Data – The Voronoi Approach. *CISM Journal*, 45,1, 65–80.

101 Peucker, Thomas K., Robert J. Fowler, James J. Little, and David M. Mark. 1979. The Triangulated Irregular Network. *Proceedings, Auto-Carto 4*, Reston, VA. Bethesda, MD: ACSM and ASPRS, 96–103.

Gold, Christopher M. 1979. Triangulation-Based Terrain Modelling: Where Are We Now? *Proceedings, Auto Carto 4.* Bethesda, MD: ACSM and ASPRS, 104–11.

Collins, Stanley H., and George C. Moon. 1979. A Unified System for Terrain Analysis and Mapping from DEM and DTM. Proceedings, *Auto Carto 4.* Bethesda, MD: ACSM and ASPRS, 124–131.

102 Douglas, David H. 1992. The Proper Distributions of Tasks to Digitize a Clean Boundary Network. *Cartographica*, 29, 2, 37–45.

103 Peucker, The Impact of Different Mathematical Approaches to Contouring, 2.

Gold, Christopher M. 1984. *Common-sense Automated Contouring: Some Generalizations.* In David Douglas. 1984. *Auto-Carto 6, Selected Papers. Cartographica*, monograph nos. 32, 33, vol. 17, nos. 1 and 2. Toronto: B.V. Gutsell, 121–9.

104 Furuya, H. 1973. Automating the Marine Chart: Production Processes. In LeBlanc, *Computer Cartography in Canada*, 23–36.

Anderson, Neil. 1980. Computer-Assisted Cartography in the Canadian Hydrographic Service. Tenth International Conference, ICA, Tokyo.

105 Boyle, A. Raymond. 1976. The Requirements of an Interactive Display and Edit Facility for Cartography. *Canadian Cartographer*, 13, 1, 35–59.

106 Yan, Joel Z., and D. Ross Bradley. 1983. Computer-Assisted Cartography for Census Collection: Canadian Achievements and Challenges. In Barry Wellar. *Automated Cartography: International Perspectives on Achievements and Challenges. Proceedings, Sixth International Symposium on Automated Cartography*, vol. 2. Ottawa: CIS, 135–146.

107 Castonguay, Jean, and Jean-Pierre Thouez. 1977. Cartographie automatique et geographie sociale. *Canadian Cartography*, 14, 2, 139–51.

108 Siekierska, Eva M. 1984. Toward an Electronic Atlas. *Cartographica*, 21, 110–20.

Siekierska, Eva M., and D.R.F. Taylor. 1991. Electronic Mapping and Electronic Atlases: New Cartographic Products for the Information Era – The Electronic Atlas of Canada. *CISM Journal*, 45, 1, 11–21.

109 Eaton, R.M., N.M. Anderson, and T.V. Evangelatos. 1983. The Electronic Chart. *The Canadian Surveyor*, 37, 4, 235–45.

110 Taylor, D.F.R. 1982. The Cartographic Potential of Telidon. *Cartographica*, 9, 3–4, 18–30.

111 Taylor, D.F.R. 1985. The Educational Challenges of a New Cartography. In D.R.F. Taylor, ed. 1985. *Education and Training in Contemporary Cartography.* Toronto: John Wiley, 3–25.

112 Lagacé, M. 1982. Le programme d'information intégrée sur la faune: télématique cartographique. Paper read at the *Colloque Graphise Numérique et Banks de Données*. Association Canadienne des Sciences Géodésiques, Montreal.

113 Tomlinson, The Impact of the Transition from Analogue to Digital Cartographic Representation, 259.

114 Ruggles, Richard I. 1987. The Next Step Forward: A Further Review of Research on the History of Cartography and Historical Cartography in Canada. *The Canadian Surveyor*, 41, 3, 291–312. In Barbara Farrell and Aileen Desbarats, eds. 1988. *Explorations in the History of Canadian Mapping*. Ottawa: Association of Canadian Map Libraries and Archives, 1–19.

115 Verner, Coolie, and Basil Stuart-Stubbs. 1979. *The Northpart of America: An Atlas of Facsimile Maps*. Toronto: Academic Press.

Nicholson, Norman L., and Lou M. Sebert. 1981. *The Maps of Canada: AGuide to Official Canadian Maps, Charts, Atlases and Gazetteers*. Folkestone, Kent: Wm. Dawson & Sons.

Armstrong, Joe C.W. 1982. *From Sea unto Sea: Art and Discovery Maps of Canada*. Scarborough, ON: Fleet.

116 Spink, John, and D. Wayne Moodie. 1972. Eskimo Maps from the Canadian Eastern Arctic. *Cartographica*, monograph no. 5. Toronto: B.V. Gutsell.

117 Moodie, D. Wayne. 1985. Indian Map-making: Two Examples from the Fur Trade West. *Bulletin, Association of Canadian Map Libraries*, 55, 32–43.

118 Pentland, David H. 1975. Cartographic Concepts of the Northern Algonquians. *Canadian Cartographer*, 12, 2, 149–60.

119 Beattie, Judith. 1985. Indian Maps in the Hudson's Bay Company Archives. *Bulletin, The Association of Canadian Map Libraries*, 55, 19–31.

120 O'Day, Fabian. 1971. *The Seventeenty Century Cartography of Newfoundland*. *Cartographica*, monograph no. 1. Toronto: B.V. Gutsell.

121 Heidenreich, Conrad E. 1976. *Explorations and Mapping of Samuel de Champlain, 1603–1632*. *Cartographica*, monograph no. 17. Toronto: B.V. Gutsell.

122 Heidenreich, Conrad E., and Edward Dahl. 1979. The Two States of Champlain's Carte Géographique. *Canadian Cartographer*, 16, 1, 1–16.

123 Jost, T.P. 1967. Voyages of Discovery: Hugh Say Alias John Day, The Men of Bristol and Joao Fernandes. *The Cartographer* 4, 1, 1–12.

O'Day, Fabian. 1988. Cabot's Landfall – Yet Again. In Farrell and Desbarats, *Explorations*, 55–70.

124 Prichard, J.S. 1979. Early French Hydrographic Surveys in the Saint Lawrence River. *International Hydrographic Review*, 56, 1, 125–42.

Prichard, J.S. 1981. French Charting of the East Coast of Canada. In Deric House, ed. *Five Hundred Years of Nautical Science 1400–1900*. Greenwich: National Maritime Museum, 119–29.

125 Trudel, Marcel, ed. 1948. *Collection de cartes anciennes et modernes pour servir à l'étude de l'histoire de l'Amérique et du Canada*. Quebec: Tremblay and Dion.

126 Ruggles, Richard I., and John Warkentin. 1970. *Historical Atlas of Manitoba*. Winnipeg: Historical and Scientific Society of Manitoba.

127 Gentilcore, R. Louis, and C. Grant Head. 1984. *Ontario's History in Maps*. Toronto: University of Toronto Press.

128 For example Ruggles, Richard I. 1977. Hospital Boys of the Bay: The Hudson's Bay Company Surveying and Mapping Apprentices. *The Beaver* (Autumn), Outfit 308:2, 4–11.

Ruggles, Richard I. 1980. Hudson's Bay Company Mapping. In Carol M. Judd and Arthur J. Ray. *Old Trails and New Directions*. Papers of the Third North American Fur Trade Conference. Toronto: University Toronto Press, 24–36.

Ruggles, Richard I. 1984. Mapping the Interior Plains of Rupert's Land by the Hudson's Bay Company to 1870. *Great Plains Quarterly*, 4, 3, 152–65.

129 Ruggles, Richard I. 1991. *A Country So Interesting: The Hudson's Bay Company and Two Centuries of Mapping 1670–1870*. Montreal: McGill-Queen's University Press.

130 Verner, Coolie. 1971. The Arrowsmith Firm and the Cartography of Canada. *Canadian Cartographer*, 8, 1, 1–7; and in Farrell & Desbarats, *Explorations*, 47–53.

131 Verner, Coolie with the assistance of Frances Woodward. 1972. *Explorers' Maps of the Canadian Arctic 1818–1860*. Cartographica, monograph no. 6. Toronto: B.V. Gutsell.

132 McEwen, Alec. 1983. The Township System of Surveys in Newfoundland. *The Canadian Surveyor*, 37, 2, 39–50.

133 Dawson, Joan 1985. Putting Acadia on the Map: The Transitional Cartography of Nova Scotia. *Cartographica*, 22, 2, 79–91.

134 Morrison, W.K. 1975. The Other Revolution in 1775. *Proceedings, Ninth Annual Conference of the ACML*. Ottawa: ACML, 59–82.

Morrison, W.K. 1982. The 'Modern Mapping' of Nova Scotia. *Map Collector*, 18, 28–34.

135 Charbonneau, André. 1972. Cartobibliographie de Jean-Baptiste-Louis Franquelin. *Papers of the Bibiographical Society of Canada*, 11, 39–52.

136 Garant, Jean-Marc. 1973. Jacques-Nicolas Bellin, 1703–1772. Cartographe, hydrographe, ingénieur de Ministère de la Marine: sa vie, son œuvre, sa valeur historique. Master's thesis, Université de Montréal.

137 Koerner, Wood. 1973. Joseph-Gaspard Chaussegros de Lery and His Maps of Detroit. Master's thesis, University of Michigan.

138 Heidenreich, Conrad E. 1966. Maps Relating to the First Half of the Seventeenth Century and Their Uses in Determining the Location of Jesuit Missions in Huronia. *The Cartographer*, 3, 2, 103–26.

Heidenreich, *Explorations and Mapping of Samuel de Champlain, 1603–1632*.

139 Olsen, Marilyn J.M. 1968. Aspects of the Mapping of Southern Ontario. Master's thesis, University of Western Ontario.

Gentilcore, R. Louis, and Kate Donkin. 1973. *Land Surveys of Southern Ontario: An Introduction and Index to the Field Notebooks of the Ontario Land Surveyors 1784–1859*. Cartographica, monograph no. 8. Toronto: B.V. Gutsell.

140 Clarke, John. 1971. Mapping the Lands Supervised by Colonel The Honourable Thomas Talbot in the Western Districts of Upper Canada. *Canadian Cartographer*, 8, 1, 8–18.

Clarke, John. 1971. Documentary and Map Sources for Reconstructing the History of the Reserved Lands in the Western District of Upper Canada. *Canadian Cartographer*, 8, 2, 75–83.

141 Heidenreich, Conrad E. 1981. Mapping the Great Lakes: The Period of Imperial Rivalries, 1700–1760. *Cartographica*, 18, 3, 74–109.

Sandilands, R.W. 1982. Hydrographic Surveying in the Great Lakes During the Nineteenth Century. *The Canadian Surveyor*, 36, 2, 139–63.

142 Ray, Arthur. 1972. Early French Mapping of the Western Interior of Canada. *Canadian Cartographer*, 9, 2, 85–98.

143 Oppen, William A. 1978. *The Riel Rebellions: A Cartographic History*. Cartographica, monograph nos. 21, 22. Toronto: B.V. Gutsell.

144 Pearson, D.F. 1974. An Historical Outline of Mapping in British Columbia. *Canadian Cartographer*, 11, 2, 114–24.

145 Woodward, Frances. 1981. Exploration and Survey of the Kootenay District. In Farrell and Desbarats, *Explorations*, 223–38.

146 Morse, Eric W. 1981. Modern Maps Throw New Light on Samuel Hearne's Route. *Cartographica*, 18, 4, 23–35.

147 Wonders, William C. 1982. The Mapping of Canada's Arctic Islands. *The Canadian Surveyor*, 36, 1, 89–102.

148 Woodward, Frances. 1974. The Influence of the Royal Engineers on the Development of British Columbia. *B.C. Studies*, 24, Winter, 3–52.
Woodward, Frances. 1976. The Royal Engineers' Mapping of British Columbia. *Information Bulletin, Western Association of Map Libraries*, 7, 3, 28–42.

149 Nagy, Thomas. 1974. *Ottawa in Maps: A Brief Cartographical History of Ottawa, 1825–1973.* Ottawa: National Map Collection, Public Archives of Canada.

150 Dahl, Edward H. et al. 1975. *La Ville de Québec, 1800–1850: un inventaire de cartes et plans.* Ottawa: Musée Nationale de l'Homme.

151 Artibise, Alan F.J., and Edward H. Dahl. 1975. *Winnipeg in Maps 1816–1972.* Ottawa: Public Archives of Canada.

152 Hayward, Robert. 1974. Charles E. Goad and Fire Insurance Cartography. *Proceedings, Eighth Annual Conference of the ACMLA.* Ottawa: ACMLA, 51–72.
Hayward, Robert J. 1977. *Fire Insurance Plans in the National Map Collection.* Ottawa: National Map Collection, Public Archives of Canada.

153 Woodward, Frances, and Robert J. Hayward. 1974. *Fire Insurance Plans of British Columbia Municipalities: A Checklist.* Vancouver: Special Collections Division, UBC Library.

154 Farrell and Desbarats, *Explorations*. See note 114.

155 McGrath, Gerald. 1977. The Surveying and Mapping of British East Africa 1890–1946. *Cartographica*, monograph no. 18.

156 Bagrow, Leo. 1975. *A History of the Cartography of Russia up to 1600,* vol. 1. Ed, Henry W. Castner. Wolfe Island, ON: Walker Press.
Bagrow, Leo. 1975. *A History of Russian Cartography up to 1800*, vol. 2. Ed. Henry W. Castner. Wolfe Island, ON: Walker Press.

157 For example Gibson, James R., trans. 1975. Essays on the History of Russian Cartography, Sixteenth to Nineteenth Centuries. *Cartographica,* monograph no. 13.

158 McGrath, Gerald. 1983. Mapping for Development. The Contributions of the Directorate of Overseas Surveys. *Cartographica,* 20, 1 & 2.

159 Godlewska, Anne. 1988. The Napoleonic Survey of Egypt. *Cartographica*, monograph nos. 38, 39.

160 Winearls, Joan. 1976. Cartobibliography and Map Cataloguing in Canada. *AB Bookman's Yearbook,* part 1: 63–70.
Winearls, Joan. 1979. Progress in Bibliographical Theory and Control for Maps. *Bibliographic Society of Canada*, colloquium 3: 106–14.

161 Kidd, Betty. 1988. Maps as a Source of Historical Evidence. In Farrell and Desbarats, *Explorations*.

162 Gentilcore, R. Louis. 1988. The Use of Maps in the Historical Geography of Canada. In Farrell and Desbarats, *Explorations*, 21–32.

163 Wood, Clifford H. 1985. Tonal Reproduction Processes in Map Printing from the Fifteenth to the Nineteenth Centuries. *Cartographica*, 22, 1, 78–92.

164 Gridgeman, N.T., and M. Zuker. 1978. Mercator, the Antigudermannian, and a Fluke. *Canadian Cartographer*, 15, 1, 50–7.
165 Smyth, David. 1981. David Thompson's Surveying Instruments and Methods in the Northwest, 1790–1812. *Cartographica*, 18, 4, 1–17.
166 Sebert, Lou M. 1981. David Thompson's Determination of Longitude in Western Canada. *The Canadian Surveyor*, 35, 4, 405–14.
167 Mackay, Daniel S.C. 1982. James White: Canada's Chief Geographer, 1899–1909. *Cartographica*, 19, 1, 51–61.

CHAPTER THIRTEEN

Education

Angus C. Hamilton

It is only the ignorant who despise education

Publilius Syris, 1st century B.C.

In this chapter "education" will be viewed in the Webster's dictionary sense of "preparation for one's life work." Because until quite recently there were no programmes specifically for those entering careers in surveying and mapping, self-education has played a major role in the training of the majority of those in the profession. To limit discussion to formal education would be a rank injustice to all those who have identified the learning they needed and then persevered to find the books and, if possible, to find a coach to enable them to acquire the needed knowledge and experience.

For those who aspired to explore, to establish coordinates, and to make maps and charts there was not until the last couple of decades an institutional structure setting out the knowledge requirements. Thus a review of the avenues followed by this group in getting the knowledge they needed is a significant part of the education story; it is presented in the section "Informal, Semi-formal, and General Education."

For those who aspired to be commissioned as land surveyors the knowledge requirement has long been set out by boards of examiners. The first board was established in the middle of the last century, and others followed shortly thereafter. Needless to say the evolution of these boards is a significant part of the education story.

The first continuing engineering programme in the country started at McGill in 1871 with one professor of civil engineering and one professor of assaying and mining on the faculty. Many of the early engineering programmes were often referred to as "civil engineering and surveying" because almost half of the specialized courses were in surveying. In that era there was no doubt whatever that the academic home for surveying was in civil engineering. By the turn of the century the proportion of time allotted to surveying subjects had declined significantly, and it continued to decline as the many other phases of civil engineering evolved. By the late 1950s the rationale for continuing to consider civil engineering as the academic home for surveying was being questioned. At a colloquium in 1959 it was recognized that in Canada the time had come for surveying to become an independent academic discipline.

Immediately following the 1959 colloquium the University of New Brunswick (UNB) established a research-oriented baccalaureate programme that became the Department of

Surveying Engineering. At the same time Laval University began developing a programme of graduate studies and research to complement the undergraduate teaching in surveying that it had carried out since 1908. The last act in the "surveying as a component of civil engineering" story was the closing in 1970 of a surveying option that had been offered at the University of Toronto (U of T) since 1955. In 1972 a programme in survey science was established on the Erindale campus of the U of T within the Faculty of Arts and Science. In 1980 the University of Calgary established a programme that became the Department of Geomatics Engineering.

Concurrent with the evolution of these four strong, research-oriented baccalaureate programmes there has been a steady increase in interest in cartography, remote sensing, and Geographical Information Systems (GIS) in many university geography departments, both at the undergraduate and the graduate level. Developments in these fields at the university level are discussed in chapters 12, 14, and 15. Complementing all the university-level activities there has been a strong surge in technician and technologist courses in surveying, cartography, and GIS studies at community colleges.

In view of the fact that nowhere in the three volumes of *Men and Meridians* is education *per se* discussed, this chapter will start at the beginning: it will start with the education of those intrepid individuals who first delineated the shape of what is now Canada.

INFORMAL, SEMI-FORMAL, AND GENERAL EDUCATION

The story of education for surveyors and mappers in Canada begins, of course, with Samuel de Champlain, the Brouage Voyageur, the dean of surveyors in Canada. The record shows that, in surveying, Champlain was self-educated.[1,2] He decided what skills he needed and then went to someone who could teach him and give him the necessary books to study by himself. Champlain was self-educated in the sense that he sought out good tutors and learned from them. In this regard he was the first of many great explorer-surveyors to receive their education this way.

Champlain's successor was Jean Bourdon (1601–68) who Pelletier describes as "Le premier professeur d'hydrographie et d'arpentage à Québec."[2] Bourdon's career as a surveyor in New France began in 1634 and continued until his death in 1668. Between 1635 and 1660 he completed twenty-nine *bornages*. Pelletier lists four of Bourdon's successors who were granted the title "hydrographe du roi": Martin Boutet, 1671–83; Jean-Baptiste-Louis Franquelin, 1683–93; Louis Jolliet, 1697–1700; and Jean Deshayes, 1702–06. After these royal appointments ended there was generally one of the members of the Jesuit College capable of providing instruction in hydrography and surveying.

The Hudson's Bay Company's (HBC) penetration into Canada was at first timid. Trading posts were set up on the coast of Hudson Bay, and the Indians were encouraged to bring their furs down to the posts. When the North West Company forced the HBC to compete by moving inland, the gentlemen in London realized that if they were to make correct decisions regarding the location of supply routes and trading posts in central Canada, they needed accurate maps. To meet this need the company hired a competent surveyor, Philip Turnor. He had the necessary skills to take observations on the sun and stars for both latitude and longitude. By using these points as a framework he was able to draw route maps of commendable accuracy. Although he did good fieldwork himself, his most valuable contribution was the tutoring he gave to two young apprentices, David Thompson and Peter

Fidler. Both had long and productive careers, and their explorations and maps did much to open the Canadian west.

The North West Company also had its surveyor-explorers. One of the best of these was Alexander Mackenzie, who saw that exploration was useless unless a record of the explorer's travels could be laid down on accurate maps. As the North West Company had no resident surveying instructor, he had to return to England to obtain the necessary skills.

Thus by a combination of self-study and on-the-job training, the early travellers of western Canada acquired the skills to survey and draw accurate route maps. These, when compiled into a broader scope by the map makers in London, resulted in the first reasonably accurate maps of western Canada.

Topographic maps are much more detailed than those of the explorers, and require a surveyor-cartographer with a different training. In Canada this was provided, in the main, by the semi-formal channel of military engineering. The Murray Map (the map of New France compiled after the fall of Québec), the extensive mapping of Samuel Holland, and Des Barres' charts in the Atlantic Neptune all reflect the teaching in surveying and mapping at European military academies. Later, in the 1800s, the influence of military engineering continues. The work of Colonel By in surveying and mapping for the Rideau Canal is one example.[3] In what is now British Columbia the Royal Engineers provided men for the British half of a team to locate and to mark the western part of the International Boundary. When the 1858 gold rush occurred they were on the spot and took responsibility for much of the road construction and all of the surveying in that region.

The British military tradition in surveying and mapping was certainly maintained at the Royal Military College (RMC) in Kingston. Surveying, field sketching, and mapping were given a prominent place in the curriculum right from the opening of the college in 1876. Although no calendar was issued at that time, copies of the examinations available from the Massey Library show that in December 1895 and in June 1896 there were six examinations in surveying and eleven in civil engineering in all three years of the programme. In other words about one-third of the engineering part of the college's curriculum was surveying. The impact of this programme on surveying and mapping in Canada has been far reaching and long lasting. Thomson has listed many of the more distinguished alumni who have contributed to surveying and mapping in Canada prior to the Second World War.[4] If he were compiling that list today he would certainly add the name of Samuel Gamble. Gamble graduated from RMC just prior to the war, served overseas, and returned to a distinguished career directing Canada's federal mapping programme.

When systematic mapping at the One-Mile scale was initiated by the Department of Militia and Defence just after the turn of the century, a nucleus of Royal Engineers was loaned from the British army.[5] After the First World War the Canadian army carried on the topographic mapping of south-eastern Canada without British assistance. Military training in mapping reached a peak during the Second World War. Many Canadians received extensive training in the use of air photos and stereoplotters, and because many of these men wanted to stay in mapping, their availability made possible the rapid postwar expansion of federal and provincial mapping programmes.

Parallel with this semi-formal military education channel there has always been a very informal, entrepreneurial, artisan-based education system in cartography and in cartographic reproduction. This channel manifested itself in the many county and city atlases that were produced by the private sector in the 1870s and 1880s,[6] and in the many small-scale maps produced by private enterprise and countless government agencies throughout the twentieth century.

In hydrography although one of Bourdon's titles was "professeur d'hydrographie," the title was not granted to his successors nor could it be claimed by anyone until baccalaureate programmes were established at the UNB in the late 1970s. The Canadian Hydrographic Survey Branch was established in the Department of Marine and Fisheries in 1904. Prior to this move some Canadian hydrography was done on inland waters, but the coastal waters were left to the British Admiralty. Even for a long time after the establishment of a Canadian hydrographic agency, it was assumed that ex-officers of the Royal Navy or ex-mariners were the best candidates for this work. In the mid-twentieth century, when such officers were no longer available, the Canadian Hydrographic Service (CHS as it was by this time known) had to recruit candidates with no formal education in hydrography. Thus civil engineers, mining engineers, foresters, and others were hired. Although a few in-house courses were provided, for the most part this generation was indeed self-educated in hydrography. After the war when acoustic devices began to replace the lead line and electronic positioning began to replace the sextant, in-house courses were expanded and continued until the universities took over with baccalaureate programmes, and community colleges provided courses for technologists.

In geodesy the first generation of members of the Geodetic Survey of Canada were drawn mainly from among the graduates of the astronomy and geodesy option in the Civil Engineering Department at the U of T. The second generation, those recruited after the war, were drawn from a wide range of university programmes such as civil engineering, electrical engineering, engineering physics, and mathematics and physics. It was assumed that they had a sufficiently strong education in mathematics to be able to absorb geodesy on the job.

At the technician level, until recently virtually everyone became qualified by on-the-job learning. Almost all of these persons started as rodmen or chainmen and learned how to use a level, a transit, or a theodolite by asking questions and being coached by their party chief. When survey parties were large there were frequent opportunities for an interested survey apprentice to fill in and learn to do the work of another member of the party. As more sophisticated instruments became available the number of persons on most survey parties decreased, with a corresponding decrease in opportunities for learning on the job. This has led to a proliferation of programmes at the technician and technologist level.

THE EVOLUTION OF EDUCATIONAL REQUIREMENTS
FOR LAND SURVEYORS

With minor exceptions a license or a commission to practise land surveying has always been required to survey property boundaries in Canada. Initially those so authorized were called "deputy surveyors." Later they came to be called, for example, Dominion Land Surveyors or Ontario Land Surveyors.

In the colonial period it was customary for the governor to have a surveyor general as a full member of his council. The surveyor general was responsible for ensuring that a satisfactory survey had been done before letters patent were issued granting land to a settler. To facilitate his work the surveyor general was usually authorized to appoint deputy surveyors or, at least, to recommend appointees to the governor. Generally speaking the first generation of surveyors general were highly competent themselves, and insisted on a high level of competence and integrity in those appointed as deputy surveyors. Later, as the pressure for land decreased, the office of surveyor general became less critical to the success of an administration, and political considerations began to outweigh professional competence when surveyors general were being appointed.

In the mid-1800s, when the quality of surveying being done by incompetent deputy surveyors became a scandal, the provinces began to authorize the establishment of boards of examiners charged with setting standards and examining applicants before a license or commission was granted. Initially these boards were appointed by, and were responsible to, a senior government official. But gradually as the self-governing associations became established the responsibility for the boards was assumed by the associations.

For many years the general level of the examinations was equivalent to one or two years of post-secondary education. During the 1960s, however, the level of the examinations was gradually raised and the scope of the subject matter was broadened. By the late 1980s all jurisdictions were requiring either a bachelor's degree from an accredited programme or were setting examinations at the bachelor level. In table 13-1 the evolution of education requirements over the last 250 years is summarized for all the jurisdictions in the country. Each phase of this evolution will be discussed in more detail.

Deputy Surveyors by Appointment

Under the British regime the appointment of a surveyor general was one of the first actions taken by the Colonial Office when a new colony had been established. In turn among the first challenges addressed by a newly appointed surveyor general was the appointment of deputy surveyors.

The first colony in what is now Canada to appoint a surveyor general was Nova Scotia. Charles Morris was installed in 1749 at a time when the colony was responsible for all territory north of the American colonies that was not under French jurisdiction. After the American Revolution, when thousands of Loyalists were clamoring for land in what was then the hinterland of Nova Scotia (now New Brunswick), it is reported that Morris had only fourteen deputies to meet all the demands on his office. There is no record of the educational qualifications of Morris's deputies but, Halifax being mainly a military and naval outpost at that time, it can be assumed that most, if not all, of his deputies had been trained as military engineers or navigators.

Maj. Samuel Holland, one of General Wolfe's best military engineers, was appointed "Surveyor General of the Northern District of America" (i.e., all British territories north of the Potomac) in 1764.[7] It is not clear what authority Holland had in the already-established British colonies, but it is clear that he had full authority in all the territory ceded by the French, namely Québec, Acadia, Cape Breton, and St John's Island (Prince Edward Island). Holland was a very competent individual capable of handling both the administrative duties and the fieldwork. He knew what work needed to be done, and he knew the qualifications needed by deputy surveyors. He insisted that all appointees had satisfactory qualifications and were trustworthy men. In general one can say that the first generation of deputy surveyors in British North America were well qualified.

In 1784 one of Governor Thomas Carleton's first actions in the new colony of New Brunswick was to appoint George Sproule as surveyor general.[8] Sproule had been a military

Table 13-1
The Evolution of Educational Requirements for Admission to the Practice of Land Surveying in Canada

Jurisdiction	Surveyor general's office established*	Establishment of a board of examiners	Association of Land Surveyors granted legal status**	Responsibility for board assumed by association	Adoption of degree or degree-equivalent admission level*****
Nova Scotia	1749	1910	1959 (1951)	1959	1980
Québec	1764	1849	1882	1882	1975
Prince Edward Island	1770	1884	1968	–	1986
New Brunswick	1784	1874	1954	1954	1978
Ontario	1792	1849	1892 (1886)	1892	1969
Newfoundland	1821	1951	1953	1963	1980
British Columbia	1866 (1851)	1891	1905	1905	1980
Canada (Federal lands)	1871	1872	(1985)	***	1978
Manitoba	–	1881	1881	1881	1980
Saskatchewan	–	1909	1913	****	1980
Alberta	–	1910	1910	1910	1980

*   There was a surveyor general for Vancouver Island appointed in 1851 but it was 1866 before there was a surveyor general for all of British Columbia. The Prairie provinces were never colonies and hence had neither a surveyor general nor deputy surveyors.

**   Date in brackets is the date that the association first became active.

***   It was expected that in 1995 the federal Government would pass legislation giving the Association of Canada Land Surveyors responsibility for the CLS board.

****   The Saskatchewan association had the responsibility for its board of examiners from 1913 until 1923 when the responsibility was given to the University of Saskatchewan.

*****   The associations in the four Atlantic provinces established the Atlantic Provinces Board of Examiners for Land Surveyors in 1978, and the associations in the four western provinces established the Western Canadian Board in 1980. When each of the participating provinces adopted the degree-equivalent level for admission it contracted with its regional board for the administration of the technical and professional examinations.

engineer and, prior to the American War of Independence, had been surveyor general of New Hampshire. In his first few years as surveyor general of New Brunswick Sproule appointed at least thirty deputies. Some fourteen of these worked more or less full time for his office; the others could be considered as casuals. All, however, were relatively well educated and most had another profession or trade to fall back on.

A few decades after the Loyalists and the disbanded British soldiers had been settled in the loyal British colonies, the importance of the surveyor general's office diminished and, along with the trend to responsible government – or in some cases, to irresponsible government – political considerations overrode professional competence when Surveyors General were being appointed. The political appointees, having no significant competence themselves, had no particular interest in the qualifications of their deputies, and tended to view the appointment of a deputy as an opportunity to practise political patronage. There is one story of a politically well-connected individual who lost his appointment as post-master because he was illiterate; as compensation he was appointed a deputy surveyor.[9] This story may be apocryphal but, in the old files, there is ample evidence of surveyors who could chain fairly well but could not run a straight line, and of others who could run a straight line but could not chain well.

The redeeming virtue of responsible government is that when a problem becomes so bad that the public complains vigorously about it, something will be done. By the mid-1800s the calibre of deputy surveyors had become so low that something had to be done. In the Legislature of the Province of Canada an act was passed in 1849 authorizing the establishment of a board of examiners.[10] Whether or not there had been several "studies" prior to the passage of this act, there is no record. In any event the act designated the criteria for the members of the board, and even listed the subjects in which the board was to set examinations.

With Confederation the provinces of Ontario and Québec retained responsibility for land and hence for their boards of examiners. In 1882 an act entitled Land Surveyors and the Survey of Lands was passed creating the Corporation of Land Surveyors of Québec.[11] The council of the corporation was called the Board of Management, and, among other duties, it was given the responsibility for the "conditions required to be admitted to practice." Although an association was formed in Ontario in 1886, it was 1892 before the Act to Incorporate the Association of Ontario Land Surveyors was passed.[12] The act gave the association legal status and therewith the responsibility for the board of examiners.

In 1867 the new Dominion of Canada had little additional need for surveyors, but when it took over the responsibility for Rupert's Land from the HBC in 1870 it had an urgent need for both surveys and surveyors. To meet this challenge the government established the office of surveyor general in 1871. The following year it passed the Dominion Lands Surveys Act establishing a board of examiners with the surveyor general as chairman.[13] This act, however, was not implemented until 7 May 1975 when an order in council named the members of the first board. In 1874 the act was amended and, among other things, the title Deputy Surveyor was changed to Dominion Land Surveyor. From its inception the DLS board set high standards that were followed by most of the provincial boards for many decades.

There were two sets of examinations. The first set was "examination for articles as pupil"; the subjects were penmanship, orthography, arithmetic and logarithms, algebra, plane geometry, plane trigonometry, spherical trigonometry, and mensuration of superficies. The second set was the "full examination for admission as surveyor" with the following subjects: plane geometry and mensuration, solid geometry, spherical trigonometry, dividing and laying off of land, measurement of areas, description for deeds, astronomy, practical surveying, and Manual of Survey and Dominion Lands Act. A complete syllabus and set of examination papers for the year 1886 can be found in the *Annual Report* of the Department of the Interior for that year.[14]

At this time, also, a higher-level syllabus called a Dominion Topographic Surveyor's Certificate was introduced.[15] Although it was never a prerequisite for carrying out legal surveys, it did recognize that "surveying" included geodesy, astronomy, and topographic mapping as well as cadastral surveys. When baccalaureate degree programmes were established almost a century later, their curricula spanned a similar range of activities.

In 1874 New Brunswick followed the Dominion's example and established a board of examiners, but it would be 1954 before an association was formed and given the responsibility for appointing members to this board.[16] In Prince Edward Island a board of examiners was first authorized in 1884.[17] In 1968 the Prince Edward Island Land Surveyor's

Act established the provincial association and also restructured the board of examiners.[18] Although the association may name two members to the board, the other three must still be appointed by the government. In Nova Scotia a board was established by The Act in Relation to Provincial Land Surveyors in 1910,[19] but it would be 1959 before the Provincial Land Surveyors Act gave the Association of Nova Scotia Land Surveyors the responsibility for the province's board of examiners.[20] Even then, although the majority of board members were to be appointed by the association and the association was responsible for the expenses of the board, the deputy minister of Lands and Forests was, and still is, designated as a member of the board.

A board of examiners was established in British Columbia in 1891 but it was not until 1905 that the Association of British Columbia Land Surveyors received legal status and was given the responsibility for its board.[21]

In Newfoundland the Lieutenant-Governor in Council was authorized by the Crown Lands (Amendments) Act, 1951[22] "to appoint a Board to examine applicants for appointment as surveyor and to issue certificates to such applicants as satisfy the Board of their competence." The Association of Newfoundland Land Surveyors received formal approval in 1953, and ten years later became responsible for its board of examiners.

In Manitoba the Association of Land Surveyors was given responsibility for the board of examiners when the association was established in 1881. Thus Manitoba was the first province to entrust a self-governing association of surveyors with control of those admitted to practice. It is not known where the initial impetus originated, but it is clear that the act authorizing the establishment of the association also gave the association responsibility for the board of examiners.[23] This was a breakthrough. It is interesting to note that the first president of the association, and presumably the leader in working to get the legislation passed, was J.S. Dennis Jr, who at that time was only twenty-five years old.

Similarly, in 1910 The Alberta Land Surveyors Act established the Association of Alberta Land Surveyors and gave it responsibility for the board of examiners.[24] As a matter of convenience, or perhaps of economy, the Alberta board for many years required its candidates to pass the DLS board examinations rather than setting examinations itself.

The story of the Saskatchewan board differs significantly from that of the other boards.[25] The responsibility for the Saskatchewan board was given to the Association of Saskatchewan Land Surveyors in 1913, but in 1923 it was transferred to the University of Saskatchewan, where it still remains.

Although the boards of examiners, by themselves, have rarely offered courses of instruction leading to their examinations, they have had a significant impact on the courses offered by the academic institutions. Several of the first civil engineering programmes included almost as many courses in surveying as in engineering, and many of the civil engineering programmes emphasized in their calendars that parts of their curricula were designed specifically to prepare candidates for the examinations set by the various boards of examiners. Several departments continued this practice beyond the middle of the twentieth century.

The practice of setting standards but leaving the candidates to prepare themselves for the examination has been maligned from time to time. The criticism generally directed at the boards had been for emphasizing how things had been done in the past without any consideration being given to alternative methods. This made for stability but it did not encourage progress. On the other hand the candidates who, in effect, were educating themselves had to become self-reliant. They had to have the initiative to settle down and prepare themselves without input from lectures and the external discipline of weekly assignments in a structured course of studies.

The next, and presumably the final, step in the evolution of educational requirements for admission to the practice of land surveying was the raising of admission standards to the level of a bachelor's degree (see table 13-1). This upgrading of standards has been an incremental process. Although Québec, by virtue of its long-established degree programme at Laval University, had been in the forefront in raising standards, it was in Ontario that this step was first formalized.

The Ontario board, influenced in part by a sustained effort within the Civil Engineering Department at the University of Toronto (U of T), began raising standards and offering courses to meet these standards shortly after the end of the Second World War. This process culminated in what became known as By-Law 95, approved by the association in 1969. This by-law was the result of a prolonged campaign for an "expanded profession." This concept meant the inclusion of geodesy, photogrammetry, and hydrography as part of the profession under the aegis of the association. By-Law 95 called for examinations in the above-mentioned fields of surveying, which had not heretofore been included with traditional land surveying. A candidate did not have to sit for all examinations, of course, but he or she could only practise in the fields where competence had been demonstrated. Although the by-law did not specify that a degree was required, it was quite clear that the examinations were to be at the level of the upper years in a bachelor's programme. Québec was the next jurisdiction to require a degree or degree-equivalent standards.[26]

It is interesting to note, too, that the expanded profession and the higher academic standards are, in actuality, the culmination of the vision of those who established the Dominion Topographic Surveyor certificate in the 1870s. Although the general level of examinations is now roughly equivalent to those in a baccalaureate programme, most boards maintain a complete schedule of examinations so that through home study or through some other avenue, candidates can still qualify and be admitted to the practice of land surveying.

At the federal level, in order to respond to the new need for legal surveys offshore in support of oil and gas exploration, the DLS Act was superseded by the Canada Lands Surveys (CLS) Act in 1978. Among other things this act replaced the DLS board with a new board called the Canada Lands Surveys board, and gave it a mandate for surveying offshore as well as on land. The CLS board has introduced geodesy, hydrography, photogrammetry, and several other subjects at approximately the baccalaureate level. Although the act changed the title "Dominion Land Surveyor" to "Canada Land Surveyor," it left the responsibility for the board with the surveyor general of Canada Lands. Subsequently there was agreement in principle that the responsibility for the CLS board would be given to the Association of Canada Lands Surveyors in 1995.

Concurrent with the movement for changes at the federal level, the New Brunswick association initiated the formation of the Atlantic Provinces Board of Examiners for Land Surveyors (APBELS).[27] APBELS undertook to set a series of examinations at approximately the baccalaureate level in all the technical and professional subjects required by the provincial boards. New Brunswick made the commitment to APBELS standards in 1978, and the other Atlantic provinces followed suit as soon as they overcame various administrative and legal problems. Nova Scotia and Newfoundland formally joined the board in 1980, and Prince Edward Island in 1986.

Having much in common due to their roots in the DLS system, the four Western provinces were able to form the Western Canadian Board of Examiners for Land Surveyors in 1980, and adopt standards similar to those of the CLS board and APBELS. With Prince Edward Island's adoption of the APBELS standards in 1986, the minimum education required by all land surveyors, anywhere in Canada, was approximately equivalent to the bachelor degree in an accredited programme.

COURSES AND PROGRAMMES AT ACADEMIC INSTITUTIONS[28]

Civil Engineering and Surveying as "Courses" or "Options" in Arts: 1854–63

The first course in civil engineering and surveying on record at an academic institution in what is now Canada would, currently, be classified as an "extension" course. It was presented by McMahon Cregan at King's College, now UNB, between mid-February and the end of April 1854.[29] There were three lectures a week together with "instructions in the field once a week or as often as may be expedient." The course was open to the general public as well as to the full-time students in the arts programme. Cregan was a British consultant working on the plans and design for a proposed railroad between Halifax and Portland, Maine. The announcement indicated that the greater part of the time would be spent on surveying topics although some "engineering" subjects were also listed. It can be assumed that the full-time students in the college, and also most of the others, would have been well prepared by having taken Professor Brydone-Jack's lectures in astronomy-related mathematics. Twenty-six students took the course.

The act establishing UNB in 1859 included provision for a three-term diploma programme in civil engineering. Although at least one student qualified for this diploma, it would be 1889 before the university established a chair in civil engineering and surveying, and began offering an ongoing diploma programme.

In 1857, three years after Cregan's course at King's College, the Arts Faculty at McGill appointed Mark Hamilton as professor of civil engineering and road and railroad engineering, and offered a civil engineering diploma programme as an option in the Faculty of Arts.[30] Students studying for this diploma took courses in drawing and surveying in the first year, and similar courses the following year. They were exempted from classics but were required to fulfil the other faculty requirements. Two students registered for the 1857–58 year and six the next year, but just as the programme was beginning to gain acceptance the enthusiasm for railroads faltered. The McGill board faced one of its more severe financial crises and it terminated the programme.[31] Hamilton's appointment was cancelled at the end of the 1862–63 academic year. Sixteen students had completed the programme.

Each of these universities had an observatory – a status symbol in that era – and each consisted primarily of a Faculty of Arts in the classical European model. However within each university, and within each colonial/provincial legislature, there were strongly held views on the need for "practical science," but in the 1850s there were even more strongly held views on the merits of a classical education. As always the debate came down to funds and, as noted above, the initial efforts to introduce some practical science courses were short-lived due to the lack of money. Nevertheless the campaign for practical-science programmes steadily gained support, and it began to bear fruit in the 1870s.

The Surveying Component of Civil Engineering Programmes: 1871–1970

The story of civil engineering as the academic home for surveying in Canada starts at McGill in 1871 and ends at the U of T in 1970. In February 1871 President Dawson at McGill, having heard of plans to start an engineering programme at the U of T, received approval from his board to establish a Department of Practical Science, on the condition that he raise the initial cost of $7500. He raised the money and recruited G.F. Armstrong as professor of civil engineering and B.J. Harrington as lecturer in assaying and mining. The name was soon changed to the Department of Applied Science, and new degrees of Bachelor and Master of Applied Science were established. In 1875 the department became a faculty.[31] The first graduating class in 1873 included Willis Chipman, who played a leading role in the founding of the Association of Ontario Land Surveyors.[32] Also in that first class was Clement Henry (Bunty) McLeod, who very soon became superintendent of the observatory and a lecturer, and went on to a distinguished career as Professor of Surveying and Geodesy at McGill. McLeod collaborated with scientists at Harvard and at Greenwich in refining the longitude of the McGill observatory. He was then able to provide a time service to the railroads. In recognition of this and other work McLeod[33] was elected a Fellow of the Royal Society of Canada, and had the distinction of being the only Canadian elected a Fellow of the Royal Astronomical Institute. He had become a Québec Land Surveyor in 1877.

At McGill in the 1895–96 academic year there was one full-year course in surveying in second year, and another in third year. In the fourth year there was a full-year lecture course as well as a laboratory course in geodesy. The first sentence in the preamble to the descriptive notes for the courses headed "Surveying and Geodesy" states "This course is designed to qualify the Student for admission to the practice of Provincial and Dominion Land Surveying."[34] The content left no doubt that this was advanced material. Among a long list of exercises to be completed was "Determination of longitude by telegraphic method and by moon culminations." All the students in civil engineering took these courses: at that time McGill did not allow electives or options.

In 1873, two years after the start of the McGill programme, the province of Québec authorized the establishment of l'École Polytechnique, and in January 1874 the first class of twelve students began their studies in its three-year diploma programme.[35] The curriculum initially included several courses in surveying and "dessin topographique."[36] Like McGill, l'École Polytechnique did not offer any electives or options. The only other engineering programme being offered in Canada during the 1870s was at RMC, as was mentioned previously.

Although agreement in principle had been reached in Ontario in the early 1870s, it was not until 1878, seven years after McGill's programme was launched, that the School of Practical Science (SPS) opened its doors in Toronto.[37] It was an independent institution until 1889 when it became part of the U of T. From 1878 to 1892 SPS offered only a three-year diploma programme. In the syllabus all civil engineering students took one course in surveying in their first year, and a course in "engineering and surveying" in their second and third years. This covered topics such as levelling, railway location, hydrographic surveying, theory of surveying instruments, geodesy, and practical astronomy. Louis B. Stewart was appointed lecturer in 1888, became a full professor in 1901, and continued until his retirement in 1932.[38] In 1892 the degree of Bachelor of Applied Science (BASc) was approved. It was open to students who had successfully completed the three-year diploma programme and had prepared a thesis based on the results of their fourth-year work. They also had to pass written and oral examinations on any one of four groups of subjects. "Astronomy and geodesy" was one of the four groups. In this group there was a two-hour lecture period in astronomy, a two-hour lecture period in geodesy, and twenty-three hours of laboratory time, each week. With this depth in astronomy and geodesy it is not surprising that many of the first generation of the staff of the Geodetic Survey of Canada were graduates of this programme. This astronomy and geodesy option continued to have the same time allotment for almost fifty years.[39] It was replaced by a photographic surveying elective in 1941 that continued until 1948. There were no electives or options until 1955 when a strong surveying option was introduced that continued until 1970.

By 1915 there were ten universities in Canada offering degrees in civil engineering. In order of their appearance they were: McGill, l'École Polytechnique, U of T, UNB, Queen's, Manitoba, Nova Scotia Technical, Alberta, Saskatchewan, and UBC. Of these, the U of T was the only one that allowed specialization. The others insisted that their students become generalists competent in all the fields of civil engineering.[40] Nevertheless, like McGill's, the U of T Civil Engineering Department and most of the other civil departments claimed that their curricula would prepare students for the examinations of the DLS board and for those of one or more of the provincial boards. Thus in the English-speaking part of the country it was accepted without question that civil engineering was the academic home for surveying. The establishment of an independent "surveying" programme at Laval in 1908 did not have any impact on this perception.

Prior to the turn of the century and for quite a few years thereafter the norm was three full-year courses including at least one course in astronomy, plus at least two survey camps. However as the national priorities shifted from railroads to a much more complex engineering infrastructure, there was strong pressure for more and more "engineering" courses within civil engineering. Because the surveying required for day-to-day engineering was becoming less complex, civil departments began reducing the time allocated to surveying. Surveying professors could sometimes delay but could not prevent this reduction. As an alternative many did succeed in getting one or two elective courses approved. After the Second World War there were many valiant efforts to introduce options, but only one such effort was successful.[41] In 1955 Oscar Marshall, Professor of Surveying in the Civil Engineering Department at U of T, in collaboration with K.B. Jackson, professor and head of the Applied Physics Department, developed a strong survey option.

The establishment of this U of T option was not enough to reverse or even to delay the general trend. As shown by the data in a paper by Sybren de Jong, in 1958 the average surveying component of some sixteen civil engineering programmes was less than 6 percent of the total curriculum.[42] Despite the reductions most civil engineering departments in Canada – and in the United States – still considered themselves as the academic home for survey education. As is explained in the next section, in Canada this perception was changed rather quickly. The U of T option programme was terminated in 1970 when the Department of Civil Engineering decided to end all its option programmes. This formally ended a century of "surveying as a component of civil engineering" in Canada.

The Turning Point: The 1959 Colloquium on Survey Education

In human affairs the natural tendency is to follow along with the established way of doing things. As discussed above, in Canada the academic way of getting an education in surveying during the first half of the twentieth century was to enrol in a department of civil engineering. It was understood, and sometimes explicitly stated, that the programme would prepare the student for the examinations to become a land surveyor.

In the United States this civil engineering model was reinforced by the *Report of a Task Committee on the Status of Surveying and Mapping*, sponsored by the American Society of Civil Engineers.[43] In February 1959 the board of direction voted to adopt, as society policy, the following statement: "The American Society of Civil Engineers ... declares the following four major categories in the field of activity commonly designated as surveying and mapping are a part the Civil Engineering profession: I, Land Surveying; II, Engineering Surveying; III, Geodetic Surveying; IV, Cartographic Surveying."[44]

Although the American Society of Civil Engineers has no jurisdiction in Canada nor, for that matter, in the United States, it did spell out very clearly that in the academic battle for surveying and mapping in the United States, the civil engineering departments were not going to throw in the towel. In general the civil engineering faculties in both the United States and Canada were doing a reasonable job with engineering surveying, but they were only giving lip service to the other three activities identified by the task committee. Even more significantly they were virtually ignoring the foundation sciences for surveying and mapping, namely geodesy and photogrammetry. During the 1950s a sense of unease with this state of affairs led to the heretical thought that, perhaps, surveying should be considered as a discipline separate from civil engineering.

To focus attention on the education issue in 1958 Angus Hamilton, in his capacity as chairman of the editorial committee of the Canadian Institute of Surveying (CIS), asked Gamble, chairman of the education committee, for help in putting together a special issue of *The Canadian Surveyor* on surveying education. Gamble responded by proposing a special conference on education with proceedings that would be published as a special issue. The conference became the "Colloquium on Survey Education" that was held in Ottawa on 29–30 October 1959, and the proceedings were published as a special issue of *The Canadian Surveyor.*[45] This colloquium is recognized as the turning point for surveying and mapping education in Canada.

The colloquium was organized and chaired by Gamble. He invited E.H. Thompson, head of the Department of Civil Engineering at University College, London, and a distinguished photogrammetrist, to be the keynote speaker. Gamble and Col. C. H. Smith had talked to Thompson during the Conference of Commonwealth Surveyors and, without the approval of CIS council, had invited Thompson and committed the institute to paying $500 for his travel expenses. Both were on council and both were quite contrite in being so presumptuous. Council approved the funds, and there is no doubt that it was one of the best investments the institute ever made.

In the best British tradition Thompson laid it on the line and did not mince words. He bluntly accused civil engineering departments of holding on to, but not doing justice to, surveying education. He said "I want to be frank about the effects of being linked with civil engineering. Surveying education has been grossly retarded by contact with the dead hand of civil engineering. The major advances in surveying have been made by people who had nothing to do with civil engineering."[46] His phrase "the dead hand of civil engineering" drew an analogy with the deceased person whose will restricts the actions of the heirs to an estate. It was widely quoted for years afterwards. This colourful phrase dramatized the fact that, in general, civil engineering was not serving the needs of surveying but, as documented by the above-cited action of the American Society of Civil Engineers, it would not let it go.

Leslie Howlett, Head of the Physics Division of the National Research Council, reinforced the case for a new approach: "As a consequence of what I have said it seems crystal clear that some Canadian university has the magnificent challenge and opportunity of putting together the kind of course in surveying which will best develop a highly qualified professional who will be able to face modern problems with the confidence that a store of fundamental knowledge always gives." Howlett continued to elaborate on what that store of knowledge should include and then finished by saying: "One last thought – a vital one – must be left for the university that takes up the challenge. Let me plead that it not improvise and make over what is left from the rundown past. The solution is not in the addition of an extra hour of instruction here and another one there. It is not in the modification of this and that. Surveying must not be a minor subject in another discipline – a poor relation as it were – but it must be a discipline in its own right. As such it should be as independent as any other discipline."[47]

The colloquium proceedings include a profile of surveying and of surveying education in Canada, in the Commonwealth, and in the United States.[45] There were presentations by many representatives of civil engineering departments and, to their credit, most of them conceded, in principle, that Thompson was right, that surveying should have an academic home of its own. In the final discussion Ira Beattie, the forward-looking young head of the Department of Civil Engineering at UNB, speaking from the floor, introduced himself by saying "I'm one of those terrible civil engineers." He continued by stating that there was hope. He said "Two years ago we realized that we were not filling the needs of the engineer going into surveying. After some study we felt that it would be impossible to properly prepare all civil engineers for specialized surveying. We decided that the first step was to obtain the services of a qualified surveying engineer to upgrade our present courses and to guide us in setting up a specialized curriculum. We now have such a person on our staff. Our President and Dean are sympathetic in principle to the idea of higher education in surveying. A group of our graduates and others in the profession have encouraged us. We feel therefore that the time is near when we may introduce survey education at a more advanced level."[48] The "person on our staff" was Gottfried Konecny.

Beattie had been prepared for this occasion. On the way to Ottawa for the colloquium he had travelled on the train with Konecny, William Hilborn from the Faculty of Forestry at UNB, and Willis Roberts, director of the Survey, Title, Record and Draughting Branch in the Provincial Department of Lands and Mines. Accounts of this trip differ in detail, but all agree on two facts: (1) there was a generous supply of rum in their compartment, and (2) the plans for what became the Department of Surveying Engineering at UNB were put together between Fredericton and Ottawa. Although the energy and leadership that brought the Department of Surveying Engineering into existence came from many people, there is no doubt that the recognition that "its time had come" was established at the colloquium. The established way of doing things had been challenged and a new model had emerged.

The colloquium set the stage for the three programmes in surveying that evolved in English Canada during the next twenty-five years: (a) the above-mentioned surveying engineering programme that was started at the UNB in 1960 and became the Department of Surveying Engineering; (b) the survey science programme at the Erindale campus of

Figure 13-1
Participants at the Colloquium on Survey Education, Ottawa, 29–30 October 1959.
Photo: SMB, EMRU

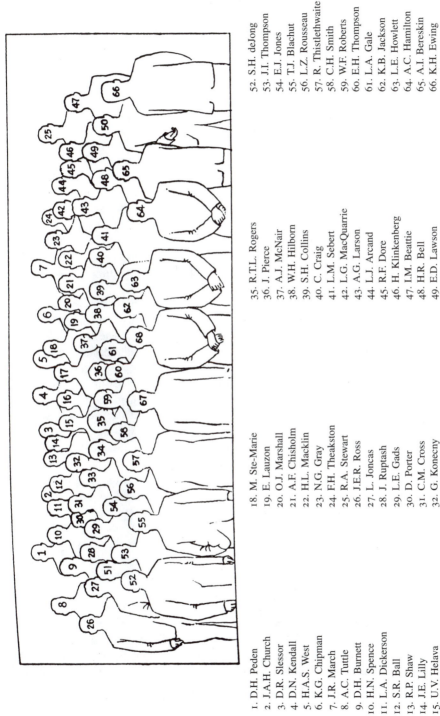

1. D.H. Peden
2. J.A.H. Church
3. D.R. Slessor
4. D.N. Kendall
5. H.A.S. West
6. K.G. Chipman
7. J.R. March
8. A.C. Tuttle
9. D.H. Burnett
10. H.N. Spence
11. L.A. Dickerson
12. S.R. Ball
13. R.P. Shaw
14. J.E. Lilly
15. U.V. Helava
16. P.E. Lachance
17. A.P. Bill

18. M. Ste-Marie
19. E. Lauzon
20. O.J. Marshall
21. A.F. Chisholm
22. H.L. Macklin
23. N.G. Gray
24. F.H. Theakston
25. R.A. Stewart
26. J.E.R. Ross
27. L. Joncas
28. J. Ruptash
29. L.E. Gads
30. D. Porter
31. C.M. Cross
32. G. Konecny
33. F.W. Lambert
34. F.J. Doyle

35. R.T.L. Rogers
36. J. Pierce
37. A.J. McNair
38. W.H. Hilborn
39. S.H. Collins
40. C. Craig
41. L.M. Sebert
42. L.G. MacQuarrie
43. A.G. Larson
44. L.J. Arcand
45. R.F. Dore
46. H. Klinkenberg
47. I.M. Beattie
48. H.R. Bell
49. E.D. Lawson
50. I.W. Tweddell
51. A.M. Floyd

52. S.H. deJong
53. J.I. Thompson
54. E.J. Jones
55. T.J. Blachut
56. L.Z. Rousseau
57. R. Thistlethwaite
58. C.H. Smith
59. W.F. Roberts
60. E.H. Thompson
61. L.A. Gale
62. K.B. Jackson
63. L.E. Howlett
64. A.C. Hamilton
65. A.I. Bereskin
66. K.H. Ewing
67. A. Dumas
68. S.G. Gamble

the U of T that became the Centre for Survey Science; and (c) the programme in survey engineering that became the Department of Surveying Engineering at the University of Calgary. All three programmes went through several name changes.[49]

While surveyors in most of the English-speaking countries of the world were bemoaning the dead hand of civil engineering, Laval University had years earlier (1907) adopted the European model of a school of surveying. At the colloquium L.-Z. Rousseau, dean of the Faculty of Surveying and Forestry, summarized the history of the Laval programme, which as of 1959 was an equal partner with forestry in his faculty.[50]

Baccalaureate Programmes

In most institutional matters major change is an agonizingly slow process. In normal times the major changes called for by Thompson and Howlett might not have happened for ten, twenty, or even thirty years, if ever. Fortunately the early 1960s were not normal times; change, renewal, and "progress" were the order of the day – and governments were prepared to spend money on new ideas. Immediately after the colloquium one completely new programme was established (in surveying engineering at UNB), and an existing programme (in surveying at Laval University) was transformed from a traditional undergraduate teaching model to a research-oriented model along the lines spelled out by Howlett.

The Laval programme had an advantage in that it was established, with a flow of students through it to careers as Québec Land Surveyors; it had a disadvantage in that it had a staff of tenured professors with a long-established way of doing things. The UNB programme had an advantage in that it was starting with a clean slate, but it had a disadvantage in that it did not yet have a place – it was not part of an established pattern with an external support system. Both programmes made the most of their inherent advantages, and persevered with their disadvantages. The results of their efforts – graduates at both the undergraduate and post-graduate levels – are shown in tables 13-2 and 13-3 together with the results of the two other programmes that became established a few years later.

Many, probably the majority, of the graduates from the four baccalaureate programmes article with practising land surveyors and receive their commissions as land surveyors from one or more of the eleven boards of examiners. A significant number of the graduates from UNB and the University of Calgary become registered as professional engineers, and quite a few become both commissioned land surveyors and registered professional engineers.

Some, however, whose careers are in the technical rather than the legal side of the profession, do not concern themselves with registration at all. Recently, that is since the advent of remote-sensing and GIS technology, this group has been supplemented by graduates from several of the university geography departments that have offered a significant number of courses in cartography, remote sensing, GIS, and related topics.

During the 1960s and 1970s a significant number of bachelor graduates were international students. The first wave was from Africa, primarily Nigeria, along with some from the Caribbean. As noted under "The University of New Brunswick" below, one class consisted only of African students. In the 1970s and early 1980s there were some from the Middle East and quite a few from Pacific Rim countries, especially Hong Kong and Malaysia. By the 1990s this had become a negligible number because by then there was an undergraduate survey programme in virtually every developing country.

Table 13-2

Baccalaureate Degree Programmes and Graduates from 1908 to 1993

	Laval	U of T	UNB	U of C	Total	
1908–17	28				28	In 1907 a chair in surveying was established at Laval
1918–27	20				20	University and J.-N. Castonguay was appointed to it.
1928–37	31				31	The first student graduated in 1908. Average number of
1938–47	37	C.E.			37	graduates during the first forty years was three. From
1948–56	67	option			67	1946 to 1952 the average was eleven.
1957	5	7			12	In 1955 a surveying option in civil engineering at the
1958	2	2			4	University of Toronto was started under the direction of
	8	0			8	Oscar Marshall.
1960	9	5			14	In 1960 a surveying engineering degree programme was
	7	3			10	started at UNB under the direction of Gottfried Konecny.
1962	6	4	4		14	
	16	3	6		25	
	24	4	3		31	
1965	21	6	4		31	
	24	8	5		37	
	17	3	5		25	
1968	29	8	5		42	
	41	6	14		61	The surveying option programme at the University of
1970	28	6	9		43	Toronto was closed; the last class graduated in 1970.
Subtotal	420	[65]	55			
1971	31		16		47	
	27	Erindale	15		42	In 1972 a survey science programme was established on
	10		17		27	the Erindale campus of the University of Toronto under
1974	28	1	24		53	the direction of Gordon Gracie.
1975	28	1	15		44	
	36	16	14		66	
	39	13	31		83	
	62	18	16		96	
	82	21	26		129	In 1979 a surveying engineering programme was
1980	58	19	38		115	established at the University of Calgary under the
	71	19	26	8	124	direction of Edward Krakiwsky.
1982	65	29	28	10	132	
	56	24	37	20	137	
	51	17	20	14	102	
1985	27	29	33	13	102	
	21	19	30	13	83	In 1986 the name of the Laval programme was changed
	20	20	19	23	82	to "Geomatics."
	33	18	24	22	97	In 1988 the Centre for Surveying Science was
	34	17	21	20	92	established at Erindale.
1990	47	25	16	17	105	
	56	14	20	17	107	
	58	31	21	24	134	In 1992 the name of the U of C programme became
1993	52	29	14	14	109	"Geomatics Engineering."
Subtotal	992	[380]	521			In 1994 the name of the UNB programme became
Totals	1412	445	576	215	2648	"Geodesy and Geomatics Engineering."

Table 13-3
The Number of Master's and Doctorates Awarded in Surveying, Mapping, and Related Fields between 1950 and 1993

	Master's								Ph.D.						
	Laval	UNB	U of T	U of C	U of S*	Sub-total	Geog. Depts**	Grand Total	Laval	UNB	U of T	U of C	Sub-total	Geog. Depts**	Grand Total
1950			1			1		1							
51			1			1		1							
53			1			1		1							
55			1			1		1							
58			1			1		1							
59			3			3		3							
62	1					1		1			1		1		1
63	1	1				2	1	3							
64	1					1		1							
65	1	2				3		3							
66	1	2	1			4	1	5	1				1		1
67	2	3				5		5							
68	4	3	3		2	12	1	13							
69	1	1	2		1	5	1	6	3				3		3
70	3	9	3		1	16	1	17		3			3		3
71	7	5	4		1	17	1	18	1	1			2		2
72	4	9				13	5	18			1				
73	3	5			1	9	5	14							
74		5	1		1	7	5	12	1	2			3	1	4
75	4	4	1			9	7	16		3			3		3
76	1	3				4	5	9		2			2		2
77	2	6	1		1	10	9	19		1			1		1
78	2	5				7	5	12							
79	4	9	1			14	2	16		2			2	1	3
80	2	11	1		1	15	4	19		1			1		1
81	4	8				12	6	18	1	2			3		3
82	5	3	1			9	2	11		2			2		2
83	9	12				21	2	23		1			1		1
84	8	8	3			19		19		3			3		3
85	3	6		4		13		13	2	1			3		3
86	9	11	1	5		26	6	32	1			1	2		2
87	4	8	2	3		17	4	21	3	1			4		4
88	5	9	1	4		19	12	31		5		2	7		7
89	14	15	2	3		34	10	44	1	3		2	6		6
90	4	13		3		20	1	21	1	1			2		2
91	9	14	4	10		37	2	39	3	1	1	2	7		7
92	2	12	2	5		21	2	23		2	1	2	5	2	7
93	6	13		6		25		25		1		3	4		4
	126	215	42	43	9	435	100	535	18	38	4	12	71	4	75

* Nine master's degrees were awarded by the Faculty of Engineering at the University of Saskatchewan for work on automated cartography under Professor Ray Boyle.

** Geography department data is from tables 12-1 and 12-2, compiled by Henry Castner. It is the total number of graduate degrees in cartography and related fields awarded by geography departments in Canada.

Joseph-Narcisse Gastonguay and his fellow directors of the Québec Land Surveyors Corporation campaigned for many years for a School of Surveying at Laval University, and in 1907, when Gastonguay was president of the corporation, their efforts were rewarded. The parliament of the province of Québec created a "Chaire d'arpentage, en vue de favoriser l'étude des sciences naturelles et mathématiques." At the general assembly of the Québec Land Surveyors Corporation of 10 April 1907, the following resolution was approved concerning the admission requirements to study surveying at the university: "Il est résolu que tout élève, avant d'être admis à l'étude de l'arpentage, ait des connaissances équivalentes à l'inscription en réthorique, sauf le latin et le grec." In the minutes of this assembly one can find the following comment by President Gastonguay: "Aujourd'hui, la perspective devient plus belle pour nos enfants et nous pouvons compter que ceux qui nous remplaceront seront des arpenteurs instruits, capables de faire honneur à la patrie, à leur province et de faire aux exigences de leur temps."

In March 1908, at the request of the Québec Land Surveyors Corporation and the provincial government, the School of Surveying was affiliated with the Faculty of Arts of the university. Eleven years later in 1919 the School of Surveying and the School of Forest Sciences, which had been created in 1910, were merged to form the School of Surveying and Forest Engineering. In 1963 the name of the faculty was changed to the Faculty of Forestry and Geodesy. On 15 August 1989 the name of the faculty was finally changed to the Faculty of Forestry and Geomatics in order to reflect better the evolution and modernisation of the curriculum.

Before 1921 no degree was awarded by the university for the programme. The purpose of the curriculum was to prepare the student for the examinations required by the Québec Land Surveyors Corporation and for a Dominion Land Surveyor's commission. After 1921 those who completed the course successfully received the degree of Bachelor in Surveying. Until 1968 the duration of the programme was dependent on the student's previous education. For those students who were coming from the "classical course" (a course of eight years including humanities and sciences) the duration of the study was four years, while the others had to complete a preparatory year. Following the introduction of the CEGEP (Collège d'Éducation Générale et Professionnelle) system in 1968 it became a four-year course for all students. In 1972 the credit system was introduced. The four-year curriculum had 126 credits and led to the degree of Bachelor in Applied Sciences – Geodesy/Surveying.

The curriculum was restructured for the start of the 1986–87 academic year. The change was made because of the maximum of 112 credits that had been imposed by the provincial Department of Education. It has a duration of three and a half years and leads to the degree of Bachelor in Applied Sciences – Geomatics. The study consists of a common core of 68 credits plus two options, geomatics management and geomatics engineering, each of 38 credits. It is completed by six credits that are of the student's choice. The curriculum tends to achieve a balance between three levels: basic courses, discipline-specific courses, and courses in social sciences and humanities. The engineering option places more emphasis on the exact sciences and measurements and less on the liberal, legal, and management aspects, while in the management option the emphasis is placed more on the liberal, legal, and management aspects.

In the early 1960s the emphasis of technical development was put on photogrammetry. Major equipment such as Wild A7 and B8 plotters were acquired, as well as an analytical plotter. This development was initiated by André Frechette and resulted in the creation of a Department of Photogrammetry in 1965. In the mid-1960s on the initiative of Robert St Arnaud the technical emphasis was placed on cartography, which culminated in the establishment of a cartographic laboratory and a cartography service. Also in the mid-1960s under Louis Joncas there was a major expansion in the field of metrology with the acquisition of equipment such as a Keufel & Esser calibration bench for optical instruments, and a Michaelson Interferometer for the calibration of tapes, levelling rods, and other measuring devices. This, along with the acquisition of a Lacoste-Romberg gravimeter, EDM instruments, and theodolites resulted in the formation of a geodesy/metrology laboratory in 1967. In the mid-1970s on the initiative of Guy Rochon a DIPIX Remote Sensing system was acquired and in 1979 a remote sensing laboratory was established in partnership with the provincial SCANIQ (Systéme Conjoint d'Analyse Numérique d'Image du Québec). In the 1980s developments were focused on the fields of GPS, video photogrammetry, and GIS applications. These efforts resulted in the formation in 1989 of a major research centre, Centre de Recherche en Géomatique (CRG).

University of Toronto: The Option Programme in Civil Engineering: 1955–70

In 1955 a strong option programme became established in the Civil Engineering Department at the U of T. As indicated in table 13-2 there were several graduates each year from 1957 through 1970.[52] Although the enrolment was never large the graduates were well received; many became leaders at the provincial and national level. John Barber became the president of one of the largest practices in Ontario, J.D. Barnes and Associates, and he served as president of the Ontario Association of Land Surveyors and of the Canadian Institute of Surveying; Gary Sawayama became director of the Surveys and Mapping Branch in British Columbia and Peter Finos became surveyor general of Ontario. Nevertheless, as has been mentioned, the Department of Civil Engineering decided to terminate all option programmes in 1970. This left the Association of Ontario Land Surveyors (AOLS) in an awkward position. It had recently approved By-Law 95, which in effect made a degree a prerequisite for admission. This by-law was the culmination of a long and controversial dialogue aimed at broadening the scope of activities of the association to include geodesy, photogrammetry, and hydrography. Fred Pearce, a surveyor practising in Stratford who had led the association's drive for educational programmes at both the technical college and university level all through the 1960s, was not willing to give up when the option programme was closed. He and his colleagues met with several university presidents and eventually, after talks with J. Tuzo Wilson, the distinguished geophysicist, who was at that time principal of Erindale College, they found a home for surveying on the Erindale campus of the U of T.

University of Toronto: Survey Science at Erindale:[53] 1972–

One of the final steps leading to the establishment of the Erindale programme had been the Conference on the Surveying Profession – its Structure and its Home. The conference was sponsored jointly by the AOLS and Erindale, and had focused on the need for an undergraduate surveying programme in Ontario. It was held in October 1970.

An implementation plan was made in 1971 following appointment of Gordon Gracie to the Erindale faculty. The new discipline was identified as survey science, and the plan was endorsed by the AOLS in January 1972. Shortly thereafter the proposed programme was accepted by the university, and financial support was approved by the Ontario Ministry of Colleges and Universities.

Instruction during the first two years was provided by Gordon Gracie and by Robert Gunn who transferred to Erindale from the Department of Civil Engineering. David Lambden and Hans Klinkenberg joined the faculty in 1974. However the programme suffered a serious setback in December with the sudden death of Klinkenberg. His position was filled in 1975 by Louis Gale who continued teaching until his retirement in 1979. He was followed by Sol Cushman, a visiting professor, who served until 1981. Jack Young joined the faculty in 1980 and Petr Vaníček was with the programme from 1981 to 1983.

The undergraduate programme underwent considerable development during the 1970s. This was accompanied by steady growth in student enrolment – from 23 in 1972 to 150 in 1979. By 1979 a total of 70 students had graduated from the programme. In the early 1980s elective streams were created and new courses were added, and several adjunct appointments were made including those of Robert Clipsham, Izaak de Rijcke, Ross Douglas, Hugh O'Donnell, and Tom Seawright. There was a significant decrease in undergraduate enrollment in the 1980s, but this was followed by full recovery to the 150-student level by 1990.

The 1980s also witnessed considerable effort toward the development of a solid research capability and a curriculum of graduate studies. This was accomplished with the full cooperation of the U of T Department of Civil Engineering, under which surveying was a major field of study at the graduate level. In 1987 the undergraduate specialist programme was granted full accreditation by the Canadian Council of Land Surveyors. It was also revised in anticipation of changes in the surveying profession in Ontario that were subsequently implemented under the Surveyors Act of 1989. Also instituted in 1987, and continuing annually at Erindale until 1992, was a special seven-week course on maritime boundary delimitation that attracted participants from over forty countries of the world.

In 1988 the university created the Centre for Surveying Science. Until then the discipline known as survey science was free-standing, that is it was under direct administration of the college. With the establishment of the centre, surveying science was given its own administrative home. The year 1988 also saw appointment of V.B. Robinson to the faculty and to the directorship of the newly created Institute for Land Information Management, a research and consultative facility that complements the activities of the centre. In recent years the research activities of surveying science have focused more and more on land information studies, a field that is very much shared by geographers. In a move to unite and strengthen graduate studies in land information, the graduate programme in surveying science was transferred in 1993 from the Department of Civil Engineering to the Department of Geography.

In January 1993 Rear Admiral Darshan Kapoor, who had been appointed in 1983 to develop a hydrographic programme, died suddenly. As a result courses in hydrographic surveying are no longer offered. Also in 1993 Gunn retired and Ferenc Csillag was appointed to teach and do research in remote sensing, cartography, and GIS.

Ever since 1976, when the first class of graduates entered the workforce, surveying science at Erindale has been the primary source of recruits for the surveying profession in

Ontario. As of 1993, 348 men and women had completed their undergraduate studies in surveying science, 20 had completed their studies for master's degrees, and two had been awarded Ph.D. degrees.

The University of New Brunswick: 1960–

Following the 1959 colloquium Konecny took full advantage of the opportunity provided by Beattie and supported by the young dean, Jim Dineen, at UNB. The plans developed on the train to the colloquium were put into a brief to the president, and in the fall of 1960 a Bachelor of Science in Engineering (surveying engineering) programme was initiated under the wing of civil engineering. The last two years of the five-year programme were devoted to surveying, which was taught by three faculty members, (Konecny, Peter Wilson, and Gerhard Gloss) to students who had completed three years in civil engineering. In 1961 a first-order stereoplotter, a Wild A5, was acquired and a Master of Science in Engineering (MSCE) programme was begun. In 1962 four students received their BSCE (surveying engineering) degree: Peter Berghuis, Cyril Carlin, Lorne Pelton, and Ted Pond.

A year later, still under the aegis of civil engineering, the Division of Surveying Engineering was established and a Ph.D. programme was authorized. Also in 1963 the first Master of Science in Engineering (MSCE) degree was awarded to Eugene Derenyi. In 1964 a research programme was started in engineering and mining surveys. In November 1965 the Department of Surveying Engineering was formally established as an entity completely separate from the Department of Civil Engineering. Thus in just six years from the time that Howlett had identified the need for it, an independent teaching and research unit in surveying and mapping had been established. Also in 1965 a one-year practice-oriented diploma course began with ten students from Africa and Central America. By the time this programme was discontinued in 1970 thirty-eight students had completed it. In 1966 undergraduate and graduate courses in engineering and mining surveys were started by Adam Chrzanowski who, after an appointment as a post-doctoral fellow, had been appointed to the faculty. In 1968 a Master of Engineering programme was started. This differed from the MSCE curriculum in that more course work and less research were required. Also in 1968 the undergraduate curriculum was revised to provide three years of specialization following two years of courses common to other departments in the faculty. In the same year an analytical plotter was acquired through a major equipment grant from NRC, supplemented by funding from the Donner Foundation and from the Defence Research Board of Canada. This plotter, one of the first delivered, was made by the OMI Corporation in Italy under license from the National Research Council in Ottawa (see chapter 12). The International Symposium on Land Registration and Data Banks, co-sponsored by CIS and the National Advisory Committee on Control Surveys and Mapping, was held in November.

Although there were new initiatives every year as indicated above, there were still teething problems, not the least of which was low enrolment. The department was caught in a chicken-and-egg situation: students were not enrolling in surveying engineering because jobs were not being advertised, and employers were not advertising jobs because they did not know what to expect from a surveying engineering graduate. Had it not been for CIDA-sponsored African students the department might not have survived. One graduating class of five, in 1968, had no Canadians and another had only one. This absence of

Canadian students caused the university to question the viability of the programme. University officials held a closed meeting with Gamble, Howlett, and one or two others. No minutes of this meeting were kept, but Konecny must have been persuasive. Instead of having his programme terminated or his staff reduced he received approval to increase his faculty to ten and his support staff to five. Shortly thereafter enrolment picked up, and since then the department has never looked back.

Edward Krakiwsky joined the faculty in 1968 with the responsibility for developing a research and graduate programme in geodesy. In 1969 a Doppler satellite receiver was acquired as part of this initiative. Also in 1969 the department hosted a symposium on mining and rock deformation, as is described in chapter 16. In 1970 the first Ph.D.s were awarded to F.A.E. Ahmed, E.E. Derenyi, and D.M.J. Fubara. At the same ceremony Gamble, director of the Surveys and Mapping Branch, Ottawa, received the first Surveying Engineering–sponsored honorary degree. In 1970 first-order Wild A10 and Kern PG2 stereoplotters were acquired, and in 1971 the cartographic laboratory was equipped with an overhead camera and accessories, and cartographic courses were expanded. Also in 1971 Petr Vaníček joined the department and initiated a research thrust in physical geodesy. In the same year Wolfgang Faig arrived to conduct research and supervise graduate studies in aerotriangulation and close-range photogrammetry. In 1972 a cadastral studies research programme was started under John McLaughlin.

In 1975 the surveying engineering curriculum was reduced from approximately 210 credit hours to 180 credit hours to conform to a standard adopted by the faculty. This was achieved by pruning non–surveying Engineering courses, and by compacting or dropping some of the older surveying engineering material. In 1976 Donald Thomson joined the department and a hydrographic research programme was initiated. In 1977 the Ninth National Surveying Teachers Conference was hosted by the department, whilst in 1978 undergraduate enrolment peaked at 181.

A graduate programme in land information management was introduced in 1979. Two years later a fully interactive digital mapping facility was acquired, as was a digital analysis system that gave the department the most advanced remote sensing facility in the Atlantic provinces. In 1983 a graduate diploma course in mapping, charting, and geodesy, developed in collaboration with Mapping and Charting Establishment of the Department of National Defence, was approved. An exchange agreement was signed with Wuhan Technical University of Surveying and Mapping, People's Republic of China.

The year 1985 marked the twenty-fifth anniversary of surveying engineering at UNB, and as part of the celebration Konecny was awarded an honorary Doctor of Science for his contribution to the university. He had served as chairman until 1971 when he accepted the chair in photogrammetry and engineering surveys at the University of Hannover, Germany. He was succeeded by Angus Hamilton, who had been with the Department of Energy, Mines and Resources in Ottawa for twenty years. Hamilton stepped down in 1985 and was succeeded by John McLaughlin. McLaughlin was followed by Adam Chrzanowski in 1991. In 1990 a chair in ocean mapping was announced, and Larry Meyer was appointed to fill it in 1991.

The University of Calgary:[54] *1979–*

At the University of Calgary (U of C) a surveying engineering programme was started in 1979 under the leadership of Edward Krakiwsky as a division of the Civil Engineering

Department. It achieved departmental status in 1986. Compared to the other courses the programme at U of C got off to a flying start. This was possible because the need for surveying engineers had been recognized and there were qualified teachers available. During the 1979–80 academic year five full-time faculty appointments were made: E.G. Anderson, J.A.R. Blais, G.D. Lodwick, K.-P. Schwarz, and W.F. Teskey. Krakiwsky had earned his degree in geodesy at The Ohio State University and subsequently had helped to build the geodesy component of the UNB surveying engineering programme. At U of C he served as chairman of the division of surveying engineering until 1986, and then continued as head of the programme after it achieved departmental status. In 1989 he was succeeded by Klaus-Peter Schwarz who had earned a master's degree at UNB in 1967 and served there as a senior research associate prior to joining U of C in 1979.

In 1981 the division hosted its first major international conference on the use of inertial technology in surveying and geodesy. The response to this initiative was enthusiastic, and a conference on this theme has been held every four years since. Also in 1981 C.S. Fraser joined the division.

In 1982 the division received approval to offer graduate programmes at both the master's and Ph.D. levels. The first master's student, R.V.C. Wong, received his degree that year. In 1983 the department initiated a continuing education series. The first of this series was a two-day conference, Land Information: Concepts, Terminology and Impact. Rod Blais organized the conference and edited the proceedings for publication as *Lecture Notes In Digital Mapping and Land Information* published jointly by the department and the CIS.

The year 1985 saw the acquisition of an image processing facility, an inertial laboratory, and two GPS receivers. An externally funded position in digital mapping and spatial data management was added. Also in 1985 the first Ph.D. was awarded to A.A. Vassiliou. Research in kinematic geodesy under Schwarz and Krakiwsky was augmented when Gerard Lachapelle joined the department in January 1988.

The department hosted the Thirteenth North American Surveying and Mapping Teachers' Conference in 1990. Also in that year a Distinguished Lecturer Series was established. This series enabled the department to strengthen its graduate studies by bringing outstanding scientists from around the world to give two two-week graduate courses each summer.

The department has a truly distinguished record in awarding doctorates to women. In 1990 Elfriede Knickmeyer received her Ph.D.; she was the first woman to earn a doctorate in surveying engineering in Canada. She was closely followed by Elizabeth Cannon (1991), and by Angela Rauhut and Elly Rasdiani (1992).

Two new positions were established in 1991. One of these, in cadastral studies, was filled by A.C. McEwen, formerly the International Boundary Commissioner for Canada. This position was made possible through the encouragement and financial support of the Western Land Surveying Associations. The other position was filled by M.E. Cannon, winner of a prestigious NSERC (Natural Sciences and Engineering Research Council) Women's Fellowship, the first at the U of C. In 1992 the department obtained approval from the university to change its name to Geomatics Engineering.

Accreditation of Baccalaureate Programmes

The Canadian Council of Professional Engineers (CCPE) has had an accreditation programme since 1965. Under this system the academic credentials of the graduates of accredited programmes are accepted without question by all provincial associations, whereas graduates of non-accredited courses are reviewed individually and are usually required to write additional examinations. To be accredited a department must submit a comprehensive list of all its resources, records, examination papers, etcetera. Subsequently a peer-group team, usually one or two faculty members from an accredited programme and one or two senior practitioners, make a two-day on-site inspection of the facilities. Programmes may get full accreditation or conditional accreditation; full accreditation is valid for five years but conditional accreditation for only three years. The surveying engineering programme at UNB was accredited in 1972 and that at U of C in 1982. Both have had their full accreditation status renewed at each five-year re-accreditation since.

In 1985 the Canadian Council of Land Surveyors (CCLS) established an accreditation programme for surveying programmes similar to that of the CCPE. The surveying engineering programme at UNB was accredited by CCLS in 1985, that at the U of T in 1987, at Laval in 1988, and at U of C in 1991. Also in 1985 the UNB hydrographic option became the first university programme to receive academic accreditation from the International Hydrographic Organisation.

Cartography/GIS Education in Geography Departments

Geography departments in Canada are relatively new participants in surveying and mapping education. In 1972 when Canada was host to the International Cartographic Association there were still only a few "academic" cartographers in the country. However that was the year that Landsat 1 was launched and, in effect, it was the year that remote sensing from space made its formal debut. Soon thereafter virtually every geography department began to develop some teaching and research capability in this new sub-discipline.

In addition to the interest in remote sensing there was rapid growth in automated cartography and data storage and manipulation by computer during the next 15 years. The natural evolution from these technologies was GIS. Thus by 1987, when Chris Gold prepared a report on cartographic education in Canada that summarized the involvement of geography departments in cartography, there had obviously been a major expansion.[55] Specifically Gold said: "Two departments [of twenty-eight that responded to his questionnaire] have a low involvement in cartography, giving either zero or one course in the subject. Nineteen universities fall in the medium category giving two to four courses with nine of these providing three courses in cartography. Seven universities fall in the high category offering five or more courses; three of these being classified as very high having eight or more courses available … The high category (Alberta, Carleton, Memorial, Queen's, Simon Fraser, and Western Ontario) in general coincides with those universities … that specifically mention graduate programs."

This expansion is confirmed by the number of post-graduate degrees (see table 13-3) awarded in cartographic topics by geography departments during this period: fifty master's and two Ph.D.s compared to eleven master's and no doctorates in all the years prior to 1972.

In 1990 Jacqueline Anderson[56] and Peter Keller[57] examined the *Guide to Departments of Geography in the United States and Canada* and analyzed the results of a questionnaire sent to fifty-four departments in Canadian universities and colleges "thought to have an interest in cartographic graduate research." Although their questionnaire included much more detail than Gold's had, there is no indication of significant differences from Gold's analysis above, showing that only a few geography departments offer a "concentration" in the mapping sciences.

Many graduates from these geography programmes have found rewarding careers in mapping; most notable in this category is Gabriella Zillmer, a graduate from Queen's, who became director of the Surveys, Mapping and Remote Sensing Branch of the Ontario Ministry of Natural Resources in 1991. Generally, however, the geography graduates who have had a strong concentration on mapping sciences are working in some aspect of remote sensing, or they are using mapping databases for some statistical analysis.

To what extent are geography departments contributing to surveying and mapping education? The answer to this question depends largely on how surveying and mapping are defined. If the old and rather narrow definition is used then the answer has to be "modestly"; however if a broad definition is used then the answer will be "significantly." This is because the traditional boundaries are being blurred – there is no longer a clear distinction between those who collect, those who compile, and those who use spatial data. With high technology the distinction between field and office, and between producer and user, is no longer sharply defined. This blurring, in turn, is leading to a reduced distinction between the activities of those in traditional surveying and mapping and many of those in geography.

Graduate Studies

As mentioned earlier, by 1875 McGill had established a Faculty of Applied Science authorized to award bachelor's and master's degrees. The first "surveyor" to receive a master's degree was C.H. McLeod who received an M.E. degree in 1878. Although the topic of his dissertation has not been found, it can be assumed that it had some connection with his work at the observatory. The next graduate degree of record was awarded to John B. Baird at McGill in 1909; his dissertation was entitled "Approximate Methods of Longitude Determination: An Investigation of Personal Equation in Astronomical Observations with the Respold Micrometer Eyepiece." His supervisors were C.H. McLeod and J. Cox. No other records of graduate studies prior to the Second World War have been found.

In 1950 the first postwar master's degree was awarded to Shi-Liu Kao by the Department of Civil Engineering at the U of T. His thesis was "Astronomic Positioning by Ball's Method for Photogrammetric Control (With a Comparison of Graphical and Analytical Solutions)." Six more master's degrees were awarded at the U of T between 1951 and 1959.[58] Some of these were awarded by the Department of Civil Engineering under Oscar Marshall and some by the Department of Applied Physics under K.B. Jackson. At that time the Department of Applied Physics was responsible for photogrammetry and air photography.

The first doctoral degree was awarded in 1962 to Deszo Nagy for his research on geoidal contours at the U of T. At Laval the first doctorate was awarded to André Frechette in 1966; the title of his dissertation was "Étude sur les levés cadastraux dans la province de Québec avec considération spéciale des méthodes photogrammétriques."

In table 13-3 the number of master's and doctorates awarded by each of the four ongoing surveying programmes is shown together with the cumulative total for all of the cartography-related master's and doctorates awarded by geography departments. In view of the fact that the number of graduate degrees awarded by a programme is a rough measure of research activity, this table can be considered a measure of the research done by the faculty members in these programmes.

In the 1960s a sustained effort in research and graduate studies began at both Laval and UNB. At the U of T the Erindale programme gradually took over the responsibility for graduate studies from the Department of Civil Engineering, and the U of C programme quite quickly developed a strong graduate studies programme. It should be noted, however, that quite a large proportion of these degrees were earned by international students. Many of the first wave of foreign students applied for and were granted landed immigrant status in Canada. However when the supply of Canadian graduates was sufficient to fill the available Canadian positions, only those who qualified as refugees were admitted to Canada without delay. Most of the international students returned to their home countries as faculty members or as administrators, and a few became "citizens of the world" and took positions in a Third World country.

Technician and Technologist Programmes

Compared to Europe Canada has, with minor exceptions, been decades behind in developing curricula that bridge the gap between secondary school and university. This is as true for surveying and cartography as for other occupations. Prior to the Second World War there was only one survey technician programme in the country. This was at the Provincial Institute of Technology and Art, now the Southern Alberta Institute of Technology (SAIT) in Calgary. That programme, modified many times, continues and is now called surveying and mapping technology (see table 13-4).

The next initiative was started during the war when Maj. James Church, in Halifax, was asked to set up a course in surveying for servicemen. At the end of the war Church reasoned, logically, that if a course was needed in wartime there must also be a need for one in peacetime.[59] He argued persuasively for the expansion of his wartime course into the programme that became the first building block of the Nova Scotia Land Survey Institute in Lawrencetown. The institute has always been innovative and flexible. When it identified a need it moved quickly to meet that need, and when there was no further need for a course it moved quickly to cancel it. In 1986 it was renamed the College of Geographic Sciences (COGS).

In St John's the Newfoundland College of Trades and Technology began in 1963 to offer a solid two-year programme in survey technology under the direction of Peter Berghuis. In 1981 the college expanded this programme to three years and added hydrographic surveying to the curriculum. In 1986 it changed its name to the Cabot Institute of Applied Arts and Technology.

In the west the British Columbia Institute of Technology began in 1964 to provide a strong two-year technology course under the direction of Dave Mason. The following year a photogrammetry option was introduced, and in 1987 a two-term GIS advanced diploma programme was established.

In his presentation to the Second Colloquium on Survey Education in 1966 R.D. Thompson, at that time an instructor in civil technology at Ryerson, claimed that there were no technology courses given in central canada.[60] Thompson had already alluded to the courses in Newfoundland, Nova Scotia, Alberta, and British Columbia. (Although there were no "survey technology" courses being given in Ontario, some surveying was being taught in civil technician and technology courses.) This state of affairs changed very soon after the colloquium. Under the indefatigable Fred Pearce, the AOLS pressed for, and obtained, a three-year survey technology programme at Ryerson Polytechnical Institute and, in addition, several survey technician programmes at newly established community colleges (see table 13-5). Thompson himself left Ryerson shortly after the colloquium, and started a three-year technology programme at Humber College.

The Ryerson Polytechnical Institute is a one-of-a-kind institution. In 1948 it was assigned to develop technology programmes that would fill the gap between the vocational courses in high schools and degree studies at universities. In many ways it was given a mission similar to that of the SPS in 1878. As noted elsewhere the SPS evolved into the Faculty of Applied Science and Engineering at the U of T. In 1971 the Ryerson Polytechnical Institute became the Ryerson Polytechnic University with authority to extend its three-year technology programmes to four years and to give Bachelor of Technology degrees. The programme in geodetic sciences was one of those extended to four years, and it became the only institution in the country giving the degree of Bachelor of Technology in geodetic science. In 1982 its name was changed to Bachelor of Survey Engineering Technology. Needless to say this programme has had difficulty finding its niche in the professional world, but today there is no doubt that it is firmly established. It has met the two essential criteria for survival: it has been able to attract students, and its graduates have been able to find employment.

Starting in 1966, as shown in table 13-4, there was a virtual explosion of technician and technology programmes across the country. At this point it may be relevant to discuss the terms "technician" and "technologist." It is generally agreed that a technologist is more advanced than a technician, but there the consensus ends. Three-year curricula are always specified as "technology" while one year curricula are almost always called "technician" programmes. But two-year courses can be termed either one or the other, apparently at the discretion of the college authorities. One approach followed by several provinces has been to add three or four weeks to the normal twelve- or thirteen-week term and offer a technology programme in four terms. Generally the objective across the country has been to offer the "technology" programmes. However, as noted above, when the CAATs (Colleges of Applied Arts and Technology, later renamed Community Colleges) in Ontario first burst onto the scene they all offered two-year technician programmes, in name and in content. As indicated by a comparison of the data in Tables 13-4 and 13-5, Ontario took a much more aggressive approach than the other provinces in expanding its facilities. Within four years of the introduction of the first survey technology programme at Ryerson, eight four-term technician programmes had been started, as well as the six-term technology programme at Humber. By 1993 considerable rationalization had occurred. Four of the colleges were no longer offering any surveying, two were offering both four-term and six-term programmes, and three were offering only four-term programmes. In 1993 there were only thirty-four graduates from the five four-term courses and six graduates from the two six-term courses.

The evolution of studies in the mapping technologies lagged behind the evolution in surveying. This may have been because map compilation was generally done by governments, and governments could and did develop in-house training. The first programmes in the mapping technologies were offered in 1962 by the Nova Scotia Land Survey Institute (now the College of Geographic Sciences). In that year two-term courses were offered for photogrammetric and cartographic technicians (see table 13-6).

Table 13-4
Technician and Technologist Programmes in Surveying

Province/Institution/Programme	Place	First offered	Status 1993*	Length (Terms)	Number of graduates Low/High	Average
BRITISH COLUMBIA						
BC Institute of Technology	Burnaby					
Surveying and mapping technology		1964	C	4T	18/68	≈ 35
Surveying technician			C	2T		
Camosun College						
[Students transferred to BCIT	Victoria	1971	1983	2T		
for their 3rd and 4th terms]						
ALBERTA						
SA Institute of Technology	Calgary	1925	C	4T		≈ 10
NA Institute of Technology	Edmonton	1966	C	4T		≈ 15
SASKATCHEWAN						
Pallister Institute	Moose Jaw	1969	C	4T + WT	5/12	≈ 8
		1991	C	5T + WT		
MANITOBA						
Keewatin Community College	The Pas	1971	1982	4T	3/10	≈ 5
Red River Community College	Winnipeg	1970	C	4T		≈ 9
ONTARIO						
Ryerson Polytechnical Institute	Toronto	1966	1976	6T	1/21	≈ 10
Ryerson Polytechnic University		1971	C	8T	3/17	≈ 9

At one time nine community colleges in Ontario were offering programmes in surveying; by 1993 only five were offering any surveying programmes. Data on these programmes are shown in table 13-5.

QUÉBEC						
Limoilou College	Québec	1976	C	6T		≈ 20
Ahuntsic College	Montréal	1971	C	6T		≈ 20
NOVA SCOTIA**						
College of Geographical Sciences	Lawrencetown					
Survey Technology [12 mo.]		1945	1958	3T		≈ 16
Survey Technology		1958	1989	4T	15/30	≈ 20
Survey Technology [2nd yr]		1989	C	(2T) + 2T		≈ 23
Survey Assistant		1975	1993	2T		≈ 11
Survey Office Technician		1974	1989	2T	/18	≈ 10
Survey Technician Certificate		1989	C	2T	/40	≈ 30
NEWFOUNDLAND						
Cabot Institute of Applied Arts and	St John's	1963	1981	4T	5/22	≈ 17
Technology		1981	.C	6T	8/19	≈ 15

*   This column shows the year of termination for closed programmes; ongoing programmes are shown as C for Continuing.
    WT = work terms.

** This data provided by John Wightman, principal of the college from 1986 to 1994.

Table 13-5
Ontario Community College Programmes in Surveying

College	Place	First offered	Status: 1993*	Length (Terms)	Number** of graduates for years 1981 through 1993	
					Low/High	Average
Algonquin	Ottawa	1967	C	4T	4/29	15
		1971	C	6T	0/17	9
(There were no graduates from Algonquin's four-term programme in the years 1985 through 1990)						
Confederation	Thunder Bay	1971	1990	4T	2/11	6
Fanshawe	London	1967	C	4T + WT	4/13	8
George Brown	Toronto	1967	1982	4T	4/5	5
(Formerly the Provincial Institute of Trades)				The enrolment had peaked in 1972–73 at 55.		
		1971	1983	6T	3/7	5
Georgian	Barrie	1969	C	4T + WT	3/27	11
Humber	Toronto	1983	1990	4T	5/10	4
		1969	1989	6T	2/13	8
Loyalist	Belleville	1968	C	4T	1/9	5
Niagara	Welland	1968	1989	4T	4/12	8
Northern	South	1967	C	4T	0/12	6
	Porcupine	1973	C	6T	0/7	3

*   This column shows the year of termination for closed programmes; ongoing programmes are shown as C, for continuing.

** Data on the technology and technician programmes in Ontario for the academic years 1980–81 through 1992–93 were provided by Margaret Wieser of the Ontario Ministry of Education and Training.

As indicated in Table 13-6, by 1993 there were seven institutions offering programmes in one or more of the mapping technologies. It is interesting to note that in 1993 there were more graduates from the two Ontario institutions offering programmes in the mapping technologies than from the five institutions offering surveying programmes. Specifically, from Algonquin and Sir Sandford Fleming there were thirty-eight graduates from the four-term programmes and twelve graduates from those of six-terms. Nationally it is apparent that the long-standing shortfall in educational facilities bridging the gap between secondary school and university has been corrected.

CLOSING REMARKS: THE HUNDRED YEAR CYCLE

In retrospect it appears that the need for surveyors builds up to a peak once every hundred years. In each era, as the need builds up, there is an educational response, then after the peak demand has subsided there is a long, slow levelling-off period.

The first peak was in the 1780s. In 1783 the largest of several groups of Loyalists arrived in the Maritime provinces, the Eastern Townships, and Upper Canada expecting land as a reward for their loyalty. Concurrently, British soldiers who had fought against the rebellious colonies were being encouraged to settle in Canada. The urgent need for deputy surveyors to lay out lots for all these people was met by on-the-job training under the direction of former military surveyors such as Samuel Holland, Charles Morris, and George Sproule.

Table 13-6
Technician and Technologist Programmes in Photogrammetry, Cartography, Remote Sensing, Geographic Information Systems, and Related Activities

Province/Institution/Programme	Place	First offered	Status: 1993*****	Length [Terms]	Number of graduates Low/High	Average
BRITISH COLUMBIA						
BC Institute of Technology*	Burnaby					
Photogrammetry option (first term is common with surveying technology)	Lawrencetown	1964	C	2T + 2T	1/10	5
GIS advanced diploma		1987	C	2T	10/30	25
Camosun College	Victoria					
Map drafting		1973	1983	10 mon.		≈15
ALBERTA						
SA Institute of Technology	Calgary					
Mapping technology (first semester is common with surveying technology)		1972	C	2T + 2T		7
ONTARIO**						
Algonquin College	Ottawa					
Cartography technician			1986	4T	1/12	4
Cartography/photogrammetry			1984	4T	7/14	10
S & M mapping		1984	1989	6T	3/9	6
S & M photogrammetry		1984	1986	6T	1/5	3
GIS technician		1989	C	4T	7/14	11
GIS technologist		1991	C	6T	9/9	9
Seneca College	Toronto					
Cartographic technician		1969	1988	4T	8/24	16
Sir Sanford Fleming College	Lindsay					
Cartographic technician		1973	C	4T***	15/53	31
Cartographic technologist and GIS application specialist		1973	C	(4T) + 2T	10/17	13
QUÉBEC						
Limoilou College	Québec					
Geomatics: cartographic technology		1976	C	6T		≈20
L'Outaouais College	Hull					
Cartographic technology		1971	C	6T	15/25	≈18
NOVA SCOTIA****						
College of Geographical Sciences	Lawrencetown					
Photogrammetry technician		1962	1967	2T		≈8
		1967	1978	4T		≈6
Photogrammetric operator		1980	1983	2T		
Cartographic technician		1962	1985	2T	6/12	≈9
		1985	1989	3T		≈8
		1989	C	4T		≈7
Property mapping technician		1974	1981	2T		≈14
Remote sensing		1978	1982	4T		≈4
		1982	1992	3T		≈9
Remote sensing certificate		1992	C	2T*		≈5

Table 13-6 (cont'd)
Technician and Technologist Programmes in Photogrammetry, Cartography, Remote Sensing, Geographic Information Systems, and Related Activities

Province/Institution/Programme Place	First offered	Status: 1993*****	Length [Terms]	Number of graduates	
				Low/High	Average
Computer graphics	1985	1988	3T	2/10	≈6
GIS	1985	1992	3T		≈13
GIS certificate	1992	C	2T*		≈17
Integrated RS/GIS diploma	1992	C	(2T*) + 2T		≈11

*   This data provided by Ken Schuurman.

**   This data provided by Margaret Wieser of the Ontario Ministry of Education and Training.

***   Those who graduate from the 4T programme at Fleming may continue for two more terms and complete the cartographic technologist/GIS applications programme, and those who graduate from either of the two 2T programmes at the College of Geographical Sciences may continue for two more terms in the integrated remote sensing/geographic information systems programme.

****   This data provided by John Wightman, principal of the college from 1986 to 1994.

***** This column shows the year of termination for closed programmes; ongoing programmes are shown as C, for continuing.

Holland, Morris, and Sproule were well qualified and those trained under their direction did good work, but subsequently standards declined and by the 1840s the situation became so bad that something had to be done.

The next peak was in the 1880s. In 1883 Dominion Land Surveyors surveyed twenty-seven million acres in the Prairie provinces. The build-up to this peak had begun with the construction of railroads in eastern Canada some forty years earlier and it surged in the 1870s and 1880s as the authorities prepared for widespread settlement following the construction of the transcontinental railway. The first step in the educational response was the establishment of boards of examiners starting in 1849. The second step was the establishment of several programs in civil engineering and surveying starting with McGill in 1871. The early graduates of these programs had well-paying jobs for a few years but the demand, and the salaries, gradually declined. As Otto Klotz, the president of the DLS Association, put it in his 1886 report: "We have surveyed our heads off ... [We] devoured ... the whole country with instrument and chain."[61]

The third peak was in the 1980s. In 1983 the number of baccalaureate degrees awarded in surveying peaked at 137 (see Table 13-2). The decline in activity following the 1880s had continued to the end of the Second World War. The four civil engineering programs that got under way before the 1883 peak continued to include surveying as part of their civil engineering programmes – albeit as a gradually diminishing percentage of the curriculum. Similarly, other engineering programs as they came on stream followed suit. When the need for more surveyors and for better-educated surveyors exploded after the Second World War, the pressure on civil engineering led to a parting of ways and by 1979 there were surveying degree programmes at four universities: Laval, UNB, U of T, and U of C. In 1984 the number of graduates declined to 102 and it has been hovering around this level since then.

This review leads to an interesting question: Will it be another hundred years before the need for surveyors peaks once again?

1 Armstrong, J.C.W. 1987 *Champlain.* Toronto: MacMillan of Canada.

2 Pelletier, J. Roland. 1982. *Arpenteurs de Nouvelle-France.* Québec: Ordre des arpenteurs-géomètres du Québec.

3 Smithers, A.J. 1991. *Honorable Conquests.* London: Leo Cooper.

4 Thomson, Don W. 1967. *Men and Meridians,* vol. 2. Ottawa: Queen's Printer, 256–7.

5 Ibid., 251.

6 Nicholson, N.L., and L.M. Sebert. 1981. *The Maps of Canada: A Guide to Official Canadian Maps, Charts, Atlases and Gazetteers.* Folkestone, U.K.: William Dawson and Sons Ltd.

7 Thomson, Don W. 1966. *Men and Meridians,* vol. 1. Ottawa: Queen's Printer, 100.

8 Fellows, Robert. 1971. The Loyalists and Land Settlement in New Brunswick 1783–1790: A Study in Colonial Administration. *Journal of the Archives Section, Canadian Historical Association,* 2, 2, 5–15.

9 Roberts, W.F. 15 March 1994. Private conversation.

10 Upper and Lower Canada, 1849, 12 Vic., c.35.

11 Québec, 1882, Cap. 16 S., 28–9.

12 Ontario, 1892, 55 Vic., c. 34.

13 Canada, 1872, 35 Vic., c. 23.

14 Annual Report of the Department of the Interior. 1886. Ottawa.

15 Ross, J.E.R. 1943. The Dominion Land Surveyor. Some Historical Facts, His Training and Qualifications. *The Canadian Surveyor,* 8, 1, 12–22.

16 New Brunswick, 1874, 37 Vic., c. 21, s. 4.

17 Prince Edward Island, 1884, 47 Vic., c. 3.

18 Prince Edward Island, 17 Eliz. II, c. 43, s. 8.

19 Nova Scotia, 1910, 10 Edwd VII, c. 5, s. 3.

20 Nova Scotia, 1959, 8 Eliz. II, c. 6, s. 8.

21 MacInnes, A. 1942. Paper presented at the BCLS Annual General Meeting in 1942. *BCLS Archives.*

22 Newfoundland, 1951, no. 86, s. 3B.

23 Manitoba, 1881, 44 Vic. c. 29.

24 Holloway, J.H. 1964. *A History of the Alberta Land Surveyors' Association.* Edmonton: The Alberta Land Surveyors Association, 2.

25 Seis, Morley J. 1974. *The History of the Saskatchewan Land Surveyors Association and the Board of Examiners for the Saskatchewan Land Surveyors Association.* Regina: Archives, Association of Saskatchewan Land Surveyors.

26 Minute 1.01. 27–8 Aug. 1975. Board of Direction, Ordre des arpenteurs-géomètres du Québec.

27 Faig, Wolfgang, Angus Hamilton, and James Doig. 1994. The Atlantic Board of Examiners for Land Surveyors. *Focus,* November, 30–5.

28 In older academic calendars the word "course" is often used where "programme" would be correct today. Because of the complexity of modern post-secondary education, "course" now refers to a particular study within a programme. In non-academic writing, as in this text, the two words are used interchangeably. Where a misunderstanding might exist, an explanation is added in brackets.

29 Baird, A. Foster. 1950. *The History of Engineering at the University of New Brunswick.* In A.G. Bailey, ed. *University of New Brunswick Memorial Volume.* Fredericton: UNB.

30 Prospectus of the University of McGill College: session of 1857–58.

31 Frost, Stanley B. 1980. *McGill University, Vol. 1. 1805–1895*. Montreal: McGill-Queen's University Press.

32 Ladell, John. 1993. *They Left Their Mark*. Toronto: Dundurn Press, 138, 201.

33 Obituary for Clement Henry McLeod in *Proceedings and Transactions of the Royal Society of Canada*, 3rd Series, 12, 14.

34 Calendar, Faculty of Applied Science, McGill, 1895–96, 71–83.

35 Audet, Louis-Phillipe. 1965. La Fondation de l'École Polytechnique de Montreal. *Les Cahiers des Dix*, no. 30, 147–91.

36 École Polytechnique calendar for the year 1886.

37 Although the School of Practical Science became the Faculty of Applied Science in 1900, it continued to be known as SPS for many decades.

38 See Thomson, Don W. 1969. *Men and Meridians,* vol 3. Ottawa: Queen's Printer, 40 for the highlights of Professor Stewart's career.

39 The old calendars listed four groups of "electives"; in modern terminology they would be called "options."

40 A three-year diploma programme had been established at UNB in 1889, and a Faculty of Practical Science at Queen's in 1893. After the turn of the century engineering programmes were established at: the University of Manitoba in 1907; the Nova Scotia Technical College in 1908; the University of Alberta in 1909; the University of Saskatchewan in 1912, and the University of British Columbia in 1915. Stirling, J.B. 1954. *The First Hundred Years*. Founders Day Address, 15 February 1954. Fredericton: UNB.

41 One example of the effort to establish a surveying option programme was at UBC where Sybren de Jong and Harry Bell tried for years to establish such an option.

42 de Jong, Sybren. 1960. The Present Status of Surveying Education in Canada. *The Canadian Surveyor*, 15, 1, 54–60.

43 Report of the Task Committee on the Status of Surveying and Mapping. *Journal of the Surveying and Mapping Division, American Society of Civil Engineers*, 85, Surv. 1, 1959.

44 McNair, A. 1960. Survey Education in the United States. *The Canadian Surveyor*, 15, 1, 48–54.

45 1960. *The Canadian Surveyor*, 15, 1.

46 Thompson, E.H. 1960. The Education of the Surveyor in the British Commonwealth. *The Canadian Surveyor*, 15, 1, 40–4, 60.

47 Howlett, L.E. 1960. The Crisis in Survey Education. *The Canadian Surveyor*, 15, 1, 67–70.

48 Beattie, I.M. 1960. Discussion. *The Canadian Surveyor*, 15, 1, 78.

49 At UNB the Survey Option was started in 1960, became the Department of Surveying Engineering in 1965 and the Department of Geomatics Engineering in 1994. The survey science programme at Erindale began in 1972 and became the Centre for Surveying Science in 1988. At Calgary the programme in surveying engineering started as a division of the Department of Civil Engineering in 1979, became the Department of Surveying Engineering in 1986, and the Department of Geomatics Engineering in 1992.

50 Gagnon, Pierre. 7 January 1994. Fax to author.

51 Gagnon, Pierre. 3 August 1994. Fax to author.

52 Gunn, Robert. 13 September 1994. Fax to author; and Jerry Vlcek, personal communication.

53 Gracie, Gordon. 20 December 1993. Letter to author.

54 Schwarz, Klaus-Peter. 12 July 1994. Fax to author.

55 Gold, Christopher. 1987. Cartographic Education in Canada. *The Canadian Surveyor*, 41, 3, 466–76.

56 Anderson, Jacqueline. 1991. Undergraduate Cartographic Education in Canada. *CISM Journal,* 45, 1, 157–60.

57 Keller, C. Peter. 1991. Trends and Opportunities for Graduate Studies in Cartography in Canada. *CISM Journal,* 45, 1,126–35.

58 The six master's degrees were awarded to Angus Hamilton (1951), Trevor Harwood (1953), William Carr (1955), Deszo Nagy (1958), and Jerry Vlcek and Robert Gunn (1959).

59 Doig, James F. 1990. *A Life Worth Living: Major James A.H. Church.* Lawrencetown NS: Geographics Press. Also Thomson, Don W. *Men and Meridians*, vol. 3, 1969. Ottawa, Queen's Printer, 257–66.

60 Thompson, R.D. 1967. Objectives and Problems of the Institutes of Technology. *The Canadian Surveyor*, 21, 1, 84–6.

61 Thomson, *Men and Meridians*, vol. 2, 65.

CHAPTER FOURTEEN

Remote Sensing in Canada

Leo Sayn-Wittgenstein, Robert A. Ryerson, and Frank Hegyi

INTRODUCTION

This chapter places Canada's activities and successes in remote sensing within the context of the general development of the field on a worldwide basis. It recounts the evolution of remote sensing in Canada from its beginnings in postwar air photographic interpretation to the present situation by reviewing four stages. It also discusses the public and private sector cooperation that has resulted in the creation of a new industry that, to date, has been very competitive internationally. The chapter concludes with illustrations from British Columbia of the contribution that remote sensing has made to automated cartography and Geographic Information Systems (GIS), and the growing integration of these fields.

A Canadian Definition of Remote Sensing

Remote sensing is the collection of natural resource and environmental information using imagery acquired from aircraft and spacecraft. This "Canadian" definition of remote sensing reflects the attention within Canada to collecting information, which by definition is useful. Data, on the other hand, do not have utility until they are processed and information has been extracted from them. This has been the hallmark of Canadian remote sensing – it has tried to make the data useful.

THE FOUNDATION: THE POSTWAR PERIOD TO THE LAUNCH OF LANDSAT, 1945–1972*

Background

This period spans the transition from the interpretation of aerial photography to the first applications of satellite remote sensing. The launch of Landsat 1 in July 1972 marks the

---

* This part of the chapter was contributed by L. Sayn-Wittgenstein.

end of the period. Landsat was launched by NASA and was initially designated as an Earth Resources Technology Satellite (ERTS). It was the first satellite intended for research and practical use in the survey of natural resources and the environment. It gave Canadian companies an excellent opportunity to establish themselves as leaders in remote sensing technology and applications. Landsat was also the focus of the Canadian government's attention when it established the Canada Centre for Remote Sensing in 1971, along with a policy "to make remote sensing useful."

Canadian success in remote sensing was influenced by its geography and history, and can be traced to developments and attitudes to technology during the postwar period. Canada has a land area of 9.22 million km², a fresh-water area of 755 000 km², and a coastline of 96 026 km. Approximately 90 percent of its population is located within 150 km of its southern border. Large areas of the country are rich in natural resources, virtually uninhabited, and characterized by severe climate and inaccessibility. Obtaining reliable information on the nation's natural resources, and monitoring those resources, required aerial photography and later remote sensing. Canadian success began with the boom in aerial photography during the 1950s and 1960s, building on advances in aircraft and cameras, and on practical experience in airborne missions, photointerpretation, and mapping accumulated during military reconnaissance. Canada's successes and proven competence in domestic and international projects were based on practical experience supported by strong research and development programmes. As a result Canadian industry soon became a world leader in mapping and natural resource surveys.

Photogrammetry and Photo Interpretation

Soon after the Second World War the Canadian community involved with aerial photography began to diverge along two paths that were often not as closely connected as they perhaps should have been. On the one side was the science of photogrammetry and its application in engineering and topographic mapping, with strict requirements for accurate measurements on aerial photographs. On the other side was photo interpretation with its applications in thematic mapping and the description of natural resources. Whilst the first was a quantitative science, the second was more qualitative, at times an art and not a science.

Photogrammetry was the senior and more highly regarded; it built on professional knowledge that had been in place well before the war. Photo interpretation was the junior partner. It had glamour and excitement, derived from success in military reconnaissance and in the exploration for resources. However photogrammetry, with its systematic, quantitative measurements, appeared more solid and scientific than the less precise but more versatile field of photo interpretation, with its often only loosely defined methods and standards.

Skilful interpreters were always highly regarded, but in scientific and professional organizations photogrammetry took precedence over photo interpretation. The leading international society concerned with aerial photography was the International Society for Photogrammetry (ISP), and its senior commissions dealt with photogrammetry. Photo interpretation was a recent addition.

Influential Organizations

In the first ten to twenty years after the war, the American Society for Photogrammetry provided an important forum for Canadian photo interpreters. Canadian interpreters took an active part in its affairs, and annual visits to its convention became almost routine for leaders in Canadian photo interpretation. The exchange of scientific information between Canadian and American organizations involved in photo interpretation was taken for granted. Contacts established in the early days of photo interpretation research and development were maintained later as the United States developed its programme of remote sensing from space.

In the 1960s the federal Interdepartmental Committee on Air Surveys provided a focal point for photo interpreters. Its 1964 and 1967 symposia, Air Photo Interpretation in the Development of Canada, were benchmarks in the progress of Canadian photo interpretation.

The Canadian road from aerial photography to remote sensing leads through the photo interpretation community. It was not a clear and direct progression: there were a few blind alleys and barriers to remote sensing, especially in the early years of low-resolution satellites. Obstacles to change usually arose when methods were standardized; fixed procedures mean resistance to change.

The photo interpretation community was more varied in its objectives than the photogrammetrists. It involved every subject concerned with the description of the earth's surface, including agriculture, archaeology, forestry, geology, glaciology, land-use planning, and military reconnaissance. With few exceptions procedures were subject to frequent changes. The attitude to innovation was positive and the overall objective, the study of the earth's surface, was the same as that of later remote sensing programmes.

Canadian Forestry and Photo Interpretation

Forestry provided some of the strongest Canadian photo interpretation groups. Half of Canada is covered by forests and most development projects occurred in forested areas. One had to understand trees, no matter whether one was a forester, a geologist, a civil engineer, a wildlife scientist, or an hydrologist. In forestry the lead came from the federal Forest Branch, which already before the war had established operational competence and a small but lively research programme.

Initially the Forestry Branch, then known as the Dominion Forest Service, was responsible for the forest resources of the western provinces. Though this responsibility was transferred to the provinces in 1929, the branch kept substantial obligations for surveys on federal lands. This led to early applications of aerial photography because senior forestry officials, such as H.E. (Si) Seely, understood its potential for forest surveys. They had conducted tests of photo interpretation and photogrammetric tree and stand measurements in the late 1920s and 1930s, only to be interrupted by the Depression and the war. In 1945 when Seely and his colleagues returned from military service they began where they had left off before the war.[1]

The early trials of tree-species interpretation relied on aerial photography acquired near the Petawawa Forest Experiment Station, and elsewhere in the Ottawa Valley. Low aircraft speed, large scales of photography, and, in some cases, fall photography, which increased tonal differences between tree species, compensated for slow shutter speeds and low resolution. The results were encouraging: tree species could be identified by tone, crown shape, and branching habit. In addition tree height could be obtained by parallax measurement, by direct measurement on oblique photographs, and, occasionally, by measuring the length of tree shadows.[2] Key characteristics such as the star-shaped crowns of white pine, the spherical, symmetrical crowns of red pine, and the dense cone-shaped tops of balsam fir were noted quickly.

Perspective grids were drawn, to be used with vertical and oblique aerial photography in estimating tree dimensions and in transferring information from aerial photographs to maps. Photographs were used to map the boundaries of tree stands; supplementary information came from field surveys, aerial sketching, and observation from aircraft.

The experience in mapping stands and identifying species was of lasting value, but perspective grids and shadow measurements ultimately proved of little use. The net effect was a capability to use aerial photographs for interpreting tree species, stand history, ecology, and the relationships between tree cover, soils, land-form, and topography. This comprehensive approach to photo interpretation became the guiding philosophy of Canadian photo interpreters for decades to come.

Photo interpretation activities in the federal Forestry Branch were divided between the Forest Inventory Operations Section under J.M. (Jack) Robinson and the Research Section under Seely. As veterans of the early days of forestry photo interpretation, both Seely and Robinson bridged the gap between the pre-war period and the rapid expansion of research and development after the war.

The Operations Section was assigned to the survey of federal lands: national parks, Indian reserves, military areas, and the forests of the Northwest Territories and Yukon, particularly at Watson Lake and along the Peace, Slave, Liard, and Mackenzie rivers. Field sampling was less intensive than in the forest inventories of the large pulp and paper companies further south. Northern surveys were often "reconnaissance inventories," less precise than the "management inventories" and "operating surveys" required for more intensive exploration and management practised on provincial and private lands.

The standard goals of all Canadian forest photo interpreters became the completion of "forest type maps" that showed the boundaries of forest stands as seen by the interpreter, and described stands by tree species, average stand height, and tree canopy density. There were variations on this: estimates of density, stand age (derived by the photo interpreter!), site conditions, and other variables might be added, and canopy density might be dropped. However species composition and stand height were always required. The preparation of forest type maps became a dogma in Canadian forestry; it was the approach taught in all Canadian forestry schools.

The preparation of new forest type maps for each inventory was by no means traditional. European foresters relied on accumulated records of stand growth, stand history, soil productivity, and silvicultural treatments, while large American forest surveys were often completed using a network of field samples, without detailed forest cover maps.

Photo interpretation in Canada became the core of forest inventory. The speed of photo interpretation allowed rapid surveys of inaccessible territory. Photo interpretation provided the first systematic descriptions of areas for which no previous records existed. This also satisfied the requirements of large international development projects. Canadian competence in aerial-photo interpretation did much to establish Canada's excellent reputation in the survey of natural resources.

Photo Interpretation in Other Disciplines

Canada's competence covered the full range of natural resource disciplines. In addition to forestry there was an active agricultural programme. At the Department of Agriculture Laurie E. Philpotts succeeded in the interpretation of crop diseases on panchromatic and infrared photography, and in using aerial photography to monitor land-use changes.[3] His work was complemented by A.R. Mack's studies of the reflectance properties of agricultural crops and, at the University of Waterloo, by D.K. Erb's analysis of fruit orchards using aerial photographs.[4] Harold Wood and R.A. Ryerson contributed through research in farm classification and crop survey.[5]

Canadian professionals were experts in the classification of mapping of land-forms, terrain characteristics, and soils. John D. Mollard began his work in interpreting surface features and soils from aerial photographs early in the 1940s. He became a well-known consultant, highly successful in the use of aerial photography in engineering studies, pipeline location, and the search for groundwater and gravel. He also published several editions of an atlas of land-forms interpreted from aerial photographs, and a major work on photo interpretation and the Canadian landscape.[6] In 1989 he received the Massey Medal for his personal achievements in using air-photo interpretation and remote sensing in landscape interpretation.

John T. Parry at McGill University completed leading research in northern mapping and in the use of photo interpretation for terrain analysis and trafficability studies, some of which was undertaken for the Defence Research Board in the mid-1960s.[7] N.W. Radforth led in the classification of organic terrain, and provided important information for the design of equipment and transportation routes over muskegs.[8] Roger J.E. Brown at the National Research Council received international attention for his work in the interpretation of permafrost, and the relationship between vegetation and northern soils.[9]

J.D. Heyland of the Québec Wildlife Service obtained and interpreted spectacular aerial photographs, showing how they could be used in wildlife census, particularly for migratory birds, caribou, and beluga whales.[10] Parry has published an excellent account of the history of Canadian photo interpretation.[11] A good overview of Canadian competence in the early 1970s can also be obtained from the proceedings of the First Canadian Symposium on Remote Sensing, held in 1972. These proceedings include detailed accounts of the work of many of those mentioned above.

The Practice of Photo Interpretation

The effectiveness of any photo interpretation organization obviously depended on the skill of its photo interpreters. Interpretation demanded curiosity, a sharp intellect, and good stereoscopic vision. All photo interpreters did their work with a stereoscope, even if stereoscopic measurements were not required; shape, size, and texture could not be appreciated properly in two dimensions.

Before interpreters were allowed to work independently, they usually completed two years in training as apprentices of a senior interpreter. They also had to acquire and maintain a theoretical background and practical experience in the discipline that they were serving. For this reason interpreters always took part in reconnaissance surveys and fieldwork.

Interpretation in agriculture, forestry, and geology required quick decisions, combining direct observation of size, shape, tone, and texture with indirect clues from neighbouring areas and background knowledge including the history of the area. The observations finally recorded on a map were an educated guess based on many sources, eliminating the unlikely and accepting the most probably correct description.

The standards of performance were set by senior interpreters, who were highly regarded by their colleagues and often had national reputations. Senior forestry photo interpreters in the federal government, such as Russell J. Dewe, Fred W. Kippen and James Peaker, who had started their careers under Robinson and Seely, always worked as a team, exchanging information and comparing the results of their work. This cooperation and the interaction with junior interpreters and forestry officers provided the critical mass essential for a strong organization.

The 1956 Hungarian revolution proved a significant event for photo interpretation and forest inventory practice in Canada, because many individuals involved in forest surveys had been among the hundreds of students, graduates, and faculty members of Sopron University who had emigrated to Canada. For years to come every large forestry office in Canada seemed to contain at least one Sopron graduate. Victor Zsilinsky was among those who made prominent contributions to forest inventory practice, as was Frank Hegyi who, as director of the British Columbia Forest Inventory Branch, took the lead in establishing the first GIS in a Canadian forestry organization.

In the late 1950s and the 1960s strong photo interpretation groups also developed in the resource management departments of provincial organizations and the large forestry companies. One of the leaders was in the Forest Resource Inventory organization of the Ontario Department of Lands and Forests, later the Ontario Ministry of Natural Resources. Under Zsilinszky Ontario developed precise standards for forestry photography and interpretation procedures. This set a pattern that was followed widely elsewhere. Ontario photography was panchromatic, at a scale of 1:15 840, obtained in mid-summer, and processed to low contrast. Interpreters had their own requirements that could not be met by topographic mapping photographs. Previously they had had to cope with mapping photographs that showed sharp contrasts between land and water, but at the expense of details in land cover. Zsilinszky, who later headed the Ontario Centre for Remote Sensing, produced a comprehensive manual describing photo interpretation of Ontario tree species using the new standard Forest Resources Inventory photography.[12]

Summer photography was an acknowledgement of the importance of common standards in large operational projects; it ensured that similar forest conditions would have similar appearance on all photographs. Research had shown that the most precise interpretation could often be obtained with spring and fall photography. This, however, was an unacceptable condition for large projects involving many interpreters, because it required exact timing of photo missions and detailed knowledge of local phenology.

The move to low-contrast photography, championed by K.B. Jackson at the University of Toronto and by Zsilinszky, was strongly resisted by some photo interpretation pioneers who had become accustomed to working with strong highlights and shadows and who found that the usual patterns used in photo interpretation had apparently disappeared. In retrospect the change to low-contrast photography seems obvious, but it generated intense, often personal, debate at the time.

Parallel with developments in Ontario, Leo Sayn-Wittgenstein at the federal Forestry Branch published several reports on the identification of Canadian tree species on aerial photographs.[13] These publications, which were summarized in a 1978 revision,[14] drew on the accumulated knowledge of federal forestry photo interpreters and on the systematic collection of significant aerial photographs held by the federal forestry organization.

The Canada Land Inventory

The 1960s also saw the beginning of the Canada Land Inventory (CLI), a national programme to map current land use and land capability for agriculture, forestry, wildlife, and recreation in the populated areas of Canada. This, and the earlier work of the Geographical Branch in land-use mapping, have been described in chapter 11. Further information is available in a valuable overview by Coombs and Thie.[15] The CLI programme was led by R.J. McCormack of the Lands Directorate, Department of Forestry and Rural Development, and employed earth scientists and photo interpreters under the technical leadership of Lee Pratt. In 1963, as part of this initiative, the Geographical Branch of the Department of Mines and Technical Surveys began to prepare land-use maps at a scale of 1:50 000. Proven interpretation methods were applied. It may have seemed dull from a research perspective, but as McClellan has indicated it was a typical example of the ability to find immediate, practical applications for a new methodology.[16] The CLI also led to the first geographic information system, the Canadian Geographic Information System, developed under the leadership of Roger F. Tomlinson and described in chapter 15.

Closely related to the methods and philosophy of the CLI were initiatives to use aerial photographs for ecological classifications, biophysical mapping, and integrated resource surveys. One of the most prolific proponents of these approaches was Philip Gimbarzevsky, who applied these approaches on behalf of various federal departments involved in environmental impact assessments and the planning of national parks.[17]

Canadian Research and Development in Photo Interpretation

During the 1960s provincial governments, universities, and federal organizations built up forward-looking research units involved in aerial surveys. The Canadian Forestry Service, successor of the Forestry Branch, established the Forest Management Institute by combining its inventory activities with other forest management research programmes. This institute, under the directorship of Arthur Bickerstaff and later Sayn-Wittgenstein, led federal forestry research in aerial photography, sampling, and later remote sensing. Priorities included large-scale photography, ultra-small-scale photography, comparison of different film and filter combinations, and preparations for Landsat experiments.

Canadian research enjoyed unprecedented support and freedom of action. Young scientists were given opportunities that were beyond the reach of their counterparts in Europe and larger organizations in the United States. They also derived much benefit from cooperation with international colleagues, particularly in the United States. Canadian advances were well received, and there was ample opportunity for international exposure.

The combination of operational programmes with research provided an excellent basis for progress. Advances and benefits from new technology were easily demonstrated. Success in photo interpretation had come early and often, and had produced a receptive audience and a positive attitude to innovation that later did much to advance remote sensing.

The technical progress of the Second World War was soon followed by developments that covered the full range of photo interpretation activities. For example 1948 forestry tri-camera tests in northern Québec resulted in oblique views that provided outstanding opportunities for the identification of tree species. In 1950 and 1951 Forestry Branch experiments at Marmora and Petawawa, Ontario, using continuous-strip, image-motion-compensating Sonne cameras produced large-scale (1:500 to 1:1300) stereo photographs that were sharp enough to be a match for anything obtained during the next two decades. Sonne photography revealed the fundamental characteristics of crown shape and branching habit important for interpretation at all scales.

Canadian air survey companies delivered outstanding aerial photography. Standard forestry photography in most provinces was panchromatic at a scale of 1:15 840. Scales in the range of 1:20 000 to 1:38 000 were widely used in northern surveys. One spectacular set of photographs used in many displays and exhibits was 1:38 000 panchromatic photography obtained by Spartan Air Services in 1955 over Wood Buffalo Park. (A sample stereo pair is A15204: 38 and 39.) Black-and-white, infrared film became well-known in the late 1950s for its ability to increase tonal contrast between broad-leaved trees and evergreens.

Initially, normal colour aerial photography was received only with reluctance. Cost, low resolution, poor haze-penetrating ability, and narrow exposure latitude were cited as problems. The real reason for objections was probably that photo interpreters had simply become very proficient with panchromatic photography: colour brought little new information, especially for the relatively uniform vegetation of the boreal forest.

Camouflage detection film, small samples of Russian spectrazonal film, and later Kodak's colour infrared films were tested successfully and applied for vegetation damage in agriculture and forestry, especially in the large spruce budworm outbreaks in eastern Canada. At the Forest Management Institute Peter Murtha compiled a manual documenting the state of the art in vegetation damage surveys.[18]

Starting in 1959 fast-cycling, 70 mm Vinten military reconnaissance cameras were tested for forest sampling using low-altitude, large-scale photography. The first photographs for civilian experiments were obtained from test runs during military manoeuvres at Petawawa. These trials were run in parallel with U.S. Forest Service experiments using 70 mm Hulcher cameras, during which the American scientists were in close contact with Canadian colleagues.[19]

There is a direct line from these early Vinten trials to the sophisticated large-scale photography forest sampling system that is still in operation in the 1990s. The scientists leading this development were Alan H. Aldred and Udo Nielsen at the Forest Management Institute. Progress included the development of a foliage-penetrating radar altimeter to determine aircraft height above ground, and the testing of this system in Canada, Guatemala, and Suriname. This altimeter was designed and constructed by R.L. Westby at the National Research Council at the request of the Canadian Forestry Service.[20] The system was later refined and brought to its present operational status by Dendron Resource Surveys, which replaced the radar altimeter with a laser profiler, and coupled the camera and profiler to a navigation system.

Other approaches included the development of a twin-camera boom carried by helicopter.[21] This system was used by the British Columbia Forest Service, and was developed further by Hunter and Associates and others. Parker Williams of Integrated Resource Photography Ltd in British Columbia tested an alternate system based on 70 mm cameras mounted in the wing tips of light aircraft. There was no shortage of ideas, and competitiveness assured progress.

Not all developments in aerial photography were as successful as photo interpretation, stand mapping, and sampling by large-scale photography. One relatively unsuccessful initiative was the attempts to develop "stand volume tables," that is to estimate timber volume from tree heights and measures of crown closure or tree density. Much was written on this subject in Canada and the United States. In the end the results were too inaccurate to be useful.

Advances in statistical sampling theory were a major influence on the use of aerial photography during the postwar years. All major Canadian forest and agricultural surveys used statistical sampling design, and the calculation of sampling errors was mandatory. Important advances in survey techniques followed. However when it came to the transition from aerial photography to remote sensing, statistical practices became a barrier to progress. Professionals in agriculture and forestry had developed a firm belief that the only way to obtain information for large areas was to take precise measurements on carefully selected sample locations. When the early satellites failed to produce the required precision for selected samples, they were set aside or relegated to minor roles in multi-stage sampling designs. Forestry and agriculture at first had little use for low-resolution data. In this they lagged behind their colleagues in geology, geography, and environmental studies who quickly understood the value of the synoptic views obtained by satellite.

Modern remote sensing and computer methods have largely circumvented this problem. It is now possible to obtain information for each pixel (30 m × 30 m, 10 m × 10 m) in a satellite image, and thus to collect data for each basic unit in a population, even if this involves millions of pixels. The dependence on field samples for the exploration of large, inaccessible areas has diminished as satellite and data-processing technology have advanced.

Preparations for the Satellite Era

During the late 1960s and early 1970s preparations for Landsat accelerated in the United States. Space photography, especially 70 mm Hasselblad photographs obtained during the Apollo missions, was tested in agriculture, forestry, and geology, as was ultra-small-scale photography obtained from U-2 and other high-altitude aircraft.

The Canadian photo interpretation community followed developments closely. Canadian experiments with non-photographic sensors began with trials of thermal infrared scanners for applications in forest fire detection, mapping of thermal effluent, heat loss from buildings, and vegetation damage surveys. Civilian experiments were carried out with military side-looking airborne radar. The Forest Management Institute, in cooperation with the Aeronautics Experimental and Testing Establishment of the Royal Canadian Air Force, evaluated small-scale photography for forestry application. A CF-100 aircraft was equipped with several 70 mm cameras using different film and filter combinations, and flew a transect from Kingston, Ontario, up the Ottawa Valley, past Cochrane and Fraserdale, to James Bay/Moosonee.[22] Experienced photo interpreters evaluated the resulting 1:160 000 photographs and found them surprisingly useful.

These early plans and experiments in preparation for satellite remote sensing coincided with a peak in Canadian competence in aerial photography. The Canadian air survey industry, resource management organizations, and government planners all had established efficient procedures for photo interpretation and mapping, while the research community continued to refine these procedures. The rate of progress, however, had slowed down, although there was a steady flow of incremental improvements from tests of new films, filters, and scales of photography.

The established air photo technology was so successful that some of its users were sceptical of the new scanners, radar, and digital interpretation of image data. Space and airborne remote sensing were, therefore, largely confined to research and operational trials. Military reconnaissance and the application of thermal scanners in forest fire detection and thermal mapping were among the exceptions. Progress in remote sensing had to rely initially on new technology from foreign space and remote sensing organizations and, in Canada, from the national and provincial sensing programmes established by government.

THE EARLY DAYS – A SOLUTION LOOKING FOR A PROBLEM: 1971-78[23]*

The early days, or second stage, in the growth of remote sensing saw the link being developed between the user's needs and the technology to develop new applications and identify new research problems. At the same time the foundation was being laid for Canada to assume a position of leadership in the international community. The emphasis was on the development of the technology to acquire and disseminate remote sensing imagery from both satellites and specialized airborne systems and to try to apply those data to the real problems of the resource manager. This period lasted from the events that resulted in the founding of the Canada Centre for Remote Sensing (CCRS) through the launch and acqui-sition of Landsat with its Multispectral Scanner (MSS) to the development of an airborne radar remote sensing programme.

The Founding of CCRS and the Development of the Remote Sensing Advisory Structure

The CCRS was established officially on 1 April 1971 in the Department of Energy, Mines and Resources (EMR). That event can be traced back to a May 1967 meeting between various federal agencies (including EMR, National Research Council, Forestry, Defence Research Board, and Agriculture) when participation in the U.S. EROS project was consid-ered. At a series of meetings over the next three years, outside interests from industry and universities were consulted by federal agencies, various proposals were discussed, formal documents were prepared, and subsequently the remote sensing programme was approved.[24]

In retrospect the manner in which the programme was established can be seen to have played an important role in its subsequent success. From the outset, and rare for that time, the participants were the various government departments that could use remote sensing, industry, and the universities. This ensured that the community of potential users was involved both as users of services and supporters of the programme. Since there was an insufficient budget to do everything, it was essential that remote sensing enlisted the assistance of partners. The early emphasis on partners resulted in much of the later success.

On 22 July 1969 an ad hoc interdepartmental committee was struck to steer the pro-gramme, and a Program Office for Resource Satellite and Airborne Remote Sensing was established under L.W. Morley of the Geological Survey, EMR as founding director. At its second meeting on 28 October 1969 the interdepartmental committee endorsed participa-tion in the NASA ERTS programme. A memorandum to the Federal Cabinet Committee on Science and Technology dated 24 November suggested consideration of four urgent projects: (1) hyper-altitude aircraft experimental earth sensor operation, (2) research and development on remote sensors, (3) study of incidence of cloud free-areas, and (4) study of a reproduction system for resource satellite data. The funding requested was $550,000. This was approved by the cabinet on 11 December. That these four topics were enunciated

---

* This part of the chapter, and the following two, were contributed by R.A. Ryerson.

Table 14-1
Directors General of CCRS

| Dr L.W. Morley, 1971–80 |
| Mr E.A. Godby, 1980–86 |
| Dr L. Sayn-Wittgenstein, 1987–95 |
| Dr E. Shaw, 1995–present |

so clearly a quarter-century ago explains a great deal of Canada's later success in the use of satellite imagery and in the development of sensors, radar, and ground receiving stations.

At this stage while CCRS had not yet been created formally, its predecessor had a leader of vision and a budget, and something unusual and quite marvellous in the history of science and technology in Canada had begun to take shape.

On 24 December 1969 the third meeting of the Interagency Committee on Remote Sensing (IACRS) took the next major step. It approved appointments of seven ad hoc working groups in (1) Forestry, (2) Hydrology, Oceanography, Limnology, Fisheries, and Meteorology, (3) Data Reproduction and Distribution, (4) International Cooperation, (5) Sensor and Data Systems, (6) Remote Airborne Sensing, and (7) Wildlands and Geology.

Subsequently these were expanded into fourteen groups that made up the Canadian Advisory Committee on Remote Sensing (CACRS) with a mandate to "advise and assist the Government of Canada ... in meeting the objectives of the national program on remote sensing of the surface environment."[25] The advisory duties included coordination of existing and proposed new programmes and recommendation of priorities; advising on platforms (satellites, aircraft, and balloons) and sensor development; data processing, cataloguing, reproduction, and marketing; regional involvement; and research grants and contracts. It was to assist by generating requests for airborne remote sensing surveys, evaluating projects, and by organizing conferences, seminars, and training courses for the diffusion of remote sensing into Canada.

It is significant that CCRS was located in EMR with a staff complement of approximately 100 person-years and a budget of $6 million. Most of the other neophyte remote sensing agencies around the world were located within space agencies or departments of defence. In the case of CCRS there was a conscious effort to place remote sensing expertise within an agency that had a close association with prospective users. It was believed that only through such close liaison with users would remote sensing be developed rapidly enough to pay for itself. This has proven to be the case.

To provide imagery for evaluating the possibilities of the ERTS imagery, and to meet its other mandate of developing sensors and an airborne sensing capability, the Canadian Forces established an airborne sensing unit (CFASU) on 1 July 1971. This was under under the leadership of Maj. Ernie McLaren, who was to play a prominent role in marketing remote sensing across Canada and also in education and training.

In 1972 the meetings of the advisory groups came to be known officially as the CACRS meetings, the first of which was held in March of that year. After moving from a resort in Montebello to the spartan facilities of an old airbase in Arnprior, CACRS meetings took on a special charm. No one could have been accused of attending the meetings to enjoy the luxury of the antiquated plumbing, draughty rooms, and questionable heating. In spite of the facilities the CACRS meetings became something to be looked forward to for their interesting and open discussions on remote sensing and a variety of related topics. In the early years CCRS was the major employer in the field and important enough to dominate all activities within the country. It cannot be denied that CCRS did dominate, but it was confident and competent enough to relish the bear-pit sessions into which CCRS management and staff entered at CACRS. There they received both brickbats and bouquets from their stakeholders in government and academe, and then increasingly over the years from industry. Much of this approach was developed by the early leaders of CCRS, founding Director Gen. L.W. Morley, Associate Director Gen. E.A. Godby, and management consultant D.J. Clough of the University of Waterloo.

CACRS produced reports annually beginning in 1973 that totalled over 1500 pages on the activities of CCRS, the working groups, other laboratories in the federal system, universities, and provincial centres. These document the growth and changes in the field of remote sensing in Canada in a depth not available for any other programme. A rereading of all of these reports at one time is instructive in seeing the development of the field. A rather vague recommendation often appears one year, only to disappear without much discussion. If the recommendation had merit, it might return the next year in a more clearly defined manner – often from more than one group. In turn the meritorious recommendation might be followed by a much stronger recommendation in the succeeding year, or it might simply appear in the next CCRS plan. The beginnings of Radarsat, the industrial development policy, virtually all of the technological innovations, much of the applications work, and international activities can be seen to have evolved over time from recommendations made at CACRS, and discussion with and within CCRS. It should be noted that many of the recommendations were not acted upon by CCRS but by other organizations in the field. The CACRS structure and exchange of information also ensured that the overlap and duplication found elsewhere was not common in Canada.

In 1976 one of the recommendations from Québec, which presented its report in English and French, focused on the English nature of the centre and its publications. In essence the complaint was that Québec could not easily make use of much of what had been done in CCRS or in the rest of Canada. At the same time it became apparent to those working strictly in an English milieu that there was also a loss to the programme since a great deal of good work was being done in Québec to which anglophones did not have access. Foremost among applications was the innovative monitoring of the 135 000 square miles of the James Bay Hydro Development. By 1976 only a few francophones occupied senior scientific and managerial positions. Shortly afterwards a number of Francophones joined the applications division of CCRS, greatly enriching the quality and range of work to which CCRS had access and that it could disseminate in what was by then a truly national programme. Eventually CCRS was to make working in French a viable option for its staff, and young scientists from Québec could feel at home in at least part of the organization.

In 1988 CACRS was restructured into a council to advise the minister, and much of the networking and direct contact within the community was lost. In addition only a subgroup of the council actually ever met with the minister. At the time of writing, a restructuring is being planned to recapture the strengths of the past system coupled with current realities.

The ERTS satellite was launched on 23 July 1972, the first image of Canada received on 26 July, and on the following day a copy was presented at the ISP congress. This unusually rapid turnaround later became a hallmark of Canada's reception and image production capabilities. By the end of 1973 130 computer-compatible tapes had been produced, and

Table 14-2
Canadian Remote Sensing Symposia

1st	Ottawa	February 1972
2nd	Guelph	April 1974
3rd	Edmonton	September 1975
4th	Québec	May 1977
5th	Victoria	August 1978
6th	Halifax	May 1980
7th	Winnipeg	September 1981
8th	Montréal	May 1983
9th	St John's	August 1984
10th	Edmonton	May 1986
11th	Waterloo	June 1987
12th	Vancouver	July 1989
13th	Fredericton	July 1990
14th	Calgary	May 1991
15th	Toronto	June 1992
16th	Sherbrooke	June 1993
17th	Saskatoon	June 1995
18th	Vancouver	March 1996

by 1991 Canada had received one million Landsat images. With airborne sensing and data reception, two of the major components of CCRS were in place. In January of 1973 CCRS established the third plank in its programme – an applications division to focus on applications research and development.

While CCRS was the most active agency in the field of remote sensing, a number of other "specialty centres" existed with interests in specific areas. These contributed significantly to the development of remote sensing in Canada – particularly in the domain of applications. Specialty centres in this period included the Canada Centre for Inland Waters, the Lands Directorate of the Department of Environment, the five Canadian Forestry Service Institutes and Research Centres, Ocean and Aquatic Affairs (Fisheries and Oceans), and Statistics Canada.

The first national remote sensing symposium was held in Ottawa in 1972, and the second two years later at Guelph as table 14-2 shows. The Canadian Remote Sensing Society (CRSS) was born during the meeting at Guelph under the presidency of Morley (see table 14-3). Beginning in 1986 the CRSS promoted excellence in remote sensing through the presentation every two or three years of a Gold Medal for outstanding achievement (see table 14-4). The Ontario Association for Remote Sensing began a full year earlier, and the Association Québécoise de Télédétection was founded at the same time as CRSS. All have remained largely independent, although occasionally co-sponsoring meetings.

The Provinces and Their Early Role in Remote Sensing

Since natural resources are the constitutional responsibility of the provinces, it was appropriate that their monitoring with remote sensing spawned a number of provincial and territorial remote sensing centres or offices. The first were established in Manitoba (April 1973), British Columbia (July 1973), Ontario (September 1973), and then Alberta (June 1974).

Table 14-3
Presidents of the CRSS

Dr L.W. Morley	1974–1975
Dr R.W. Nicholls	1976–1977
Dr D.J. Clough	1978–1979
E.A. Godby	1980–1981
J. Thie	1982
Dr S. Pala	1983
Dr F. Bonn	1984–1985
Dr P.A. Murtha	1986–1987
Ms D. Thompson	1988–1990
Dr R.A. Ryerson	1990–1992
Ms. N. Prout	1992–1994
Dr S. Franklin	1995–1996

Table 14-4
CRSS Gold Medal Winners

Dr L.W. Morley	1986
E.A. Godby	1987
Dr J. MacDonald	1989
Dr F.J. Ahern	1991
Dr P.J. Howarth	1993
Dr J.R. Miller	1996

Eventually each province or territory had at least a remote sensing committee, and centres or offices were established in Québec, Saskatchewan, Northwest Territories, and Yukon. The provincial and territorial centres contributed greatly to grass-roots marketing and programmes of public awareness. While the centres varied from province to province according to each province's needs, there were certain basic characteristics. All were involved in education and training. The most active in the early years was the Alberta Centre, which developed a popular training course with the Faculty of Extension, University of Alberta. Most centres had rudimentary equipment whilst some others, including those in Newfoundland and Manitoba, borrowed equipment from CCRS. Most provided advice, some offered microfiche copies of satellite imagery, and all could help users obtain CCRS airborne imagery.

A number of the best-known and most effective proponents of remote sensing came from the ranks of the early provincial offices or centres of remote sensing. These included Victor Zsilinszky of Ontario, Cal Bricker of Alberta, Hervé Audet of Québec, and Bill Best of Manitoba. All shared a common desire to make remote sensing effective, and all made a considerable personal commitment to the field.

The centres varied greatly with respect to their perceived role or philosophy. There were those that supported the activities of industry through technology transfer, and others that actively entered the marketplace with the intention of recouping their costs – often in competition with industry. Over the years the different approaches have had their adherents. However one thing remains clear: where the provincial or federal agencies competed or seemed to compete with what the private sector could or did do, there were negative consequences. Either a private sector failed to develop, or what did exist withered, employment remained low, primarily in government, and no export capability developed.

In 1970 four southern-Ontario universities cooperated to offer what was called the Inter-University Course on Integrated Aerial Survey. The schools involved were Waterloo (under Dieter Steiner in Geography), McMaster (Phil Howarth in Geography, who later moved to Waterloo), Guelph (Stan Collins in Engineering), and the University of Toronto (Jerry Vlcek in Forestry). The course ended after a few years. At the same time John Parry of the Department of Geography at McGill University was actively engaged in some of the first radar work in a Canadian university.

The first Canadian known to have received a Ph.D. degree in the field of remote sensing was Peter Murtha, who received it in 1968 from Cornell University in the Department of Conservation, Faculty of Agriculture. Murtha later began a remote sensing specialization in the Department of Forestry and Soil Science at the University of British Columbia (UBC), which granted its first Ph.D. degree in 1981 to Don Leckie, now of the Canadian Forestry Service. The first Ph.D. degree to have been granted in Canada with a specialization in remote sensing was awarded to the present author from the Department of Geography, University of Waterloo in 1975.

A variety of courses, programmes, and graduate degrees began or evolved soon after those noted above in surveying (UNB), photogrammetry and forestry (Laval), soil science (Alberta and later Guelph), engineering (Memorial and Ryerson), physics (York), electrical engineering (Saskatchewan and Ottawa), landscape architecture (Calgary), and geology (Manitoba). Most of those that have developed since have been based in departments of geography. They include Sherbrooke, Laurentian, Université du Québec à Montréal, Carleton, Winnipeg, Western Ontario, Ottawa, Calgary, Victoria, Windsor, and most recently (in 1994) a new specialization in Earth observation at Manitoba. The largest of the current academic programmes in remote sensing was started in the mid-1970s by Ferdinand Bonn at the University of Sherbrooke. Sherbrooke's CARTEL was formed in 1985 as a result of the collaboration of Bonn, Jean-Marie Dubois, and Hugh Gwyn. CARTEL began a Ph.D. programme in 1990. Now there are eight full-time faculty members in the Department of Geography and Remote Sensing involved in remote sensing, and some fourteen countries are represented among its graduate students and visiting scholars. Others that grant the Ph.D. degree with specialization in remote sensing, as distinct from being it a tool studied in the context of another major discipline, are Waterloo, Laval, and UBC. Now most of the new professors are graduates of Canadian schools, whereas the original faculty members were almost all from other countries.

Technical programmes were also developed. The first began in 1977 under the leadership of John Wightman with Ernie McLaren as the first instructor in remote sensing at the Nova Scotia Land Survey Institute (now the College of Geographic Sciences) in Lawrencetown, Nova Scotia. Other programmes are offered at the British Columbia Institute of Technology and elsewhere as part of GIS or photo interpretation courses.

The Early Role of the Airborne Remote Sensing Programme

With the establishment of CFASU, CCRS had a tool that could be offered with both research and operational implications. On 1 November 1971 a Falcon jet was purchased to provide a high-altitude platform and to complement the two DC-3 aircraft. In addition a CF-100, which was retired in October 1974, was used for the acquisition of high-altitude images. The first airborne project accepted by CCRS after it assumed responsibility for CFASU was given the designation 71-1. The formal request was sent to Lee Godby on 15 February 1971. The project was to acquire multitemporal and multiband imagery over Wawa and Sudbury, Ontario, during the late summer for Peter Murtha to assess damage to vegetation caused by sulphur dioxide fumes. Like the rest of the programme the intent was to get imagery into the hands of potential users for evaluation and use. As it turned out the first project CCRS accepted provided outstanding results in an environmental/forestry application.[26]

The early Airborne Operations (AirOps) activity saw the collection of a large amount of high-altitude colour and colour infrared aerial photography, particularly in Ontario for the then Ministry of Transportation. The imagery proved its worth in many ways, including the updating of CLI land-use maps for the International Commission for the Great Lakes where Landsat (then ERTS) imagery proved not to be equal to the whole task.[27] This represents one of the dilemmas associated with the airborne activity. It was begun in part to provide simulations and justification for using satellite imagery. While it was successful, it often demonstrated that airborne sensing was a useful tool in its own right, albeit one rarely supported within CCRS by the same aggressive development of applications as the satellite programme.

The one airborne area that was well supported in applications development was the use of thermal infrared imagery for the mapping of heat loss. In one flight over $15–20 million worth of roof damage was identified.[28] Thermal imaging for forest-fire mapping and heat-loss detection were commercialized later by Intera. Other applications were also developed by external users and in-house within the data acquisition division of CCRS, working with the technology suppliers and data providers – analogous to the aerial camera and aerial survey companies discussed in chapter 6.

Beyond flying a large number of complex projects, often for investigators who rarely understood the complexities of data acquisition, one of the major accomplishments of the AirOps in the early years was the development of a clear understanding of how to expose and process Kodak colour infrared film. Jack Fleming, AirOps's quality-control specialist, noticed that there appeared to be three different appearances for this type of film. He was able to explain and correct for these variations in various batches of the film. His methods were used for exposure control and processing for all such film used in Canada, and later were adopted for use elsewhere.

To simplify the problem of data acquisition AirOps developed a guide known as "The Blue Book." It contained useful tables and information on airborne data acquisition with different sensors, films, flight line spacings, image motion characteristics, sun angles, and area coverages at different scales.[29] Several thousand copies of the document were distributed across Canada and around the world.

By 1974 the number of projects being flown had started to drop. The CF-100 was decommissioned and the Convair 580 aircraft was purchased. According to plans made at the start of the programme, Innotech Aviation was brought in as a commercial contractor in April 1975 with Intera as subcontractor to take airborne sensing into a more businesslike environment. The plan was to phase in the private sector, and phase out the public sector, over a three-year period. During the first year there was to be a plan for commercialization of airborne sensing.

Between 1971 and 1978 some 1062 projects were flown, 192 for internal work and sensor tests, and 870 for external users. A benefit-cost analysis of the programme showed clearly that it had paid for itself[30]. Benefits were measured in the millions of dollars, and ranged from reduced costs associated with data acquisition to the provision of information not available previously at any price.

The Early Landsat Era: Technology and Applications

Landsat MSS imagery was oversold. Both the applications and technology associated with the interpretation of MSS were at best rudimentary, and needed a great deal of development before they could meet any reasonable expectations of a reliable data source. Indeed after the launch of the far more useful Landsat Thematic Mapper (TM) sensor, advertising had to take into consideration the fact that many in the forestry and geology communities did not trust claims made for remote sensing. Even so the period was marked by enthusiasm, rapid development of methods, and the solution of many simple problems.

In the Landsat era the first technology developed in Canada was for data reception and processing. That CCRS was able to produce an image and deliver it to Ottawa during the ISP conference within days of the launch caught the imagination of staff, contractors, and clients alike. For them remote sensing was not just an intellectual challenge, but an opportunity to shine on the world stage. And shine they did.

The focus in the first years was, and to a certain extent has remained, technology. However it is very difficult to divorce the development of both technology and applications from the development of the fledgling industry, discussed in the next section. Industry was seen as a key player from the beginning. Early CACRS meetings continually referred to the need for industrial involvement, marketing, and product development. They also called for work in the development of image-processing algorithms, geometric corrections, side-looking airborne radar, and low-cost image-processing systems; for participation in the Seasat programme; and for a variety of sensor and applications development relating to the specific interests of the various working groups.

There were many early papers and presentations on image-processing algorithms, geometric corrections, reception systems, and data formats. There was also a large amount written on the potential of a number of different sensors, many of which were never built. Of those sensors that were built, many were abandoned for a lack of resources and committed users to see them brought to commercial use.

In applications development the problems were quite different from those faced in technology development. The costs were lower, the lead times shorter, results were easier to assess (and good results easier to obtain), and the number of willing cooperators with resources to invest was considerably larger. As a result the researcher could, in theory, be more selective about what was done. But as a result of both cost-benefit studies and work being done in the U.S., much more time and effort were spent on developing agricultural applications than the user demand would have indicated at the time. This work did pay off with excellent results in rangeland monitoring,[31] methods for estimating the area under potatoes,[32] and, much later, methods of assessing crop conditions.[33] While less money and effort appeared to be spent in forestry (particularly within CCRS), the successes there were also impressive. Forest-fire mapping, ecological mapping, and forest-fire fuel mapping all came from the Landsat MSS era. Other topics addressed included topographic map updating,[34] ice mapping, water quality monitoring, and land-use mapping.[35] Between 1973 and 1975 the world's first large-scale operational integration of information derived from remote sensing and GIS was performed by CCRS and Environment Canada for the Canadian portion of the Great Lakes Basin – an area about half the size of France.[36]

One constant amongst most applications was that each scientist could and did work with a number of different cooperators on a number of projects, thereby spreading the impact of each remote sensing specialist. There was a great emphasis within CCRS at that time on developing "real" or "useful" applications, and less on publishing results. CCRS also worked hard to ensure that it developed applications in association with agencies that have the responsibility for mapping and reporting on resources. CCRS has been very clear in its mandate and expertise – it is remote sensing. The user agencies such as the Geological Survey, Statistics Canada, British Columbia Forest Inventory Branch, and the Canadian Wheat Board provided the expertise in a particular discipline, while CCRS contributed its expertise in remote sensing. Another important factor is funding. CCRS has usually *not* underwritten all (or even the majority) of costs for the development of an application, though this has been criticized by some who wanted more grants. Much of Canada's early Landsat work was summarized in a special publication produced under the aegis of the geography working group of CACRS to mark Canada being host to a meeting of the Committee on Space Research (COSPAR).[37]

The Birth of an Export Industry

A number of public documents, including CACRS reports, draw attention to the international need for remote sensing, especially in developing countries. At the same time the possibility of using exports of technology to help pay for their development in Canada was also discussed.[38] From the beginning Canada looked outside its own borders for ideas, data, management structures, advice, and markets. Consistent with this attitude the United States, France, the Netherlands, and the European Space Agency (ESA) provided speakers to the early CACRS meetings.

The first Canadian to work in an international organization outside Canada was Ralph Chipman, who joined the UN after being one of the first employees of CCRS. Denny Kalensky served for a year in Indonesia, and then later headed remote sensing at the UN Food and Agriculture Organisation (FAO) until 1994. Several other key players in the international arena were at one time post-doctoral fellows at CCRS. These included Ade Abiodun of the UN and Victor Odenyo, who has worked for the FAO and other organizations. Three other former post-doctoral fellows now head their own companies: David Horler, Geoff Tomlins, and in 1994 George Xu. In 1994 Claire Gosselin joined the UN's ESCAP remote sensing programme in Bangkok after working with Photosur Geomat and Intera. While not charged with helping Canada to export its services, Canadian nationals active in the international community are certainly useful in keeping up Canada's profile and in providing contacts with and access to the international community.

Remote sensing received a big boost when a small company started by UBC professor John MacDonald to keep the best and brightest of his graduates in British Columbia turned its attention to the reception of ERTS/Landsat data. In December 1974 MacDonald Detwiller Associates (MDA) received a contract to build a second processing system for the short-lived receiving station CCRS established in Newfoundland. That system was put into operation in June 1977. CCRS was innovative in obtaining funds from another government programme. The Department of Supply and Services (DSS) Unsolicited Proposal (UP) Program provided much of the early funding for the acquisition of capital equipment, and contracts that helped both the technology and service industries to begin.

At that time there were three Canadian companies said to be able to build reception stations: Computing Devices, SED Systems and MDA. Computing Devices built the first processing system in Italy, and then several of their key staff left to form the company DIPIX. While SED and Computing Devices moved to other aspects of remote sensing and related business areas, MDA went on to capture 80 percent of the world market for remote sensing satellite receiving stations.

Soon after the inception of the CCRS applications division in 1973, a team under the leadership of D.G. Goodenough planned the first commercial purchase of an image analysis system. Two systems were considered, including General Electric's Image 100. While the other system was judged superior on many counts, the source code was not available and subsequent modification would not be possible. Thus it was decided to buy the Image 100.[39] Shortly after CCRS took delivery of the Image 100 in April 1974, Computing Devices, like MDA, used the UP Program to obtain funds for a contract to develop a system for the Forest Management Institute. A contract was awarded in September 1976. The result was the ARIES system, and the growth of DIPIX, which became one of the best-known (and largest) suppliers of image analysis systems in the world up to the second half of the 1980s.

With the formation of Intera in Calgary under the late Robert M. Holmes and Diane Thompson, F.G. Bercha Associates under Frank Bercha in Calgary, and Gregory Geoscience under Alan F. Gregory in Ottawa, a fledgling service sector was born by 1975 that was to employ well over 1000 people within twenty years. CCRS and Canadian industry were now on the international map with firsts in airborne sensing, the development of a service industry, data reception, and then image processing. The end of the period was marked by the development of technology that could be exported to allow more routine reception and use of imagery elsewhere in the world.

COMING OF AGE IN CANADA AND AROUND THE WORLD: 1978–84

The third era saw dramatic growth worldwide in interest in remote sensing, and the coincident development of a Canadian industry to serve that growing market based on expertise demonstrated in Canada. A popular refrain of the day was that Canada was the largest and most difficult remote sensing test site in the world.

This period saw the growth of the private sector, and solidified Canada's interest in radar remote sensing. The industrial policy developed in the previous period was consolidated, and the major players explored and captured international markets. At the same time there were many scientific successes leading to awards, breakthroughs in applications, and increase of use. It was also the time during which the airborne programme began to decline relative to spaceborne remote sensing. At the end of this period satellite imagery was priced on a more commercial basis without any loss in revenue. With the launch of Landsat TM in 1982 and more commercially oriented prices, the market entered a phase of rapid growth now that the new imagery could meet many more needs than the older Landsat MSS.

Airborne Radar and SURSAT

Radar had been a topic of discussion within Canada for some years. In 1976 cabinet approved a submission titled Microwave Surveillance Satellite Initiative. It entailed participation in the U.S. Seasat Program, renting a radar, developing a side-looking radar, and exploring international cooperation in a radar satellite. At the same time Keith Raney joined CCRS from the Environmental Research Institute of Michigan (ERIM) and continued his work in airborne and spaceborne radar processing and applications. In 1976 Intera identified Synthetic Aperture Radar (SAR) as the best opportunity for commercialization of airborne remote sensing. As a result the ERIM X/L band radar was rented and placed on the CV 580 aircraft, and Intera became the industrial partner in the SURSAT activity sponsored by CCRS and the DSS UP Program. A call for proposals that went out to the Canadian remote sensing community resulted in 101 submissions. Within a relatively short time the value of radar for ice reconnaissance was understood, and was demonstrated in 1980. Intera, which had borrowed Ray Lowry from CCRS to provide additional expertise in radar, went from this activity to the design and construction of its own system in cooperation with ERIM. The result was introduced as Star-1 in 1983. At the time Brian Bullock, the young entrepreneurial engineer who took over the leadership of Intera after the death of its founder, was quoted as having said that "he bet the company" on its radar development. In 1984 Star-1 was used in the first major export sale. From that beginning, which involved the investment of some millions of dollars, Intera was to dominate the world market that had previously been the province of American-based companies.

Other promising applications areas that were well studied under SURSAT included geology and oceans. Less promising were results in the traditional areas of information to which Landsat imagery had been applied in forestry, agriculture, and land use.

While Seasat's L-band SAR sensor lasted only about 100 days, from a Canadian stand-point it was very successful. Intera staked out a major new business area, MDA developed the first digital radar image processor based on Raney's research, and the first digitally processed SAR image was produced. The first image produced by the radar image processor was a Seasat image of Trois Rivières, published in November 1978 by *Aviation Week*. Canada had begun to take the first concrete steps down the road to Radarsat and a major role in airborne radar remote sensing after years of discussion and studies.

Building the Canadian Industry

The importance of industry and the role of the export market in paying for Canadian developments in remote sensing was articulated as early as 1973, and was reinforced at every subsequent meeting of CACRS. While the roles of the various players have been, and are still, evolving as the technology changes, essentially the private, public, and academic sectors have mutually supportive roles.

The government's role in the process has been clear. It is to undertake high-risk research and development that leads to practical products and services. It also serves as a beta market or test site for new Canadian products and services, or as an early user. Government is a window on international remote sensing activities, and displays Canadian remote sensing expertise to the world. The government also coordinates the national programme, under-takes intergovernmental negotiations, and receives and archives data.

The role of industry includes the development of commercial products and services, taking these products and services to market, advising government on research directions, and marketing. Academia has a role in basic research and development, and of course in education. There is also a role for academia in the spin-off of commercial products and services from their research and development activities. As noted earlier several academics have successfully entered the business sector to found companies.

In Canada there has been a good working partnership between the three sectors. This was facilitated in part by the exchange of information at CACRS. The primary mode of operation has been the letting of contracts to the private sector for products and services, based on the needs (and sometimes the technology) of government agencies. Some contracts are for the development of operational products and services derived from research and development in government laboratories or within universities. In most cases the award of contracts has been based on competitive bids. The resulting products and expertise have usually been sold abroad.

At first the service industry was largely based on providing information and support to research and development organizations, primarily in the federal government. Those companies that concentrated on research and development without trying to serve the user market tended to stagnate, and some died. Similarly those who saw the primary product to be remote sensing also usually failed. Those who have approached the market more aggressively using remote sensing as a tool to provide information have typically prospered.

CCRS involvement with the private sector has included initiatives with virtually all of the Canadian companies whose names are well-known in the world of remote sensing, and with many more who will become well-known.* The basis of the Canadian approach has been to maximize the potential of the private sector as a vehicle for technology transfer and marketing of remote sensing applications.

To ensure that this process is effective CCRS has assumed a role that differs from that of other national agencies involved in remote sensing. CCRS has tried to avoid the commercial domain. For this reason it does not actively seek contracts overseas, although it will work overseas in support of Canadian industry or government initiatives under narrowly defined conditions that do not involve competition with the private sector.

Where it has seen itself in a position of competition with industry it has moved out of the way. For example at one point use of the Image 100 was offered to those outside CCRS. It became evident that the private sector would not buy image-processing systems to provide a commercial service as long as CCRS offered its services without charge. When CCRS stopped providing such services two private-sector companies in Ottawa immediately bought systems, and several companies are now exporting based on their local experience. Similar growth can be seen in southern Ontario after the Ontario Centre for Remote Sensing stopped offering services for fees to external clients. In another example CCRS had begun to release a series of free public relations posters of all of the capital cities of Canada using Landsat TM. A private company appeared with a better product and better marketing. By withdrawing CCRS not only saved the cost of producing the posters. It derived income from selling the imagery, *and* received even more free publicity than if it had proceeded to distribute free posters. The happy result is that Worldsat International has become the best producer of satellite posters in the world, with significant exports and an international clientele.

This *modus operandi* has had several benefits. It has allowed industry to develop the commercial products and take them to market, which has resulted in a more efficient

---

* To date CCRS has contracted with an estimated 58 of 162 companies on the CCRS industry list, including all those active in the international market.

industry with a better opportunity to export. The government laboratory has been able to meet its mandate without worrying about generating income or competing with those whose tax dollars support its activities.

A number of companies have had their products and services purchased and used by CCRS and other government agencies and several have resulted in the development of follow-on sales. Included in the latter is Intera Technologies, which has provided services supporting a full range of applications. Others have won service contracts that have been, or are being, spun off into new offerings. They include Bercha and Associates (for airborne operations and applications), Noetix (ice remote sensing), Geomatics International (environmental monitoring), MIR Télédétection (geology applications), AERDE (hydrology and ocean applications), and Dendron Resource Surveys (forestry remote sensing).

Other companies have been involved in the National Research Council's Industrial Research Assistance Program (IRAP) by which they can draw on CCRS for advice in order to develop capabilities. For example Terrain Resources developed a GIS and image-analysis capability under IRAP, and later won a CCRS contract for work on soil salinity. This resulted in an increased capability that was applied recently on an operational basis in Thailand and elsewhere. A second example is Itres Research, which developed its Compact Airborne Spectral Imager (CASI) airborne imaging system under IRAP, with most of the subsequent sales being exports.

Scientific Successes on the International Stage

There have been international successes in remote sensing in the domains of applications and technology. The latter often resulted in products that were subsequently sold, while the former were sometimes taken up by users. Successes in applications were as varied as the Canadian geography over which they were developed. With hundreds of projects completed over a number of years, any attempt to identify the most important is subject to error and bias. What follows is a summary of several that seem to have caught the attention of the international community.

Ground spectroscopy, airborne imagery, and satellite imagery were used in research on assessing rangeland, and then in developing a Landsat MSS–based method.[40] The detailed report on this work won the American Society of Photogrammetry and Remote Sensing Autometric award for the best paper in English on image interpretation for 1983. The world's first operational summer estimation of a major crop area was made in 1981 using satellite imagery.[41] The approach has since been refined by Statistics Canada. Surveying, mapping, and remote sensing expertise were brought together for the first time in 1980 when Landsat was used operationally to update topographic maps. This experiment proved most beneficial – resulting in savings of over $10 million.[42]

The first operational use of NOAA AVHRR weather-satellite imagery for assessment of crop condition was done in Canada.[43] Radar remote sensing of ice has been the topic for a number of researchers, with much successful research and operational work completed prior to Radarsat.[44] Geology and hydrology have also been studied widely using radar, with interesting results.

Research and development in technology has also seen much success, but publication of the results has been limited because of the proprietary nature of the work. Unlike the applications area, which is less easily transportable to other environments, the technology has tended to be moved easily to other regions of the world by Canadian industry. The first laser bathymetry system was used operationally in Canada for aerial hydrography in 1985.[45] Major successes in the design of radar sensors began in the 1970s and continue to the present, culminating in Radarsat.[46] Work on the geometric correction of satellite data resulted in the Digital Image Correction System (DICS) and then the Multi-Observation Satellite Image Correction System (MOSAICS). Without this foundation the integration in a GIS of satellite imagery and results obtained from the interpretation of images would not have advanced as far and as quickly as it has in Canada.[47] Work on atmospheric corrections was also important in creating imagery that could be used more effectively and understood.[48]

Commercial Development in Ground Stations and Image Analysis

Very early in the remote sensing programme it was recognized that to make the data useful they had to be obtained in an efficient manner from the satellite or aircraft and processed into a useful format, and then useful information extracted. The first suppliers in any industry usually experience rapid growth. This was the case for MDA in ground receiving systems, and for DIPIX in image analysis. Both companies took advantage of government contracts to build a capability that could be exported. OVAAC8, another early player in the image analysis-market and a predecessor company to PCI, was less agile than PCI was to become, although it did sell systems to both Poland and Mongolia in the mid-1970s. Ten years later both MDA and DIPIX were beginning to sell a considerable number of image-analysis systems around the world, from the Asia-Pacific region to Latin America. MDA had few serious competitors, in part because there were significant barriers, both techno-logical and financial, to market entry. Unlike MDA, DIPIX had a number of competitors including firms based in the United States (I²s and ERDAS being among the survivors), and PCI in Canada. The stage was set either for growth or failure, as the market dictated, in two of the market niches that Canada had selected.

The Beginnings of Marketing

Marketing and sales have been, and to a certain degree are still, weak points in the field of remote sensing. This was recognized in the 1974 CACRS report that called for a marketing position in CCRS. The weakness was particularly evident in satellite data and sales of services. As recently as March 1994 this weakness was brought up again at a NASA-sponsored meeting in Denver on commercialization of remote sensing. CCRS tried to address this problem with the temporary assignment of Ernie McLaren to a new marketing unit in 1977. A permanent position was filled in 1979 by Paul Hession, who had experience in the private sector of computer sales and marketing. Hession, together with Fred Peet, who was then at the Forest Management Institute, were among the first to advocate the use of personal computers for image processing. Hession broadened the CCRS perspective and understanding of marketing and sales, and led Canadian participation in several interna-tional events, including the ISPRS Commission VII meeting in Toulouse in 1982. This meeting was pivotal for DIPIX, which exhibited with CCRS. None of the other vendors, American and French, could make their systems work in the heat of the exhibit hall. The DIPIX representatives drove in with a system they had demonstrated to FAO in Italy, plugged it in, and it worked. A senior Chinese official said later that "if a system could not work in the heat in Toulouse, how could one expect it to work in Nanjing or Wuhan? Hession left after several years, eventually to be replaced by the present author.

COMMERCIAL DEVELOPMENT: 1984–94

The 1984 meeting of CACRS was devoted to marketing and as a result domestic and international marketing was begun with the cooperation of other government departments and industry. The earlier focus on the increased use of remote sensing in Canada gave way to a greater emphasis on the international field.[49] In this period the market for satellite imagery, the number of companies, the number of employees, the international market, and Canada's reputation in the international community all reached what may come to be regarded as a zenith – if the unlikely is assumed that Canadian commercial development does not keep pace with the demands of the marketplace. Reliance on governments has both diminished and grown. It has diminished in the sense that industry needed less ongoing scientific advice from government, and the larger companies needed reduced financial support. They did, however, require more strategic assistance such as political support and marketing in order to continue to be effective in the market arena of large complex projects to which the industry's capability and size had taken it. Moreover there have been changes in the nature of the competition. With the fall-off in military spending, large U.S. defence contractors have moved rapidly (but not always successfully) into civilian remote sensing and environmental monitoring. Similarly Russia has entered the market actively. This was also the last year before Canada became a member of the full remote sensing club with its own satellite.

Landsat Thematic Mapper and the New Era of Applications

The launch of Landsat 4 with its 30 m resolution, seven-band TM sensor moved satellite remote sensing from the fringes of being useful to the resource manager to being an important tool. For example an operational forest monitoring system was developed in British Columbia based on TM imagery.[50] Ducks Unlimited developed a wetland mapping project that at its peak consumed over 20 percent of all data sold in Canada. Land-use, ecological, and geological mapping at a regional level could all be achieved with TM. In 1986 SPOT imagery became available with 10 m resolution in the panchromatic mode and 20 m in multispectral. This did not catch on in Canada as it did elsewhere, partly because of cost and partly due to the lack of the shortwave infrared band that was found to be so useful in both geology and forestry applications.

A combination of the availability of Landsat TM imagery and the marketing plan developed at the 1984 CACRS meeting resulted in sales increasing by approximately 400 percent over five years to about $1.25 million per annum. The marketing plan included new promotional material directed to foresters, geologists, and others, an aggressive public awareness campaign, an increased number of exhibits, and a targeted advertising campaign. Radarsat International took over marketing and sales from CCRS in 1990.

It was during this period that CCRS research largely moved from supporting electro-optical sensing in the visible, near-infrared, short-wave infrared, and thermal infrared bands to radar imaging. It was also during the early part of this period that the airborne linear array, multispectral electro-optical imaging scanner known as MEIS was turned over to Innotech Aviation for commercial operation. But the size of the system, the resulting cost of the large aircraft, difficulties in delivering data, and the limited swath the sensor offered all combined to make MEIS as it was then configured not commercially viable. Accordingly Innotech ceased to operate MEIS in March 1994. However the company had demonstrated the effectiveness of such sensing for monitoring events as different as forest fires in Yellowstone National Park and the beach cleanup after the *Exxon Valdez* oil spill. The MEIS system was the first linear array flown in a civilian system, and predated by some years the use of such arrays by SPOT. Smaller and lower-cost systems built by Itres Research of Calgary have been sold, and are operated commercially by a number of organizations.

Technology Development, Industrial Growth, and the International Market

As noted previously the scientific successes have often, but not always, been tied to commercial successes, and to Canada's needs. One of the best examples has been airborne radar remote sensing, which was a response to Canada's need for all-weather, day-and-night monitoring of ice. While originally developed for use in Canada's high Arctic, Star-1 had a number of attributes that made it useful elsewhere. It was on a small aircraft that could land on short runways. It was designed to function in extremes of temperature. It could collect images in the dark or through clouds. When the market in Canada declined another was found in South-east Asia. Star-1 was first flown there by Intera in 1985, and by 1986 the company had established an office in Indonesia. Star-1 imagery contributed in a major way to a significant oil find in Papua New Guinea, as well as to a range of other resource management and mapping applications.

Another Canadian need is associated with its long coastline and requirement for rapid hydrographic charting. The most notable of the early successes in sensors involved the development of a laser to measure depths of up to 40 m in clear water. The method was first tested operationally in 1985.[51] Tests made in 1994 showed accuracies could be achieved within a few centimetres of the most precise alternative measurements available. The early work was done by CCRS in cooperation with the Canadian Hydrographic Service, with the instrument designed and built by Optech. Development of other sensors has been done by MPB Technologies (for a microwave radiometer) and Itres Research.

Perhaps the exports most often associated with the Canadian remote sensing industry are the MDA products used for satellite data reception and processing. In the 1980s MDA was contracted by CCRS to provide MOSAICS which was mentioned earlier. Systems based on that technology were installed around the world – some even before CCRS took delivery of its system. Another innovation was the development of the world's only one terabyte optical tape recorder by CREO, under contract to CCRS and other government departments. The new tape recorder packs 1 MB of data per millimetre of long-lasting and rapidly accessible tape, thus leading to great savings of time, tape used, and storage space required. In the image-analysis market PCI has also been active in working with government to enhance its image-analysis systems, which have been installed in over eighty countries.

As a result of the growth in the domestic market and the more substantial growth of international markets, the number of companies and employees has grown dramatically since they were first tracked in the early 1980s, as is indicated by table 14-5.

Table 14-5
Canadian Remote Sensing Companies by Region

	1987	1989	1991	1993	1994
British Columbia	8	21	18	20	20
Prairies	17	24	30	27	30
Ontario	14	19	18	19	19
National Capital	15	21	24	25	29
Québec	14	19	18	28	30
Atlantic	5	14	14	16	33*
Territories				1	1
Total	73	118	122	136	162

Source: Ryerson, 1991 and 1993

* This includes a dramatic increase of companies involved in remote sensing identified through the Atlantic Centre for Remote
  Sensing of the Oceans in Halifax. It is here considered that this represents at least in part an improved accounting, not
  necessarily a large single-year increase.

Radarsat

One of the most important dates in the history of remote sensing in Canada came in June 1987 when the Radarsat satellite received approval and funding. Launched on 4 November 1995, it carries a C-Band radar with a nominal ground resolution in the order of 25 m. Unlike other satellite systems it has been designed to produce imagery quickly to meet the operational needs of users. It will, therefore, be the first fully operational radar remote sensing satellite.

CCRS and the Canadian Space Agency (CSA) are partners in the Canadian Space Program, which includes Radarsat. CSA is responsible for the space segment, while CCRS handles the ground segment in remote sensing. Each then concentrates on what it does best. This approach appears to be working to the benefit of both the remote sensing community in Canada and those using Canadian technology overseas.

Radarsat has been described elsewhere.[52] Of interest, and not normally discussed, is the long history behind it. In 1974 the CACRS working group on data handling was charged by the Interagency Advisory Committee to "look at the feasibility and practicality of a Canadian remote sensing satellite system."[53] Canadian Astronautics was given a contract, and reported that an ocean and ice reconnaissance all-weather radar satellite was necessary. At the same time, the sensor working group noted that radar sensors were increasingly attractive.

Though the concept of Radarsat was born, it faced a rough road to its eventual approval, design, and construction. It took years of discussions, airborne simulations, and evaluations before a preliminary concept was put in place. Originally there were plans for a system with both radar and optical sensors. These were reduced to a single C-Band radar sensor as a result of budget limitations. The original international partners included the U.S. (for launch) and Great Britain (providing the platform). When Great Britain withdrew, many assumed that Radarsat was dead. From where would the necessary $150 million to replace the platform come? Ed Shaw, then director of the Radarsat project office at CCRS, and his team went to work at a feverish pace to save Radarsat. They put together an innovative package that brought together sufficient funding and support from the provinces and private sector to cover the shortfall in the budget. In addition SPAR Aerospace, the prime contractor for Radarsat, developed some ingenious solutions to lower the build costs.

The first preparatory phase for Radarsat was the Radar Data Development Program (RDDP), which was begun in 1987 within CCRS with an annual budget of $5 million for up to fifteen years. This covered the cost of airborne radar data acquisition, technology development, and applications support. Scores of researchers across Canada from academia, government, and industry are involved. The RDDP has as its objective the development of the tools and applications to ensure that the highest and best use of Radarsat data are made in Canada. Many of the same tools and knowledge base are being applied internationally as well.

A third partner in Radarsat is Radarsat International (RSI). It has been marketing SPOT and Landsat imagery in Canada since 1990, and will undertake the commercial distribution of Radarsat imagery, returning funds to the government to defray at least the operating costs of the satellite. RSI has embarked upon an aggressive training and education programme, coupled with marketing activities in the key markets of Asia and Latin America.

Canadian expertise was applied in Latin America during 1992, with the support of ESA, through the Tropical Forestry Initiative. SAR imagery of Brazil, Venezuela, Costa Rica, and Guyana was acquired for cooperating agencies such as Instituto Nacional de Pesquisas Espaciais (INPE) in Brazil using the CCRS C/X airborne SAR.[54] Canada then became involved in a second airborne radar programme, GlobeSAR, funded by Canada with in-kind support from partner countries. The CCRS C/X SAR was flown in Morocco, Tunisia, Jordan, Kenya, Uganda, Thailand, Malaysia, Vietnam, and China. The objective was to introduce both airborne and simulated spaceborne SAR to the participating countries and the regions in which they are found to prepare for the availability of Radarsat. GlobeSAR was the first foreign sensing of Chinese territory to be approved since before 1949. The project was funded by CSA, IDRC, and CCRS and contained a significant component of technology transfer and training.

Research, Commercial Applications Development, and the Role of Government

In Canadian remote sensing in the early 1970s there were a large number of relatively easily solved problems. Governments were growing and funds were easy to obtain. Over 80 percent of the small remote sensing workforce was in government, and most of the work was done in government laboratories. Around the world this is still the most common situation. One government agency could cover much of technology and applications development. There were few in industry to take advantage of the opportunities, let alone do their own research. The government did a great deal of what was then called applications development but would now be called product development – part of marketing or business development. Researchers were seldom content to do "me-too" research, that is repeating what someone else had done to prove that it could be replicated. Most often work from outside Canada was used as a departure for a new innovation, method, or development.

The situation has changed. Funds are hard to obtain. Governments are shrinking. The easy research problems have been solved. Those remaining require a significant expenditure of funds and close cooperation between teams from a variety of groups, public and private.

One agency cannot cover the whole of remote sensing. Now well over 80 percent of the workforce is outside government. Those in government are now doing more background research. There is more me-too research, often as part of international collaborative efforts. There is less product or service development, which is being left to industry.

How is industry responding? In many cases very well. For a number of years MDA has had one of the largest private sector commitments to research and development in Canada. It has also been moving ideas and technologies from government to the marketplace. Others that appear to be spending significant portions of their income on research, development, and commercial product or business development include PCI, MPB, Intera, Itres Research, Optech, Satlantic of Halifax, and Geomatics International of Burlington, Ontario, to name but a few. While they are not all spending on what may have traditionally been called "research," they are looking to product and market development. And they are all growing and making a niche for themselves in the international marketplace. At the same time, while the market is growing governments are not and their overall impact, at least from a Canadian perspective, has recently been lessening.

The Growth of International Aid in Remote Sensing

Remote sensing technology and applications developed in Canada have been designed to work under the conditions of Canada's large land mass, small population, harsh climate, and extensive natural resources. Canadian technology can often be counted upon to meet the needs of those outside Canada as well as, or better than, they meet the needs of Canada itself. To help meet the requirements of other nations for Canadian technology and knowledge, Canada has developed a significant outreach activity. Since remote sensing was first used in Canada, commercial and aid activities have touched countries on all continents, providing a full and exciting range of applications. Remote sensing has been particularly important in developing countries where the information infrastructure was weak or, in some cases, altogether lacking.

Canadian aid activities through both the Canadian International Development Agency (CIDA) and the International Development Research Centre (IDRC), as well as other agencies, have contributed to remote sensing in the developing world. The countries that have received aid include those shown in table 14-6. Canadians have participated actively in international advisory groups, provided both short- and long-term consulting, and served worldwide as resource people in remote sensing. To date, CCRS staff alone have worked directly with over 750 people in and from more than forty countries. Canada has had direct remote sensing contacts with more than eighty countries, most for technology transfer, commercial reasons, or both. Through Canadian participation in international committees, presentation of papers, and other international activities less intensive contacts have been even more numerous.

Under the umbrella of international organizations many more have been assisted through the use of Canadian technology and know-how. In addition to aid activities there have also been joint projects between Canadian agencies and those of other countries. These usually result in the sharing of knowledge and experience to the benefit of all. Such projects have been undertaken with many of the countries noted above, as well as with the UN/FAO, Denmark, France, Japan, Norway, Russia, and the United States.

Table 14-6
Canadian Aid in Remote Sensing

Brazil	Malaysia
Burkina Faso	Mali
Cameroon	Morocco
China	Peru
Costa Rica	Slovakia
Czech Republic	Tanzania
Egypt	Thailand
Guyana	Tunisia
Indonesia	Uganda
Jordan	Venezuela
Kenya	Vietnam

The Increase of International Competition

Throughout the past decade Canadian success has been quite evident internationally at conferences and exhibitions; the Canadian model for the development and use of remote sensing has been studied; and efforts have been made to copy it by developed and developing countries alike. Because of its success Canada has often been regarded as a useful partner in international collaboration. In some cases this collaboration has resulted in an outright purchase of a Canadian company by a foreign firm.

It is equally obvious to the rest of the world that the Canadian companies most active and visible internationally have been growing successfully for much of the past twenty years. This fact, and the tremendous growth posted in the past and projected for the future, has resulted in a number of U.S. military contractors and large multinational companies in the aerospace industry entering the market in various ways. At the other end of the spectrum some of the less developed countries have entered the market with sales of software, hardware, and services.

Until recently, Canadian industry has had a number of competitive advantages. It was seen as a middle power, with little political attachment to purchases from its industry. In addition Canada was not a player in the early overselling of technology and, lastly, Canada has used the technology or services it was trying to sell overseas.

At one point in the mid-1980s, for every image analysis system Canada had imported, it had exported thirty-five. However those advantages have not held. There may be fewer competitors, but they are the survivors. DIPIX, whose name was once used in China to mean digital image processing, based its technology on a very impressive hardware solution at a time when software was slower and computers very expensive. It had as much as 25 percent of the world market. Changes in the marketplace resulted in highly competitive pricing, decreasing hardware costs, and the increased speed of software. DIPIX sold its remote sensing business to PCI in the early 1990s. The number of companies competing successfully in the international market for full-service digital image processing in remote sensing decreased from at least ten based in five countries in 1984 to three or four today from three countries, including PCI of Canada.

Compared to the past, the competition is now better equipped and uses new technologies and higher-resolution imagery, both airborne and spaceborne. The competition is also better educated, and is starting with the support of aggressive governments. Indeed some of the players most active in competing in the Canadian market – such as the Swedish Space Corporation – are owned by foreign governments. While Canada has enjoyed tremendous success over the past twenty years, and may well continue to do so, the pressure of competition is growing in what is truly a global marketplace.

The Current Situation: An Industry Studied from Every Angle

Remote sensing activities are spread from coast to coast in Canada. That geographic dispersal has made remote sensing stand alone from virtually all of Canada's other technology-driven industries. This and the industry's success have resulted in it becoming one of the most studied in the country. A number of private studies have been commissioned by those in the industry, as well as those by the CSA, Industry Canada, Foreign Affairs, and CCRS.

The status of remote sensing in Canada has been reviewed elsewhere.[55] Much of what was said still holds. However since 1991 there have been a number of significant changes within all sectors. Employment and budget allocations in governments have dropped. The number of companies from coast to coast who maintain that they are involved in remote sensing has grown significantly, as shown in table 14-3.

The most rapid growth of remote sensing–related companies has occurred in Atlantic Canada, followed by Québec. Atlantic Canada has benefited from the activities of the Atlantic Centre for Remote Sensing of the Oceans (ACRSO). Between 1991 and 1994 the number of companies in the region has grown from fourteen to thirty-three. Most of this growth is in the field of ocean-related services in remote sensing. In effect ACRSO has introduced remote sensing as a business area to a number of companies whose product and service mix readily accepts remote sensing as a complementary area. The addition of remote sensing to an existing product mix appears to have been an effective way in which to increase the activity. In Québec in 1991 there were eighteen companies said to be active in remote sensing: today there are thirty. It is believed that this growth is associated, at least in part, with the large and entrepreneurial graduate programme in remote sensing at the University of Sherbrooke.

There is growing evidence that the Canadian remote sensing industry is becoming more mature and self-sustaining.[56] The fact that a number of government departments are actively involved in promoting trade, foreign investment, and technology development in remote sensing and related areas is both an indication of and contributing factor to the industry's success. There is a growing industry association that has taken an active role in both government relations and the development of international trade and associated strategies. There are a number of independent consultants based in Canada who serve both Canada's industry and that of other countries. Also there has been a growing trend to foreign investment and globalization of the larger companies. The latter trend has seen significant business units developed outside Canada through purchase, joint ventures, or development. At the same time it appears that governments and academia have begun to change focus from developing operational applications to undertaking more fundamental research than was the case five to ten years ago. It is hoped that this research will lead to the theoretical and technological underpinning of Canada's remote sensing industry as it moves into the next century.

Introduction

This part examines the contributions of remote sensing to automated mapping and GIS through a case-study of the developments in British Columbia. An overview is given of the early remote sensing applications to forestry and resource inventories, and then of the processing of interpreted data through manual drafting, automated mapping, and GIS. A case-study shows that the need to process information acquired by remotely sensed techniques accelerated the development of automated mapping into GIS. Finally, the next stage of technological developments is discussed: the downloading of integrated remotely sensed data to mobile units through wireless transmission.

Applications of Remote Sensing to Forestry

Prior to the 1940s traditional forest inventory practices consisted of ground surveys. During the late 1940s and 1950s the operational use of aerial photographs was introduced for the purposes of subdividing the forest into relatively homogeneous strata and measuring their areas, as well as for controlling ground sampling. Forest inventory and monitoring techniques have experienced some dramatic changes during the past thirty years, driven by needs, local conditions, technology, and public pressure for information on resources other than forestry. The longstanding leadership of the European practices of using ground samples has been challenged by the rapidly evolving technology. Faced with extensive areas of unknown forests, North American foresters have turned to remote sensing, computers, and GIS to aid in the design of forest inventory and monitoring forest projects.

The Inventory Branch of the British Columbia Forest Service was one of the pioneers in the application of remote sensing data and techniques to forest inventory and environmental monitoring, especially with automated mapping and GIS. The British Columbia approach, which represents practices now used by several other Canadian provinces, can be summarized as follows:

- The first step in the implementation of a forest inventory is the preparation of base maps. A planimetric map provides the base on which parcel and administrative boundaries are superimposed. Automation of this process is cost-effective, and provides the opportunity to store the various sources of information as separate levels. This facilitates further manipulations with thematic and topographic information. In cases where planimetric base maps are not available, geometrically corrected satellite imagery can provide a practical alternative.
- Most forest management unit inventories require the acquisition of vertical aerial photographs. Initially 1:15 840 scale vertical black-and-white air photos were used, but in 1978 the scale was changed to 1:15 000 and 1:20 000. These photographs must be interpreted to provide descriptions of forest cover. For example in areas where the number of species within homogeneous strata are less than five, individual species may

---

* This part of the chapter was contributed by Frank Hegyi.

be determined to the nearest 10 percent. Otherwise groups of species or other relevant ecological units may have to form the description of the forest cover. The date of stand establishment or age, if available, and the total height (i.e., average height of the 100 largest stems per hectare) of the leading species are estimated next. In order to improve the estimation of volumes of individual stands, some measure of the density of stocking is important, such as crown closure to the nearest 10 percent or stems per hectare. In addition other relevant information may be included in the list of attributes, such as site index or site type, estimated timber volume, or stand history.

- Using ground control information and field samples, the interpretation of aerial photographs is confirmed. The photograph centres and the boundaries of the homogeneous forest types are transferred onto the base maps, either photogrammetrically or, since the late 1980s, directly into the GIS. High-quality forest maps can then be prepared manually or with the aid of the computer.
- A sampling system that was found to be most cost-effective and efficient involves both large-scale photograph and ground samples. Experience indicates that 70 mm stereoscopic photographs at 1:500 scale are highly suitable for the estimation of the volume of timber. A random distribution of photo samples is preferred, with the aim of representing adequately the major population groups. A sub-sample of the areas selected for photo samples is chosen randomly, and is visited on the ground for detailed measurements. Ground and photo samples can then be analysed according to procedures outlined under multiphase sampling techniques.
- In addition to the formal statistical analysis, volume equations are derived from the sample database, using independent variables that are compatible with the classification system. This approach allows estimation of volume on the basis of the individual stand, a capability that is becoming increasingly important in multiple and integrated resource management.
- The major advantages of using automated mapping or GIS for processing the inventory data are that the thematic forest cover and multi-resource levels can be combined with parcel and administrative boundaries, and other relevant levels of information that are available in digital or geo-referenced forms. Using either vector- or raster-based overlay procedures, areas of the resultant polygons can be determined and the results displayed graphically, including colour-enhanced thematic maps. In addition the statistical data may be manipulated in a flexible manner to provide a wide range of summaries of descriptive statistics.
- An integral part of the British Columbia forest inventory programme is the projection of growth. The approach adopted for this purpose is the use of deterministic volume equations, with time as one of the independent variables.

Due to the complex technical nature of the application of remote sensing to resource inventories, manual methods of drafting fell short of being able to meet the needs of users. Therefore it was decided in 1977 to introduce auomation through computer-assisted mapping (CAM). As commercial GIS were in their infancy at that time, the emphasis was placed on capabilities to produce high-quality maps during the process of acquiring a CAM system.

Automated Mapping in British Columbia Resource Inventories

An important justification for the acquisition of a CAM system to automate the resource inventory process in British Columbia was the need to convert 7000 forest cover maps to metric units, and to change the scales from 1:15 480 to 1:20 000. The processing of forest inventory data was considered to be a bonus rather than necessity when justifying the purchase of a CAM system. After examining over twenty possible systems, the M & S Computing (now Intergraph Corporation) Interactive Graphics Design System (IGDS) was acquired by the Inventory Branch of the Ministry of Forests, mainly due to its superior graphics capabilities. It is interesting to note that the hardware on which the original system resided consisted of one PDP 11/70 computer with 0.75 MB of memory, and another with 1.0 MB of RAM. There were two disk storage devices, one of 80 MB and one of 300 MB. The two PDP 11/70s provided the computing power for ten design and digitizing stations, and the output was processed on a CalComp 960 plotter. A line printer and card reader completed the necessary input and output devices. In 1978 this configuration cost approximately $1 million. The technology has certainly expanded since 1977 to the point at which laptops generally contain at least eight times more RAM than the original mainframe CAM system provided.

A major development in British Columbia occurred in 1978 when the new Forest Act was enacted. This legislation required that the inventory systems provide descriptive statistics that are reliable in terms of individual forest stands or homogeneous strata. Furthermore these descriptive statistics must relate not only to timber, but to all the resources that the public insist be considered in land-use allocation and multi-resource management. Clearly this new requirement called for a different tool than CAM. It needed a GIS. Consequently the original CAM system was upgraded to include capabilities for data management and retrieval.

However the initial decision to acquire a computer-assisted mapping system was proven to be correct. Staff who previously were skilled in manual drafting were retrained in the CAM technology. This resulted later in a relatively simple transition into the world of GIS. At the same time several thousands of forest cover maps were converted into digital form, which alone had proven to be cost-effective.

Development of GIS Applications

In British Columbia the operational implementation of GIS progressed gradually. While some provinces opted to wait until GIS was proven to be fully operational, British Columbia made a gradual transition from CAM to various levels of GIS implementation, even though the technology was not mature. GIS developments worldwide went through difficult stages, influenced largely by user needs. At the same time, user requirements were changing continuously, forcing vendors to provide solutions to a wide range of problems within unrealistic time constraints. In addition users were also inconsistent in documenting their requirements, prompting vendors to provide different solutions to fundamentally the same problems. During these developments the perceptions of vendors seemed to have been focused upon functionality, at times at the expense of cost-effectiveness and rate of output.

In the late 1970s commercial GIS systems barely qualified as computer-aided mapping tools. Raster-based systems produced poor-quality maps, while those using vector technology to improve cartographic capabilities encountered major problems in the rate of production. In an attempt to satisfy user requirements, vendors developed different strategies for solving operational problems. These strategies included the combination of vector and raster technologies, the development of relational database approaches, as well as enhancements to the specific solutions. The functionality expected of GIS by perhaps the largest sector of users, the resource managers, was initially computer-assisted mapping and the calculations of the areas of polygons. Even before these tasks could be perfected or at least implemented operationally, the general requirements were expanded to include the handling of polygon overlays. Vendors perceived this in time, and in some cases anticipated it, but not without miscommunication. For example vendors offering vector-based polygon overlay procedures were overwhelmed by the large number of resultant polygons in forest cover map processing, 10 000 or more being typical. On the other hand systems with relational database techniques showed limitations in terms of map quality as well as production rates, especially when large numbers of unique overlays were required.

In British Columbia it was found that the vector-based overlay processes and associated database management system of Intergraph Corporation could not keep up with operational requirements. In order to solve this major difficulty, Pamap Graphics Ltd was contracted to produce a raster-based data management system. A specific requirement was to mimic the old-fashioned "dot-counting" method for calculating area. The experiment was successful, and the entire resource inventory database was set up on a combined Intergraph-Pamap GIS.

Integration of Remote Sensing and GIS

Conventional aerial photographs have been the basis of resource inventories in British Columbia since the 1950s. Boundaries of homogeneous forest and natural resource types were marked on the photographs under stereoscopic examination, and a description of each stratum was entered on the back of the respective photograph. The photo interpretation relied heavily on field work where a sub-sample of forest stands was visited on the ground for detailed examination and measurements. Following the completion of fieldwork the descriptions of homogeneous strata were confirmed or finalized, and the information was transferred from the photographs to the base map using optical instruments such as the Sketchmaster or Transferscope.

The automation of the above procedure has been slow and is still ongoing. Initially the digitization of the resource inventory types occurred only after the transfers to the base maps were completed. The actual automation consisted of entering the descriptions of homogeneous types directly into the computer, referencing them through unique numbers and text nodes, then placing them in the design file prior to plotting. Experiments to enter the boundaries directly from aerial photographs to the GIS database met with some measure of success, although a fully operational and affordable workstation that could process this functional requirement is still to be developed.

The most significant influence of remote sensing on automated mapping and GIS developments occurred in the area of monitoring the depletion of the forest. Previously resource inventory projects in British Columbia, as well as in most Canadian provinces, were implemented on a twenty-year cycle. New legislative requirements reduced this cycle to at least five years or less. The costs of implementing updates on a two- to five-year cycle with conventional aerial photographs was found to be prohibitive. Therefore resource inventory specialists started to experiment with spaceborne remote sensing techniques for the update of changes due to disturbances such as harvesting, strong winds, and fire.

In British Columbia these experiments started with early Landsat products, and were followed by those of Thematic Mapper and SPOT. Satellite image analysis techniques indicated clearly that this was a cost-effective alternative for the detection of change and the monitoring of depletion. The next challenge was how to integrate the remote sensing technology into the world of GIS. Again users clearly influenced developments, and vendors started to provide conversion algorithms for raster-to-vector and vector-to-raster transfer of information. The first operational integration of remote sensing and GIS technology in British Columbia involved the Meridian System of MacDonald Dettwiler and Associates Ltd and the Intergraph GIS. The integration process was a joint venture betwen the Inventory Branch and CCRS, and was known as the SEIDAM project. Subsequently GIS vendors started to supply integrated GIS/image-analysis capabilities with their products, or formed a strategic alliance with image analaysis vendors to meet this important requirement.

Future Trends

The new Forest Practices Code that was released recently in British Columbia requires that information be available at the local level. Once again GIS vendors are being influenced strongly by users to modify their products. Because of this new requirement the following functional capabilities need to be incorporated into GIS:
- to download integrated imagery and GIS databases to portable laptop computers operating in mobile units in the field
- to interface GPS receivers and portable GIS to facilitate the determination of locations and to display these on GIS files interactively in mobile units during navigation
- and to update spatial and administrative information in the field, as well as to facilitate consultation between field staff and those in district and regional offices

Thus the next major requirement of users in resource inventory and environmental management is to have a mobile office with capabilities for wireless data transmission. Currently this is being developed as a joint venture between industry and the Technical and Administrative Services Branch of the British Columbia Ministry of Forests. This mobile office will be able to be navigated in the field with an electronic GIS database and GPS receiver, will determine its exact position, and, when given the task of moving to a new location, will automatically obtain data from its base in the district office through wireless transmission.

A future development in GIS will involve the presentation of spatial information in the field, combined with relevant administrative data and consultation services. The need for continuous monitoring of depletion, renewals, and environmental changes will continue to have further impact on the development of GIS-related systems. Finally, being able to interface with voice will present another challenge to the developers of GIS. The advent of multi-media technology facilitates narrative descriptions of spatial databases manipulated in a GIS. Navigation in the field will be occurring with voice communication, and the next generation of GIS will be able to evaluate specific information needs at a selected destination based on the purpose of the visit. This will all be done under the control of a knowledge-based expert system with capabilities of communicating verbally.

THE FUTURE OF CANADIAN REMOTE SENSING*

A new era is now beginning with the launch of Radarsat and continued competition. How well Canada's government, industry, and academic community has reacted to the challenges

---

* The concluding part of this chapter was contributed by R.A. Ryerson.

of the future during the previous period of commercial development will determine whether or not Canada will continue to play a key role in the future.

The Challenges and Opportunities for Canadian Government, Industry, and Academia

Remote sensing will continue to be driven by technical developments and by special needs in certain topical areas. It will remain as a major source of information for both government and the private sector. It can therefore be expected that decisions of public policy will affect the market for remote sensing products and services. The discussions concerning the commercialization of Landsat and the approval of high spatial resolution imagery from Worldview and Lockheed are cases in point.

In all probability there will be further rationalization in the marketplace. In the near term this process will be confused by the entry of large companies whose business was formerly in military remote sensing. Many of these large companies will probably team with those now in the field of natural resource management and remote sensing. A key factor in the competitiveness of these new entrants will be cost. The costs that are acceptable in identifying and dealing with a military threat are believed to be substantially higher than the costs acceptable to a forestry company mapping its trees. How well the new entrants deal with the cost differentials between their former and future markets will dictate how long they survive in civilian remote sensing, and how well those now in the market can compete.

Canada's focus in remote sensing has been on making the data useful. This has resulted in a concentration on practical issues such as data reception and data storage, real-time processing, sensor development, image analysis, GIS, radars, and data integration; and applications such as thematic and topographic mapping, the sensing of water depths, updating maps, and oil-spill monitoring. These areas will likely provide the basis, if not the substance, of most of the opportunities of the future.

The major technical factors affecting the future of remote sensing will include improved digital information storage, retrieval, and processing, and better integration of different data sets including information from a growing range of satellites. This will be accomplished through wider use of more sophisticated but easier-to-use GIS, a greater range of data formats, and faster data delivery through global networks. Expert systems and artificial intelligence will be applied routinely in a new generation of image analysis systems and GIS. There will be improved understanding of the interaction between radar and ground targets, and wider use and understanding of high spectral and spatial resolution airborne and spaceborne electro-optical sensors. The integration of GPS and other aids will lead to more precise location of sensing activities over both land and water.

If history repeats itself factors that are not envisioned here will probably be just as important as those identified. It can be assumed that the more developed and less developed countries will converge in their use of remote sensing as the costs diminish and the process of transferring technology is accelerated. In some ways this is an expected by-product of the globalization of economic activity. There will also be convergence between remote sensing and mapping, and *in situ* environmental monitoring and remote sensing.

Expanded and intensified use of remote sensing is anticipated in local land-based environmental management and monitoring, using high resolution electro-optical sensors for routine monitoring and for clean-up monitoring. This will also be the case with ocean monitoring and management (particularly in tropical areas that rely for their protein on the sustainability of fishing on coral reefs), disaster assessment and mitigation (because of typhoons, volcanoes, floods, and forest fires), and support to peace-keeping activities. This list will vary considerably by country and region. It can be expected to change as technologies are developed that permit remote assessment for applications now associated with either *in situ* testing or detailed field inspection.

Much of this chapter has outlined the many reasons for Canada's industrial success in remote sensing, particularly in a number of niche markets. But what does the future hold for the industry? To remain competitive in its niche markets and in the broader marketplace, Canada must continue to do both basic and applied research that is market oriented and the results of which can be commercialized. A delicate balance will have to be maintained within government research between the more esoteric work that will lead to tomorrow's technology and the more practical product or service development work. There must also be a market-driven industry with a global perspective. As a trading nation Canada must develop its talents in marketing. Will Canada maintain its current important position in the major niches it has developed for itself? It will depend on how governments, industry, and the academic sector work together, and how well its industry can respond to the changing conditions in the marketplace.

CONCLUSION

Canada's role in remote sensing has been far greater than Canada's population and economic base would lead one to expect. There are many reasons for this. Some of these include the infrastructure developed, the competitive nature of the domestic marketplace, and the approach to technology transfer and international development. Most of those involved in remote sensing have also added a personal dimension: they have tried to leave behind friends and colleagues, rather than just clients.

NOTES

1 Seely. H.E. 1949. *Air Photography and its Application to Forestry.* Forest Air Survey publication no. 6. Ottawa: Dominion Forest Service.

2 Nash, A.J. 1949. *Some Tests on the Determination of Tree Heights from Aerial Photographs.* Forest Air Survey publication no. 5. Ottawa: Dominion Forest Service.

3 Packman, D.J., and L.E. Philpotts. 1955. *Elementary Agricultural Air Photo Interpretation.* Ottawa: Economics Division, Department of Agriculture.
Philpotts, L.E. 1963. *Aerial Photo Interpretation of Land Use Change in Fourteen Lots in Prince Edward Island. 1936 to 1958.* Ottawa: Economics Division, Department of Agriculture.

4 Erb, D.K. 1967. The Identification of Fruit Trees by Aerial Photograph Analysis and "Interpretation" for Census Purposes. In *Proceedings, Second Seminar on Air Photo Interpretation in the Development of Canada.* Ottawa: EMR, 87–114.

5 Wood, Harold A. 1967. Accumulated Data Used in the Airphoto-Interpretation of Agricultural Land Use. In *Proceedings, Second Seminar on Air Photo Interpretation in the Development of Canada.* Ottawa: EMR, 100–14.
Ryerson, R.A., and H.A. Wood. 1971. The Air Photo Analysis of Beef and Dairy Farming in Ontario. *Photogrammetric Engineering,* 37, 2, 157–69.

Ryerson, R.A., and J.L. Ryerson. 1976. "Farm Income from Aerial Photography." Presented to the Fifth Annual Meeting, Agricultural Working Group, Canadian Advisory Committee on Remote Sensing.

6 For example Mollard, J.D. 1973. *Landforms and Surface Materials of Canada. A Stereoscopic Airphoto Atlas and Glossary*, 3d ed. Regina: J.D. Mollard.
Mollard, J.D., and J. Robert Janes. 1984. *Airphoto Interpretation and the Canadian Landscape.* Ottawa: Energy, Mines and Resources Canada.

7 Parry, J.T. 1968. Terrain Evaluation in Mobility Studies for Military Vehicles. In G.A. Stewart, ed. *Land Evaluation*. Sydney: Macmillan of Australia.

8 Radforth, N.W. 1955. *Organic Terrain Organisation from the Air*. Handbook no. 1, DR. no. 95; and 1958. Handbook no. 2, DR. 124. Ottawa: Defence Research Board.

9 Brown, R.J.E. 1966. The Influence of Vegetation on Permafrost. In *Proceedings, Permafrost International Conference*. NRC Publication 1287.
Brown, R.J.E. 1974. *Some Aspects of Airphoto Interpretation of Permafrost in Canada*. Technical paper no. 409. Ottawa: National Research Council, Division of Building Research.

10 For example Heyland, J.D. 1972. Vertical Aerial Photography as an Aid in Wildlife Population Studies. In *Proceedings of The First Canadian Symposium on Remote Sensing*, vol. 1, 121–36.

11 Parry, J.T. 1973. The Development of Air-Photo Interpretation in Canada. *The Canadian Surveyor*, 27, 4, 320–51.

12 Zsilinszky, V.G. 1963. *Photographic Interpretation of Tree Species in Ontario*. Toronto: Ontario Department of Lands and Forests.

13 Sayn-Wittgenstein, L. 1960. *Recognition of Tree Species on Air Photographs by Crown Characteristics*. Research Branch technical note 95. Ottawa: Department of Forestry.
Sayn-Wittgenstein, L. 1961. *Phenological Aids to Species Identification on Air Photographs*. Research Branch technical note 104. Ottawa: Department of Forestry.

14 Sayn-Wittgenstein, L. 1978. *Recognition of Tree Species on Aerial Photographs*. Information report FMR-X-118. Ottawa: Canadian Forestry service, Department of the Environment.

15 Coombs, Donald B., and J. Thie. 1979. The Canada Land Inventory System. In *Planning the Uses and Management of Land*. Agronomy series no. 21. Madison, WI: Soil Science Society of America, 909–33.

16 McClellan, John, 1967. Air-Photo Interpretation in the Present Land-Use Sector of the Canada Land Inventory. In *Proceedings, Second Seminar on Air Photo Interpretation in the Development of Canada*. Ottawa: EMR, 27–31.

17 Gimbarzevsky, P. 1967. Land Forms and the Productive Capacity of Forest Land. In *Proceedings, Second Seminar on Air Photo Interpretation in the Development of Canada*. Ottawa: EMR, 32–56.

18 Murtha, P.A. 1972. *A Guide to Air Photo Interpretation of Forest Damage in Canada*. Publication 1292. Ottawa: Canadian Forest Service.

19 Aldrich, R.C, W.F. Bailey, and R.C. Heller. 1959. Large-Scale 70 mm Colour Photography Techniques and Equipment and Their Application to a Forest Sampling Problem. *Photogrammetric Engineering*, 25, 5, 747–54.

20 Westby, R.L., A.H. Aldred, and L. Sayn-Wittgenstein. 1968. The Potential of Large-Scale Air Photographs and Radar Altimetry in Land Evaluation. In Stewart, *Land Evaluation*, 376–83.
Aldred, A.H., and L. Sayn-Wittgenstein. 1968. *Development and Field Tests of the Forestry Radar Altimeter*. Information Report FMR-X-14. Ottawa: Department of Fisheries and Forestry.

21 Lyons, E.H. 1966. Fixed Air-Base 70 mm Photography, a New Tool for Forest Sampling. *Forestry Chronicle*, 42, 420.

22 Wightman, J.M. 1972. High Altitude Photography Records and Monitors Logging Operations. In *Proceedings of The First Canadian Symposium on Remote Sensing*, vol. 1. Ottawa: EMR, 137–43.

23 Much of the material in this and the following two parts of this chapter draws on Canadian Advisory Committee on Remote Sensing. 1973–86. *Report*. Ottawa: Canada Centre for Remote Sensing. Various pagination.

Ryerson, R.A. 1991. Remote Sensing in Canada. *Geocarto International*, 6, 3, 79–83.

Ryerson, R.A. 1993. Canada's International Role in Making Remote Sensing Operational. In *Proceedings, International Symposium on Operationalisation of Remote Sensing*, vol. 1. Enschede, Netherlands: International Training Centre, 19–27.

24 Canadian Advisory Committee on Remote Sensing. 1973. *Report*. Ottawa: Canada Centre for Remote Sensing, 14–15.

25 Canadian Advisory Committee on Remote Sensing. 1974. *Report*. Ottawa: Canada Centre for Remote Sensing, 1.

26 Murtha, P.A. 1973. ERTS records SO$_2$ Damage to Forests, Wawa, Ontario. *Forestry Chronicle*, 49, 6, 251–52.

27 Gierman, D., R.A. Ryerson, G. Moran, and W.D. Switzer. 1975. Remote Sensing and The Canada Geographic Information System for Impact Studies. In *Proceedings of the Third Canadian Symposium on Remote Sensing*. Ottawa: EMR, 235–41.

28 Ryerson, R.A. 1981. *Results of a Benefit Cost Analysis of the CCRS Airborne Program.* CCRS research report 81–1. Ottawa: Canada Centre for Remote Sensing; Energy, Mines and Resources Canada.

29 CCRS. 1977. *Information Bulletin. Airborne Operation.* Ottawa: Canada Centre for Remote Sensing; Energy, Mines and Resources Canada.

30 Ryerson, *Benefit Cost Analysis.*

31 Brown, R.J., F.J. Ahern, K.P.B. Thomson, K. Staenz, J. Cihlar, C.M. Pearce, and S.G Klumph. 1983. *Quantitative and Qualitative Applications of Remotely Sensed Data to Rangeland Management.* CCRS research report 83–1. Ottawa: CCRS; Energy, Mines and Resources Canada.

32 Ryerson, R.A., R.N. Dobbins, and C. Thibault. 1985. Timely Crop Area Estimates from Landsat. *Photogrammetric Engineering and Remote Sensing*, 51, 11, 1735–43.

33 Brown. R.J., M. Bernier, G. Fedosejevs, and L. Skretkowicz. 1982. NOAA-AVHRR Crop Condition Monitoring. *Can. J. of Remote Sensing*, 8, 2, 110–17.

34 Gauthier, J. 1987. Topographic Mapping from Satellite Data: A Canadian Point of View. *Geocarto International*, 2, 3, 61–6.

35 Thompson, M.D., ed. 1982. *Landsat for Monitoring the Changing Geography of Canada*. Special publication for COSPAR. Ottawa: CCRS; Energy, Mines, and Resources Canada.

36 Gierman et al., Remote Sensing.

37 Thompson, *Landsat.*

38 See Canadian Advisory Committe on Remote Sensing. 1974. *Report.* 7.

39 Economy, R., D.G. Goodenough, R.A. Ryerson, and R. Towles. 1974. Classification Accuracy of the Image 100. In *Proceedings of the Second Canadian Symposium on Remote Sensing*. Ottawa: EMR, 277–87.

40 Brown, R.J. et al., *Quantitative and Qualitative Applications.*

41 Ryerson, R.A. et al, Timely Crop Area Estimates.

42 Gauthier, Topographic Mapping.

43 Brown. R.J. et al., NOAA-AVHRR.

Brown, R.J., W.G. Best, and G.K. Walker. 1990. Satellites Monitor Global Vegetation Conditions. *GEOS*, 19, 2, 12–16.

44 Ramsay, B., T. Hirose, M. Manore, J. Falkingham, R. Gale, D. Barber, M. Shokr, B. Danielowicz, B. Gorman, and C. Livingstone. 1993. Potential of Radarsat for Sea Ice Applications. *Can. J. of Remote Sensing*, 19, 4, 363–71.

45 Banic, J., R. O'Neil, and S. Sizgoric. 1987. Airborne Scanning Lidar Bathymeter Measures Water Depth. *Laser Focus* (adapted from SPIE Proceedings, vol. 663). Washington: SPIE, 2.

46 Luscombe, A.P., I. Ferguson, N. Sheppard, D.G. Zimcik, and P. Naraine. 1993. The Radarsat Synthetic Aperture Radar Development. *Can. J. of Remote Sensing*, 19, 4, 298–310.

47 Friedel, J.P., and T.A. Fisher. 1987. MOSAICS – A System to Produce State-of-the-Art Satellite Imagery for Resource Managers. *Geocarto International*, 2, 3, 5–12.

48 Ahern, F.J., D.G. Goodenough, S.C. Jain, V.R. Rao, and G. Rochon. 1977. Use of Clear Lakes as Standard Reflectors for Atmospheric Measurements. In *Proceedings, Eleventh International Symposium on Remote Sensing of the Environment*. Ann Arbor, MI: Environmental Research Institute, 731–55.

49 1987. *Remote Sensing Products and Services for World Markets*. Ottawa: External Affairs Canada.

50 Pilon, P., and R. Wiart. 1990. Operational Forest Inventory Applications Using Landsat TM Data: The British Columbia Experience. *Geocarto International*, 5, 1, 25–30.

51 Banic, J. et al., Airborne Scanning.

52 1993. See *Can. J .of Remote Sensing*, 19, 4.

53 Canadian Advisory Committee on Remote Sensing. *Report*. 1974.

54 Ahern, F.J., F.H.A. Campbell, C. Elizondo, H.J.H. Kux, E. Novo, W. Paradella, R.K. Raney, R. Salcedo, Y. Shimabukuro, and V. Singhroy. 1993. C-Band SAR for Resource Management in Tropical Environments: Lessons from SAREX-92 Investigations in Brazil, Costa Rica, Venezuela, and Guyana. In *Proceedings of the SAREX-92 Final Results Symposium*. Paris, France, December 6–8. Paris: European Space Agency, 235–46.

55 Ryerson, Remote Sensing in Canada.
   Ryerson, Canada's International Role.

56 Thompson, M.D., and D.R. Inkster. 1990. The Commercialization of Remote Sensing in Canada 1972–1990. In *Proceedings, Twenty-third International Symposium on Remote Sensing of Environment*, ERIM, Bangkok, Thailand.

CHAPTER FIFTEEN

GIS and LIS in Canada

Roger F. Tomlinson and Michael A.G. Toomey

INTRODUCTION

Perhaps the most significant technical development in the world since 1947 is the advent and widespread use of the digital computer. It now influences almost every aspect of human endeavour and, as can be imagined, has transformed the making and using of maps. In the last thirty years several sets of procedures using computer systems have been devised to produce or handle maps. This chapter will deal with two of these, Geographic Information Systems (GIS) and Land Information Systems (LIS).

There are other systems, such as automated cartography systems, computer-aided drafting systems, and image-processing systems that have some of the same characteristics. Some of these terms are defined briefly in the glossary, but it will be useful here to expand the definitions somewhat so that the reader can understand the important differences between systems that otherwise might appear to be quite similar. In particular the different purposes of using each type of system will be made clear.

To grasp the scope and wide application of the systems to be described in this chapter, it is necessary to discuss some basic terminology. Geographical data are the facts that describe the earth, resulting from observations of the phenomena on the earth. The spatial distribution of such phenomena are usually displayed on maps, charts, or images. These can describe any aspect of the earth's topography, surface geology, soils, climate, water, vegetation, land values, land ownership, tribal lands, lease boundaries, administrative boundaries, agriculture, land use, environment, transportation and communication networks, census districts, population distribution, income distribution, incidence of disease, and so on. Alternatively, geographical data may be in the form of lists of variables that are grouped by location and related to places shown on maps, that is they are spatially referenced statistics. Note this important reference to the multitude of statistical data describing the earth, because the power of GIS includes the ability to handle these data as well as those that originate from maps.

A GIS is a system for capturing, storing, integrating, analysing, and displaying data about the earth that are spatially referenced. It is normally taken to include a spatially referenced

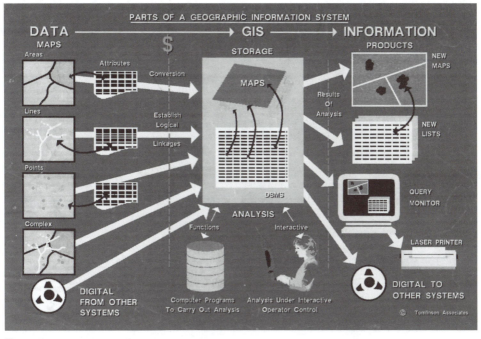

Figure 15-1
The principal components of GIS and LIS systems and the year of their development.
Source: Tomlinson Associates Ltd

database and appropriate applications software. The primary purpose of such systems is to be able to read geographical data from one or many digital maps or statistical sources, and selectively measure, combine, compare, and analyse those data to produce information for use in decision-making purposes. In essence they are analysis engines designed to make use of geographical data. Figure 15-1 shows the principal components of a GIS.

Decisions using geographical data are made in many agencies, and hence GIS have wide application. They are found in government agencies at local, municipal, regional, provincial, federal, international, and global levels. They are used by workers in disciplines ranging from archaeology to zoology, they are found in business and commerce from the retail level to multinational corporations, and they are an integral part of modern military operations.

LIS are a very important and special type of GIS. One of their main purposes is to handle data concerning the subdivision of all land into parcels of ownership, rights, tenure, and title, and to underpin the transfer of those rights. They are designed to facilitate cadastral survey, and to establish registers of land parcels and the attributes of those parcels. There is a requirement for high precision in these systems because they must meet the juridical and fiscal decision-making needs placed on them by society. They must be able to handle extremely complex historical problems of land ownership. They must be able to deal with and create databases from the measurements resulting from land surveys. They are fundamentally important systems in all matters concerning the ownership of land.

LIS are able to relate spatially defined ownership parcels and taxation parcels; these in turn relate to cadastral plans filed with a land register. The land registers dealing with privately owned land are usually described as title or deeds registers. Chapter 7 on cadastral surveys provides further information. The building of an LIS attempts to tie various forms of information related to the ownership parcel to the digital property mapping base, and uses modern database technology to store, select, present, and disseminate the data. Other complex operations can be performed on the data, but the above functions have to be performed as a minimum. The production of maps from the database is just one form of presentation that is available; a listing of titles in a selected area could be another.

Automated cartography is the preparation and presentation of maps using machines controlled by computers. The purpose of automating the cartographic process is to produce new maps more swiftly, economically, and accurately than by previously available hand and photo-mechanical procedures. The design and implementation of these systems have been pursued vigorously by agencies that are primarily responsible for making maps and charts. The reader should note the difference in purpose between these systems and GIS and LIS mentioned above. While there are similarities in the computers and the peripheral hardware, for example printers and plotters, used in all of these systems, their objectives and functions are different. Automated cartography focuses on the process of compiling maps. The emphasis is on map production and not necessarily on the problems of map utilization. In general, early automated cartographic systems were not established to facilitate geographical analysis, and in some cases they severely inhibited such analysis.

Digital maps, a seemingly simple term, refers to maps that have been recorded in digital (numerical) form, and hence can be stored in digital computers. They may result from the map having been produced by digital photogrammetry and automated cartography, or may result from an existing hard-copy map having been digitized. In its simplest form the digital map is a numerical representation of the graphic features to be seen on the source map. At its most sophisticated a digital version of a map can include highly structured sets of codes in the digital form that identify specific objects or sets of objects on the map, and the topological relationships between them such as inside, outside, adjacency, connectivity, and so on. There can be further differences resulting from the ways in which the digital maps were created, for example by the process of line tracing or by a scanning process, which may result in widely differing forms of digital map. In short there could be several digital versions of the same map sheet, each form being suitable for a different use. Simply because a map is in digital form does not mean that it is suitable for use on all computers for all purposes. The task of converting from one digital map form to another can vary from the easy to the cumbersome to the impossible, all workable cases taking time and resources to accomplish and sometimes losing information in the process.

Image processing and analysis is the processing and interpretation of pictures held in digital form. The most widely used source of such pictures is satellite images that originate in digital form, although conventional air photographs can be scanned and turned into digits for subsequent image processing. The purpose of image-processing systems is to interpret and recognize features and conditions in the pictures that are of interest to the observer. The pictures may be stretched or squeezed, geometrically reoriented, made to simulate three or four dimensions, and coloured in different ways to allow for better interpretation of features upon them. Such pictures can be used as an image backdrop to mapped information in GIS and LIS, but their use as map data sources relies on the identification of specific features that can then be added to maps.

Computer-aided drafting is a set of systems used to automate the process of drawing. Their purpose is to allow a draftsperson to produce more economically and efficiently any variety of drawing, particularly where repetitive elements are involved. These systems have a wide variety of uses such as the creation of engineering drawings, architectural designs, machine designs, and printed circuit designs. They result in a digital version of the drawing that can be readily edited, amended, updated, and distributed. They have exciting capabilities of simulating three-dimensional structures from planar sources. Computer-aided drafting systems are typically part of a Computer-Aided Drafting (or Design)/Computer-Aided Manufacturing process (CAD/CAM) where a computer is used to help design and produce a product.

The above families of systems frequently use the same type of computers and peripheral devices, but have widely different purposes, operations, and functionality. The situation becomes even more confusing as time goes on because the manufacturer of one type of system typically tends to expand its capabilities into those of another family. A computer-aided drafting system may be extended to include automated cartography for the drawing of maps, and subsequently claim to be an LIS or even a GIS. Conversely GIS and LIS may be enhanced to include automated cartographic functions so that their output can match the skill and artistry of a traditional map product. Similarly GIS and LIS are being designed to accept digital versions of images that can be displayed simultaneously with their map contents. Undoubtedly this integration of system functions will continue in future, but as of 1994 there was not one system that performed all functions well, and the optimal use of any one system was still related to its original design objectives. Nevertheless the most observable trend is the move in many agencies from the simpler forms of digital maps and automated cartography to GIS that can analyse the digital data and produce useful information.

This chapter will concern itself mainly with GIS and LIS. It will describe the characteristics of GIS in the context of the political and economic needs for their development and the technical opportunities that allowed that development. The history of this Canadian innovation will be described, as will the spread of the technology and the variety of systems and applications that ensued. It will examine the growth of Canadian commercial system developments, and the growth in demand and production of digital geographic data in Canada. Other parts of this book are devoted to modern forms of automated cartography and computer-aided drafting, particularly chapters 3 and 4, which cover national and provincial topographic mapping. Image-processing systems are covered in chapter 14, "Remote Sensing in Canada."

THE NEED FOR GIS

Most technological advances come about because there are limitations in the existing methodology, coupled with an economic incentive to move forward, a technical opportunity that allows the change, and a concept of how to overcome the limitations. These components of the GIS innovation are examined below.

Limitations of Existing Methodology

Although hard-copy maps can be an efficient way to store and display data concerning the earth's surface, there are two basic limitations to their use. The first is the limitation on the amount of descriptive data that can be stored and displayed on one map sheet. The current problem is not so much one of what to put on the map, but what has to be left off, and it can be argued that this influences the type of observations that are made. Any single map only contains a very limited subset of the features on the surface of the earth. If more features or more detailed data need to be portrayed, more map sheets are required for the same area. Alternatively the data may be classified, simplified, and symbolized, but this may cause a loss of detail in the transition to a more generalized form. Either way the size of recording surface available, coupled with the demand for legibility, is a constraint to the data content of hard-copy maps.

The second limitation is that data in hard-copy map format have to be retrieved visually and manually. While the human eye and brain can scan and interpret map data more rapidly than the best of current software can process the equivalent digital data, the human process of reading a large volume of map data is overwhelming. Human map measurement is laborious, and quantitative comparisons are slow and expensive. This is intuitively understood by many practitioners today, but rarely do they know just how slow and expensive it is because they are wise enough not to attempt using those same techniques. Thirty years ago there was little alternative. In summary, storing a large amount of data on maps results in many maps. Many maps present a formidable task of reading and measurement if the information is to be extracted from them visually and manually.

Economic Incentive to Move Forward

The geographical data for which a government has a need are related to the type and level of economic development of the country, and to its political and social activities. Canada in the late 1950s and early 1960s was a country feeling, perhaps more acutely than before, that its natural resources were not limitless. Rural depopulation was accelerating. There was an increasing competition among the potential uses of land within the commercially accessible zones. Various symptoms of this situation were apparent. As noted in chapter 11, a special committee of the Senate was established in 1958 to examine land use in Canada. A "Resources for Tomorrow" conference, involving most of the country's senior resource scientists, was held in 1961. Government perceived that it had an increasing role to play in decisions about land management, planning the utilization of natural resources, and monitoring change. Geographical data in sufficient detail to be useful for the types of land-management decisions of concern to national (federal) and regional (provincial) governments are at map scales between 1:250 000 and 1:20 000. In a country of Canada's size many such map sheets are required. Canada was a relatively wealthy country at the time. It could afford to gather the data and make the maps, but the necessary manual techniques of map analysis required thereafter were extremely labour-intensive and time-consuming. Canada needed to understand these geographical data to guide programmes of land adjustment and regional economic development, but quite simply did not have the trained people needed to make full use of such data using manual methods of map analysis. Canada had an economic incentive to develop GIS.

Technical Opportunity

The critical factor enabling technical opportunity at that time was the transistor. It replaced the vacuum tube in computers and allowed computers to be faster, more reliable, cheaper, and, most importantly, to have larger memories. Computers could become information storage devices as well as calculating machines. Thus for the first time computers could economically store and handle comparatively large volumes of digital data. The technical challenge was to put maps into these computers, and to convert shapes and images into numbers so that they could be used by the digital computers then available.

The recording of shapes and lines in numerical form was not new. Coordinate descriptions of lines had existed for centuries. Francis Galton, the secretary of the Royal Geographical Society in the late 1800s, had devised methods for compact digital encoding of line direction (later called Freeman codes) to record line shapes, and had anticipated their use for encoding maps. By the late 1950s rudimentary digitizing instruments were used regularly to create numerical records of such curves as missile trajectories, ships lines, bubble chamber traces, and highway alignments. The late 1950s and early 1960s also saw photogrammetric instruments starting to be equipped with digital encoders registering x, y, and z coordinates and heights on paper tapes or punched cards.

New Concepts Required

The missing concepts were those that subsequently underpinned the development of GIS. The fundamental idea was that of using computers to ask questions of maps, to be able to read them, to measure, combine, compare, and analyse the data that they contained or could be related to them, and to produce useful information from them. This implied that the maps had to be in digital form, and that digital rather than paper maps were required as the product of map making. This in turn led to the idea that many maps in digital form could be linked together across Canada and be available for analysis and, further, that the digital maps could be linked intelligently to digital databases of statistics. In this set of ideas the limitations of paper maps are addressed, both with respect to their ability to store detailed data and with respect to using the data that they contain. These were Roger Tomlinson's ideas; they arose from Canadian needs and led to the development of the first GIS.

CANADIAN INNOVATION – EARLY ACHIEVEMENT IN THE 1960S

In 1960 Spartan Air Services (Spartan) of Ottawa was a large, high-technology surveying and mapping company using airplanes, helicopters, and advanced photogrammetric machines, active in topographic mapping, geophysical surveys, and land-resources surveys worldwide. Some of the proposed projects required manual analysis of mapped data, including the maps that Spartan had produced themselves. Careful estimates of the costs involved in manual analysis were found to be excessive, almost as much as those for the initial survey, and were firmly rejected by the management and clients. The management of the company, particularly George Brown, chief in the land resources division, gave Tomlinson time and encouragement to try digital methods. Two small test maps (5 × 5 inches, each containing five polygons) were created in numerical coordinate form, and it was determined that these could be overlaid graphically and that areas could be measured from the digital record. Initial contacts were made with the main computer companies that had offices in Ottawa at the time (Computing Devices of Canada, IBM, Sperry, and Univac) with a view to a joint venture to develop the methodology further. These were unsuccessful.

Later John Sharp, a consultant to IBM in Washington, D.C. introduced Spartan to the digital photogrammetric research being done at IBM Poughkeepsie in the United States. Subsequent contacts were made with the staff in the IBM office in Ottawa, and that was the beginning of a relationship that was to grow significantly over the years. Tomlinson could see the need and had the geographical training to formulate the new concepts. IBM brought early experience of computers and programming to the task.

The economic support for GIS development was sparked by a chance meeting between Tomlinson and Lee Pratt in 1962. In response to the pressure on natural resources and low incomes of marginal farmers, Canada had passed the Agricultural Rehabilitation and Development Act into law in June 1961. The initial administration of the act was under the auspices of the federal Department of Agriculture. It created a need for an inventory of land use and land capability across Canada, and thus the Canada Land Inventory (CLI) was established in 1962. With the cooperation of provincial governments, the CLI was planning to create about 1500 maps of the commercially productive parts of Canada at scales of 1:50 000 to 1:250 000, showing the capability of land for agriculture, forestry, wildlife, and recreation, as well as maps showing present land use and the boundaries of census subdivisions. This huge and successful effort to map the resources with consistent classifications across a continent is described in chapter 11. Pratt was the new head of this CLI. He was also faced with the problem of analysing the maps when they had been created, and the idea of using computers to do this was very attractive. At Pratt's urging Tomlinson wrote a paper entitled "Computer Mapping; an Introduction to the Use of Electronic Computers in the Storage, Compilation and Assessment of Natural and Economic Data for the Evaluation of Marginal Land," which proposed the ideas to the National Land Capability Inventory Seminar in Ottawa in November 1962. It was well received. Spartan was given a contract from the Department of Agriculture in 1963 to carry out a technical feasibility study for a "computer mapping system" for the CLI. Tomlinson wrote the report[1] that was delivered to government in early August 1963.

It is interesting to note the functional requirements for a GIS that were clearly established in that seminal report. The purpose of the system was to carry out analysis of geographical data over any part of a continent-wide area. The results of those analyses were to be provided in statistical (tabular) or graphic (map) form, or both. Many maps of different kinds needed to be put into the system. A seamless, nationwide data structure was specified. The data file organization was regarded as critical. The structure recommended separating the descriptor data and the image (boundary) data, and thus was not to be a system for automated cartography. The task of converting many maps to a digital form was addressed. The optimum input process was recognized as being different for each fundamental data form, that is automated scanning for polygon boundaries, digitizing for selected points as identifiers inside polygons, and keypunching (typing) for input of descriptor and statistical data. These data types were to be input separately and linked logically later. The coordinate system (map projection) requirements were examined, and the concepts of error in subsequent area calculation considered. Image data compaction requirements were identified to reduce the data volumes that needed to be stored on magnetic tape. The need to combine socio-economic data with mapped data was prescribed. Data analysis (assessment) capabilities were to include area measurement and multiple topological overlays. Many different assessments over time on all or any part of the database were prescribed. It is clear that the concept of a comprehensive GIS had arrived.

The Department of Agriculture (Pratt and Al Davidson) accepted the proposal. An economic feasibility study, and contracts with IBM and Spartan for development work, then followed. Tomlinson was asked to join the Agricultural Rehabilitation and Development Administration (ARDA) team and direct the development of the system. Over forty people worked on the development teams in the rest of the decade.[2] There was a considerable migration of ideas and people between government and industry. A very key role was played by Guy Morton, who designed a brilliant tessellation schema now known as the Morton Matrix, which was fundamental to the data structure. Don Lever was central to most of the logic and converting the scanner data to topologically coded map format. It was the first use of the arc-node concept of line encoding incorporated in a GIS. Bruce Sparks and Peter Bédard made major contributions to the automatic map sheet edge-matching capability, which topologically maps polygons and contents seamlessly over a continent. Art Benjamin played a major part in designing the automatic topological map error recognition capability, and in designing the links between image data and descriptor data. Bob Kemeny developed the essential map data compaction methods using the eight-directional coding originated by Galton and later called Freeman codes. Frank Jankaluk devised the reference coordinate system and made the calculations of error in system calculation algorithms. Bob Whittaker designed the system for error correction and updating. Also incorporated in the system were map projection change, rubber sheet stretch, scale change, line smoothing and generalization, automatic gap closing, area measurement, dissolve and merge, circle generation, and new polygon generation, all operating in the topological domain. A computer command language that recognized geographical analysis terms that could be understood by a wide range of potential users was a very important part of the system. Peter Kingston was responsible for the overall design of the data-retrieval system and the efficient polygon-on-polygon overlay process. The command language was designed by Kingston, Ken Ward, Bruce Ferrier, Mike Doyle, John Sacker, Jankaluk, Harry Knight, and Peter Hatfield.

The Canada Geographic Information System (CGIS) was responsible for several developments in cartographic instrumentation. The first automated cartographic size scanner was engineered for the project by D.R. Thompson at IBM Poughkeepsie. It was delivered in 1967 at a cost of approximately $180,000, and worked well for fifteen years until replaced by a newer model. The original is now in the National Museum of Science and Technology in Ottawa. The digitizing tables were the first high-precision 48 × 48 inches free cursor digitizing tables ever produced. They were designed and manufactured especially for the project by Ray Boyle, then working for Dobbie McInnes (Electronics) Ltd in Scotland.

The term "computer mapping" became clearly inappropriate for the system by the end of 1963. It was then being loosely referred to as the ARDA Data Coordination System. After some discussion, in which the term "spatial data system" was rejected as being far too general, and the term "land information system" was rejected as being far too restrictive considering the data types that were to be involved, the term "geographic information system" came into use. The system was referred to as a "geo-information system" or "Geo-IS" by the working teams, and more officially as the "Canadian Geographical Information System." Later, in 1966, a wise politician in the cabinet shortened it to "Canada Geographic Information System" to reflect the then popular use of Canada as a synonym for the federal government. On reflection the name "geographic information system" defines the system's capabilities perfectly. It has been widely adopted for other systems of the same kind throughout the world since that time.

The development of the CGIS continued during the 1960s. The National Film Board of Canada made a movie of the progress in 1967, entitled "Data for Decision." Papers[3] describing the GIS were published in 1968. All the capabilities referred to above were demonstrated in 1969, and the system became fully operational in 1971. Interactive graphics were added in 1974, and a new scanner and related scanner software were adopted in 1983. Links to commercial systems (SPANS) were developed in 1986. Input of additional data to the system ceased in 1989, but in 1994 it had over 10 000 sheets of more than 100 different types of geographical data in digital storage, representing the largest national archive of digital geographical data in Canada.

Developments outside Canada led to other innovations in Canada in the second half of the 1960s. Automated cartography took a significant step forward when Ray Boyle came to Canada in 1966, having had previous experience with the Oxford system of automated cartography in the United Kingdom. Working at the University of Saskatchewan in conjunction with the Canadian Hydrographic Service (CHS), he developed a program for hydrographic charting called CART-8.[4] In 1972 this research work was moved into the CHS in Ottawa under the direction of Tim Evangelatos to become a fully functional automatic cartographic system for producing hydrographic charts. The system migrated to the PDP-11 computer and became known as GOMADS in 1974. The early software was sold to Universal Systems in 1979, where it was developed into CARIS (Computer-Aided Resource Information System), which was sold back to the CHS in 1985 to form the basis for modern hydrographic charting and digital hydrographic chart development.

The grid cell–based map display package SYMAP was developed in the United States under the direction of Howard Fisher at the Harvard Laboratory for Computer Graphics and Spatial Analysis in the mid-1960s. Both SYMAP and the subsequent DIME package for street centreline coding, which grew out of the 1966 U.S. Bureau of Census small area data research study, spurred related developments in Canada in the second half of the decade. In 1967 the Dominion Bureau of Statistics started research leading to development of its own street centreline software, the Geographically Referenced Data Storage and Retrieval (GRDSR) system, to allow census data to be related to block face centroids on digital representations of streets in the urban areas of Canada.[5] Ivan Fellegi, later to become the chief statistician of Canada, was instrumental in getting this project started, with John Weldon acting as project manager. The first Area Master Files (AMF) for cities in Canada that resulted from this software were produced and used in the 1971 census. A by-product of GRDSR was an innovative way to store all individual census responses as string files in the database (called RAPID), and to have a generalized tabulation system (called STATPAK) retrieve such string files for ad hoc tabulation requests. Both RAPID and STATPAK were developed in Statistics Canada by Mel Turner and Martin Podehl and their development teams. This ability to manipulate and analyse geographical data with respect to precise location clearly establishes this as an early GIS.

The same interest in relating street addresses to street locations was taken up by the National Capital Commission in 1966. Working in conjunction with the Dominion Bureau of Statistics, Hugh Calkins developed a prototype urban geocoding system for the Ottawa region in 1967.[6] More importantly the commission had acquired a large number of land parcels in the process of implementing the greenbelt and the Gatineau regional park elements of the 1955 Greber Plan for the National Capital Region. Managing this land had become a problem, and early work by Dave Symons resulted in the construction of a prototype parcel database for the city of Hull in 1969. These are the first digital representations of property boundaries to be evidenced in Canada. While they were regarded simply as digital mapping, they could probably be considered to be a first attempt at an LIS in Canada in that they set out to represent digitally property boundaries and their attributes. The city of Vancouver was also an early entry in the work of digital urban mapping.

In 1968 the Surveys and Mapping Branch of Energy, Mines and Resources (EMR) established a research and development project to accelerate the production and maintenance of maps through the use of computer graphics. This automated cartography development team was led by Brig. L.J. Harris (who had come to Canada from military survey in the United Kingdom), with G. A. Montagano as the cartographer and J. Linders of the Computer Science Faculty of the University of Waterloo. The design specifications were developed by 1969, and work began on the AUTOCARTO system for the digitization of existing graphics. Another parallel but independent project was undertaken by a team at Topographical Survey Division with the objective of developing a system for digital stereocompilation. There were also plans for a more advanced system called XCM (X Cartographic Monitor), and some preliminary work was started. These early efforts were abandoned in 1975. In 1977 the total responsibility for digital mapping was assigned to the Topographic Division under the direction of J.M. Zarzycki, which had acquired an interactive stereo digitizing and map editing system from M&S Computing, later to be renamed Intergraph.[7] The combined resources were directed to the development of an integrated digital terrain information system that comprised such aspects of digital mapping as data acquisition, data handling, and representation, and the creation of the Digital Topographic Data Base (DTDB).

By the end of the 1960s there was some interest in academic circles. Tom Poiker, at the Department of Geography at Simon Fraser University, added trend surface routines and point distribution indexes to SYMAP. In Ottawa David Douglas and Fraser Taylor used SYMAP to create an atlas of the city.[8] Dieter Steiner had created his own grid cell mapping program, GEOMAP, at the Department of Geography at the University of Waterloo, and a similar grid cell – based system named was created at the University of Western Ontario in 1967. There was to be a continuing series of map data manipulation algorithms from these workers that made significant contributions to the development of systems by others in the decades that followed.

In summary the decade of the 1960s was one of Canadian innovation and early achievement. GIS were the first on the scene and were under active development in the ARDA and in the Dominion Bureau of Statistics. LIS had at least been addressed initially in the National Capital Commission. Automated cartography was well represented by the CHS and the Surveys and Mapping Branch of EMR. The primary difficulties encountered were the limited size and great expense of early computers. Only very large institutions with nationwide responsibilities had the justification or the funds to pursue the development of the technology. A major constraint was the lack of people who could program computers. Most worked for computer vendors or universities; few knew much about maps or geographical analysis.

There was surprisingly little communication between agencies working on essentially the same problems, and very little cross-fertilization of ideas even in Ottawa, where most of the work was going on. This was more than the usual competition for federal government dollars, and had its roots in the departmental views that each was expert in the technology related to their own mandate. It was only much later that the generic capabilities of GIS and the widespread application of the technology became apparent.

Spread of Technology from the 1970s

The spread of GIS and LIS technology in Canada resulted in hundreds of systems eventually being put in place by 1994. Tracing each of these is clearly beyond the scope of this chapter. The examples mentioned will be illustrative of developments, but will make no attempt to be a comprehensive description of activity. A chronological diagram of the examples mentioned is provided in figure 15-2.

Communication between workers in the field of GIS took a large step forward when the First International Conference on Geographic Information Systems was held in Ottawa in 1970. All of the Canadian agencies mentioned so far in this chapter attended, as did representatives of all known GIS activity in the world. There were forty-nine participants. The conference was organized by the International Geographical Union (IGU), with the support of the Canadian government and Unesco, and was chaired by Tomlinson. This five-day conference was tape recorded, and from it resulted a book[9] that described the current status of the field with respect to categories of systems, digital data input, digital data use and manipulation, digital data display, and presentation.

In 1972 the Second International Conference on Geographic Information Systems was held in Ottawa under the auspices of the IGU, the government of Canada, and Unesco, again chaired by Tomlinson. Working groups from the first conference had produced and published a two-volume, 1300-page text. This work[10] covered geographical data sensing (including remote sensing input to information systems), equipment for geographical data processing, the techniques of geographical data manipulation and analysis, geographical data display, current systems for handling geographical data, and the economics of geographical data handling. Each of the 300 participants received a copy of the text, and over 1000 more were printed and distributed, before it was given to the United States document distribution service and made widely available for the cost of reproduction. Regrettably Canada had no such facility. It became the basic text on GIS for the decade that followed, and established Canada as a leading player in the technology.

Canada can rightfully regard 1972 as its earth sciences year because four major conferences in geology, photogrammetry, geography, and cartography were held individually or jointly in the provinces of Ontario and Québec. The cartographic conference consisted of the Fourth General Assembly and the Sixth International Conference of the International Cartographic Association. Sessions were held on automation in cartography. Another important conference in 1972 was the Second National Conference on Urban Surveying and Mapping, organized by a subcommittee of the National Advisory Committee on Control Surveys and Mapping (NACCSM). In several of the papers[11,12,13] the term "information system" was linked to urban surveying and mapping. The concept of using computers to handle land-title textual data and representations of cadastral parcel boundaries was introduced. Later the term "land information system" was adopted at the Canadian Council on Surveying and Mapping (CCSM) in October 1974.

The 1970s saw the adoption of the new digital technologies by municipal authorities, by utilities for power, telephone, water, sewer, and oil pipelines, for topographic and cadastral mapping by provincial authorities, for soil maps, and for provincial forest inventories.

Examples from across Canada that originated in the 1970s are given below, though no attempt is made to give a complete listing. The emphasis is on early or innovative examples.

Early Examples of LIS

The Atlantic Provinces Surveying and Mapping Program (APSAMP)[14] was supported by provincial and federal funding, and as chapters 4 and 7 have noted, was designed to make four sub-programmes available to the Atlantic region. They were a second-order network of coordinated control monuments; a mapping programme using orthophoto and line map techniques; a modified Torrens land title system utilizing disk and microfilm storage; and a data bank specializing in the location of specific data. It was clearly the intent of this programme to use computers in the later stages of the project. The programme was transferred to the new Maritime Land Registration and Information Service (LRIS)[15] in 1972. The preliminary phases of this programme used conventional survey methodology, and resulted in the mapping of 450 000 land parcels by the late 1980s. Using resources at the University of New Brunswick, a computer-based land title system was designed by Cyril B. Carlin[16] starting in 1971. This text-based system incorporated a unique parcel identifier that, coupled with the hard-copy cadastral mapping system, sufficed until 1990 when the newly formed New Brunswick Geographic Information Corporation undertook the digitizing of existing conventional property maps to create digital property map files. It is interesting to note that this quintessential LIS is now called a GIS.

Other provinces moved somewhat more swiftly than New Brunswick into the implementation of LIS in the 1970s. The City of Edmonton Planning Department[17] had already digitized the centroids of all land parcels in the late 1960s. In 1971 it used the AMF created by Statistics Canada to describe urban street networks for transportation studies and traffic accident location. The same engineers and planners used SYMAP to display transit patron origin-destination data. In 1977 the city authorized the purchase of a PDP-11/70 computer and the in-house development of a geographic-base information system for assessment, planning and building, power, telephones, engineering, water, and sanitation. In 1979 the city acquired Intergraph systems and PDP-11/70 computers. A VAX 780 was added in 1983. Massive databases were stored in ORACLE in 1989. The city was making widespread use of Intergraph microstations by 1990 and, under the direction of Dale Rhyason, Edmonton's system stands as a major urban LIS today.

Mention has also been made in chapter 7 of the Ontario Law Reform Commission report that, in 1971, made far-reaching recommendations for changes in the province's land registration systems. Two specific aspects were that a coordinate control system should be established and used for indexing parcels and to record the location of monuments, and a computer system should be used for land registration.[18] Subsequent studies by the Ministry of Consumer and Commercial Relations led to the submission of the Province of Ontario Land Registration and Information System (POLARIS) report, which received cabinet approval in 1979. It was recognized at the outset that two POLARIS digital databases were required – the property-mapping database and the title records database – to form the basic components of the LIS for Ontario. An Intergraph system was adopted in 1980. A prototype land registration office containing approximately 35 000 properties was established in Woodstock, and a business case was presented to Ontario Management Board in 1987. There were approximately fifty municipalities within the province that were involved in

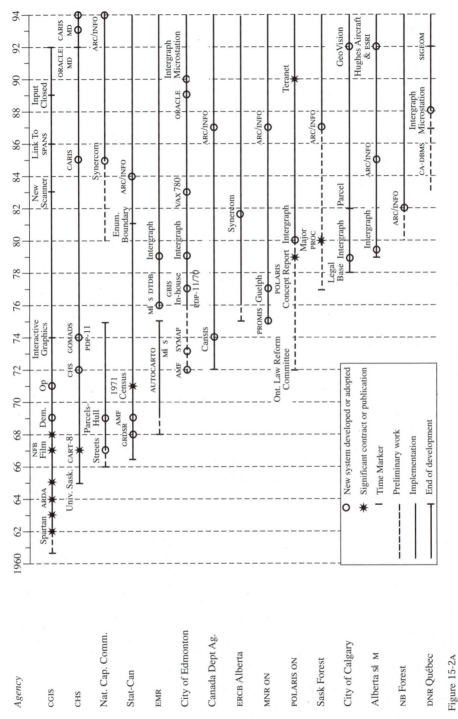

Figure 15-2A

A chronological diagram showing the emergence of GIS and LIS systems in Canada.

Source: Tomlinson Associates Ltd

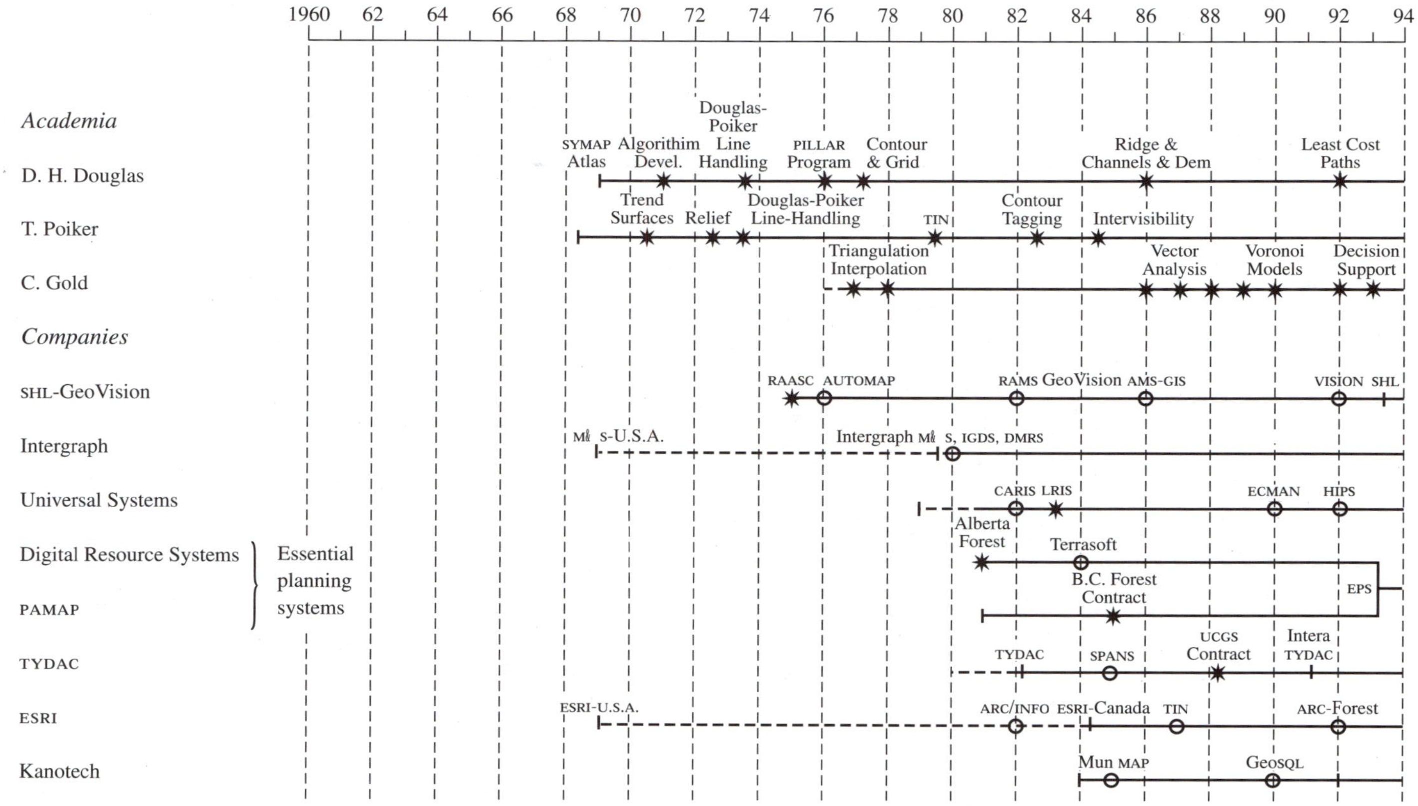

Figure 15-2B

A chronological diagram showing the emergence of GIS and LIS systems in Canada.

Source: Tomlinson Associates Ltd

some aspect of developing automated municipal LIS by 1990. The POLARIS activity within government was effectively privatized through a strategic alliance when the company Teranet was formed in 1991, as described in chapter 7.

Several other initiatives in western Canada had their origins in the 1970s. The Energy Resources Conservation Board (ERCB) pipeline graphical database was automated in 1975.[19] A Synercom Corporation INFOMAP system was selected to maintain the digital graphical database. This province-wide digital network with related attributes now contains about 220 000 km of pipeline. This is from 95 to 98 percent of all energy-related pipelines ever built in Alberta, although rather than being a map they are a schematic representation related to the Alberta township system.

Computerized legal base map production started in Calgary in late 1978,[20] followed closely by computerized parcel base map production in 1981. Digital mapping of the base products was completed in 1984. Since that time a broad range of departments in the city and city-owned utilities added data elements and incorporated attribute data associated with the graphic data. Later in the 1980s the city laid plans to develop a corporate GIS, and in recent years has developed the CalSIM system under the direction of Don Evans to provide the data needed to support the city's businesses and to provide the technology to manage the data.

The activity in LIS in Edmonton, Calgary, and ERCB must be viewed within the provincial context under the guidance of Wally Youngs and Ed Kennedy. The Alberta Bureau of Surveying and Mapping commenced digital base mapping of Alberta with an Intergraph system in 1979. The programme focused on cadastral mapping in the urban areas through cost-sharing agreements with the cities of Edmonton and Calgary, and seventy-one of Alberta's larger communities. The commencement of the Land-Related Information System (LRIS) project in 1980 within the Treasury Department was based on the understanding that the digital mapping would ultimately enable the development of a cadastral parcel database to which attribute data could be related. Mike Toomey followed Kennedy as head of the provincial surveying and mapping agency, and concluded a cost-sharing agreement with the gas, electricity, and telephone companies. This enabled the digital mapping of the cadastral fabric for the remainder of the province outside the urban programme to be started as the Parcel Mapping Project in 1991. Sixty percent of the province was completed by March 1994. The LRIS project is developing a spatial database using ARC/INFO tools, and all cadastral mapping throughout the province will be converted to a topologically structured database. An innovative project to achieve the integration of Intergraph files and ARC/INFO data is being undertaken by Hughes Aircraft. The Land Titles Office titles will be referenced by a LINC number to ownership parcels based upon the survey parcels. The geodetic survey control, ownership parcels, title files, and crown land ownership records form the primary system components of the LRIS project, providing an excellent example of an LIS. By February 1994 some 200 subscribers could obtain remote access to the LRIS network by direct dial-up.

It can be seen that LIS related to ownership parcels flourished in Canada in the 1980s, particularly within large cities. Typically a property mapping base has been compiled over a period of ten years from registered survey plans, and has been converted into a digital map base. Often the initiative came from a service department, such as data processing or surveying and mapping, but the engineering department with access to large public works budgets was usually a major player. The early champion of a system quite often gave a natural priority to its major interests. Thus systems could be seen based on property mapping of high accuracy, for example an absolute accuracy of 10 or 15 cm, promoted by city engineering departments but not by city planners. When Dale Rhyason, representing the city of Edmonton, was asked at the 1990 URISA conference how the city could afford such an expensive property base map, he replied that it was only rich enough to do the job properly the first time. The accuracy of the base map also enabled an extra stage of engineering planning to be performed without further field survey.

As the city systems mature into the middle of their second decade, it is apparent that the first decade focused on a digital map base of property boundaries and utility information. The efforts in the second decade are now directed to increasing their efficiency. Typically the systems are being enhanced by purchasing GIS from suppliers other than those involved in the initial digital base map creation. These changes are required to satisfy the needs for geographical analysis of a rapidly growing community of users within the large municipalities. A similar situation exists at the provincial level of government, although few cases exist where the level of integration is as great as in the leading cities. Alberta expected to have its digital property mapping essentially complete in 1995, converted to a topologically structured database, linked to the Land Titles and the Crown Lands databases, and made available for remote access and random searches. Given this combination it might claim to be the current provincial leader. After ten years of effort Laurel McKay was the principal architect of the provincial LRIS project and was also the 1993–94 president of URISA.

The Resource Evaluation and Planning Division of Alberta Energy and Natural Resources started the planning of a Natural Resource Information System in 1979. Intergraph provided the initial mapping system, and the 1:20 000 scale digital mapping programme was used as the basis for referencing thematic data. The ARC/INFO GIS product was purchased in March 1985 to add geographical analysis capability in a wide variety of pilot projects.

As GIS/LIS projects become successful they satisfy a widening group of customers within the participating institutions and outside. Greater expectations are created for enhancements, and the systems place a strain on early institutional arrangements. More formal system functions become essential, as do full-time positions for the administration of data and databases, and the modelling of geographic data and processes. The payback from well-designed systems covers the costs of such expansion, but the high up-front costs of GIS/LIS projects, especially for data creation and conversion, requires well-argued support.

The most successful large projects in the 1990s have in common the existence of layers of supporting committees of experts and internal customers. In this sense GIS technology is a catalyst for causing institutional cooperation. Without such cooperation the successful application of the digital mapping technology has at best given limited benefits and at worst has brought the project to a halt.

This trend of digital mapping programmes and LIS moving towards more advanced GIS capabilities is well exemplified in the activities of the Ontario Ministry of Natural Resources (MNR).[21] In 1972 the Ontario Government Committee on Productivity recommended that a coordinated approach be taken to geographic referencing, and MNR was given a mandate to create such a referencing system for Ontario. Early collaboration with the Waterloo Research Institute resulted in a Province of Ontario Mapping Information System (PROMIS) being initiated. Subsequent work with the University of Guelph did not lead to a production mapping system for MNR. A major provincial and municipal user-needs study was conducted in 1983 to determine the requirements of GIS, and the applications that users required from a GIS. This led to the acquisition of ARC/INFO software in 1984, the development of LIS applications in Oxford County and Cambridge, an Ontario Basic Mapping digital production system, and the development of capabilities for ambulance dispatch. In 1985 the MNR Forest Resource Branch acquired a similar GIS for digital forest resource inventory. In the late 1980s the MNR entered into joint GIS application development with the Environmental Systems Research Institute (ESRI) for a series of forest-planning software programs based on the Plonski Decision Support System. This successful joint venture has resulted in commercial software that is useful to the MNR, and can be used worldwide in forest resource management. The MNR has recently completed a major procurement process to select GIS software as a standard to support an Integrated Natural Resource Information System (INRIS). The ARC/INFO family of products was acquired after much deliberation.

Early Examples of GIS

Several important examples of direct GIS implementation occurred in the 1970s. The sub-committee on data handling of the Canada Soil Survey Committee recommended to the federal Department of Agriculture in 1970 that a national soil data bank be established. Work on this began in 1972, resulting in the development of the Canada Soil Information System (CanSIS).[22] Although computerized provincial soil test files of textual data had already been established in Canada since the mid-1960s, this was the first attempt to establish a national system of data collection and data comparability within and between data-gathering units, and to create a GIS to store, manage, analyse, and display soil boundaries. Early work by Julian Dumanski, Bruce Kloosterman, and S.E. Brandon developed in-house software that achieved this objective. In 1987 the system migrated to ARC/INFO software.

The need to acquire GIS capability by the Saskatchewan Department of Tourism and Renewable Resources for forest inventory resulted in an assessment of the state of development of GIS. This was published[23] and had a significant impact on the subsequent development of commercial GIS capabilities. From June 1979 to March 1980 the department, under the direction of James Benson and with the assistance of Tomlinson Associates Ltd. prepared specifications for a GIS to meet its requirements. This departed from prevailing common practice in Canada, which usually saw system implementation begin with minimal assessment of the technical needs. For the first time a natural resource management agency had determined its precise requirements for the functions to be performed, the data to be processed, and the output to be prepared. This allowed the province to benchmark test five systems (by Systemhouse, M&S Computing, Earth Satellite Corporation, Comarc, and ESRI) and to determine that in 1980 none of the systems was capable of carrying out more than 40 percent of the operations needed. Some of the companies ignored the results; some increased their sales staff; others improved their system capabilities to meet the needs. The province went on to redefine its needs and broaden the GIS application requirements, and acquired an ARC/INFO system in 1987.

In New Brunswick[24] the catalyst for forestry GIS acquisition was the 1980 Crown Lands and Forests Act that required a sophisticated information system to allow the level of management envisaged. A search team was struck to recommend a system for purchase, the systems of several vendors were benchmark tested in 1982, and ARC/INFO was selected. This was actually the first sale of the now well-known ARC/INFO software anywhere in the world. The complete Forest Inventory has been entered into the database since that time. The initial database required 1.5 gigabytes of computer storage. Increasing users and subsequent applications currently require 20 gigabytes. The system provides updated inventory data for input to wood supply models and, most importantly, allows the mapping of the twenty-four-year wood-supply. Additional applications include identifying suitable forests for budworm spray planning, the mapping of forest site productivity, the monitoring of annual and cumulative defoliation, and forest habitat supply analysis. It is this analysis of geographical data to provide vital information for decision making that typifies the use of GIS.

In Québec an emphasis has been placed on natural resource development. The Department of Natural Resources Geological Research Unit added mapping capability to a Computer Associates relational database by adding Intergraph Microstation in 1988. Under the current direction of Charles Roy, this innovative system, named SIGEOM,[25] supplies available information on geochemistry, geophysics, mineral deposits, geology, mining activities, documents, assessments, and geographical referencing on floppy disk or magnetic tape to the mining industry and to the public on request.

Early Academic Work

The academic community in Canada was very active in the 1970s. David Douglas developed a suite of spatial data-handling algorithms, published in 1971,[26] and went on to develop perspective modelling and line handling capabilities. The latter resulted in the now-famous 1973 Douglas-Poiker algorithm[27] for the reduction in the number of points along a curve. His widely used PILLAR program[28] was developed in 1976, and a contour-to-grid algorithm in 1977. His many contributions have included a ridge and channel identification algorithm for digital elevation models,[29] and recently a least-cost path algorithm.[30]

Tom Poiker developed relief-shading algorithms[31] in 1972 and cooperated with Douglas in the line information reduction algorithms of 1973. These have been adopted in GIS worldwide. In 1976 Poiker developed the concept and the name of Triangulated Irregular Networks (TIN).[32] This algorithm was later taken up by commercial vendors to provide a digital representation of three-dimensional surfaces. Poiker continued to develop valuable spatial analysis algorithms in the 1980s, including one for contour tagging[33] in 1982, and for the determination of intervisibility[34] in 1985.

Chris Gold developed smooth interpolation over a triangulation[35] in 1977, and enhanced the modelling over a triangulation base during the next decade. In the late 1980s he moved to work on vector spatial data structures,[36] and then to the development of Voronoi spatial models.[37] Recently he has made significant contributions to dynamic spatial data structures[38] for managing map history, and to decision support systems.[39] Many of these Canadian innovations went south of the border and are incorporated in U.S. systems on the market today.

COMMERCIAL DEVELOPMENTS IN CANADA

The availability of lower-cost minicomputers in the mid-1970s allowed small companies to acquire computing capacity and develop commercially viable software systems. Sometimes a company was contracted to develop a system for a particular client. On other occasions companies were in a related business such as environmental analysis, and developed software for their own use. Sometimes ideas migrated from government systems and were developed further for sale. The following companies are examples of those established in Canada, described in approximate order of appearance. The authors consider it likely that other commercial systems have been developed in Canada, and emphasize that any omission is due only to constraints of time and space.

In 1975 SHL Systemhouse received a $1.5 million contract from the Royal Australian Army Survey Corps to produce an automated cartography system for topographic mapping.[40] Brian Giles, who had gained experience working with CGIS, had written the proposal. The resulting AUTOMAP software was built in less than a year by an Ottawa-based team that included Doug Seaborn. The applications began to broaden from topographic mapping to hydrographic charting, land information, and forest inventory. An ice charting/forecasting system was developed with AES in 1982. A substantial automated mapping business grew within Canada, primarily for sales to surveying and mapping companies who for the first time were offering digital map products to their respective provincial and federal governments. In 1984 the graphics system division of SHL became GeoVision Corporation, with Seaborn as its first president. After 1986 GeoVision introduced new product lines, including AMS/GIS and VISION, which became the first major GIS offering to use relational database technology. By 1992 GeoVision was established worldwide, with over 250 staff and yearly revenues in the order of U.S.$25 million, but in 1993 ownership of GeoVision reverted to SHL Systemhouse in Ottawa.

In 1977 the Intergraph Corporation was established in Canada[41] and offered software from the M&S Computing Company in the United States, notably an interactive graphic design system (IGDS) and a data management and retrieval software (DMRS). It worked closely with clients requiring automatic cartography and digital urban mapping. The first client was the Department of Energy, Mines and Resources in Ottawa for cartographic map production. The governments of Québec, British Columbia, and Alberta followed suit. The cities of Edmonton and Calgary were early municipal users, and the Ministry of Forests in the province of British Columbia pioneered the use of Intergraph technology in natural resource mapping applications. Utility companies in Alberta, TransAlta Utilities, Nova Corporation, SaskTel, B.C. Hydro, and B.C. Gas followed as Intergraph applied their technology to the utility environment.

The second all-Canadian system emanated from Universal Systems Ltd,[42] which was formed in 1979 by Sam Masry from the University of New Brunswick. Initial company research into data structures, and the acquisition of the CART-8 system from the CHS, developed into CARIS. The first commercial sale of CARIS was made in 1983 to LRIS, the Maritime agency responsible for digital base mapping. A succession of sales followed, principally to agencies concerned with digital mapping, LIS, and particularly hydrographic charting throughout the world.

PAMAP Graphics was formed in 1981 by Peter and Pamela Sallaway[43] of Victoria, British Columbia. The product was produced initially to add raster-based GIS analysis capabilities to the Intergraph mapping system located at the Ministry of Forests (BCMOF). As early as 1985 BCMOF was using an Intergraph system for its mapping and the PAMAP software for its GIS and topographic analysis. The PAMAP product was developed into a fully functional GIS and has been exported to over twenty-five countries.

Digital Resource Systems (Canada) Ltd[44] was also established in 1981 by Dan Lemko and Jim Spencer, who had both been involved in developing forest planning systems for MacMillan Bloedel in Nanaimo, British Columbia. Their objective was to sell GIS on low-cost computer platforms to the forest sector, and to provide support. These programs developed into a generic GIS named Terrasoft in 1984. Both the PAMAP and Terrasoft systems are now owned by Essential Planning Systems Limited (EPS) of Vancouver. This company is maintaining those product lines and also introducing innovative modular system GIS capability that can be added to relational database technology for users not wishing to acquire proprietary GIS.

In the early 1980s the DPA Group Inc. consulting organization in Ottawa required a GIS for resource-management consulting projects in Canada and overseas. The owners of the DPA Group, Giulio Maffini and Richard Higgins, founded TYDAC Technologies Inc. in 1982 to develop such capability.[45] The core idea behind the development was to provide a suite of spatial analytical tools that could be used on a personal computer by anyone without their having to become an expert in GIS. Menus should be used to access all functions, and effort should be concentrated on functions that solved commonly experienced problems. The idea of using the quadtree structure to represent area maps was developed by Wolfgang Bitterlich with Maffini. The resulting system, SPANS, was launched at the URISA conference held in Ottawa in 1985. There are now over 3000 users of SPANS in at least sixty-five countries. An early customer was the CGIS in 1986, which added an interface to SPANS to make its huge databases available to many users. TYDAC also created the not-for-profit Canada Centre for GIS Education in 1991, through which the company provided low-cost software to universities around the world. Most of SPANS customers are involved with the management and study of natural resources, including water resources, forestry, agriculture, geology, and the oceans. A smaller but growing number are users who are in the business sector and who analyse economic activity. The company passed through the hands of several owners until, in 1994, TYDAC was purchased by PCI Enterprises Ltd, a Toronto company specializing in remote sensing.

ESRI was established in the United States in 1969. It had a long history of GIS development before establishing ESRI Canada in 1984.[46] The new product coming onto the market at that time was the first version of ARC/INFO. This very successful software development has over 500 installations in Canada in 1994. ESRI Canada, under president Alex Miller, has developed several all-Canadian products that are now finding markets worldwide. The first of these was built on Poiker's TIN algorithm, which was developed into a digital terrain modelling system called TIN. Research work in conjunction with the Ontario Ministry of Natural Resources resulted in a new application software product called ARC/FOREST.

A significant event was the sale of ARC/INFO software to the County of Oxford in Ontario, and the related direct involvement of ESRI in developing the concepts of integrated land-records management at both provincial and municipal levels. This has recently led to an offshoot of ESRI Canada called Alex Miller and Associates, in partnership with Geoplan Consultants, Fredericton, EastCan Group from Dartmouth, Nova Scotia, and Atlantic Geomatics Research from Sydney Mines, Nova Scotia, to develop a land-records management infrastructure product for sale in Canada and overseas. The funds committed for the development of this product during the period 1994–97 are nearly $6 million. It is an important and all-Canadian integration of LIS and GIS capabilities, and a forerunner of such developments worldwide.

Typical of the smaller companies basing developments on CAD capabilities is Kanotech Information Systems, which began in 1984 under the direction of Lance Maidlow.[47] The Central Surveys and Mapping Agency (CSMA) in the province of Saskatchewan had just completed a pilot project using CAD technology to map a small city in the province. The limitations and high cost of this approach had become apparent, and Kanotech proposed an alternative approach using the emerging personal computer platform. By 1987 the software had been commercialized under the MunMAP trademark. This first product was AutoCAD-based with the ability to link entities to an external database. By 1990 the software was being used in projects ranging from the clean-up of the Valdez oil spill to oil-field management and pipeline management, as well as an inventory system for a large warehouse. The core technology was renamed Geo/SQL, which has subsequently been relaunched under the name Spatialist. The company has been actively licensing its base technology to third parties around the world.

The rapid development of attractive and capable commercial systems in the late 1970s and 1980s is reflected in the fact that nearly all of the early government initiatives to develop software in Canada have either been developed into commercial software products or have died out. This concentration of system development capability in the private sector has resulted in an intensely competitive environment, and undoubtedly the concentration of expertise will continue as companies consolidate and acquire dominant market share in future. An existing fully developed GIS in 1994 has over 1000 person-years of effort invested in software writing. This makes it difficult for new companies to enter the marketplace unless they offer extremely innovative products.

OVERALL TRENDS

Proliferation of Users

The competition resulting from the proliferation of systems and users has forced prices down. Both hardware and software prices have been lowered significantly. System capabilities that had development costs amounting to $10 million in 1970 could be purchased for $1 million in 1980, and for $100,000 or less in 1990. The purchase price in the foreseeable future is likely to be $10,000 or less. This has resulted in a proliferation of users over a wide range of applications. It is impossible to list all types of users, or to identify those that are being added daily. Since 1980 GIS have been adopted for national defence, ice forecasting, natural gas pipelines, pulp and paper industry, tile drainage management in agriculture, *The National Atlas of Canada*, oil lease management, oil-spill clean-up, tourism management, railway yard management, Elections Canada, pollution monitoring, crime analysis, postal service planning, the provision of highway information, school bus routing, municipal assessment, native land management, and retail business analysis, to mention just a few.

Geographic Data Inventories

This variety of applications has led to a growing demand for digital map data in a form suitable for analysis, and for information on what geographical data are available. Inventories of geographical data in Canada were developed in the 1980s. The first was probably undertaken in 1980 by the Department of Indian and Northern Affairs and the Yukon government, which created a directory of data types and sources in the Yukon Territory. This included descriptions of all data (hard copy or digital) for agriculture, archaeology, climate, fisheries, forestry, geology, ecological zones, land, minerals, recreation parks, soils, terrain, tourism, vegetation, water, and wildlife.

In 1983 EMR created a directory of all small-scale (smaller than 1:10 000 scale) mapped data in digital form in federal, provincial, municipal, and commercial agencies across Canada. This directory described 248 digital data sets, and gave an analysis of their data characteristics and utilization.[48] The directory was produced in digital form to enable searches by computer.

In 1990 EMR carried out a survey of federal government digital geographic databases by an extensive questionnaire. The categories of data included agriculture, archaeology/ heritage, boundaries (political, regulatory, statistical, and cadastral), climate, coastal zone, communications, engineering, fisheries, forestry, geodesy, geology, geomorphology, geophysics, hydrography, hydrology, land use, natural resources, oceanography, planning, recreation, remote sensing, socio-economic, soils, topography, toponomy, utilities, and wildlife. This directory described 314 federal digital data sets. Responses were verified, indexes created, and a report was produced on the rate of growth of geo-referenced data, trends, the balance of data sets across thematic categories, and the availability of data by digital format.[49] The directory was created in a machine-readable form that can be searched, and has been made available to the public. All of the above directories were created by Tomlinson Associates Ltd under contract to the government agencies concerned.

Interchange Standards

The creation of digital geographical data on different systems resulted in many varieties of data being available in different digital formats. The 1990 federal data inventory identified data available in thirty-five different digital formats. Early commercial vendors had no interest in data formats other than their own. They had a proprietary self-interest in maintaining the status quo. The competitive pressures of second-generation system procurements meant that if one vendor was to replace another, the former had to be able to translate the existing data into its system format. Hence digital data interchange standards were created. Governments, being major purchasers of systems and seeing the need to exchange data between departments and agencies, had a vested interest in creating common standards.

In Canada there are currently five related activities that are attempting to provide the basis for one or more solutions.[50]

- Digital topographic data standards, organized under the auspices of the CCSM, now the Canadian Council on Geomatics (CCOG), has developed a successful standard for the exchange of topographic data between the federal government and several provincial governments.
- Map Data Interchange Format (MDIF), developed by the Ontario Ministry of Natural Resources, uses the same model as the CCSM format, but employed other international telecommunications standards for its implementation.
- Map and Chart Interchange Format (MACDIF) is similar to MDIF, but has a broader context that includes special applications such as the exchange and updating of nautical chart data.

- The Committee on Geomatics was created in 1989 under the Canadian General Standards Board, with the objective of establishing a broad range of spatial standards.
- Geographical Document Architecture (GDA) was intended to be a general interchange format for all types of geographic information between two communicating entities, in a manner similar to the definition of the Office Document Architecture for interchange between office systems. The work is supported by the Directorate of Geographic Operations of National Defence.

It is fair to say that none of the Canadian standards had been widely adopted outside Canada by 1994. Exchanges of digital geographic data between most systems across Canada in 1994 tended to be carried out via vendor-designed interchange formats. As can be imagined, there is intense international pressure to create and adopt internationally recognized standards. Canada is actively cooperating in these efforts. In particular the geomatics unit of the Surveys and Resources Mapping Branch, British Columbia Ministry of Environment, Lands and Parks, submitted a series of four papers on behalf of Canada for consideration by the International Standards Organisation (ISO) database language multimedia working group. Included in this submission was a framework for the development of part 3 of SQL3/MM based directly on the British Columbia Spatial Archive Interchange Format (SAIF) standard. This proposal was accepted,[51] and will be the basis for all future ISO work regarding spatial/temporal data management in SQL/MM.

DEVELOPMENT OF TRAINING FACILITIES

While Canadian education and training for geodesy, photogrammetry, cartography, digital mapping, cadastral surveying, and LIS are described in chapter 13, it should be mentioned that there is a current and foreseeable deficiency in the supply of persons who can make full use of GIS, and probably of the future developments of LIS. To solve geographical problems requires a knowledge of the techniques of geographical analysis appropriate to the problem concerned. This is true regardless of whether the person is a city planner, a detective, a forester, the manager of a public utility, or, in fact, any person who uses a GIS. These techniques can range from simple spatial comparisons (e.g., map overlay) to more complex procedures (e.g., network analysis). Clearly there is a need for people with such training who also know how to make a GIS work to carry out the problem-solving procedures appropriate to their data.

The supply of trained persons competent in both GIS technology and in quantitative methods for geographical analysis is critically short. This may be the limiting factor in the rational development of the field. In the 1960s and 1970s the system capabilities fell short of user needs. The crossover came in the late 1980s when systems exhibited capabilities in advance of those required by first-time users. Now the gap between system capabilities and user ability to take full advantage of those capabilities can be quite substantial. There is frequently a lack of usage of advanced system capabilities by the people who have bought those systems.

An estimate of the size of the problem can be attempted. Using investment in hardware, software, and data conversion as a rough guide to the need for trained people, and assuming conservatively that each $1 million of investment requires the services of only one trained person, then the field of spatial information systems in North America is facing a requirement for 1000 to 3000 newly trained persons each year in the 1990s. Even a cursory examination of existing training facilities and student enrolment in universities, colleges, and vendor-training centres shows a massive shortfall. There are shortages of teachers and facilities, inadequate research effort and funding, and, with some notable exceptions, difficulty in moving conservative academic departments to new curricula.

The situation has implications beyond those of the academic community. The principal users of GIS are already in the workplace. Their skills for geographical analysis may be reaching the limits of improvement possible through self-learning. If the knowledge gap between system capabilities and user abilities is to be reduced significantly, then a substantial increase in post-university training may be envisaged. This has implications for all geographical educational institutions, for improved in-house training programmes, and for public and private continuing education programmes designed to enhance geographical skills.

An important aspect of improving communication of knowledge between workers in the field has been the recent development of publications and the increasing number of major conferences. The GIS field is well served with scientific journals of record (e.g., *International Journal for Geographic Information Systems*), popular magazines (e.g., *GIS World*, *Mapping Awareness*, *Business GIS*), numerous textbooks (over thirty titles on GIS in 1994 from one publisher, Longmans, alone), and vendor user conferences and conferences of national scope that attract thousands of participants. Important among the latter in Canada is the National Conference on Geographic Information Systems held in Ottawa, usually in the spring of each year since 1989. This well-organized conference, established by the Canadian Institute of Surveying and Mapping (now the Canadian Institute of Geomatics) with substantial support from Energy, Mines and Resources Canada, was successful in its first year in producing a 1400-page set of proceedings[52] that represented the major publication of GIS-related papers in Canada. The conference was a significant educational event. It was attended by over 1000 people, and helped to establish lines of communication between vendors and clients and between agencies across Canada.

Similarly a major GIS conference, partly funded by Forestry Canada and focusing on natural-resource development, has been held in the west of Canada since 1987. The first meeting was in Winnipeg, the second in Edmonton, and those since 1989 in Vancouver.

Two earlier conferences can be noted. The U.S.-based URISA held a conference in Ottawa in 1985, and in Edmonton in 1990. The latter had 2700 in attendance, 50 percent from outside Canada and 25 percent from Alberta. It was particularly useful in introducing applications to municipal and provincial government elected officials who attended the conference and were able to talk to practitioners and listen to the most recent developments. The Ontario Ministry of Natural Resources has been holding a major yearly conference on GIS since 1983. The original purpose was to brief members of the department on the ongoing GIS activities in the department, and to provide an educational experience in the technology to these potential users. The conference has grown in scope to the point at which it attracts 500 people, is self-supporting financially, and is recognized as the most important GIS event in Ontario each year.

It is evident from this level of activity that there is an increasing interest and rapid growth in the fields of GIS and LIS. It is frequently said that they are the fastest-growing area in the field of computing. Certainly the conferences are significant educational opportunities in the field, and continue the tradition of the original GIS conferences held in Ottawa in 1970 and 1972.

As early as 1976 the Unesco publication *Computer Handling of Geographical Data*[53] observed that "there are just as many problems, and possibly more, on the management side of implementing a geographic information system as there are on the technical side." Canada, with its extensive history of GIS implementation, had accumulated a great deal of experience in the management processes associated with putting a system in place and maintaining its effectiveness. This pool of experience was drawn upon by numerous agencies in Canada, and resulted in early and satisfactory implementations occurring across the country. The Canadian Forestry Service had a major role in this process in the 1980s. Federal-provincial forestry agreements of the time included funding for GIS but, most importantly, for the planning process to manage adequately the implementation of such systems. These funds were used in practically every province in Canada to plan carefully for GIS implementation, and resulted in the establishment of world standards for system procurements, benchmark testing, and vendor development of system capabilities to meet Canadian requirements.

The components of a sound geographic information planning process start with determining what information the system has to produce as output to meet the needs of the agency requiring the system. This leads to the identification of the data sets and data elements that are required to be input, and the system functions that must be used to generate the information. At this time the logical linkages between data elements that will have to be established in the system database are identified, so that an intelligent database design can be established at an early stage in the project. These considerations lead to an analysis of the volume of data that will be processed by the system, and setting priorities to the effort required so that the size of the eventual system and the rate at which specific data must be made available can be determined. The role that can be played by existing agency hardware and software can then be assessed. The requirements must be established for institutional interaction between local, provincial, and federal data sources and the recipients of information. This leads to concerns of data accuracy (resolution, integration requirements, update requirements, level of error, and requirement for information products), which in turn lead to the data standards that must be put in place to ensure the reliability of the information to be produced. The focus is, and must be, on the information that the agency needs for its business purposes. With the above knowledge in hand it is then possible to establish the functional requirements of the system and the need for interfaces, data conversion, data communications, and thus the hardware and software that need to be acquired.

A well-managed GIS is integrated into the working processes of the institution in which it is placed. This may entail a system security plan, legal opinions on new methods of handling vital source data, cost-benefit analysis, risk analysis, examination of management issues, a comparison of alternative implementation strategies including possible pilot projects, and eventually an agreed strategy of implementation. A major procurement will benefit from a written definition of system requirements in the Request for Proposals (RFP), clearly established system procurement procedures, selection criteria, and the design of a benchmark test with the related methodology for monitoring and evaluation. In parallel there will be an analysis of departmental budgeting requirements, staffing requirements, and training by categories of personnel. Systems that are carefully planned in this manner are usually satisfactory. Systems that are acquired without such preparation have proved to be high-risk investments.

Canadian development of new tools to assist in the GIS planning process is very advanced. A group of researchers at the Centre for Research at Laval University, under the direction of Yvan Bédard, has designed and developed a new computer-assisted system engineering (CASE) tool to accelerate the design and set-up of GIS databases.[54] This CASE tool is called ORION, and helps to create the data schema and an integrated data dictionary that can automatically translate the user's needs into instructions to set up a commercial GIS. The data-modelling technique is called MODUL-R2.0, which is a combination of object-oriented and entity relationships concepts with extensions for both spatial and temporal conditions. The project was financed by Intergraph Corporation.

Rigorous cost-benefit analysis techniques for GIS have been developed under the direction of Douglas Smith, head of the Department of Economics at Carleton University in Ottawa, and Tomlinson Associates Ltd Consulting Geographers, resulting in software embedded in GISPLAN, a comprehensive GIS planning support system. The cost-benefit analysis procedures are a significant improvement over 1980s economic theory, which prescribed that data had no value other than the cost of acquisition. An examination of the costs and benefits of previously established GIS indicated that this was not the case. Moreover it suggested that the benefit of information produced by a GIS can be assessed by measuring the impact that the new information has on the operations of the agency concerned, and on improvements in the effectiveness of investment decisions in those agencies. The first full use of this methodology was employed in the GIS planning for the city of Ottawa in 1991.[55] With extremely conservative benefit estimation it was possible to show that a cost-benefit ratio of 1:2.5, fully discounted over a ten-year period, could be achieved. The approach has now been used worldwide with extremely satisfactory results, most recently in the state of Victoria in Australia where GIS planning was carried out for thirty-nine different departments and agencies of state government in a two-year period ending in September 1993.

CONCLUSIONS

There is no doubt that in the last thirty years GIS have come of age. This Canadian innovation is now spread worldwide. There are probably in excess of 1000 current system licenses in Canada alone. The implementation of GIS started in the context of specific projects that provided a raison d'être for the high level of investment required to create a GIS in the early days. As their capabilities increased they became department-wide in scope; all activities in a forestry department, for example, would be reliant on data from a departmental GIS. In 1994 the trend is to enterprise-wide systems wherein all departments in an enterprise, such as a major corporation or a state government, plan to have integrated GIS using shared databases. The step thereafter will be broad societal use of GIS where their use is commonplace. There are few agencies who do not make decisions that concern place. Those that do so deal with elections, land values, planning, education, environment, health, transportation, navigation, fire, ambulance, crime, industrial locations, sales, retail outlets, direct mail, water, gas, electricity, telephones, cable TV, extractive industry, agriculture, forests, geology, oil exploration, irrigation, urban management, and advertising. All of these agencies, and many more, will be GIS users making demands for access to geographical data and inexpensive and easy-to-use GIS in the foreseeable future. Wise governments are striving to provide low-cost geographical data as the underpinning to the broad societal need for economic development. Vendors are moving rapidly to lower-cost systems, and to improving the user-friendliness of GIS. The recognition is slowly growing that GIS are a generic technology for handling many types of geographic data, and that their use is not, and cannot be, the domain of any narrowly focused discipline. Don Thompson noted that "when mapping by means of computers becomes common procedure, a development that now appears to be inevitable, there is every prospect that information for all types of thematic maps will be stored in data banks for retrieval and use when required. This process of digitising cartographic information and for the 'storing' of maps is certain to lead to the production of a greater number and variety of up-to-date thematic maps."[56] That has certainly been the case, and Canada has led the way in developing the vital and exciting field of geographic information systems and land information systems.

NOTES

1 Spartan Air Services. 1963. *Feasibility Report of Computer Mapping System*. Report to the Agricultural Rehabilitation and Development Administration, Department of Agriculture, under project 14007. Ottawa: Dept of Agriculture.

2 Tomlinson, R.F. 1988. The Impact of the Transition from Analogue to Digital Cartographic Representation. *The American Cartographer*, 15, 3, 249–61. Extract used with the kind permission of the American Congress on Surveying and Mapping.

3 Tomlinson, R.F. 1968. A Geographic Information System for Regional Planning. In G.A. Stewart, ed. *Land Evaluation*. Sydney: MacMillan of Australia, 200–10.

4 Boyle, A.R. 1970. Automation in Hydrographic Charting. *The Canadian Surveyor*, 24, 5, 519–37.

5 1972. GRDSR: *Facts by Small Areas*. Ottawa: Statistics Canada.

6 Calkins, H.W. 1967. Ottawa Street Address Conversion System. *Highway Research Record*, 194, 96–102.

7 Zarzycki, J.M. 1978. An Integrated Digital Mapping System. *The Canadian Surveyor*, 32, 4, 443–52.

8 Taylor, D.R.F., and D.H. Douglas. 1970. *A Computer Atlas of Ottawa-Hull*. Ottawa: Carleton University, Department of Geography.

9 Tomlinson, R.F, ed. 1970. *Environment Information Systems*. Ottawa: International Geographical Union, Commission on Geographical Data Sensing and Processing.

10 Tomlinson, R.F., ed. 1972. *Geographical Data Handling*. 2 vols. Ottawa: International Geographical Union, Commission on Geographical Data Sensing and Processing.

11 Symons, D.C. 1972. Automated Mapping and Its Relation to Urban Information Systems. *The Canadian Surveyor*, 26, 5, 545–57.

12 Larsen, H.K. 1972. On the Economics of Land and Property Information Systems. *The Canadian Surveyor*, 26, 5, 587–90.

13 McLaughlin, J.D. 1972. Survey Data in an Information System of the Urban Physical Environment. *The Canadian Surveyor*, 26, 5, 567–70.

14 Larsen, H.K. 1971. *An Economic Study of the Demand for, and Gains Associated with, the Atlantic Provinces Co-ordinate Control, Mapping, Land Title and Data Bank Programme*. Report to the Management Committee for the APSAMP Programme. Fredericton, NB: Dept of Surveying Engineering, UNB.

15 Larsen, H.K. 1972. A New Approach in the Maritimes. *The Canadian Surveyor*, 26, 5, 606–7.

16 Carlin, C.B. 1971. Program Development for a Computer-Based Land Titles System. *The Canadian Surveyor*, 25, 2, 188–90.

17 City of Edmonton. 1993. Memo to M.A.G. Toomey, 8 December. History of geographic information systems in the city of Edmonton.

18 R. Scott. 1994. Memo to R.F. Tomlinson, 2 January. Land records management within context of Ontario GIS requirement.

19 K. Sharp. 1993. Memo to M.A.G. Toomey, 22 December . ERCB pipeline graphical database.

20 Don Evans. 1993. Memo to M.A.G. Toomey, 13 December. Automated mapping to GIS/AM/FM: the city of Calgary adventure.

21 G. Zilmer. 1994. Memo to R.F. Tomlinson, 14 January. Chronology of geographic referencing activity and expenditures, Ministry of Natural Resources, Ontario.

22 Dumanski, J., B. Kloosterman, and S.E. Brandon. 1975. Concepts, Objectives and Structure of the Canada Soil Information System. *Canadian Journal of Soil Sciences*, 55, May, 181–87.

23 Tomlinson, Roger F., and A. Raymond Boyle. 1981. The State of Development of Systems for Handling Natural Resources Inventory Data. *Cartographica*, 18, 4, 65–95.

24 D. MacFarlane. 1994. Memo to R.F. Tomlinson, 7 January. Short history of Timber Management Branch GIS installation.

25 DNR, Quebec, C. Roy. 1994. Memo to R.F. Tomlinson, 14 March. Notes on SIGEOM.

26 Douglas, D.H. 1971. *Collected Algorithms*. Harvard Laboratory for Computer Graphics and Spatial Analysis. Cambridge, MA: Harvard University.

27 Douglas, David H., and Thomas K. Peucker. 1973. Algorithms for the Reduction of the Number of Points Required to Represent a Digitized Line or Its Caricature. *The Canadian Cartographer*, 10, 2, 112–22.

28 Douglas, D.H. 1979. The PILLAR Mapping Program: Two Common Tasks of the Thematic Cartographer. In *Harvard University Mapping Collection, Mapping Software and Cartographic Data Bases*, vol. 2. Cambridge, MA: Harvard Laboratory for Computer Graphics and Spatial Analysis, 51–62.

29 Douglas, D.H. 1987. Experiments to Locate Ridges and Channels to Create a New Type of Digital Elevation Model. *The Canadian Surveyor*, 41, 3, 373–406.

30 Douglas, D.H. 1993. Least Cost Path in Geographic Information Systems. *University of Ottawa Department of Geography Research Notes*, 61, 1–22.

31 Peucker, T.K., and D. Cochrane. 1973. The Automation of Relief Representation – Theory and Application (translation of German title). *International Cartographic Yearbook*, 14, 128–39.

32 Peucker, T.K., R.J. Fowler, J.J. Little, and D.M. Mark. 1976. *Triangulated Irregular Networks for Representing Three-dimensional Surfaces*. Technical report no. 10, "Geographic Data Structures" to Office of Naval Research Contract N00014–75–0886. Washington, DC: ONR.

33 Roubal, J., and T.K. Poiker. 1985. Automated Contour Labelling and the Contour Tree. *Proceedings, Auto-Carto VII*. Washington, DC: American Society of Photogrammetry, 472–81.

34 Poiker, T.K., and L. Griswold. 1985. A Step Toward Interactive Displays in Digital Elevation Models. *Proceedings, Auto-Carto VII*. Washington, DC: American Society of Photogrammetry. 408–15.

35 Gold, C.M., T.D. Charles, and J. Ramsden. 1977. Automated Contour Mapping Using Triangular Element Data Structures and an Interpolant over Each Triangular Domain. *Computer Graphics*, 5, 2, 170–5.

36 Gold, C.M. 1988. PAN Graphics; An Aid to GIS Analysis. *International Journal of Geographic Information Systems*, 2, 1, 29–42.

37 Gold, C.M. 1989. Voronoi Diagrams and Spatial Adjacency. *Proceedings, GIS: Challenge for the 1990s*. Ottawa: Canadian Institute of Surveying and Mapping, 1309–16.

38 Gold, C.M. 1993. An Outline of an Event-Driven Spatial Data Structure for Managing Time-Varying Maps. *Proceedings, The Canadian Conference on GIS*. Ottawa: CIG, 880–8.

39 Gold, C.M. 1993. Forestry Spatial Decision Support System Classification and the "Flight Simulator" approach. *Proceedings, Seventh Annual Symposium on Geographic Information Systems in Forestry, Vancouver*. Vancouver: British Columbia Dept of Environment and Natural Resources, 797–802.

40 D. Seaborn. 1993. Memo to R.F. Tomlinson, 24 December. GeoVision – historical notes.

41 J. Cromie. 1994. Memo to R.F. Tomlinson, 27 January. History of Intergraph Canada.

42 D. Garey. 1993. Memo to R.F. Tomlinson, December. A brief history of Universal Systems Ltd.

43 S. Hill. 1994. Memo to R.F. Tomlinson, 13 January. Product PAMAP GIS.

44 S. Hill. 1994. Memo to R.F. Tomlinson, 13 January. Background information on DRS.

45 M. Simmons. 1993. Memo to R.F. Tomlinson, December. Background on INTERA TYDAC Technologies Inc.

46 A. Miller. 1993. Memo to R.F. Tomlinson, 14 January. ESRI Canada history.

47 L. Maidlow. 1994. Memo to R.F. Tomlinson, 14 January. Brief history of MunMAP and related software.

48 Energy, Mines and Resources Canada. 1984. *Report on Current Status and Users of Digital Cartographic Data Bases in Canada*. DSS contract no. 03SQ.23246–4–5508. Ottawa: EMR.

49 Inter-Agency Committee on Geomatics. 1991. *Report on Current Status and Trends in Federal Geographic Data in Canada*. DSS contract no. 19CB.23246–9–7644. Ottawa: EMR. Available at http://www.geocan.nrcan.gc.ca/iacg/.

50 Evangelatos, T.V., and M.M. Allam. 1992. Canadian Efforts to Develop Spatial Data Exchange Standards. In H. Moellering. *Spatial Database Transfer Standards: Current International Status*. London: ICA/Elsevier, 45–67.

51 G. Sawayama. 1993. Internet message forwarded by M. Sondheim to G. McGrath and R.F. Tomlinson, August. ISO acceptance of Canadian SQL3 multi-media "spatial proposal."

52 Canadian Institute of Surveying and Mapping. 1989. GIS: Challenge for the 1990s. *Proceedings, National Conference on GIS*. Ottawa: CISM.

53 Tomlinson, R.F., H.W. Calkins, and D.F. Marble. 1976. *Computer Handling of Geographical Data*. Natural resource research series 13. Paris: Unesco Press, 20.

54 Y. Bédard. 1994. Memo to R.F. Tomlinson, 11 February. Notes on ORION-CASE tool.

55 Smith, D.A. and R.F. Tomlinson. 1992. Assessing costs and benefits of geographical information systems: methodological and implementation issues. *International Journal of Geographical Information Systems*, 63, 247–256.

56 Thomson, Don W. 1969. *Men and Meridians*, vol. 3. Ottawa: Queen's Printer, 239.

CHAPTER SIXTEEN

Engineering and Mining Surveys

Adam Chrzanowski

INTRODUCTION

The term "engineering surveys," as it has evolved over the last fifty years, deals with special survey and precision measurement techniques developed for three purposes: (a) setting out (positioning) the construction elements of large engineering works such as dams, tunnels, and bridges; (b) the stability control (deformation measurement) of these works and their surroundings (ground subsidence and slope stability); and (c) the positioning and aligning of machinery and scientific apparatus. The term "mining surveys" retains its age-old connotation, to which have been added rock stability control and the protection of underground and surface structures that may be influenced by ground subsidence.

In the years before the Second World War Canada managed very well without precision survey specialists. Such work was covered by certain civil and mining engineers who, on their own, studied the instruments and methods being developed for surveys of high precision. With experience and intuitive common sense these men provided the survey control needed in complicated engineering enterprises. The many bridges over the St Lawrence, the mine shafts almost a mile in depth, and the high-rise office buildings that were beginning to appear in the 1930s were just a few of the projects requiring their skills.

Probably the one project that best illustrates the proficiency of Canadian surveyors in this line of work are the surveys conducted before and during the construction, in 1908–09, of the two connected spiral tunnels built on the CPR main line near Field, British Columbia. These tunnels were needed to reduce by half the "frustrating" 4.2 percent grade through the Kicking Horse Pass. The first tunnel enters Mount Ogden from the west, and circles and crosses its own line fifty feet above its point of entry, as is seen in figure 16-1. The track then crosses the Kicking Horse River and enters Cathedral Mountain where a second tunnel circles and again crosses its own line with a gain in elevation of fifty feet. The two tunnels together compose a gigantic figure eight more than 1.1 miles in length with a manageable gradient of only 1.7 percent.[1] As can be imagined the precise survey of this complicated enterprise was absolutely essential to its successful completion. When

Figure 16-1
Canadian Pacific freight train passing through the lower spiral tunnel, Yoho BC.
Photo: N. Morant. Source: Canadian Pacific Limited

design and construction requirements of engineering projects have demanded precision surveys, Canadian engineers have always been able to provide them.

Having said that, the development of new and remarkable survey instruments and techniques since the Second World War has shown that precision surveys are no longer the field for a dedicated amateur; they now require the educated specialist. By 1960 Electromagnetic Distance Measurement (EDM) of great precision had become commonplace. Laser beams to provide reference lines and planes were coming on the market. Gyroscopic theodolites were available to provide accurate azimuths in the depths of Canada's mines. The measurement of position (latitude and longitude) to a high degree of precision by signals from satellites was just around the corner. These inventions, and the study of phenomena such as the effects of the earth's gravity and atmospheric conditions on angle and distance measurements, were making it impossible for the non-specialist to keep abreast of developments. The time had come for the establishment of courses on these matters in specialized engineering departments in selected Canadian universities. The first of these was established by Gottfried Konecny at the University of New Brunswick (UNB) in 1960.

Although this important development started in 1960, Konecny's interest was mainly in photogrammetry, and serious research in survey engineering did not start until 1964 when

Adam Chrzanowski joined the programme. The first undergraduate courses covering advanced engineering surveys began in 1966. Other universities had noticed the need for research in this field. Laval University, which had for many years offered formal education in cadastral and forestry surveying, in 1965 developed a laboratory and research programme in the theory of measurement under Louis Joncas, but engineering surveys as such were not included. In 1965 the University of Toronto introduced an option in surveying, with courses in engineering surveys given in the final two years of its civil engineering programme. In 1980 the University of Calgary set up a new programme in survey engineering, which in 1993 changed its title to "Geomatics Engineering" to indicate the modernization of the role of the surveyor.

Thus it can be seen that certain Canadian universities are providing the required courses to train competent survey engineers. The impact that these men and women have made on Canadian engineering is best shown by describing some of the major engineering projects that have employed their skills during the last fifty years.

PIPELINE SURVEYS

Canada has a long history in oil and gas production. Oil was first discovered in Lambton County in Southern Ontario in 1858. In 1913 Calgary Petroleum Products found oil in Alberta, and by 1950 there were 2025 oil wells and 401 gas wells in production in that province.[3] Throughout this period oil was transported to market by railway tank cars, but these were soon to be replaced by pipelines. (It is an interesting coincidence that in the decade following 1850 there was an explosion of railway construction in Canada, and 100 years later there was an equivalent explosion in pipeline building.)

Pipelines are as sensitive to grades as railways, and the shortest distance between two fixed points (oil well and refinery) may not be the most efficient route. In addition to grades the pipeline location surveyor must consider right-of-way acquisition, possible ground subsidence, presence of geological fault lines, safety regulations at all government levels, environmental impact, and a host of other considerations. The survey of the Trans Mountain Pipeline (TMPL), one of Canada's first major lines, is typical of this form of engineering. It has been described by John H. Webb, former president of the Canadian Institute of Surveying, in his book *The Big Inch*. The following abbreviated description is based on his book.

The pipeline was designed to transport oil from the oil fields near Edmonton to Vancouver. The project was organized in the following manner: TMPL would make an estimate of the cost, a consortium of oil companies would be assembled to share the construction costs with TMPL, and together they would apply to the Board of Transport Commissioners for permission to build the line.

The vital step was the selection of the route. From the beginning an all-Canadian route was preferred rather than one through the United States. Naturally the passage through the mountains was the critical route decision, and several alternatives were selected. Each was studied on National Topographic System (NTS) maps and newly flown aerial photography. The most promising of these was selected, and a prominent Canadian surveyor, Guy Blanchet, was retained to make a thorough on-the-ground investigation of this first choice. His commission was to explore the route in detail, examine all "difficult passages," and supply TMPL management with a comprehensive report.

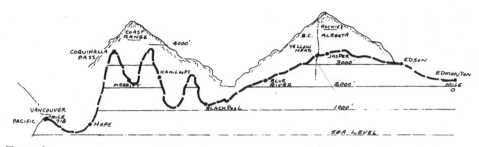

Figure 16-2
Vertical cross-section of the Trans Mountain Pipeline route.
Source: Webb, John H. *The Big Inch*

Blanchet's report indicated that the selected route was difficult in places but feasible overall. On the strength of this, tenders were called for its construction. Canadian Bechtel Limited was chosen to carry out construction, and their pipeline specialists started the marking of the right of way on the ground. The legal survey followed the initial marking, but the right of way was changed only if insurmountable legal problems were encountered.

The pipeline route started from Edmonton with 50 miles of good farmland on undulating ground, then 200 miles of timber country, 400 miles of rugged mountain terrain, and finally 70 miles of flat Fraser Valley land. Figure 16-2 shows the various elevations along the route and the major towns adjacent to the line. The critical passage from the construction point of view was west from the summit of Coquihalla Pass where the line drops 3640 feet in 28 miles. Ties were made to the legal survey fabric along the way and, in all, 2700 land titles were affected. The legal surveyors were also responsible for the levelling of the line. As grades are very important in the calculation of pumping facilities and hydrokinetic pressures, the levelling was done to the very close tolerance of one-tenth of a foot per mile. By September 1951 a close estimate of the cost was made and various oil companies were invited to join the project. Imperial Oil Limited as the major producer was the first to give its approval, and then twenty other companies joined the consortium. The Board of Transport Commissioners gave its approval on 13 December 1951, and the "Big Inch" was officially on its way.

Despite many local engineering problems, some of which required minor route changes, the work went well. Just like the driving of the last spike on the CPR at Craigellachie in 1885, the TMPL became a reality when the first oil arrived at the Burnaby Tank Farm on 17 October 1953.

THE ST LAWRENCE SEAWAY SURVEYS

The St Lawrence Seaway project was one of the major engineering projects of the 1950s. It led to a major improvement of the St Lawrence waterway, which made a highly important interior section of North America accessible for the first time to deep-draught, ocean-going vessels. It also permitted the large Great Lakes freighters to extend their range of operations to ports on the lower St Lawrence. The waterway was completed for the opening of the navigation season in April 1959.

The seaway project in the St Lawrence River consisted of constructing seven locks, dredging long sections of the channel, constructing protective dykes, digging canals, and building bridges. The related power project stretched from Cornwall on the east to Galop Island on the west. Its main components were the Long Sault Dam, the Iroquois Dam, and the Canadian and U.S. power houses that joined at the International Boundary, whose combined total of thirty-two generating units had a capacity of 18 MW. A headpond was created to produce an average operating head of 25 m.

An excellent account of various survey problems encountered on the project was given at the annual meeting of the Canadian Institute of Surveying in 1958 by W.H. Williams, who at the time was the chief surveyor of the Hydro-Electric Power Commission of Ontario. Extracts from his presentation[4] are given below by permission of the Canadian Institute of Geomatics (CIG).

Our work on the St Lawrence was governed by the fact that both engineering and cadastral surveys had to be conducted by the same group. Its stock in trade consisted of plane rectangular coordinates, and it was required to integrate and control these surveys over a five-year program.

The job of the Ontario Hydro Survey and Generation Departments at the St. Lawrence falls into three categories: hydrographic, topographic and cadastral.

The hydrographic surveys were conducted to provide data for the construction of a hydraulic model of the entire project. It is a matter of interest that the basis for the construction of Hydro's hydraulic model (a model, I might say, that was used with equal benefit by Hydro's contractors and those of the United States) was the considerable hydrographic and hydrometric surveys carried out by Ontario Hydro on the St Lawrence in the early 1920s. Plans were prepared from these surveys at 1″ = 400′, and to provide a modern check on these plans it was necessary to set up a system of horizontal and vertical control from Cornwall to Prescott, a distance of some 45 miles. International Boundary monuments were already established and co-ordinated to the North American Datum. International Waterways Commission monuments were in existence as a result of previous triangulation, and were similarly co-ordinated. It was deemed expedient, therefore, that wherever possible the existing triangulation net be extended.

Topographic surveys, the second of the three categories I have mentioned, were conducted for the purpose of producing plans to serve as a base for the design and construction of all phases of rehabilitation and replacement of essential services.

Thirdly, cadastral surveys were essential to the provision of the data that enabled us to acquire 20 000 acres of land, and to re-allocate that land to its new uses.

Even before the "green light" was given to the St Lawrence dream, Hydro crews were in the field. Early in 1953, three reference monuments were chosen, and three local grids were established. These controlled the work in the most active localities. To bring about uniformity of result, it was eventually agreed between Canada and the US that the co-ordinates for the entire project would be plane rectangular on the one origin, referred to the meridian of longitude 78 degrees, 48 minutes, and 0.618 seconds through International Boundary Monument No. 11.

Hydro's surveyors carried out approximately 80 check soundings across the river, at right angles to the direction of flow, and at half-mile intervals. Horizontal control was extended to each by selecting sides of triangles of the existing net at two-mile intervals. Second- and third-order triangulation was then run between the sides, tying in each sounding line in succession. Certain channels of the river remote from the International Boundary, and hence not monumented, proved uneconomical to triangulate. In those cases, high-order traverses were carried out.

A convenient series of triangles was selected for computation between bases, and a random traverse was carried through the triangles. Closures showed a general error of 1:20 000 or better, and the transit rule of adjustment was therefore applied to the co-ordinates. Towards the end of the job, the method of least squares was used to adjust several series of triangles, but the difference in adjustment between the two methods was not sufficient to warrant changing from the first.

However, to take soundings in the Long Sault Rapids would daunt the most venturesome. Our Hydro engineers evolved a method of suspending a weight and counter-weight by piano wire from a helicopter, hovering at an altitude of 900 feet. A flag was fixed to the wire 70 feet above the weight. By means of portable radios at four ground stations and in the helicopter, a simultaneous fix was taken on the flag as it came to rest.

All work was related to the United States Lake Survey Datum 1953 Adjustment. It was decided to adhere to standard precise levelling procedure, as closely as personnel, availability of equipment, time, and atmospheric conditions would permit. For this purpose, working rules were devised, based on the assumption that errors of levelling are accidental only and thus obey the usual square-root law.

These surveys, of course, preceded the actual start of the St Lawrence Seaway and Power Project, but the fact that they were done gave the job a most satisfactory head start.

In all, some 6500 men, women, and children, living in eight urban communities and four townships on the Canadian side of the river, had to be moved, together with their homes and goods, from areas that would be flooded by the vast headpond of the powerhouse to new locations beyond the flood-waters – a far different affair from surveying a power project in the wilderness.

Contributing to the success of this ticklish venture in human relations we find the Hydro surveyor. It was his task to lay out and monument new townsites, and to do so with the highest degree of accuracy. Slip-ups in such a venture would, to put it mildly, have been embarrassing. Those of our citizens affected by the venture had every right to expect us not to make mistakes.

Five hundred and twenty-five homes have been moved from their previous locations to their lots in the new towns, and I am happy to say that there is not a single case on record of a citizen putting the right key in the wrong keyhole – at least through any fault of a Hydro surveyor!

In proceeding with our St Lawrence surveys, topographic maps at a scale of $1'' = 400'$, showing five-foot contours, completed planimetry, and referred to the original grid, were required. It was decided to produce such maps by photogrammetric techniques, relying on extensive ground control for accuracy.

Co-ordinates were carried by high-order traverse on the re-established centre of side and concession roads, using the river triangulation as a base. This provided both for the extension of horizontal control and the retracement of the original township pattern. Secondary control was later extended by additional traversing over relatively short distances from the nearest control point, thus pin-pointing photogrammetric control. Notwithstanding the fact that basic control was available in close proximity to the points chosen, this work still entailed 113 miles of traverse to establish 700 control points to an accuracy of 1:5000.

To establish vertical control, Hydro surveyors ran 130 miles of levels to second and third order; these tied in 350 vertical control points. When added to the same 700 elevations previously obtained through the extension of primary control, they yield an over-all distribution of eight vertical control points per square mile. This later proved to be an excellent density. We found, by the way, that this operation was ideally suited to the use of the automatic spirit level, and we employed this instrument almost exclusively. As a result, we acquired all necessary vertical control for the photogrammetric work in seven weeks ...

The widespread and successful application of the plane rectangular co-ordinate system to our St Lawrence surveys provides confirmation of the many advantages others have claimed for this system ...

Sometimes the lament is heard that the St Lawrence should have been started years ago. In sober truth, I am very glad that we did not begin this monumental work twenty years back. If we had started in, say, 1935, the survey program alone would have taken ten years, or else we would have had to triple our staff to do what we did with our present staff over the past three years!

This talk was given in 1958, just as electronic survey instruments were coming on the scene. Williams' work would have been at least cut in half if GPS receivers and total station theodolites had been available to his survey parties.

MINE SURVEYING

The Techniques of Mine Surveying

Mine surveying is an important branch of engineering surveying, but one that is little understood by the general public. Most underground mines have concurrent operations at several levels. The actual work consists of the undermining and controlled caving of the ore, and it is of course imperative that the position of the workings at one level be known precisely at the next level above. This, in essence, is the job of mine surveyors, and their work must be kept up to date throughout all active areas of a mine.

Mine surveyors work under several handicaps. The most obvious is the lack of a reference object, such as the sun or a star, to provide them with an azimuth. Nevertheless it is essential that the mine's reference azimuth line be established on each new level opened. In former times, and even today at smaller mines, this line was obtained by hanging plumb-wires down the shaft to provide a very short line of known azimuth at each shaft station. Recent technical advances, as will be mentioned below, have provided mine surveyors with the tools to overcome this difficulty.

Another major disadvantage is the fact that most of the mine surveying must be carried out in cramped quarters, in three dimensions, and must follow the turns, twists, and rises of the works of the miners who are themselves following the meanderings of the ore-bearing veins. Dust, deafening noise of drilling and excavating machinery, transportation traffic in narrow tunnels, poor illumination, and very often knee-deep water add to the misery of the working conditions. Despite these disadvantages mine surveyors are often required to do very precise work, particularly in large tunnelling projects.

Systematic research work on the development of new techniques for mine surveying was started at UNB in 1966. This included the first post-graduate specialization in engineering and mining surveys; the first Ph.D. degree (Fouad Ahmed) was granted in 1970.

Canada's contribution to the development of new methods and techniques for mine surveying during the late 1960s and 1970s was immense. The Engineering and Mining Surveys Research Group at UNB developed and patented prototypes of instruments for laser shaft plumbing[5] and for tunnel profiling,[6] developed specifications and guidelines for the optimal design of tunnelling surveys,[7] and implemented in practice a new concept of integrated monitoring surveys for ground subsidence studies in which terrestrial surveys were combined with geotechnical measurements and aerial photogrammetry.[8] Significant research was also conducted at the Surveys and Mapping Branch in Ottawa on the evaluation and improvements of gyro azimuth determination.[9]

Today azimuths are established by very accurate gyro-theodolites that can establish true bearings by sensing the rotation of the earth, and thus the direction of the pole. Laser beams are used to establish horizontal and vertical lines. Electronic total station theodolites (i.e., capable of electronic angle reading and distance measuring) are now standard in most mines, and GPS is used for many types of surface surveys. Though the precision demanded from mine surveyors has increased, the new tools of the trade make their lives much easier than fifty years ago.

The Foundation of the International Society of Mine Surveying (ISM)

Soon after the Survey Engineering Department was opened at UNB, Chrzanowski conducted an evaluation of the state of mine surveying in North America. Visits were made to certain mines and questionnaires were sent to others. In all, forty-five mines were covered. The questionnaire asked about the educational background of survey personnel, the instruments being used, the methods being employed, and the technical difficulties being encountered. The picture obtained was not bright. In many cases the instruments and methods had not progressed beyond those of pre-war days, despite the impressive advances that had been made in other fields of surveying.

Data had been obtained from the above-mentioned forty-five mines at which some 380 persons were employed in surveying. The following is a summary of the data received:[10]

1 In 67 percent of the mining companies, no one in the survey section held a university degree.
2 In the remaining 33 percent there was no one with a degree in surveying; those with degrees included mining and civil engineers, foresters, and even one economist.
3 In 31 percent of the companies all survey personnel had been trained entirely on the job, without any formal education in surveying at the technician or technologist level.

These rather disheartening statistics were brought to the attention of Angus Hamilton, who at the time was the president of the CIS and later to be a professor at UNB. Sam Gamble, director of the Surveys and Mapping Branch, was also informed. During his student days, Gamble had worked as an assistant to a mine surveyor and thus was particularly interested in this situation. They agreed that as a first step a symposium should be organized to bring this state of affairs to light. The result was the First Canadian Symposium on Mining Surveying and Rock Deformation Measurements, held at UNB from 22 to 24 October 1969. Over 100 delegates participated. Being the first symposium of its kind in North America, it attracted not only Canadian surveyors and specialists in rock mechanics but also representatives from Australia, Austria, Czechoslovakia, Germany, Hungary, South Africa, Switzerland, the United Kingdom, and the United States. A total of twenty-six papers were presented[11] covering developments in such subjects as applications of photogrammetry, gyro technology, laser techniques, and electronic distance measuring. Problems in measuring rock deformation were an important feature on the programme. Rock bursts are an ever-present danger in many Canadian mines, and their prediction by exceedingly precise measurement and other techniques is of continuing interest to mining engineers.

Three important resolutions were drafted during the symposium:

1 The CIS and the National Advisory Committee on Control Surveys and Mapping (NACCSM) were both urged to make the Canadian mining industry aware that their survey

methods were by and large antiquated, and that in general their survey personnel were not trained to the standards of other survey activity.

2 The CIS was encouraged to extend its activities in the mine surveying field, and thus attract new members from the mining industry.

3 The CIS was encouraged to take the lead in establishing an international society on mining surveying.

The CIS took these resolutions to heart. Resolution 1 involved informal education and "missionary work," which over the years has had a subtle but beneficial effect on the mining industry. Resolution 2 was acted upon almost immediately. In April 1971 the CIS established a committee on Engineering and Mining Surveying, with Chrzanowski as chairman. During subsequent years this committee has organized symposia every three to five years. Papers from most of these meetings have been published by the CIS or its successor, the CIG. The 1993 meeting attracted representatives from twelve countries.

Resolution 3 was taken just as seriously as the other two, but the results were slower in appearing. In 1972 the Second International Symposium on Mining Surveying was held in Budapest. At this gathering, with strong support from the Canadian representative, an "organizing presidium" was established charged with the task of establishing an international society on mine surveying. This presidium met several times between 1972 and 1975, and finally, at the Third International Symposium on Mining Surveying, held at Leoben, Austria, in 1976, the International Society on Mine Surveying (ISM, from the German translation) was officially established with fourteen countries signing the constitutional protocol.

This six-year support by Canadians, and in particular by the survey engineering group at UNB, has meant that there is now a worldwide forum for the exchange of scientific and technical information on mine surveying and rock mechanics. When one considers the advances that have been made in survey instruments since the Second World War, it is apparent how quickly one could get out of touch if there were no societies, both national and international, charged with keeping their members up to date.

HYDROELECTRIC MEGA-PROJECTS

Construction and Survey of Large Dams

The postwar need for electric energy resulted in huge hydroelectric projects in the 1960s and 1970s. Hundreds of large dams and thousands of kilometres of power lines had to be constructed in a comparatively short time to satisfy the energy needs. The Churchill Falls project in Newfoundland in the late 1960s and the harnessing of rivers in northern Québec (Manicouagan-Outardes and James Bay projects) can be classified as world-class engineering mega-projects. New survey techniques had to be developed for construction and deformation monitoring of large dams and for the alignment of generating machinery. Both the dam construction and the building of the long power lines were under very tight schedules.

According to the International Commission on Large Dams (ICOLD) any dam over 15 m in height or any dam between 10 and 15 m in height with a reservoir capacity of over 10 000 000 m^3 is classified as a large dam. In 1988 there were over 36 000 registered large dams in the world. Canada, with over 600 such dams, is ranked seventh.[12] Between 1947 and 1981, due to the aforementioned demand for hydroelectric energy, 431 large dams were constructed in Canada. Twelve of these dams exceeded a height of 100 m and two dams (Mica in B.C. and Daniel Johnson in Québec) were over 200 m in height. By 1988 hydroelectric power accounted for 60 percent of all electric power generated in Canada.

Survey engineers are required at every stage of dam construction. Preliminary reconnaissance for a power dam is normally made using federal 1:50 000 scale maps or, if available, provincial maps at larger scales. When a tentative site is selected, very large-scale topographic maps of the reservoir and tailwater areas are ordered. The terrain configuration beneath the dam must be mapped at high precision for use both in design and for quantity estimates. Permanent survey control stations must be established around the dam site, and these must be surveyed to high precision. All surveys must be designed to satisfy the structural accuracy tolerances. In the case of power dams, mapping of the corridors for the layout of power lines is also done.

Additional surveys are needed for the drawing of general layout plans and the setting out of concrete forms. Surveys are required to monitor the ground stability during construction and during the initial settling. Other surveys are needed for the positioning of the generating equipment, and the related penstocks and outflow conduits. Finally, very precise surveys are needed to monitor the dam's behaviour, first during the loading period and then, long into the future, to detect and measure any deformation.

According to the world statistical data of 1993, one or two large dams fail every year. Theoretically, through post-analysis, each failure should teach us a lesson about the mechanism of the deformation or subsidence that led to the disaster. In reality, however, according to a study conducted at UNB for the U.S. Army Corps of Engineers in 1992 (see note 12), failures do not provide the expected quantitative information because of notoriously insufficient or ill-designed monitoring schemes and antiquated methods of deformation analysis. Hydro-Québec was the first hydroelectric company in Canada to recognize the importance of providing precise monitoring of dam deformations. Faced with the construction of the immense Daniel Johnson Dam, engineers Richard Moreau, Benoit Boyer, and Raymond Hamelin at Hydro-Québec realized that the design behaviour of the dam had to be verified by precise geodetic measurements aimed at the accuracy of 2 to 3 mm. An examination of this project follows.

The Manicouagan-Outardes Hydroelectric Project

Early in the 1950s Hydro-Québec, confronted by rapidly increasing needs for power, expanded the capacity of the existing Beauharnois plant south of Montreal and exploited the Belsiametes River north of Forestville. But these were only stopgap measures, and a much greater source of power was needed. Thus began the major effort of developing the Manicouagan and Outardes Rivers north of Baie Comeau. Seven power stations (Outardes 2, 3, and 4 and Manic 1, 2, 3, and 5) were put into service progressively during the 1970s. An additional station, Manic 5A, was added at Manic 5 in the 1980s for peak power needs. The total power available in 1994 from all these stations was 8200 MW. Both Manic 5 and Manic 5A depend on the same reservoir, ranked sixth in the world for its volume created by the very large concrete Daniel Johnson Dam (figure 16-3). With a height of 214 m and a length along its crest of 1314 m, this dam is the largest multiple-arch and buttress dam in the world.

Figure 16-3
The Daniel Johnson Dam.
Photo: *The Canadian Surveyor*, 26, 1, 23.

As implied above, very precise methods are required for measuring the absolute and relative displacements of concrete structures, since a few millimetres of movement (sometimes even a fraction of a millimetre) becomes significant. At the Daniel Johnson Dam a triangulation network of eighteen pillars, well anchored to the bedrock, with two baselines measured with invar tapes, served as the reference network. The network served two purposes: it permitted multiple angular measurements by intersections to targets attached to the downstream face of the dam, and it detected relative deformations of the bedrock surface within a 200 to 300 m band at the foot of the dam. Horizontal measurements of displacements of selected points were completed by alignment surveys along the crest. High-quality spirit levelling was performed along three lines: along the crest, inside the lowest gallery, and, perpendicular to the dam, to a benchmark nearly four kilometres downstream. The best commercially available instruments were chosen at the outset: Kern DKM3 precision theodolites, precision levels, invar tapes and staves, and forced centring devices. Some equipment was specially designed, such as sliding targets[13] for the optical alignment procedure. In the early 1970s EDM instruments were added to the observation scheme. The geodetic surveying techniques were complemented by plumb-lines and inverted pendulums.

An inverted pendulum, sometimes called an inverted plumb-line, requires some explanation. A normal pendulum consists of a weight swinging below a fixed pivot. An inverted pendulum consists of a fixed point below a moving pivot, as illustrated in figure 16-4. At the Manicouagan project the typical use was to have a wire fixed to the centre of the bottom of a 3-inch (7.5 cm) borehole that had been drilled as much as 30 m into the bedrock. The top of the wire was attached to a float that kept it both taut and absolutely vertical. Any

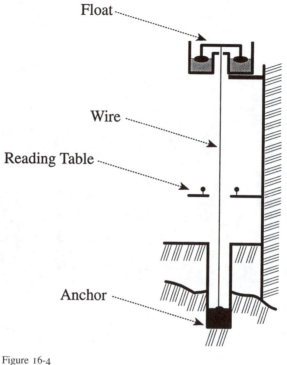

Float

Wire

Reading Table

Anchor

Figure 16-4
An inverted plumb-line.
Source: A. Chrzanowski

relative movement between the bottom of the borehole and the surface structure was reflected in the position of the wire at the top. This movement could be measured precisely, and gave valuable information on the stability of the structure.

Standard plumb-lines were hung in shafts in the four major buttresses of the dam, permitting the relative determination of displacement to about 0.1 mm accuracy between the different levels. This was done by taking periodic measurements with optical micrometers of the distance between the wire of the pendulum and reference marks on a reading table embedded in the wall of the shaft. Absolute displacements were obtained by means of the inverted pendulums anchored, as has been mentioned, at the bottom of vertical boreholes drilled 30 m into the bedrock. It was assumed that the foundation bedrock at that depth would no longer be affected by the combined weight of the dam and the water in the reservoir. (The inverted pendulum principle was adopted from an earlier development by Alfredo Morazio at the Electric National Energy of Italy [ENEI], an institution that is still one of the world's leading centres in dam deformation studies.)

At the Daniel Johnson Dam an inverted pendulum was installed underneath the two central buttresses, which permitted a link with the standard suspended plumb-lines and thus allowed absolute measurements to be extended to the crest. A third inverted pendulum was installed near the middle of the central arch. Finally, seven of the eighteen triangulation pillars were also equipped with inverted pendulums providing references for the determination of absolute displacements of observed points.

The triangulation and intersection data were subjected to least-squares adjustment, which at that time was still a novelty among most practising surveyors. During the second half of the 1960s the COSMOS program written in FORTRAN by Michael Perks of British Columbia became available. It was modified at Hydro-Québec by Richard Moreau[14] in order to adapt it to the particular circumstances in Québec relating to mapping control, setting-out surveys, and deformation surveys. The modified COSMOS, and an error ellipse estimation program called ERQUAM, which was developed in- house, were used on large computers at Hydro-Québec until the 1980s when the program KASPER, suitable for microcomputers, became available from the Geodetic Survey.

The use of inverted pendulums became the norm for establishing reference points at other projects requiring high-accuracy measurements of bedrock movement such as at the Super Collider Project in Texas, described below.

The implementation of inverted pendulums at the Daniel Johnson Dam had its share of difficulties, particularly in the drilling of nearly vertical boreholes. Neither had means been planned for the replacement of the wire in the same axis in case of accidental damage to the original wire. Solutions to these problems and others were found at Hydro-Québec in the early 1970s.[15] These included development of a methodology for the rapid drilling of small-diameter (typically 3-inch) almost truly vertical holes as deep as 50 m; the design of special anchors; and an apparatus for easy installation of the pendulum wire and, if need be, its removal and replacement. In addition an improvement was made in the monitoring system by adding a second wire, of invar, near the edge of the plumb-line hole for deter-mining vertical displacements at ground level. A travelling pendulum was developed later, which permits the monitoring of the variations in the profile of the borehole over time. Readings of the plumb-line positions have since been automated by electric transducers. Between 1975 and 1985 total station theodolites, a Hewlett-Packard 5526A interferometer, and the Kern ME3000 Mekometer were added to the monitoring survey equipment.

Needless to say the pioneering work done at the Daniel Johnson Dam has resulted in a greatly improved methodology for dam construction in Canada, and to a certain extent in other parts of the world. The James Bay project is a case in point. On this project the deformation monitoring techniques, so carefully documented at the Daniel Johnson, were employed meticulously. It is also safe to say that they are being adopted on many major dam projects worldwide. This should ensure a reduction in the number of dam failures in the future.

The James Bay Project

Between 1964 and 1970, predicting that the installations in the north-east would not be sufficient to meet the power needs of the 1980s, Hydro-Québec began examining the hydroelectric potential of several rivers flowing into James Bay. In 1972 La Grande Rivière was selected as the preferred initial site, and construction began in 1973. The colossal task, *La complexe La Grande*, was completed in 1985. All told, 215 dikes and dams were needed to create the reservoirs and their completion required 156 million cubic metres of fill. The outcome is the production of 10 300 MW from three power plants installed along the 800 km east-west course of La Grande Rivière. The power is transmitted to southern Québec by five power lines of 1100 km average length. A sixth line, completed in 1990, links La Grande 2 (LG2) power station to Sandy Point near Boston. Its length is 1500 km. The project required construction of 1600 km of roads, five field airports, seven permanent camps, and five settlements for about 14 000 workers and administrators. Surveyors had their hands full establishing geodetic control and laying out construction sites. Although the surveys were performed in wilderness and often in very isolated areas, helicopters, radios, and the comparative comfort of the permanent camps provided less "frontier adventure" to the surveys than the earlier surveys for the transcontinental railway or the transmountain pipeline.

A very tight time schedule was established for the Hydro-Québec surveyors, especially concerning the design and alignment of the power lines. Two years were needed to gather the preliminary terrain data, mostly by 1:20 000 mapping of a wide band of territory between La Grande and Montreal. This was needed so the most efficient route for the power line corridors could be found. Initial power production was needed in 1979, so this left only five years for the engineering surveys and the final design and construction of the first three 1000 km lines. Traditional setting-out methods for the corridors were considered too time and labour consuming for such a deadline, and would have entailed almost insurmountable logistical problems. The region crossed by the corrridors was heavily forested and almost completely devoid of access roads. In order to overcome the lack of intervisibility (an eternally limiting factor in ground-based surveys), hovering helicopters were used as targets. These were the equivalent of towers up to 2000 m in height, which served for establishing both horizontal and vertical control points needed to orient the clearing of the vegetation and for laying out each tangent of the right of way. They also provided geodetic control for large-scale photogrammetry that was needed to provide accurate profiles of the proposed paths of the power lines. Such profiles were required for the final design and optimization of the conductors. The large-scale photogrammetry (1:2400) for the power line corridors posed a challenge because the specified accuracies were 18 cm vertical and 50 cm horizontal (at one standard deviation) for the control points.

Unfortunately the equipment available for assuring the precise horizontal location of the hovering helicopter was not suitable to meet the 50 cm requirement. Therefore a new centring apparatus[16] (patented in the U.S. and Canada) was designed by Richard Moreau for this purpose. In short it consists of a centring device attached ahead of the helicopter cabin, at floor level, directly in view of the pilot. This allowed the pilot to keep the centring device in contact with a laser beam emitted vertically from a laser lamp set over the ground point being surveyed in. During precise hovers at heights chosen to provide intervisibility, angle and distance measurements were taken from known base points to the helicopter. Instruments included the Kern DKM2A theodolite, an MRB201 Tellurometer, and devices to correct for the eccentric position of the visibile target (i.e., the Tellurometer anntena) with respect to the middle of the pilot's centring device.[17]

The first power line for the La Grande project was completed on schedule. It was estimated that the cost of the engineering surveys was half of that for traditional ground-based methods.

SURVEY ENGINEERING DURING THE CONSTRUCTION OF THE OLYMPIC STADIUM

Setting out surveys for the Montreal Olympic Stadium have been selected as being representative of construction surveys for large buildings during the 1970s. Naturally other

Figure 16-5
The Montreal Olympic Stadium under construction.
Photo: M. Brunet

examples could have been used, but this one was chosen because of the complexity of the structural design. It tested the ability of the engineers and surveyors who participated in its construction during 1975 and 1976. Each element of the stadium was made of concrete, and all individual components were precast separately and brought to the site to be positioned in their exact designed location. The construction aspect resembled a huge three-dimensional jigsaw puzzle (see figure 16-5).

The geometry of the stadium called for a pseudo-ellipse at its base. The geometric centres of the four arcs of circles that defined this near ellipse were marked on the floor of the stadium and used by surveyors during the construction. The geometry of the ribs that defined the stadium would change in time because of the cantilever aspect of those ribs. Different geometries had to be calculated for the different epochs. These would take into account the stage of construction with the weight of the various concrete components and the effect of tightening by the post-tensioning of the cables inside the concrete components.

On all major construction projects the contractor has the task of positioning all components of the structure, and the consulting engineer has the task of verifying and accepting the work done. Such was the procedure followed by surveyors at the Montreal Olympic Stadium in order to eliminate gross and costly errors. Specific concrete components of the ribs called for precise positioning in three dimensions, and that procedure was delicate and time consuming.

Minor errors in precasting of the components could cause problems. If the component was too short, this could be compensated for by increasing the thickness of the joints between the components. But if it was too long, it could not be shortened. Distances were measured from known points inside the stadium to the positions of those specific components. These distances were calculated and compared to their theoretical values according to the overall design. The components were then moved by hydraulic jacks along x, y, and z axes, according to the derived increments computed at the site. The components were often moved several times before an acceptable position was agreed upon by the contractor and the consulting engineer. These acceptable positions were painstakingly reached using the survey technology available at that time. EDM with tracking devices came into use in 1978, three years after the time when they would have tremendously simplified the procedures for positioning those enormous ribs and beams. Today small positioning errors can be detected around the "technical ring" atop the stadium, but to the credit of the surveyors who worked on the project, these small errors are quite acceptable.

Construction started in the summer of 1974, and at the peak of activity required 125 survey technicians who worked both at the Olympic site and at the different factories that were producing the concrete components for the stadium. Work was around the clock and seven days a week. The pressure of the deadline of July 1976 provoked much tension among the workers, the union, and senior management. No problems were too big and a solution was always found. Michel Brunet, who was responsible for the surveying aspect of the construction, will always cherish the experience he gained whilst part of this audacious project. "To be able to visualise day to day the results of your surveying effort is a unique pleasure derived from working in the construction industry."[18]

THE ROGERS PASS CPR TUNNEL

Surveys for long railway and highway tunnels differ considerably from routine underground surveys performed by mine surveyors along the mine's drifts and crosscuts. The long tunnels are usually constructed simultaneously from two opposite directions to meet at a predesigned breakthrough point. Since tunnelling is expensive, accuracy requirements for the control surveys are usually high. The underground geodetic control is limited to long traverses with little or no checks on the accumulation of errors in the observed angles and distances. The possibility of directional deviation due to atmospheric refraction and other systematic errors is always present. Though the advent of precision gyro-theodolites, mentioned previously, has significantly reduced the accumulation of errors in guiding tunnels to their breakthrough point, the utmost care is required in the design and execution of the surveys. This is shown in the surveying for the CPR tunnel at Rogers Pass.

On 26 November 1982 the CPR invited bids for the fulfilment of a contract to cover the complete design, analysis, and survey for a proposed 14.5 km railway tunnel at Rogers Pass, British Columbia. The survey work would include a surface control network, two open-ended tunnel traverses, and control for a vertical ventilation shaft. The tunnel was to be driven from both sides simultaneously. According to the contract specifications the surveys were to be designed to achieve lateral and vertical breakthrough errors of less than 15 cm and 5 cm respectively at a 95 percent confidence level. In addition the positioning of the 8.5 m diameter and 350 m deep vertical ventilation shaft (to be located about halfway along the tunnel) was to be achieved with an accuracy of 15 cm.[19]

The purpose of the proposed tunnel was to decrease the gradient of the westbound railway track from the 2.6 percent through the Connaught Tunnel (built in 1916) to less than 1 percent.

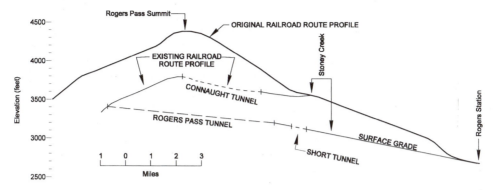

Figure 16-6
Condensed profiles showing the original Connaught Tunnel and the Rogers Pass Tunnel.
Source: Canadian Pacific Railway contract specifications

To make this grade improvement CPR decided to build 34 km of a new track for westbound traffic, including the 14.5 km tunnel and a second 1.6 km tunnel, as shown in figure 16-6.

The contract for the survey services was won by Nortech Surveys in the spring of 1983. The accuracy requirements called for extreme care in designing both surface and underground geodetic control. This was due to expected large changes in the deflection of the vertical in the area and to atmospheric refraction, particularly in the tunnel traverses.

Gerard Lachapelle of Nortech Surveys (now a professor of geodesy at the University of Calgary), a renowned expert in the geodetic aspects of control surveys, and Mark Dennler (currently president of WildCAT Precision Measurements Limited) designed the surface network with conventionally observed horizontal directions, vertical angles, and a few EDM distances. Robert Simmering was the chief surveyor on behalf of the CPR. Extreme care was taken with the observations. For example the horizontal directions were observed over two nights with sixteen sets each, using the precision theodolite Wild T3. The distances were observed four times over several hours with two different Hewlett Packard HP3808 instruments. Due to the expected large differences in the deflection of the vertical, and to differences in the elevation between observing stations of up to 1600 m, astronomic observations for latitude, longitude, and azimuth were made with a Wild T4 theodolite at stations 33, 38, and 30. These were intended to strengthen the network and provide information for the reduction of observations for the effects of the deflection of the vertical.

The horizontal network adjustment contained 69 degrees of freedom. No observation was rejected during the adjustment. The final result gave 4.4 cm relative accuracy between the two portals of the tunnel at a 95 percent confidence level as compared to the design requirement of 7 cm.

Special-order spirit levelling was carried out along the Trans-Canada Highway between the entrances to the tunnel using a Zeiss NI-1 precision level. The Special Order Canadian Accuracy specifications were followed in the levelling, and no problems were encountered. The observations were transformed into geopotential number differences, and the effect of real gravity along the route was taken into account. Adjusted geopotential numbers were transformed into Helmert orthometric heights. The accuracy of the height difference between the tunnel portals was estimated at 10 mm.

The underground tunnelling surveys were carried out during the period 1984–86. David Neufeldt was in charge of the field operations. The long tunnel was excavated from both sides simultaneously using the conventional drill-and-blast technique in the west section and a tunnel-boring machine in the east section. In the west section the concrete lining members were poured some 600 m behind the excavation face. In the east section the boring machine drilled a circular tunnel that had to be adjusted later to its actual design shape.

It was obvious from the pre-analysis of the long tunnel survey that if the accuracy requirements were to be met, gyro-azimuth observations had to be included in the traverse measurements. Otherwise there would be no check on the accumulation of random errors and errors caused by refraction. Another basic rule in tunnelling surveys is to run the traverse either along its centre line or in a zigzag manner in order to make the effects of refraction random. Due to unavoidable local conditions, neither of the two rules could be fully satisfied. A MOM GiB-11 Gyro-theodolite, which has an accuracy of about 5 seconds of arc, was acquired for the project. In April 1986, when each tunnel section was 3 km from the breakthrough point, the gyro-theodolite broke down, and it was found to be impossible to obtain a working replacement instrument in time to complete the surveys.[20] Thus the last 3 km of each tunnel section could only be guided by angle and distance measurements. The associated risks were known by all parties involved, but evidently the excavation could not be put on hold. The traverse in the east section was run along one wall of the tunnel because cables, pipes, and other obstacles prevented the establishment of monuments on both sides to satisfy the zigzag rule.

The breakthrough occurred in October 1986. The vertical breakthrough error was 1 cm, well within the 5-cm limit specified by CPR. The corresponding lateral error was 35 cm versus the 15 cm limit specified by CPR. A post-breakthrough analysis confirmed that the lateral error specification was exceeded due to the lack of a gyro-theodolite during the last few kilometres of each tunnel section.

ANALYSIS OF DEFORMATION SURVEYS

Deformation measurements in engineering and geoscience projects, along with precision alignment and the setting out of structural components, are the most demanding tasks of survey engineers. Even the most precise measurements of displacements and deformations may lead to a disastrous misinterpretation of the observation results if the repeated measurements are not properly evaluated for their accuracy, or if unstable points in the reference monitoring network are not identified. Full advantage must be taken of the integration of all types of deformation observations whether obtained by geodetic or geotechnical measurements. The problems of deformation analysis have preoccupied the minds of survey engineers all over the world for the past twenty years. Canadian developments in this field can be classified as being among the most significant international contributions in the whole field of surveying. Therefore a few words should be said about these developments and their practical applications.

The Development of the Generalized Method of Deformation Analysis

One of the first problems recognized in the technical literature, as early as the 1950s, was the identification of stable reference points. At the second International Symposium on

Deformation Measurements in 1978, organized in Bonn by Working Group 6c of FIG, an ad hoc committee on deformation analysis was created to investigate problems in this field, and to compare various methods for the identification of unstable points. Chrzanowski of Canada was asked to chair this committee. Several research centres including UNB initiated intensive research leading to significant developments and improvements in deformation analysis. During the first few years the focus was on the geometric analysis of deformations, that is on the determination of change in shape and dimensions of the object under investigation, including the problem of the identification of unstable reference points.

Confirmation of the stability of reference points is one of the main problems in deformation analysis. To obtain the absolute displacements of the object points, the stability of the reference points must be ensured and any unstable points identified. Naturally reference points are supposed to be located outside the deformation area but some may move due to local instability, inappropriate monumentation, or even the forces causing the deformation of the object affecting the surroundings over a wide area.

By 1983 the UNB team had developed a method for identifying unstable reference points by applying an iterative weighted transformation that resulted in a displacement pattern that would reveal the stable and unstable points.[21] At the same time UNB proposed a generalized approach to geometric deformation analysis that has become known as the UNB Generalized Method of Deformation Analysis, which is supported by DEFNAN software.[22,23] The method permits the carrying out of a simultaneous analysis of any type of geodetic or geotechnical/structural observations even if the observations are scattered in space and time. The method is applicable to deformation studies, not only in engineering but in the geosciences, for example in the analysis of tectonic plate movement, ground subsidence, and slope stability studies.[24]

Perhaps a non-technical explanation of the working of the UNB Generalized Method and DEFNAN would be appreciated by the reader who is not intimately involved with deformation studies. In elementary statistical analysis a trend line or curve is often calculated to pass through points plotted on a graph so that the sum of the squares of the distances from each point to the line is a minimum. On more complicated issues the graph can be three-dimensional, and a smooth surface could be calculated to pass through the points, this time with a least-squares sum of the distance of the points to the surface.

In deformation the changes in a structural state that occur at or among selected observation points are fitted by a function that, in some respects, may be considered as a surface. But this surface is of the changes, not the initial or subsequent state of the structure. This fitted function (i.e., "surface") is then used to generate a regular field of displacement or of strain. This more readily reveals the deformation. DEFNAN is a suite of programs that together can perform all possible analyses encompassed by the UNB Generalized Method. This includes finding the best-fitting displacement function as is illustrated in the practical example below.

The development of the UNB Generalized Method was a breakthrough in geometric analysis. At the eighteenth congress of FIG in Toronto in 1986 all members of FIG Working Group 6c agreed that the problems of geometric analysis had been solved. It was recommended that the international effort should now be directed toward an optimal design of integrated monitoring schemes and toward interdisciplinary physical interpretation of deformations (i.e., the analysis of load-deformation relationships).[25] At the congress Canada agreed to chair Working Group 6c. Between 1986 and 1994 three international symposia were organized by the group: in 1988 the fifth symposium in Fredericton, Canada; in 1992 the sixth symposium in Hannover, Germany; and in 1993 the seventh symposium in Banff, Canada.

Between 1986 and 1994 the UNB team (consisting of Chrzanowski, Chen Yong-Qi, Anna Szostak-Chrzanowski, James Secord, and several graduate students) worked vigorously on further developments in deformation monitoring. Some of the more important achievements were:

- Development of program FEMMA (Finite Element Method for Multi-purpose Applications) for the interpretation and numerical modelling of deformations using the finite element method (FEM)[26]
- Development of a method for an optimal design of integrated monitoring networks[27]
- Development of a method (known as the S-C Method) for the modelling of ground subsidence in mining areas[28]

The UNB Generalized Method was expanded into an integrated system in which the geometric analysis is combined with the physical interpretation of deformations. This gives a better understanding of the mechanics of deformation. A similar approach has been taken at the University of Calgary, led by William Teskey who joined the community researching deformation surveys in the mid-1980s.[29]

The Canadian developments have gained a high international reputation and Canada has been recognized as a leading force in all aspects of deformation monitoring and analysis. The UNB Generalized Method has gained popularity and has been applied in many international problems dealing with complex deformations. One application, the integrated analysis of deformation at the Mactaquac Dam, is briefly described below.

Deformation Analysis at the Mactaquac Power Generating Station

The UNB Generalized Method was applied to an integrated analysis of a concrete gravity dam and powerhouse at the Mactaquac power generating station in New Brunswick (figure 16-7). In the mid-1970s abnormal deformations in both structures were noticed in the form of cracks, opening of vertical construction joints (annual rates of up to 3 mm in the powerhouse), and leakage through horizontal construction joints in the intake.[30] Numerous theories were put forward by various consultants to explain these abnormal structural deformations. At first the theories included regional and local rock movements, transfer of water load through the penstocks to the powerhouse, effects of alkali reaction in the concrete, residue stress, and squeeze and/or rebound in the foundation.

In order to better understand the mechanisms and causes of the deformations, an extensive monitoring scheme was established by N.B.Power in the early 1980s. This included precision geodetic surveys (horizontal and vertical) and measurements with geotechnical instruments such as multi-point borehole extensometers, invar tape and rod extensometers, suspended and inverted plumb-lines, strain gauges, tiltmeters, and various joint meters and tell-tales across joint openings and structural cracks. Figure 16-8 shows a typical instrumental cross-section of the intake dam and powerhouse. In 1994 the Mactaquac Dam and its generating station were probably the best instrumented structures in North America.

Since 1987 the UNB Survey Engineering Group has been involved in the analysis and redesign of the monitoring surveys. A trend analysis of all observations was performed,

Figure 16-7
The Mactaquac Dam.
Photo: A. Chrzanowski

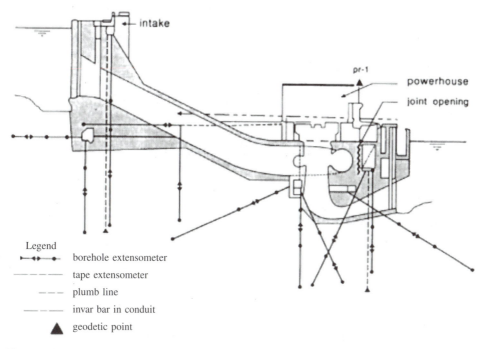

Legend

- ▶◀▶● borehole extensometer
- ––––– tape extensometer
- – – – plumb line
- — · — invar bar in conduit
- ▲ geodetic point

Figure 16-8
Typical instrumentation in a cross-section of the dam and powerhouse at Mactaquac.
Source: NB Power

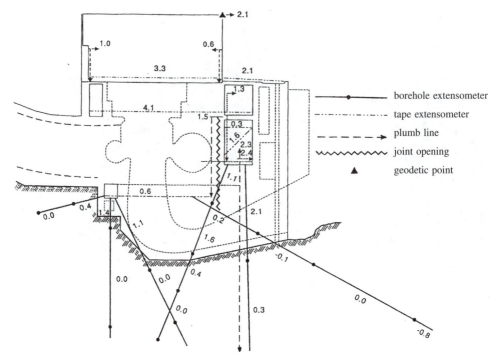

Figure 16-9
Rates of deformation (mm per year) derived from measurements in a cross-section of the Mactaquac powerhouse.
Source: A. Chrzanowski

and this indicated that the deformations were fairly linear in time, after the observations were compensated for seasonal periodic variations (temperature and water-level changes). Therefore the average rates of observation change could be taken for the spatial trend analysis. Figure 16-9 gives an example of rates of deformation (mm per year) derived from a sample of measurements taken at frequent intervals (most of the observations were taken biweekly) over a period of three years (1988–91) in one upstream-downstream cross-section of the powerhouse.[31]

The absolute displacement of points obtained from geodetic and inverted pendulums, when compared with other relative deformations, indicated clearly that the powerhouse was expanding. Examination of borehole extensometer results showed that the bedrock, at least under the upstream portion of the powerhouse, seemed to be either stable or was moving as one solid block. The plumb-line and joint meter measurements indicated a possible relative rotation of the structural blocks. Examination of the individual observables could not give the overall picture of the deformations. Therefore a generalized integrated analysis was performed using the aforementioned UNB Generalized Method.

Several different functions (full or partial polynomials) were attempted in fitting observation data, including relative rotations and translations between structural blocks and

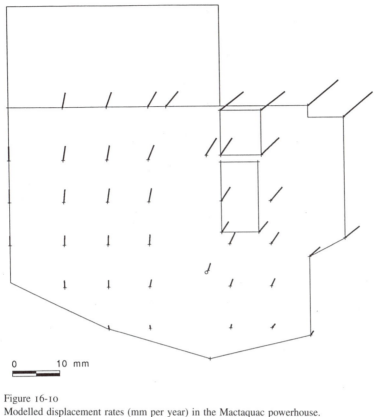

Figure 16-10
Modelled displacement rates (mm per year) in the Mactaquac powerhouse.
Source: A. Chrzanowski

different deformations in each block. After eliminating all the statistically insignificant coefficients of the selected displacement functions, the final model appeared to be quite simple, and led to the displacement field (rates per year) shown in figure 16-10. The displacements, and the strain parameters derived from them, clearly indicated a volumetric expansion of the whole structure. The results of the integrated analysis supported the earlier postulated hypothesis concerning the swelling of the concrete due to an alkali-aggregate reaction. To further corroborate this finding, a finite element analysis of the deformation was performed using the FEMMA software mentioned previously, and applying the average expansion coefficient from the geometrical analysis as the initial strain. A comparison of the geometrical analysis and the finite element modelling confirmed that the main cause of the deformation was the swelling of the concrete. In addition, the analysis indicated that the swelling had resulted in the creation of a discontinuity between the foundation of the structure and the bedrock under the downstream portion of the structure. This was a new finding that could not have been discovered without using the generalized integrated analysis.

Once it was determined that the deformation of the structure was being caused by the swelling of the concrete, remedial action was taken. This consisted of cutting through the concrete dam, top to bottom, with a powerful diamond-wire cutting apparatus. In all, six so produced have been sufficient to reduce the pressure (stress) in the concrete. The gaps have been sealed off on the upstream face of the dam to prevent leakage. The strength of the dam has not been materially impaired because of its firm foundation on bedrock. Monitoring of the whole structure will continue indefinitely.

THE MONITORING OF GROUND SUBSIDENCE

Ground subsidence due to mining activities and the withdrawal of oil, gas, and water is of major concern in densely populated areas, mainly in Europe. In North America, however, the problem was practically ignored until the 1960s due to the fact that most mining activities were in sparsely populated areas and thus did not threaten public safety or the safety of sensitive structures on the surface. In recent years, however, the problem of ground subsidence has become one of major importance in certain areas.

Knowledge of ground subsidence has been important not only for surface protection but also for a better understanding of the mechanism of rock deformation, and for better planning and safer operation in mines. Development of prediction methods for modelling ground subsidence and the development of new techniques for modelling rock deformation became a subject of intensive studies at CANMET (Canada Centre for Mineral and Energy Technology) in Ottawa and at several universities in the late 1970s. The UNB development of the prediction method (the s-c Method mentioned previously) was based on a combination of empirical methods together with an iterative finite element analysis, and was one of the more important achievements in this field. In monitoring techniques the concept of the integration of terrestrial and satellite geodesy, photogrammetry, and geotechnical techniques, all joined in an integrated analysis, has been put into practice. Two examples follow.

Subsidence at the Sparwood Coal Mining Operation

Between 1975 and 1983 CANMET was involved in the development of survey methods for surface subsidence in the rugged terrain and difficult winter conditions of south-eastern British Columbia.[32] The project was part of a study on strata mechanics in connection with the hydraulic mining operation of B.C. Coal near the town of Sparwood. The coal seam, known as the Balmer Seam, is very thick (12 to 14 m) and has a steep angle of dip of 30° to 50°. The surface terrain rises steeply from the outcrop of the seam resulting in a rapid change in the depth of cover. The seam has been extracted in its entire thickness by an hydraulic mining method with roof caving. This was done because the strata above the seam, being affected by faults, folds, and washouts, made normal underground mining quite difficult (see figure 16-11).

No previous knowledge on the behaviour of rock strata in similar conditions was available to use for comparison or prediction. Thus the subsidence in the Sparwood area was of major importance, not only for B.C. Coal but generally for the future application of the knowledge gained in other mining areas. Limited monitoring of the surface subsidence above the extraction panels had been carried out by CANMET in cooperation with B.C. Coal since 1975 when the first surface movements and cracks in the ground were noticed. Initial surveys by angular intersections to fixed targets on the hillside were replaced by a three-dimensional (3D) positioning method using an AGA 700 total station.

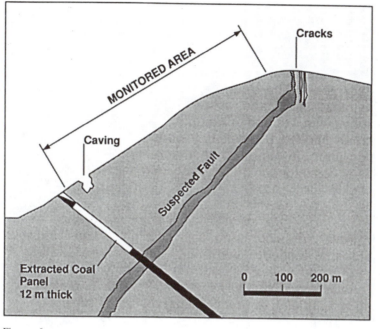

Figure 16-11
Coal Mine at Sparwood, British Columbia.
Source: A. Chrzanowski

These surveys were not easy. In addition to difficult topographic conditions, the snow cover of up to 5 m made access to, and visibility of, the targets practically impossible between October and mid-June. Therefore normal geodetic methods were of very limited use, being available only during the short summer season. This lack of continuity of measurements was of particular concern because the time factor in a study of subsidence is of prime importance. The development of a continuous monitoring system with telemetric data acquisition was given priority in the CANMET research programme. This was to be augmented by photogrammetry to give general "static" evaluation of the subsidence area. In 1978 CANMET issued a nationwide call for proposals with the following conditions:

1 The system must be capable of monitoring surface stations within a radius of 5 km having elevation differences of up to 1000 m.
2 No power lines would be permitted between the stations due to difficult topography and possible interference by wildlife.
3 The system must be capable of continuous, or at least twice-a-day, automatic monitoring of ground movements in temperatures down to −40°C.

The UNB team consisting of Chrzanowski, Faig, Kurz, and Makosinski, in cooperation with Ecological and Resources Consultants, submitted a proposal and won the contract in March 1979.

The proposal was based on the concept of using electronic bi-axial tiltmetres of the servo-accelerometer type as sensors, and radio transmission of the ground-movement signals at preselected time intervals. The system consisted of slave units directly linked to each tilt

Figure 16-12
Tiltmeter and slave station for the telemetry monitoring system at the Sparwood Coal Mine.
Photo: A. Chrzanowski

sensor, and a master unit with a microcomputer that served as a controller and handled the data from the slaves.[33] It also provided data storage and a limited capability for data analysis. The required low operating temperature placed severe restrictions on the selection of compo-nents. In order to ensure that the system would work unattended through the winter, it was designed to turn itself off (to a stand-by mode) after being interrogated by the master set. The design allowed up to ten interrogations per day for one year without recharging the batteries.

In August 1980 the prototype system consisting of five tiltmeters and their slave stations (figure 16-12) was installed in the area of the expected maximum ground tilts produced by the extraction of a coal panel that had started a month earlier. The extraction of the panel was completed in August 1981, but the ground movements continued until mid-1982. The system worked very well except for one slave station that was damaged (perhaps by a grizzly bear) in May 1981. Useful information was continuously recorded on time-related rock movements. A step-wise ground movement was observed with some evident rock bursts at the beginning of May 1982, almost ten months after the extraction of coal was completed. During the same period (1980–82) B.C. Coal continued conventional ground surveys with the AGA 700. In addition three aerial photogrammetric surveys were carried out at a photo scale of 1:700, providing material for a truly integrated deformation analysis.

The analysis was performed using the UNB Generalized Method. The maximum ground displacement was 2.5 m. The tilt data proved essential for the evaluation of ground movements. The existence of the suspected underground fault was confirmed through a

Figure 16-13
General view of oil rigs on Lake Maracaibo and the dykes that prevent the flooding of the adjacent land.
Photo: Maraven Oil Company of Venezuela

comparison with the finite element prediction model using the aforementioned numerical method developed at UNB. This fault was one of the reasons for the termination of operations at Sparwood two years later.

The Use of GPS in Ground Subsidence Studies in Venezuela

In 1984 the UNB survey engineering research group was approached by the Maraven Oil Company of Venezuela to design a scheme to monitor the subsidence in the very large dykes that prevent flooding of low-lying areas adjacent to Lake Maracaibo (figure 16-13). The subsidence is caused by the extraction of oil from the relatively shallow (300 to 1000 m) reservoir under the lake. Extraction was started in 1926 and has from the first caused subsidence that has been monitored over the years by standard levelling techniques. In 1984 Maraven decided to expand the monitoring to include horizontal displacement and strain components along the dykes. UNB was invited to make a proposal, including the addition of GPS observations to replace the costly levelling surveys and provide horizontal as well as vertical measurements.

The GPS measurements were started in 1988 using Wild/Magnavox WM101 single-frequency receivers, and repeated in 1990 using Trimble 4000ST single-frequency receivers. In 1988 the constellation of GPS satellites was only half complete, and the geometrical distribution of the satellites was quite different from the geometry in 1990. This is perhaps the reason why a significant rotation (over 1″ of arc) and a scale change of the GPS network was noticed between the two surveys. Similar rotation was observed between the 1990 and 1991 surveys.[37] Maraven purchased dual-frequency receivers in 1992 and repeated the surveys then and in 1994. By 1994 the full constellation of GPS satellites became available, providing an improved geometry and the analysis of the two campaigns has shown much smaller rotation (only about 0.3″ of arc) than in the earlier surveys. The experience gained in Venezuela has led to the development of a method for modelling systematic errors of GPS in integrated surveys. The method has been used in designing GPS densification control surveys[38] for the Super Collider project, and in 1994 was being used in studies of ground subsidence in two potash mines in New Brunswick.

INDUSTRIAL ALIGNMENT AND METROLOGY

One of the important tasks often faced by survey engineers is the alignment of machinery components or structural members where tolerances are acute. In the highest-precision alignment and in quality checks of prefabricated elements (e.g., in the auto and avionic industries), special measuring techniques have been developed creating a new field of surveying known as industrial metrology. These techniques, based mainly on special mechanical and optical tools such as jig transits, optical squares, aligning telescopes, optical micrometers, and, recently, laser interferometry have been used by mechanical engineers, millwrights, and even physicists. The first impact of Canadian surveying engineers came in the late 1960s with the developments of laser instruments at UNB. The UNB research team made significant progress in the studies on laser propagation in a turbulent atmosphere,[39] development of new techniques for precision alignment surveys using laser diffraction methods and self-centring targets,[40] and construction of the aforementioned laser plummets. These new techniques were still distinctly different from those used in conventional geodetic surveys. It was not until the advent of precision electronic theodolites in the 1980s that the gap between the geodetic and industrial methods narrowed. By interfacing two or more electronic theodolites with a portable computer, conventional geodetic methods in the form of 3D micro-triangulation surveys could be utilized in real-time positioning of industrial components with accuracies satisfying the requirements of industry.

One of the first practical applications of a 3D coordinating system with electronic theodolites was the alignment of a cyclotron at the Chalk River Nuclear Laboratory of the Atomic Energy of Canada in 1987.[41,42] The UNB team (Chrzanowski, Secord, and Wilkins) developed for the project a 3D coordinating system consisting of two electronic theodolites interfaced with the Macintosh Plus computer. Over forty magnets (figure 16-14) were aligned in a cramped laboratory space over a distance of about 40 m with accuracies better than 0.1 mm in the transverse and vertical directions and better than 0.2 mm in the longitudinal direction. The whole job took three weeks despite an estimate that it would take about three months using conventional mechanical and optical tooling of industrial metrology. Usher Canada Ltd has successfully used the UNB system for additional alignments at Chalk River.

Following the application of electronic theodolites, other geodetic and photogrammetric techniques entered into the industrial metrology applications. Beginning in 1989 the University of Calgary has conducted two interesting industrial projects – the Industrial Alignment Project (IAP) and Dynamic Alignment Project (DAP) – which have been funded jointly

Figure 16-14
Alignment of magnets at the Chalk River Nuclear Laboratory of the Atomic Energy of Canada Limited.
Photo: A. Chrzanowski

by the Natural Sciences and Engineering Research Council (NSERC) and a number of industrial firms in western Canada. The aim of the projects has been to develop advanced techniques in the field of precise alignment. Four members of the Department of Geomatics Engineering at Calgary (Schwarz, Teskey, Sideris, and Chapman) and several graduate students carried out research in the IAP (1989–92), and in 1994 were undertaking research in the DAP field, which was to be completed in 1996. Two researchers from NRC in Ottawa (El-Hakim and Rioux) were also at work on DAP.[43]

The applications of three relatively new technologies to align machinery have been investigated in IAP: the 3D coordinating systems (mentioned previously) with electronic theodolites, inertial survey systems, and digital imaging systems. The main accomplishment, in terms of system development, is the expansion of the two-theodolite coordinating systems to a multiple-theodolite system for determining alignment and changes in the alignment. This system has been in production and use since 1991. In addition a fast gyrotheodolite technique was developed for parallel alignment of rollers in pulp and paper mills; and in the field of industrial photogrammetry there has been extensive testing of digital array cameras for the monitoring of point movement.[44]

One of the most interesting applications of the systems developed was the use of a ring-laser gyro strapdown inertial system for the measurement of displacements caused by the

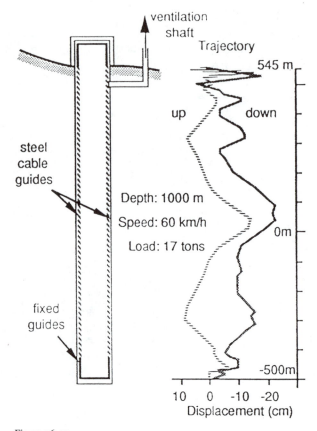

Figure 16-15
Trajectory of skips in a one-kilometre-deep mine shaft
in Saskatchewan.
Source: Department of Geomatics Engineering, University of Calgary

moving hoist skips in a 1000-m-deep mine shaft owned by the Saskatchewan Potash Corporation. The system permitted the plotting of the trajectory behaviour of the skips, which would have been a very difficult and time-consuming task if conventional methods had been used (see figure 16-15).

Two types of alignment-vibration monitoring systems are under development in the DAP project. The alignment component is being monitored by both digital array cameras and a laser scanner developed at NRC. The vibration component of both systems is being provided by Kadon Electro-Mechanical Services. The IAP/DAP projects at the University of Calgary utilize the most advanced technologies, which, together with the developments at UNB, will provide new measuring systems for the industrial metrology of the twenty-first century.

THE SUPERCONDUCTING SUPER COLLIDER PROJECT

In 1990 the U.S. Department of Energy began a $10 billion project to construct the Superconducting Super Collider (SSC) in Texas. This was to be the world's largest accel-

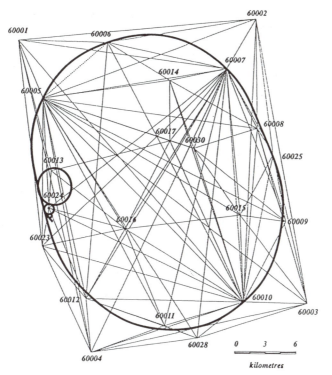

Figure 16-16
Layout of tunnels at the Superconducting Super Collider (heavy black line)
and the GPS surface control network used in the survey.
Source: A. Chrzanowski

erator of subatomic particles (protons). Its primary and mainly scientific task was to accelerate counter-rotating beams of protons to a very high energy, and then cause these beams to collide in large detector halls, up to 100 million times per second, and to produce for direct observation subatomic particles that had been postulated but not yet observed. These experimental events were expected to advance an understanding of the fundamental properties and the origin of energy and matter.

The main SSC collider ring was designed to be placed underground, south of Dallas, Texas, in a 4.2 m diameter, 87-km-long tunnel. Additional tunnels, including energy boosters and injectors, making up another 27 km of tunnelling were included in the design (see figure 16-16). The main collider tunnel as well as the tunnels for the energy boosters were to be connected to the surface by a number of vertical shafts of various sizes based, on average, every 4.3 km along the main collider ring. Over 12 000 magnets in the main collider alone were to be used to accelerate and guide the particle beams within the 50 mm beam tubes at the centre of the supercooled ($-269°C$) magnet assemblies (cryostats). To have the accelerator working efficiently the magnets in the main collider would have to be aligned in a perfect geometric plane (not a horizontal surface) to better than one part per million of distance (1 mm per kilometre) in order that the two counter-rotating beams should collide at the designed locations.

Tunnelling for the SSC project was to be accomplished using up to six Tunnelling Boring Machines (TBM) equipped with fully automatic guidance systems working simultaneously along different sections of the SSC ring. After completing the excavation of each 4.3 km section of the tunnel, a final invert would be poured and the installation and alignment of the magnets would begin without waiting until the entire tunnelling work was completed and checked for the closure of the geodetic control.

The above requirements presented unprecedented geodetic challenges for the design and execution of the control surveys. The construction of the tunnels and other conventional facilities was contracted to the PB/MK team, a joint venture of Parsons Brinckerhoff and Morrison Knudsen engineering companies. The geodetic control surveys for the SSC project were subcontracted to John E. Chance and Associates of Lafayette, Louisiana, and to Measurement Science Inc. of Denver, Colorado, who were required to work in close cooperation with the geodetic section of the SSC laboratory.

A total of twenty geodetic engineers were employed to design and supervise the geodetic control surveys for the project. Of the twenty engineers, fifteen were former students of UNB (with Trevor Greening, Greg Robinson, and Rick Wilkins holding key positions) and two came from the University of Calgary. This was certainly a victory for Canadian education in engineering surveys.

In addition the Engineering and Mining Surveys research group at UNB (Chrzanowski, Secord, Szostak-Chrzanowski, Chen, and Grodecki), and several graduate students, were invited by John E. Chance and Associates to be the main consultants for the geodetic and tunnelling surveys as well as for software development.

The survey tolerances for the excavations of the main collider tunnel and tunnels for the energy boosters were not to exceed ±108 mm error in the relative positioning of any two points located anywhere in the tunnel. Due to the strict alignment guidelines the specified relative positioning tolerance was taken as the maximum permissible error at the 99 percent confidence level, rather than the usual 95 percent. For vertical control surveys the tolerance for relative positioning was decreased to ±12 mm to accommodate the strict requirements for placing the final concrete inverts on which the magnets were to be installed.

Difficulties were encountered in predicting the influence of systematic errors arising from atmospheric refraction (particularly in the tunnelling surveys), uncertainties in the deflection of the vertical, and calibration errors of the survey instruments. Thus only half (54 mm) of the error budget of 108 mm for the relative positioning tolerance could be assigned to accommodate the propagation of random observation errors in the horizontal control surveys. The remaining part of the error budget was reserved for the accumulation of possible systematic defects. The SSC survey system was designed using least-squares simulation techniques following the procedures of the breakthrough analysis. For practical reasons the design was split between surface control, shaft transfer survey, and underground control networks. The horizontal surface control was provided by precision GPS surveys (figure 16-16) with dual-frequency Ashtech receivers yielding the average standard deviation of horizontal baseline components equal to $\pm(3 \text{ mm} \pm 10^{-7}\text{K mm})$ where K is the length of the baseline component in kilometres. Specially designed monumentation with inverted plumb-lines anchored deeply in the bedrock assured the stability of the control network. The vertical control was established by geodetic levelling of special order yielding the standard deviation of $\pm(0.56 \text{ mm}^2\text{K} + 0.13 \text{ mm}^2\text{K}^2)$ for one-way levelling over a distance K kilometres. The transfer of control to the tunnel (see figure 16-17) was provided by vertical shafts (spaced on average every

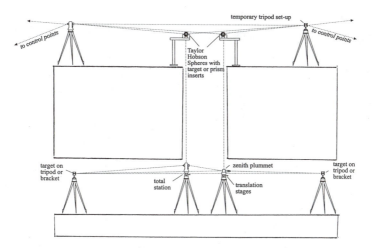

Procedure for the transfer of horizontal control

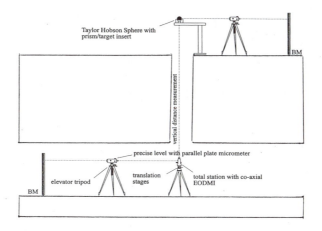

Procedure for the transfer of vertical control

Figure 16-17
Method for the transfer of surface geodetic control to the tunnel.
Source: A. Chrzanowski

4.3 km) using spherical Taylor-Hobson targets adapted from industrial metrology, Leica precision optical plummets, and total stations TC2002. With these instruments accuracies of 1 mm in height transfer were obtained. The underground control was run with double zigzag traversing (to reduce refraction errors) using GYROMAT 2000 precision gyro-theodolites and TC2002 total stations placed on specially designed wall brackets spaced at 150 m intervals.

By September 1993 over 20 km of the main tunnel (five sections between shafts spaced at 4.3 km), and several shafts, had been excavated. Figure 16-18 shows the exciting moment just after breakthrough for the first 4.3 km portion of the tunnel. The results of the tunnelling surveys exceeded expectations. The horizontal breakthrough errors of the five tunnel sections

Figure 16-18
Just after the exciting moment of the breakthrough. The crew are standing in front of the one of six Tunnelling Boring Machines.
Photo: PB/MK Team

were well within the given tolerances as they ranged from 5 mm to 24 mm, and the vertical errors ranged from 2 mm to 6 mm, after correcting for the upheaval of the tunnelling floor. This proved that the designed methods and techniques worked as expected.[45]

In October 1993 work on the SSC project was stopped by the U.S. Congress after about $3 billion had been spent. Thus one of the largest scientific projects of this century, which could have led to a simulation of the Big Bang theory of the origin of the universe, has not materialized. Nevertheless the project has supplied a wealth of geodetic data and helped in developing some new survey techniques and methods. The project gave Canada a tremendous boost in self-confidence, and was a convincing example that Canadian education and research in engineering and mining surveys has, within thirty years, exceeded the world standard. It has placed Canada in the lead in this highly specialized field.

CONCLUDING REMARKS

Many of the techniques of engineering surveys have been practised in Canada by certain civil and mining engineers who were interested in such work, and specialized in it. But it was not until the 1960s that formal courses in this science were offered to engineering students. Also in the 1960s research was started in Canada in the meticulous measuring technology that is required in engineering surveys. This research was started at the University of New Brunswick and was augmented, a short time later, at the University of Calgary. As has been illustrated in the case-studies included in this chapter, Canada has come a long way in this field. Today, due to the work at these two universities, the Canadian practitioners in this field are considered in most engineering circles to be among the best in the world.

NOTES

1 Mankin, J.H. 1978. Rocky Mountain Surveyors 100 Years Ago. *The Canadian Surveyor,* 32, 3, 370–3.

2 Blachut, T.J. 1957. What Should an Academic Education for Survey Engineers Be, and Why? *The Canadian Surveyor,* 13, 8, 523–7.

3 Hamilton, G.C. 1951. Surveying for the Oil Industry. *The Canadian Surveyor,* 10, 9, 36–7.

4 Williams, W.H. 1958. Surveys on the St Lawrence Power Project. *The Canadian Surveyor,* 14, 5, 185–90.

5 Chrzanowski, A. 1970. New Techniques in Mine Orientation Surveys. *The Canadian Surveyor,* 24, 1, 23–46.

6 Chrzanowski, A., and S. Masry. 1969. Tunnel Profiling Using a Polaroid Camera. *The Canadian Mining and Metallurgical Bulletin,* March, 1–3.

7 Chrzanowski, A. 1981. Optimization of the Breakthrough Accuracy in Tunnelling Surveys. *The Canadian Surveyor,* 35, 1, 5–16.

8 Chrzanowski, A. 1968. Role of Surveyors in the Mining Industry. *Surveying and Mapping,* 28, 1, 93–6.

9 1969. *Proceedings of the First Canadian Symposium on Mine Surveying and Rock Deformation Measurements.* Ottawa.The Canadian Institute of Surveying.

10 Chrzanowski, A., Y.Q. Chen, P. Romero, and J.M. Secord. 1986. Integration of Geodetic and Geotechnical Deformation Surveys in Geosciences. *Tectonophysics,* 130, 369–83.

11 Gregerson, L.F. 1982. Report from Experiments with the MOM B23 Gyroscopic Theodolite. *Proceedings, Fourth Canadian Symposium on Mining Surveying and Rock Deformation Analysis,* Banff, Alberta. Ottawa: The Canadian Institute of Surveying, 43–51.

12 Chrzanowski, A., S.L. Frodge, and S. Avella. 1993. The Worldwide Status of Monitoring and Analysis of Dam Deformations. *Proceedings, Seventh International FIG Symposium on Deformation Measurements,* Banff, Alberta, 3–5 May. Calgary: Dept of Geomatics Engineering, University of Calgary, 77–88.

13 Moreau, R.L., and B. Boyer. 1972. Les Methodes Topographiques Appliquées a L'Ausculation du Barrage Daniel Johnson (Manicouagan 5). *The Canadian Surveyor,* 26, 1, 20–37.

14 Moreau, R.L. 1969. Colloque sur L'Emploi de Programme COSMOS. *Hydro-Québec, Relevés Techniques.* 13 November.

15 Boyer, B., and R. Hamelin. 1985. Ausculation Topographique, Progress Réalisés dans L'Emploi des Pendules Inversés, Amélioration de la Fiabilité. *Proceedings of the Fifteenth Congress of the International Commission on Large Dams,* Lausanne. Q56, R4, 79–106.

16 Moreau, R.L. 1975. Method and Apparatus for Determining Geodetic Measurements by Helicopters. U.S. patent 3 918 172.

17 Moreau, R.L. 1977. Techniques MGH de Precision, Analyse des Résultates de 1974 et 1975. *Hydro-Québec, Relevés Techniques.* June.

18 Brunet, M. 1994. Letters to and telephone conversations with author.

19 Lachapelle, G., M. Dennler, J. Lethaby, and E. Cannon. 1984. Special Order Geodetic Operations for a Canadian Pacific Railway Tunnel in the Canadian Rockies. *The Canadian Surveyor,* 38, 3, 163–76.

20 Lachapelle, G., M. Dennler, D. Neufeldt, and R. Tanaka. 1988. Positioning of the CP Rail Mount MacDonald Tunnel. *CISM Journal ACSGC,* 42, 1, 7–16.

21 Chen, Y.Q., A. Chrzanowski, and J. Secord. 1990. A Strategy for the Analysis of the Stability of Reference Points in Deformation Surveys. *CISM Journal ACSGC,* 44, 2, 39–46.

22 Chen, Y.Q. 1983. Analysis of Deformation Surveys, A Generalised Method. *Technical Report no. 94, Department of Surveying Engineering, UNB.* Fredericton, NB: Dept of Surveying Engineering, UNB.

23 Chrzanowski, A., Y.Q. Chen, and J. Secord. 1983. On the Strain Analysis of Tectonic Movements Using Fault Crossing Geodetic Surveys. *Tectonophysics,* 97, 1–4, 297–315.

24 Chrzanowski, A., Y.Q. Chen, P. Romero, and J.M. Secord. 1986. Integration of Geodetic and Geotechnical Deformation Surveys in the Geosciences. *Tectonophysics,* 130, 1–4, 369–83.

25 Chrzanowski, A., and Y.Q. Chen. 1986. Report of the Ad Hoc Committee on the Analysis of Deformation Surveys. *Proceedings of the Eighteenth Congress of FIG.* Toronto, 11 June 1986. Paper 608.1. Ottawa: Canadian Institute of Surveying and Mapping.

26 Szostak-Chrzanowski, A., and A. Chrzanowski. 1991. Use of Software FEMMA in 2D and 3D Modelling of Ground Subsidence. *Proceedings of the Second Canadian Conference on Computer Applications in the Mineral Industry.* UBC Vancouver, 15–18 September 1991. Vancouver: Dept of Mining and Mineral Process Engineering, UBC.

27 Kuang, S.L., and A. Chrzanowski. 1994. Optimization of Integrated Survey Schemes for Deformation Monitoring. *Geomatica,* 48, 1, 9–22.

28 Szostak-Chrzanowski, A., and A. Chrzanowski. 1991. Modelling and Prediction of Ground Subsidence using an Iterative Finite Element Method. *Proceedings of the Fourth International Symposium on Land Subsidence.* Publication no. 200. Wallingford, Oxfordshire, U.K.: International Association of Hydrological Sciences, 419–432.

29 Teskey, W.F., and T.R. Porter. 1988. An Integrated Method for Monitoring the Deformation Behaviours of Engineering Structures. *Proceedings of the Fifth International Symposium (FIG) on Deformation Measurements.* UNB, Fredericton. Ottawa: Canadian Institute of Surveying and Mapping, 536–45.

30 Hayward, D.G., G.A. Thompson, R.G. Charlwood, S.J. Rigbey, and R.R. Steele. 1988. Engineering and Construction Options for the Management of Slow/Late Alkali Aggregate Reactive Concrete. *Proceedings of the Sixteenth Congress of the International Commission on Large Dams,* San Francisco.

31 Chrzanowski, A., Y.Q. Chen, J.M. Secord, and A. Szostak-Chrzanowski. 1991. Problems and Solutions in the Integrated Monitoring and Analysis of Dam Deformations. *CISM Journal ACSGC,* 45, 4, 547–60.

32 Fisekci, Y.M., A. Chrzanowski, B.M. Das, and G. LaRocque. 1981. Subsidence Studies in Thick and Steep Coal Seam Mining. *Proceedings of the First Annual Conference on Ground Control in Mining.* University of West Virginia, 230–238.

33 Chrzanowski A., A.W. Faig, M. Fisekci, and B. Kurz. 1982. Telemetric Monitoring of Ground Subsidence over a Hydraulic Mining Operation in the Canadian Rocky Mountains. *Proceedings*

of the Fifth International Symposium for Mine Surveying. ISM, Varna, Bulgaria, vol. 3. Sofia: Scientific Union of Geology and Mining, 249–56.

34 Armenakis, K., and W. Faig. 1982. Subsidence Monitoring by Photogrammetry. *Proceedings of the Fourth Canadian Symposium on Mining Surveying and Deformation Measurements.* Banff, Alberta. Ottawa: Canadian Institute of Surveying, 179–208.

35 Chrzanowski A., and A. Szostak-Chrzanowski. 1987. Some New Developments in Monitoring, Analysis and Prediction of Ground Subsidence. *CIMM Bulletin,* 80, 901, 46–50.

36 Murria J., and A. Saab. 1988. Engineering and Construction in Areas Subjected to Subsidence Due to Oil Production. *Proceedings of the Fifth International Symposium (FIG) on Deformation Measurements.* UNB, Fredericton, 367–73.

37 Chrzanowski A., and Y.Q. Chen. 1994. Modelling of GPS Systematic Errors in Monitoring and Control Surveys. *ASCE Journal of Survey Engineering,* 120, 4, 145–55.

38 Chrzanowski A., W. Greening, J. Robins, and G. Robinson. 1994. Geodetic Control for the Superconducting Super Collider Project. *Proceedings of the Twentieth FIG Congress.* Melbourne, Australia. Vol 6, paper 601.5.

39 Chrzanowski A., and F. Ahmed. 1971. Alignment Surveys in a Turbulent Atmosphere Using Laser. *Proceedings of the Thirty-first ACSM Annual Meeting.* Washington, DC: American Congress on Surveying and Mapping, 494–513.

40 Chrzanowski A., A. Jarzymowski, and M. Kaspar. 1976. A Comparison of Precision Alignment Methods. *The Canadian Surveyor,* 30, 2, 81–96.

41 Wilkins, F.J. 1989. *Integration of a Coordinating System with Conventional Metrology in the Setting out of the Magnetic Lenses of a Nuclear Accelerator.* Technical report 146. Fredericton, NB: Dept of Surveying Engineering, UNB.

42 Wilkins, F.J., A. Chrzanowski, M.H. Rohde, H. Schmeing, and J.M. Secord. 1988. A Three Dimensional High Precision Coordinating System. *Proceedings of the Fifth International Symposium (FIG) on Deformation Measurements.* UNB, Fredericton, 580–92.

43 Teskey, W. 1994. Letters to and telephone conversations with author.

44 Schwarz, K.-P. 1993. *Industrial Alignment Project. Description of Case Studies.* Available from Dept of Geomatics Engineering, University of Calgary.

45 Chrzanowski, A., W. Greening, and J.S. Robins. 1994. Control Surveys for an 87 Mile Ring Tunnel. *Proceedings of the Ninth Congress of the International Society for Mine Surveying.* Prague: Society of Mining Surveying and Geology, 203–9.

CHAPTER SEVENTEEN

Marketing Spatial Information

Gerald McGrath

INTRODUCTION

"Marketing" has become an established term in the vocabulary of Canadians during the past 40 years, both for the professional and general public alike. It is, however, less easy to define in such a way that the result is agreed by everyone. Indeed it has been suggested that "there are almost as many definitions ... as there are basic marketing textbooks."[1] The following definition of Marketing was proposed by Stanton and Summers,[2] and is chosen because of its relevance to the activities described in this volume: "Marketing is a total system of interacting business activities designed to plan, price, promote and distribute want-satisfying products and services to present and potential customers."

It can be seen that marketing consists of a number of functions. Not mentioned explicitly in the definition, but of central importance, is *market analysis*. Here the market for the current products and services of the organization or company is defined, and the identities of the users and uses are established. An understanding is developed of the way in which the market is segmented and is changing. This may lead to conclusions on what new products and services might be offered, and estimates of the size of the potential market for a particular new product or service. At this point the first element of the *Marketing Mix*, the *product*, is introduced. The concept of the new product has to be described, and detailed specifications of its form and means of production have to be drawn up. The proposed new product may be given test marketing. Decisions must be made about the *price* that will be charged for the product. This will require the economic and other objectives of the organization or firm to be taken into account, as well as external factors. General or directed advertising may be used as forms of *promotion* to ensure that the new product is made known to potential customers, and the effectiveness of advertising may be measured. National campaigns and educational programmes may be used to increase public awareness of the product or service. Finally existing or new distribution channels will be utilized to deliver the suitably packaged product to the *place* where it will be used. There is a wide variety of users of Canadian aerial photographs, satellite images and digital tapes, hard-copy and digital topographic maps, aeronautical and hydrographic charts, thematic maps, atlases, and gazetteers. The users include those concerned with defence, emergency services, and the exploration and exploitation of natural resources. Included in the last are geological prospecting parties, soil surveyors, foresters, and mining companies. Others are businesses, farms, schools and universities, the navigators of vessels and aircraft, and the general public in outdoor recreation and other pastimes.

THE MARKETING OF SPATIAL INFORMATION

The past forty years have seen a substantial expansion in the range of products that contain spatial information, and in the provision of related services. Table 17-1 shows that such products may be divided into two main groups, textual and graphical. The former is a varied collection. Examples are listings of survey stations and benchmarks with their coordinates and heights; specifications of control surveys; copies of documents held in land registries; the "pilots" for marine and aeronautical navigation; selected census statistics; and gazetteers of names. Increasingly these products may be available in electronic format recorded on magnetic tapes and diskettes, as well as the long-established hard-copy, paper format. Graphical products are, of course, characterized by graphic or photographic images. In this group are diagrams showing the locations of survey stations and benchmarks; aerial photographs and topographic maps; reproduction material from which topographic maps are printed; satellite and radar images; cadastral survey plans and index maps; hydrographic and aeronautical charts; and thematic maps and atlases. During the past ten years electronic graphical products have been made available to professional users, and gradually they will be used also by the general public. This chapter will not attempt to deal with the marketing of information in Canadian land registries (the cadastral textual records), Canadian hydrographic products (which are discussed in chapter 8), and Canadian census materials.

There are a number of special factors that must be kept in mind when considering the marketing of spatial information in Canada.

1 Initially the Department of National Defence was the prime customer for national topographic mapping in the postwar years. Its influence declined gradually as the needs of other government departments grew, and when its own participation in the national mapping programme came to an end in the mid-1960s.

2 The collection of data for the production of topographic maps, hydrographic charts, and aeronautical charts was initiated mainly by the federal government, and was financed from tax revenues. The data collected were, and still are, protected by Canadian copyright law.

3 For a long period the federal government controlled the methods of data manipulation and presentation. The specifications for topographic mapping were influenced by the needs of the Department of National Defence, and by international agreements with Canada's defence partners. To a greater extent aeronautical and hydrographic charting specifications were governed by international conventions and agreements.

4 In the circumstances there was apparently very limited need for market research. This did not change until the mid-1960s and later.

5 There was slow but steady growth in the civil market for topographic mapping, and for both aeronautical and hydrographic charts. The growing needs were for natural resource exploration and exploitation, urban and regional planning, emergency measures, policing, land management, secondary and higher education, administration, and recreation. The natural resource industries include mining, oil and gas, and forestry.

Table 17-1
Textual and Graphical Spatial Information Products

Type of Information	Textual Products		Graphical Products	
	Hard-copy	Electronic	Hard-copy	Electronic
Geodetic	x	x	x	x
Topographic			x	x
Cadastral	x*	x*	x	x
Hydrographic[1]	x*		x*	x*
Aeronautical[2]	x		x	x
Thematic	x	x	x	x
Statistical	x*	x*	x	x
Toponymic	x	x		

[1]   Federal government responsibility

[2]   Predominantly federal government responsibility

*   Not addressed in this chapter

6 The promotion of graphical and textual products was also affected by the circumstances that have been described. Indeed there was little promotion of federal map products until the 1960s.

7 A central feature in pricing federal topographic map products has been the concept of the full costs of the first copy of the map or chart being paid for from general tax revenues. It was expected that only the costs of reproducing the additional copies of the maps and charts would be recovered from the sales of those copies. There has been, then, a strong element of the "public good" in the pricing of federal maps and charts. Notable exceptions have occurred in the atlases produced and published for civil uses by governments and the private sector.

8 A significant fact in the marketing of spatial information in Canada has been the small numbers of each product that have been sold or issued without charge. For example in 1974 the 1:250 000 map sheet with the largest number of sales and free issues was the Montreal sheet. Over 11 000 copies were sold and issued in that year. Conversely not a single sale was recorded for more than 150 of the 918 sheets then needed to cover Canada at that scale. The system for distributing maps and charts has had to respond not only to the highly concentrated population along the southern boundary, but also to the needs of important users in isolated small settlements in this large country. Given the time-sensitive nature of aeronautical and hydrographic chart information, which must reflect changes to navigational aids and new surveys as soon as they occur, effective management of map and chart distribution has been essential. During the 1970s and 1980s the federal government gave special attention to this subject.

THE CHANGING CONTEXT FOR MARKETING SPATIAL INFORMATION

Maps and related products published by the federal and some provincial governments have been available *for sale* to government and private sector users throughout the period covered by this volume. *Marketing* spatial information has been a relatively recent innovation for

Canadian governments, though private sector publishers of maps and atlases have had to market their products aggressively for a much longer period. Technological, economic, and political circumstances have caused the shift from simple sales to the complexities of marketing. What are some of these factors? First, throughout the 1970s and 1980s the federal government made major capital investments in new technology for control surveys, computer-assisted cartography, and digital mapping to ensure that the national mapping programme was sustained and modernized. In the period 1978–80 the average annual capital expenditure of the Surveys and Mapping Branch, EMR* was $1.12 million, of which Topographic Survey accounted for over 40 percent. Capital expenditures increased significantly during the first half of the 1980s, rising to a maxiumum of $6.29 million in the 1984–85 fiscal year.[3] Such expenditures increased the readily apparent imbalance between the expenditures and revenues of this agency. *Second*, for the past twenty years the federal government – and more recently provincial governments – has experienced growing and recurrent financial pressures. Public sector borrowing requirements have been increased substantially. Forecasts of revenue from taxation have not been achieved during the recessionary years of the 1980s, and again in the period 1990–93. Financing government operations from general taxation has become much more difficult, and has resulted in greater scrutiny of proposed departmental expenditures. In turn the demands for increased cost recovery have become more vocal and strident. Departments responsible for surveying and mapping have consistently produced revenues from sales of their products and services, though modest in relation to their budgeted expenditures. They have become a focus of attention in governments' search for enhanced cost recovery. Almost inevitably conflict has arisen between the public-good element of government surveying and mapping and the search for enhanced revenues from increased user fees.

Third, partially associated with issues of financing government operations and partially separate, was the matter of producing and printing maps and charts within government departments. The corollary was the capacity of private industry to undertake much of this work. One component of federal surveying and mapping, that is aerial photography of Canada, had been contracted successfully to the private sector commencing in 1953. In 1977 the Surveys and Mapping Branch, EMR submitted a proposal to the Treasury Board to contract to the private sector a proportion of field surveys, new 1:50 000 topographic map compilation, map printing, and the production of aeronautical charts. The staffing of the branch would be reduced by 240 person-years over a ten-year period.[4] By 1987 all new topographic mapping was contracted to industry,[5] as was a substantial proportion of map printing. The latter was shown subsequently not to be cost-effective relative to in-house printing, or having map and chart printing undertaken by Supply and Services Canada.[6] In provincial governments the general practice has been to contract topographic mapping to private industry from the inception of the mapping programme. In such cases the appropriate government department is responsible for drafting programmes of work, arranging funding, and specifying the work to be done; conducting tender procedures; and supervising the execution of the contract.

A *fourth* factor is the growing orientation to users in product design, packaging, and distribution. One illustration is the co-publication of the fourth edition of *The National Atlas of Canada* with Macmillan of Canada, which was mentioned in chapter 10. The

---

* Refer to chapter 1 for the organizational changes that have occurred to the Branch.

company brought to this venture its wealth of experience in packaging and marketing books. During the first eighteen months after publication of the bound version, 63 percent of the long print run were sold. Conversely loose-leaf base and thematic maps from the atlas were not as successful. The lessons learned were noted by the Advisory Committee on the National Atlas, which recommended in 1974 that for the fifth edition "the public market be kept in mind in developing and designing readable maps, [and] that expert knowledge outside [the] Geography Division be obtained in developing the atlas."[7]

Fifth, as commercial Geographic Information Systems (GIS) software became widely available in the mid-1980s, federal digital topographic data assumed greater significance as a potential base on which thematic data could be overlaid. The topographic database was being built gradually with data obtained during 1:50 000 topographic mapping. The first sales of such data were made in 1984. Since the data received little customizing whilst it was being collected and processed, and specifically had not been structured topologically, criticisms were soon heard. The need for structured digital data has been confirmed in a recent study.[8] Provincial topographic databases were in their infancy, and they also were subject to similar limitations. *Sixth*, the development of GIS and the changing nature of the market for spatial information have together encouraged SMRSS to re-evaluate the business in which it is engaged. A task force within the sector concluded that one of its two primary businesses should be to collect, develop, manage, set standards for, and distribute geographically referenced data, but leave to private industry the use of the data and the development of value-added applications.[9] The task force also favoured a strong concentration on marketing and the development of a marketing plan for the sector. Though the focus here is upon the federal government, similar views prevail in provincial government departments. Evaluations of this kind have stimulated new government initiatives. These include licensing private industry to resell government topographic data in its original or a modified form, which would apply when topographic data is combined with thematic data.

Seventh, to a large extent efforts to improve the marketing of spatial information and enhance sales during the period 1977–90 were inhibited by a longstanding practice of the federal government. This is the transfer to the government's general revenue fund of the proceeds from the sale of SMB products and services. It has been a disincentive to increasing the number of staff allocated to map production and printing, has prevented a higher volume of sales, and has dampened creative marketing. The practice was criticized by the Task Force on National Surveying and Mapping whilst examining the functions and products of the branch in 1978,[10] and was given further attention in a subsequent evaluation of programmes in 1981.[11] It was not until 1991 that agreement was reached with the Treasury Board that permitted the sector to retain a portion of the revenues earned from the sale of products and services. *Finally*, government surveying and mapping agencies have been considered for privatization. Given the nature of their production operations, and the fact they are characterized by expenditures that greatly exceed their modest revenues from sales of products and services, such consideration is hardly surprising. The options have ranged from full privatization of the agency to privatization of one or more working units within the agency. Although the term "privatization" was not used in 1977, the federal map distribution function was the first to be reviewed in this manner.[12] Eleven years later privatization or a "Government-owned, Company-operated" arrangement were considered for both the printing and air-photograph distribution functions of SMRSS[13]. The decision of the federal government to transform the sector into a special operating agency on a trial basis, to take effect at the opening of the 1994–95 fiscal year, reflects the continuing government interest in privatization. Notable are the references to "enhanced revenue generation, cost reduction activities, [and] the creation of a marketing office."[14] The founding of the New Brunswick Geographic Information Corporation in 1989, and the province of Ontario entering into a strategic alliance with Real Data (Ontario) for the creation of a jointly owned company called Teranet, attest to similar interests in the provinces.

MARKETING SPATIAL INFORMATION IN EMR

During the postwar period three major periods of marketing spatial information within EMR can be recognized. Each will be discussed in this chapter.

1947–76

ORGANIZATION AND RESPONSIBILITIES
At the conclusion of the Second World War the federal Department of Mines and Resources included the Surveys and Engineering Branch, of which Legal Surveys and Map Service was one division. Amongst the division's responsibilities was the production, distribution, and sale of topographic maps, plans, and publications. In 1946–47 the 350 000 items distributed were nearly 250 percent greater than at any time prior to the war. This substantially increased distribution was attributed to a wide variety of civilian users. It was not, however, due to advertising as there had been no publicity since 1939. There was a small network of dealers, to whom a 40-percent discount was given for resale of the maps. In the same year the service assumed responsibility from the Department of Transport for the preparation and circulation of the two volumes of the *Canada Air Pilot*. Distribution increased rapidly during the following two years (figure 17-1), part of which was said to be due to "an awakening of the public's map interest," which "has been more strongly stressed in the demand for those maps covering the summer playgrounds of the nation."[15] More important were the increasing needs for maps and charts due to the expansion of the Canadian economy (particularly the rapid growth of the mineral industry), and defence requirements with their focus upon the North. The Map Distribution Office (MDO) was first mentioned in 1950, and was moved several times during the period. The first was in 1953 when map sales were transferred to the Map Compilation and Reproduction Division. This and subsequent organizational changes resulted in fewer items being distributed by MDO. After the transfer of MDO to the Map Design/Printing Division, above-average increases in demand were experienced. The most significant change occurred in 1966 when, after a major review of policy, the map storage and distribution functions of the SMB and the Army Survey Establishment (ASE) were integrated; and the Marketing and Information Office was also established.[16] The Canada Map Office (CMO) was created in 1972, and in 1974–75 its substantial stock was moved into a new building on Bentley Avenue in Ottawa. Increased demands brought pressure to revise and print maps more frequently, and consequently the printing facilities had to be expanded on several occasions.

THE MARKET
In 1966 the first federal Map Users Conference was held in Ottawa under the sponsorship of the National Advisory Committee on Control Surveys and Mapping (NACCSM). This

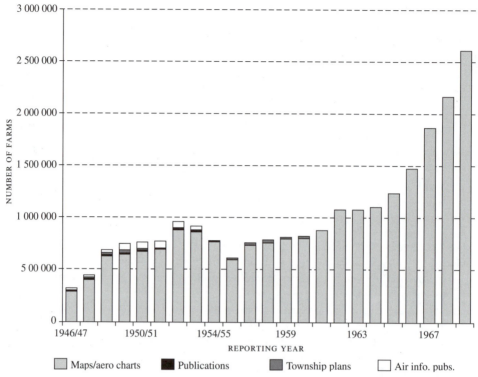

Figure 17-1
Maps, charts, plans, and publications distributed by Surveys and Mapping Branch.
Source: SMRSS, EMR

form of *market research* may have been influenced by similar ventures in the U.S. and the U.K. at about the same time. A systematic attempt was made to collect data on federal and provincial mapping requirements and map uses, and representatives from governments and Crown corporations discussed their mapping-programme requirements. Unfortunately the occasion was not repeated. This may have been due to criticisms of aspects of the National Topographic Series (NTS) map specifications, for example the UTM grid and road symbols without casings, slow updating, and the need to extend map coverage more rapidly than SMB could achieve. That "the delegates were asking for everything but the moon"[17] was one comment on the conference. Although a second conference was not convened, there are indications that in 1974 thought was given to doing so.[18] Instead a sub-committee of the NACCSM was set up under Tuzo Wilson, which included map users and producers. Its task was to examine the needs for maps of the North, and the possibility that new styles of mapping might be developed. Another attempt to define map requirements in a semi-public forum was the Northern Mapping Study in 1974. Nonetheless the Branch *was* willing to explore the needs for change. The *product definition* study on tourist mapping of the Waterton Lakes National Park, undertaken by McGrath in 1969 using sample surveys, is one example.[19] The results were reflected in a new design for a map of the park, which was published in 1974. The SMB was also concerned about the future of the 1:250 000 NTS

Series, completed in 1971. McGrath and Castner were contracted to investigate the situation in 1974, on which they reported in 1975[20] prior to a second phase being authorized.

PROMOTION AND PRICING

The modest *promotional* activities during the early years of the period were intensified in 1963 when information kiosks were opened at the National Sportsmen's Show, Toronto, and the Central Canada Exhibition in Ottawa. The National Boat Show in Toronto was added subsequently, and by 1969 there were booths staffed at nine regional and sportsmen's shows. As part of the enhanced public relations effort the MDO organized tours of the SMB which in 1969 were attended by over 1500 students, teachers, and officials. Illustrated talks were given at local schools, and a publicity film was prepared for this purpose. Advertising was placed in newspapers and magazines, and articles about the work of the SMB and its units appeared in professional and other journals. After the first printing of a brochure on the history of the National Air Photo Library in December 1962, of which 10 000 copies were distributed, a second edition was necessary in April 1963. Central principles in *pricing* the products of the SMB were allocating the costs of map compilation and preparation to its operating budget, and recovering the costs of reproduction and distribution from the purchasers. Exceptions to the latter were large map orders from federal and provincial government departments, which were sent free of charge until 1966, when the practice of selling with a 70-percent discount was introduced. In 1972 this was used as an inducement to provincial governments to centralize orders for NTS maps through a single agency in each province. It was also suggested that distribution centres be set up in the major cities, which would be map stores for the general public and would service local dealers. Recovering the full and growing costs of reproduction and distribution was a recurrent problem that threatened the core mapping programme of the SMB. It led to the Treasury Board directive and order in council during 1972 that full recovery should be accomplished within three years, partially through progressively increased prices for maps and further reduction in free issues.[21] Prices of products were therefore increased in 1973, 1975, and 1976.

DISTRIBUTION

Although the map stocks of more than 9 million copies had been consolidated in a map depot at the new Booth Street headquarters of the SMB in 1961, a more significant change occurred in 1966. This was the integration of the separate civilian and military map distribution facilities, which was noted earlier. At the same time the building of a dealer network was begun to meet the objective of bringing sales of NTS maps closer to the public. Separate dealers were appointed for the sale of topographic maps and aeronautical charts respectively; and provision was made for a modest level of support to the dealers through visits in alternate years. By 1970–71 there were 345 approved topographic map dealers in Canada, and 246 aeronautical chart dealers. The numbers of both grew annually such that by the end of this period there were 475 topographic and 304 aeronautical chart dealers. Another element of decentralizing map distribution was utilizing federal and provincial agencies across the country, thereby relieving pressure on the resources of CMO and the SMB. The earliest arrangement was with the Geological Survey of Canada (GSC) for the Institute of Sedimentary and Petroleum Geology in Calgary to be a new distribution centre for NTS maps covering the four western provinces and the territories. A third element of ensuring wider dissemination of topographic maps was the map depository. University map libraries and large public libraries were selected as depositories for full or partial collections of federal topographic maps. By 1973–74 there were 138 such depositories. They required constant liaison and, in 1973, a review of their nature, expansion, significance, and arrangements.

The need for management information systems in Surveys and Mapping Branch was recognized by Jack Davidson, who in 1963 was appointed consultant to the director after retirement from the U.S. Geological Survey. Davidson arranged for Fred Silk from P.S. Ross and Partners to undertake several studies, one of which recommended that a Map Inventory Control System (MICS) be created for the MDO. John A. McArthur guided the development of the system, which utilized punched cards prepared from hard-copy data listings, and batch processing at two-week intervals on the Treasury Board IBM mainframe computer. The system became operational in May 1968, and continued until it was integrated into a more modern system in 1985. About the same time methods of inventory control used in industry were investigated to see whether they could be applied to maps and charts so that customer demand and printing requirements could be estimated more accurately.[22] However the forecasting of Economic Order Quantities proved to be a recurrent difficulty. After CMO was created in 1972, the Department of Supply and Services (DSS) recommended to EMR that an order-processing system should be introduced based on an NCR accounting machine. This was implemented and also remained in service until 1985. Other developments at CMO in handling orders for maps included conversion of the mailing lists from Addressograph to Alphatext; introducing a self-mailer type of renewal notice; and the commencement of an after-hours answering service in 1974–75. The many improvements in map distribution increased the number of orders received by CMO, but equally important the average number of maps per order also rose. With the enlarged dealer network and new distribution centre in Calgary, more purchases were made and orders submitted through the network than directly to CMO. Nevertheless the effectiveness and cost of the map distribution system continued to exercise the minds of SMB managers, and led in 1976 to the commissioning of a study on an optimal distribution system.

1977–89

ORGANIZATION AND RESPONSIBILITIES

The Reproduction and Distribution Directorate (RDD) was created under the management of John McArthur during a reorganization of Surveys and Mapping Branch early in 1977. For the first time units with interlocking responsibilities were brought together. These were the reproduction and printing of maps, aeronautical charts, and hydrographic charts, the reproduction of air photographs and other images, and the storage and distribution of maps and photographs. This significant step allowed McArthur to take new initiatives. The first of many was in October 1977 when he raised the possibility of integrating the distribution of federal and provincial maps in a single system of outlets,[23] and sought advice from the provinces on how distribution through the dealer network could be improved, to which Alberta and Manitoba responded. In May 1977 the task force was established to report on national surveying and mapping. In the course of its work it also addressed issues of printing, distribution, revenue from sales, and marketing. Ten years elapsed before further reorganization occurred after SMRSS was established in April 1987. The directorate was closed and replaced by the Cartographic Information and Distribution Centre, to which new responsibilities were assigned for digital cartographic products and the provision of common services to the sector.

THE MARKET

Market research was reflected in several studies during the period. Prior to 1982 all topographic maps had been distributed to dealers in flat form. Storing and handling flat maps was troublesome to some dealers. The situation was reviewed by CMO, which recommended that folded topographic maps should be introduced after appropriate folding and wrapping machines were bought. These changes were implemented successfully. A second study was undertaken for the directorate by McGrath and Silic.[24] This utilized a large sample survey to examine the use of topographic and other maps by visitors to provincial parks in Ontario.

PRINTING

Printing maps and charts proved to be a challenging activity for several reasons. The first was contracting printing to private industry, consistent with government policy that work should be contracted wherever possible. This was begun in 1974–75 when some 3.5 percent of printing (measured by the number of copies) was contracted out. It rose to 8 percent in subsequent years; increased to 20 percent as a result of an in-house study made in 1979–80; and then accelerated rapidly to 27 percent in 1980–81 and 42 percent in 1981–82. These achievements were not without difficulty, in part because industry viewed map and chart printing unenthusiastically. The number of copies of each map or chart to be printed was small. Very careful registration of the colour separations was essential. And many of the charts required a large-format press. The situation was also influenced by what may be described as a running battle fought with DSS between 1975 and 1983. The SMB planned to modernize the printing plant by retiring old two-colour and purchasing new larger-format, multi-colour presses. DSS contended that it had the mandate to approve all purchases of printing machinery, and claimed the right to print maps and charts. Neither the task force in 1978, nor a subsequent modernization plan devised by Brig. L.J. Harris, was successful in changing the position of DSS. After an observation of the auditor general a decision was left to Treasury Board ministers who approved the purchase of a wide-body four-colour press in 1983, and a forty-inch seven-colour press in 1985. The gain in productivity from the latter was nine times that of the two-colour machines that had been retired.

PRODUCTS AND PROMOTION

An important *product change* that followed an earlier initiative in topographic mapping was begun in 1980 and concluded ten years later. This was the change in format of aeronautical charts. It reduced the previous national coverage of 219 CPC charts to 51 VNC charts, and in turn the number of charts to be printed and the number of charts sold. The major improvements that were made in other aspects of marketing were not matched in *promotion*. For a time the SMB curtailed visits to dealers and attendance at shows because the visits were not considered to be cost-effective. Yet the SMB cooperated with the Ontario Department of Education in the production of a booklet of aerial photographs and topographic maps for use in schools. It began to advertise its maps in the Yellow Pages in 1981 under the name of each full-map dealer. Interest in a comprehensive catalogue and brochure as part of a public information programme led to the study undertaken by McGrath and Silic in 1985. And world and Canada maps were offered as premiums in association with a MacLean-Hunter magazine.

PRICING

The central issue in pricing was the cancellation of "vote netting" in 1977–78 after which all revenues from sales had to be deposited in the government's Consolidated Revenue Account. This, the task force argued, reduced the incentive of the SMB to sell more maps and charts as it would divert resources from the core mapping activities. In a significant statement the task force contended that "the objective of map distribution should be to maximise distribution, not to maximise the return on distribution investment."[25] There were, nevertheless, major price increases in June 1980 consistent with the Treasury Board directive. This saw the price of a topographic map rise from $1.50 to $2.50, and the total volume of maps and charts sold to customers fall by 9.5 percent in the following fiscal year (though there had also been a decline of 7.5 percent from peak sales in 1979–80). Further price increases occurred in 1982, 1985, 1986, and 1988. By 1985 digital data were available for purchase. As the outcome of research and development they were priced in an ad hoc manner in order to encourage experimentation by users, and to stimulate demand. Judged by the increasing number of requests received, which rose from nine in 1984–85 to fifty-three in 1987–88, this approach seems to have been successful. The agreement that the purchaser signed required a report to be submitted on each project which utilized digital data. The requests trebled in 1988–89, during which new pricing and distribution policies were published. These dealt with digital data explicitly, and stated that prices would include the tape, the cost of copying the data onto tape, shipping, and appropriate taxes. The price for a standard magnetic-tape map file was then increased from $140 to $160. Only months later a draft policy directive was written for the distribution of electronic information. This included the objective of recovering "… a modest amount of revenue from the users of this information for [the government] which has made a major investment in assembling and maintaining this geographic information …" This marked a significant departure from the pricing policy that had prevailed, and from the principle that only the costs of repro-duction and distribution should be recovered. The directive gave warning that the price of a standard topographic map sheet digital file would become $500. In the 1989 draft policy statement the change was made more explicit in these terms: "the user should be called upon to bear an increased share of the costs of the generation and maintenance"[26] of the digital data.

DISTRIBUTION

The greatest changes occurred in distribution. They began in 1976–77 with the decision to contract the distribution of aeronautical information publications to ARC Industries Ltd. Woods, Gordon were then asked to study the overall system for distributing topographic and special-interest maps in Canada. Amongst the specific tasks were identifying options for wholesale and retail distribution, and defining the role of the CMO in distribution. The far-ranging study visualized the distribution of maps to dealers being contracted to a national wholesale distribution firm rather than regional organizations. Although several recommendations of the study were to guide later developments, the overall view of RDD

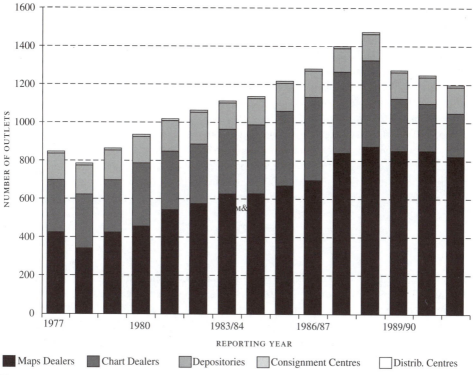

Figure 17-2
Map/aero chart distribution network, Surveys and Mapping Branch.
Source: SMRSS, EMR

was one of disappointment that an economically viable alternative to in-house distribution had not been found. Nevertheless McArthur pursued the twin goals of transferring the bulk of retail operation to the dealer network, and cooperating with provincial agencies in decentralized distribution through regional sales arrangements. In 1981 agreements were signed with the Surveys and Mapping Branch of Manitoba, and the Maritimes Resource Management Service in Nova Scotia. Alberta, British Columbia, and Saskatchewan signed similar agreements in 1985, 1987, and 1988 respectively. Attention was also turned in 1981 to the subject of full-map depositories, usually university libraries that received a copy of each published map, and partial depositories that received maps of the specific province. After a study by Sauer, RDD revised the depository arrangements and agreements substantially to ensure that the public would have clear access to the map collections. The opportunity was also taken to place limited map deposits in several regional library systems. A further review of all agreements with depositories was undertaken in 1988, and forty-four were not renewed as they failed to meet the required specifications. These and other fluctuations in the distribution network are shown in figure 17-2.

The design of an integrated and computerized inventory control, order processing, and accounting system was begun in 1978. The objectives were to shorten the response time on orders to CMO, and facilitate the automatic distribution of maps. Despite bureaucratic delays over the computing hardware to be bought, the system was eventually installed early in 1985.[27] In addition it offered the potential for creating and analysing customer profiles, though it appears this has not been utilized fully. Later expansion of the system allowed it to be used by anyone with a desktop computer and an appropriate modem, and specifically allowed direct access from four regional sales centres. In a paper on strategies for promoting, pricing, and distributing digital data the authors discussed a variety of possibilities for distribution.[28] Several of these were reflected in the 1989 policy directive on distributing electronic information. This recognized, for the first time, that in addition to end users of digital data there could be licensees. The latter might resell the digital data purchased from EMR, either as a whole or selectively, and with or without value being added to the original data. Thus the directive included controls on use by end users, audit of licensees, and a disclaimer. Discussion of the draft directive at the annual meeting of the Canadian Council on Surveying and Mapping in 1989 resulted in a decision to consider the matter from a Canada-wide perspective.

1990 Onwards

CHANGE AS THE CONTEXT

Several critical changes have dominated the period that opened in 1990. After substantial growth in the economy during the 1980s, a deep and lengthy recession reduced tax revenues. The federal government has had to limit budget allocations to departments. It has also had to insist on the costs of products and services being recovered through new or increased user fees. Improved business practices and marketing have become essential to offset declining sales. Government policy has increasingly favoured joint ventures with the private sector for the delivery of products and services. And by no means the least, privatization of government programmes has been given serious consideration. These factors provide the context for several important developments within the Surveys, Mapping and Remote Sensing Sector.

The first was the agreement with Treasury Board over sharing revenue. It was signed late in 1989 as the Increased Ministerial Authority and Accountability Accord (IMAA). This long-overdue agreement allowed the sector to retain a portion of the revenue earned from the sale of products, and relaxed some controls and regulations that would encourage it to operate in a more business-like fashion. Retention of revenues varied from 100 percent of the revenues from the sale of intellectual property, to 50 percent of all increased revenues beyond the level of sales of conventional map and chart products in 1989–90. Second, the Products and Services Task Force was set up in 1990 as an outcome of IMAA. Its terms of reference gave it the freedom to view products, services, integration of efforts within the sector, and improved coordination up to the year 2000. Its analysis included developments within the provinces and opportunities for Canada overseas. The report also reviewed the situation in several other countries, though the last was uneven in quality. Amongst the recommendations was the formation of the Marketing Office, which would "be the focal point for the sale and marketing of all Sector products and services,"[29] and would promote, support, and coordinate marketing throughout the sector. It did not foresee the office playing the central role in identifying products and services required by clients, and shaping the sector's responses. It was decided later, however, that the office would indeed be responsible for the marketing of all sector information. The federal government's decision to form a special operating agency that would undertake all government printing led to DSS taking over the map and chart printing operations of the Sector on 1 April 1990. This third development brought the longstanding jurisdictional dispute to an abrupt end in a solution that was uniquely Canadian. It did, however, allow a further reorganization that resulted in the Products and Services Division being formed in 1991, including the Marketing Group as proposed by the task force.

Fourth, and arguably the most influential factor, the auditor general identified a number of fundamental elements of the sector's activities in his 1990 annual report to Parliament. The central themes were the cost-effectiveness of producing printed maps by digital methods, and the compatibility of the largely unstructured digital data with users' needs. The outcome was the major user-needs study contracted to Georef Systems in 1991. The primary objective was to seek information and advice from more than 800 current and potential users in government, industry, and academia on their needs and preferences for topographic data and information. But the study also discussed possible roles for the sector, considered cooperation with the provinces, and addressed issues of structuring and maintaining digital data. Much of this might have been unnecessary if there had been regular liaison in earlier years with a broader range of users than the provinces alone.

PROMOTION AND PRICING

The new Marketing Office was established in 1991, and early attention was given to improving promotion. Placing orders to CMO by 1–800 telephone numbers was introduced. A distinctive logo was designed to complement the sector's printed maps and new brochures. Advertisements were placed more widely in outdoor magazines, and during the winter of 1993 TV was used sparingly, with anglers in the Toronto and Montreal areas as the target. Participation with dealers in outdoor shows was increased, and support to map dealers was enhanced through regular visits. Promoting the wider use of digital data was helped by the creation of four demonstration sets, copies of which were released to clients who intended to purchase data. Major increases in *pricing* conventional products were approved in 1990 when a standard topographic map was increased from $4.50 to $8.00. The volume of sales dropped by about a half-million items in the first full year after the increase. To what extent this reduction represented elasticity in demand, or rather reflected the general effects of the recession, is unclear. Pricing of conventional products was reduced in 1991 so that the newly introduced Goods and Services Tax could be included, but there were further increases in 1992 and 1993. A new distribution policy for digital data was adopted in April 1990 that resembled closely the recommendations made in 1989. Further price increases in line with inflation occurred in 1992 and 1993. The new distribution policy encouraged the licensing of firms that could resell the data directly or add value to the data as a whole or in part. By 1993 licenses had been issued to thirty large public sector utilities, systems integrators, GIS consultants, and mapping firms. Finally, revisions to the policy were made in 1993. These introduced volume discounts of up to 30 percent based on the number of digital files purchased in one order, and a sliding scale of royalties based on the volume of digital data resold.

MARKETING SPATIAL INFORMATION IN THE PROVINCES

The evolution in the federal government from sales of spatial information to marketing has had its parallels in the provinces. To some extent the federal Surveys and Mapping Branch has been a model for the provinces on aspects of marketing. This is most clear in the distribution of conventional products, on which there was close liaison and cooperation between the federal and provincial governments from 1977. It also applies to the pricing and distribution of digital data in the late 1980s. But because topographic mapping in the provinces commenced at different times, there have been significant differences in emphasis and some interesting innovations by specific provinces. These will be illustrated by discussion of marketing in several provinces.

Manitoba

DISTRIBUTION

Manitoba Surveys and Mapping Branch (MSMB) has been selling maps since it was created in 1930. The Air Photo Library was added in 1948–49 when the inventory consisted of 65 000 prints of oblique and vertical air photographs. As the CMO increased its marketing thrust during the 1970s, MSMB recognized that "such innovations as sole regional distributorships for federally produced map sheets had considerable appeal, especially when coupled with the distribution of provincially produced map products."[30] Accordingly the Manitoba government decided to distribute its map products through authorized dealers, both government and private. An economic study of the operations of the Map Office and the Air Photo Library was made in 1980 within the context of recovering all costs. A scale of fees was established for wholesale and retail sales, and a standard agreement with private sector dealers was drawn up. In May 1981 agreement was reached with the federal government on recognizing MSMB as the sole distributor of federal maps and charts in Manitoba. By late 1981 there were five regional map offices supplied with bulk stock from Winnipeg. The number rose to seven in 1986–87 before two were taken over by the private sector. All products were supplied on consignment, and the revenue from sales was credited to the MSMB. Some thirty private dealerships had also been awarded by 1982. The number was increased to forty-two in 1986, seventy-five in 1990, and ninety-one in 1993; and sales coverage was extended into north-western Ontario, Saskatchewan, and the nearby states in the U.S. as the sources of many visitors to the province. Approval was also received to allow the reproduction of provincial map products for non-commercial use under a license with MSMB. The first was issued in 1982.

PROMOTION

Other means of reaching the public were coupled with promotion. These included highly successful booths at the annual sports show and the International boat shows, the latter jointly with CMO. Advertisements have been placed in fishing regulations and Travel Manitoba publications, and for over ten years each dealer has been identified by MSMB in the Yellow Pages. This emphasis upon outdoor recreational users of maps and charts has continued, and has been expanded to include the Chicagoland Sport Fishing Show and the Mid-Western Sport Show in Minneapolis. A self-service system of map indices was an early initiative of the Manitoba Map Office, and a new map catalogue was published. MSMB has provided workshops and seminars for sports groups within the province, and has displayed its 1:20 000 scale photographic township maps in municipal offices throughout the area covered by this series. These various steps helped to increase both the volume of sales and the average monthly revenue, which rose from $6100 in 1978 to $8500 in 1980 and $17,000 in 1981. Sales to government departments were additional. Annual sales of hard-copy publications peaked at $580,000 in 1990–91. The subsequent decline can be attributed partially to the substantial increase in the selling price of federal topographic maps, but the severe recession may also have taken its toll. A similar growth pattern occurred in sales of aerial photographs and remote sensing images. Currently between 1 and 2 percent of revenue from sales is used to promote and market products. Manitoba is considering a policy for the distribution of digital data. A draft licence agreement has been prepared for the reproduction and sale of digital data. This defines the rights of the province in the data, protection by copyright, and a sliding scale of royalties for reproduction of the data. A draft purchase and sale agreement has also been written for end-use of digital data. This is explicit on a royalty being charged when there is more than one user in the company.

Québec

ORGANIZATION AND RESPONSIBILITIES

The government of Québec began producing maps in 1962, and the Service de la Cartographie was created three years later. Although the Société de Cartographie du Québec was founded in 1969, it lapsed and was not revived until 1973 when the then Department of Lands and Forests was reorganized. To this agency was assigned the responsibility for the provincial mapping programme at scales 1:20 000 and larger. Within the context of cadastral reform a legal fund was set up in 1985 with an initial advance of $5 million from the Minister of Finance. It was intended that this fund would be maintained with revenues from the sale of maps throughout a ten-year programme of mapping, and that any surplus should revert to the Consolidated Revenue Fund. This was the context for establishing the Centre d'Information Géographique et Foncière. Its mandate included the distribution and marketing of land and geographic information, and the administration of a revolving fund. Photocartothèque Québécoise is the corporate name for the centre. Law 55 of 1988, and decrees 470 and 471 of 1989, defined the form and operation of Le Fonds d'Information Géographique et Foncière. Specific reference was made to the expenses of sales and promotion.

PROMOTION

The Photocartothèque Québécoise's predecessor became a dealer in federal NTS maps in 1967. A map index and price list for the 1:20 000 topographic series was produced as early as 1976, and has been revised regularly. In recent years it has been supplemented by indices of 1:15 000 scale aerial photographic cover (on the reverse of the index of printed topographic maps), and 1:20 000 digital topographic and cadastral maps. These forms of promotion have been complemented by publicity directed towards municipalities and specialized customers on the one hand, and to the general public on the other. A product catalogue, and a variety of separate leaflets and announcements, serve the former. For the latter an attractively designed and informative instructional booklet has been published on the construction and use of topographic maps in Québec.[31] This resembles closely a publication of Institut Géographique National of France. The Photocartothèque Québécoise logo has been used on hard-copy products since 1991, and is also used for point-of-sale advertising. The Photocartothèque Québécoise has also targeted hunters and fishermen in its promotional campaigns by staffing a booth at the annual Soirée Chasse et Pêche, and

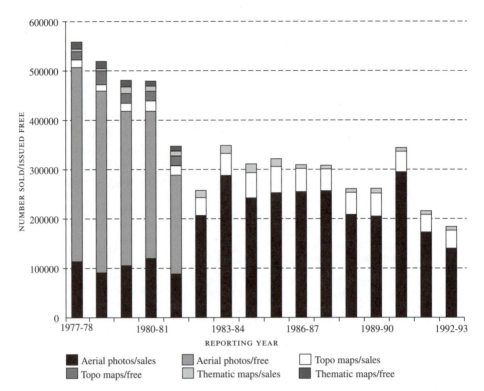

Figure 17-3
Photocartothèque Québécoise, sales/free issues of products.
Source: Photocartothèque Québécoise

presenting maps and aerial photographs at the Clinique Pêchatout. The tourist guidebook project has been a significant contribution to the promotion and use of hard-copy topographic maps. The printing of the 1:20 000 topographic series is contracted to the private sector, whilst in common with other provinces copies of large-scale topographic maps are produced on demand by the diazo process or electrostatically.

DISTRIBUTION
Free issues of aerial photographs and topographic maps were made annually from 1962–63 until 1981–82 when this practice was ended. In the peak year of 1969–70 over 414 000 photographs and 41 000 topographic maps were issued free. Although data on sales are not available prior to 1977–78, figure 17-3 shows clearly the positive effect on sales of the termination of free issues. The distribution network for hard-copy maps was increased significantly in 1990. It now consists of sixty-eight dealers well distributed throughout the settled area of Québec, and two dealers in Montreal for photographic products. The sale of digital maps began in 1986, and the first thematic digital data file was also sold in the same year. Digital data are available for 1:1000 and 1:20 000 topographic maps, large-scale cadastral maps, and alphanumeric data of cadastral parcel detail. The distribution policy for digital data announced in 1992 established clearly both the government's rights to the data, and

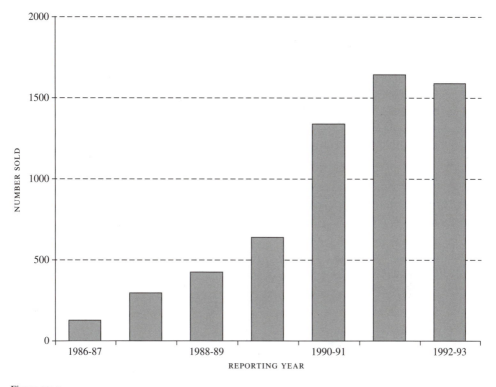

Figure 17-4
Photocartothèque Québécoise, sales of digital maps.
Source: Photocartothèque Québécoise

its obligations. It created a user's licence and a comprehensive agreement. This recognized that if the licensee had more than three business sites at which the digital data were used, a communal use licence would be applied with a sliding-scale tariff. The policy also created a distribution licence. This permitted the licensee to distribute the data as a whole or in part, established the tariff, and defined the obligations of the distributor to its clients and to the government. A special agreement with municipalities was drawn up covering municipal use of provincial large-scale digital topographic and cadastral data, and the sale of digital data by the municipality. Some sixty such agreements have been made since 1989. The impact of these initiatives on the sales of digital maps is illustrated in figure 17-4.

New Brunswick

ORGANISATION AND DISTRIBUTION

The programme of producing topographic and cadastral mapping of New Brunswick, initially part of the Atlantic Provinces Surveying and Mapping Programme and after 1972 under the Land Registration and Information Service (LRIS), has been reviewed in chapter 4. This created a growing inventory of 1:10 000 scale orthophotomaps for sale in the contoured Topographic and uncontoured Property Map series. During the latter part of the

1970s the Lands Branch served as the provincial map distribution centre, with the supporting network of registry and mapping offices across the province as points of sale. The aerial photographic library was also a point of sale for federal NTS maps and provincial aerial photography. The registries have remained essential parts of the distribution network, particularly the five regional offices. The modest gross revenue was $86,000 in 1976 and $88,770 in the following year, with just over 40 percent coming from the sale of aerial photographs. After the commencement of 1:10 000 digital contoured resource mapping in 1984, printing copies of maps on demand was started in map sales offices. In 1985 the Office of Government Reform recommended that a consolidated surveys and mapping service should be established within the Department of Municipal Affairs and Environment, and the proposal was approved early in 1986. Unfortunately a provincial election intervened, and the proposal became inactive. The decision in 1989 to disband LRIS was accompanied by the establishment of the New Brunswick Geographic Information Corporation (NBGIC).

PRODUCT DEVELOPMENT AND PRICING

The NBGIC gave early attention to product development. One new product was the *Cartes NB Maps*, a book of maps based on the 1:10 000 digital data and incorporating additional data from the Department of Natural Resources and Energy. User needs for such a product were investigated by surveys conducted in government agencies, and with outdoor recreational associations and other prospective users. In 1992–93 *Cartes NB Maps* earned nearly $36,000 from sales in the five regional registry and mapping offices, and new digital topographic and property mapping data generated revenue of over $128,000. The Fredericton office recorded the most dramatic increase, largely due to purchases by one government department. The corporation was also able to improve its retailing of NTS maps, for which it is the wholesale distributor in New Brunswick, and aerial photographs. In the period 1989–93 the revenue earned from the sale of NTS maps in the five offices more than doubled. Overall, sales of maps and data increased from $580,824 to $1,063,586 between 1990–91 and 1992–93 – despite the recession that has been mentioned earlier as a possible cause of reduced sales. In 1991 consultants were asked to prepare guidelines for a policy on pricing digital data within the context of the corporation having to become financially self-sufficient by 1995–96. The resulting policy statement contained two important principles: that the use of land-related information should be encouraged, and duplication of effort should be discouraged. The policies recognized the need for multi-site uses of data, discounts for volume purchases, and the possibility of licensing arrangements. The approaches to pricing treated five categories of products and services in different ways – those required by law, existing infrastructure such as topographic base mapping, future infrastructure, standard cadastral products, and retail products and services. The visible results[32] of what clearly was a penetrating and analytical exercise are a timely reminder of how the pricing of goods and services concerned with spatial information is changing in response to severe financial pressures on governments.

CONCLUSIONS

The postwar period in Canada has seen a slow evolution from the free distribution and modest sales of government maps, charts, and related publications to marketing of spatial information in the widest sense. The evolution is continuing and accelerating. Initially the maps and other products were created primarily for use by governments. Expanded sales can be attributed partially to views in the 1960s and 1970s that map information should be made available more widely. The introduction of digital data in the second half of the 1980s emphasized the need for new approaches. Changed financial circumstances recently have made the generation of increased revenue essential.

The policy that required revenue from sales to be deposited to the Consolidated Revenue Fund was, by itself, a significant deterrent to innovative and aggressive marketing. It was not until the 1980s that various initiatives were taken in several provinces for the creation of revolving funds. And the sector's agreement with the federal Treasury Board on revenue sharing was not reached until 1989. For most of the last twenty years the federal government and, more recently, the provincial governments have concentrated on improving and widening the distribution of hard-copy products. A critical factor has been decentralizing distribution at both levels of government, and this has prompted successful cooperation between them. Concern over the storage, management, and cost of inventory, and the handling of orders, led to the development of computerized distribution management systems and controls. This was begun by the federal government with a successful system designed in Canada and installed in the CMO. There have been parallels in several provinces. Overall the federal government has undertaken rather limited market research into the requirements for and use of hard-copy maps. Efforts to understand the Canadian market have been made only intermittently since the one federal map users' conference in 1966. The most recent has been driven by the need to reconcile the production of printed maps and digital data. Current pricing of spatial information, hard-copy and digital, reflects a radical change in policy. Pricing used to be based on the costs of reproduction and distribution, but it now includes a contribution to the capital investment. Finally, although promotion of hard-copy products was minimal during the first twenty years of the period, it was given greater emphasis thereafter. In the current economic circumstances, and those that are likely to face government geomatics organizations in the future, promotion is a necessity.

NOTES

1 McDermott, M.P. 1987. Marketing and the Cartographic Industry. In *The Cartographic Enterprise. Markets and Marketing.* International Cartographic Association, Working Group on The Cartographic Enterprise, 3.

2 Stanton, W.J., and Montrose S. Summers. 1973. *Fundamentals of Marketing.* Toronto: McGraw-Hill Ryerson.

3 Annual Reports, Surveys and Mapping Branch, and EMR.

4 1980. Report of the Task Force on Contracting Out. Internal report. Surveys and Mapping Branch, EMR.

   1986. *Minutes of Proceedings and Evidence of the Standing Committee on Research, Science and Technology. House of Commons.* 8 December 1986. Ottawa: Canadian Government Publishing Centre, 7:8

5 1988. Our New Direction. Internal report. Surveys, Mapping and Remote Sensing Sector, EMR.

6 1988. *Make or Buy Study.* Cartographic Information and Distribution Centre. Report by Price Waterhouse, ii.

7 1977. National Atlas and Map Information/Reference Library Sub-activities. Earth Sciences Services Program. Internal Evaluation Report, Corporate Evaluation Group, EMR.

8 1992. Defining the Essential Federal and National Topographic Data Requirements and Associated Costs and Benefits. Report of Georef Systems Ltd to Surveys, Mapping and Remote Sensing Sector, EMR, ii.

9 1990. Products and Services in the Year 2000. Report to the Assistant Deputy Minister by the Task Force on Products and Services, Surveys, Mapping and Remote Sensing Sector, EMR, 2.

10 Lapp. P.A., A.A. Marsan, and L.J. O'Brien. 1978. *Report of the Task Force on National Surveying and Mapping.* Surveys and Mapping Branch, Energy, Mines and Resources Canada, 148, 158.

11 1981. *Program Evaluation of the Surveying and Mapping Activity. Department of Energy, Mines and Resources.* Philip A. Lapp Ltd, 52–3.

12 1977. A Study of the Distribution of Topographical Maps in Canada. Report by Woods, Gordon and Co. to Surveys and Mapping Branch, EMR, 8.

13 1988. *Make or Buy Study,* ii.

14 Dept. of Finance. 1993. *Federal Budget.* Ottawa: Queen's Printer.

15 1949. *Annual Report of Mines, Forests and Scientific Services Branch, 1948–9.* Ottawa: Dept of Mines and Resources.

16 1970. Phase I Environmental Study. Surveys and Mapping Branch. Systems Analysis. Map and Chart Sales and Distribution. Annex L.

17 1966. Proceedings of the 1966 Map Users Conference, NACCSM, 2–3 November, Ottawa.

18 1974. Report to the Canadian Council on Surveys and Mapping. Topographic Survey, Surveys and Mapping Branch, EMR.

19 McGrath, Gerald. 1969. Interim Report on the Waterton Lakes National Park Map Information Survey, 1969. Report to the director, Surveys and Mapping Branch, EMR.

20 McGrath, Gerald, and H.W. Castner. 1975. An Evaluation of the 1:250,000 Map Series of the National Topographic Map System and Possible Modifications to the Series. Interim report under contract OSU 3–0551 to Topographical Survey Directorate, Surveys and Mapping Branch, EMR.

21 *P.C. 1972–724,* C. Gaz. 1972. 1.

22 Clemmer, G.A., and L.M. Sebert. 1969. *Inventory Control in the Map Distribution Office.* Technical report 69-3. Ottawa: Surveys and Mapping Branch, EMR.

23 McArthur, J.A. 1977. Map Distribution Operations of the Federal Government. Presented to Canadian Council on Surveying and Mapping.

24 McGrath, Gerald, and Barry A. Silic. 1983. An Investigation of the Role of Official Maps in Outdoor Recreation. Report to the director, Reproduction and Distribution Division, Surveys and Mapping Branch, EMR.

25 Lapp, Marsan, and O'Brien. *Report,* 155.

26 1989. *Draft Policy Directive 3–89. Policy on the Distribution of Electronic Information.*

27 McArthur, J.A., and G. McGrath. 1991. Some Current Issues in Cartographic Distribution and Future Prospects. *Cartographic Journal,* 28, 2, 200–7.

28 McGrath, Gerald, J.A. McArthur, and M.P. McDermott. 1989. Issues in Marketing Digital Cartographic Data by Government Agencies. In *Proceedings, National GIS Symposium,* 818–32.

29 1990. Products and Services in the Year 2000, 51.

30 Roberts, A.C. 1981. Report to the Canadian Council on Surveys and Mapping.

31 1986. *Initiation à la carte topographique.* Québec: Centre d'information géographique et foncière.

32 Gamble, Robert W., and Donald Shiner. 1993. Pricing Policy of the New Brunswick Geographic Information Corporation. In *Proceedings, The Canadian Conference on GIS,* 918–25.

CHAPTER EIGHTEEN

Canada's International Role

Gerald McGrath

INTRODUCTION

During the past forty years Canada has made many contributions internationally through its surveying, mapping, remote sensing, and geographical information sector. Economic development overseas, the western defence alliance (noted in chapter 5), international organizations, and the vitality of international professional associations have all benefited from Canada's participation. In the process Canada has achieved international recognition and a professional stature out of all proportion to the sizes of its industry and professional ranks. The private sector has been a flag bearer. It has won numerous contracts outside Canada for the supply of surveying, mapping, and remote sensing services, often in highly competitive bidding. Canadian industry has also earned an enviable reputation for advanced design and high quality in the equipment, hardware, software, and systems that it has supplied worldwide. In addition, private sector firms have helped to implement Canada's external aid and international development pro-grammes overseas. This is the arena in which Canadian firms have been highly visible, and highly successful, throughout a period that began in the late 1940s. Delivering such services has involved the support and services of the federal Surveys and Mapping Branch (SMB) of Energy, Mines and Resources (EMR) as technical advisor, contract supervisor, and the source of training for numerous overseas personnel. Significant contributions have been made by several universities and colleges, starting with students from the Caribbean enrolled at the University of Toronto after the Second World War. Then in the 1960s the University of New Brunswick became known throughout the English-speaking world, and beyond, for its undergraduate and graduate programmes in survey engineering (see chapter 13). Finally, diverse Canadian professionals have made vital contributions to international associations and societies concerned with surveying, geodesy, photogrammetry and remote sensing, and cartography. Indeed since 1960 Canada has provided many senior officers of these professional groups, and continues to do so.

CANADIAN INDUSTRY AND
ITS INTERNATIONAL ACTIVITIES

The Beginnings

At the end of the Second World War the requirements for surveying and mapping in the then colonial dependencies were urgent, massive in scope, and costly to satisfy. Existing control survey frameworks had to be improved and expanded. There was very little standard medium-scale mapping in national series for most of Africa, the Caribbean, portions of South-East Asia, and those parts of South America administered by France, Netherlands, and the U.K. What existed was largely out of date due to the diversion of limited resources to the war effort. Large-scale mapping of the cities barely existed. In addition there were new infrastructure projects for which basic mapping was needed. These included the hydroelectric power dam proposed for the Volta River in the Gold Coast (now Ghana); the rail link between the port of Dar es Salaam in Tanganyika (now Tanzania) and the Copperbelt in Northern Rhodesia (now Zambia); and the proposed Kariba Dam on the Zambesi. Consequently major programmes to create or expand the basic surveying and mapping infrastructure were initiated shortly after the war by Belgium, France, Netherlands, Portugal, Spain, and the U.K. Soon afterwards, newly independent countries such as Ceylon, India, and Pakistan commissioned aerial photography for resource surveys and other purposes. And non-Commonwealth countries in Latin America were much in need of aerial photography and airborne geophysical surveys.

Don Thomson has recorded that early in the postwar years "Canadian air survey companies were aggressive in seeking work beyond Canada's borders."[1] Don McLarty has shown in chapter 6 that as early as 1946 the Photographic Survey Corporation (PSC) of Toronto commenced aerial photography of Colombia, and subsequently obtained contracts in other South American countries. The company was also contracted in 1951 to provide aerial photography of 768 840 km^2 of West Pakistan for geological mapping. In 1955 it began photographing the whole of Ceylon (now Sri Lanka) at 1:40 000 scale. In the same year Spartan Air Services (SAS) of Ottawa was commissioned to undertake an airborne geophysical survey of 51 600 km^2 of Rajasthan in India, and of part of the Ganges valley. Other aeromagnetic and aerial photography tasks were undertaken for Malaya (now part of Malaysia). None of these projects was funded by the Canadian government. Canada's first major surveying and mapping project overseas was begun in 1959 after a feasibility study had been carried out in the previous year by G.S. Andrews, then surveyor general of British Columbia. This was for the project of flood control, irrigation, and hydroelectric power generation on the lower Mekong River in Cambodia, Laos, Vietnam, and Thailand. Canadian industry played a central role in the project, with PSC leading a successful consortium of Canadian companies in the production of almost 800 topographic map sheets during the period 1959–64. This sterling achievement was assisted by a new Canadian instrument, the Airborne Profile Recorder (APR), which had been developed by the National Research Council and is described in chapters 3 and 12. This project also introduced SMB, EMR as the technical advisor and contract monitor, ostensibly to the government of Canada but in reality to the UN, which was the executing agency for this project funded by a group of twenty-one national donors.[2] The project is also summarized in appendix C, together with other overseas mapping projects supported by Canadian government funding.

Expansion of activities overseas after the commencement of the Mekong project was relatively rapid. The first two projects were in Africa for blocks of standard topographic mapping under agreements between Canada and the overseas governments. Both were financed by the Special Commonwealth African Assistance Plan (SCAAP). The project in Nigeria, which has been mentioned in chapter 6, consisted of topographic mapping and an airborne magnetometer survey. Canadian Aero Service Limited (CAS) was contracted to provide the overall technical direction under J.M. (George) Zarzycki, and to compile the photogrammetric mapping, whilst Pathfinder Engineering of Vancouver was responsible for the ground surveys. The project was notable for its ingenious use and integration of instruments and film. These included the super-wide-angle lens aerial camera so that 1:40 000 photography could be obtained from an altitude lower than the prevailing harmattan haze layer at 12 000 feet above ground level; infrared film to allow the haze to be penetrated; and APR, horizon cameras, and the Radan-Doppler navigational system so that aerial triangulation could be done with the minimum of ground control.[3] The Nigerian project employed the SMB experience of using Aerodist for increasing the density of ground control from the air. It also brought a Nigerian officer to Canada to be trained at SMB, the first in what became a steady stream. One of the later projects, Nigeria 3, involved the establishment of a national control network in the Northern Region by Marshall Macklin and Monaghan (MMM) of Toronto. A field complement of 30 Canadians and 250 Nigerians levelled over 9000 km of precise and lower-order traverses; observed twelve Laplace stations, and fixed fifty-one stations by Doppler satellite during the five-year project. The second African country that Canada assisted was Tanzania.The project involved the provision of 120 multi-coloured 1:50 000 map sheets covering 85 149 km² of south-eastern Tanzania. SAS as contractor began work in 1965, though again SMB provided staff to undertake an Aerodist survey. It was not intended that printing of the map sheets should be part of the agreement with the Tanzanian government, but this was decided subsequently and printing was contracted to the private sector in Ottawa. This project was followed immediately by a second in an adjacent area of southern Tanzania. Infrared aerial photography, extending the primary network with second-order traversing, vertical control by APR, and the production of 126 multi-coloured 1:50 000 sheets were components of this project.[4] Five more blocks of standard mapping were completed in due course. Thus Canadian private industry was responsible for much of the basic topographic mapping of Tanzania, and complemented the work of the U.K. Directorate of Overseas Surveys and Italian, Finnish, and Polish mapping companies.

Commonwealth countries in the Caribbean and on the South American mainland were the second locus of activity funded by the Canadian government. They also introduced Lt Col J.I. (Bing) Thompson as the newly appointed representative of SMB responsible for its external aid programmes, in which he served with distinction until his retirement in 1979. The first request for Canadian assistance was received from Trinidad and Tobago. This was for aerial photography of both islands at several scales, to be used in land reform and for planning. Aerial photography, and the preparation of photo-mosaics, were completed in 1965 by General Photogrammetric Services of Ottawa with Aero-Photo as subcontractor. A second phase followed almost immediately in which further photo-mosaics, and large-scale mapping of specific areas on the two islands at 1:2500 and 1:5000 scales, were produced by Survair of Ottawa. An important element of the support given to Trinidad and Tobago was in training local staff. This included on-the-job training in the necessary field survey techniques needed to control photogrammetric mapping; photogrammetric compilation of manuscript maps; the field completion of the manuscripts in Trinidad prior to cartographic preparation; map drafting; and photo-mechanical procedures. The provision of training in this case, and in many others, was to be a central contribution of SMB rather than the contractors. Mapping assistance given to Guyana began in 1966, and occurred in a very difficult physical environment for conventional surveying and aerial photography. Ingenuity was needed and was provided, again, by Zarzycki of Terra Surveys. He utilized Aerodist for increasing the density of the sparse control survey framework, and the statoscope, APR, and Doppler navigation system for obtaining data that could be used in aerial triangulation.[5] The success achieved in the first block of mapping north of 4° N led to the remaining parts of the country being tackled in two blocks. In the case of Jamaica, aerial photography of the whole island was exposed by SAS during 1967–68 for topographic mapping to be produced by the Jamaican Survey Department under a UN-funded project. In addition Tellurometer measuring instruments were supplied and training was provided by SMB. Finally, the mapping requirement for Barbados stemmed from a land valuation project in which large-scale base maps and property index maps were needed. General Photogrammetric Services produced the mapping from aerial photography that had been flown by a British company in 1964. It was, however, only the first of several requests for Canadian assistance in producing large-scale mapping by conventional and computer-assisted methods.

Changes in the Export Markets

Throughout the 1970s Canada's aid programme emphasized capital assistance. It was directed to the countries that have been mentioned and other Commonwealth nations, and contributed to the expansion of their basic surveying and mapping infrastructure. Support was also provided by CIDA to several non-Commonwealth countries, including Ethiopia, Haiti, and Nepal. In addition the services of Canadian firms were contracted directly by overseas governments. For example MMM of Toronto created a national geodetic network of over thirty horizontal control points in the Sultanate of Oman using Doppler satellite positioning techniques and astronomical azimuths. During the period 1978–83 projects that were not funded by CIDA accounted for an average of 60 percent of annual export sales by members of the Canadian Association of Aerial Surveyors (CAAS), though as figure 18-1 shows, the percentage fluctuated rather widely from year to year. Taken overall, the 1980s brought significant changes to the export markets in which Canadian companies competed. Most aid donors and development banks reorientated substantial parts of their aid to structural adjustment programmes to help overcome shortcomings in national economies. Donors and banks began to emphasize projects that integrated economic, social, and environmental themes, especially in the rural environment but also in the urban. Infrastructure projects suffered to some extent as a result. In a significant change the development banks increased their support to projects concerned with land reform, land registration, property taxation, and land information management. Though a number of Canadian companies (and provincial agencies) were well qualified, few competed for the new opportunities in these fields. To make matters worse, competition from other donor countries in the field of geomatics was intensified, particularly in land reform and land information. In some cases this was attributed to foreign companies being subsidized by their

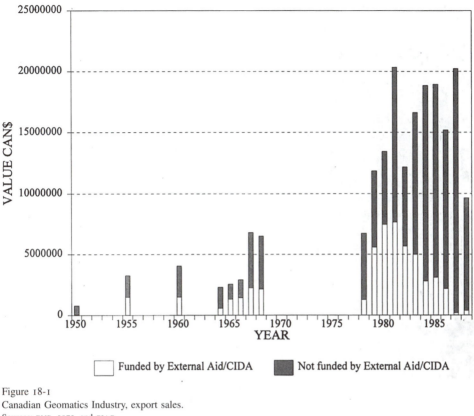

YEAR

| | Funded by External Aid/CIDA | ■ Not funded by External Aid/CIDA |

Figure 18-1
Canadian Geomatics Industry, export sales.
Sources: EMR, 1973, and GIAC

governments. At home in Canada there was a marked recession during the period 1982–84, which caused the overall domestic market for surveys and mapping to contract. Furthermore the price of oil fell by 50 percent or more due to declining demand worldwide. This caused a rapid reduction in exploration within Canada that affected the surveying and mapping industry. And throughout the 1980s there were relentless technological changes. Software for microcomputers and work stations made image processing more accessible. Digital mapping, spatial information systems, and specifically GIS were expanded rapidly. And by no means the least, GPS began to have substantial effects upon geodetic and control surveys.

The National Task Force

It was these changes which led in 1983 to the establishment of the influential Task Force on the Surveying and Mapping Industry in Canada, and to its report in 1985.[6] In this it recommended that the level should be raised at which government contracted work to the private sector under longer-term programmes. It also suggested that increased support should be provided to private industry for competing in export markets, and communication with External Affairs should be improved for identifying opportunities abroad. Moreover it argued that a unified strategy for export markets was needed. One of its most significant recommendations was that the activities of the private sector should be reorientated to the management of spatial information. In December 1986 a national conference was convened on the economic development of the industry, both at home and overseas. In a penetrating paper John McLaughlin identified the changing nature of export markets, the market for new services, and the implications for Canadian private industry and governments. Roy Depper's entertaining yet serious contribution gave insights into the difficulties in dealing with export promotion programmes, and advice to the uninitiated on undertaking projects overseas.[7] Figure 18-1 shows clearly that there *has* been significant growth in the private sector's work overseas despite increasing international competition. Contributing factors included the efforts of Canadian industry to adopt state-of-the-art technologies and innovative methods, the support of the Surveys, Mapping and Remote Sensing Sector of EMR, and the developments in the Middle East, Central and Eastern Europe, and more recently in the Americas.

Another outcome of the task force's work was the decision taken by the CAAS, in 1987, to change its name and scope of activities to encompass all of the surveying, mapping, remote sensing, and land/geographical processing disciplines. The resulting organization, the Geomatics Industry Association of Canada (GIAC), expanded its membership from thirty to more than ninety member firms between 1988 and 1994. GIAC has played an increasingly proactive role in supporting its members' international business development efforts, and has done this by being a partner with several government agencies on specific initiatives. Its accomplishments have included preparation of an export strategy for the industry; various forms of promotion; the organization of several technical missions to the U.S., the Middle East, Asia, and Latin America in cooperation with the Surveys, Mapping and Remote Sensing Sector of EMR and other departments of government; and completion of several market studies.

Land Information Management Projects

Reference was made earlier to new opportunities that were created in land reform, land registration, property taxation, and land information management during the 1980s. Though the number was small, Canadian companies and consultants did respond. For example McElhanney Geosurveys of Vancouver was contracted by the ministry responsible for agrarian reform in Brazil to supervise ground-control surveys in the north-east, and to help execute them. These were needed as the foundation for the immense land administration project funded by the World Bank. In 1985 McElhanney provided staff and GPS receivers for positioning and computing the coordinates of the control stations, on which new 1:10 000 orthophotomapping was based. The significance of Canadian experience in GPS positioning for other than cadastral purposes is also illustrated by the events after the eruption of Mt Pinatubo in the Philippines. In 1991 the company assisted an American engineering consultant by providing GPS control of the area after the volcano had erupted and mud flows had begun. Another example from the cadastral field is the work of the Montreal-based company Photosur Geomat in several French-speaking African nations. During 1988–90 it undertook a feasibility study for the government of Senegal into aspects of a proposed fiscal cadastre (or property assessment and taxation system) for nine cities.

These included the design, staffing, computerization, and financial returns from the property tax system. In Yaounde, the capital of Cameroon, the company investigated titles, demarcated parcels, made cadastral surveys, and produced large-scale digital cadastral maps of the centre of the city during 1984–85. Later it integrated geomatics and cadastral management in a new computing centre for the cadastre, and trained system managers and technicians. Between 1984 and 1986 Charles Weir (of Stewart, Weir and Company) and Denis Hosford (of North West Survey Corporation International), both of Edmonton, designed and implemented a Land Information System for the Bangkok Metropolitan Authority in Thailand when such systems were in their infancy. This demonstration LIS was the second phase of a two-part project partially financed by CIDA, the first phase being a study of the feasibility of a national GIS for Thailand. The demonstration LIS was created for a part of the downtown area of Bangkok, and integrated data on zoning for planning purposes, buildings, and utilities (sewers, water, hydro, and telephones) with the land parcel base. In Indonesia SNC-Lavalin of Montreal was the consultant to the Land Resources Evaluation Project, Phase 1, in which the foundations of a nationwide GIS were laid. Canadian consultants have also been commissioned to advise and assist overseas governments. John McLaughlin's recent work in Peru has addressed conceptual issues in land reform. Roger Tomlinson of Ottawa was consultant to a government committee of inquiry investigating the handling of spatial data in the U.K., and recently led comprehensive detailed and strategic planning for GIS within five key programme areas of the government of Victoria, Australia. Even with this vignette it can be seen that Canadian contributions to countries overseas have grown from aerial photography into full mapping projects and, more recently, to the rich diversity of cadastral, land, and geographic information systems.

SURVEYS, MAPPING AND REMOTE SENSING SECTOR, EMR SINCE 1987

The Changing Context of Canadian Aid

At the time the sector was created a major review of Canadian official development assistance was under way. This had been preceded by lengthy hearings on the matter held by a Standing Committee of Parliament. One topic that was debated keenly was reducing the portion of aid tied to the purchase of Canadian goods and services (but not food) under bilateral, or direct government to government, agreements. On this the committee stated that "we also want to encourage Canadian firms to seek out development challenges in the Third World and to bid aggressively on multilateral as well as bilateral contracts."[8] The new CIDA strategy announced in 1987 allocated 50 percent of CIDA funding to bilateral assistance. Other important changes were the broad shift in priority from large capital projects to a wider range of initiatives; an increased emphasis upon human resource development in developing countries; the introduction of sustainable development; a commitment to environmental protection; and a reduction in tied aid.[9] To counterbalance the last, the new strategy offered a partnership with Canadian industry. Initially this was called General Lines of Credit, but was later renamed the Private Sector Development Initiatives Fund. It encouraged industry to identify potential development projects overseas in up to twenty countries in which Canada had long-term interests. A proposed project should be consistent with the development plan or strategies of the recipient country, and should meet

Canada's overseas development assistance goals.[10] This, then, was the changed context of development aid in which the new sector should operate.

The Sector and Overseas Markets

The newly appointed assistant deputy minister of the sector, J. Hugh O'Donnell, moved quickly to sign a Memorandum of Understanding (MOU) with the CAAS (now the GIAC). The MOU was essentially a framework within which cooperation on matters of mutual interest could take place. It included support for industry in international projects, the exchange of information, research and development, and other significant topics. It reflected "our increased desire to work with the private sector."[11] O'Donnell also set in motion an assessment of the future role of the sector, and that of the private sector as a whole. It was concluded that the value of foreign projects had been $50 to $60 million per annum during the previous five years; and that the principal markets were in South-East Asia (particularly for remote sensing), Africa, South America, and the Middle East.[12] The inclusion of South America at that stage reflected the potential in remote sensing and GIS. There were three immediate tasks. Canada's presence in increasingly competitive export markets had to be enlarged. Additional projects that would be financed under bilateral arrangements other than through CIDA had to be identified. And Canada had to bid successfully for projects funded by multilateral donors and development banks. O'Donnell chose to use the MOU as the instrument for the first and second tasks, and thereby forge bilateral links with similar agencies in overseas governments. In these cases the MOU had to establish the terms under which agencies of two sovereign states could cooperate and contribute to projects of mutual interest without a formal treaty being required, or a contractual relationship being necessary. Thus the MOU should deal with areas of cooperation between the two agencies, and provisions for the assessment and transfer of technology, exchange of information, education, and training. Should a specific programme be agreed, it would be covered by a separate implementing agreement. There were precedents for such arrangements in MOUs that covered a variety of technical subjects: redefining the North American Datums (with the U.S.), the development of a rapid precision levelling system (U.S.), the receipt of satellite data (U.S. and France), and research and development in cartography (France). These, and the MOUs that were signed subsequent to the creation of the sector, are listed in appendix D.

In each MOU with a foreign agency there was the potential for one or more cooperative projects. A project would require considerable discussion both at home and overseas, coordination of inputs from the sector and private industry, and administrative support. Competing successfully in international markets required the development of a national export strategy. In turn this increased the need for promotion of Canada's achievements in geomatics, the sector, Canadian industry, and Canada's academic institutions. Liaison with External Affairs, CIDA, Canadian industry, and academia was central to success in the international markets. There were also the long-standing links with international organizations. In view of these growing commitments an office of external relations was opened within the sector in 1989. One outcome, noted earlier, was a strategy for Canadian industry to compete in domestic and international markets. This was developed by the Geomatics Industry Competitiveness Working Group, established jointly by GIAC and the sector. The well-conceived and carefully structured report referred to "more innovative financing of geomatics projects,"[13] and the potential for cooperation with municipalities. It also focused strongly upon what would be needed to improve Canada's competitiveness overseas, and noted that where necessary a partnership might be developed with a competitor.

The first MOU was signed in 1988 with the Fundação Instituto Brasileiro de Geografia e Estatistica of Brazil. This led in 1991 to an implementing agreement for the training of photogrammetric staff, both in Ottawa at the sector and in Brazil. In 1989 the sector opened a major new thrust with the objective of helping the Canadian geomatics industry develop export markets. The Middle East was the first target, an area to which Canadian industry had already supplied services. A series of export development missions visited several countries in the region, with Saudi Arabia and Egypt being the principal targets. After the visit of an assessment team and the submission of a detailed proposal, the sector worked closely with the Military Survey Department of the Ministry of Defence and Aviation, Kingdom of Saudi Arabia, on aspects of the modernization of its surveying and mapping facilities, and in personnel development. In the case of Egypt, where a project funded by CIDA had recently been completed, an MOU was signed in 1989 with the General Authority for Surveys and Mapping in the Ministry of Public Works and Water Resources. The aftermath of the Gulf War in 1991 brought other challenges for Canada in assisting Kuwait and Qatar. Late in 1990 O'Donnell led a mission to Moscow, which was followed in 1991 by the sector giving GIS seminars there and in Leningrad. Private industry made a number of presentations on Canadian hardware and software for digital mapping, remote sensing, and GIS. Discussions on technical cooperation between the two countries that occurred at these meetings led to an MOU being signed with the Main Administration of Geodesy and Cartography of the USSR. This was replaced by an MOU with the new Russian Federation in 1992, and an MOU with the Ukraine in 1993. There were also trade missions to Latin America (Mexico, Venezuela, and Chile) and South-East Asia (Indonesia, Thailand, Malaysia, and the Philippines) during 1991. Remote sensing and GIS were the main thrust of the mission to Latin America, whilst surveying companies also participated in the Asian mission. The MOU signed with the Instituto Nacional de Estadistica, Geografia e Informatica (INEGI) of Mexico in 1992 was probably one of the most important developments for Canadian industry. Egypt was visited twice during 1992 as its government was interested in environmental monitoring, and the role of an information system for that purpose. The second visit consisted of a feasibility study of the proposed project. A trade mission also visited the Caribbean (Jamaica and Trinidad) in 1992 during which eleven Canadian companies made presentations. Later trade missions in 1993 to Thailand, Korea, Japan, Mexico, and Saudi Arabia included the Minister of Energy, Mines and Resources (Hon. Bill McKnight).

Cooperation with Mexico

These missions and MOUs have indeed led to the Canadian geomatics industry becoming more visible in export markets, and to new business opportunities being created. Important contributors to these processes have been External Affairs and International Trade (EAIT), and the industry association GIAC. INEGI of Mexico provides one example of potential being turned into achievement. This department, and ten others, had been visited by O'Donnell, Denis Beaulieu, and Marcel Frigon in May 1991 within the general context of the North American Free Trade Agreement providing Canada with new opportunities. From discussions it became clear that the senior management of INEGI was interested in cooperation with, and support from, the sector on several subjects. They included the use of GPS and Active Control Stations to increase the density of the Mexican control network; the design and use of a geodetic database; converting conventional mapping to digital format by scanning the paper maps; designing a GIS model for municipal cadastral applications; and strengthening INEGI as an institution through appropriate coordinating mechanisms and further training in geomatics. When staff from INEGI visited centres within the sector during June 1991, they were impressed particularly by the work being done within the Canada Centre for Geomatics (CCG) at Sherbrooke. The MOU signed in October 1992 referred explicitly to several of the subjects discussed in 1991. In due course a Canadian consortium led by SNC-Lavalin of Montreal won a contract of $22 million to provide a unique digital mapping system at INEGI that would be a parallel to that created at CCG. The sector contributed by seconding several staff to the project. In May 1993 a project implementing agreement was signed with INEGI to cover the sector's participation in the Latin America Seminar on Digital Mapping and GIS, which occurred late in 1993. The two organizations also agreed to explore a partnership for developing an integrated database concept for the management of GIS data, and for joint marketing of training services through Latin America. The former requires the integration of textual and graphic data, often in large databases, a topic that is still challenging and is of considerable interest worldwide. It would be very difficult, if not impossible, for Canada to achieve the latter by itself. Thus in the space of three years Canadian links with Mexico, which had not previously been a client or partner in the field of geomatics, were built and expanded to the mutual advantage of both parties.

Cooperation with Russia

The Russian Federation provides a second and final illustration. When it was created as a partial successor to the USSR, an early decision was made to privatize both agricultural land and urban properties. This occured after more than seventy years of state ownership of land and buildings. Consequently there was an urgent need to strengthen the federation's capability, and to expand its capacity, for registering legal interests in land parcels. In addition it was necessary to introduce effective means of assessing the values of land and buildings for the purpose of property taxation. This provided much of the context for cooperation between the sector and the USSR Main Administration of Geodesy and Cartography, and the MOU signed in April 1991. Several themes emerged in discussions during the first two visits to Moscow. They included demonstration of a cadastre and title system using Moscow as a test site; environmental monitoring in the Chernobyl region where the nuclear power station meltdown had occurred in 1986; and a system for environmental monitoring of the Aral Basin. With the demise of the USSR, it was necessary for a new MOU to be signed with the Russian Federation in 1992; and for the Chernobyl theme to be taken up with the government of the Ukraine. The sector undertook the initial two pilot projects in Russia. The first was a demonstration for the State Geodetic Enterprise in Leningrad (now Sankt Petersburg) of the new cadastral information system RESULTS developed by the sector's Legal Surveys. It was used for managing surveys, mapping, and land registration data; and integrated the INGRES relational database management system for textual data and the CARIS digital mapping system developed in Canada. The latter could accept a variety of inputs from field surveys and photogrammetry. The second project took place in the Ryazan region, and demonstrated methods of creating and updating large-scale digital maps. Both projects were financed by the External Affairs Bureau for Assistance to Central and Eastern Europe. As cadastral organizations from Australia, Germany, Sweden, and other countries were also to undertake pilot projects in Russia, the first of Canada's two pilot projects could be described as an investment in a potential future – the more so as any major cadastral project would have to receive external funding from donors or development banks. The second had the greater chance of long-term success through the adoption of proven Canadian technology and methods.

CANADA'S SUPPORT TO INTERNATIONAL AND REGIONAL ORGANIZATIONS

Conference of Commonwealth Surveyors

Strictly speaking, this organization that Canada has supported is not a standing body. It is, rather, a forum in which senior managers have discussed matters of interest to management. They have come from departments in Commonwealth countries that are responsible for surveys, mapping, lands, and hydrography. The first conference was convened in London in 1928, and there were two subsequent meetings before the war. Twelve years elapsed before the first postwar meeting in 1947. Since then the conferences have been held at four-year intervals, and all but the first have been housed in one of the colleges at the University of Cambridge. The fact that most delegates lived in college and dined together has been a distinctive feature of the conference, as it has provided many opportunities for informal discussion. A second unusual feature was the ample opportunity for recreation – often golf – at which business was also transacted. A third was the practice for all papers to be printed and circulated to delegates before the conference convened. This allowed the maximum time for discussion of the papers or related topics. Finally, recommendations were debated and adopted before the conference dispersed. From 1947 to 1983 the conference was chaired by the Director of Colonial (later Overseas) Surveys of the U.K. There has been Canadian representation at each conference, with the senior representative from the federal SMB (now the sector) leading the delegation. Senior managers from federal government agencies, provincial departments, and private industry, and usually one or two academics, have been members of the delegation. Though this has grown in size it has rarely exceeded fifteen members. Canadian papers to the conference have reported on challenges that have been encountered in surveying and mapping, solutions that have been devised, and achievements. It is clear that reporting Canadian experience has been valued by other delegates, particularly those from developing countries. It is also clear that informal discussions at the conference have resulted in formal requests to Canada from overseas governments for technical assistance and training. In addition, the director of the SMB has been a member of the standing committee of the conference since it was created, and has represented Commonwealth countries in the Western hemisphere. Conference matters have been discussed during occasional visits to Caribbean island states and Guyana when the requirements for development assistance in those countries has been the principal topic.

Pan-American Institute of Geography and History (PAIGH)

The second organization supported by Canada is, in most respects, significantly different from the first. The institute was founded in 1928, and today has commissions on cartography, geography, history, and geophysics – though "cartography" is defined broadly to include geodesy, topographic mapping and photogrammetry, aeronautical charting, hydrography, thematic cartography, and large-scale surveys. The objectives of the institute are to enourage, coordinate, and publicize studies in these fields, and to promote cooperation among appropriate institutions in the Americas. Canada's minimal attention to PAIGH before 1944, Canadian participation as observers in the meeting of the commission on cartography that year, and the official invitation to join PAIGH have been described by Mougeot.[14] For complex political and other reasons, Canada had only observer status in the commissions on cartography and geography until 1960. Nevertheless senior staff of several federal departments participated actively in the work of each commission.

When Canada became a member of the institute in 1960, a national section was formed. Initially Mines and Technical Surveys, National Defence, and the National Research Council (NRC) played key roles. Subsequently Surveys and Mapping Branch provided most of the Canadian members, with others coming from the Canada Centre for Remote Sensing, Fisheries and Oceans, and academia. In 1965 S.G. Gamble, director of the SMB, convened a seminar on cartography in Ottawa at which professionals from Latin America were present, and obtained funding for a training course for cartographers from the region. He also became chairman of the national section, an event that saw his already strong commitment to the work of the institute being intensified. That year also marked the beginning of Lou Sebert's longstanding participation in PAIGH, which led to the formation of the committee on special maps. In 1969 T.J. Blachut of NRC organized a meeting on urban surveying and mapping. From this ensued the committee on large-scale and cadastral surveying and mapping, and ultimately the jointly authored book on the subject.[15] In the same vein he formulated in 1975 a pilot project in cadastral surveys for Bogota, Colombia, which utilized instruments developed in Canada. Projects of the commission on geography, which for some years was chaired by H.A. Wood of McMaster University, included seminars held in Ottawa on national and regional atlases[16] in 1979, and urban information systems in 1980. A manual on Doppler surveying was written by SMB personnel in the same year, and was then translated into Spanish. Despite these and other achievements there have been recurrent doubts about the role of the institute and Canada's participation. These have centred on matters of political friction, organization and protocol, adequate financing, the relevance of projects undertaken by the institute, and its technical accomplishments. On balance, however, the views have prevailed of those who have considered the institute as an important and unique interdisciplinary forum for meeting, and working with, their counterparts in Latin America.

United Nations

Encouragement of national surveying and mapping programmes began in 1948 with a formal resolution of the Economic and Social Council. A committee of experts advised that regional conferences should be held, and thus was initiated a series that began in Asia, then spread to Africa in 1963, and finally to the Americas in 1976. The first was held in

India in 1955, at which Canada was represented by the director of Surveys and Mapping Branch, W.H. Miller. Canada's Shoran programme was reflected in a resolution of the conference, and Miller offered to provide training in Canada for technicians. Subsequent conferences were convened at three- or four-year intervals. Canada was represented at almost every conference, and the delegation was led by the current director of the branch or his delegate. Those conferences for the Americas that were held in New York were well attended by Canadians. All technical presentations to the conference were in the form of papers submitted by national governments, and most were written by civil servants. Only recently have there been papers from private industry. The papers fell into two main categories: those on recent advances in techniques and technology, and national reports on progress since the last conference. Most came from western countries, and to a large extent were statements of national achievements. Only in more recent years have papers addressed the difficult subject of how techniques and technology might be applied in developing countries, and management issues. Each conference concluded with the adoption of formal resolutions. Canada's presentations were numerous and varied: from Aerodist through aerial triangulation by independent models to digital topographic data banks and automated cartography. Cadastral reform and land information systems were included. Canadians also served as the chairmen of ad hoc committees and conference rapporteurs. As with all conferences, the UN regional conferences provided opportunities for senior managers from Canadian departments to have informal discussions with their counterparts on matters of mutual interest.

The UN also held inter-regional seminars in different locations, one of which occurred in Aylmer, Québec, in 1985. This was organized by the SMB and attended by senior managers from surveys and mapping departments overseas.[17] Another distinctive contribution of the UN has been the continuing investigation of the status of topographic mapping throughout the world. This was first done in 1968, and has been repeated at regular intervals. A.J. Brandenberger of Laval University has been consultant to the UN on these matters. On behalf of the UN he has collected data and information from national governments by questionnaire survey; created and maintained a database; analysed the data and determined correlations with various demographic and economic variables; and reported the results and conclusions in UN publications.[18] A second study of the human resources engaged in surveying and mapping, and the training facilities available, was added later. The reports on the status of mapping have been cited widely, and doubtless have been used to support proposals for modernization and expansion of mapping programmes. Despite their considerable value, they may in some cases have contributed to mapping policies that today could hardly be justified on economic grounds.

Commonwealth Association of Surveying and Land Economy (CASLE)

The concept of the future association was discussed informally during the Commonwealth conference in 1967, and again in 1968. The association was founded under the auspices of the Commonwealth Foundation in 1969, and embraced three groups of professionals: those concerned with land economy (covering appraisal, land management, and town planning), surveyors in the broadest sense (aerial, hydrographic, land, and mining), and quantity surveyors. Canada took part from the earliest discussions, and its interests have been represented by the Canadian Institute of Surveying (now Geomatics) and the Canadian

Institute of Quantity Surveyors. The association has pursued professional development in a variety of ways. Seminars have been held in many locations on the status of the professions, the development of land surveying, and land management. Much attention has been given to human resources, education and training through forecasts of needs, the establishment of degree programmes, and the publication of standards in education. Indeed the Commonwealth Board of Surveying Education was set up in 1973 to advise on these matters. Canada's principal contributions have been to seminars in the Atlantic region, with which it was associated formally and through longstanding political and economic ties, and in hosting the 1981 general assembly in Ottawa. Trinidad, Barbados, and Jamaica were the sites of seminars in 1975, 1978, and 1979 respectively, at which there were Canadian papers. In commenting on the Barbados seminar the secretary-general stated "I should like to say how much we have all appreciated the input that has been made to this meeting by our colleagues from Canada, who have demonstrated why we tried so hard for so long to get Canada involved in CASLE."[19] Shortly afterwards T.D.W. McCulloch of the Canadian Hydrographic Service was elected to the executive committee. At the general assembly held in Kuala Lumpur in 1985, CASLE decided to sponsor a book on land information management that would be designed for managers and students in the developing countries. Peter Dale and John McLaughlin (of the University of New Brunswick) co-authored the volume, which rapidly became an established work of reference.[20] McLaughlin later became vice-president of the association and its educational advisor. Between 1986 and 1990, however, the nature of the association's activities was changed, and there was expansion. Several lecture tours were made on behalf of the association, including one by Y.C. Lee of UNB to member organizations in South-East Asia. There were many regional workshops on a variety of subjects. But the expanded activities were accompanied by increased membership fees. In 1990 this prompted the sector to ask the Canadian Institute of Surveying and Mapping whether it wished to continue its subscription to the association. Given the magnitude of the fee, and the straightened circumstances of the times, the response was negative. Canada then withdrew from CASLE in 1991.

CANADA'S PARTICIPATION IN INTERNATIONAL PROFESSIONAL ASSOCIATIONS

Canadian organizations, private firms, universities, and colleges have encouraged their staff to participate in the affairs of international professional associations in diverse ways. There have been Canadian presidents or vice-presidents for a fixed term; chairmen, other officers, and members of commissions and working groups; corresponding members or rapporteurs; presenters of papers; organizers of meetings held in Canada; and editors of the papers presented at such meetings. Some have led groups of visiting lecturers to foreign institutions. Others have participated in the association's research programmes and the writing of reports. Many have helped to bring an association's bureau or commission to Canada for a specified period. There have been two vital catalysts in these processes. The NRC represented Canada during the early postwar years in the International Society of Photogrammetry and other bodies. Subsequently the responsibility for international representation was transferred to the Canadian Institute of Surveying (now Geomatics). Eventually the institute represented Canada's interests in the associations concerned with photogrammetry, surveying, cartography, geodesy, and mining surveying. It has often co-sponsored professional meetings with international professional associations; sometimes advanced funds to enable immediate expenses to be met; and has occasionally devoted a special issue of its journal to publishing selected papers.[21] Given the breadth of professional involvement, and the many distinguished Canadians who have progressed across the international stage during the course of almost fifty years, only glimpses can be provided here of Canada's interaction with several international associations – those concerned with photogrammetry and remote sensing, surveying, cartography, and geography, and the union concerned with the first three. Canadian contributions to other international associations have been mentioned elsewhere in this volume.

International Society for Photogrammetry and Remote Sensing (ISPRS)

This is one of the older professional associations in the field of geomatics, having been founded in 1910 as the International Society for Photogrammetry. In the immediate postwar years the NRC undertook fundamental research on camera calibration under the direction of L.E. Howlett, the results of which won international recognition. An early outcome was the award to Canada of the chairing of Commission I of ISP on Aerial Photography, which Howlett held for five years. Chapter 3 has shown that Canada's photogrammetric experience during the Second World War was adapted quickly to the federal mapping programme, which began in 1947. Before long Canadian innovations in topographic mapping also became recognized in international photogrammetric circles. This was reflected in the ISP award to Canada of Commission IV on Mapping from Photographs in 1952, which carried with it the presidency of the commission for the four-year term (see table 18-1). That year also marked the beginning of T.J. Blachut's long association with ISP. Initially he was secretary of Commission IV. Subsequently he chaired one of the commission's working groups throughout the period 1956–64, from 1972 was chairman of the working group concerned with the international orthophoto experiment, and later chaired the groups investigating on-line analytical aerial triangulation and compiling a history of photogrammetry. The Canadian presence at the congress in Stockholm during 1956 was substantial. Four of the six Canadian papers were contributed by staff from NRC, with the balance from SMB and private industry. There was also a strong showing of Canadian papers at the 1968 Congress. At that meeting Brandenberger was elected president of Commission VI on education; and thirty-four Canadians were present to support Canada's formal invitation for the 1972 congress to convene in Ottawa, which was accepted. The 1972 congress was an outstanding professional success, and also saw the logistical accomplishment of feeding more than a thousand delegates at a memorable barbeque held in perfect summer weather. The congress marked the opening of Gamble's term as president of ISP for the period 1972–76. To make the year even more memorable, the Brock Gold Medal was awarded to U.V. Helava, who has been described as a leading inventor in this century, for his creative scientific work in the design and development of analytical plotters. Further recognition of Canada's contributions came in the election of Leo Sayn-Wittgenstein, then of the Canadian Forestry Service, as president of Commission VII on photo interpretation.

Gamble's untimely death in 1977 cut short his term as first vice-president. In a tribute to him and to his country it was said that "during the 1960's Canada's activities in the professional survey field have become remarkable in the international scene. Sam Gamble therefore recognised the importance of international exchanges supporting concentrated activities in such organisations as ... the International Society of Photogrammetry."[22] At the 1976

Table 18-1
International Society for Photogrammetry and Remote Sensing

Term	Venue and Year of Congress	Canadian Office Holder	Meeting Held in Canada
1948–52	The Hague 1948	Commission I: Dr L.E. Howlett (Chairman) from 1951	
1952–56	Washington 1952	Commission I: L.E. Howlett (Chairman) Commission IV: G.S. Andrews (Chairman)	
1956–60	Stockholm 1956		
1960–64	London 1960		
1964–68	Lisbon 1964		
1968–72	Lausanne 1968	Commission IV: Dr A.J. Brandenburger (Chairman)	
1972–76	Ottawa 1972	President, ISP: Dr S.G. Gamble Commission VII: Dr L. Sayn-Wittgenstein (Chairman)	1972: ISPRS, Ottawa
1976–80	Helsinki 1976	1st Vice-President: Dr S.G. Gamble Commission IV: Dr J.M. Zarzycki (Chairman)	1978: Commission IV, Ottawa
1980–84	Hamburg 1980	1st Vice-President: Dr J.M. Zarzycki Commission II: Z. Jaksic (Chairman)	1982: Commission II, Ottawa
1984–88	Rio de Janeiro 1984	1st Vice-President: Dr J.M. Zarzycki Commission V: Dr V. Kratky (Chairman)	1986: Commission V, Ottawa
1988–92	Kyoto 1988	Commission VII: F. Hegyi (Chairman)	1990: Commission VII, Victoria
1992–96	Washington 1992	Commission II: Dr M.M. Allam (Chairman)	

congress Zarzycki was elected president of the commission responsible for topographic and cartographic applications. His many contributions to photogrammetry and ISP were recognized later by his election as first vice-president for two terms. The 1976 meeting also saw Canadians elected to chair seven working groups; and the Canadian delegation propose that remote sensing should be added to the name of the society – from which derives the present name and acronym of ISPRS. The many photogrammetric patents in the name of Gilbert Hobrough, and his development of the Gestalt Photomapping System, were recognized in 1980 when he received the society's Brock Gold Medal. Canada's substantial contribution to the professional health of the society has remained throughout the 1980s, and continues today. These are reflected in table 18-1. It cannot reveal, however, the substantial time spent in organizing and hosting the ISPRS symposia that have been held in Canada at four-year intervals since 1978, and the associated technical tours to local institutions. Nor does it disclose the numbers and diversity of Canadian technical presentations to these symposia, the co-sponsorship of the symposia by the federal government and the Canadian Institute of Geomatics, and the venture of publishing the papers for the opening of each meeting.

Fédération Internationale des Géomètres (FIG)

FIG was founded in 1878. Canada had observer status prior to the Second World War, though its membership began only in 1961. As a new member its initial contributions were in the form of national reports on Canadian developments and achievements in surveying, and the work of the Canadian representatives to all commissions of FIG with the exception of valuation and management of real estate. Not surprisingly some representatives were also active in commissions and working groups of ISP, for example G. Konecny in the field of education and training. A significant change in the conduct of meetings took effect during the London congress in 1968, when the practice of presenting national reports, reports of the commission chairs, and special reports on the work of the commissions, was discontinued. It was accepted that commission chairs could invite papers to be presented, and thereafter invited papers and papers offered by authors became the normal practice. Canadian surveyors adapted to these changes quickly, with the number of Canadian papers presented increasing from nine in 1971 to twenty-eight in 1986. The Appraisal Institute of Canada also became a member of FIG in 1975 to represent Canada in the commission dealing with that subject, but it withdrew early in 1979.

Several major symposia have been held in Canada in connection with FIG (see table 18-2). The first was the International Hydrographic Technical Conference organized in conjunction with the International Hydrographic Bureau, which occurred in 1979. In the same year Blachut chaired an FIG symposium on modern technology for the cadastre and land information systems. The papers included a contribution by the director of the Geographical Institute of Colombia on the photogrammetric cadastral techniques suggested to the Colombian cadastre by Canada. The theme of land information was repeated during 1984 in the symposium entitled The Decision Maker and Land Information, which was co-sponsored by the Edmonton branch of CISM. One of the sessions was devoted to the modernization of land information in Alberta and its major cities to demonstrate the progress that had been made. Canada was host to the eighteenth FIG congress, which was convened in Toronto during June 1986 under the presidency of Charles Weir of Edmonton, who was FIG president for the period 1985–87. This marked only the second time an FIG congress had been held outside Europe. Some 1500 persons attended the opening ceremony, which was followed by about 300 papers and fourteen technical tours to eight locations. Again there was an outdoor barbeque, attended by over 1000 guests, which was endowed with the good fortune of perfect weather. Canada's contributions to FIG have continued, particularly in the fields of land information systems and hydrography. An aspect of the latter is the close cooperation that has been required with the International Hydrographic Organisation on coordinating technical assistance to developing countries on hydrographic matters.

International Cartographic Association (ICA)

This association is one of the more recent to be formed, and had its origin in the so-called Esselte Conference on Applied Cartography held in Stockholm during 1956.[23] Although the participants did not include a representative of Canada, one of the names suggested for the small organizational committee was Janusz Klawe who was then working in Edinburgh and had previously been employed by SMB, Ottawa. Further meetings were held in 1958, one of which was attended by Brig. D. Baldock of SMB, before the formal inaugural meeting of ICA in 1959. It was agreed then that the new association should seek affiliation with the International Geographical Union (IGU). Klawe returned to an academic post at the University of Alberta in 1964, and subsequently was elected to be the first Canadian office holder in the association as a vice-president. Canadians presented papers to some of the

Table 18-2
Fédération Internationale des Géomètres

Congress/Venue/Year	Canadian Office Holder	Meeting Held in Canada
VII Lausanne 1949		
VIII Paris 1953		
IX Scheveningen (Holland), 1958		
X Vienna 1962		
XI Rome 1965		1967: Permanent Committee meeting no. 34, Ottawa
XII London 1968		
XIII Wiesbaden 1971		
XIV Washington 1974	Commission 2: H. Klinkenberg	
XV Stockholm 1977	Commission 4: T.D.W. McCulloch (Chairman) Commission 5: C.H. Weir (Vice-Chairman)	1979: Commission 4, 1st International Hydrographic Technical Conference (with IHB), Ottawa 1979: Commissions 3 and 5, Ottawa
XVI Montreux 1981	Commission 4: T.D.W. McCulloch (Chairman)	
XVII Sofia 1983	Vice-President, Group A: C.H. Weir Commission 3: Prof. A.C. Hamilton (Vice-Chairman)	1984: Commission 3, Edmonton
XVIII Toronto 1986	President: C.H. Weir Vice-President, Group A: T.D.W. McCulloch Secretary General: C.W. Youngs Commission 3: Prof. A.C. Hamilton (Chairman) Ad Hoc Commission on Surveying and Mapping in Developing Countries: C.H. Weir (Chairman) Ad Hoc Commission on Regional Structure and Initiatives: T.D.W. McCulloch (Chairman)	1986: FIG Congress, Toronto
XIX Helsinki 1990	Vice-President, Group A: C.W. Youngs Commission 4: G.R. Douglas (Secretary)	
XX Melbourne 1994		1994: Commissions 3 and 7, with Geomatics Atlantic, Fredericton

ICA conferences prior to Canada being host to the fourth general assembly and sixth conference in Ottawa during 1972. Baldock chaired the organizing committee for the Ottawa meetings, which were attended by 390 participants and were preceded by a joint session with the IGU at its congress in Montreal. The working group (later commission) on oceanic cartography was an outcome of the Stresa conference, but it met first at the Ottawa conference with A.J. Kerr of the CHS as chair. For a period of twelve years, with a change of name in 1980, it pursued an active programme of research and publishing.[24] The latter used *Cartographica*, the well-known and highly respected Canadian journal

Table 18-3
International Cartographic Association

Venue and Year	Type of Meeting	Canadian Office Holder	Meeting Held in Canada
Wabern (Switzerland) 1959	Foundation meeting		
Paris 1961	1st Gen. Assembly and Conference		
Edinburgh 1964	2nd Gen. Assembly and 2nd Conference		
Amsterdam 1967	3rd Conference		
New Delhi 1968	3rd Gen. Assembly and 4th Conference	Vice-President: Prof. J. Klawe	
Stresa (Italy) 1970	5th Conference	Vice-President: Prof. J. Klawe	
Ottawa 1972	4th Gen. Assembly and 6th Conference	WG, Oceanic Cartography: A.J. Kerr (Chairman)	Gen. Assembly and Conference, Ottawa
Madrid 1974	7th Conference	WG, Oceanic Cartography: A.J. Kerr (Chairman)	
Moscow 1976	5th Gen. Assembly and 8th Conference	Cartographic Technology: R. Groot (Chairman) Oceanic Cartography: A.J. Kerr (Chairman)	
College Park (U.S) 1978	9th Conference	Cartographic Technology: R. Groot (Chairman) Oceanic Cartography: A.J. Kerr (Chairman)	
Tokyo 1980	6th Gen. Assembly and 10th Conference	Marine Cartography: A.J. Kerr (Chairman) CTTTW: R. Groot (Chairman)	
Warsaw 1982	11th Conference	Marine Cartography: A.J. Kerr (Chairman) CTTTW: R. Groot (Chairman)	Ad hoc meeting, Marine Cartography: Ottawa
Perth (Australia) 1984	7th Gen. Assembly and 12th Conference	Vice-President: Dr D.R.F. Taylor WG Cartographic Enterprise: Prof. G. McGrath (Chairman)	
Morelia (Mexico) 1987	8th Gen. Assembly and 13th Conference	President: Dr D.R.F. Taylor WG Marketing: Prof. G. McGrath (Chairman) Task Force on Women in Cartography (1989): Dr E. Siekierska (Co-Chair)	
Budapest 1989	14th Conference	President: Dr D.R.F. Taylor WG Marketing: Prof. G. McGrath (Chairman) Task Force on Women in Cartography (1989): Dr E. Siekierska (Co-Chair)	
Bournemouth (U.K.) 1991	9th Gen. Assembly and 15th Conference	President: Dr D.R.F. Taylor WG Marketing: V. Glickman (Chairman) WG Gender in Cartography: Dr E. Siekierska (Chair)	
Cologne 1993	16th Conference	President: Dr D.R.F. Taylor WG Marketing: V. Glickman (Chairman) WG Gender in Cartography: Dr E. Siekierska (Chair)	

edited and published by Bernard V. Gutsell of York University, to maximum advantage. Dick Groot of SMB assumed the chair of the commission on cartographic technology in 1976, four years after its formation at Ottawa. An important but later result of the commission's sustained international cooperation to clarify techniques in cartographic production was a compendium edited in Ottawa by J. Curran of SMB.[25]

A resolution accepted at the Moscow conference called for seminars to be held in developing countries so that knowledge of current cartographic techniques could be shared widely. This programme was begun in 1978 with a seminar in Nairobi. Two years later Groot accepted the chair of the experimental Committee on the Transfer of Technology to the Third World (CTTTW). In this capacity he organized a team of lecturers to present seminars in Wuhan, China, in 1981 and the following year in New Delhi. Both he and N. Anderson of the CHS gave lectures. In 1981 Gutsell began a long and fruitful association with the ICA publications committee. He played a major role in implementing a resolution of the Tokyo general assembly that there should be a regular ICA newsletter. The first issue of the twice-yearly newsletter appeared in June 1983 with Gutsell as co-editor. His innovation was to publish it in such a way that it could be reproduced in national cartographic journals, thereby ensuring wide dispersion of ICA news. For his contributions to the newsletter and as editor of *Cartographica* he was awarded an honorary fellowship of ICA in 1991, and an honorary doctorate by York University subsequent to his retirement. Gerald McGrath was elected chair of the new Working Group on the Cartographic Enterprise in 1984, which he continued to chair until 1991. Canada's second vice-presidency was conferred on D.R. Fraser Taylor at the Perth meeting, and at the next general assembly in 1987 he was elected president. In this role he has travelled extensively to increase the visibility of ICA, and to build sound working relationships with sister associations, international agencies, and PAIGH. An equally important contribution was his creation of a presidential task force on women in cartography, co-chaired by Dr E. Siekierska of Ottawa.

International Union for Surveys and Mapping (IUSM)

Technological innovations and computer applications in geomatics expanded rapidly during the 1970s. A parallel development saw photogrammetric, remote sensing, and cartographic processes overlapping increasingly. As a consequence, previously well-defined boundaries between the professional interests of the sister associations that have been described in this chapter, and the International Association of Geodesy, began to lose their sharpness. The promotion of inter-disciplinary studies of problems in surveying and mapping assumed greater significance. In addition, efforts to coordinate the scheduling of conferences and symposia by the respective organizations became a necessity. The first experimental meeting of the presidents and secretaries of the associations to explore the possibilities of a union was held in Stockholm during the FIG congress in 1977. Regular meetings began in 1979, and eventually led to the founding of the International Union of Surveying and Mapping in Harrogate, U.K., in September 1985 – unfortunately without the associations of geodesists and mining surveyors. The former joined the union later. Canada was well represented in the founding of the union by Charles Weir, then president of FIG. Fraser Taylor was elected the first president of the union in 1989 prior to its first general assembly, which was held concurrently with the ICA conference in Budapest; and J. Hugh O'Donnell of Ottawa was elected executive secretary.

International geographical congresses were held at three- or four-year intervals starting in 1871, each one being independent until the formation of the union as a permanent body in 1922. In the early postwar years the union encouraged cooperative research and communications on a wide range of geographical subjects, many of which are not pertinent to this volume. They did, however, include early maps, national atlases, the world population map, and air-photo interpretation. N.L. Nicholson was Canada's first corresponding member of the commission on national atlases, which concluded that a comparative study should be made. This was undertaken by a team of Soviet geographers and cartographers, and at the request of IGU the report and recommendations were later translated and published in Canada[26]. When discussions were held in Stockholm during the union's 1960 congress on the affiliation of ICA with the IGU, the latter established a special commission on cartography. This convened in July 1964 at the IGU congress in London to which Canadians read papers on cartographic topics and air-photo interpretation. ICA and IGU held a joint session in London before ICA opened its conference in Edinburgh. The special commission was discharged at the conclusion of the London congress, and thereafter ICA assumed responsibility for fostering international cooperation in investigating and reporting on most cartographic subjects. As time progressed remote sensing applied to mapping and GIS were added, though they had been represented strongly in IGU since 1964 and 1968 respectively. The two associations maintained close relationships and coordinated their conferences until 1984, when the respective conferences ceased to be held in the same city and ICA sought to harmonize its conference schedule with those of ISPRS and FIG. Nonetheless cooperation between IGU and ICA continued.

At its 1968 congress IGU created a commission on geographical data sensing and processing, which has proved to be highly influential and which, for twelve years, was chaired by R.F. Tomlinson of Ottawa. The first symposium on GIS was held in Ottawa in 1970 withm forty participants.[27] With the IGU congress in Montreal and the ICA conference in Ottawa, both in July 1972, the opportunity was taken to convene the second international conference on GIS in Ottawa. This was attended by 300 people, and witnessed the publication of a two-volume text on the subject – the first of its kind.[28] Canadian leadership in this emerging field continued with the publication in 1977 of the first world directory of persons who were active in geographical data handling. This was published on behalf of IGU by the Lands Directorate of Environment Canada, as were the revised editions of 1979 and 1981. The Canada Geographic Information System was one case-study described by the commission in a later publication.[29] Subsequently the commission undertook a comprehensive worldwide review of all existing software used in spatial data handling. During 1984 the commission presented in Zurich the first of a series of international symposia on spatial data handling, at which there were several Canadian papers (by J.-C. Muller, M.F. Goodchild, and R.M. Defoe).[30] Canadian contributions to this increasingly significant field have continued in the subsequent biennial meetings. Tomlinson also chaired the IGU Global Database Planning Project, which held the primary meeting on global GIS at Tylney Hall, U.K., in May 1988.

FOUR DECADES OF INTERNATIONAL ACHIEVEMENTS

In the interests of brevity, only glimpses of Canada's many international achievements in geomatics could be provided in this chapter. From these it is apparent that the origins in the immediate postwar years were modest, and were due largely to research undertaken at NRC and vigorous promotion of photogrammetric services overseas by two private sector companies. Canada's international contributions became more visible after 1951 when Canada was awarded a commission by ISP, and later undertook the Mekong project in South-East Asia. International visibility and reputation increased rather rapidly throughout the 1960s. The private sector developed creative solutions to difficult problems in control surveys and photogrammetric mapping as part of Canadian technical assistance to Commonwealth countries. Canada became a member of PAIGH, a Canadian was elected as a vice-president of ICA, and Canadian cities were selected as the venues for the 1972 conferences of ISP, ICA, and IGU. Canadian prominence reached its peak in the 1970s and early 1980s. The tempo of Canadian technical assistance to countries overseas was increased, and the scope of aid in geomatics was broadened. Canadians were senior officers of ISP and commissions of ISP, ICA, FIG, and IGU; several commission meetings were held in Canada; and Canada contributed substantially to the work of CASLE in the Western hemisphere. During the past ten years the Canadian position has been maintained. The presidencies of FIG and ICA came to Canada, and Toronto was host to the FIG congress. Despite the impact of two economic recessions, a re-orientation of CIDA aid, and greatly increased competition in export markets for geomatics, the private sector has managed to diversify its services overseas. Viewed from the present it can be said that strength of commitment, variety, and innovation have been the hallmarks of Canada's international role in the surveying, mapping, remote sensing, and geographic information sector throughout the past four decades. Canada's international position in geomatics has been secured, whilst the professional reputations of many Canadian companies, public sector organizations, institutions, and individuals have been enhanced.

NOTES

1 Thomson, Don W. 1983. Window on the Third World. The Role of the Federal Surveys and Mapping Branch in Canadian Air Survey Overseas. Unpublished report. 10.

2 Brocklebank, R.A. 1961. Mekong River Survey. *The Canadian Surveyor*, 15, 7, 402–10.

3 Zarzycki, J.M. 1963. Super-Infragon Photography and Auxiliary Data on a Mapping Program for Nigeria. *The Canadian Surveyor*, 17, 1, 13–26.
Zarzycki, J.M. 1963. Experience with a New Mapping System Employed on a Topographical Survey in Nigeria. *Proceedings, Conference of Commonwealth Survey Officers*. Paper 50. London: HMSO.

4 Gaffney, A.I. 1970. A Survey in Tanzania. *The Canadian Surveyor*, 24, 5, 576–80.

5 Zarzycki, J.M. 1971. The Use of Airborne Equipment in Surveying and Mapping in Guyana. *Proceedings, Conference of Commonwealth Survey Officers*. Paper D2. London: Foreign and Commonwealth Office, Overseas Development Administration.

6 Usher, W.D., ed. 1985. *Report of the Task Force on the Surveying and Mapping Industry in Canada*. Ottawa: Department of Regional and Industrial Expansion.

7 McLaughlin, John D. 1987. Export Opportunities for the Canadian Surveying and Mapping Industries; and Depper, Roy. In Pursuit of Export Markets. In *Proceedings, National Conference on the Economic Development of the Surveying and Mapping Industry*. Ottawa: Canadian Institute of Surveying and Mapping, 84–90; 91–4.

8 1987. *For Whose Benefit? Report of the Standing Committee on External Affairs and International Trade on Canada's Official Development Assistance Policies and Programs*. Ottawa: Queen's Printer.

9 1987. *Sharing Our Future. Canadian International Development Assistance*. Ottawa: Ministry of Supply and Services Canada.

10 For example, 1991. *Invitation Call for Proposals on Private Sector Development Initiatives Fund. For Colombia, Morocco, Pakistan and Zimbabwe*. Ottawa: CIDA.

11 1989. *Annual Review, 1988–89*. Ottawa: Energy, Mines and Resources Canada; Surveys, Mapping and Remote Sensing Sector, 1.

12 1988. Our New Direction. Surveys, Mapping and Remote Sensing Sector. Unpublished report, 17.

13 1993. *Competitiveness Strategy for the Canadian Geomatics Industry*. Ottawa: GIAC, 3.

14 Mougeot, Luc. 1977. *The Canadian participation in the PAIGH. 1944–1971*. Ottawa: Surveys and Mapping Branch, EMR.

15 Blachut, T.J., A. Chrzanowski, and J.J. Saastamoinen. 1979. *Urban Surveying and Mapping*. New York: Springer-Verlag.

16 Gutsell, Barbara J., ed. 1979. The Purpose and Use of National and Regional Atlases. *Cartographica*, supplement no. 1 to *The Canadian Cartographer*. Toronto: B.V. Gutsell.

17 1985. *Proceedings of the UN Inter-Regional Seminar on the Role of Surveying, Mapping and Charting in Country Development Programming*. Ottawa: Surveys and Mapping Branch, EMR.

18 Brandenberger, A.J. 1970. The Status of World Topographic Mapping. In *World Cartography*, vol. 10. New York: UN, 1–96.

Brandenberger, A.J. 1976. The Status of World Topographic Mapping. In *World Cartography*, vol. 14. New York: UN, 3–96.

Brandenberger, A.J. 1980. Study on the World's Surveying and Mapping Manpower and Training Facilities. In *World Cartography*, vol. 21. New York: UN, 3–72.

Brandenberger, A.J. 1983. World Topographic Mapping, 1980. In *World Cartography*, vol. 17. New York: UN, 3–38 and 45–115.

Brandenberger, A.J., and S.K. Ghosh. 1990. Status of World Topographic and Cadastral Mapping. In *World Cartography*, vol. 20. New York: UN, 1–116.

Brandenberger, A.J. 1993. Study on the World's Surveying and Mapping Human Power and Training Facilities. In *World Cartography*, vol. 22. New York: UN, 72–138.

19 Steel, R. 1978. *Surveying and Land Economy in the Atlantic Region: Facing the Challenges of the 1980s*. London: CASLE.

20 Dale, Peter F., and John D. McLaughlin. 1988. *Land Information Management*. Oxford: OUP.

21 For example, 1980. Special Edition. FIG International Symposium on Modern Technology for Cadastre and Land Information Systems. *The Canadian Surveyor*, 34, 1.

22 1980. *Proceedings of Hamburg Congress*. International Archives of Photogrammetry and Remote Sensing, 23, part A. Bonn: Committee of the Fourteenth International Congress for Photogrammetry/Photogrammetrisches Institut de Universität Bonn.

23 Ormeling, F.J. Sr. 1984. *International Cartographic Association. 25 years. 1959–1984*. Enschede, The Netherlands: International Cartographic Association.

24 Kerr, A.J. and A. Kordick, eds. 1972. *Oceanographic Cartography*. ICA.

Kerr, A.J., ed. 1980. *The Dynamics Of Oceanic Cartography. Cartographica*, 17, 2. Monograph 25. Toronto: University of Toronto Press.

Perrotte, Roland. 1985. *Coastal Zone Mapping. Cartographica*, 23, 1/2, monograph 34–5. Toronto: University of Toronto Press.

25 Curran, J.P., ed. 1988. *Compendium of Cartographic Techniques*. London: Elsevier.

26 Fremlin, G., and L.M. Sebert, eds. 1972. National Atlases. *Cartographica,* monograph no. 4.

27 Tomlinson, R.F., ed. 1970. *Environment Information Systems. Proceedings of the UNESCO/IGU First Symposium on Geographical Information Systems.* Ottawa: IGU Commission on Geographical Data Sensing and Processing.

28 Tomlinson, R.F., (ed.) 1972. *Geographical Data Handling*, 2 vols. Ottawa: IGU Commission on Geographical Data Sensing and Processing.

29 Tomlinson, R.F., H.W. Calkins, and D.R. Marble. 1976. *Computer Handling of Geographical Data.* Natural Resources Research, monograph 13. Paris: Unesco Press.

30 1984. *Proceedings of the International Symposium on Spatial Data Handling.* Zurich: Geographisches Institut, Universität Zurich-Irchel.

CHAPTER NINETEEN

Retrospect and Prospects

Gerald McGrath

THE PERIOD IN RETROSPECT

As these pages are being written, Canada is preparing to enter a new century and a new millenium. The mood of the country today is certainly different from that one hundred years ago. In 1896 George Washington Carmack had discovered gold in quantity on the Klondike River. Men had left their banks, abandoned their farms, forgotten their fisheries, and headed north-west to fame and fortune. Of course this ebullience was short-lived, and reality set in long before many of these adventurers reached the Yukon. The twentieth century has had its full share of disillusionment. Two terrible wars and a series of soul-destroying recessions have left their mark. It was once thought that Canada's great natural resources would always be a buffer against difficult times, but resource extraction has its sombre aspect. Mines inevitably cause pollution, at least locally. Timber harvesting becomes a sardonic phrase if unrestricted over-cutting is permitted. There are too many examples of the way in which over-fishing can ruin a viable industry. But there is ample evidence that these lessons have been learned. The fields of endeavour outlined in the chapters of this book illustrate how science can foster resource development. Many of these same fields have provided monitoring systems and information storage facilities that will allow correct long-term development strategies to be followed. It is in this spirit that we make a final review of the past fifty years, and present a glimpse into the future.

In the immediate postwar world both external and internal factors forced the federal government to take a new view of the national requirements for surveying, mapping, and charting. The federal Surveys and Mapping Branch (SMB) was the agency responsible for the new nationwide programmes of surveying and mapping. It was given the full assistance of the Army Survey Establishment (ASE) of National Defence, which worked hard on the basic mapping series until it was assigned other international military commitments in 1966. The control survey network was extended by taking advantage of each succeeding technological innovation so that truly national coverage could be achieved for the first time. The expanded network was re-computed during the 1980s in cooperation with the U.S. and the provinces to provide a coherent continental coordinate system known as NAD83. Aerial triangulation as the basis for photogrammetric mapping was completed for the whole country. The first national topographic mapping coverage at 1:250 000 scale was finished in 1971, and almost all of the 12 990 map sheets at 1:50 000 scale had been published by 1994. Moreover the metrication of the map series has been accomplished. Digital versions of the 1:250 000 maps are now available, and the 1:50 000 digital programme is advancing steadily. Aeronautical charting has responded to the innovations in air navigation installed on the ground and in successive generations of aircraft, and is now operating in a digital environment. The substantial growth of SMB as the responsible federal agency came to a halt in the late 1970s, and was then reversed as more of its production work was contracted to the expanding and dynamic private sector. But the agency has also played a central and vital role in the national coordination of surveying and mapping, and continues to do so. The Canadian Hydrographic Service (CHS) assumed responsibility for national hydro-graphic charting, initially as an entity within SMB and then in Fisheries and Oceans. It also has applied evolving technology to positioning hydrographic vessels, and to gathering data on water depths and the seabed. In addition it has commissioned the development of sensors and vessels that are appropriate to Canadian waters and harsh environments, particularly in the North. Hydrographic charting has been expanded greatly and metricated, and special-purpose charting for resource inventories, fishing, and recreational boating have become standard products.

Wartime inventions were adapted to help meet the challenges of early postwar Canadian surveys and mapping. As George Babbage has indicated, the Shoran technique of position-ing control stations by airborne radar was the means of extending control throughout the North at a rate that could not have been equalled by any other current surveying technique. Several authors have referred to the role of the Airborne Profile Recorder (APR), which became an established method of determining heights for topographic mapping by photo-grammetry, and was used extensively in Canada and overseas. From 1952 the National Research Council's Photogrammetric Research Section was a prolific source of creativity and inventions, primarily but not exclusively in photogrammetry, throughout its thirty-five year life. Procedures for the numerical adjustment of aerial triangulation, the invention of the analytical plotter, and stereo-orthophotographs are but three of many successes from NRC. Beginning in the 1960s the universities added their contributions in satellite position-ing, photogrammetry, computer-assisted cartography, digital mapping, remote sensing, and deformation analysis. Reference to research would be incomplete without mentioning private industry and its achievements, particularly in remote sensing where Macdonald Detwiller of Vancouver has become synonymous with the reception and processing of satellite data.

Canada took an early lead in the development of geographical and land information systems, the former in the federal CGIS and the latter in the LRIS of the Maritimes provinces. Both achieved international recognition and were studied closely by other countries. There were also early and significant initiatives in automated cartography within SMB and CHS. Though the former was overtaken by the development of digital photogrammetric mapping techniques within the same organization during the mid-1970s, the latter was the first step in a series of improvements leading to the automation of most phases in the construction of hydrographic charts. Douglas and Poiker became well-known for their algorithm on cartographic generalization, which was followed by others from these and other researchers.

From these beginnings has arisen the widespread use of computer-assisted cartography in Canada, and subsequently GIS, at all levels of government, in the private sector, and in academia. Neither GIS nor computer-assisted cartography has yet had a major impact on the design, production, and publication of federal, provincial, school, and special-purpose atlases – of which many have been published since the Second World War. This is consistent with experience in other countries. The production of thematic maps has, however, been affected to a much greater extent by computer-assisted cartography, and latterly by GIS. The late 1970s saw the birth of a Canadian private sector capability in computer-asssisted cartography, and later GIS, which has resulted in worldwide use of Canadian software such as GEOVISION, SPANS, PAMAP, and CARIS. Perhaps the only serious shortcoming was the delay in recognizing that structured topographic digital data would be highly significant to users of GIS. In this Canada was not alone.

Although there had been an earlier provincial topographic mapping capability in British Columbia, the onset of provincial mapping programmes intended to achieve coverage of the provinces at map scales larger than those of the federal government occurred during the 1970s. There were two principal requirements for such mapping: as a general-purpose tool for the operating departments of municipal governments and resource managers in rural areas, and as a base for land registration and property valuation. Urban and rural coverage required many thousands of hard-copy map sheets and, subsequently, the introduction of digital mapping. In several provinces the mapping was contracted to the private sector, thus contributing to the strengthening of an industry that had already distinguished itself overseas. Mention has been made of the Maritimes LRIS as the first provincial land information system. This was followed in the 1980s by major land information programmes in other provinces, and the building of land and engineering information systems in many cities. Today the principal centre of activity in initial or new topographic mapping lies in the provinces, as does the burden of ensuring that the mapping and digital databases are kept up to date. This has significant implications for the future of federal topographic activities.

Canada's participation in surveying and mapping overseas is both a postwar phenomenon and a story of continuing success. Canadian aerial survey companies were pioneers in exposing aerial photography for governments and private sector clients overseas. The interpretation of the photographs was soon added as a service, and by the late 1950s a consortium of Canadian private companies was providing topographic and engineering mapping services to a major development project in South-East Asia. The creation of the External Aid Office, and later CIDA, resulted in numerous surveying and mapping projects overseas being funded by the federal government but executed by Canadian private industry. The principal contributions of SMB throughout the 1960s and 1970s were liaison with overseas governments, technical advice to the aid agency, and the technical supervision of aid contracts. This Canadian response to the provision of overseas aid in surveying and mapping was markedly different from that in the U.K. Throughout the period the private sector continued to find clients in need of control surveys, aerial photography, and mapping. Its more recent expansion into cadastral and spatial information systems was a response to changing technology and an emerging overseas market for such services. From the late 1980s the efforts of the federal and some provincial governments have been directed jointly with industry to winning contracts overseas in what has become a fiercely competitive market. Nevertheless success continues.

The same aerial survey companies were also involved in early postwar air-photo interpretation projects within Canada, as was the federal Forestry Branch. The latter was joined by such federal departments as Agriculture and ARDA in extensive use of photo interpretation in agriculture, resource and land-use mapping, and terrain evaluation. Private sector consultants and academics also made important contributions. As Leo Sayn-Wittgenstein has indicated, the first half of the postwar period was marked by a growing and wide range of Canadian capabilities in interpreting aerial photography. A pivotal element in the Canadian response to the U.S. programme of satellite remote sensing was the founding of CCRS. This helped to ensure a national role for remote sensing in Canada, largely but not exclusively based on the reception, processing, analysis, and classification of data from the U.S. earth-orbiting resource satellites. The many achievements of CCRS have ranged from innovations in data processing to the development of sensors and creating a wide variety of applications. Amongst the last there have been important connections with initial medium-scale topographic mapping and map revision, and with shallow-water bathymetry for nautical charting. Remote sensing has not by any means been confined to the federal government. Provincial remote sensing centres were also established in the 1970s. Most have made substantial contributions to the development of applications, and the transfer of technology to prospective users of remote sensing. At least one has also assisted overseas governments. Private industry has been an essential partner with government in the expansion and full utilization of remote sensing in Canada and, since the early 1980s, in a growing number of countries overseas.

Angus Hamilton has described the perceptions of the postwar need for higher education in surveying and mapping independent of other disciplines. During a period of twenty years three university undergraduate degree programmes in surveying and mapping were added to the existing offering at Laval University. Graduate degrees followed in close association with the research activities of the academic staff. Most of these relatively youthful academic departments have achieved national and international recognition for the high standards of their education, research, and professional activities. So also has post-secondary training in surveying, photogrammetry, cartography, remote sensing, and, more recently, Geographic Information Systems been introduced in institutes and colleges of applied arts and technology across Canada. Several departments of geography began to offer undergraduate courses in surveying, photogrammetry, and cartography during the 1960s. Graduate degrees in cartography, remote sensing, and GIS were added later. As spatial information has become more readily available, users and applications have become more diverse, and the measurement sciences of surveying and photogrammetry have been broadened, interdisciplinary boundaries have become less significant. This is especially the case in remote sensing and GIS. These developments have been partially responsible for the replacement of "surveying engineering" and "surveying" in the titles of academic programmes by "geomatics engineering" and "geomatics."

Perhaps one of the most significant factors of the postwar period has been the manner in which recent governments have come to view their purposes, responsibilities, and activities. Although there were earlier indications of growing concern, effectively the process of fundamental review began outside Canada in 1980. It was emulated later by successive governments in Canada, and gathered momentum during the balance of the decade. No part of Canada has been exempted. Nor have geomatics organizations in government. In these cases the starting point was the capital and recurrent costs of the organization, and the very modest revenues that were then collected from the sales of products and services. It was concluded that the recovery of costs should be increased, although it would still remain partial. In some cases government set specific financial targets for cost recovery. Whether or not this was the case, almost all geomatics organizations have reviewed the pricing of their products and services within the context of increasing revenues. The resulting price increases have occasionally been startling, and have raised the question of whether the organization is still intended to serve the public good. In some situations there has been pressure upon the geomatics organization to be more sensitive to actual and potential users of its data, products, and services. Amongst the responses have been the development of new products, a greatly increased emphasis on digital data and customizing those data to meet the requirements of specific customers, increased promotion of products and services to more clearly defined groups of customers, and improved means of distributing the products. These processes are far from being completed.

Canada in the 1990s is responding to a change that is continuing and applies equally to other countries. It is the transformation of the economy from one in which the creation of wealth has arisen mainly from the extraction of resources and manufacturing to the increasingly significant contribution of wealth created from ideas, information, and innovation. The latter offers geomatics unprecedented opportunitities for diversification and growth, both domestically and abroad.

THE FUTURE PROSPECTS?

In an age of predictions by many soothsayers, Canadians can be sure of one thing: change will continue. Indeed it may well accelerate. This concluding section will provide a glimpse into the future of geomatics to complement the forecasts made by several authors in this volume.

Due to ubiquitous and increasingly "user-friendly" computer-based technology, the users of digital spatial data will become more and more independent of the traditional collectors, processors, and packagers of such data – that is the government agencies that have acted in this capacity since the 1970s and 1980s. These agencies will have to become increasingly orientated to corporate and individual users of spatial data, and to understanding and responding to their needs. The number of small firms in the private sector that process and add value to basic spatial data will rise, though the continued success of such firms will depend upon their being efficient, responsive, and competitive. Arguably the most important development will be the swelling population of individual users of spatial data. They will obtain the data they require from both government and private sector wholesalers and retailers, and will combine, manipulate, and extract from the data sets using proprietary software.

There are precedents for the integration of positioning, remote sensing, and spatial information systems. The integrated electronic nautical chart and marine navigation system is already operational. There are several car navigation systems in limited use. And to some extent the integration of remotely sensed digital data with data sets in geographic information systems is established. In all cases of integration there will be continued expansion of capabilities (which will include multi-media), enhancement of analytical functions, greater simplification of use, and increased accessibility to a wider community of users.

The last will depend mostly upon careful market research and innovative marketing, particularly in pricing the product so that there is not a significant barrier to acceptance. It is clear that the multinational companies that manufacture computer and electronic systems understand the factor of competitive pricing. So also must those who integrate positioning, remote sensing, and spatial information systems, and who supply data that integrated systems can utilize.

The quality of spatial data has always been of concern to public and private sector surveying, mapping, charting, and cadastral organizations. It has been reflected in such features as error ellipses for survey control stations, map reliability diagrams, classifications of overall map accuracy, revision patches on nautical charts, revision or replacement of topographic and cadastral maps, and precise timing on documents deposited in land registries. As spatial data become more readily available, accessible, and widely used, there will be increased emphasis on quality. This will include detailed identification of the source of the data, clear statements on their currency or up-to-dateness, and careful assessments of the reliability of the data. It will apply to all spatial data, both in graphic and textual form. The management of quality will assume greater significance to organizations and individuals concerned with the collection, delivery, and use of spatial data. To some extent this will be influenced by the International Standards Organisation and its ISO 9000 or succeeding standards. Programmes of Total Quality Management will become routine in organizations that handle spatial data. This renewed focus on quality will also require the producer to specify the extent of liability for the data that are released.

With the increased availability of digital spatial data it might be expected that hard-copy topographic maps, charts, atlases, and thematic maps will be replaced in their entirety by digital versions. Such predictions have been made in the past. Given the nature of developments during the past fifteen years, it is clear that these hard-copy products will endure well into the twenty-first century – though high-quality electrostatic printing in colour may gradually replace conventional lithographic printing of many maps. The life of a personal vehicle means that car navigation systems will not replace the compact and inexpensive road atlas overnight. Despite government regulations that require hydrographic charts to be carried on small boats used for recreational purposes, the number and diversity of boats is such that electronic chart and navigation systems will remain inappropriate or beyond the financial means of many boat owners. Nor will the avid hiker replace standard topographic maps – even outdated maps – with GPS and digital topographic maps at current prices. Nevertheless the pace of technological innovation and declining prices of hardware, software, and data will increase the penetration of digital services and products. As this happens, conventional hard-copy products will gradually become rare in the same manner as tape cassettes are being superseded by compact discs.

Electronic access to records and indexes in computerized land registries is already available to approved users in several Canadian provinces. The electronic transfer of spatial files between producers and users has also become routine, though the specific standards to be employed in the transfer of data have been the subject of much discussion. These closely controlled situations are not, however, representative of the so-called information highway. This will have diverse branches with a multitude of possible interconnections. For spatial information it can be said that Canada has only recently commenced its journey along this highway. But there are indications that the highway will become more and more relevant to the identification, promotion, and especially distribution of digital and non-digital spatial information products to a wider range of users. The Internet and the World Wide Web are already being used for these purposes in an exploratory way. There will be new openings for the education of actual and prospective users on the nature, characteristics, and applications of spatial data in both hard-copy and digital forms. Indeed there will be unprecedented opportunities for ingenuity and creativity in the use of the highway by agencies, companies, and individuals that have data to offer and needs to be satisfied.

Most of the current "capital" programmes for creating the federal and provincial control survey networks and digital databases, both topographic and cadastral, will be completed before the end of the century. The federal and provincial surveying, mapping, and land information agencies will, therefore, have to readjust to the ongoing function of maintaining the networks and databases. In all probability the widespread use of GPS for positioning will result in only a selection of the stations in the control networks having to be maintained permanently. Organizational and technical means of transferring spatial data between federal, provincial, and municipal agencies will become more critical in maintaining digital databases. The overall context for these challenging readjustments will be continued government financial stringency, and renewed pressures to contract out much of the work of maintenance to the private sector. Given these circumstances it is highly likely that the staff of the surveying, mapping, and land information agencies will be reduced even further. Additional steps will be taken towards privatization of the agencies, and one or more may be privatized. The exception may be those agencies that have statutory responsibilities for the accuracy and integrity of land records.

Faced with the challenges described above, there will be a growing need for surveying, mapping, and land information agencies to define more clearly the nature of their ongoing business. The physical and mathematical maintenance of the network or selected points within it may be a part. The agency may also continue to be responsible for the currency, accuracy, and integrity of data in its textual and graphic databases. It may publish hard-copy maps. But overall, the future emphasis is likely to be more on the supply of services than the provision of products. The agencies will become integrators of data from different data sets, knowing the characteristics and quality of each set. They will design new products but not necessarily produce them, this task falling more and more to the private sector under contract. They will facilitate data exchange with other levels of government so that databases at all levels can be maintained properly and cost-effectively. And by no means the least, the agencies will be advisors to a wider group of users of spatial information, many of whom will be less sophisticated users than in the past.

Over the years Canada has achieved an enviable reputation for the quality of the assistance in geomatics it has given to overseas clients. Competition in the international market for geomatics has been intensified of late as additional countries and private sector firms have entered the arena. All indications point to increased competition continuing into the next century. Yet the opportunities for Canadian governments, industry, and academia have already been diversified. They include demonstration projects in the modernization of surveying, mapping, and spatial information systems; the transfer of Canadian technology and methodology; and human resource development through education and training on a greater scale than before. The number of surveying, mapping, and land information systems that are still to be modernized worldwide exceeds what has been accomplished thus far. These represent the future opportunities to which Canadian institutions and companies must respond. Whilst Canada has generally been able to meet the requirements of an overseas project without the participation of a government or private firm from another country, this may well change. Indeed what is known colloquially as "networking" with non-Canadian organizations may become essential to ensure that the opportunities of the future are realized.

This, then, is one view of the future for geomatics at the beginning of the twenty-first century. In some aspects of geomatics change will be accelerated, and in some it will be profound. Public institutions, private firms, and academia will all be affected. New opportunities will be created. And if the record of the past fifty years is indicative of future prospects, Canada's responses to new opportunities will be positive, creative, and innovative.

APPENDICES

Authors

GEORGE BABBAGE was born in Cape Town, South Africa. He graduated from the University of Cape Town (BSc. 1950). He emigrated to Canada in 1953, and was employed by EMR until his retirement in 1991. He served with Legal Surveys, Branch Headquarters, and Geodetic Survey. He was appointed dominion geodesist in 1988 and director general, Canada Centre for Surveying in 1989.

TEODOR J. BLACHUT, Dr.Sc.Techn, Dr.h.c., FRSC, F.PAN. was born and educated in Poland. In the Second World War he served with the Polish army in Poland and France. He is a researcher, inventor, and author of numerous publications. From 1951 until 1980 he was head of the Photogrammetric Research Section at NRC. After his retirement he continued to be active as a consultant to the Canadian mapping industry and foreign governments. He travelled extensively conducting studies and organizing pilot projects. His textbooks have been translated into many languages.

HENRY CASTNER, B.Sc., M.A., Ph.D., is Emeritus Professor of Geography at Queen's University where he spent twenty-five years teaching and conducting research on map design, map perception, and the relationship between mapping and geographic education. He is the author of *Seeking New Horizons: A Perceptual Approach to Geographic Education*. He is now living in North Carolina.

ADAM CHRZANOWSKI is chairman of the Department of Geodesy and Geomatics Engineering at UNB. He received B.Sc., M.Eng., and Ph.D. degrees from the Technical University of Mining in Krakow, Poland. He is leader of the FIG Study Group 6C on Deformation Surveys, and is a presidium member of the International Society of Mine Surveying. He is the author of numerous books on engineering surveying

GEORGE FALCONER, B.A., M.A., is a geographer. He did research in the physical geography of northern Canada for EMR from 1958 to 1967, after which he joined the National

Atlas Project. He became chief of the Geography Division, and later senior advisor in the National Geographic Information Division. From 1975 to 1989 he was editor-in-chief of *The National Atlas of Canada*.

DAVID GRAY, M.A.Sc, P.Eng., CLS, transferred in 1971 from Geodetic Survey to the Canadian Hydrographic Service where he is at present the geodesy and radio positioning specialist. He is the author of papers on radio propagation, maritime boundaries, toponymy, and geodetic positioning. He is associate editor (Hydrography) for *Geomatica*.

ANGUS HAMILTON, M.A.Sc., was chairman of the Department of Surveying Engineering (now the Department of Geodesy and Geomatics Engineering) at UNB from 1971 to 1985, and is now a professor emeritus in the department. From 1951 he held various surveying and mapping positions in what is now Natural Resources Canada.

FRANK HEGYI has a B.Sc. degree in forestry from the University of Edinburgh and an M.Sc. in biometrics from the University of Toronto. He started his career in remote sensing in Guyana (1961–64), and then worked with the Canadian Forestry Service for eleven years. From 1978 to 1990 he was director of the B.C. Forest Inventory Program. Currently he is president of Hegyi Geotechnologies International.

HELEN KERFOOT, B.Sc., is executive secretary of the Canadian Permanent Committee on Geographic Names, and is currently vice chief of the United Nations Group of Experts on Geographical Names. She is the author of various articles and papers on place-names and related subjects.

GERARD LACHAPELLE, P.Eng., CLS, is a professor in the Department of Geomatics Engineering at the University of Calgary. He holds a B.Sc. from Laval, an M.Sc. from Oxford, an L.Ph. from the University of Helsinki, and a Ph.D. from the Technical University at Graz. He is past president of the Canadian Institute of Geomatics and the Association of Canada Lands Surveyors. He is the author of many papers on geodesy and related subjects.

ALEC McEWEN, LL.D., Ph.D., CLS, is Professor of Cadastral Studies at the University of Calgary. Previously he served for fifteen years as Canada's International Boundary Commissioner. He is qualified as an OLS, CLS, and NLS, and has spent over forty years as a surveyor in Canada and overseas. Among his many publications are two books, *International Boundaries of East Africa* and *In Search of the Highlands*.

GERALD McGRATH served the Directorate of Overseas Surveys (DOS) in East Africa after undergraduate and graduate work in surveying in the U.K. He then taught at Makerere University in Kampala before being appointed to Queen's University at Kingston in 1962. He has published four books and numerous papers, was Professor of Cartography at ITC in The Netherlands during the 1980s, and has undertaken land information investigations in Saudi Arabia, Indonesia, Kenya, Romania, Moldova, and India.

DONALD McLARTY was president of the Canadian Association of Aerial Surveyors (now the Geomatics Industry Association of Canada) from 1968 until his retirement in 1988.

Prior to 1966 McLarty held senior management positions with the Photographic Survey Corporation of Toronto and Spartan Air Services of Ottawa. He was first appointed vice-president (overseas) and later president of Spartan.

LESLIE O'BRIEN, B.Sc., M.Sc., had a long career in surveying and mapping in the federal government, beginning as a military survey officer in 1951, and concluding with his retirement in 1991 as the director general of the Canada Centre for Mapping, Department of Energy Mines and Resources (now NRCan).

ALLAN ROBERTS, now retired, was formerly director of surveys in the Manitoba Department of Natural Resources from 1969 to 1983. He qualified as a New Zealand Land Surveyor before emigrating to Canada where he qualified as a Manitoba Land Surveyor in 1953.

ROBERT RYERSON was chief, Industrial Cooperation and Communications at the Canada Centre for Remote Sensing. He received his M.Sc. at McMaster and his Ph.D. in environmental studies at Waterloo. He has been chairman of the Canadian Remote Sensing Society, secretary of Commission 7 of ISPRS, and is editor-in-chief of the third edition of the *Manual of Remote Sensing*.

LEO SAYN-WITTGENSTEIN was director general of the Canada Centre for Remote Sensing, a position he held from 1987 to his retirement. He graduated from U of T (B.Sc. forestry 1957), and received his Ph.D. from Yale (1966). He has served as research scientist and later as director of the Forest Management Institute, and was a founding principal and then president of Dendron Resource Surveys. He has published extensively on air-photo interpretation and remote sensing.

LOUIS SEBERT, B.A.Sc, P.Eng., DLS, graduated in mining engineering from the University of Toronto in 1940. He remained in the army after the war, transferring from the Armoured Corps to the Army Survey Establishment in 1947. In 1965 he retired from the army and joined the Surveys and Mapping Branch, EMR. He retired once again in 1981.

IAIN TAYLOR was chief geographer, Canada Centre for Mapping, and has degrees in geography from the Universities of Leeds, Toronto, and Liverpool (Ph.D. 1976).He was research coordinator on the *Economic Atlas of Ontario*, teacher at Seneca College, tutor for the Open University, U.K., and head, Social Sciences and later director of northern region at Athabasca University. He was appointed chief geographer in 1991.

ROGER TOMLINSON, Ph.D., F.R.G.S., is president of Tomlinson Associates Ltd Consulting Geographers of Ottawa. He originated GIS and named the field. He is editor of *Geographical Data Handling* and four other GIS books, and is the author of numerous papers on GIS. He has now had over thirty years of worldwide consulting experience in GIS planning and management.

MICHAEL TOOMEY was born in England, and spent the first half of his career working in the surveys and mapping industry in Africa and the Middle East. He came to Canada in

1967 and worked in the photogrammetric mapping industry before joining the Alberta Bureau of Surveying and Mapping in 1984. He is now the executive director of information resource management services for the Alberta Department of the Environment.

LILLIAN WONDERS, B.A. (U of Washington), M.A. (Syracuse University) is now retired after an active career as a lecturer in cartography at the Universities of Washington, Toronto, and Alberta. She has been a member of the United Nations Cartographic Unit, and is co-editor of the *Junior Atlas of Alberta*, published in 1979.

GEORGE ZARZYCKI, Ph.D., P.Eng., has held the positions of director, Surveys and Mapping and Remote Sensing Branch of the Ontario Ministry of Natural Resources, and director of the Topographical Survey Division of EMR. He was one of the founders of Terra Surveys Ltd and then executive vice-president of Canadian Aero Service Ltd. While working in both the Ontario and federal governments he pioneered the application of digital methods in photogrammetry and the integration of digital mapping with remote sensing and GIS.

The Canadian Permanent Committee on Geographical Names and Canada's Toponymy

Helen Kerfoot

INTRODUCTION

At a brief meeting in Ottawa's Langevin Block on 15 May 1946 seven members of the Geographic Board of Canada regrouped after a lack of such gatherings during the years of the Second World War. This rebirth of the board increased the level of geographical naming activity in Canada, following the very limited duties undertaken by the secretary, J.H. Corry, and a small executive committee in the Depression and war years.

The next five decades would bring extensive changes to the operation of the board, with increased provincial and territorial participation, and the creation of advisory committees to address particular areas of toponymic concern. They would herald major strides forward in methods of record keeping and communication with the use of computers, and witness Canadian participation internationally in geographical names standardization. Field collection of geographical names would increase in importance, principles and procedures for naming would be updated, and dissemination of data in printed and digital form would increase in importance.

THE FIRST FIFTY YEARS OF CANADA'S NAMES AUTHORITY (1897–1947)

The roots of Canada's national names authority[1,2] can be traced back to the 1880s. For years surveyors, geographers, geologists, and map makers had recognized the need for a single body to which questions of geographical nomenclature and orthography could be referred for decision. Inconsistencies in spelling and application of geographical names, particularly on federal government maps, marine charts, and other documents, could then be avoided. At the 1888 annual meeting of the Dominion Land Surveyors Association in Ottawa feature names given by Lt Frederick Schwatka's American military reconnaisance in the Yukon River basin (1883) drew considerable negative reaction. He had applied "... entirely new names to features which were well known and had already been named by miners." The resulting *Report of Proceedings* notes "... the numerous conflictions and absurdities in geographical names that were to be met with in all parts of the Dominion."[3] A

Table 1

Chairs of the Geographic Board of Canada, the Canadian
Board on Geographical Names, and the Canadian
Permanent Committee on Geographical Names

Name	Dates in office
Gourdeau, François F.	1898–1910
Anderson, William P.	1911–13
Deville, Édouard G.	1913–24
Anderson, William P.	1924–26
White, James	1927–28
Craig, John D.	1928–31
Boyd, Walter H.	1932–40
Dickison, Alexander	1940–45
Peters, Frederic H.	1946–48
Chipman, Kenneth G.	1948–49
Palmer, Philip E.	1949–54
Smith, Cyril H.	1954–59
Nicholson, Norman L.	1959–64
Drolet, Jean-Paul	1964–88
O'Donnell, J. Hugh	1988–90
Dorion, Henri	1990–91
O'Donnell, J. Hugh	1991–92
Price, E. Anthony	1992–present

month later the DLS Association president, E.J. Rainboth, submitted to the Minister of the Interior six recommendations concerning the standardization of geographical names and the compilation of an authentic reference dictionary.

In 1890, through the work of A.H. Whitcher, the Department of the Interior made efforts to ensure uniformity of nomenclature on federal government publications and issued a list of existing feature names to surveyors in north-western Canada. Early in 1892, at the request of the deputy minister of the Interior, acting surveyor-general W.F. King submitted a recommendation for the appointment of a Board on Geographical Nomenclature. It was pointed out in 1897 that "... in consequence of our inaction ... the United States Board is now ruling upon Canadian names."[4] Only then was prompt action taken by order in council of 18 December 1897 to establish the first national names authority – the Geographic Board of Canada.

The early days of the board were ones of federal authority with six members from different departments, F. Gourdeau, deputy minister of Marine and Fisheries, as chairman, and A.H. Whitcher of the Department of the Interior as secretary (see tables 1 and 2). Rules of nomenclature were drawn up, the Royal Geographical Society rules of orthography (R.G.S. II System) were adopted, and departments were directed to use the names and orthography as approved by the board. Quickly it was realized that participation of the provinces was desirable. A new order in council in 1899 gave each province and the North-West Territories (as it existed at the time) the right to appoint a member to advise the board, provided that their government accepted board decisions. Québec declined this arrangement; the province did provide names to the secretary of the board, and Ottawa referred questions to the Québec Geographic Board established in 1912. Despite assurance to provincial members that they had equal status with federal members, the recommendations they made to the Geographic Board of Canada were not always accepted without amendment, and on several occasions

Table 2
Secretaries of the Geographic Board of Canada,
the Canadian Board on Geographical Names, and the
Canadian Permament Committee on Geographical Names

Name	Dates in office
Whitcher, Arthur H.*	1897–1916
Douglas, Robert	1916–30
Corry, J. Harry	1931–46
Palmer, Philip E.	1946–48
Skinner, Lyman B.	1948–53
Munroe, G. Max	1954–62
Fraser, J. Keith	1962–68
Delaney, Gordon F.	1968–73
Rayburn, Alan	1973–87
Kerfoot, Helen	1987–present

* Also acted in secretarial capacity from 1892 to 1897, prior to
the establishment of the Geographic Board of Canada.

board meeting minutes indicate that the functioning of the board was being questioned and that better cooperation with the provinces was being urged.

At monthly board meetings[5] members discussed names proposed for inclusion on particular topographic and geological maps, and hydrographic charts of various scales. Local usage became of prime importance, and new names to be considered for approval were divided between "established" and "contentious," usually based on the criterion of usage. Names for post offices and railway stations came before the board, as did public submissions such as lists of names supplied by explorers.

Between 1900 and 1928 the board published nineteen reports containing principles of nomenclature and decisions on names. Two were of particular significance: the Ninth Report of 1910, which included maps and origin information on names in the Northwest Territories, as well as lists for Québec and the Thousand Islands; and the Eighteenth Report of 1924, which contained a cumulative list of decisions since the inception of the board in 1897. Various names studies were published by the board prior to the Second World War. James White (board member 1898–1928) wrote the studies in the Ninth Report; Robert Douglas (board secretary 1916–30) produced place-name booklets, including those for Prince Edward Island, Alberta, and Manitoba. In the late 1930s the board was only able to meet on an occasional basis, and as the war years drew on most of the work was carried out at the clerical level, with names lists for a large number of maps being circulated to available executive committee members for their concurrence.

POSTWAR DEVELOPMENTS (LATE 1940S AND 1950S)

After the war, meetings of the board were restarted on a monthly basis[6] and the purpose and functions of the board discussed. A new order in council was passed in 1947 providing the board with staff and a publications budget; the board's name was then altered to the Canadian Board on Geographical Names (CBGN). Representation from the provinces was encouraged by holding annual spring meetings in collaboration with meetings of the Canadian Institute of Surveying.

The board continued standardizing post office, railway, and national park names, as well as approving names for an increased number of federal maps being compiled for publication. Various

Table 3
Gazetteer Production

* Répertoire géographique du Québec

issues required resolution, including increased emphasis on local usage, map sheet titles, alphabetizing standards, the use of possessive forms of names, and generic terminology.

With a larger staff the new board was able to address the need to publicize official names. The *Gazetteer of Canada* series was initiated in 1952 with the production of a volume on Southwestern Ontario. Since then volumes in the series have been published on a province-by-province basis, with several editions completed for each jurisdiction except Québec. The Commission de toponymie du Québec (CTQ) has maintained its own detailed records and has published three editions of its own repertoire. The Canadian Hydrographic Service has produced two editions of a *Gazetteer of Undersea Feature Names* for the CPCGN (see table 3).

Soon after the Second World War, one of Canada's most contentious name changes brought forth public outcry in support of established names and provincial names management. In 1946 Castle Mountain near Banff, Alberta, was renamed on instruction from the prime minister's office to recognize the contributions of Gen. Dwight D. Eisenhower to the Allied victory. Copious files of correspondence from the public accumulated on this single name change, until in 1979 a decision was reached that would satisfy the supporters of both names. Castle Mountain was restored and Eisenhower Peak was designated for the most prominent summit on the mountain.

The postwar years were also busy days in the mapping and naming of Canada's North – many islands were individually identified, for example those of the Borden–Mackenzie King group. The later stages of this phase of "completing the map of Northern Canada" led to the "discovery" and naming (in 1949) of an island in Foxe Basin for Prince Charles. Subsequently, one of the last features to be named for the royal family was the archipelago north of Parry Channel, which in January 1954 received the appellation Queen Elizabeth Islands.

In the 1940s the first steps were taken to commemorate Canadians who had given their lives in the Second World War. This programme, which was to blossom in later years, started with the assignment of the names of decorated war casualties to features in the northern Prairie provinces and the Northwest Territories. Still now in the 1990s Manitoba, Saskatchewan, and British Columbia, in particular, continue to name geographical features for war casualties and to present commemorative scrolls to their families in association with these programmes.

The original rules of nomenclature of the board had been written in 1898. They received minor modifications through the years until, in 1955, the CBGN undertook a complete revision[7] of the principles and procedures and outlined the duties and responsibilities of the board, its three-member executive committee, and the secretary. In later years the publication *Principles and Procedures for Geographical Naming* would be updated on a regular basis.

A NEW APPROACH (1960S AND 1970S)

The board was again reorganized in 1961 to create the Canadian Permanent Committee on Geographical Names (CPCGN). In accordance with a recommendation from Prime Minister Diefenbaker, appropriate federal and provincial ministers were given the authority to decide on names within their jurisdictions. Responsibility for names in the Northwest Territories and Yukon Territory, however, would still remain with the federal Department of Indian Affairs and Northern Development until devolution of these functions in 1984. No longer was there in the 1960s a need for the executive committee in the decision-making process, but the position of executive secretary for the CPCGN was formally designated. Initially the chair of the CPCGN was the director of the Geographical Branch, but in the mid-1960s this respon-sibility was assigned to the senior assistant deputy minister of the federal Energy, Mines and Resources. With great interest, enthusiasm, and integrity Jean-Paul Drolet provided strong leadership in this role and chaired the CPCGN annual meetings[8] for over twenty years, from 1965 to 1988. In recent years the position of CPCGN chair became a ministerial appointee from the private sector.

The methods of collecting and verifying toponyms changed quite considerably in the 1960s and 1970s. Prior to the mid-1960s the process of updating nomenclature on federal maps and charts depended to a large extent on the survey crews of Topographical Survey and Canadian Hydrographic Service. Other sources of new names information came from the CBGN members and from the public. However collection and verification of names at that time[9] could not be considered either systematic or comprehensive.

Several field studies were then undertaken by federal-provincial cooperation. The first comprehen-sive survey, in Renfrew County (Ontario) in 1964, revealed that some 20 percent of existing names on federal maps needed correction when reviewed by local inhabitants for contemporary relevance. The fieldwork essentially doubled the existing stock of toponyms in current use. Several systematic studies of complete provinces followed: New Brunswick (1967–69); Prince Edward Island (1966, 1970–71); Nova Scotia (1972–74); and Manitoba (1975–76). These detailed projects added substan-tially to the toponymic records for Canada, they reinforced the importance of local usage, and, particularly in the case of Manitoba, the studies laid the ground work for recognition of aboriginal names from unwritten languages.

In conjunction with the fieldwork considerable archival research was undertaken, either by the individuals leading the projects or by contractors. After perusal of various archival map collections they gathered a wealth of historical toponymic material. For Nova Scotia and Manitoba most of this documentation remains in manuscript form. The information from the Prince Edward Island and New Brunswick work, however, was prepared by Alan Rayburn for the first two (and only two) *Toponymy Studies*, published by the Surveys and Mapping Branch for the CPCGN (Prince Edward Island 1973; New Brunswick 1975).

While some provinces entered into federal-provincial projects where costs and expertise were shared, others developed and implemented their own independent studies. Québec, Ontario, and Alberta were among the latter group, each gaining its own experience in establishing programmes in urban, rural, or remote settings, and developing ways of resolving questions on such subjects as the language treatment of names or urban area names.

Several years later, in the early 1980s, federal-provincial cooperation was again possible to initiate comprehensive fieldwork in the Avalon Peninsula of Newfoundland. For several years summer projects added to the bank of locally collected names and helped improve the toponymy on topographic maps, many of which still showed only the names from the early British Admiralty charts. Another item of interest from Newfoundland – by virtue of its relatively recent discovery in 1976 – Landsat Island, off the coast of Labrador, could be considered noteworthy in Canadian geographical naming. After several name proposals were made the current name was selected as this small piece of land had been identified through the use of Landsat satellite imagery.

During the late 1960s and the 1970s the CPCGN appointed several advisory committees to provide expertise in areas of special interest to members. Two committees established at that time still have ongoing responsibilities – undersea features and toponymy research. A third has recently changed its focus from the original nomenclature of glaciological and alpine features to the wider scope of nomenclature and delineation of geographical features.

In 1967 an advisory committee under the direction of the dominion hydrographer was created to deal with undersea features in maritime areas of interest to Canada. Over 4000 names have been endorsed since the inception of the committee; information brochures have been printed and two editions of the *Gazetteer of Undersea Feature Names* have been published from the database, now (in the 1990s) stored in digital format and maintained by the Canadian Hydrographic Service for the CPCGN.

The Advisory Committee on Toponymy Research (ACTR) was organized in 1975 to advise on issues and priorities of geographical names research. The committee has played a strong role in the promotion of workshops on gazetteer production, creation of toponymic databases, recording and treatment of Native names, and development of procedures for transboundary naming. In the late 1980s the ACTR was also responsible for preparing the first strategic plan for the CPCGN, encouraging the production of the CPCGN video *What's in a Toponym? The Story of Canada's Geographical Names*, and holding working sessions on alternate names, Native names, and urban names.

Also in 1975 the Advisory Committee on Glaciological and Alpine Nomenclature (ACGAN) was established to develop guidelines for the treatment of names relating to permanent ice features and alpine regions. This committee has been particularly useful in resolving jurisdictional questions in alpine areas. In considering appropriate generic terminology for alpine features, the committee cooperated with the translation bureau of the Department of Secretary of State to produce, in 1987, Terminology Bulletin 176, *Glossary of Generic Terms in Canada's Geographical Names*. In addition ACGAN developed the text for a pamphlet[10] to assist the general public in submitting name proposals. Later, in 1991, this committee, as the Advisory Committee on Nomenclature and Delineation, had its terms of reference widened to deal with more general questions of feature delineation.

In 1975 the CPCGN secretariat started producing *Canoma*, a twice-yearly publication of news and views in Canadian toponymy. Now [1994] in its twentieth year this journal has become a useful collection of toponymic material about Canada, providing administrative and policy information on the CPCGN and provincial and territorial programmes, as well as historical material on Canadian names. One particular series carried in the journal in the late 1970s and 1980s provided information on place-names gathered early in the century. In 1905 James White, chief geographer of Canada, had sent a circular letter to postmasters across Canada requesting information on the origins of the names of their communities. Responses were received from some 3000 locations, some of which are detailed in *Canoma*.

DAYS OF LANGUAGE ISSUES AND DATABASE DEVELOPMENT (1980s AND 1990s)

In the early 1980s the Office of the Commissioner of Official Languages exerted strong pressure to have both English and French forms of geographical names recognized for official federal use on maps and in documents. Considerable discussion was held with the Official Languages Branch of Treasury Board (TB), culminating in the policy *Official Languages and Geographical Names on Federal Government Maps*[11] documented in TB circular 1983–58. This includes a list of some eighty "pan-Canadian" names (provinces, territories, and well-known major features) endorsed by the CPCGN for use in English and French on federal maps.

The Translation Bureau of the Department of Secretary of State extended this policy to develop guidelines for the use of geographical names in English and French in federal texts. In the late 1980s this was followed up by the Translation Bureau's CUENGO committee, which elaborated on some elements of translation policy, and the CPCGN secretariat prepared a document listing all features in Canada that for a variety of reasons carry more than one official name.

Increasingly the CPCGN secretariat has been called upon to provide geographical names not just for maps of Canada, but also for international maps. As a result, in 1982, the CPCGN approved guidelines[12] for "names outside Canada for official Canadian use." This action has meant increasing Canadian acceptance of geographical names approved by names authorities of other countries, and Canadian use of names in keeping with Romanization systems recognized by the United Nations.

The years of the 1980s and 1990s have seen considerable progress in the conversion of geographical names record card collections into digital databases, which include official and cross-reference names with some twenty to thirty fields of locational and cultural attribute information. This step was first taken in 1979 at the federal level within the Department of Energy, Mines and Resources, primarily to facilitate the production of gazetteers and to improve the process of names compilation for National Topographic System (NTS) maps. Since then enhancements to the system have led to a national-coverage toponymic database, the Canadian Geographical Names Data Base, which contains records of some 500 000 names of which about 65 percent are currently official, as approved through the CPCGN. In addition several provinces and territories – notably Québec, Manitoba, Alberta, Northwest Territories, British Columbia, and Ontario – maintain their own files in a digital environment. Newfoundland, New Brunswick, Nova Scotia, and Yukon Territory were (in 1994) also moving towards their own digital storage systems.

To facilitate the development of a "vision" for Canadian digital toponymy, to develop national standards, and to guide CPCGN members in this aspect of their work, the CPCGN established the Advisory Committee on Canadian Digital Toponymic Services in 1992. Its leadership will be crucial in the expansion of digital exchange and dissemination.

The 1980s and 1990s have also brought considerable increase in awareness of the toponyms used by Native people of Canada. In 1979 the CTQ had held a workshop on the writing and terminology of Québec Amerindian names. In 1986 the CPCGN sponsored a symposium on Native geographical names, with presentations and workshops on collection, writing, funding, and future prospects. Twenty-seven resolutions from the symposium were subsequently endorsed by the CPCGN, and have formed the basis for activity in later years. Many names of Native communities in Québec (in the 1970s) and in the Northwest Territories (in the 1990s) have been changed to reflect local preferences. Particular efforts in the field collection of Native names have been made in Québec, Ontario, Manitoba, Northwest Territories, Alberta, Yukon Territory, and British Columbia. The CPCGN has also published reference tools such as the *Guide to the Field Collection of Native Geographical Names* and *Native Canadian Geographical Names: An Annotated Bibliography*.

In the 1990s the tasks lying ahead of the CPCGN centre on collection, recording, and dissemination of authoritative geographical names information. In March 1990 a new order in council (P.C. 1990-549) gave more appropriate recognition to the decision-making responsibilities of the provinces and territories within the CPCGN framework. The technical and cultural roles of geographical names authorities in the preservation of Canadian heritage have now been expressed, and the CPCGN has reviewed its mission, responsibilities, and goals while developing a strategic plan for the 1990s.

A major technological breakthrough has helped the CPCGN make geographical names information available worldwide. In the summer of 1994 the CPCGN records on the Canadian Geographical Names Data Base, maintained at Natural Resources Canada, were launched as the core of the GeoNames World Wide Web site. The CPCGN became the first national names authority to provide on-line search capabilities on the Internet. Access to the database and information about the committee, its publications, and toponymic issues are now readily available to a rapidly growing Internet community.

The thrust of Canadian toponymy into the twenty-first century will be to achieve at least a basic field coverage of names collection across the country, to develop suitable names policies and procedures to recognize standard versions of geographical names, to provide appropriate tools for those working in this field of endeavour, and to continue the development of widely available digital toponymic data. With these goals must go the dissemination of accurate geographical names information for Canada, as well as outreach to other countries, to increase the consistency of toponymic usage throughout the world.

PROVINCIAL AND TERRITORIAL NAMES BOARDS AND ACTIVITIES

Now the CPCGN has federal, provincial, and territorial government members. Federal participation comes from departments involved with mapping and charting, archives, defence, national parks, statistics, and translation/terminology – all significant users of geographical names. In addition to one representative from the departments responsible for the geographical names programmes in each province and territory, the chairs of advisory committees have membership on the CPCGN during their terms of office. In 1994 there was a total of twenty-five CPCGN members.

The orders in council for the CPCGN have quite clearly placed decision-making authority in the hands of provincial ministers, and since 1984 also with territorial ministers. Decisions in federal lands (national parks, Indian reserves, and military bases) within the provinces and territories are the joint responsibility of federal and provincial/territorial jurisdictions. This was discussed at CPCGN meetings in the 1970s and formally agreed in 1979.

Geographical-names activity varies in degree and intensity from jurisdiction to jurisdiction. In some provinces and territories the responsibility for names authorization rests with one person or a few people who recommend decisions for their minister's signature. More sophisticated procedures exist in jurisdictions where a committee or board has been established, in most cases by provincial or territorial law. In 1994 five provinces and one territory had names boards (with public and private sector participants) to provide recommendations; the other provinces and territory had various bureaucratic structures for this purpose. In addition the degree of digital data storage and processing currently varies considerably across Canada.

Québec

Québec has one of the world's most sophisticated toponymic authorities. Stemming from the Québec Geographic Board created in 1912, the CTQ was established in 1977 within the framework of the Charter of the French Language. The commission, a seven-member board that meets every two months to authorize name decisions, is supported by a full-time staff that, since 1977, has maintained a level of twenty to thirty staff. The CTQ has had a prolific publishing programme and systematically has addressed standardization issues: publishing guides for editors and cartographers, developing general toponymic guidelines and methodologies, a research series, Native-language names manuals, and *Noms et lieux du Québec : dictionnaire illustré* (1994). The CTQ has produced three editions of the *Répertoire toponymique du Québec*, together with regular cumulative supplements. Digital data storage became a fact of life of the CTQ in the 1980s with the development of the TOPOS database. The commission has provided continuing leadership in initiatives in geographical names standardization at the United Nations level; Québec hosted the 1988 UN-sponsored toponymy training course and Henri Dorion, president of the commission, was chair of the United Nations Group of Experts on Geographical Names from 1987 to 1991.

Ontario

The Ontario Geographic Names Board (OGNB) was established by provincial legislation in 1968. Membership consists of five appointees from the private sector, the surveyor-general for Ontario (ex-officio), and the executive secretary by ministerial appointment. In 1975 Ontario published its *Principles of Geographical Naming*, subsequently updated in 1977 as *Naming Ontario*. The Ontario government has published jointly with the Québec government (in 1987) *A Manual for the Field Collection of Geographical Names*, based on the original French *Méthodologie des inventaires toponymiques* published by Québec in 1986. During the past two decades Ontario has been very involved in geographical naming in a bilingual context; of particular interest has been Ontario's ability to provide advice to other countries in the treatment of minority languages at a provincial level. Also notable has been the province's work with Native groups, including support for the 1993 publication of the *Historical Map of Temagami*. The Ministry of Natural Resources provides support for the OGNB; it maintains names for mapping purposes and recently has put resources into establishing the extents of features (i.e., geographical names applications) for its digital mapping programme.

Newfoundland

A names authority was first established in 1904, over forty years before Newfoundland joined Confederation. The programme saw years of feast and famine in the amount of geographical naming activity undertaken. A new act was passed on 21 May 1974 establishing the Newfoundland Geographical Names Board consisting of six members (including chair and secretary); in 1991 its name was changed to the Newfoundland and Labrador Geographical Names Board. In the 1980s Newfoundland undertook extensive field recording of geographical names, largely under the direction of the Department of Geography at Memorial University and especially in the Avalon Peninsula, Trinity

Bay, and parts of Labrador. As a result several thousand locally used names were approved and added to the official names of the the province.

Alberta

Alberta set up its own geographical names authority immediately after the Second World War, followed in 1975 by establishment of the Historic Sites Board as part of the Alberta Historical Resources Act. A geographical names committee makes recommendations to this board, which then reports to the minister (in 1993, the Minister of Alberta Community Development). Alberta has developed its own principles, procedures, and policies, which were published in its *Geographical Names Manual* in 1987. With a strong emphasis on cultural aspects of geographical names, Alberta has produced publications for students, tourists, and the public in general. In the late 1980s work started on a four-volume reference series *Place Names of Alberta*, with the first three volumes published between 1991 and 1994. Very valuable support has been provided by the Friends of Geographical Names of Alberta Society, formed in 1988; the group has been instrumental in the computerization of Alberta's geographical names data and in the very active publication programme. A considerable amount of fieldwork has been undertaken in the province, and recently emphasis has been placed on Native cultural studies.

Saskatchewan

The Saskatchewan Geographical Names Board was established in 1974. The board is chaired by the general manager of the Central Surveys and Mapping Agency, and has developed a structure that over the years has represented the interests of aboriginal groups, the Canadian Legion, the Provincial Archives, the Saskatchewan Natural History Association, and the Multicultural Advisory Council. The Saskatchewan geographical names programme is closely tied to provincial mapping, and it has strong support for commemoration of war casualties with over 3600 features named in this way.

Yukon Territory

In 1984 the responsibility for geographical names in Yukon Territory devolved from the federal government (DIAND) to the government of Yukon; the Yukon Geographical Names Board (YGNB), with government and public membership, was then established in 1987. Land claims settlements in the early 1990s have given rise to equal Native/non-Native participation on the six-person board. Yukon concerns in the past ten years have been with Native language toponymy, as well as with other names of historical interest. The Yukon Native Language Centre has been closely linked with the Heritage Branch of the Ministry of Tourism in encouraging geographical names fieldwork and standardized approaches to recording names in Native languages, such as Tlingit and Northern Tutchone. An information brochure on the programme has been produced.

Other Provinces and Territories

In other provinces and the Northwest Territories geographical names decisions are made by a government minister, with the support and recommendations of office staff but without recourse to the advice of a geographical names board. British Columbia has had an active names programme over the last half-century. Thousands of detailed names records were collected on index cards, which became the source of names data for provincial mapping. Although no comprehensive fieldwork has been undertaken in the province, special attention has at various times been given to the hierarchy of mountain nomenclature. In 1991 the Ministry of Crown Lands published a brochure entitled *Geographical Names in British Columbia*, presenting the policies, principles, and procedures for naming features in the province. Today's programme is now supported by a digital toponymic database with strong ties to digital mapping and increasing cooperation with Native language groups in the province.

Manitoba's geographical names programme is also located within the provincial mapping branch. In the mid-1970s the federal/provincial field survey provided some 8000 decisions on names in local use, including many in Chipewyan, Saulteaux, and Cree. The province has an active commemorative naming programme, with over 2000 geographical features named for Manitobans who died in war service. During the 1970s Manitoba produced its own *Annual Directory*, but discontinued this with the production of the 1981 *Gazetteer of Canada: Manitoba*. Provincial names data were converted to digital files in the 1980s and a brochure, *Manitoba's Geographical Names*, was first published in 1988.

The Northwest Territories government's cultural heritage programme took over responsibility for geographical names from DIAND in 1984. Since that time considerable emphasis has been put on field collection of toponyms and associated oral history from elders and various communities across the North. Thousands of new records have been created and a tiered names authorization system has been established to cope with both straightforward and controversial situations. Greater recognition of the indigenous forms of names for Native communities was initiated with the change of Frobisher Bay to Iqaluit in 1987. The current approach of the Northwest Territories to the preservation and promotion of traditional names is documented in the 1993 publication *NWT Geographic Names Program Manual*.

In New Brunswick, Nova Scotia, and Prince Edward Island authority for names has fallen variously under mapping or executive council offices. Fieldwork studies were undertaken by federal-provincial agreement in the late 1960s and early 1970s; for each province this meant several thousand new names records – a work effort that has provided a good base for the decades to follow. Although the names programmes have not been particularly active at the provincial levels, all have contributed to the work of the national names authority and are now increasingly becoming involved with digital names data and questions relating to the language of official names.

INTERNATIONAL LEADERSHIP AND COOPERATION

Canada has been active on the international scene in efforts to promote the global standardization of geographical names. Canada sent a delegation of five, under the leadership of Jean-Paul Drolet, then chairman of the CPCGN, to the first United Nations Conference on the Standardization of Geographical Names, held in Geneva in 1967. Since that time a further five conferences and sixteen meetings of the Group of Experts on Geographical Names (UNGEGN) have been organized. Although not by any means having the largest number of delegates, Canada is one of the few countries that has participated in every meeting (see table 4).

In 1987 Canada had the honour of hosting the fifth conference in Montréal. Drolet was elected president of the conference; Alan Rayburn was rapporteur; Helen Kerfoot was assistant editor; Henri Dorion a committee chairman; and Jean Poirier a committee rapporteur. In the work of the UNGEGN, Canada has contributed in a number of areas – for example, national programmes, gazetteers and toponymic data files, toponymy training courses, toponymic terminology, and toponymic guidelines for map and other editors. Papers presented at each conference have been published in the two-volume

Table 4
United Nations Conferences on the Standardization of Geographical Names

Number	Year	Location	Canadian participation
1	1967	Geneva	J.-P. Drolet; J.K. Fraser (chair, committee 4); J. Poirier, E.J. Holmgren (rapporteur, Committee 1); R. McKinnon
2	1972	London	J.-P. Drolet; G.F. Delaney; J. Poirier (rapporteur, Committee 1); M.B. Smart (rapporteur, Committee 4); H. Dorion; J.B. Rudnyckyj
3	1977	Athens	J.-P. Drolet; H. Dorion; J. Poirier; M.B. Smart; Y. Slavutych; A. Rayburn (rapporteur, Committee 1)
4	1982	Geneva	J.-P. Drolet; A. Rayburn (rapporteur); F. Beaudin (rapporteur, Committee 2); P. Millman; L. Fillion; J.B. Rudnyckyj
5	1987	Montréal	J.-P. Drolet; A. Rayburn (rapporteur); H. Dorion (chairman, Committee 3); J. Poirier (rapporteur, Committee 1); H. Kerfoot; T. Jolicœur; L. Fillion; R. Freeman; G. Holm; A. Karamitsanis; M.B. Smart
6	1992	New York	H. Kerfoot (editor-in-chief); A. Lapierre; J. Revie

UN reports. In addition Canada produced English and French versions of Canadian papers for the first five conferences.

UNGEGN is responsible for the programme of the conferences held every five years, and for implementation of conference resolutions. Three Canadians have held leadership roles in UNGEGN: Alan Rayburn, rapporteur (1977–87); Henri Dorion, chairman (1987–91); and Helen Kerfoot, vice-chair (1991–). Within the divisional framework of UNGEGN Canada participates in two linguistic/geographic divisions, namely the U.S./Canada and Romano-Hellenic divisions.

One very important element of the UN geographical names standardization activities is the support of toponymic training programmes. To further these goals the CTQ hosted a session in Québec in 1988. This two-week course, including field collection and office treatment of toponyms, was designed for participants from French-speaking African countries. The CTQ has also been in the forefront of providing assistance programmes, for example to Morocco and Cameroon. Five other UN training courses have been held up to 1994. Canada has participated by providing teaching staff in Cipanas, Indonesia (1989), and in Pretoria, South Africa (1992 and 1993).

Apart from the work in UN activities, Canada has contributed in various ways to the international exchange of toponymic knowledge. Frequent collaboration has existed with the United States Board on Geographic Names since the early years of the century, and in 1990 representatives from the CPCGN participated in the USBGN's celebration of their centennial. Canada has often provided toponymic information and policy advice – from Greenland (Kalaallit Nunaat) to New Zealand, and from China to Venezuela.

THE ROAD AHEAD

The year 1997 marks the 100th anniversary of a national names authority in Canada. Quite clearly many steps forward have been taken since the first efforts to standardize the use and spelling of Canadian geographical names. Ahead still lie many challenges in policy development, toponymic heritage preservation, and the dissemination of data files through new and exciting electronic media, increasingly reaching out to a wider public. Cooperation between federal, provincial, and territorial governments will remain crucial to the authority and effectiveness of the work of the Canadian Permanent Committee on Geographical Names.

NOTES

1 Kerfoot, Helen. 1988. Towards the Formation of the Geographic Board of Canada in 1897. *Canoma,* 14, 2, 16–21.

2 Kerfoot, Helen, and Alan Rayburn. 1990. The Roots and Development of the Canadian Permanent Committee on Geographical Names. *Names,* 38, 3, 183–92.

3 1888. *Report of Proceedings of the Association of Dominion Land Surveyors, Fifth Annual Meeting.* 15–16 March, Ottawa. Montreal: John Lovell and Son, 65.

4 Ibid.

5 Geographic Board of Canada. 1897–1947. *Minutes of Board meetings.* Ms at CPCGN, Natural Resources Canada.

6 Canadian Board on Geographical Names. 1948–1961. *Minutes of Board meetings.* Ms at CPCGN, Natural Resources Canada.

7 Canadian Board on Geographical Names. 1955. *Revision of Regulations, Principles of Nomenclature and By-laws.* Ms at CPCGN, Natural Resources Canada.

8 Canadian Permanent Committee on Geographical Names. 1962–present. *Proceedings of Committee meetings.* Ms at CPCGN, Natural Resources Canada.

9 Munro, M.R. 1979. Toponymic Fieldwork and Related Office Procedures: Federal and Provincial Perspectives. III. Government Participation in Toponymic Fieldwork. *Canoma,* 5, 1, 20–3.

10 Canadian Permanent Committee on Geographical Names. 1990. *Naming Canada's Geographical Features* (pamphlet). Ottawa: Energy, Mines and Resources Canada.

11 Canadian Permanent Committee on Geographical Names. 1993. *Principles and Procedures of Geographical Naming.* Ottawa: Energy, Mines and Resources Canada, 17–19.

12 Ibid., 15.

Tables

APPENDIX C
Surveying And Mapping Projects Funded by Government of Canada

Country	Type of Project	Area	Contractor
Bangladesh 1974–75	Complete 1:30 000 scale aerial photographic coverage	Entire country Approximately 56 000 square miles	Capital Air Surveys Ltd
Barbados 1 1968–70	1:1250; 1:2500, and 1:5000 mapping for land valuation base and index maps		General Photogrammetric Services Ltd
Barbados 2 1973	Aerial photos at 1:12 500 and 1:20 000 for 1:2500 mapping: horizontal control targeted		Capital Air Surveys Ltd
Barbados 3 Land Mapping and Registry Project 1983–89	1st phase, 1983–84, mapping: 33 × 1:5000 scale sheets with 10 ft CI and 36 × 1:2500 sheets with 5 ft CI 2nd phase, 1986–89, supply of computer-assisted mapping system and COGO, training	North-east and East of Barbados	Western Photogrammetry Geovision
Cameroon 1982–1984	Black-and-white aerial photos, 1:20 000 of 5,000 km² and 1:40 000 for 110 000 km²; aerial triangulation; 1:50 000 mapping with 20 m CI of 60 000 km²; 4-colour printing; training. Changed to monochrome mapping, ultimately by enlargement of existing 1:200 000 maps	South of 5° N and West of 12°45' E	Photosur Inc.
Egypt ISAWIP 1985–88	Mapping control surveys, aerial triangulation, orthophotomapping at 1:25 000, 1:10 000, and 1:2500	Daqahliya Governorate, Integrated Soil and Water Improvement Project	North West (Survey) Geographic Services Ltd
Ethiopia 1972–1973	Provide technical services necessary to produce 1:50 000 semi-controlled mosaics	Approximately 31 000 square miles, Omo River area	Spartan Aero Ltd
Ghana 1971–1980	Aerial photos, mapping control surveys, and 3-colour 1:50 000 topo mapping	South from 7°30' N	Terra Surveys Ltd

APPENDIX C *(cont'd)*
Surveying And Mapping Projects Funded by Government of Canada

Country	Type of Project	Area	Contractor
Guyana 1 1966–74	Aerial photos, mapping control surveys, and topo mapping	North from 4° N	Terra Surveys Ltd
Guyana 2 1968–73	Aerial photos, mapping control surveys, and topo mapping	South from 4° N	Terra Surveys Ltd
Guyana 3 1974–79	Extension of Guyana 2		Terra Surveys Ltd
Haiti 1976–1980	Colour aerial photos	Approximately 4000 line km in certain areas of Haiti	Aero Photo Inc.
Indonesia REAP I Doppler 1979–81	Resource Evaluation Aerial Photography (REAP) Project; establish horizontal control points using Doppler satellites as a database for 1:50 000 mapping of natural resources, primarily forestry. Purchase of receivers	Approximately 210 stations in Kalimantan and Sulawesi; 28 in Bali, Nusatenggara Barat, Nusatenggara Timur, Maluku, Sumatera Selatan, and Riau	McElhanney Surveying and Engineering Ltd CMC
Indonesia REAP Phase 2 Photography 1981–82	Black-and-white 1:100 000 aerial photos of Kalimantan and Sulawesi; remainder super-wide angle at 1:60 000; simultaneous wide-angle, colour infrared photos; Training	Kalimantan, Sulawesi, Java, Bali, and Nusatenggara	Kenting Earth Sciences Ltd
Indonesia REAP Phase 3 APR 1985–90	a) Assess suitability of Seasat and GOES-3 Satellite Radar Altimeter data for 1:50 000 mapping b) APR of 12 000 line km (net), and aerial triangulation of 4500 models for 1:50 000 topo mapping; horizontal block adjustment of 1:100 000 photos; Training	Parts of Kalimantan, all of Sulawesi, and part of Irian Jaya	Algonquin College, Wild Heerbrug a) Kenting Earth Sciences Ltd b) McElhanney Surveying and Engineering Ltd, Kenting Earth Sciences Ltd., Terra Surveys Ltd
Jamaica 1967–68	2350 line km aerial photos for topo mapping; supply of EDM equipment; Training		Spartan Air Survey SMB

APPENDIX C (*cont'd*)
Surveying And Mapping Projects Funded by Government of Canada

Country	Type of Project	Area	Contractor
Kenya 1 1969–74	Aerial photos, mapping control surveys, and production of 5-colour 1:50 000 topo maps and photo mosaics	39 × 1:50 000 sheets, Kenya-Tanzania boundary	General Photogrammetric Services Ltd
Kenya 2 1970–71	Provide technical services necessary to produce semi-controlled mosaics at 1:50 000 and 1:25 000; aerial film supplied by the Survey of Kenya	Southern portion of coastal belt, approximately 2400 square miles	International Mapping
Mekong 1959–64	Air survey of Mekong River area: aerial photos, mapping control surveys, and photogrammetric compilation of maps Main Stem 1:20 000 ci 5m Dam Sites 1:2000 ci 1–2m Tributaries 1:20 000 ci 5m	In Cambodia, Laos, Vietnam, and Thailand 779 Sheets	Hunting Survey Corp. Ltd
Nepal 1978–79	Aerial photos, approximately 8400 line km, 1:20 000, super-wide angle; and approximately 700 line km, 1:50 000, super-wide angle	Western Development Region	Capital Air Surveys Ltd
	Approximately 6500 line km, 1:50 000, super-wide-angle photos	Central and Eastern Nepal	
Nigeria 1 1962–69	Aerial photos, mapping control surveys, photogrammetry, and drafting 1:50 000 topo maps	96 × 1:50 000 sheets Approximately 28 400 square miles southern Nigeria	Canadian Aero Service Ltd
Nigeria 2 1965–69	Aerial photos, APR, and 96 × 1:50 000 sheets Mapping cities of Ibadan at 1:1250 and Benin at 1:2500, ci 2–5 ft		Canadian Aero Service Ltd
Nigeria 3 1975–82	Mapping control surveys and topo maps (108 colour line maps and 68 photo maps)	North-eastern Nigeria	Photosur Inc.

APPENDIX C (cont'd)
Surveying And Mapping Projects Funded by Government of Canada

Country	Type of Project	Area	Contractor
Pakistan 1978–79	Horizontal and vertical control surveys	For the development of a deep sea port at Port Qasim, near Karachi	McElhanney Surveying and Engineering
Tanzania 1 1965–70	Aerial photos, airborne survey control, compilation and production of 1:50 000 colour line and photo mosaic maps	120 × 1:50000 sheets South-east Tanzania 31 500 sqare miles	Spartan Air Services Ltd
Tanzania 2 1969–73	Aerial photos, APR, mapping control surveys, and production of 5-colour topo maps and photo mosaic maps	126 × 1:50 000 sheets Southern Tanzania	Spartan Air Services Ltd
Tanzania 3 1973–74	Geodetic Survey by Aerodist of certain regions of Tanzania and training of Tanzanian personnel	Approximately 94 000 square miles	Terra Surveys Ltd
Tanzania 4 1974–79	Aerial photos, mapping control surveys, and 1:50 000 map production	Western Tanzania 190 × 1:50 000 sheets Approximately 56 000 sqare miles	Kenting Earth Sciences Ltd
Tanzania 5 1977–78	Aerial photos at 1:50 000 Black-and-white infrared 1:20 000 photos for areas totalling 1000 km² Colour infra-red 1:20 000 photos for area of approximately 150 km²	Approximately 33 400 km² for Bagamoyo, Kisorawe, Rufiji, and Mofia Island districts	Capital Air Surveys Ltd
Tanzania 6 1979–82	Aerial photos, APR, and mapping control surveys; aerial triangulation and numerical adjustment in Canada		Terra Surveys Ltd
Tanzania 7 1980–	Field interpretation of aerial photos; collection of geographical names; 1:50 000 colour map production	Mbeya-Iringa and Selous areas, 365 × 1:50 000 sheets	Terra Surveys Ltd
1982–83	Wheat Research and Production Project; aerial photos, horizontal control targeting, vertical control, aerial triangulation, and block adjustment; 1:10 000 photomaps	410 km² 23 map sheets	Photocan Surveys Ltd

APPENDIX C *(cont'd)*
Surveying And Mapping Projects Funded by Government of Canada

Country	Type of Project	Area	Contractor
Trinidad-Tobago 1965	a) Aerial photos, 1:10 000, of approximately 675 square miles b) Aerial photos, 1:5000, of approximately 75 sqare miles c) Semi-controlled mosaics, 1:2500, of approximately 675 square miles (see [a] above) d) Enlarged prints of the aerial negatives taken under (a) and (b) above		General Photogrammetric Services Ltd
Trinidad-Tobago 1966–71	Aerial photos at scales 1:2500, 1:10 000, 1:1250, 1:5000 Semi-controlled mosaics at 1:10 000 (built-up areas) Mapping at 1:2500 with and without contours Approximately 425 square miles 1:2500 with c_i 5 ft Approximately 625 square miles 1:5000 with c_i 10–20 ft Training of 6 draftsmen	675 square miles in Trinidad 57 square miles in Tobago 80 square miles in Trinidad and Tobago	Survair Ltd SMB
Zimbabwe Phase I 1982	Provide 17 000 line km of aerial photos covering approximately 185 000 km² at 1:65 000; provide 18 000 line km of photos covering approximately 18 000 km² at 1:80 000	To cover the entire country	North West Survey Corporation
Zimbabwe Phase II 1983–84	Responsibility for all operations required to establish a database for orthophotomapping including the inertial and doppler control, and aerial triangulation	Eastern portion of country	Consortium Geo-Carto

APPENDIX C (*cont'd*)
Surveying And Mapping Projects Funded by Government of Canada

Country	Type of Project	Area	Contractor
Zimbabwe Phase III 1984–89	Provide CIDA with all orthophotomapping services necessary for 569 photomaps of areas "A" (1st priority, 288 × 1:80 000 sheets) and "B" (2nd priority, 281 × 1:65 000 sheets)	Eastern portion of country	McElhanney Group Ltd
Zimbabwe Phase III 1984–89	Provide CIDA with all orthophotomapping services necessary for 327 × 1:25 000 photomaps in Area "C"; photography at 1:65 000	Eastern portion of country	Western Photogrammetry Ltd
Zimbabwe Phase IV 1983–84	To engineer, furnish, install, and maintain a computer-assisted mapping system complete with ancillary equipment and services including training		Systemhouse Ltd

APR: Airborne Profile Recorder
CI: Contour Interval
Topo: topographical
Photo, photos: photography
SMB: Surveys and Mapping Branch, EMR
Sources: Trenholm (1985); Surveys, Mapping and Remote Sensing Sector files

Appendix D
Bilateral Arrangements of the Surveys, Mapping and Remote Sensing Sector, EMR

With Country/Organization	Title of Arrangement	Subject Matter	Start/Expiry
Brazil – Fundaçao Instituto Brasileiro de Geografia e Estatistica (IBGE)	MOU between SMRSS and IBGE	Cooperation in surveys, mapping, remote sensing, and GIS	1988 1993
Ecuador – Centro de Levantamientos Integrados de Recursos Naturales por Sensores Remotos (CLIRSEN)	MOU between CCRS and CLIRSEN	Cooperation in remote sensing	1991 1996
Ecuador – Instituto Geografico Militar (IGM)	MOU between SMRSS and IGM	Cooperation in surveys, mapping, and GIS	1991 1995
Egypt – Survey Research Institute, Ministry of Public Works and Water Resources (EGASM/WRC-SRI)	MOU between SMRSS and MPWWR	Cooperation in surveys, mapping, remote sensing, and GIS	1989 1994
France – European Space Agency (ESA)	MOU between CCRS and ESA	Development and exploitation of ERS-1 satellite data	1985 open
France – European Space Agency (ESA)	Arrangement between CCRS and ESA	Reception, archiving, processing and distribution of ERS-1 data	1991 1994
France – Institut Géographique National (IGN)	MOU between IGN and Surveys & Mapping	Research and development projects in cartography	1985 open
France – Institut Géographique National (IGN)	MOU between IGN and SMRSS	Installation de balises d'orbitographie à Yellowknife et Ottawa, re: Projet DORIS	1988 1991
France – SPOT Image	MOU between CCRS and SPOT Image	Reception and distribution of SPOT data	1989 1992
Hungary – Ministry of Industry	MOU between SMRSS and Ministry of Industry	Cooperation in surveys, mapping, remote sensing, and GIS	1990 1995
Indonesia – National Coordination Agency for Surveys & Mapping (Bakosurtanal)	MOU between SMRSS and Bakosurtanal	Cooperation in surveys, mapping, remote sensing, and GIS	1990 1995
Japan – National Space Development Agency of Japan (NSDAJ)	MOU between CCRS and NSDAJ	Reception and distribution of MOS-1 satellite data	1988 open
Jordan – Royal Jordanian Geographic Centre (RJGC)	MOU between SMRSS and RJGC	Cooperation in surveys, mapping, and remote sensing	

Appendix D (*cont'd*)
Bilateral Arrangements of the Surveys, Mapping and Remote Sensing Sector, EMR

With Country/Organization	Title of Arrangement	Subject Matter	Start/Expiry
Kuwait – Survey Department, Muncipality of Kuwait	MOU between SMRSS and Municipality of Kuwait	Cooperation in surveys, mapping, remote sensing, and GIS	1989 1994
Mexico – Instituto Nacional de Estadistica, Geografia e Informatica (INEGI)	MOU between SMRSS and INEGI	Cooperation in surveys, mapping, remote sensing, and GIS	1992 1997
Mexico – Instituto Nacional de Estadistica, Geografia e Informatica (INEGI)	Projects Implementing Arrangement between SMRSS and INEGI	Participation in seminar, and feasibility studies	1993
Peru – The National Commission for Aerospace and Research Development of Peru (CONIDA)	MOU between CCRS and CONIDA	Cooperation in remote sensing	1991 1994
Qatar – GIS Steering Committee	MOU between SMRSS and State of Qatar	Cooperation in surveys, mapping, remote sensing, and GIS	
Russia – Russian Federation Committee for Geodesy and Cartography (CGC)	MOU between SMRSS and CGC	Cooperation in surveys, mapping, GIS, and remote sensing	1992 2002
Ukraine – Main Administration of Geodesy, Cartography, and Cadastre (GUGKK)	MOU between SMRSS and GUGKK	Cooperation in surveys, mapping, GIS, and remote sensing	1993 1998
U.S.	International Boundary treaty	International Boundary with the U.S.	1925 open
U.S. – NASA	Crustal Dynamics Project	Geodesy, geophysics	1982 open
U.S. – National Mapping Division, U.S. Geological Survey (USGS), Dept. of Interior	Implementing Arrangement between USGS and SMRSS	Coordination of mapping activities along International Boundary	1990 1993
U.S. – National Mapping Division, U.S. Geological Survey (USGS), Dept of Interior	Statement of Intent (SOI) between SMRSS and USGS	Cooperation in surveys, mapping, remote sensing, and GIS	1991 1996
U.S. – National Oceanic and Atmospheric Administration (NOAA)	Agreement between Surveys & Mapping Branch and National Geodetic Survey	Redefinition of the North American Datum (NAD83)	1977 open

Appendix D (cont'd)
Bilateral Arrangements of the Surveys, Mapping and Remote Sensing Sector, EMR

With Country/Organization	Title of Arrangement	Subject Matter	Start/Expiry
U.S. – National Oceanic and Atmospheric Administration (NOAA)	MOU between Surveys & Mapping Branch and National Geodetic Survey	Redefinition of the North American Vertical Datum re: NAVD88	1982 open
U.S. – National Oceanic and Atmospheric Administration (NOAA), International Union of Geodesy and Geophysics (IUGG), and the International Association of Geodesy (IAG)	MOU between the Surveys & Mapping Branch and the National Geodetic Survey, the IUGG, and IAG	Development of a Rapid Precision Levelling System	1985 open
U.S. – National Oceanic and Atmospheric Administration (NOAA)	MOU between NOAA and Geological Survey of Canada and Geodetic Survey Division, SMRSS	Cooperative programme in geodesy and geodynamics	1990 1995
U.S. – National Oceanic and Atmospheric Administration (NOAA)	MOU between CCRS and NOAA	Reception and distribution of Landsat data	1984 1991
U.S. – SPOT Image Corp. (SICORP)	Agreement between SICORP and CCRS	Agreement for reception and distribution of satellite data	1989 1992
U.S. – Truview International Inc.	Licence Agreement between SMRSS and Truview	Reproduction and distribution of *National Atlas of Canada*	1990 1993
USSR – Main Administraion of Geodesy & Cartography GUGK	MOU between SMRSS and GUGK	Cooperation in surveys, mapping, remote sensing, and GIS	1991 1996
Venezuela – Ministry of Environment and Non-Renewable Resources	MOU between CCRS and MENR	Cooperation in remote sensing	1992 1997
Yemen – Ministry of Oil and Mineral Resources (MOMR)	Multisectoral MOU, EMR and MOMR	Cooperation in earth sciences and mining	1989 1994

Glossary*

Term	Explanation
A0 Paper	Designation given to the size of paper sheets measuring 1189 × 841 mm.
Accelerometer	A device for measuring acceleration. A particularly sensitive accelerometer embodies a mass suspended by electrostatic or electromagnetic forces. It is used to sense movement in Inertial Survey Systems.
Accuracy	Closeness of an estimated (e.g., measured or computed) value to a standard or accepted value of a particular quantity.
Active Control Stations	Stations that monitor the orbits of survey satellites and furnish Canadian GPS units with more precise data.
Additional Secondary Factor (ASF)	The additional delay in the arrival time of a low-frequency radio wave (usually Loran-C) that passes over the actual ground from the transmitter to receiver as opposed to the theoretical travel time for the same distance over an all sea water path. In an hyperbolic situation the ASF is the difference between the ASFs for the two transmission paths.
Adjudication	The determination of rights in land.
Adjustment	The process of finding, from a set of redundant observations, a set of "best" values, in some prescribed sense, for the observed quantities or for quantities functionally related to them.
Adverse possession	Occupation of land by a person that conflicts with the rights of the true owner of the land.
Aerial (or air) survey	The process of producing maps from aerial photographs.

---

* One-quarter of the terms in this glossary are taken from P.F. Dale and J.D. McLaughlin, 1988. *Land Information Management*. Oxford: Clarendon Press, and are published by permission.

Aerodist	An airborne version of the Tellurometer.
Aeromagnetic survey	An airborne method of sensing and mapping anomalies in the earth's magnetic field. The resulting maps can be used to predict and locate mineral resources and to add to knowledge of geology.
Aerotriangulation, aerial triangulation	A process for extending horizontal and vertical control from measurements of points on overlapping stereo-photographs.
Air/Ground Communication Box	A small rectangle on a chart near an airfield enclosing the airfield name, radio frequency, etcetera.
Altimeter	An instrument that determines its distance above a particular surface.
Altimeter, surveying	A barometric altimeter used to determine approximate differences of altitude or elevation between points.
Anaglyph	A composite image formed by superimposing the projection of one photo of a stereo-pair, filtered in red, over the other, filtered in cyan. When viewed through spectacles with red and cyan lenses, a three-dimensional image is seen.
Analogue plotter	A photogrammetric plotter in which the three-dimensional model is formed by rays of light, space rods, etcetera, and not by using digital means.
Analytical plotter	A plotting instrument on which the three-dimensional image is formed by digital calculation rather than by rays of light, space rods, etcetera.
Angle, horizontal	An angle between two directed lines in an horizontal plane.
Appraisal	The estimation of the market value of a property.
Arctic Circle	The parallel of latitude, in the Northern hemisphere, corresponding to latitude 66°33′ N.
Assessment	Determining the tax level for a property based upon its relative value.
Astrofix	A position whose latitude and longitude are found by sun or star observations.
Astronomy, geodetic	The determination of longitudes, latitudes, and azimuths by observations of the directions of stars and other celestial bodies. Coordinates so determined are called astronomic coordinates or astrogeodetic coordinates.
Atmosphere	The envelope of gas surrounding the earth.
Atmosphere, refractive index of	The ratio of the wavelength of the radiation of a given type in the atmosphere to the corresponding wavelength in a vacuum.

Attribute	A characteristic of an object that may be used in its classification.
Automated cartography	The preparation and presentation of maps using machines controlled by computers. Automatic cartography focuses on the processes of compiling maps and not necessarily on the problems of map utilization.
Azimuth, astronomic	At the point of observation, the angle between vertical planes passing through the celestial pole and the observed object.
Azimuth, Laplace	A geodetic azimuth derived from an astronomic azimuth by means of the Laplace Equation.
Backsight	In levelling, a reading on a levelling rod held on a preceding point. See also Foresight.
Backup copy	A duplicate that is made in case original data or software become destroyed.
Base, gravity	A point at which gravity has been measured with sufficient accuracy for use in calibrating gravimeters or as a reference in gravimetric surveys.
Base map	An outline or topographic map on which information may be added to form a thematic map.
Baseline	In a control survey net, the baseline is a precisely measured distance from which other lengths are computed by trigonometry. In a radio navigation system, the baseline is the line between two transmitters. In the context of the Law of the Sea, the baseline is the line from which the territorial sea and other maritime areas are defined. It can be the low-water line or straight line joining headlands, islands, or rocks.
Baseline, calibration	A line on which markers are placed at intervals so accurately measured that they can be used for calibrating distance-measuring instruments or equipment.
Batch processing	A procedure whereby the computer collects tasks and then processes the data at one time rather than as each task arises.
Beach landing site	A suitable location to off-load supplies by lighter for northern installations such as DEW Line sites and Arctic communities.
Benchmark	A relatively permanent, natural or artificial, material object bearing a marked point whose elevation above or below an adopted surface (or datum) is known.
Benchmark test	The measurement and evaluation of system capabilities, typically a comparison of competing systems, using the same data, the same exercises of system functions, and the same prescribed outputs in each case. The analysis of the results of the benchmark test

	determine whether a system can carry out the required functions and the level of performance of the software on a proposed hardware configuration.
Benchmark, tidal	A benchmark whose elevation has been determined with respect to mean sea level at a nearby tide gauge; the tidal benchmark is used as reference for that tide gauge.
BIONAV	An integrated navigation system developed at the Bedford Institute of Oceanography. It incorporated Doppler satellite fixes, rho-rho Loran-C measurements, cesium frequency standard data, Doppler sonar log, gyrocompass, and ship's speed log data.
Boundary	Either the physical objects marking the limits of a property or an imaginary line or surface marking the division between two legal estates.
Bridging	The technique whereby a photogrammetric model is orientated to ground control, and then additional overlaps are added until more ground control is reached. The whole bridge is then scaled and orientated to fit the control at both ends of the bridge.
Cadastral map	A map, normally forming part of a provincial or national series, that shows the correct size, shape, and location of all land parcels within the map limits and gives a unique identifier for each parcel.
Cadastral plan	A large-scale plan showing the boundaries of one or more land parcels and their relationship to adjoining parcels, prepared for the purpose of illustrating or creating legal title. Normally a cadastral plan shows the bearing and distance of each boundary, the area of the parcel, and an identifying number or letter for each parcel.
Cadastral survey	A legal survey conducted to show the definition and boundaries of real estate.
Cadastre	Juridical – a register of ownership of parcels of land; fiscal – a register of properties recording their value; multi-purpose – a register of attributes of parcels of land.
Cardinal buoy	A navigation buoy that is laid either north, south, east, or west of the navigation hazard that it marks. The direction to the hazard is indicated by painted stripes, top features, and flash characteristics of the light.
Census tract	A statistical areal unit used in the Census of Canada to group data at the enumerator area level.
Cesium frequency standard	A highly accurate timing device (sometimes known as a cesium clock).
Chain survey	A simple method of survey relying solely on measures of distance by a survey chain or tape.

Chart	A map used for navigation on water or in the air.
Chart Datum (vertical)	Chart Datum is the lowest level that water is expected to achieve. In Canada, Chart Datum is usually defined as the Lower Low Water, Large Tides.
Chart scheme	The geographical arrangement of charts for navigation given the expected size of ships, intended routes of most marine traffic, complexity of the hydrography, geographical features, size of paper, completeness of surveys, and the needs of adjoining charts.
Choropleth maps	A type of thematic map that employs the boundaries of data-collecting areas to map data divided into appropriate classes or values. The classes are usually represented by a sequence of colour tones or patterns.
Chronaflex (master)	A stable plastic medium on which a map can be plotted for reproduction by photocopying.
Clearance, bridge or overhead wire	Usually the distance from high water to the lowest point on the obstruction.
Clipping	A graphic process of cutting map lines and symbols off at the edge of a display area.
Comparator	A device for taking precise measurements of the position of points on single (mono-) or overlapping (stereo-) photographs.
Compiled map	A map assembled from a variety of sources such as published maps at various scales, railway and highway plans, and other engineering and geographical documents (compare Derived map).
Cone (or bar) check	The lowering of an acoustically reflective cone or bar to various known depths to calibrate the echo sounder for a zero error and for an error proportional to the depth.
Configuration	The way that a computer and its peripherals are linked together as one system.
Continental drift	The hypothesis that the continents of today were at one time integral parts of a single large continent (Pangea) or of a northern continent (Laurasia) separated by the Tethys Sea from a southern continent (Gondwanaland).
Continental shelf	The submarine extension of the continental land mass. According to the 1982 Law of the Sea Convention there are several conditions by which a state can claim a continental shelf beyond 200 nautical miles from the coast.
Control, geodetic	A synonym for control. A set of control stations established by geodetic methods.
Control, horizontal	Control stations whose horizontal coordinates have been determined with respect to a specific datum.

Control, vertical	Control stations whose elevations have been determined with respect to a specific datum.
Course	A series of lectures with or without laboratories presented during one academic term or one academic year.
Crown lands	Land, or land covered by water, the ownership of which is vested in her Majesty in right of Canada or of a province. In a more restricted sense, Crown land is land that originally belonged to, and has never been disposed of, by the Crown.
Crustal motion	A movement of the Earth's surface, horizontally or vertically, resulting in the displacement of monuments or benchmarks. Crustal motion can be episodic as caused, for example, by earthquakes, or continuous as caused, for example, by plate tectonic motion.
Cyan	A blue-green colour that is complementary to dark red.
Dappled screen	A printing screen with an irregular pattern of lines drawn to represent a forested area on a monochrome map.
Data	A raw collection of facts.
Database	An organized, integrated collection of data.
Database management system (DBMS)	A set of programs for managing a database.
Datum, geodetic	A set of constants specifying the coordinate system used for geodetic control, that is for calculating coordinates of points on the earth.
Datum, horizontal	A mathematical representation of the shape and size of the earth and the accurate computation of geographic coordinates on that surface.
Datum, North American 1983	The horizontal control datum for the United States, Canada, Mexico, and Central America, based on a geocentric origin and the Geodetic Reference System 1980. This datum, designated as NAD83, is the most recent geodetic reference system.
Datum, sea level	An equipotential surface passing through a specified point at mean sea level that is used as a reference for elevations.
Datum, vertical	The vertical datum for charts is often selected to be the lowest water level that is reasonably possible, or more precisely, the Lower Low Water, Large Tides.
Decca	A phase comparison range or range difference (hyperbolic) low-frequency system of positioning developed in the U.K. during the Second World War. The system uses transmitters broadcasting

continuously on fixed, but harmonically related, frequencies. The phase is measured at the frequency of the lowest common multiple of the two frequencies. The distance between one phase comparison and the next is called a lane.

Decca-Lambda
A modification of the original Decca system by which the absolute number of lanes can be identified.

Decca Navigator
The version of Decca that is available for general public navigation and includes lane identification possibilities.

Density
The storage capacity of magnetic media such as disks or tapes.

Derived map
A map drawn from map detail taken from larger-scale map coverage of its area (compare Compiled map).

Diazo printing
A printing method that involves placing an original (map, drawing, etc.) in contact with paper that has been sensitised with a dye made from a diazonium compound. The original is illuminated, and the exposed paper is then treated with an ammonia gas to bring out the image.

Digital Elevation Model (DEM)
A numerical model of the height of points on the earth's surface.

Digital mapping
The processes of acquisition (capture), transformation, and presentation of spatial data held in digital form.

Digital Terrain Model (DTM)
A numerical model of the earth's surface in which the third dimension may be height or some quantity other than height (for instance, gravity or land value).

Digital video plotter
A plotter that uses a video display of aerial photos or satellite images in place of aerial photographs. The lines of pixels, and the pixels on each line, are used as coordinates for the forming of a digital model.

Digitizing
The process of recording map data in digital form. Also the conversion of a photograph from a graphic to a digital display.

Direct access storage device
A device such as a magnetic disk that allows data to be accessed directly, unlike sequential access where all data must be scanned until the item sought is found.

DOLPHIN
The Deep Ocean Logging Platform with Hydrographic Instrumentation and Navigation. It is a remotely controlled, seven-metre long submersible with a snorkel for air for the diesel engine, a base for the radio antenna, and a deep fin for stability.

Doppler Satellite Navigation System
The periodic positioning of a vessel by means of the Doppler TRANSIT Satellite System. For ship navigation the over-the-ground speed and direction of the ship must be known for accurate position determination.

Doppler sonar log	The determination of the true ground speed and direction (relative to the ship's head) by measuring the Doppler shift that occurs to acoustic transmissions aimed 45° downwards in the forward and aft directions, and to both sides.
Doppler TRANSIT Satellite System	A system for fixing position on the earth's surface from measurements to satellites.
Double projection instrument	A photogrammetric plotter in which the images of a stereo-pair are projected down on a table for viewing stereoscopically, either anaglyphically or by a rapidly alternating system (left image, right image).
Drying Rock	A shoal that is exposed above the chart vertical datum but is submerged at high tide.
Earth anchor	A device that may be driven into the ground to form a firm mark or monument.
Easement	The right of a landowner to use land belonging to another person for a specific purpose; also a right of way exercised under statutory authority, for example by a public utility.
Echo sounder	Measures the depth of water by converting the time of travel of acoustic transmissions to and from the bottom The apparatus that sends and receives the transmissions is called a transducer.
Ecozone	A major division of the earth's ecosystem in which distinctive interacting landforms, soils, vegetation, and climatic and hydrologic characteristics and life-forms occur. Ecozones are the largest division in a hierarchy of nested and progressively smaller ecological units.
Edge matching	The process of ensuring that detail along the edge of two adjacent map sheets matches correctly.
Elective	A course that a student may choose as part of a programme.
Electromagnetic Distance Measurement (EDM)	The determination of distance from precise measurements of intervals of time taken by an electromagnetic wave to pass between two points.
Elevation	The distance of a point above a specified surface of constant potential; the distance is measured along the direction of gravity between the point and the surface.
Elevation, orthometric	The distance between the geoid and a point, measured along the plumb-line and taken positive upward from the geoid.
Entity	An object about which information is stored in a database.

Enumerator Area	A fundamental building block in the collection of census information. An enumerator area is descriptively defined and mapped for use in the actual collection of census data.
Feature	Another word for an entity (q.v.).
Field sheet	The manuscript of the hydrographic survey in graphical or digital form. It includes depth measurements taken from the sounding profiles, bottom samples, the coastline, all navigation aids found, the survey control points used, and all conspicuous objects. Field sheets are the detailed originals that are then generalized for chart construction.
File	(1) An organized collection of related records. (2) In digital mapping, a category of related features (contours, forest cover, drainage, etc.) coded while being digitized so they can be plotted by a single computer command
Fish (towed)	A streamlined object that is towed behind the ship, helicopter, or hovercraft and is submerged to a specific depth from which any side-looking sounder will display the strong and weak responses caused by the unevenness of the sea bottom.
Fixed boundary	A boundary that is mathematically defined in terms of its bearing and distance or by its coordinates.
Flare triangulation	An obsolete triangulation system in which parachute flares are dropped from an aircraft, and simultaneous observations (triggered by a radio signal) are made on them by observers with theodolites at both known and unknown positions. The former intersect the flares while the latter resect their positions.
Foresight	In levelling, a reading on a levelling rod held on a succeeding point. See Backsight.
General boundary	A boundary that is defined by a physical feature such as a fence, hedge, or wall, without specifying its mathematical measurement or its precise location within the feature.
Geodesy	The scientific study of the size and shape of the earth and determination of positions upon it.
Geodetic framework/network	A spatial framework of points whose position has been precisely determined on the surface of the earth.
Geographic Information System (GIS)	A system of capturing, storing, checking, integrating, analysing, and displaying data about the earth that is spatially referenced. It is normally taken to include a spatially referenced database and appropriate applications software.

Geoid	The equipotential surface of the earth's gravity field that best fits mean sea level.
Geomatics	A field of activity that, using a systematic approach, integrates all the means used to acquire and manage spatial data required as part of the scientific, administrative, legal, and technical operations involved in the process of production and management of spatial information.
Gimbal	A ring carrying, along a diameter, an internal axis about which the ring can rotate, and a pair of internal or external trunnions on a diameter perpendicular to that on which the internal axis lies. Gimbals are often nested one inside the other so that there can be free, rotary movement in three mutually perpendicular directions.
Global Positioning System (GPS)	A system for fixing positions on the surface of the earth in real time by measuring the ranges to a special set of satellites orbiting the earth.
Graphic Kernal System (GKS)	A system for allowing graphics software to be used on a range of different devices.
Graphical cadastre	A cadastral system in which the cadastral map shows the correct size, shape, and location of land parcels, together with each parcel identifier, but does not show boundary dimensions or parcel areas.
Graphics terminal	A device with a cathode ray tube for displaying digital spatial data.
Graticule	A network of lines on a map representing certain parallels and meridians.
Gravimeter	An instrument for determining either the value of gravity at a point, or the difference in gravity between that point and another point.
Gravimetry	In geodesy – the science or technique of measuring gravity.
Gyrocompass	A compass based on the principle that a gyroscope will align itself with the spin axis of the earth.
Gyroscope	Any device using a spinning mass to establish or maintain a direction. Gyroscopes can therefore be used to maintain the orientation of an instrument (such as an inertial navigation system).
Hard copy	The physical media (typically paper or stable base materials) on which maps and other documents are printed and stored.
Height, geodetic	The perpendicular distance from an ellipsoid of reference to a point. It is a geodetic coordinate.

Hi-Fix	A phase comparison range or range difference (hyperbolic) electronic positioning system that uses medium frequency transmissions.
Horizon camera	A camera directed to photograph the horizon at the same instant that a connected vertical camera is exposed.
Hydrodist	A marine version of MRA-2 Tellurometer.
Hyperbola	In electronic navigation the line of position in which there is a constant difference in distance (or signal travel time) between two separated transmitters.
Hypsometric tints	Tints of a colour, generally brown or green, indicating areas on a map of a given elevation.
Image	The picture of the external form of an object, frequently used to refer to pictures of the earth's surface produced by sensing devices in satellites (satellite images). May be used to describe the graphic portion and symbols on a map as opposed to spatially referenced statistics relating to the map.
Image analysis	The processing and interpretation of graphic images held in digital form.
Inertial surveying	The determination of position through the use of gyroscopes and measurements of acceleration.
Information	Data transformed into a form suitable for the user.
Infrared film	Film sensitive to the visible part of the spectrum and to light rays that are just beyond the visible spectrum (to 0.9 micrometers wavelength).
INT chart	A chart produced by one nation to certain international standards set by the International Hydrographic Organization and then supplied to other countries for minor modification and printing.
Interface	The connection between two devices that handle data in different ways.
Interferometer, Very Long Baseline	A pair of radio telescopes separated by a great distance – usually 1000 km or more – that act as radio interferometers on signals of common origin. The ability to determine the location of one telescope relative to the other within a few centimetres makes the device important geodetically. Often referred to as a VLBI.
Invar	An alloy of nickel and steel that has a very low coefficient of thermal expansion (about 1/25 that of steel). In geodesy, used for very accurate measuring tapes and for scales in levelling rods.

Lambert Conformal Projection	A map projection in which the graticule is formed by meridians of longitude projected as straight lines and by parallels of latitude drawn as circular arcs. It is used extensively to map areas that have a greater extent from east to west than from north to south.
Land	The surface of the earth, the materials beneath, the air above, and all things fixed to the soil.
Land administration	The functions involved in implementing land management policies.
Land information management	The managing of information about land
Land Information System (LIS)	A system for acquiring, processing, storing, and distributing information about land.
Land management	The management of all aspects of land including the formation of land policies.
Land parcel	A tract of land, being all or part of a legal estate.
Land registration	The recording of rights in land through deeds or as title.
Land tenure	The mode of holding rights in land.
Land title	The evidence of a person's rights to land.
Land transfer	The transfer of rights in land.
Land use	The manner in which land is used, including the nature of the vegetation upon its surface.
Land value	The worth of a property, determined in a variety of ways that give rise to different estimates of value.
Landsat	A series of earth resource scanning satellites.
Lane jumps	When signals are weak or there is interference from skywave reflections, the odometer-like lane counter can "flip" to the next lane, thus losing or gaining a lane.
Lanes	The distance between lines of position having the same phase comparison in such positioning systems as Decca and Hi-Fix.
Layer	A subset of spatial data, selected on a non-spatial basis, such as all objects in the same category, for example contours or vegetation.
Lead line	Used to measure the depth of water by lowering a lead weight to the bottom, and possibly to obtain a sample of the bottom for analysis.
Least squares, method of	If corrections are to be made to observed quantities to satisfy given theoretical conditions, then the sum of the squares of these corrections must be a minimum. An example is the adjustment of a braced quadrilateral in which all corner angles have been read. The

adjustment ensures that all triangles in the quadrilateral contain exactly 180 degrees, and that the sum of the squares of the corrections to bring this about was a minimum.

Legal cadastre

A systematic public register of individual land parcels for ascertaining the location and extent of each parcel within a particular jurisdiction, and for recording the creation, transfer, or extinguishment of the ownership of, or other legal interests in, the parcel.

Legend

The information printed on a map, generally in the margin, explaining the symbols and conventional signs that are used.

Level line

A set of measured differences of elevation, presented in the order of their measurement, and the similarly ordered set of points to which the measurements refer.

Levelling

The process of finding vertical distances (elevations) from a selected equipotential surface to points on the earth's surface, or of finding differences of elevation. Usually levelling must be done either as the sum of incremental vertical displacements of a graduated rod (differential levelling) or by measuring vertical angles (trigonometric levelling).

LIDAR

A laser light beam is pointed downwards from the aircraft. The laser light reflects from the water surface (to give the height above the water) and a second reflection from the bottom (to give the depth of water). The laser light is usually swept through an arc to provide a swath of data rather than a single profile under the aircraft.

Line map

A term used to distinguish a map drawn with lines and symbols from a photomap.

Line of position

In navigation, the locus of points having a constant parameter, be it distance (i.e., an arc of a circle), an azimuth or bearing (a straight line), an angle between two points (an arc of a circle), or a difference in distance or travel time (an hyperbola).

Link

A series of consecutive non-intersecting line segments. See also Node.

Local area network (LAN)

A comunication system that allows several processing devices that are nearby to be linked together.

Loran-A

Developed by the United States during the Second World War as a medium-frequency, pulse-matching hyperbolic (range difference) navigation system.

Loran-C

United States low-frequency, cycle matching within groups of transmitted pulses navigation system. It is generally used in the

	range difference (hyperbolic) mode, but can be used in a range mode if the user has an accurate clock.
Lot	A land parcel (q.v.).
Magnetic declination	The deviation of a compass needle from true north caused by slow and continuous changes in the earth's magnetic field. Maps of the current deviation are required to ensure accurate navigation by compass.
Manuscript map	The original drawing of a map, by hand or on a plotting machine, before any steps have been taken to reproduce it.
Map	A diagrammatic representation of the earth=s surface or part of it showing the positions of natural and artificial features, or the geographical distribution of population, natural resources, or other attributes.
Map sheet	The geographic extent of a geographic data set specified by a minimum bounding rectangle. Typically a single hard-copy map from a map series, or a single portion of a digital map database.
Mechanical projection plotter	A plotter in which the optical model is formed in the mind of the operator when he or she views a stereo pair that has been set up in the machine. The viewing system involves space rods that guide the optics of the viewing system and that generally are moved by hand-wheels. Later designs of some instruments allowed scanning by the simple movement of a handle at the junction of the space rods.
Metes and bounds	A property description by reference to the bearings and lengths of the boundaries and the name of adjoining properties.
Microfiche, microfilm, microform	Storage media based on photographic processes.
Military Town Plan	A large-scale (1:25 000 or larger) gridded map of a built-up area. Such a map may or may not be contoured. Specifications for MTPs may require the showing of features of military interest such as power generating stations, telephone exchanges, lumber yards, etcetera. MTPs are sometimes called Military City Maps.
Mini-Ranger	A microwave direct wave ranging system.
Minor control	Points of known horizontal position (and at times elevation) obtained by photogrammetric techniques such as radial line plotting, slotted template assembly, and strip and block adjustment.
Modem	A "modulator-demodulator" device that allows data to be converted into a form whereby they can be transmitted as a set of pulses down a cable and then reassembled at the other end.
Mortgage	The transfer of the ownership of, or a legal interest in, land to a lender for the purpose of providing security for a debt.

Nautical mile	A length of 1851.9 m. This approximates the average value of 1 minute of latitude.
Network (computer)	A system consisting of a computer and its connected terminals and devices. The term is also used to describe two or more interconnected computer systems.
Network (survey)	A series of connected survey points that provide a spatial framework for an area.
Node	The start or end of a link.
Notices to Mariners	Issued weekly by Canadian Coast Guard to provide mariners with information to keep their nautical charts and other publications current.
Numerical cadastre	A cadastral system in which the cadastral map shows the correct size, shape, and location of land parcels, individual parcel identifiers, parcel areas, boundary dimensions, and boundary monuments. Boundary corner coordinates may either appear on the map or be available from separate records.
Optical disc	A computer storage device that uses laser technology to store and read data from disks coated in light-sensitive material.
Option	A group of courses within a programme.
Orthophotograph	A composite aerial photograph from which height and tilt displacements have been removed.
Orthophotomap	A photomap (q.v.) made from orthophotographs.
Orthophotoscope	A photogrammetric device that produces photographs from which photographic distortion has been removed.
Overlap	The duplicated coverage along a strip of aerial photographs. An aerial photograph overlaps its neighbour by at least 60 percent in the direction of flight (forward overlap), and between 20 and 30 percent with each of the adjacent flight lines (lateral overlap or sidelap).
Parcel	See Land parcel.
Pass point	A synonym for a minor control point.
Photogrammetry	The science and art of taking accurate measurements from photographs.
Photo mosaic	An assembly of air photos to produce a rough photomap.
Photomap	A map made by printing photo images rather than using abstract conventional signs and symbols.

Pingo-like feature (PLF)	Features on the bottom of the ocean (notably in the Canadian western Arctic) caused by ice wedges forcing up the bottom into an oval mound.
Pixel	One of a regular array of cells (picture elements) on a grid, within which data are stored.
Place-name	A name applied to a geographic feature, either natural or man-made.
Plane tabling	A simple method for plotting surveys in the field by using a portable drafting table.
Planimetric	A map that does not have contours to represent relief, or any other representation of relief such as layer tinting or hill shading.
Plate tectonics	A geophysical theory that ascribes large-scale crustal changes, such as folding and faulting, to the movement of large, continent-sized crustal segments (called "plates") and explains such changes in terms of the relative movements of the plates and the consequent pressures of plate upon plate.
Plot	A land parcel (q.v.).
Plotter	Any device for drawing maps and figures.
Polygon	A closed plane figure having three or more sides. Typically a multi-sided figure that represents an area on a map. Polygons have attributes that describe the geographic feature they represent.
Polygon overlay	A process that merges spatially coincident polygons and their attributes from two or more maps.
Potential, gravity	The potential attributable to the earth's gravitational field and centrifugal force. It is equivalent to the work done in bringing a body of unit mass from infinity to a point attached to or rotating with the earth. The term is also used for the potential attributable to the gravitational field and rotation of any other body.
Premarking	The marking of points on the ground prior to the taking of aerial photographs so that the points can be of certain identity.
Presignalization	Premarking (q.v.).
Private conveyancing	The transfer of rights in land without any public record of the transfer.
Programme	A sequence of courses and other tasks that when completed will earn the candidate a degree, diploma, or certificate.
Property map	A map showing the extent and ownership of parcels of land.

Provisional map	A map that does not conform to the standards set by the publishers for the series in which it occurs. It may lack contours, vegetation cover, etcetera.
Quadrangle	The map, figure, or area enclosed by two parallels and two meridians.
Quadtree	An organization of raster data that minimizes data storage.
Radial line plotting	A graphic system for removing photographic distortion from pass points.
Radio Aids to Marine Navigation	A series of annual publications issued by the Canadian Coast Guard that provides radio information to the mariner.
Radio range	A radio navigation system whereby a pilot is kept on a given course by audible signals when the pilot strays to the left or right of the course.
Range holes	The occurrence of destructive interference to signals emanating from a transmitter, principally with a microwave positioning system.
Range lights	Navigation lights that are physically separated and are designed to give a line of direction of safe navigation when the two lights appear superimposed.
Raster	A cellular data structure composed of rows and columns. Groups of cells represent features. The value of each cell represents the value of the feature. Image data are stored using this structure.
Real estate	See Real property.
Real property	Land, including land covered by water, and anything permanently affixed to land, such as buildings and fences. The term is generally synonymous with real estate.
Reference plan	A cadastral plan showing part or parts of a registered lot, block, or parcel.
Refraction, atmospheric	The bending of electromagnetic radiation by the atmosphere. Light and infrared radiation are refracted principally by temperature inversions in the troposphere, the lowest part of the atmosphere.
Refresh rate	The frequency with which the image on a cathode ray tube is redrawn.
Refresh tube	A cathode ray tube in which the image is continuously being redrawn.
Registration of deeds	A system whereby a register of documents is maintained relating to the transfer of rights in land.

Registration of title	A system whereby a register of ownership of land is maintained based upon the parcel rather than the owner or the deeds of transfer.
Remote sensing	The technique of determining data about the environment from its spectral image as seen from a distance.
Rental value	The value of a property in terms of the rent that may be derived from it.
Reprints	Nautical charts that are printed with only the information provided in *Notices to Mariners* since the last new edition of the chart. Reprints do not cancel previous versions of the same chart, whereas a new edition of the chart would since it contains more information than is provided in *Notices to Mariners*.
Resection angles	In marine navigation the angle measured with a sextant at the ship between two fixed objects (usually control survey points). A second line of position can be obtained by a second resection angle, bearing line, or distance.
Rho-rho Loran-C	Rho-rho (for range-range) Loran-C uses the Time of Arrival of Loran-C signals. The Time of Transmission of each signal is predicted by a computer using a cesium frequency standard as a timing device.
Right of way	The right of a person to pass over the land of another person. A private right of way is a form of easement.
Road casing	The parallel lines on a map representing the sides of a road.
Rubber sheeting	The transformation of spatial data to stretch or compress them to fit with other data.
Run length encoding	A method for storing raster data in a database
Satellite, artificial	A man-made satellite, as distinguished from natural satellites such as the planets and their moons.
Satellite geodesy	The process of obtaining geodetic information by the observation of artificial satellites.
Satellite image	See Image.
Scale	The ratio between the distance between two points on a map and the distance between the same two points on the ground. Maps are generally classified into one of three classes, that is large-scale, medium-scale, and small-scale, but there is no general agreement on the boundaries between classes. To the military, a 1:25 000 is a large-scale map, but to the town planner it is a small-scale map.

Scale error	The difference between the stated scale of a map and the actual scale at a given point or area on the map. The error is caused by the imperfections of the projection, and generally increases with the distance from the standard parallel(s) or meridian.
Scalloped line	A line consisting of small circle segments resembling the edge of a marine bivalve. It is used on monochrome maps to represent the edge of a forested area. The points of the line point toward the trees.
Scanning	The process of data input in raster format with a device called a scanner. Some scanners also use software to convert raster data to vector data.
Scribe coat (plastic)	A clear plastic film with an opaque, wax-like coating that is scratched off by a scribing tool. The scribe coat is then a temporary negative from which a permanent photographic negative can be made.
Seasat	A NASA satellite placed in orbit in June 1978 that carried an imaging radar system in the L-band for oceanographic studies, and that in its working life of 3.5 months achieved coverage of 100 million km^2.
Sextant	An angle-measuring device with which the user superimposes the image of the two distant objects on top of one another.
Slack water	Slack water is the time when there is no perceptible current.
Slotted template	A fibre-board card that has been punched with a hole at its centre to represent the principal point of an aerial photo, and with radial slots cut to represent the rays from the principal point out to the minor control points. The template is assembled with others, representing the other photos in a block, by the use of studs in the centre holes and in the radial slots (see figure 3–4).
Software	A set of instructions that causes a computer to perform specified functions. It may be complex and sophisticated as in geographic information system software.
Spatial referencing	The association of an entity with its absolute or relative location.
Spider template	A mechanical system for block adjustment similar to the slotted template method but using metal arms instead of a slotted card, as shown in figure 3-5.
SPOT	A series of high-resolution earth resource satellites (Système Pour l'Observation de la Terre)
Spot height	A dot on a map showing the elevation of that point.
Stamp duty	A levy charged on the transfer of property.

Station, control	A point on the ground whose horizontal or vertical location is used as a basis for obtaining locations of other points.
Station, gravity	A point at which gravity has been measured.
Station, Laplace	A control station at which both astronomic longitude and astronomic azimuth are observed.
Station pointer	A three-armed protractor used in marine navigation to plot the position of the vessel.
Statoscope	A precise barometric device for recording the changes in altitude of a plane.
Stereographic projection	A type of conformal projection in which the projection plane is normal to a line connecting the earth's centre with a viewpoint at the opposite side of the earth.
Storage tube	A cathode ray tube that stores graphic data on the screen without having to continuously redraw it.
Strata title	Title to land that is not necessarily divided horizontally, such as in high-rise buildings or for mining rights.
String, 2D, and 3D	A set of line elements such as x, y coordinate pairs, that go to make up a continuous whole.
Strip chart	A nautical chart printed on long narrow paper so that it can be folded for easy use on small craft.
Subdivision	The partition of a parcel of land into two or more parcels.
Super-wide-angle lens	See under Wide-angle lens.
SWATH vessel	Small Waterplane Area Twin Hull vessel after a concept patented by Frederick G. Creed of Nova Scotia. The vessel is essentially a catamaran, but its buoyancy is in two submerged, streamlined pontoons with only thin, almost fin-like, connections to the hull that are above the surface.
Syledis	An ultra-high-frequency (UHF) pulse matching, multi-ranging positioning system for vessels.
Tenure	Tenure is the system in place in a given jurisdiction for owning rights to land.
Tesselation	A mosaic structure of closely fitting parts. Typically used to partition the earth's surface into regular arbitrary units to facilitate storage of relevant data. Often referred to as "tiling" structures in geographic information systems.

Thematic map	A map displaying a particular theme such as geology, population distribution, etcetera. The term excludes topographic maps, general maps at small scales, and navigation charts for air and marine uses.
Theodolite	A precise surveying instrument consisting of an alidade with a telescope mounted so it can be rotated about horizontal and vertical axes; the amount of rotation is measured on an accurately graduated, stationary circle.
Thiessen polygon	A polygon around a sampling point that has the property that all points within it are nearer to that point than to any other sampling point.
Tide gauge	A device for measuring the rise and fall and the current height of the tide.
Tide Table	A publication that provides mariners with the time and height of high and low waters for each day at various primary ports. Tidal conditions at secondary ports are predicted and related to primary ports by fixed offsets of time and heights. Tide tables also predict times of slack water (zero velocity) in channels where there are very strong currents.
Title to land	See Land title.
Topographic map	A map showing a portion of the surface of the earth in as much detail as the scale of the map will permit.
Topography	The physical features of the earth's surface.
Topology	The study of properties of a geometric figure that are not dependent upon absolute position, such as connectivity.
Torrens	A name given to the land titles registration system in Canada and some other countries. It derives from Sir Robert Torrens who introduced the system in south Australia in 1857.
Tower, Bilby	A tower used in triangulation and consisting of two tripods, one within the other. The Bilby tower is constructed (according to the design of J.S. Bilby of the U.S. Coast and Geodetic Survey) so that an observer on a platform at the top of the outer tripod can move about without disturbing an instrument mounted on the top of the inner tripod.
Tower, Lambert "twin"	A tower used primarily in surveying for horizontal control, consisting of a 9-inch-diameter vertical pipe supporting the instrument and a separate vertical, triangular prism, 12 inches on a side, that surrounds the pipe and supports an observing platform at the top.
Township fabric	The system of survey used to lay out a township. The pattern is disclosed by the roads, fences, etcetera resulting from the survey.

Transducer	The transmitter and receiver for acoustic transmissions used in sounding. Multi-beam sounders have very directional transducers.
Transistor	A semiconducting device that has replaced the more fragile radio tube. It is capable of amplification, reduction of radio frequencies, etcetera.
TRANSIT	See Doppler Satellite Navigation System.
Transverse Mercator projection	A conformal cylindrical projection in which the features of a map are projected onto the cylinder wrapped around the spheroid tangent to a chosen central meridian or secant to two small circles equidistant from the central meridian. In the Universal Transverse Mercator system the mapping is normally limited to 3 degrees each side of the central meridian. Some provinces use a TM projection in which the mapping is restricted to 1.5 degrees on either side. This restriction is to keep the scale error of the projection to less than 1 part in 10 000.
Traversing	A land survey technique of measuring successive angles and distances to establish new positions.
Triangulated Irregular Network	A surface representation derived from irregularly spaced sample points with x, y coordinates and a surface or z value. The points are connected by lines to form a set of non-overlapping triangles used to represent the surface.
Triangulation	The method of extending control by measurement of the angles in a series of connected triangles, quadrilaterals, and other polygons.
Trilateration	The method of extending horizontal control by measuring the sides rather than the angles of triangles. Some angles may also be measured. See Triangulation.
Trimetrogon	A mapping system using air photographs from three cameras each having a metrogon lens.
Trisponder	A microwave direct wave ranging system.
Troposphere	The lowest layer of the atmosphere, which extends from the earth's surface to an average height of some 12 km.
Valuation	The determination of the value of property.
Vector	(1) A quantity having both magnitude and direction that in a spatial database is usually stored as a pair of coordinates. (2) A coordinate-based data structure commonly used to represent linear map features. Attributes are associated with the feature as opposed to a raster data structure that associates attributes with a grid cell.
Visual display unit (VDU)	A computer terminal with a cathode ray tube used for displaying data.

Voronoi spatial model	Uses the concept of nearness for subdividing parts of the earth's surface. A Voronoi spatial model (also called Dirichlet regions or Thiessen polygons) consists of polygons the interiors of which consist of all points in the plane that are nearer to a selected sample point than to any other selected sample point.
Wide-angle lens	A wide-angle aerial camera lens has a focal length of 152.4 mm as compared to a super-wide-angle camera lens with a focal length of 85 or 88 mm. The shorter focal length produces smaller-scale photography, and thus fewer photos are needed to cover a given area. In general, however, the wide-angle photography is clearer, and more suitable for mapping under Canadian conditions.
Wilderness Line	An arbitrary line drawn across a map of Canada (see figure 3-15) that separates the area south of the line where full-colour 1:50 000 maps are drawn from the northern area where monochrome maps are produced.
Windowing	Selecting by area a section of a spatial database. Also the facility in some systems to display several functions together on one screen.
Workstation	A graphic screen, keyboard, and (in digital mapping) digitizing tablet all on one desk and linked together with a computer.
Zooming	Proportionally enlarging or reducing an area of a map displayed on a screen.

ANNEX: ORDERS OF CONTROL SURVEYS

Mention is made in several chapters of various orders of surveys such as first order and second order. These orders refer to orders of accuracy according to *Specifications and Recommendations for Control Surveys and Survey Markers*, a booklet published in 1978 by the then Surveys and Mapping Branch, Department of Energy, Mines and Resources, Ottawa. Theere are two sets of specifications, one for levelling and the other for horizontal control, as follows:

Levelling

Orders are assigned based on the maximum allowable difference between independent forward and backward levellings between adjacent benchmarks (usually about 2 km apart). Five different orders are recognized, with individual allowable limits as follows:

Special Order	3 mm × K
First Order	4 mm × K
Second Order	8 mm × K
Third Order	24 mm × K
Fourth Order	120 mm × K

where K is the one-way distance between the adjacent benchmarks in kilometres.

The orders refer to the accuracy of position of individual control stations, and are based on the concept of a confidence region surrounding the station. A confidence region is an area bounded by an ellipse, and is derived from a least squares computational adjustment of a set of horizontal control measurements. The true position is expected to lie within this elliptical area with a certain probability.

For the assignment of orders, a 95 percent confidence region has been selected as the criterion for determining the station accuracy. The true position of the control station is expected to lie within this ellipse with 95 percent probability (see sketch below). The station is classified by order according to whether the semi-major axis of this ellipse (with respect to other stations of the network) is less than or equal to *r* centimetres, where

r = C (K + 0.2)

K = the distance in kilometres to any other station

C = an order coefficient assigned according to the following table

Order	C
1	3
2	5
3	12
4	30

For example if two stations are 10 km apart, they will be classified first order if *r* is less than or equal to 2 (10 + 0.2) or 20.4 cms. They will be classified second order if *r* is less than or equal to 5 (10 + 0.2) or 51 cms, but exceeds 20.4 cms (the first-order limit).

For a more detailed explanation of the specifications that describe orders of control surveys, please refer to the booklet mentioned above.

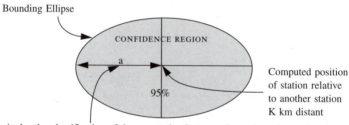

Bounding Ellipse

CONFIDENCE REGION

a

95%

Computed position
of station relative
to another station
K km distant

For a required order classification of the connection between the stations the semi-major axis a must be less than r = C (K + 0.2) cm where C has the value assigned for the order.

List of Acronyms and Abbreviations

Acronym	Definition
ABSM	Alberta Bureau of Surveys and Mapping
ACGAN	Advisory Committee on Glaciological and Alpine Nomenclature
ACND	Advisory Committee on Nomenclature and Delineation
ACP	Active Control Point (part of ACS)
ACRSO	Atlantic Centre for Remote Sensing of the Oceans
ACS	Active Control System
ACSM	American Congress on Surveying and Mapping
ACTR	Advisory Committee on Toponymic Research
ADF	Automatic Distance Finder
ADIZ	Air Defence Identification Zone
ADM	Assistant Deputy Minister
Aerodist	Airbone Distance Measuring System
AES	Atmospheric Environment Service
AMF	Area Master File, Statistics Canada
AMS/GIS	Automated Mapping System/Geographic Information System developed by Geo-Vision Corporation
AOLS	Association of Ontario Land Surveyors
APR	Airborne Profile Recorder

APS	Aerial Photography and Survey (government flying licence)
APSAMP	Atlantic Provinces Surveying and Mapping Program
ARC/INFO	Geographic Information System software developed by ESRI Inc.
ARDA	Agricultural Rehabilitation and Development Administration
ASCII	American Standard Code for Information Interchange. It is an international standard that defines how letters and other characters are represented in a computer's storage.
ASDB	Aerial Survey Data Base
ASE	Army Survey Establishment
ASF	Additional Secondary Factor
ASPRS	American Society of Photogrammetry and Remote Sensing
ATS 77	Average Terrestial System 1977, used in Maritimes instead of NAD83
AutoCAD	computer-aided drafting software
AUTOCARTO	automatic cartography system developed at Surveys and Mapping Branch, Energy Mines and Resources Canada, 1969–75
Auto-Carto	general abbreviation for automated cartography
AUTOMAP	software developed for the Royal Australian Army Survey Corps by SHL Systemhouse Ltd
AVHRR	Advanced Very High Resolution Radiometer
BCMOF	British Columbia Ministry of Forests
CAAS	Canadian Association of Aerial Surveyors (later GIAC)
CACRS	Canadian Advisory Committee on Remote Sensing
CAD/CAM	Computer-Aided Drafting (or Design)/Computer-Aided Manufacturing
CAGS	Canadian Absolute Gravity Site
CalsIM	urban information system, City of Calgary
CANAC	Canada Air Chart (computer program used by Aeronautical Chart Service)
Cansis	Canadian Soil Information System
CARIS	Computer Aided Resource Information System, which was developed from the Canadian Hydrographic Service GOMADS system by Universal Systems Ltd
CARL	Canadian Applied Research Ltd
CART-8	Canadian Hydrographic Service hydrographic charting system developed by A.R. Boyle

CASE	computer-assisted system engineering
CASI	Compact Airborne Spectral Imager
CASLE	Commonwealth Association of Surveying and Land Economy
CBGN	Canadian Board on Geographical Names
CCG	Canada Centre for Geomatics, EMR, Sherbrooke, Québec; also Canada Communication Group (formerly the Queen's Printer)
CCM	Canada Centre for Mapping, EMR, Ottawa, Ontario
CCOG	Canadian Council on Geomatics (formerly CCSM)
CCRS	Canada Centre for Remote Sensing
CCSM	Canadian Council on Surveying and Mapping (now CCOG)
CEGEP	Collège d'Enseignement Général et Professionnel
CESAR	Canadian Expedition to Study the Alpha Ridge
CFASU	Canadian Forces Airborne Sensing Unit
CFRGS	Canadian Forest Resources Data System
CGIS	Canada Geographic Information System
CGSN	Canadian Gravity Standardisation Network
CHS	Canadian Hydrographic Service
CIDA	Canadian International Development Agency
CIG	Canadian Institute of Geomatics
CIS	Canadian Institute of Surveying (now CIG)
CLI	Canada Land Inventory
CLISP	Corporate Land Information Strategic Plan (BC)
CLS	Canada Lands Surveyor
CLUMP	Canada Land Use Monitoring Program
CMO	Canada Map Office
CMP	Council of Maritime Premiers
COGO	Coordinate Geometry
COSINE	a comprehensive Ontario database management program
COSPAR	Committee on Space Research
CPC	Canada Pilotage Chart
CPCGN	Canadian Permanent Committee on Geographical Names (formerly CBGN)

CRSS	Canadian Remote Sensing Society
CSA	Canadian Space Agency
CSMA	Central Surveys and Mapping Agency (Province of Saskatchewan)
CTP	Conventional Terrestial Pole
CTQ	Commission de toponymie du Québec
CTTTW	Committee for the Transfer of Technology to the Third World
DBF	Digital Boundary File
D Carto	Director of Cartography (now D Geo Ops)
DEM	Digital Elevation Model
DEW	Distant Early Warning (Line)
D Geo Ops	Director of Geographic Operations, DND (formerly D Carto)
DGEOS	Director General of Environmental and Operational Services
DIAND	Department of Indian Affairs and Northern Development
DIME	Dual Independent Map Encoding
DIPOP	Differential Positioning Program
DLS	Dominion Land Surveyor (later CLS)
DMA	U.S. Defense Mapping Agency
DME	Distance Measuring Equipment
DMRS	data management and retrieval software, Intergraph Corporation
DMTS	Department of Mines and Technical Surveys
DND	Department of National Defence, Canada
DOLPHIN	Deep Ocean Logging Platform with Hydrographic Instrumentation and Navigation.
DOSS	Director of Operational Services and Survey
DREE	Department of Regional Economic Expansion
DSS	Department of Supply and Services, Canada
DTDB	Digital Topographic Data Base
DTM	Digital Terrain Model
EA	Enumerator Area
EAIT	External Affairs and International Trade, Canada

ECDIS	Electronic Chart Display and Information System
EDM	Electromagnetic Distance Measurement
EMR	Energy, Mines and Resources, Canada
EPS	Essential Planning Systems Limited
ERCB	Energy Resources Conservation Board (Province of Alberta)
ERIE	grid cell mapping program developed by University of Western Ontario
ERIM	Environmental Research Institute of Michigan
EROS	Earth Resources Observation Satellite
ERTS	Earth Resources Technology Satellite
ESA	European Space Agency
ESRI	Environmental Systems Research Institute
FAO	Food and Agriculture Organisation (of the United Nations)
FIG	Fédération Internationale des Géomètres
FILS	Ferranti Inertial Survey System
GADB	Geographic Attribute Data Base
GALS	Geographic Adjustment by Least Squares
GDA	Geographical Document Architecture
GDLSAT	Geodetic Doppler Satellite
GDS 91	Canadian computer program for estimating the geoid-spheroid separation
GEBCO	General Bathymetric Charts of the Oceans
GEPDEQ	Géodésie Québec. A program for handling geodetic databases
GEODOP	Geocletic Doppler software
GEO-IS	Geographic Information System
GEOMAP	grid cell mapping program developed by D. Steiner at the University of Waterloo
Geo/SQL	Geographical/System Query Language software developed by Kanotech Information Systems
GFRD	Geographic Frame Data Base
GIAC	Geomatics Industry Association of Canada (successor to CAAS)
GIS	Geographic Information System
GITDP	Geographic Information and Technology Development Program (federal)

GOMADS	Graphical On-line Manipulation and Display System, which evolved from the CART-8 system and was developed in-house by Canadian Hydrographic Service.
GPH 200	military instrument approach procedure publication (an air navigation publication)
GROOM	Generalized Reduction of Observed Material. A comprehensive program for adjusting geodetic observations
GPS	Global Positioning System
GRDSR	Geographically Referenced Data Storage and Retrieval system, Statistics Canada
GSC	Geological Survey of Canada
GSGS	Geographical Section of the General Staff
HE	High Enroute (an air navigation chart)
HIRAN	High Accuracy Shoran
IACRS	Interagency Committee on Remote Sensing, EMR
IALA	International Association of Lighthouse Authorities
IBC	International Boundary Commission
IBM	International Business Machines
ICA	International Cartographic Association
ICAO	International Civil Aviation Organization
ICOD	International Centre for Ocean Development
IDRC	International Development Research Centre
IFR	Instrument Flight Rules
IGDS	interactive graphic design system, Intergraph Corporation
IGLD	International Great Lakes Datum
IGU	International Geographical Union
IHO	International Hydrographic Organization
IJC	International Joint Commission (concerned with boundary waters)
IMAA	Increased Ministerial Authority and Accountability Accord
INFOMAP	GIS software by Synercom Corporation
INGRES	database management software
INRIS	Integrated Natural Resource Information System (Province of Ontario)
INS	Inertial Navigation System
ISA	Integrated Survey Area

ISM	International Society for Mine Surveying
ISO	International Standards Organisation
ISPRS	International Society for Photogrammetry and Remote Sensing (originally International Society for Photogrammetry, ISP)
ISS	Inertial Survey System
ITRF	International Terrestrial Reference Frame
IUGG	International Union of Geodesy and Geophysics
JOG	Joint Operations Graphic
LandDATA	an automated land information system
LE	Low Enroute (navigation charts, sometimes called LO)
LF	Low Frequency (radio signals)
LIDAR	Light Detection and Ranging
LIFT	Lower Inventory for Tomorrow programme of the government of Canada
LINC	identifier used to reference Land Titles Office titles to ownership parcels based upon survey parcels in Alberta Land Information Network for Canada
LIS	Land Information System
Loran	Long Range Aid to Navigation
LOREX	Lomonosov Ridge Expedition
LRIS	Land Registration and Information Service (Maritime provinces); also Land-Related Information Systems (Province of Alberta)
MACDIF	Map and Chart Data Interchange Format
MANOR	Ontario computer program for survey data processing
MASCOT	Alberta database management program
MCAPP	Mapping, Charting and Air Photography Plan (U.S.-Canada joint plan for North America)
MCE	Mapping and Charting Establishment, DND (formerly ASE)
MCM	Military City Map
MCP	Mapping and Charting Plan
MDIF	Map Data Interchange Format
MDO	Map Distribution Office (later CMO)
MEF	Maximum Elevation Figure (printed in each quadrangle of an air chart)

MEIS	Multispectral Electro-optical Imaging Scanner
MF	Medium Frequency
MICS	Map Inventory Control System
MISAM	Municipal Integrated Surveying and Mapping (programme in Alberta)
MNR	Ministry of Natural Resources, Ontario
MODUL-2.0	data modelling technique supported in ORION, a combination of object-oriented and entity-relationship concepts with extensions for spatial and temporal descriptions and behaviours
MOEP	Ministry of Environment and Parks (BC)
MOU	Memorandum of Understanding
MSMB	Manitoba Surveys and Mapping Branch
MSS	(Landsat) Multispectral Scanner
MTP	Military Town Plan
MunMAP	software developed by Kanotech Information Systems
NACCSM	National Advisory Committee on Control Surveys and Mapping
NAD27, NAD83	North American Datum 1927 and 1983
NAPP	National Air Photography Plan
NASA	National Aeronautics and Space Administration, U.S.
NATMAP	National Geoscience Mapping Program
NAVD 88	North American Vertical Datum 1988
NBGIC	New Brunswick Geographic Information Corporation
NCR	National Cash Register
NDB	Non-Directional Beacon
NESS	National Earth Science Series (maps produced by CHS)
NLUIP	Northern Land Use Information Program
NOAA	National Oceanic and Atmospheric Administration, U.S.
NRC	National Research Council
NRCan	Natural Resources Canada (previously Energy, Mines and Resources Canada [EMR])
NRM	National Resource Maps (produced by CHS)
NSERC	Natural Sciences and Engineering Research Council

NSSC	National Soil Survey Committee
NTDB	National Topographic Data Base
NTS	National Topographic System
OBM	Ontario Basic Mapping
OGNB	Ontario Geographic Names Board
ORACLE	a relational database management system
ORION	case tool developed at Université Laval, Québec, to help create data schema and the integrated data dictionary (with navigation capabilities)
OSGB	Ordnance Survey of Great Britain
PAIGH	Pan-American Institute of Geography and History
PAMAP	Geographic Information System developed by PAMAP Graphics
PAT-M	Photogrammetric Aerial Triangulation – Models
PCCF	Postal Code Conversion File
PCSP	Polar Continental Shelf Project
PDBA	Provincial Digital Baseline Atlas (BC)
PDBM	Provincial Digital Base Mapping (Alberta)
PILLAR	perspective view method of illustrating an absolute geographic distribution (D. Douglas)
PJDB	Permanent Joint Board on Defence
PLF	pingo-like feature
PM	Parcel Mapping (Alberta)
POD	Print on Demand (system for printing maps as and when requested by the customer)
POGO	Processing of Gravity Observations
POLARIS	Province of Ontario Land Registration and Information System
PROMIS	Province of Ontario Mapping Information System
RAPID	software developed to store all individual census responses as string files in a database, Statistics Canada
RCAF	Royal Canadian Air Force
RCN	Royal Canadian Navy
RDDP	Radar Data Development Program

RESULTS	Registration, Survey, and Land management Triangular System of Canada Centre for Surveys, Ottawa, Ontario
RFP	Request for Proposal
SA	Selective Availability
SAIF	Spatial Archive and Interchange Format (BC)
SAR	Synthetic Aperture Radar
Shoran	Short Range Aid to Navigation
SIGEOM	Québec database for natural resource information
SMB	Surveys and Mapping Branch, EMR; also Surveys and Mapping Branch, Manitoba
SMRSS	Surveys, Mapping and Remote Sensing Sector, EMR (now Geomatics Sector, NRCan)
SNF	Street Network File
SPACE-M	photogrammetric adjustment for control using independent models
SPANS	Spatial Analysis Systems, Tydac Technologies
SPAR Aerospace	Special Projects Applied Research (a commercial company)
SPOT	Système Pour l'Observation de la Terre (French satellite)
SQL/MM	System Query Language/Multi-Media
SQRC	Systeme Québécois de Référence Cartographique
STATPAK	generalized tabulation system software for retrieval of string files stored by RAPID for ad hoc tabulation requests, Statistics Canada
SWATH	Small Waterplane Area Twin Hull
SYMAP	Synergraphic Mapping System
TAC	Terminal Area Chart (used for an instrument approach to an airfield)
TACAN	Tactical Air Navigation
TIN	Triangulated Irregular Networks
TM	Transverse Mercator projection; also Thematic Mapper sensor on Landsat 4 and 5
Transit	a Doppler satellite positioning system
TRIM	Terrain Resource Information Management (BC)
UHF	ultra-high frequency
UNDP	United Nations Development Programme
Unesco	United Nations Educational, Scientific and Cultural Organization

UNGEGN	UN Group of Experts on Geographical Names
URISA	Urban and Regional Information Systems Association
USNGS	United States National Geodetic Survey
UTM	Universal Transverse Mercator projection
VFR	Visual Flight Rules
VHF	very high frequency
VISION	Geographic Information System using relational database technology, GeoVision Corporation
VLBI	Very Long Baseline Interferometry
VNC	VFR Navigation Chart
VOR	Very-high-frequency Omni-directional Range
VTA	VFR Terminal Area Chart (Used for visual approach to an airfield. Not to be confused with TAC)
WAC	World Aeronautical Chart
WGRS	World Geographic Reference System
XCM	X Cartographic Monitor, early EMR automatic cartography system
YGNB	Yukon Geographic Names Board
ZUPT	Zero velocity and alignment updates to ISS equipment

Canadian and Foreign Companies Mentioned in Text

Private industry has played an important role in the development of technology, techniques, and applications that are recorded in this volume, and in publishing. Companies large and small, present and past, Canadian and foreign that are mentioned in the text are summarized here for the convenience of the reader.

CANADIAN

Academic Press
AERDE
Aero Photo Inc.
Aero Surveys Limited
A.E. Simpson Ltd
Alex Miller and Associates
Allmaps Canada Ltd
ARC Industries Ltd
Arctic Air Lines
Atlantic Air Survey Company Ltd
Atlantic Geomatics Research
Atomic Energy of Canada
A.V. Roe
B.C. Coal
B.C. Gas
B.C. Hydro
Brault et Bouthillier
Breakwater
Calgary Petroleum Products
Canadian Aero Service Ltd
Canadian Aero Surveys

Canadian Air Surveys Ltd
Canadian Astronautics
Canadian Bechtel Limited
Canadian Cartographics Ltd
Canadian Pacific Airways
Canadian Pacific Railway
Cannonbooks
Capital Air Surveys Ltd
Cartex Inc.
CN Marine Atlantic
Computer Associates
Computing Devices of Canada
Coome Books
Copp Clark
de Havilland
Dendron Resource Surveys
Digital Resource Systems (Canada) Ltd
DIPIX (later PCI)
DPA Group Inc.
EastCan Group
Ecological and Resources Consultants

Éditions Naaman
ESRI Canada
Essential Planning Systems
F.G. Bercha Associates
Fleet/Lester and Orpen Denis
Gaetan Morin and Associates
Gage Education Publishing (Canada)
Gage Ltd
General Photogrammetric Services Ltd
Geomatics International
Geoplan Consultants
Georef Systems
Geovision Corporation
Gregory Geoscience
Guérin éditeur
Guiness Publications
Hobrough Ltd
Hosford Publishing
Hudson's Bay Company
Hunter and Associates
Hunting Survey Corporation Limited
Hydro-Québec
I2s
Imperial Oil Limited
Infomap
Innotech Aviation
Instronics
Integrated Resource Photography
Intera Technologies
International Nickel Company
Interwest Publishers
Itres Research
J.D. Barnes and Associates
J.M. Dent and Sons (Canada) Ltd
J.M.R. Instruments Canada
Kadon Electro-Mechanical Services
Kanotech Information Systems
Kenting Aviation
La Compagnie Photo-Air Laurentides (later La
    Société de Cartographie du Québec)
Leigh Instruments
Librairie Larousse
Lockwood Survey Corporation (later Northway
    Survey Corporation
Northway Survey (Corporation)
LRIS International Corp

MacDonald Dettwiler Associates
MacLean-Hunter
Macmillan of Canada
MapArt
Marconi of Canada
Maritex
Marshall Macklin Monaghan
McElhanney Engineering
McElhanney GeoSurveys
McElhanney Group
McElhanney Surveying and Engineering Ltd
McGill-Queen's University Press
Measurement Science Inc.
Mika Publishing Co.
MIR Télédétection
Moyer School Supplies
MPB Technologies
N.B. Power
Nelson Canada
New Brunswick Geographic Information
    Corporation
Noetix
Nortech Surveys
North West Company
North West Geomatics Ltd
North West Survey Corporation International
North West Surveys Corporation (Yukon)
North West (Survey) Geographic Services Ltd
Nova Corporation
NovAtel Communications Ltd
Offshore Systems Ltd
Ontario Hydro
Optech
OVAAC8
PAMAP Graphics
Pathfinder Engineering
Pathfinder Map Inc.
PCI Enterprises Ltd
Perly's Maps
Perly's Variprint Ltd
Photograhic Survey Corporation Ltd (later
    Hunting Survey Corporation Ltd)
Photographic Surveys (Québec) Limited
Photosur Geomat
Prentice Hall (Canada) Ltd
Presses de l'Université Laval

Presses de l'Université du Québec
PSC Applied Research Ltd (later Canadian
   Applied Research Ltd, then SPAR Aerospace
P.S. Ross and Partners
Publication Centre Éducatif et Culturel Inc.
Pulsearch Navigation Systems
Québec Cartier Mining Company
Radarsat International
Reidmore Books
Renouveau Pédagogique
Saskatchewan Potash Corporation
SaskTel
Satlantic
SED Systems
Shaw Photogrammetric Services Ltd
Shell Canada
Shelltech
SHL Systemhouse Ltd
SNC-Lavalin
Spartan Air Services Ltd
Sparwood Coal Mining Co.l
Stanford Telecommunications Inc.
Stanley Associates Engineering Ltd
Stewart, Weir and Company
Sunfire Publications

Sunset Travel Guide
Survair Ltd
Talonbooks
Tellurometer
Teranet Land Information Services Inc.
Terra Surveys Ltd
Terrain Resources
Tomlinson Associates
TransAlta Utilities
Trans-Canada Air Lines
Trans Mountain Pipeline
TYDAC Technologies
Universal Systems Ltd
Université du Québec à Montréal
University of Alberta Press
University of British Columbia Press
University of Toronto Press
Usher Canada Ltd
Western Photogrammetry
Wildcat Precision Measurements Ltd
Williamson
Woods, Gordon
World Book
Worldsat International
Worldview

FOREIGN

AAA
AGA
Ashtech
Bausch and Lomb
Cessna
Comarc
Dobbie McInnes (Electronics) Ltd
Douglas (Aircraft Corporation)
Earth Satellite Corporation
ERDAS
ESRI
Fairchild Aviation Corporation
Ferranti
General Electronic
Geodimeter
George Philip and Son
Ginn and Co.
Gousha Co.

Hammond University Press
Hewlett Packard
Hughes Aircraft
Hunting Group
Hunting Surveys U.K.
IBM
Intergraph Corporation
John E. Chance Associates
Kern
Keufel and Esser
Lane Books
Leica
Litton
Lockheed
M and S Computing
Maraven Oil Company
Methuen Publishers
MOM

Morrison Knudsen
Nistri
OMI (Ottica Mecanica Italiana)
Oxford University Press
Packard-Bell
Parsons Brincker Hoff
Rand McNally
Reader's Digest
Rolls Royce
Royal Dutch Shell Group

Spartan Air Surveys Argentina Ltd
Sperry
Synercom Corporation
Texas Instruments
Thomas Nelson and Sons
Trimble Navigation
Univac
Vickers
Wild
Zeiss

Index of Persons

General Index

Certain departments, branches, and agencies listed in this index have had numerous name changes over the years while continuing to perform much the same functions. To avoid duplication, references to these groups will be made under a single headword.

Surveys and Mapping Bureau (1947–49), Surveys and Mapping Branch (1949–87), Surveys, Mapping and Remote Sensing Sector (1987–95), Geomatics Canada (1995-present). *See under* Surveys and Mapping

Department of the Interior (1873–1936), Mines and Resources (1936–49), Mines and Technical Surveys (1949–66), Energy, Mines and Resources (1966–93), Natural Resources Canada (1993-present). *See under* Canada: Energy, Mines and Resources

To facilitate the search for instruments or systems serving much the same function, certain groupings have been made. For example, most surveying instruments and systems have been consolidated under "positioning." Other similar groups are height determination and Geographic Information Systems.

air charts. *See* charts, aeronautical

aircraft: Avro Anson, 165; Canso PBY, 178; Cessna 320, 166; Cessna Conquest, 166; CF 100, 430, 437; Convair 580, 437, 441; de Haviland Mosquito, 166; Douglas DC3 (Dakota), 166, 436; Falcon Jet, 436; Grumman Goose, 179; Hudson, 166; Lancaster, 168; Lear Jet, 166; Lockheed P38, 166; Norseman, 179; Piper Apache, 166; U-2, 430; Vickers Vedette, 246

air photography. *See* aerial photography

air survey industry. *See* Canadian air survey industry

Alberta, 41, 59, 75, 196, 202, 397; Bureau of Surveys and Mapping, 184; Department of Education, 286; Department of Highways, 282; Department of Lands and Forests, 170; Environmental Protection, Land Surveys Division, 202; Metis Settlement Land Registry, 198, 202; Municipal Integrated Surveying and Mapping programme (MISAM), 133, 184; Parcel Mapping (PM), 133; Provincial Digital Mapping Programme, 132; Resource Evaluation and Planning Division, Energy and Natural Resources, 477

algorithms: Channel Identification algorithm, 479; contour-to-grid algorithm, 479; Cosandier-Chapman algorithm (close range positioning), 360; Douglas-Poiker Algorithm (line handling) 479; Poiker relief-shading algorithm, 479; TIN (Triangular Irregular Networks), 479, 481

Argentina, 166, 178–9

Army Survey Establishment (later Mapping and Charting Establishment), 17, 42, 104–5, 141, 248, 573

associations. *See* survey associations

Atlantic Provinces, 117; Atlantic Provinces Board of Examiners for Land Surveyors (APBELS), 394; Atlantic Provinces Surveying and Mapping Program, 118

atlas

– commercial: Canadian content, 287; road, 288; tourist and travel; 288; table 10–3, 288

– junior or school: Canadian content, 284; cartographic design, 286; cartographic workshop, Alberta 1970, 286; colour, 287; format, 286; layout, 286; sections, 286; symbols, 286; type styles, 286; table 10–2, 285

– National Atlas of Canada: 3rd edition, 271; 4th edition, 273; 5th edition, 273, 277; First Advisory Committee, 273; Second Advisory Committee, 275; Third Advisory Committee, 279

– other federal: Centennial Atlas of Canada, 272; Gazetteer Atlas, 276; Geographical Map Series (atlas type), 275; National Atlas Database Map Series, 277; National Atlas Information System, 275

– provincial or regional: colour, use of, 282–3; cost recovery, 280; photographs in colour, 283; process colours, 283; table 10–1, 280

– thematic: county, 294; economic and resource, 296; environmental, 289–90, 297; health and electoral, 297; historical and cultural, 293–4; physical, 295; regional development, 296; urban, 298; table 10–4, 291

automation, in cartography, 161, 371–4, 470–1

awards: Prince Albert (of Monaco) Medal, 243; Thomas O'Malley Award, 176

Barbados, 552

baseline program (for EDM equipment calibration), 46. *See also* National Geodetic Baseline (NGBL)

Bedford Institute of Oceanography, 60, 224, 227, 232, 333

Bilby tower, 29

block adjustment. *See* aerotriangulation

boat and sportsmen shows, 535, 542

Bouguer surveys, 42, 53

Brazil, 178, 554, 557

British Columbia, 1, 5, 13, 35, 133–5; Ministry of Environment, Lands and Parks, 202; Surveys Branch, Department of Lands and Forests (later Surveys and Resource Mapping Branch, Environment Lands and Parks), 135; Terrain Resource Information Management (TRIM), 134, 184

bush-pilot activity, 246

cadastral map or plan, 192; reference plan, 198

cadastral surveys: aboriginal land claims, 199; boundary descriptions, metes, and bounds, 198; boundary litigation, 198; building permit, 197; cadastral map and plan detail, 191–2; lot or parcel surveys, 197; mortgage, 197; resurveys (retracement), 194; right of way surveys, 197; subdivision surveys, 197; Surveyor's Real Property Report, 197

cadastre: deeds recording vs title registration, 191, 194; economic, 191; fiscal, 191; graphical, 191; legal, 198; multi-purpose (Land Information System), 190; numerical, 192

Caldwell Report, 158

calibration of survey equipment, 46–7

Cambodia, 185

Canada:

– Agriculture Canada, 13, 17. *See also* Canada Land Inventory

– Air Transport Committee, Air Transport Board, 181

– Army: early mapping (19th and early 20th century), 140; Joint Operations Graphics, 159; NTS mapping, 142–52; role in survey education, 388;

Second World War, 141–2; special military mapping, 152–8. *See also* Canadian Forces
– Cabinet activity, 2, 142. *See also* Federal Cabinet Committee on Remote Sensing
– Canadian Advisory Committee on Remote Sensing (CACRS) (formerly Interagency Committee on Remote Sensing), 432, 449
– Canadian International Development Agency (CIDA) (formerly External Aid Office), 179–80, 183, 449–50, 552–5, 575
– Centre for Remote Sensing: directors general 1971-present, 432; founding in 1971, 431. *See also under* Surveys and Mapping Branch
– Centre for Surveying. *See* Surveys and Mapping Branch
– Energy, Mines and Resources, Department of, 15, 99–101, 223, 432
– Environment Canada, 14, 230, 316; Lands Directorate, 16, 296
– Fisheries and Oceans Canada, 16–17, 230
– Government Publication Centre (formerly the Queen's Printer, now Canada Communication Group), 275, 278
– International Role: industry abroad, 550–5; participation in international and professional associations, 562–9; support to international and regional organizations, 559–62; Surveys, Mapping, and Remote Sensing Sector international activities since 1987, 555–9
– Land Inventory (CLI), 290, 296–7, 311, 315, 427–8, 468
– Land Use Monitoring Program (CLUMP), 317; land capability and capability maps: agriculture, forestry, recreation, wildlife, 313, 468; present land use, 314; Resources for Tomorrow Conference, 315; socio-economic classification of land, 320; Special Committee of the Senate on Land Use in Canada, 315
– National Committee for Geography, 271
– National Defence, Department of, 17
– Parks Canada, 200
– Regional Economic Expansion, Department of, 118
– Supply and Services, Department of, 174
– Treasury Board, 158, 173, 273, 536–7
Canadian Advisory Committee on Remote Sensing. *See under* Canada
Canadian air survey industry; over capacity in, 182; role in remote sensing, 430; transfer of digitizing to, 99. *See also* Geomatics Industries Association of Canada
– Canadian Coast Guard vessels: CCGS *Camsell,* 231; *C.D. Howe,* 222; *Sir John A. MacDonald,* 231
Canadian Council of Land Surveyors, 48, 211
Canadian Council on Geomatics, 48, 483

Canadian Council on Surveys and Mapping, 48
Canadian Expedition to Study the Alpha Ridge, 51
Canadian Forces Airborne Sensing Unit, 432
Canadian Forces Bases: Fort Churchill, 152; Gagetown, 154; Rivers, 152; Rockliffe, 165; Suffield, 152; Wainwright, 154
Canadian Geographic Information System, 311, 569
Canadian Government Publication Centre. *See under* Canada
Canadian Gravity Standards Network, 34
Canadian Hydrographic Service, 13, 60, 100, 574; accreditation of hydrographers as Canada Land Surveyors, 237; Atlantic Region, 223; boat shows, 229; Central Region, 223; Chair in Ocean Mapping, 243; Gazetteer of Undersea Features, 240; inland waters surveys, 230, 235; laser sounding, 446; metrication, 233–4; Newfoundland subregional office, 242; *Notice to Mariners,* 240–1; Pacific Region, 220; Québec Region, 131–2; Radio Aids to Marine Navigation, 234; *Sailing Directions,* 240; *Tide Tables,* 233; training: in drafting, 229, 235, in hydrography, 229; university-level education, 243
Canadian Institute of Surveying/Geomatics, 210, 242, 363. *See also under* survey associations
Canadian International Development Agency (CIDA). *See under* Canada
Canadian Permanent Committee on Geographical Names, 240, app. B
cartographic and geographic societies and commissions: Association of Canadian Map Libraries and Archives, 364; Canadian Association of Geographers, 364; Canadian Cartographic Association, 364; Carto-Québec, 364; National Commission for Cartography, 364; Ontario Institute of Chartered Cartographers, 363–4; Society of University Cartographers, 363
cartographic communication, 369–71
cartographic research, 357, 360 ff., 368
cartographic specifications: federal, 101–9; provincial, 118–35
cartography: defined, 361; support for: government agencies, 367, professional societies, 363, universities, 366
cases, legal: Association of Manitoba Land Surveyors v. Carefoot, 213; Association of Manitoba Land Surveyors v. Manitoba Telephone, 231; Attorney-General for BC et al. v. Infomap Services, 212; Gulf of Maine maritime boundary, 241; R. v. Robb (K.W.) & Associates Ltd, 214
Centennial Year, 223, 282
charts
– aeronautical: Aeronautical Chart Service, 262; elevation data lacking on early charts, 249; lack of charts in early Canadian flying, 246; production

during war years, 249–52; special military charts, 265–6; styles and designs, 253, 262–5; U.S. need for Canadian charts, 82, 250; use of American charts in Canada, 246–7; World Aeronautical Charts at 1:1 000 000, 253
– hydrographic: 219 ff.; Atlas of the Gulf Islands, 229; bilingual, 233; British Admiralty, 229, 592; buoyage, 238; copper-engraved, 221; correction patch, 229; digital, 240; General Bathymetric Chart of the Oceans (GEBCO), 238; INT (international) 234; legal liability for chart information, 241; Mackenzie River, 233; National Earth Science Series, 239; Natural Resource Maps, 239; print on demand, 235, 243; reprints, 231, 240; re-scheming, 234; storage, 231; strip chart, 229
Chief Geographer's Series. See map series
Chile, 178
China, 448
Colombia, 177, 179
Commonwealth Air Training Plan, 249
Commonwealth Association of Surveying and Land Economy (CASLE), 561
community colleges: British Columbia Institute of Technology, 413; Major Church's School, 413; Nova Scotia Land Survey Institute (later College of Geographic Sciences), 413; South Alberta Institute of Technology, 413; St John's College of Trades and Technology (later Cabot Institute of Applied Arts and Technology), 413. See also tables 13–4 and 13–5
compilation. See map compilation
Computer-Aided Drafting (CAD), 196, 374
computer systems and software: ARC/INFO, 478–9; APPLAC, 332; AUTOMAP, 480; CARIS, 478, 575, COGO85, 196; DIPOP, 338; DMRS, 480; FORTRAN, 332; GALS, 29, 58; GANET, 330; GDLSAT, 36; GEODOP,36; Geopan, 196; GeoVision, 575; GHOST, 58, 330; GROOM, 29, 111, 330; INRIS, 478; LEV-ELOB, 330; MANOR, 58; PAMAP, 480, 575; PILLAR, 479; RAPID, 470; SEMIKEN, 338; SIGEOM, 479; SmartCOGO, 196; SPANS, 481, 575; STATPAK, 470; SYMAP, 322; TERRASOFT, 481; TRANET, 332
computer use: in survey calculations, 1, 29; in block adjustment, 93; in cartography, 196, 305
Conference of Commonwealth Surveyors, 559
Continental Astro-Geodetic Geoid Model, 331
continental drift. See plate tectonics
Conventional International Origin, 330
Conventional Terrestrial Pole, 330, 342
coordinatograph, 90
Council of Maritime Premiers, 118
crustal movement, 32, 35, 53, 331, 341

dams for hydroelectric power, 35; deformation of, 500; definition of large, 499

databases: Aerial Survey Data Base 96; Digital Boundary File, 321; Digital Topographic Data Base, 471; Geographic Attributes Database, 321; Geographic Frame Database, 321; National Geodetic Data Base, 53; National Gravity Data Base (NGDB), 51–2; National Topographic Data Base (NTDB), 96, 137; Northern Mapping Data Base (NMDB), 96; Postal Code Conversion File, 321; RAPID Database, 470; Street Network File, 321
datums: ATS77 (Average Terrestrial System 1977), 48; GRS 80 ellipsoid, 333; International Great Lakes Datum (IGLD), 32; NAD27 (North American Datum 1927), 47, 331; NAD83 (North American Datum 1983), 47–9, 331, 341–2, 574; NAVD 88 (North American Vertical Datum 1988), 45–9
"dead hand of civil engineering," 398
dealers: assistance enhanced, 541; expanded network, 535; promotional ideas, 537; small network of in 1945, 533
Decca. See positioning
Deception Island, 178
deflection of the vertical, 331
deformation surveys, 508–14
deputy surveyor, appointments of, 390
Digital Astro Printer, 332
Digital Elevation Model, 91, 117
digital resource maps, 121
Digital Terrain Model. See Digital Elevation Model
digitizing: of hydrographic charts, 240; of topographic maps, 95, 464
Distant Early Warning, 154
Dominican Republic, 179
Dominion Land Survey, 4
Dominion Land Surveyor, 392, 394
Dominion Topographic Surveyor, 394
Doppler. See air and sea navigation equipment, height determination and positioning

Earth Physics Branch, 33, 42
earthquake prediction, 21
Economic depression, 249
Ecuador, 178
edge matching: in digital photogrammetry, 360; with maps, 373
educational requirements for licence as land surveyor, 389
Egypt, 557
Electronic Chart Display, 240–1
Electromagnetic Distance Measurement: Aerodist, 30; Geodimeter, 29; Hydrodist, 226; Macrometer, 336; Mekometer, 46; Shoran, 26–7, 102; Tellurometer, 28; theory, 28; Total Station, 195, 498, 514–16; trials on early equipment, 329; use in aircraft, 256; use in cadastral surveys, 195
Energy, Mines and Resources Canada. See Canada

engineering surveys: defined, 591; deformation surveys, 508; ground subsidence, 514; hydroelectric power development, 499; machinery alignment, 519; mine surveys, 497; Olympic Stadium, 504; pipeline surveys, 498; Rogers Pass Tunnel, 506; Superconducting Super Collider, 520

environment, 14. *See also* Canada, Environment Canada

Environmental Systems Research Institute (ESRI), 478

Ethiopia, 552

examination subjects, 392

Exxon Valdez, 241

Falkland Islands, 178

Federal Cabinet Committee on Remote Sensing, 431

federal topographic mapping programme, 99 ff.

Fédération Internationale des Géomètres, (FIG), 564–5

fire insurance mapping, 375

First Corps Field Survey Company, 81, 141

flicker viewing, 87; electronic flicker, 91

Flight Publications, 266

flying: accidents, 42, 147; in Canada in early days, 246

Food and Agriculture Organization (FAO), 177–8, 312, 439

forestry, 10, 170, 312, 424–5; age and species identification, 313; forest inventory, 164, 424–7; forest management, 313, 452; Forest Map of Canada, 313; record of insect damage, 313; tree height measurement, 359

French hydrographic surveys, 374

Gambia, 242

gauges (water level) 235

Generalized Method of Deformation Analysis, 508–10

geodesy: defined, 1; discontinuance of traditional astronomy, 15; electronic era, 3–13; geodetic network-related research, 329; in the private sector, 59; satellite era, 13–24

Geodetic Survey of Canada. *See* Surveys and Mapping Branch

Geographical Section of the General Staff, 2, 84, 140–1

Geographic Information System (GIS), 95, 371–4, 574; Canadian development, its concept and design, 469–70; Canadian origin, 467; city GIS/LIS, 476–7; commercial developments, 479; data inventories, 482; description of GIS, 462; First International Conference (1970), 472; interchange standards, 483; lack of communication between agencies during 1970s, 472; National Conference on GIS, 485; need for technology, 465; planning

and management tools, 486; proliferation of users, 482; Second International Conference (1972), 472; spread of technical data during 1970s, 472; systems and software, 467–71; training, 484–5

geoid, 53–6, 332–3

Geoid Prediction Package, 56

Geological Survey of Canada, 4, 5, 17, 120; Geophysics Division (formerly Earth Physics Branch), 42, 45; Gravity Section, 23, 53; Topographical Survey Division, 100, 111

Geomatics Canada. *See* Surveys and Mapping Branch

Geomatics Industries Association of Canada (GIAC) (formerly Canadian Association of Aerial Surveyors [CAAS]), 171, 176, 552–4, 557

glaciological research, 354

Graham Land, 178

gravimetry, 21, 23, 33, 42, 51–3

Great Lakes levelling. *See* height determination

ground subsidence, 510–18

Guyana, 181

Haiti, 552

height determination: Airborne Profile Recorder, 4, 83, 102, 252, 345, 547; by barometer, 4, 83, 102; by contract, 42; by Doppler, 21, 55; by GPS, 39–40; Great Lakes levelling, 32, 331; Ground Elevation Meter, 40; level line to Arctic Ocean, 32, 44; levelling instruments, 23, 32, 47; levelling operations, 31–2, 42–5, 331; Litton Autosurveyor 40; motorized levelling, 24; Zeiss NI-1 level, 507

helicopters, 26, 29, 33, 42, 103, 145, 429; as survey targets, 504

Hills Report, 99

history of cartography, 374–5

Hong Kong, 402

hovercraft, 231

Hudson Bay Lowlands, 118; glacial rebound, 331

Hudson's Bay Company, 387

hydroelectric power development, 499

hydrographic charts. *See* charts, hydrographic

hydrographic surveying: acoustic sounder, 227–8; DOLPHINS, 243; LIDAR sounding, 238; shallow water sounding, 238; standards, 243; sweeping, 238

hydrographic vessels: *Acadia,* 219; *Advent,* 232; *Algerine,* 222, 224; *Arctic Sealer,* 222; *Baffin,* 224, 229, 231; *Bayfield,* 232; *Cartier,* 219, 221; *Dawson,* 224; *Ehkoli,* 221; *F.G.C. Smith,* 241; *Fort Francis,* 221; *Frederick C. Creed,* 243; *Hudson,* 224; *John P. Telly,* 225, 238; *Kapuskasing,* 221, 226; *Limnos,* 224; *Marabell,* 222; *Matthew,* 226; *Maxwell,* 222; *North Star IV,* 222; *Parizeau,* 224; *Parry,* 221; *Pender,* 238; *R.B. Young,* 243;

Richardson, 224; *Theron,* 222; *Theta,* 222; *Vector,* 224; *Wm. J. Stewart,* 220, 229
Hydro-Québec, 58

ice island surveys, 51
immigration, 7
Increased Ministerial Authority and Accountability Accord, 540
India, 242
Indonesia, 242
industrial alignment, 518–20
Inertial Survey System. *See* positioning
inland waters surveys. *See* Canadian Hydrographic Service
Integrated Survey Area. *See* British Columbia
Interior, Department of. *See* Canada, Energy, Mines and Resources
international alliances and agreements: bilateral (Canada, U.S.), 6; Mapping, Charting and Air Photography Plan (later Mapping and Charting Plan), 101, 141; NATO, 6, 268; Tripartite (Canada, U.S., U.K.), 6. *See also* appendix D, 608 ff.
International Association of Lighthouse Authorities, 238
international associations, societies, and unions: Cartographic Association (ICA), 565–8; Geographical Union (IGU), 560; Geodesy and Geophysics (IUGG), 34, 329; Hydrographic Organization (IHO), 222–3, 234, 242; Society for Mine Surveying (ISM), 498; Union for Surveys and Mapping (IUSM), 568
International Civil Aviation Organization (ICAO), 268
International Commission on Large Dams, 499
International Earth Rotation Service, 338
International GPS Service for Geodynamics (IGS), 338
International Hydrographic Bureau, 222, 242
International Terrestrial Reference Frame, 338
invar: rods, 47; tapes, 29, 226
inverted pendulum, 501–2

Jamaica, 242, 552
James Bay Project, 503
Joint Operations Graphic (JOG), 159–61
journals: *Chronicle/Chronique,* 364; *Lighthouse,* 242; *The Canadian Surveyor* (later *Geomatica*), 210, 365; *The Cartographer* (later *Cartographica*), 265

Kuwait, 557

LaCoste-Romberg gravimeter, 33
Lambert Tower, 36
Land Information System: defined, 190

land parcel: in concession and lot townships, 194; irregularly shaped, 193; in rectangular section townships, 194; in seigneuries and river lots, 104
Land Registration and Information Service (LRIS), 28, 37, 118, 198, 200, 545
land survey associations vs the air survey industry, 175–6
Laos, 185
Lapp Task Force, 96, 276
laser beams, 492
laws
– international: Law of the Sea, 235
– provincial: Act to Promote the Reform of Cadastre in Québec, 208; Alberta Companies Act, 212; Alberta Land Surveyors' Act, 202, 211–2; Alberta Surveying Professions Act, 212; Alberta Surveys Act, 202; British Columbia Land Surveyors' Act, 212; British Columbia Provincial Land Surveyors' Act, 212; Civil Code of Lower Canada, 208; Civil Code of Québec, 208; Crown Lands (Amendments) Act, 393; Manitoba Real Property Act, 203; Manitoba Special Survey Act, 203; (Manitoba) The Land Surveyors' Act, 213; New Brunswick Crown Lands and Forests Act, 478; The New Brunswick Land Surveyors Act, 213; New Brunswick Land Titles Act, 201; Newfoundland and Labrador Land Surveyors Act, 214; Nova Scotia Engineering Act, 214; Nova Scotia Land Surveyors' Act, 214; Nova Scotia Provincial Land Surveyors' Act, 214; NWT Condominium Act, 205; NWT Land Titles Act, 198, 205; NWT Land Titles Plans Regulations, 205; Ontario Boundaries Act, 206–7; Ontario Certification of Titles Act, 206; Ontario Condominium Act, 206; Ontario Land Registration Reform Act, 207; Ontario Land Titles Act, 206; Ontario Registry Act, 206; Ontario Surveyors Act, 215; (Ontario) The Land Surveyors Act, 215; Prince Edward Island Land Surveyors Act, 215; Prince Edward Island Land Survey Act, 216; Québec Cadastre Act, 208; Saskatchewan Land Surveyors Act, 217; Saskatchewan Land Surveys Act, 209; Saskatchewan Land Titles Act, 209; Yukon Land Titles Act, 198
laws and regulations, federal: Agriculture Rehabilitation and Development Act, 290; Canada Land Surveyors Act, 211; Canada Lands Surveys Act, 199; Charts and Publications Regulations, 241; Dominion Land Surveyors' Act, 394; Dominion Lands Surveys Act, 216; Indian Act, 199; Land Titles Act, 198; Rockey Mountain Park Act, 318
legal cases. *See* cases, legal
LIFT Project, 175
long range mapping plan, 1–3, 141–2, 252
Loran-A, -C. *See* positioning

Mactaquac power generating station, 510–14
Malawi, 178
Malaysia, 242, 402, 448
Manicouagan-Outardes Project, 500
Manitoba, 41, 58, 131; Department of Highways and
    Transportation, 204; land information centre, 204;
    Land Titles Office, 203; Surveys and Mapping
    Branch, Department of Natural Resources, 131,
    203, 542–3
map
– communication. *See* cartographic communication
– compilation, 148; digital, 94–5; stereo, 94
– design, 360–3, 369–71
– drafting and printing, 149–50
– generalization, 368
– projections. *See* projections
– revision, 109–10
– styles, 111–13
– use, 369–71
map series:
– 1:1000–1:5000. *See also* provincial mapping,
    118–36
– 1:10 000, 120, 123, 128–9, 131
– 1:12 500, 119
– 1:15 840 (Four-Inch), 84, 120
– 1:20 000, 120–1, 125, 128–9, 131–2
– 1:25 000, 108–10, 116, 132
– 1:31 680 (Two-Inch), 120
– 1:50 000, 104, 111–12, 123, 574; half sheets, 111
– 1:50 000 monochrome, 113
– 1:50 000 provisional, 112
– 1:63 360 (One-Mile or One-Inch), 100, 104, 111,
    249, 388
– 1:125 000, 104
– 1:126 720 (Two-Mile), 2, 100, 104
– 1:190 080 (Three-Mile), 4, 104, 130, 249
– 1:250 000, 101–4, 574
– 1:250 000 U.S. Series in Northern Canada, 101
– 1:253 440 (Four-Mile), 101–4, 252, table 9–1
– 1:500 000, 247, 252, 254
– 1:506 880 (Eight-Mile), 83, originally a compiled
    series, 249; conversion to 1:500 000, 253
– 1:1 000 000 International Map of the World, 160
– Canada Land Inventory Series (1:250 000 and
    1:1 000 000), 315
– Chief Geographer's Series (1:250 000 and
    1:500 000), 4–5
– Military Town Plans/City Maps, 108, 154–7
– Northern Land Use Information Series
    (1:250 000), 315
– Wetland Mapping Series (1:50 000), 318
Mapping, Charting, and Air Photography Plan
    (MCAPP) (later MCP), 101, 141
Mapping and Charting Plan. *See* Mapping, Chart-
    ing, and Air Photography Plan

Mapping a Northern Land, organization of the book,
    18–19
Mapping and Charting Establishment. *See* Army
    Survey Establishment
mapping available in 1947, 2
mapping consortia, 174
mapping programme from 1900 to 1950, 3–6
maps, thematic, 287–94: aeromagnetic, 308–9; appli-
    cations and uses, 304; bio-physical, 308, 318;
    census, 321; choropleth, 314, 322; climate, 319;
    combined with computer assisted cartography,
    305; demographic, 321; disease mortality, 304,
    322; Ducks Unlimited, 318, 445; ecological, 317;
    ephemeral, 304; forest information mapped, 312–
    4; Forest Map of Canada, 313; forestry, 312; with
    Geographic Information Systems, 311; geologi-
    cal, 307; geomagnetic, 309; Isodemographic Map,
    323; land use, 316–18; Northern Land Use Infor-
    mation series, 316; northern reconnaissance map-
    ping, 306; parks, 318; private sector, 323;
    producers of, 305; research into tourist series,
    318; road maps, 323; sea ice surveys, 319; seis-
    mic hazards, 309; seismological, 309; socio-
    economic, 320; socio-economic disadvantage,
    305; soil, 310; Soil Landscape, 312; Soil Map of
    Canada, 312; surficial geology, 308; used to com-
    municate ideas and concepts, 204; use of terrain
    analysis, 308; users and uses, 304; Wetland Map-
    ping Series, 318; Windsor-Québec Axis, 322
marketing spatial information, 529–30; change in
    policies on revenue, printing authority and mar-
    keting, 540–1; in EMR, 533–41; map distribution,
    538–40; market, 533, 537; Marketing in Mani-
    toba, 542; Marketing in New Brunswick, 545;
    Marketing in Quebec, 543; printing, 537; promo-
    tion and pricing, 535, 537, 541
Mekong River surveys, 59, 185
memorandum of understanding (MOU), 177, 556–8
metrication, 104, 111, 113, 133, 233–4, 574
Mid Canada Line, 105
Military Geographic Information Systems, 161
military survey staff organization, 151, table 5–1
military training areas. *See* Canadian Forces Bases
Miller-Smith mapping plan, 2–3
Mines and Resources. *See* Canada, Energy, Mines
    and Resources
Mines and Technical Surveys. *See* Canada, Energy,
    Mines and Resources
mine surveying, 497–8
Morton Matrix, 469
Multispectral Scanner, 431
Municipal Integrated Surveying and Mapping pro-
    gramme (MISAM). *See* Alberta
municipal surveys. *See* surveying and mapping,
    urban

Murray Map, 388

NAD27. *See* datums
NAD83. *See* datums
Namibia, 242
National Advisory Committee on Control Surveys
and Mapping, 364
National Geodetic Baseline (NGBL), 46
National Geodetic Reference System, 21
National Research Council, 21, 47, 295, 329, 547;
Photogrammetric Section, 343–6; end of photo-
grammetric research at, 356
National Topographic System, 2, 100
Natural Resources Canada. *See* Canada, Energy,
Mines and Resources
navigation aids. *See* air and sea navigation
equipment
navigation hazards: Black Rock, 226; Bligh Reef,
241; Cerberus Rock, 241; Ripple Rock, 229;
Whaleback Reef, 224
Nepal, 552
New Brunswick, 123, 183; Geographic Information
Corporation, 18, 204, 545–6
Newfoundland and Labrador, 105, 118–19, 183;
Lands Branch, Department of Environment and
Lands, 18, 205
Nigeria, 185, 402, 551
non-cartographic photogrammetry, 354–9
Northern Domestic Airspace, 256
North West Company, 387
Northwest Territories, 42, 135; Surveys and Map-
ping Division, Municipal and Community Affairs,
18, 205
Nova Scotia, 120–3, 183; Geomatics Centre, Land
Information Management, Department of Munici-
pal Affairs, 18; Survey Division, Department of
Natural Resources, 205

Observatories Branch, 33
oil and gas exploitation, 11
Olympic Stadium, 504
Oman, 552
one-hundred-year cycles, 416–18, 493
Ontario, 31, 57, 127–9; Land Titles Office, 206;
Ontario Basic Mapping, 128–9; POLARIS, 198;
Surveys and Design Office, Ministry of Transportation, 207; Survey and Titles Services, Consumer and Commercial Relations, 206
orthophoto and stereo-orthophoto systems, 351
orthophotomaps, 120–1

pack-horse transportation, 143–5
Pakistan, 185
Pan-American Institute of Geography and History,
276, 560–1

peacekeeping operations, 159
Permanent Joint Board on Defence, 101, 141
Peru, 179
Philippines, 554
photogrammetric instruments: analytical plotter, 90–
1, 346–9; Anaplot, 347; Balplex Plotter, 87; Digital Video Plotter (DVP), 358–9; digital video photogrammetric workstation, 91; double projection
direct viewing, 85; Gamble Plotter, 87; Gestalt
Photomapper, 95, 183; improvements to, 86;
Kelsh Plotter, 86; mechanical projection, 88–9;
monocomparator, 349; Multiplex Aeroprojector,
83–5, 148; Rectoblique Plotter, 82; Stereocompiler, 352; Wild A5 Plotter, 88; Wild A7 Plotter,
88; Wild B8 Plotter, 90; Zeiss Stereoplanigraph,
344. *See also* tables 3–1 and 3–2
photogrammetric orientation (interior, relative, absolute), 86
photogrammetric systems, 76 ff.
photogrammetric test areas, 350
photogrammetry: use in mapping, 76, 84 ff., 148;
use in measuring water depths, 238
Photographic Zenith Tube, 330
photo interpretation, 423–4, 425–7; research in,
428–30
photo-topography, 103, 141
physical geodesy and astronomy, 21, 35, 53–7
"pigs," for pipeline testing, 336
pipeline surveys, 493–4
plate tectonics and crustal motion, 22, 56–7, 331
Polar Continental Shelf project, 33, 52–3
political spheres, 6
population growth. *See* immigration
ports: Come By Chance, 233; Halifax, 14; Montreal, 14; Port aux Basques, 240; Port Cartier,
222; Port Hawkesbury, 233; Sept-Îles, 222;
Vancouver, 14
positioning (instruments and systems), 21, 26–31;
astronomic positioning: Ball's Method, 412;
Black's Method, 332; Decca, 224–6; Decca-
Lambda, 226; Decca-Navigator, 224; Doppler, 35,
59, 333, 335; end of conventional methods of
geodesy, 36; flare triangulation, 145; Global Positioning System (GPS), 37–40, 329, 336–9; GPS in
aircraft, 360; GPS in cadastral surveying, 196;
GPS-ISS integration, 336–8; GPS-Loran-C integration, 240; gyro-theodolite, 332, 508, 523; HIRAN,
329; Inertial Survey System (ISS), 37, 41–2, 335–
6; ISS in Arctic, 21; Litton Autosurveyor, 40;
Litton LASS, 41; Loran-A, 224; Loran-C, 60, 232–
4; Mini-Ranger, 232; rho-rho Loran-C, 232; sextant, 232; Syledis, 232; Trisponder, 232; Very
Long Baseline Interferometer (VLBI), 48, 329–41;
Wild T3, 507. *See also* Electromagnetic Distance
Measurement

Prince Edward Island, 42, 123–4, 183, 207; Geomatics Information Centre, Fiscal Management Division, Department of the Treasury, 18; Properties and Survey Section, Transport and Public Works, 207

printing, 111, 149–50, 235, 243, 537, 540–1, 578; on demand, 235, 243

Products and Services Task Force, 540

Program Office for Resource Satellite and Airborne Remote sensing, 431

projections: 3° Transverse Mercator, 119, 121, 125, 132; Lambert Conformal, 207, 272; Modified Polyconic, 272; NB Stereographic, 123; PEI Stereographic, 124, 207; Universal Transverse Mercator, 128, 131, 135

prospecting, 4

provincial and territorial organizations, 202–9

provincial: boundaries, 67–72; mapping, 118 ff.; survey operations, 18, 57–8, 116 ff.

Qatar, 557

Québec, 35, 58, 125–7; Direction du cadastre, Ministère de l'Energie et des Ressources Naturelles, 208; Lands and Forests, 543; Service de la cartographie, Direction des Relevés Techniques, Ministère des Ressources Naturelles, 18; SIGEOM geology and geophysics information programme, 479; Système québécois de référence cartographique (SQRC), 125

radar, 224, 240; for ground clearance, 252; response simulation terrain models, 171

Radarsat, 433–41, 444–8

radial line plot. See aerotriangulation

rapid mapping exercise, 158

RCAF, 163, 430

remote sensing, 422 ff.; 1978–84, 440–51; academic involvement, 436; airborne remote sensing, 436; automated mapping and remote sensing, 452; definition, 422; future prospects, 456–8; GIS and remote sensing, 452; industry in remote sensing, 443; integration of remote sensing and GIS, 455; international work in, 443; James Bay Hydro development, 433; Landsat era, 438; marketing, 444, 446; 1945–72, 422; provincial work, 434; satellite era, 430 ff.; symposia, table 14–2, 434; universities working in, 436; working groups (forestry, fisheries, hydrology, limnology, meteorology, oceanology), 432

researchers recruited from Europe, 344

research funds: availability during Cold War, 1

resources: mapping for exploitation of, 10

Rogers Pass Tunnel, 506

Royal Australian Army Survey Corps, 480

Royal Canadian Navy: 219, 221, 226; HMCS Kapuskasing, 221, HMCS Labrador, 224

St Lawrence Seaway, 222–3, 243, 494–7

Saskatchewan, 132, 209; Central Surveys and Mapping Agency, Saskatchewan Property Management Corporation, 18, 132, 209, 482; Chief Surveyor's Office, Property Registration Branch, Department of Justice, 209

scribing, 150–1, 223–4

sea bed, 13

sea ice, 51, 295

secondary control, 40–3

Second Colloquium on Survey Education, 413

Second International Photogrammetric Conference, 347

Senegal, 242

Seychelles, 179

softcopy photogrammetry, 358

Somalia, 178

sonar, 232

Sonar Side Scan, 138

sovereignty, 33

Sparwood Coal Mine, 514–17

special operating agencies, 16

spheroid calculations, 55

spiral tunnels, 491

SPOT satellite, 91

Sputnik, 35, 232

Statistics Canada, 17

stereocompilation theory, 93–4

Superconducting Super Collider, 520–4

survey associations: Alberta Land Surveyors, 211, 393; Canada Land Surveyors, 211, 394; Canadian Hydrographic, 242; Canadian Institute of Surveying (later Canadian Institute of Geomatics), 210, 242, 363; Corporation of Land Surveyors of BC, 212, 393; Manitoba Land Surveyors, 212, 393; New Brunswick Land Surveyors, 213, 392; Newfoundland Land Surveyors, 214, 393; Nova Scotia Land Surveyors, 214, 393; Ontario Land Surveyors, 215, 392; l'Ordre des Arpenteurs-géometres du Québec, 216, 392; Prince Edward Island Land Surveyors, 215, 392; Saskatchewan Land Surveyors, 216, 393

surveying and mapping
– status of: Report of a Task Committee, 398
– texts: Geodesy, The Concepts, 329; GPS Positioning Guide, 38; Guide to GPS Positioning, 339; Historical Development of Photogrammetric Methods and Instruments, 356; Surveying Offshore Canada Lands, 331; Survey Law in Canada, 210; Urban Surveying and Mapping, 356
– urban: 30–1, 119, 122, 123, 124, 126, 128, 131, 132, 133, 135

surveyor general, 199; regional surveyor, 199

Surveys and Mapping Branch, EMR: Canada Centre for Mapping, 16; Canada Centre for Remote Sensing, 16, 431–4; Canada Centre for Surveying, 16; Canada Map Office, 278, 315, 533, 538, 542, 547; Cartographic Information and Distribution Centre, 16; Geodetic Survey of Canada, 5, 23, 26, 41; Geographical Services Directorate, 276; Geographic Information Systems Division, 16; Legal Surveys Division, 199; Map Compilation and Reproduction Division, 100; Topographical Survey of Canada (later Topographical Survey Directorate), 7, 95, 100

Synthetic Aperture Radar (SAR), 441

Système Québécois de référence cartographique. *See* Québec

Task Force on the Surveying and Mapping Industry in Canada, 553

Tennessee Valley Authority, 84

Terrain Resource Information Management (TRIM), 134

test areas (photogrammetric), 350

Thailand, 185

Thematic Mapper, 445

thematic maps. *See* maps, thematic

topographical data in digital form, need for, 96

Topographical Survey of Canada. *See* Surveys and Mapping Branch

Trans-Canada Airway, 4, 247

Trans-Canada Highway, 32

transistors vs vacuum tubes, 1, 466

Trimetrogon mapping, 82–3

Trinidad and Tobago, 179

typesetting, lead type, 223

United Nations, 560–1

United States, 21, 25, 32, 42, 101; air charts, 246; Corps of Engineers, 500; Defense Mapping Agency, 42; National Geodetic Survey, 330; Naval Surface Weapons Center, 332

United States Navy: USS *Bramble*, 224; USS *Burton Island* 224; USS *Northwind*, 231; USS *Requisite*, 224; *Spar*, 224; *Storis*, 224

universities: Calgary, 329, 336, 338, 359, 402, 409–10; l'Ecole Polytechnique, 396–7; King's College, 395; Laval, 329, 358, 367, 402, 405–6, 576; McGill, 395–7, 412; Manitoba, 397; New Brunswick, 60, 329–30, 332, 335–6, 341, 357, 395, 399, 402, 408–9, 492, 500; Nova Scotia Technical, 397; Queen's, 364, 397, 411; Ryerson, 414; Saskatchewan, 393; Sherbrooke, 451; Toronto, 367, 394, 396–7, 406, 412, 549; Toronto – Erindale, 359, 406–8; Toronto – School of Practical Science, 396; York, 340

urban centred regions, 8–10

urbanization, 8–10

urban surveying and mapping. *See under* surveying and mapping

vehicular navigation, 338

Venezuela, 178; ground subsidence in, 517–18

Very Long Baseline Interferometry. *See* positioning

Vietnam, 185

Wilderness Line, 113–14

Wild Statoscope, 186

Yukon, 42–3, 135

ZUPT (zero velocity and alignment updates for ISS equipment), 41